This book offers a detailed and comprehensive guide to contemporary sources for research into the history of individual nineteenth-century U.S. communities, large and small. The book is arranged topically (covering demography, ethnicity and race, land use and settlement, religion, education, politics and local government, industry, trade and transportation, and poverty, health, and crime) and thus will be of great use, too, to those investigating particular historical themes at national, state, or regional level.

As well as treating a wide variety of the types of primary sources, published and unpublished, quantitative and qualitative, available for the study of many places, the book also provides information on certain specific sources and some individual collections, in particular those of the National Archives. Though not intended as a guide to individual archive depositories or libraries, nor as a detailed bibliography of the history of any particular place or region, the book provides references to guides, catalogs, and bibliographies of manuscript and printed sources, and to commentaries. Included, too, is discussion of significant subjects for research into the various topics and of appropriate methodological techniques and approaches.

This will prove a valuable work of reference to a wide range of university and college students and faculty, to libraries, archivists, family historians, and schoolteachers, and to many interested amateurs who wish to pursue seriously the study of their region or community, neighborhood or family, or some particular aspect of the American past.

THE SOURCES OF HISTORY
STUDIES IN THE USES OF HISTORICAL EVIDENCE

GENERAL EDITOR: G. R. ELTON

SOURCES FOR U.S. HISTORY:
NINETEENTH-CENTURY COMMUNITIES

THE SOURCES OF HISTORY

STUDIES IN THE USES OF HISTORICAL EVIDENCE

GENERAL EDITOR: G. R. ELTON

The purpose of this series of books is, broadly, to present to students and readers of history some understanding of the materials from which history must be written and of the problems which these raise. The books will endeavor to bring out the inescapable links between historical sources and historical reconstruction, will help to define promising lines of fruitful research, and will illumine the realities of historical knowledge. Each volume is concerned with a logical span in the history of a given nation, civilization or area, or with a meaningful historical theme, and confines itself to all the primary material extant for that sector. It considers these materials from the point of view of two crucial questions: what can we know, and what have we no right to expect to learn, from what the past has left behind?

VOLUMES IN THE SERIES

Sources for Ancient History
MICHAEL CRAWFORD

Sources for Early Modern Irish History 1534–1641
R. DUDLEY EDWARDS and MARY O'DOWD

England 1200–1640
G. R. ELTON

Sources for English Local History
W. B. STEPHENS

Sources for U.S. History: Nineteenth-Century Communities
W. B. STEPHENS

Sources for U.S. History

Nineteenth-Century Communities

W. B. STEPHENS

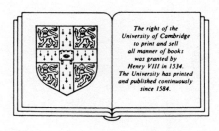

The right of the
University of Cambridge
to print and sell
all manner of books
was granted by
Henry VIII in 1534.
The University has printed
and published continuously
since 1584.

CAMBRIDGE UNIVERSITY PRESS

CAMBRIDGE
NEW YORK   PORT CHESTER
MELBOURNE   SYDNEY

Published by the Press Syndicate of the University of Cambridge
The Pitt Building, Trumpington Street, Cambridge CB2 1RP
40 West 20th Street, New York, NY 10011, USA
10 Stamford Road, Oakleigh, Melbourne 3166, Australia

First published 1991

Printed in Great Britain by
Redwood Press, Melksham, Wiltshire

British Library cataloguing in publication data

Stephens, W. B. (William Brewer), *1925–*
Sources for US history: nineteenth-century communities. –
(The sources of history).
1. United States. Historical sources
1. Title   11. Series
973.072

Library of Congress cataloguing in publication data

Stephens, W. B.
Sources for US history: nineteenth-century communities / W.B. Stephens.
p.   cm. – (The sources of history, studies in the uses of historical evidence)
Includes index.
ISBN 0 521 35315 7
1. United States – History. Local – Sources.   2. United States –
History. Local – Sources – Bibliography.   1. Title   11. Series.
E180.S74   1991
973 – dc20   90–37810   CIP

ISBN 0 521 35315 7 hardback

RP

To the memories of
E.B.S., R.M.S., C.C.B.S.,
T.E.W., and M.A.W.

Contents

Contents

Author's preface

The need for a book of this kind was suggested to me in 1979 by my friend, Ben Bloxham, who originally hoped to collaborate with me in writing it. Unfortunately other duties made it impossible for him to do so. I remain, however, deeply indebted to him for advice and encouragement, and to him and his wife, Becky, for friendship and hospitality over the years.

Completion of the book has been facilitated by generous financial assistance towards travel expenses from the British Academy and the Twenty-Seven Foundation, and by Visiting Research Fellowships at the Newberry Library, Chicago, in 1982 and 1984. I am most grateful to these organizations. I have been further helped in the work by periods as Visiting Professor at Brigham Young University, Utah, in 1979 and 1982, and as Visiting Scholar in 1986 and Visiting Professor in 1988 at the College of William and Mary in Virginia. I wish particularly to thank Dean John M. Nagle of William and Mary for his considerable support.

To Robert W. Karrow, Jr. (Newberry Library) and Elisabeth Wittman (Evangelical Lutheran Church in America Archives), who read parts of my text in draft and made valuable suggestions, I am specially grateful. My thanks are also due to Kenneth A. Krieger, my graduate assistant for a semester at William and Mary, who did sterling work in checking references and searching out material. I am particularly grateful, too, for assistance received from Peter Bunce (Chicago Regional Archives, NA), David Thackry (Newberry Library), Alan F. Zoellner and Linda F. Templeman (documents librarians, William and Mary), James N. McCord and John E. Selby (William and Mary), David Pratt and Susan

L. Fales (Brigham Young University), John Killick (University of Leeds), Donald J. Munro (Institute of Historical Research, London), Lucy P. Burgess (Cornell University), and Robert P. Swierenga (Kent State University). I have benefited greatly, too, from conversations with Thad W. Tate (Institute of Early American History and Culture, Williamsburg).

Without access to the holdings of the National Archives, Washington, DC, the Library of Congress, the Institute of Historical Research, the British Library, and the British Library of Political and Economic Science, my task would have been impossible. I wish, therefore, to thank the staffs of those institutions, and also those of the following depositories and libraries of which I made extensive use: Newberry Library, Chicago; Chicago Public Library; Chicago Historical Society; Carnegie Library of Pittsburgh; Virginia State Library; Family History Library, Salt Lake City; Bancroft Library, University of California, Berkeley; Hampton University, Virginia; and the libraries of the College of William and Mary, Chicago University, Northwestern University, Brigham Young University, University of Utah, University of Virginia, Virginia Commonwealth University, University of Pittsburgh, Carnegie-Mellon University, Pittsburgh, University of London, and University College London. To the Inter-Library Loan librarians of the Brotherton Library, University of Leeds, I owe a special debt. I have also received help in various ways from a large number of other institutions, librarians, archivists, and scholars, and am only sorry that I cannot mention them all by name here.

At a more personal level I would like to thank my friend of undergraduate days, Tran-Qui-Than, and his wife, Bach, who made several visits to Berkeley so pleasant. Similarly I owe much to Armand J. Galfo, who suggested the College of William and Mary as a base for continuing my research in 1986, and who, with his wife, Mary, has been so generous in hospitality over several years. To my son-in-law, Ian Harden, I am grateful for his patience in helping me overcome my natural antipathy to word-processing. And above all I am indebted to my wife, who has accompanied me in visiting twenty-six of the states of the U.S. and has helped me in very many ways in the completion of this work. The final version of the text and notes has been much improved by the careful vetting of Jean Field of the Cambridge University Press, to whom I am most grateful.

Finally I must record my thanks to Peter Gosden (University of Leeds) and Andrew G. Watson (University College London) for positive support at various times, and especially to the General Editor of this series, Professor Sir Geoffrey Elton, who has given unstinted encouragement, help, and advice over several years.

Despite all the help I have received there will inevitably be in a work of this kind errors and omissions, and for these I must bear sole responsibility. I may note here, too, that two National Archives and Records Administration publications appeared too late to be made use of in this volume. *Guide to the Records of the United States Senate at the National Archives, 1789–1989* (1989) (replaces PI 23 (1950)) and *Guide to the Records of the United States House of Representatives at the National Archives, 1789–1989* (1989) (supplements PI 113 (1959)) are important for a number of topics and their indexes should be searched.

W.B.S.

1989

Abbreviations

AA	*American Archivist*
AASLH	American Association for State and Local History
AgHR	*Agricultural History Review*
AH	*Agricultural History*
AHA	American Historical Association
AHR	*American Historical Review*
ALA	American Library Association
Am./*Am.*	American/*American*
AR/*AR*	Annual Report/*Annual Report*
Baker, *Finding List*	
	James M. Baker (ed.), *Finding List to Important Serial Publications by the Government in the Libraries of the United States Senate* (1901)
BHM	*Bulletin of the History of Medicine*
bibl.	bibliography/bibliographical note, essay
BPP	British Parliamentary Paper
Brock	William R. Brock, *The United States, 1789–1890* (1975)
Bull.	*Bulletin*
Bull. AASLH	*Bulletin of the [American] Association for State and Local History*
Burr	Nelson R. Burr, *A Critical Bibliography of Religion in America* (1961)
Carman and Thompson (1960)	
	Henry J. Carman and Arthur W. Thompson, *A Guide to the Principal Sources of American Civilization, 1800–1900, in the City of New York: Manuscripts* (1960)

Carman and Thompson (1962)

Henry J. Carman and Arthur W.
Thompson, *A Guide to the Principal Sources
of American Civilization, 1800–1900, in the
City of New York: Printed Materials* (1962)

CH   *Church History*

Checklist   *Checklist of United States Public Documents,
1789–1909* (1911, repr. 1953)

CHR   *Catholic Historical Review*

CIS   Congressional Information Service

DP   NA, Descriptive Pamphlet

Dubester (1948)

Henry J. Dubester, *State Censuses: An
Annotated Bibliography of Population after the
Year 1790 by States and Territories of the
United States* (1948, repr. 1969)

Dubester (1950)

Henry J. Dubester, *Catalog of United States
Census Publications, 1790–1945* (1950) (repr.
U.S. Bureau of the Census, *Bureau of the
Census Catalog of Publications, 1790–1972*
(1974)

ER   *Ecclesiastical Review*

Genealogical Research

*Guide to Genealogical Research in the National
Archives* (NA, 1983, repr. 1985)

GLO   General Land Office

GNA   *Guide to the National Archives of the United
States* (1974, repr. 1987)

Hasse   Adelaide R. Hasse, *Index of Economic
Material in Documents of the States of the
United States, 1789–1904* (1907–22)

HD   House Document

HED   House Executive Document

HEQ   *History of Education Quarterly*

Hershberg, *Philadelphia*

Theodore Hershberg (ed.), *Philadelphia:
Work, Space, Family, and Group Experience
in the Nineteenth Century: Essays Towards an
Interdisciplinary History of the City* (1981)

HG   Frank Friedel (ed.), *Harvard Guide to
American History* (2 vols., 1974)

Hist.	*Historical/History*
HM	*Historical Methods*
HMD	House Miscellaneous Document
HMN	*Historical Methods Newsletter*
Hoornstra	Jean Hoornstra and Trudy Heath (eds.), *American Periodicals 1741–1900. An Index to the Microfilm Collections* . . . (University Microfilms International, 1979)
HR	House Report
HRS	Historical Records Survey (WPA)
ICPSR	Inter-University Consortium for Political and Social Research
JAH	*Journal of American History*
JCH	*Journal of Contemporary History*
JEH	*Journal of Economic History*
JFH	*Journal of Family History*
JIH	*Journal of Interdisciplinary History*
JMH	*Journal of Mississippi History*
JNH	*Journal of Negro History*
Jnl./jnl.	*Journal/journal*
Jones	H. G. Jones, *Local Government Records* (1980)
JPH	*Journal of the Presbyterian History Society/ Journal of Presbyterian History*
JSH	*Journal of Social History*
JSoH	*Journal of Southern History*
JUH	*Journal of Urban History*
Kellogg and Walker	Jefferson B. Kellogg and Robert H. Walker (eds.), *Sources for American Studies* (1983)
LH	*Labor History*
M	NA microfilm (*followed by number*)
Mag.	*Magazine*
Makower	Joel Makower (ed.), *The American History Sourcebook* (1988)
MRR	*National Archives Microfilm Resources for Research* (1986 or current issue)

Munden and Beers
        Kenneth W. Munden and Henry P. Beers (comps.), *Guide to Federal Archives Relating to the Civil War* (1962)
MVHR   *Mississippi Valley Historical Review*
NA   National Archives and Records Administration (*formerly* Service)
NC   NA unpublished guide, etc., civil records
NM   NA unpublished guide, etc., military records
NUC   used for both: *National Union Catalog. Pre-1956 Imprints* (London, 1968–81) and Library of Congress, *National Union Catalog* (1963–)
NUCMC   *National Union Catalog of Manuscript Collections, 1959–* (1962–)
Palic   Vladimir M. Palic, *Government Publications* (1975)
PAM   NA, Pamphlet Accompanying Microfilm
PDM   NA, Pamphlet Describing Microfilm
PI   NA, Preliminary Inventory
Procs.   *Proceedings*
Prucha   Francis P. Prucha, *Handbook for Research in American History: A Guide to Bibliographies and Other Reference Works* (1987)
Q.   *Quarterly*
Rep./rep.   *Report*/report
Rev.   *Review*
RG   Record Group (NA)
RIC   NA, Reference Information Circular
RIP   NA, Reference Information Paper
SAA   Society of American Archivists
Schmeckebier and Eastin
        Laurence F. Schmeckebier and Roy B. Eastin, *Government Publications and their Use* (1969 edn.)
Schulze (1983)   Suzanne Schulze, *Population Information in Nineteenth Century Census Volumes* (1983)

Schulze (1985)	Suzanne Schulze, *Population Information in Twentieth Century Census Volumes: 1900–1940* (1985)
SD	Senate Document
SED	Senate Executive Document
ser.	series *and* Congressional publication serial number
SL	NA, Special List
SMD	Senate Miscellaneous Document
Source	Arlene Eakle and Johni Cerny, *The Source: A Guidebook of American Geneaology* (1984)
SR	Senate Report
Sweet	William W. Sweet, *Religion on the American Frontier* (4 vols., 1926–46, repr. 1964)
T	NA microfilm (*followed by number*)
Trans./ *Trans.*	Transactions/ *Transactions*
T/S	Typescript
WNRC	NA, Washington National Records Center, Suitland, MD 20409
WPA	Work Projects Administration

In addition, the postal abbreviations for state names have been used

CHAPTER 1

Introduction

The term "community" has diverse meanings.[1] In this book it is taken to mean a group of people whose composition changed over time, occupying a particular territorial area smaller than a state – like a region, a county, a township, or a city, or perhaps a distinct part of a large city – and regarded, however vaguely, as an identifiable entity. The history of urban and rural communities so defined could quite justifiably be labeled "local history." The term "community history" has, however, been preferred because of the popular connection "local history" has had in recent times in the United States with antiquarianism and boosterism, with genealogy and associated family history, and with amateurism, rather than with the main stream of historical scholarship.

Traditionally American county and other local histories have been compilations of factual (often miscellaneous and unselected) data, narrowly based on readily available local sources, tradition, and hearsay, inadequately referenced and heavily laced with genealogical information on early settlers and prominent citizens. Usually they are essentially narrative in style and often of a self-congratulatory kind. If they answer questions, these are the obvious ones of what? and when? They often fall short of being serious historical works by failing to provide analysis of the facts collected, to tackle the nature of change, or to follow up answers to the basic questions by seeking to answer more serious ones, like how? and why? The worst have been written in a sort of vacuum by those ignorant of the histories of other communities and of national and regional trends and influences. Others have

---

[1] See, e.g., Kathleen N. Conzen, "Community studies, urban history, and American local history," in Michael Kammen (ed.), *The Past Before Us* (1980), 289–90.

regarded an assumed national history as the norm and used local history as largely illustrative of supposed general developments and events.

Local history thus has the reputation of being a harmless pastime for the eccentric, and the local historian is often seen as a dabbler in the past, interested in objects and facts simply because they are old, and to whom all facts are of equal value.[2] These are the hallmarks of amateurism and antiquarianism, and as long ago as the mid 1880s professional historians in the United States had come to regard their own field as national or general history, and local history as an inferior activity to be left to amateurs.[3] Indeed the view has been expressed that it is not the professional historian who will write the history of American communities, but "If the local history of the United States is to be written at all, it will have to be done by an interested, if amateur, citizen or group of citizens in each community."[4]

But the work of "amateurs" need not be "amateurish"; the intelligent layman willing to read widely in national and regional history as well as in the history of his locality, and to spend time acquainting himself with knowledge of the requisite sources and methods of using them, can produce as "professional" work as the salaried academic, though to reach such a level is not easy nor quickly achieved. The American Association for State and Local History, formed in 1940, has, through its publications, striven to broaden the knowledge and sharpen the expertise of serious amateur historians. Yet much of the output of local historians remains at a low level.

Some of this weakness may lie in the traditional association in America of local history with genealogy. The recent upsurge in so-called "local history" has been to a considerable extent as an adjunct of the type of family history which is an extension of genealogy (as opposed to the study of the family

[2] Dixon R. Fox, "Local history societies in the United States," *Canadian Hist. Rev.*, 13 (1952), 263; Philip D. Jordan, *The Nature and Practice of State and Local History* (1958), 30; Richard Shryock, cited Carol Kammen, *On Doing Local History* (1986), 34.
[3] David D. Van Tassell, *Recording America's Past* (1960), 171–9.
[4] Donald D. Parker, *Local History* (rev. Bertha E. Josephson, 1944; repr. 1979), xi.

as an institution). Most publications aimed at the amateur local historian appear to regard genealogy (and associated family history) as almost synonymous with local history. Thus to many librarians, archivists, and professional historians an expressed interest in local history is immediately assumed to indicate a central interest in genealogy and the history of the individual family. These observations are not intended to be antagonistic to genealogy and its family-history offshoot – these are worthwhile, and serious pursuits, requiring extensive skills and knowledge, and at times they overlap in their techniques and their topics of interest with local history. But they are distinct forms of endeavor. Genealogy is not history, and family history is not the same as local history. Genealogy and family history are not necessarily, or even often, rooted in a particular community over long periods, and by their very nature they tend to be concerned principally with the accumulation of basic factual data about individuals and families rather than with a wide spectrum of topics relating to communities as a whole.

In these circumstances it is not surprising that many American academics remain antagonistic to what they see as the second-rate popularization of history at the local level. Professional historians interested in the development of local communities have, therefore, tended to avoid labeling themselves local historians, preferring to be known as "social," "urban," "political," or "economic" historians.[5] Yet the study of local communities is a task serious historians should not be ashamed of undertaking: a generation or more of serious work in British and French universities supports this. Particularly in centuries before the present, the lives of many Americans centered in their local community. They were dominated by the local economy, the social life of the county, town, city, or neighborhood, the local churches and schools, local government and political affairs, and so on – rather than by what went on in Washington or even the state capital

[5] Louis Bisceglia, "Writers of small histories: local historians in the United States and Britain," *Local Historian*, 14 (1980). Cf. Gerald George, "State and local history," *Perspectives*, 23, 3 (1985).

(though, of course, such influences were in some aspects of life important). And they had their own distinct demographic, ethnic, and racial characteristics. Indeed it has been claimed that the history of local communities is the "fundamental basis of the American story."[6] Yet for many communities a detailed history is lacking, and for many others there is still great scope for serious research.

It is, nevertheless, true that although much of the expansion of interest in local and community history has been at the popular level, concentrating on the very recent past and associated with decorating the family tree, there has been a growth also in serious work undertaken by informed amateurs, at the undergraduate level and in schoolteaching, and also associated with the so-called "public history." Perhaps more significantly there has been an increase in historical research at the local level by graduate students and by professors, and a burgeoning awareness in academic circles of the importance of the local dimension in the interpretation of the American past. Moreover, growing availability of records through photographic reprints, including microforms, combined with the existence of large and often untapped collections of increasingly well cataloged records are making serious research into the history of local communities more and more feasible. Some sound histories of local communities were, of course, published in the earlier and middle decades of the present century,[7] while many historians then and later have made good use of local evidence in works of a more general kind. And in recent decades sophisticated work on colonial communities has been undertaken.

For nineteenth-century community studies the biggest advance has been in the field of urban history. Those involved have tended to be associated with the "new" social and political history, characterized by a concern with the place of groups and classes in society (looked at from the "bottom up" rather than concerned mainly with elites), by preference for quantifiable source materials and statistical methodology, and by the

---

[6] William B. Heseltine, quot. Jones, 119.
[7] E.g., Merle Curti et al., The Making of an American Community (1959).

application of social science theory. In this development there has also been evident a tendency to reflect present-day radical political viewpoints. The influence of social science and the belief in the use of the past to provide examples relevant to contemporary problems have led some scholars to a concern with the generic attributes of cities rather than to an interest in the unique experience of individual urban communities, their investigations of particular cities being regarded as case studies of general characteristics.[8]

The contribution of these "new urban historians" to the disciplined study of urban communities has been considerable. They have in particular opened up for detailed study such topics as demography, social structure, social mobility, grass-roots politics, and ethnicity and race. Community historians generally can learn much from their exploitation of certain types of sources and from their methodological approaches.

How far the recruitment of social science theory to the investigation of past communities is valuable must, however, be debatable. It has been argued that "sociology has little to offer history," that "there is no substitute for detailed historical research in understanding social change," and that "knowledge of specific historical sequence is more useful than abstract theorising."[9] Ideally historians should base their conclusions solely on the evidence they have accumulated and in the light of their general knowledge of their subject, bearing in mind that history differs from the social sciences in being interested in the particular, the unique, as well as in recurring similarities. Historians cannot, however, be unaware of explanations and theories about aspects of past and present societies propounded by their colleagues and by social scientists. Consciously or unconsciously such ideas are likely to be in their minds when they assess their own evidence. No harm, and possible advantage, can result, providing that evidence is not forced to fit preconceived theory.

---

[8] See, e.g., Stephan Thernstrom and Richard Sennett, *Nineteenth-Century Cities* (1969).
[9] Daniel Chirot, "Sociology and history," *HM*, 16 (1983), 123.

Potentially, however, the scope of local or community history as an academic study is broader than that of a source for case studies for the sociological investigation of urbanity, and is essentially part of the discipline of history. First, the history of local communities is an ingredient (though not in aggregate the totality) of regional, state, and national history. Without continuing research into certain aspects of the history of localities the task of refining and revising the generalized history of larger entities would be impossible. Second, however, the history of local communities is not merely the history of the nation or state writ small. Where regional and local differences were great in any aspect of life the assessment of general trends and hypothetical averages can be of only limited value in re-creating the past. As well as sharing in national and regional change, each American community, urban and rural, has a unique history worth studying in its own right, and "studying a universal process of urbanization," itself a worthy pursuit, nevertheless "offers no panacea for the problem of writing the history of a particular society."[10] All the world was not Philadelphia.[11] We cannot say "for Las Vegas see Salt Lake City"; those cities, relatively close to each other, no doubt had certain common characteristics and shared common experiences, but for ascertainable reasons they were, and are, essentially very different and merit individual histories. It is as worthy a task to study uniqueness as commonality.

Nevertheless, another possible function of local community history does lie in its use for the purposes of comparative study, if not necessarily to provide or confirm universal social theory. Though different communities had distinct historical experiences, some had much in common with others, and it is a proper extension of local history to seek to examine in a comparative way various communities in a state or region: to show what, for instance, industrial or farming communities of comparable size and antiquity had in common, and how and why aspects of life in them may have differed from those of clearly different sorts of community in an area. But, again, it is

[10] Conzen, "Community studies," 290.
[11] Cf. Sam B. Warner, "If all the world were Philadelphia," *AHR*, 74 (1968).

important in the comparative approach to seek to explain why some apparently very similar communities with many characteristics in common, yet also differed from each other in certain respects: why, for example, the experience of one Western mining community was not identical with that of another.

Another characteristic of the "new" history relevant to the community historian, the place of quantification and statistical methodology in historical research, has been a matter of dispute in recent years.[12] Now, however, the more extreme claims of supporters of these approaches have become muted as common sense has blunted the enthusiasm of novelty. At the same time many who had viewed these developments with suspicion now admit that they may have some merit.[13] In some of the following chapters it will be shown that the exploitation of quantifiable evidence by means of statistical techniques may have potential value for the student of certain aspects of the history of local communities. Such methods are perhaps most useful in demonstrating the relationship between variables at a particular moment in time (as, for instance, the connection between certain ethnic or religious characteristics and political attitudes in an election) rather than in the more difficult task of explaining the complexities of change over time.[14] They can sometimes perform a useful service by destroying unfounded hypotheses based purely on subjective interpretations of qualitative evidence. They can often add more precise meanings in place of historians' traditional use of assumption as to proportions or quantity (as "few," "less," "majority," "most," "increasing," and so forth) derived impressionistically from literary sources. Moreover, computers and statistical techniques can sometimes be used to tackle data too unwieldy to be employed in

[12] Robert W. Fogel and G. R. Elton, *Which Road to the Past? Two Views of History* (1983); Richard E. Beringer, *Historical Analysis* (1978), 193–202.
[13] Fogel and Elton, *Which Road?*, 67; Roderick Floud, "Quantitative history and people's history," *Hist. Workshop Jnl.*, 17 (1984; also in *Social Science Hist.*, 8 (1984)); David Herlihy, "Numerical and formal analysis in European history," *JIH*, 12 (1981), 115.
[14] Allan G. Bogue, "United States: the 'new' political history," in Robert P. Swierenga (ed.), *Quantification in American History* (1970), 50.

traditional approaches, and so to answer previously insoluble problems.[15] More often they produce what amounts to additional evidence relating to the problems being investigated, such fresh data themselves suggesting new and perhaps interesting questions.[16] Again, in some cases large-scale quantification exercises have produced stockpiles of machine-readable data that are at the disposal of other researchers.

It is thus sensible for the community historian to consider, where appropriate, adding to traditional methods the use of such statistical evidence as has survived or may be compiled from other sources. Though initially daunting to those with a traditional humane training, useful statistical methodology may with effort be acquired.[17] Failing that, assistance may be "bought in" where appropriate. And some new to statistical methods may be encouraged by the view that "crude methods . . . often capture meaning in quantitative data that more sophisticated analysis only refines."[18]

However, such methods do have limitations. They do not, for instance, obviate the need for the traditional skills of the historian in interpretation and explanation. Application of statistical techniques to quantifiable material handed down from the past may be dangerous if used in isolation. The provenance and context of such material should be fully comprehended and the evidence from other sources relevant to the topic taken into account.[19] The apparent precision and finality of statistics should not do away with linkage of evidence from as many diverse sources as possible. This is particularly needful considering that virtually all statistical information compiled in the nineteenth century is likely to be more or less

[15] Lawrence Stone, *The Past and the Present* (1981), 18; Fogel and Elton, *Which Road?*, 80.
[16] Cf. Eric H. Monkkonen, "The challenge of quantitative history," *HM*, 17 (1984), 92.
[17] See Charles M. Dollar and Richard Jensen, *Historian's Guide to Statistics* (1971); Roderick Floud, *An Introduction to Quantitative Methods for Historians* (1973); Edward Shorter, *The Historian and the Computer* (1971); Swierenga, *Quantification in American History*, bibl.; Nancy E. Fitch, "Statistical and mathematical methods for historians: an annotated bibliography . . .," *HMN*, 13 (1980), 222–31; Robert P. Swierenga, "Computers and American history," *JAH*, 60 (1973–4), 1,045–6.
[18] Allan G. Bogue, "Numerical and formal analysis in United States history," *JIH*, 12 (1981), 166.
[19] Cf. Bogue, "United States," 47.

incomplete and often to some degree inaccurate. Thus, like other types of historical evidence, the validity of past statistics needs to be assessed. Likewise fresh statistics compiled from nineteenth-century material may themselves be subject to problems of composition and interpretation.

Again, it should be understood that establishment of a relationship between one factor and another does not explain the reason for such a relationship; certainly positive correlation does not necessarily demonstrate a causal relationship. Moreover, statistical analysis "seldom isolates particular or unique phenomena" and may, therefore, not be useful for the historian dealing with a particular event.[20]

Above all, as subsequent chapters will show, for many important topics there is no statistical evidence, and many sources of information are not amenable to quantification. If research into the history of local communities were confined to factors that can be quantified, many significant aspects would have to be ignored.[21] Fortunately that is not necessary. It would be unfair to claim, as some have, that almost no important questions can be answered by statistical methods,[22] but certainly many important questions cannot. Even where quantitative approaches are possible they seldom alone solve important problems.[23] Everything points to the wisdom of the historian using such evidence as is available and such methods as are appropriate for particular purposes but where possible linking evidence from different sources.[24]

This book seeks to introduce the reader to a variety of types of sources, both quantitative and qualitative, which may be available for a spread of aspects of the history of U.S.

[20] E.g. Stephen L. Hansen, "The illusion of objectivism," *HM*, 12 (1979), 108; Edward Pessen, "Jacksonian quantification," in Herbert J. Bass (ed.), *The State of American History* (1970), 368; Morton Rothstein *et al.*, "Quantification and American history," in ibid., 314–15.

[21] Bogue, "United States," 47; Leo F. Schnore (ed.), *The New Urban History* (1975), 6.

[22] Arthur Schlesinger, Jr., "The humanist looks at empirical social research," *Am. Sociological Rev.*, 27 (1962), 770; Pessen, "Jacksonian quantification," 368.

[23] Val R. Lorwin and Jacob M. Price (eds.), *The Dimensions of the Past* (1972), 10.

[24] Samuel P. Hays, "Scientific versus traditional history," *HM*, 17 (1984); Bogue, "Numerical and formal analysis," 139, 157; Eric E. Lampard, "Two cheers for quantitative history," in Schnore, *New Urban History*, 47.

communities in the nineteenth century. It also attempts to supply references to, and some detail of, certain specific sources and sometimes individual collections. It should be stressed, however, that though much specific bibliographical material is alluded to in footnotes and there are many references to particular types of records, the book does not set out to be a general bibliography of community-history sources nor a union catalog of record collections. It would be quite impossible, moreover, to write a definitive or comprehensive guide to the source materials historians of American communities might find of value in their researches. Aside from the inevitable lack of omniscience in any author or group of authors, history is a living subject. Both the questions historians pose and seek to answer, and the topics in which they are interested, are always changing and being extended.

The chapters in this book are arranged by subjects. Most are prefaced by suggestions for topics which might be considered for investigation, though these are not exhaustive, and new questions to answer will arise as historians' interests change. The subject divisions of the chapters, too, are naturally artificial. Many researchers will be interested in topics which cut across those divisions (as, for instance, the effects of industrialization, and the relationship between one topic and another). Others will wish to investigate as wide a spectrum as possible so as to provide a rounded picture of a community in particular decades. Yet others may wish to compare certain aspects of life in one community with the same aspects in others, or to study a region and the various communities within it.

No exclusive readership is envisaged. Professors and students of history, both undergraduates and particularly graduate students, will hopefully find the book of use, as may serious amateur historians, and schoolteachers interested in using community-source material in the classroom.[25] Again, although not written with genealogists or family historians in mind, it may be that information useful for their purposes will

---

[25] See Kathleen Roe, *Teaching with Historical Records* (1981); Fay D. Metcalf and Matthew T. Downey, *Using Local History in the Classroom* (1982); NA, *Teaching with Documents* (1989).

be found in these pages. And those sociologists interested in using historical evidence, both of a quantitative and a qualitative kind, may well find a wider array of possible source material noted here than is commonly utilized by social scientists.

Some guidance to techniques of using the evidence obtainable from the sources discussed has been provided. Lack of space, however, dictates that this cannot always be as comprehensive or as detailed as may be necessary for researchers to put the methods into practice. References have, however, been made in the notes to works which will assist the researcher by providing suggestions and outlining the strengths and weaknesses of specific types of evidence.

The subsequent sections of this introductory chapter include a survey of types of sources and of certain unique sources useful for the study of a variety of topics, as well as references to basic bibliographical sources and guides to published and unpublished records. The remaining chapters are arranged topically, but since some sources are of use for topics covered in more than one chapter, cross-referencing seeks to obviate unnecessary repetition. The index will also guide the reader to where the same sort of source material is referred to in different places.

Although great quantities of evidence are to be found in state, county, and city archives, much of it underused by historians, it is unlikely that for any particular community all the types of source material alluded to in the text will exist. The records of many counties and cities have not been well preserved, particularly for periods before 1900, and especially in the South.[26] In some cases even extant records may be difficult of access. Sometimes official records have been handed over to private individuals and institutions, in others they are in county court houses and the like (where the prime concern is not the needs of the historical researcher) or placed

[26] Leo J. Mahoney, "The state of Penn's archives," *Western Pennsylvania Hist. Mag.* NS, 69 (1986); J. M. Scammell, "Local archives and the study of government," *AA*, 2 (1939), 235; J. G. de R. Hamilton, "Three centuries of Southern records, 1607–1907," *JSoH*, 10 (1944); O. Lawrence Burnette, Jr., *Beneath the Footnote* (1969), 181–2.

in inaccessible places. "Most of the earliest city records of Wichita [Kansas]," we are told, "are stored in the salt mines at Hutchinson, and it is difficult for scholars to gain access to them."[27] Private collections may be even more difficult to trace.

For these reasons, and also because of their intrinsic value, some stress has been laid in this volume on the significance for local research of state and of federal records, published and unpublished. Few good histories of local communities can be written without the use of evidence deriving from such extra-local sources. The investigator needs, however, to be aware that, as with many records, the reports of state and federal commissions and committees and the like, together with accompanying testimony, are often political documents which may have been tailored or influenced to suit some particular interests, and should not necessarily be taken at their face value. Other records, like the censuses, may have been compiled honestly but sometimes inefficiently, and data presented in them cannot be regarded as always completely accurate.

For various reasons certain aspects of the history of individual communities receive little or no attention in this book. Lack of space has made it impossible to cover the extensive array of sources available for the study of military operations during the War of 1812, the Civil War, and the various Indian wars, though the campaigns certainly affected many communities in certain parts of the country.[28] Again, no attempt has been made to cover sources for the history of parts of America

[27] W. Craig Miller, *Wichita: The Early Years, 1865–80* (1982), 185.
[28] But see Prucha, 155–61; HG, secs. 45–6; S. Kinnell (ed.), *Military History of the United States: An Annotated Bibliography* (1986); John R. Sellers (comp.), *Civil War Manuscripts: A Guide to the Collection in the . . . Library of Congress* (1986); Dallas Irvine (comp.), *Military Operations of the Civil War: A Guide-Index to the Official Records of the Union and Confederate Armies* (NA, 5 vols., 1966–80); Munden and Beers; Henry P. Beers (comp.), *The Confederacy: Guide to the Archives of the Confederate States of America* (1968, rev. 1986); Charlotte M. Ashby *et al.* (comps.), *Civil War Maps in the National Archives* (1964, rev. 1986). For military posts, see HG, sec. 13(4). Sometimes military records contain data on local conditions: Elaine C. Everly, "State and local history sources in the Military Archives Division," in Timothy Walch (comp.), *Our Family, Our Town* (1987), 27.

before they became part of the United States. Largely omitted, too, is guidance on aspects of history which require a technical knowledge not normally at the disposal of even the trained historian – such as archaeology and geology. Also not dealt with are aspects of the cultural life of individual communities, such as folklore, drama, music, art, leisure activities, and so forth. These are topics too disparate for detailed advice in a book of this kind, however desirable it is that they should not be ignored. Oral history (or more properly the collection and use of oral evidence) has not been covered, since this volume is confined to the nineteenth century. By now the number of possible subjects able to recall life before 1900 must be insignificant. Reference to such evidence collected in earlier decades and recorded has, however, been made.

The study of local place-names may be mentioned briefly here. Place-names do not have the same significance as historical sources in the U.S. as they do in Europe, where they can be used to illuminate long-past centuries. Nevertheless they may give some clue as to the places of origin or the ethnic character of early settlers, the names of founders, the approximate dates of foundation, or the dominant features of the landscape at the time of exploration or settlement. Others recollect the existence of former Indian occupants of the land,[29] or significant past events occurring there. There are a number of bibliographies and guides, some for particular states.[30] Many records may give a clue to early names. Wills, for instance, may refer to names of fields and streams now forgotten.[31]

Family structure is given some attention in chapter 2. The whole field of family relationships, the place of women in local communities, child-rearing practices, child life, and allied subjects, which are undoubtedly proper fields for study, are

---

[29] See, e.g., Otto R. Landelius, *Swedish Place-Names in North America* (ed. Raymond Jarvi, trans. Karin Franzen, 1985); William A. Reed, *Indian Place Names in Alabama* (1984 edn.).

[30] Citations in Prucha, 129–30; *HG*, 49; Henry Gannett, *The Origin of Certain Place Names in the United States* (Geological Survey, 1905, repr. 1973); Wilbur Zelinsky, *The Cultural Geography of the United States* (1973).

[31] See, e.g., Arthur Hecht and William J. Heynen, *Records of the Post Office Department Relating to Place Names* (RIP 72, 1971); Jones, 143.

not, however, dealt with as distinct topics.[32] It would be difficult to prescribe specific and commonly available types of source for such subjects in individual communities; many of the records detailed in various chapters, however, will yield relevant evidence.

The American Association for State and Local History has published several volumes on physical sources[33] – artifacts of various kinds including museum collections, buildings and architecture, and historical sites generally – and there are other works, too, which offer similar guidance.[34] This type of source and associated topics have not, therefore, been covered in this volume, [35] though a few words may be said here on buildings.

Remarks on and descriptions and sometimes illustrations of buildings appear in many nineteenth-century publications, like guide books, newspapers, directories, travelers' writings, and so on, as well as in monographs devoted particularly to local architecture – such as Thompson Westcott's *The Historic Mansions and Buildings of Philadelphia*.[36] Other contemporary sources include bird's-eye-view maps, photographs, fire-insurance records, deeds, land records, and so forth.[37] The records of the federal Public Buildings Service in the National Archives (RG 121) contain much detail on public buildings (like court houses, post offices, customhouses) from about 1833.[38]

[32] But see citations Prucha, 174–9; *HG*, 444–6; Susan Kleinberg, "The systematic study of urban women," *HMN*, 9 (1975); Elizabeth H. Pleck, "Women's history," in James B. Gardner and George R. Adams (eds.), *Ordinary People and Everyday Life* (1983); Margaret Walsh, "Women in America," *Historian* (London), 16 (Autumn, 1987).

[33] E.g., Thomas J. Schlereth, *Artifacts and the American Past* (1981); David E. Kyvig and Myron A. Marty, *Nearby History* (1982); Thomas E. Felt, *Researching, Writing and Publishing Local History* (1976), 56–62; Kammen, *On Doing Local History*, 65–76. N.B. American Association of Museums and National Register Publishing Co., *Official Museums Directory* (1986).

[34] E.g., David Weitzman, *Underfoot* (1976); Thomas J. Schlereth (ed.), *Material Culture* (1985); Ian M. G. Quimby (ed.), *Material Culture and the Study of American Life* (1978); Makower; Burnette, *Beneath the Footnote*, 337–8. For sites, see *The National Register of Historic Places* (National Park Service, biennial).

[35] Except for educational buildings: see p. 469.

[36] John Fondersmith, "American architectural guidebooks," T/S (1980) (American Urban Guides, Box 186, Washington, DC 20044); Schlereth, *Artifacts*, 35.

[37] See pp. 33–4, 58, 59–60, 171–9, 211–13, 383–5.

[38] *GNA*, 545–6.

Introduction

A great deal of research on historic buildings and vernacular architecture has been published in recent decades, much of it relating to particular regions, states, and cities.[39] The Historic American Buildings Survey has documented over 20,000 buildings, structures, and sites in over 45,000 photographs, thousands of pages of architectural and historical information, and 34,000 measured drawings. A recent checklist (to be updated regularly) includes almost 17,000 entries for fifty states and three territories.[40] The records are held in the Library of Congress but are available in microfiche arranged by states, counties, and places.[41] For a number of states and three cities (Philadelphia, Washington, DC, and Chicago) local catalogs have been published.[42] The *National Register of Historic Places*[43] covers buildings (including churches) and industrial landmarks like old railroads, canals, furnaces, and so on. Similar registers have been prepared for individual states by state and local historical societies, heritage groups, and preservation commissions.[44] G. E. Kidder Smith, *The Architecture of the United States: An Illustrated Guide to Notable Buildings* (3 vols., 1981) is also useful. For those wishing to take such surveys further and record buildings themselves, or to trace the history of particular houses, there are a number of advisory texts.[45]

[39] See, e.g., Carl W. Condit, "Architectural history in the United States," in Kellogg and Walker; John Fondersmith, "Everything you ever wanted to know about guidebooks," *Historic Preservation* (March/April 1982); John Fondersmith, "Architectural guidebooks," *AIA Jnl.* (Dec. 1976); *American Urban Guidenotes*, 4, 1 (1985); Schlereth, *Artifacts*, 195–7.

[40] In *Historic America: Buildings, Structures and Sites* (Library of Congress, 1983): embraces also the Historic American Engineering Record. See also William L. Labovich, *America's City Halls* (1984); B. Lowry (ed.), *The County Court Houses of America* (text and microfiche, 2 vols., 1982); Richard Pare, *Court House: A Photographic Document* (1978).

[41] From Chadwyck-Healey Inc., 417 Maitland Ave., Teaneck, NJ 07666.

[42] These incl. NH, IA, ME, MA, MI, NJ, TX, UT, VA, WI, GA, AL, CA. Inf. from National Park Service, Dept. of the Interior, Washington, DC 20240.

[43] U.S. Dept. of the Interior, 2 vols., 1976 (replaces earlier vols. and supplements).

[44] N.B. National Trust for Historic Preservation in the United States, *Directory of American Preservation Commissions* (1981).

[45] E.g., Harley J. McKee (comp.), *Recording Historic Buildings* (1970); John J.-G. Blumenson, *Identifying American Architecture* (1978); Marcus Whiffen, *American Architecture Since 1780* (1969); Carole Rifkind, *A Field Guide to American Architecture* (1980); Weitzman, *Underfoot*, 156–70. And see Barbara J. Howe *et al.*, *Houses and Homes* (1987); Linda V. Ellsworth, *The History of a House and How to Trace It* (AASLH, 1976); works cited Kyvig and Marty, *Nearby History*, 182.

Finally, while urban and rural topography or landscape and townscape history is a topic not dealt with here, many of the records described in various chapters (especially cartographic sources, land-holding and settlement records, travelers' descriptions, local government records, and records relating to communications) will shed light on the subject, as will study of the landscape and townscape on the ground.[46]

It has been said that "The riches that lie in countless repositories can be mined productively only if the seeker knows what he is looking for, where he may expect to find it, and how to recognize it."[47] The remainder of this volume offers the seeker some guidance.

PUBLISHED SOURCES, SECONDARY AND PRIMARY

Before embarking on original research the historian of local communities should find out what work has already been undertaken on the place and topic he has chosen for his endeavors. The first step is to acquire a working knowledge of the older state, county, and city histories, standard modern works, and recent books and articles relating to the area being studied. For particular subjects some acquaintance with general histories of the topic and recent research on it in other localities may well be essential. Fortunately there are a number of very good bibliographies and bibliographies of bibliographies which reduce the need to provide detailed lists of titles here. In particular references to the *Harvard Guide to American History* which gives a good deal of attention to regional studies, and Francis Prucha's *Handbook*, which provides up-to-date bibliographical references, should be consulted.[48] Also useful are the American Government and Information Guide Series published by the Gale Research Company, and the

---

[46] And see, Schlereth, *Artifacts*, ch. 7; May T. Watts, *Reading the Landscape of America* (1975).

[47] Philip C. Brooks, quot. Richard S. Maxwell, "State and local history sources in the Civil Division," in Walch, *Our Family, Our Town*, 31.

[48] See *HG* and Prucha in list of abbreviations. And see Henry P. Beers, *Bibliographies in American History* (rev. 1942); Henry P. Beers, *Bibliographies in American History, 1942–1978* (2 vols., 1982); Eugene P. Sheehy, *Guide to Reference Books* (1986 edn.).

Goldentree Bibliographies, and bibliographies published by ABC-Clio. There are, too, bibliographies of secondary works relating to particular regions, states, and localities, as well as general bibliographies of local history.[49] The Writers' Program and the Federal Writers' Project of the Work Projects Administration produced in the late 1930s and early 1940s a number of useful histories of and guides to various states and individual places.[50]

During his research the investigator will feel the need to consult much secondary work. The whereabouts of many publications may be traced (by author, etc.) through the *National Union Catalog, Pre-1956 Imprints* (754 vols., 1968–81) and the supplementary and ongoing *National Union Catalog* (1963–   ).[51] The *National Union Catalogs* cover the holdings of many libraries but the most substantial are those of the Library of Congress, and it may be that serious researchers will need to visit that library on occasions. Its published subject catalogs will be of value.[52] Another library with enormous holdings is the New York Public Library.[53] Many other libraries have published catalogs.[54]

Many items of use to community historians will, however, be in the form of articles rather than books.[55] Some of these will be in the transactions of state and other local history societies,[56] and others in national or other general periodical

[49] *HG*, sec. 12; Prucha, 111–14, 215–18; Nelli Schreiner-Yantis (comp.), *Genealogical and Local History Books in Print* (2 vols., 1985).

[50] See *NUC* (see next paragraph) under "US Work Projects Administration, Writers' Program" and "Federal Writers' Project"; and below p. 45.

[51] See Prucha, 8–9 for details.

[52] See Prucha, 9–10 for details. Also useful is Library of Congress Main Catalog, 1890–1980, providing access by subject and title as well as author, etc., available in microform (K. G. Saur, 1984–8).

[53] See *Dictionary Catalog of the Research Libraries of the New York Public Library, 1911–1971* (800 vols., 1979); Carman and Thompson (1962). See also Library of Congress, *Dictionary Catalog of the History of the Americas* (37 vols., 1961, 1974).

[54] See Bonnie R. Nelson, *A Guide to Published Library Catalogs* (1982); Prucha, 12–16 (esp. [B35]), 17–18.

[55] For union lists for finding locations of periodicals, see Prucha, 41. And see Dale Steiner (comp.), *Historical Journals* (1981); Janet Fyfe (comp.), *Historical Journals and Serials* (1986).

[56] *HG*, 121–7; Milton Crouch and Hans Raum (eds.), *Directory of State and Local History Periodicals* (1977). See also *Directory of Historical Societies and Agencies in North America* (AASLH, current edn.).

publications, so that indexes to these serials,[57] and abstracting publications, like *America: History and Life* (1964–), *Historical Abstracts* (1955–),[58] and *Recently Published Articles* (1976–),[59] may prove useful. Large libraries may have facilities for computer searches. The *American Historical Review*, the *Journal of Southern History*, and other well-known historical journals publish reviews and from time to time lists of new books and articles. The series *Writings on American History* provides an index to both books and articles published in most years since 1902.[60] Much recent research exists also in the form of dissertations and theses.[61]

Biographies may be secondary material or, if written in the nineteenth century, primary sources. Autobiographies for our purpose are all likely to be primary rather than secondary evidence. It is convenient, however, to mention them together here. There are some well-known compilations of biographies,[62] as well as bibliographies for finding others.[63] Obituaries are another useful type of biography.[64] Guides to genealogies, many of which may have local significance, are too numerous to list here.[65]

For original evidence the community historian will need to

[57] *HG*, 63–6; Marie S. Ensign and Barbara H. Pope (eds.), *Historical Periodicals Directory: Volume I* (1983); Neil L. Shumsky and Timothy Crimmins (eds.), *Urban America: A Historical Bibliography* (1983). Regional guides incl. Oscar O. Winther, *A Classified Bibliography of the Periodical Literature of the Trans-Mississippi West (1811–1957)* (1961) and *Supplement (1957–67)* (1970); Gertrude C. Gilmer, *Checklist of Southern Periodicals to 1861* (1934).

[58] *HG*, 66; Prucha, 36–7, q.v. (36–43) for other indexes, union lists, catalogs, and directories of periodicals.

[59] Formerly publ. *AHR*.

[60] For details, see Prucha, 19–21.

[61] See Prucha, 63–6.

[62] See Prucha, 68–70; *Dictionary of American Biography* (20 vols., supplements and index, 1928–81).

[63] See Prucha, 72–7, and below, pp. 157, 317–18; Robert F. Sayre, "The proper study: autobiographies in American studies," *Am. Q.*, 27 (1977) (pp. 258–9 for bibls.); Susan K. Kinnell (ed.), *People in History: An Index to U.S. and Canadian Biographies in History Journals and Periodicals* (2 vols., 1988; articles from 1976); K. G. Saur, *American Biographical Archive* (1986–8) cumulates on microfiche inf. from *c.*400 biographical reference works.

[64] See Prucha, 72.

[65] But see Marion J. Kaminkow (ed.), *Genealogies in the Library of Congress* (2 vols., 1972), *Complement* (1981), *Supplements* covering 1972–6 (1977), and 1976–86 (1987); ABC-Clio, *American Family History: A Historical Bibliography* (1984).

cast his net wide to embrace both published and unpublished material, not all of which will be available locally. Three sorts of published primary sources exist. First, there are original materials which have later been put into published form. Historical societies, state and municipal governments, universities, libraries, and other institutions in many states have published nineteenth-century records of wide variety.[66] The National Historical Publications Commission (now the National Historical Publications and Records Commission) has sponsored publication of the papers of numerous eminent persons which sometimes include evidence of local significance.[67] The National Archives and Records Administration (henceforth referred to as the National Archives) has published the *Territorial Papers of the United States*,[68] consisting of extracts from various National Archives record groups relating to many aspects of life in the territories, 1787–1845, a most useful publication.[69]

A second group of published primary material exists in the shape of microform editions of originally published and unpublished records and other materials. So rapidly growing is this source that it is difficult to keep up with what is available.[70] In the following pages references are made to the existence of many microform publications, but no claim to comprehensiveness is made.

The nineteenth-century publications of federal, state, and local governments, and many contemporary private

---

[66] Many are in Marion J. Kaminkow, *United States Local Histories in the Library of Congress* (5 vols., 1975); *NUC*; *Writings on American History*, etc. For societies which have published records see Walter M. Whitehill, *Independent Historical Societies* (1962). The Library of Congress (see *NUC*) and the New York Public Library (Carman and Thompson (1962)), esp., have records for many parts of the country.

[67] *National Historical Publications and Records Commission: Publications Catalog* (1976) (includes microform edns.); Robert L. Brubaker, "The publication of historical sources," *Library Q.*, 37 (1967).

[68] Clarence E. Carter (ed.) (26 vols., 1934–64); John P. Bloom (ed.) (1969–). The first 26 vols. form M721 (and see M236). See Clarence E. Carter, "The Territorial Papers of the United States," *AA*, 8 (1945).

[69] See also David W. Parker, *Calendar of Papers in the Washington Archives relating to the Territories of the United States (to 1873)* (1911). For other collections of "Territorial Papers," see below, p. 41.

[70] See current edn. *Guide to Microforms in Print*; Hoornstra.

publications, including law reports, newspapers, pamphlets, directories, gazetteers, and the like, form a third group of original evidence available in printed form. These are a rich source of information for many localities on many topics. They are dealt with in detail later, but some general remarks may be made here.

The published and unpublished records of the federal government are one of the main sources of information on many aspects of the history of American communities across the nation. Even to experienced historians, however, their sheer bulk and complexity are intimidating. Their use may, however, be facilitated by a rudimentary knowledge of the organization of the federal government and the functions and history of its agencies,[71] and by a brief outline here of the main federal publications.

Many federal publications, or documents, may be found in large libraries in their original form,[72] or in microform.[73] There are a number of good general introductions, some of which provide bibliographical references to more detailed guides which help the researcher to identify particular documents.[74] Perhaps most useful are the official *Checklist of United States Public Documents, 1789–1909* (1911, repr. 1953),[75] and the *CIS US Serial Set Index* (see below). Some older works remain useful,[76] while from 1895 onwards the *Monthly Catalog of*

---

[71] See Donald B. Whitnah (ed.), *Government Agencies* (1983); Ann M. Boyd and Rae E. Rips (eds.), *United States Government Publications* (1949).

[72] *Directory of Government Collections and Librarians* (ALA, current edn.). Also available in NA: *Looking for an Out-of-Print U.S. Government Publication?* (NA, General Inf. Leaflet 28, 1986).

[73] *Guide to Microforms in Print*. And see James A. Downey, *U.S. Federal Government Publications* (1978), 34–40; *HG*, 109–10; CIS, *CIS US Serial Set on Microfiche* (see below).

[74] See particularly Palic (cited in List of abbreviations), esp. citations, 12–15; Joe Morehead, *Introduction to United States Public Documents* (3rd edn., 1983); Edward Herman, *Locating United States Government Information* (1983); Downey, *U.S. Federal Official Publications*; Joseph K. Lu, *U.S. Government Publications Relating to the Social Sciences* (1975); Schmeckebier and Eastin (see List of abbreviations); Baker, *Finding List*. See also Prucha, 84 [M16]; *United States Government Publications* (16 vols., 1980), reprint of *NUC, Pre-1956 Imprints*, vols. 609–24.

[75] There are commercially produced microform edns. and various published indexes: for details, see Morehead, *Introduction*, 126; Downey, *U.S. Federal Government Publications*, 36–7.

[76] See Prucha, 82–3.

United States Public Documents (known as the *Monthly Catalog*) provides a comprehensive bibliography.[77]

Numerous federal documents useful to the local historian are to be found in the so-called US (or Congressional) Serial Set. This embraces committee reports, journals, and administrative reports of the House of Representatives and the Senate, together with much executive-branch material, particularly annual reports of departments and agencies, and much miscellaneous material. Citations in following chapters will testify to the variety and value of these records. The Serial Set is divided into "Documents" and "Reports" and according to whether pertaining to the Senate or the House. Thus there are "Senate Reports" (from 1847) and "House Reports" (from 1819), and "Senate Documents" (from 1817) and "House Documents" (from 1817). Between 1847 and 1895 the "Documents" of each house were divided into "Executive Documents" and "Miscellaneous Documents." In addition the journals of proceedings of both Senate and House form part of the Serial Set.

Although not all these publications carry titles with full reference citations, such references have been allotted to them and can be found in the *Checklist*.[78] It is usual to refer to the "Documents" and "Reports" by number (as Senate Report 46), Congress and session (as 49th Congress, 1st session), and increasingly by their Congressional serial number (which indicates the volume in which bound): thus the *Report of the Senate Select Committee on Interstate Commerce* is referenced as SR 46 (49–1) (2 parts), ser. 2356–7.

Serial numbers were allotted to nearly all Congressional publications from 1817.[79] In 1895 such numbers were retrospectively applied to the *American State Papers*, a collection of executive and legislative documents selected from the manuscript and printed papers of both Houses and of various

---

[77] Recently repr.: Carrollton Press, 1647 Wisconsin Ave., Washington, DC 20007. Note, too, the periodic *Index to the Subjects of the Documents and Reports and to the Committees, Senators and Representatives Presenting Them*, known as the *Document Index* (1895–1933); Prucha, 82 [M5].

[78] Also in CIS, *CIS US Serial Set Index* and the *Tables* of 1902 (see below).

[79] But not records of debates, for which see below.

departments. These were arranged in sets of volumes (I–X) by subject matter, the most important for the community historian being sets II on *Indian Affairs* (covering 1789–1827), III *Finance* (1789–1828), IV *Commerce and Navigation* (1789–1823), VII *Post Office Department* (1790–1833), and VIII *Public Lands* (1789–1837).[80] To some extent they are being superseded for the period 1789–1817 by the *National State Papers: Texts and Documents*, a reproduction of the most important documents mentioned in the Congressional journals of proceedings.[81]

An invaluable index to the Serial Set (including the *American State Papers*) is provided in the *CIS US Serial Set Index, 1789–1969* (1975–9) and where available is to be preferred to the *Checklist* and other guides for tracking down publications.[82] It lists documents under key words and subjects (including places) and also provides means of identifying the nature of documents for which only the Congress, session, and document number are known. The CIS has reproduced all the Serial Set documents in microfiche, so that many federal documents previously difficult to locate are increasingly available for research.

Documents in the Serial Set significant for the study of community history include reports of *ad hoc* committees and commissions, and the annual reports and other publications of executive departments, bureaus, offices, and other agencies of the federal government, many of which are referred to in later chapters.[83] Very important are the published volumes, abstracts, compendia, reports, and bulletins which present the findings of the decennial federal censuses on the demography and many other social and economic aspects of local communities throughout the nation (though not all federal census publications are in the Serial Set).

The value of the censuses for various topics is examined in

---

[80] For details, see Prucha, 89; and, for various series of State Papers, Schmeckebier and Eastin, 9. Available in microfilm.

[81] By 1985, 59 vols. (to 1801) publ. (by Michael Glazier, Inc.).

[82] Publ. CIS. Pts. I–V cover the nineteenth century. The "User Guide" provides in each pt. an introduction to the set. Less detailed but still useful is the *Tables* of 1902 (see Prucha, 85 [M231]).

[83] Not all are in the Serial Set. The *Checklist* includes many official publics. that are not.

detail in subsequent chapters. There specific references to data below the level of states (counties, cities, municipalities, townships, wards, and so on) have been noted. Keys to the contents of the census volumes and their organization are provided by Dubester and in more detail by Schulze.[84] Some large libraries have complete sets but regrettably too many do not. Fortunately there is now a microfilm edition,[85] so that they should become increasingly accessible. Mention may be made here of the annual *Statistical Abstract of the United States* (from 1878) which provides statistical information on many aspects of public life – mostly at the national and state levels, but sometimes providing more local data.[86]

Detailed records of Congressional debates do not form part of the Serial Set. For the nineteenth century we do not have verbatim accounts of the debates in the Senate and House, but from the middle of the century the published proceedings become increasingly near an exact daily record.[87] Four series comprise the transactions of Congress:[88] the *Annals of Congress* (covering 1789–1824), the *Register of Debates* (1824–37), the *Congressional Globe* (1833–73), and the *Congressional Record* (from 1873).[89] More succinct records of the proceedings of Congress, omitting speeches, but including motions, actions taken, and votes or divisions, are to be found in the *Senate Journal*,[90] and the *House Journal* (which from 1817 to 1953 are not included in the Serial Set).[91] Each volume is separately indexed.[92] The passage of bills can be traced through the

---

[84] Dubester (1950); Schulze (1983); Schulze (1985) (see abbreviations). See also Carrol D. Wright and William C. Hunt, *The History and Growth of the United States Census* (1900), 911–14.

[85] See *Bibliography and Reel Index: A Guide to the Microfilm Edition of the United States Decennial Census Publications, 1790–1970* (Research Publications, Inc., Woodbridge, CT, 1975).

[86] See *Checklist*, 1,184. Supplementary is the periodically published *Historical Statistics of the United States* (from 1949).

[87] See Brock, 107–10, for deficiencies in the records of debates.

[88] For varying titles, arrangement, and indexes, see Palic, 24–5; Schmeckebier and Eastin, 134–43; Baker, *Finding List*, 8–22.

[89] Available in microfiche.

[90] There is a Library of Congress microfilm of vols. covering 1789–1965, with indexes.

[91] For reprints of earlier vols. see Prucha, 86–7.

[92] For general indexes to 1821, see Palic, 26.

Journals.[93] For the Civil War period in the South there is the *Journals of the Congress of the Confederate States of America, 1861–1865* (1904).[94]

The records of Congressional committees investigating proposed legislation or other matters form another important body of information on a wide spectrum of topics. "Hearings" contain the testimony of witnesses (including experts, members of Congress, and members of the public) before committees. Frequently, opposing viewpoints and interests are illustrated, and additional material, such as submitted letters and reports, may be appended. Hearings, therefore, contain much detailed evidence – including statistical material – of interest to historians, especially on social and economic matters.

But hearings are not always easy to track down, few having been published until the latter part of the nineteenth century, except where they appear in the Serial Set.[95] Most, however, were not technically Congressional publications, though often treated as such. They are to be found in various places including the libraries of the Senate and the House, the Library of Congress,[96] and the National Archives (discussed below). Ancillary to hearings are "Prints," which consist of studies on proposed legislation requested by committees. They have been underused by historians, but access to them has now been facilitated by a new index.[97]

Federal legislation often had specific significance for particular areas and communities. Public laws were first published as "slip laws." For the period 1789 to 1873 they were

[93] Many printed bills are in the Library of Congress and have been microfilmed: Prucha, 91.

[94] SD 234 (58–2), ser. 4610–16 (since repr.).

[95] An incomplete list of hearings (under names of committees and subjects) is in *Checklist*, 1,532–652.

[96] The most up-to-date index is CIS, *CIS US Congressional Committee Hearings Index. Pt. I* (42 vols., 1981–5) (all those listed are in microfiche: *CIS US Congressional Hearings on Microfiche Full Collection*). For older indexes, see Schmeckebier and Eastin, 166–7.

[97] CIS, *CIS US Congressional Committee Prints Index from the Earliest Publications through 1969* (5 vols., 1980).

reprinted commercially, with private laws, as *Statutes at Large of the United States*, a series continued for later years by the State Department. Laws, public and private, are presented in chronological order and there are contemporary and more recent analytical indexes.[98] The topics which were the subject for legislation were legion, covering many aspects of life in numerous localities.

For territories before they became states the annual reports of governors are federal documents (of the Department of the Interior) which contain much general information on economic, social, and demographic matters, sometimes with references to particular places.

Other published sources containing information on a variety of local matters are the reports of cases in the federal and state courts. Unfortunately the volumes in which they appear do not usually have topographical indexes so that a comprehensive survey of their content is usually not practicable. If, however, the existence of particular cases and their approximate dates[99] are known, information on them may be identified. A number of bibliographical guides exists of which the most comprehensive is that of Price and Bitner, which embraces not only compilations of cases in the federal and more important state courts but also, where they exist, those for more particularly local courts.[100]

The decisions of the United States Supreme Court, published from 1790, were named, in 1875, the *United States Reports*, and the title is usually conferred retrospectively on

---

[98] See Schmeckebier and Eastin, ch. 8. Laws of 1789–1837 are also found in *Annals of Congress* and *Register of Debates*; those of 1852–73 in *Congressional Globe*. *Statutes at Large*, vol. 8 has index for vols. 1–8, later vols. have own indexes. See also Boyd and Rips, *United States Government Publications*, 86–7. Available in microfiche.

[99] Law reps. are publ. in order of decision date.

[100] Miles O. Price and Harry Bitner, *Effective Legal Research*, App. I (1969 edn.: more recent edns. do not give this inf.). See also Charles C. Soule, *The Lawyer's Reference Manual of Law Books and Citations* (2nd edn. 1884); Mary R. Chapman, *Bibliographical Index to the State Reports Prior to the National Reporter System* (1977), a guide to the microfilm edn. of these reps.; Morris L. Cohen and Robert C. Berring, *How to Find the Law* (8th edn. 1983). app. P; Prucha, 117–20.

volumes for earlier years.[101] The two series *Federal Cases*[102] and *Federal Reporter*[103] provide annotated reports of all decisions on cases in the U.S. circuit and district courts. Since these reports were organized on a geographical basis they can sometimes be useful for local studies. There are also published reports on cases in the state courts – the *Rhode Island Reports*, for instance, began publication in 1828. From the late 1870s the National Reporter System, a private venture, has published editions of the law reports for the appellate courts of all states and the state courts.[104] For many of the series noted here (for both federal and state courts) there are digests and sometimes annotated reports.[105]

The published documents of the governments of the individual states constitute a rich source of evidence on many aspects of the history of communities within their boundaries, as will be illustrated in later chapters. As in the case of the federal government, there are state documents relating to both legislatures and executive departments, as well as reports of

[101] Vols. from 1875 are numbered 91 onwards, numbers 1–90 being accorded to earlier volumes. For details of earlier edns., see Schmeckebier and Eastin, 278–83. The *Lawyers' Edition Supreme Court Reports* may be used as an index (1st ser. covers to 1956).

[102] *Federal Cases, Comprising Cases Argued . . . in the Circuit and District Courts . . . to the beginning of the Federal Reporter* [1789–1879] (31 vols., 1894–7, since repr.). Vol. 1 has a chronological table of the various circuits with their geographic limits since 1789. See Downey, *U.S. Federal Official Publications*, 108–9. Available in microfiche.

[103] From 1880; vols. 1–104 cover to 1900; also includes selected cases (mainly relating to taxes) of the U.S. Court of Claims.

[104] *Atlantic Reporter* (1885–) (ME, NH, VT, RI, CT, PA, NJ, DE, MD); *Northeastern Reporter* (1885–) (MA, OH, IN, IL, NY); *Northwestern Reporter* (1879–) (MN, WI, IA, MI, NB, ND, SD); *Pacific Reporter* (1884–) (CA, CO, KS, OR, NV, AZ, ID, MT, WA, WY, UT, NM); *Southwestern Reporter* (1887–) (VA, WV, NC, SC, GA); *Southern Reporter* (1887–) (AL, LA, FL, MS); *Southwestern Reporter* (1887–) (MO, AR, TN, KY, TX).

[105] See Price and Bitner, *Effective Legal Research*; Soule, *Lawyer's Reference Manual*; and, e.g., *United States Supreme Court Digest, 1754 to Date* (15 vols., various impressions); *Supreme Court Reporter* (annotations) (from 1882); *Federal Digest, 1754 to Date* (72 vols., 1940–56) (for all federal court cases); *American Law Reports, Annotated* (from 1919; there is a 12-vol. digest to the first 175 vols.; the last vol. of the digest has a table of cases alphabetically arranged, incl. entries under names of some cities); *Century Edition of the American Digest . . . to 1896* (50 vols., 1897–1904); *First Decennial Edition of the American Digest . . . from 1897 to 1906* (25 vols., 1908–12). There are digests, too, for particular states (and for National Reporter System series).

special commissions, and so forth. State documents are most likely to be found in state and other large libraries.[106] For thirteen states an excellent detailed guide has been compiled by Adelaide Hasse. Some states have produced their own guides and check lists and there are some other general guides, the best of these being Bowker's.[107] There are likely to be guides, too, to the recorded proceedings of state legislatures and to the state laws and statutes, as well as digests and compilations of such legislation.[108] All of this is of potential significance for the study of the history of local communities. Publications relating to constitutional conventions may sometimes be useful, too.[109]

To federal and state documents must be added the official publications of communities within states – cities, towns, townships, counties, and other local government administrations. For the great cities these are similar in scope and complexity to those of state governments; for smaller places, where governmental functions were more restricted, they are likely to be more rudimentary, and, unfortunately, often less well preserved.[110] Given the number of local governments no comprehensive guide to them is feasible.[111] These records are, however, considered more fully in subsequent chapters.

In some instances useful evidence may be found in the

---

[106] See ALA, *Directory of Government Document Collections and Librarians* (current edn.).

[107] Hasse (see abbreviations) (for CA, DE, IL, KY, ME, MA, NH, NJ, NY, OH, PA, RI, VT); R. R. Bowker (ed.), *State Publications* (4 pts., 1899–1908). See also William S. Jenkins, *Collected Public Documents of the States: A Check List* (1947). Jerome K. Wilcox (ed.), *Manual on the Use of State Publications* (1940) provides a bibl. of bibliographies of state publications. See also Margaret T. Lane, "State documents checklists," *Library Trends*, 15 (1966); David W. Parish, *State Government Reference Publications* (1974); Palic, 89–137; Prucha, 107–9.

[108] See citations Prucha, 108; *HG*, 78 and below p. 300.

[109] A. F. Kuhlman, *Official Publications Relating to American State Constitutional Conventions* (1936); citations Prucha, 109; *HG*, 77; p. 300 below.

[110] See ALA, *Directory of Government Document Collections and Librarians* (current edn.); Peter Hernon *et al.*, *Municipal Government Reference Sources* (1978).

[111] But see James G. Hodgson, *The Official Publications of American Counties: A Union List* (1937). For the complications of local government authorities and nomenclature, see Jones, 107–13; Felt, *Researching . . . Local History*, 44–5.

official publications of foreign countries, particularly Canada and Great Britain, and in other material found abroad.[112]

Newspapers are a particularly valuable non-official published source for most communities. They are doubly significant when other local records are sparse. Luckily the nineteenth-century United States had probably the largest and most diverse array of newspapers in the world. Metropolitan dailies circulated not only within cities but in their hinterlands, and even small towns had surprisingly large numbers of papers. In rural and remote areas weekly newspapers were common, and newspapers followed the pioneer trails as settlements were established.[113] In certain places ethnic publications were significant. Specialist journalism was represented particularly in the religious and the agricultural press. There must be few topics of interest to historians of communities for which some information cannot be found in the files of local newspapers. Their news reports, editorials, features, correspondence, obituaries, notices, and advertisements, are full of information, much of it obtainable nowhere else.[114]

Newspapers are, of course, known often to be guilty of bias and inaccuracy. To guard against the former, historians need to seek out the viewpoints and background of the editor and owner and to use the evidence circumspectly.[115] Bias resulting in omission, by suppression rather than falsification, may be more difficult to deal with. About local events of a more general nature greater impartiality may prevail and greater accuracy of reporting. Follow-up accounts may, however,

[112] See *HG*, 87–92. Useful may be Leo F. Stock (ed.), *Proceedings and Debates of the British Parliaments Respecting America* (5 vols., 1924, since repr.); Irish Universities Press, *Area Studies: United States of America* (60 vols., 1971); Henry P. Beers, *Spanish and Mexican Records of the American Southwest* (1979); Lewis Hanke (ed.), *Guide to the Study of United States History Outside the U.S., 1945–1980* (5 vols., 1985).
[113] George S. Hage, *Newspapers on the Minnesota Frontier, 1849–1860* (1947). A set of microfilms, "Newspapers along America's Great Trails," is publ. by Bell and Howell, Micro-Photo Division, Old Manchester Rd., Wooster, OH 41691.
[114] See Lucy M. Salmon, *The Newspaper and the Historian* (1923); William H. Taft, *Newspapers as Tools for Historians* (1970); Carl Weight, "The local historian and the newspaper," *Minnesota Hist.*, 13 (1932); Thomas D. Clark, "The county newspaper as a source of social history," *Indiana Mag. Social Hist.*, 48 (1952); Icko Iben, "The place of the newspaper," *Library Trends*, 4 (1955).
[115] See, e.g., Roberto Franzosi, "The press as a source of socio-historical data," *HM*, 20 (1987); and pp. 327–8.

give further information and more accurate accounts than the first report of an event. Most newspapers, however, contain many inaccuracies of detail, the result of inefficiency rather than bias, and where possible they should be used in conjunction with evidence from other sources. Moreover, to paint a picture of certain aspects of local life solely from news reports is likely to result in distortion, since by their nature newspapers deal in the unusual rather than the typical. That said, newspapers remain an essential source for the history of many communities.

There are several guides to newspapers from which such details as frequency and place of publication, chronological coverage, and whereabouts of files may be discovered.[116] Some libraries have especially extensive newspaper collections.[117] Some foreign depositories also possess files of American newspapers.[118] Generally university, historical, state, city, and other local libraries in the state concerned are likely to have files of local newspapers and often there are histories and guides to the local press.[119]

One difficulty in using newspapers is their sheer bulk. Sometimes, however, the historian will have some idea of the dates he should search – for a specific or annual event, an obituary, and so on. If not, he may have to search page by page, although for some purposes he will get sufficient information by sampling. If, however, a subject or nominal index to the newspaper files exists, the newspaper becomes much more potentially valuable, though such indexes are by no

[116] See citations Prucha, 56–7; *United States Newspaper Program, National Union List* (Online Computer Center, Dublin, OH, 8 vols., 1985; 2nd edn. 1987 on microfiche).
[117] Elizabeth L. Anderson, *Newspaper Libraries in the U.S. and Canada: ASLA Directory* (1980); Makower; Library of Congress, *Chronological Index of Newspapers . . . 1801–1952 in the . . . Library of Congress* (1956).
[118] See, e.g., B. R. Crick and Anne Daltrop, *List of American Newspapers up to 1940, held by Libraries in Great Britain and Ireland* (Suppl. 7, *Bull. British Assoc. for American Studies*, 1958) (further guides publ. to 1974 by this assoc.); Stephen Rush, *Union List of Non-Canadian Newspapers held by Canadian Libraries* (National Library of Canada, 1968); O. Fritiof Ander (comp.), *Swedish American Political Newspapers: A Guide to the Collections in the Royal Library, Stockholm and the Augusta College Library, Rock Island* (Uppsala, 1936).
[119] Prucha, 58–60; *HG*, 552–3.

means faultless. The guides of Anita C. Milner and the Lathrops to the existence and whereabouts of such indexes are thus invaluable.[120] Sometimes existing newspaper offices may have indexes to their past files. And some indexes, published and unpublished, including some made in the 1930s by the Work Projects Administration,[121] may exist in local libraries. Occasionally a local enthusiast may have compiled scrapbooks of newspaper extracts, often arranged by topics. The Newspaper Indexing Center in Ohio indexes major city newspapers,[122] and the United States Newspaper Project exists to locate and make inventories of newspapers in individual states and hopes eventually to produce in microform all American newspaper files since 1690.[123] An excellent guide to microformed newspapers is available.[124]

Foreign-language newspapers produced in the United States and other ethnic papers are particularly valuable for certain places and from the 1820s there was a considerable black press and some Indian tribes had newspapers.[125] Specialist newspapers can also provide information for the community historian, and where relevant are dealt with in later chapters.

As well as daily and weekly newspapers some contemporary periodicals may contain local material. For these there are guides and indexes, including some regional ones.[126] Frank

[120] See citations Prucha, 61–2; *HG*, 131. And see *Genealogical Jnl.*, 8 (1979), 185–91.
[121] *HG*, 131.
[122] *Newspaper Index* (1972–   ), Bell and Howell, Newspaper Indexing Center, Old Mansfield Rd., Wooster, OH 41691.
[123] Inventories of holdings will be available through computer terminals in many large libraries. See *Editor and Publisher*, 116 (Jan. 15, 1983), 11; *Source*, 407–8.
[124] Library of Congress, *Newspapers in Microform: United States, 1948–1983* (2 vols., 1984): despite title, dates cover nineteenth-century newspapers; strongest coverage 1775–1815, weakest 1830–70. See also current lists of University Microfilms, 300 North Zeeb Rd., Ann Arbor, MI 48106; Bell and Howell (address above, n. 122); Microfilming Corporation of America, Hawkins Ave., Box 10, Sanford, NC 27330.
[125] See pp. 121–2, 153, 226, 230, 251–2; Prucha, 191; Angie Debo, "Major Indian record collections in Oklahoma," in Jane F. Smith and Robert M. Kvasnicka (eds.), *Indian–White Relations* (1976), 116.
[126] See *HG*, 63–6, 115–17, 121–30, 325 (Winther); Helen J. Poulton, *The Historian's Handbook* (1972), 112–13; Alvan W. Clark, *Checklist of Indexed Periodicals* (1917); Gertrude C. Gilmer, *Checklist of Southern Periodicals to 1861* (1934).

L. Mott's history and guide has sections on regional and local magazines,[127] but many of the specialist series he mentions (especially those relating to religious and agricultural topics) may contain evidence on particular localities. Access is facilitated by the existence of indexes, and the publication of some serials in microform.[128]

Directories, like newspapers, form a source of information on many topics and generally demonstrate the spread of a community's commercial, social, and topographical growth. For a community to possess local directories was often an indication that it had become well established: by 1860 the bulk of the population covered by directories was living in cities.[129] Directories are especially valuable for demographic, social, political, and administrative history. They include local government handbooks, local publications (often annual) providing official and quasi-official information for states, counties, or cities, local commercial compendia, and specialist compilations connected, for example, with a particular religious denomination or devoted to a particular sphere of interest (as education or trade). City directories which listed inhabitants are a very significant source. Official municipal and county directories or registers will usually contain accurate details of local rules and orders, the names of local government officers, and information on all the city's or county's organization and official activities as well as much other information.

Those directories listing inhabitants usually include their occupations and home and work addresses, and occasionally other information such as religious and political affiliation and the country of origin of voters and taxpayers. Such directories may complement census returns. Many local directories contain maps and street guides and give information on transportation facilities and the character of different parts of a town (as residential or manufacturing) can often be

---

[127] *A History of American Magazines, 1741–1905* (4 vols., 1957).
[128] See Clark, *Checklist*; Hoornstra.
[129] Peter R. Knights, "City directories as aids to ante-bellum urban studies," *HMN*, 2 (1969).

deduced. Collections of directories are likely to be found in local and other libraries,[130] and many are available in microform.[131]

National and other almanacs can also sometimes be of value for local research.[132] Guide books and gazetteers provide similar information to that found in many local directories. Gazetteers (sometimes called registers or dictionaries) became common about 1815. Some cover the whole country, others are regional, state, or more local. They often take the form of a description of aspects of the economic, official, cultural, and religious institutions of each town, together with demographic and other details. Many were produced to assist migrants, particularly those moving westwards.[133] William Darby's *Emigrants' Guide to the Western and Southwestern States and Territories* (New York, 1818), for example, describes the routes, climate, geography, vegetation, and the towns and population along the way. Usually, especially with earlier guides, the description was an informed one and provided also details of the routes, available lodgings, and the prices of commodities. Many guide books were more for the casual visitor or tourist, but others (some of them official publications) catered for the new settlers, as, for example, *Pacific Northwest: Information for Settlers and Others* published by the Oregon Immigration Board in various editions from 1883. Contemporary geographical and topographical works covering various parts of the country were also often designed for the emigrant and the traveler, and many give similar information. H. S. Tanner's *Geographical, Historical, and Statistical*

130 Dorothea N. Spear, *Bibliography of American Directories through 1860* (1961).
131 See *City Directories of the United States, 1860–1901: Guide to the Microfilm Collections* (Research Publications, PO Box 3903, Amity Station, New Haven, CT 06525, 1983). Despite title it includes directories in Spear, all of which are in microform. E. Kay Kirkham, *A Handy Guide to Record Searching in the Larger Cities of the United States* (1974) lists directories locally held. And see Prucha, 15 [B58].
132 See Clarence S. Brigham, "Report of the librarian," *Procs. Am. Antiquarian Soc.*, NS 35 (1925); Esther Jerebac, "Almanacs as historical sources," *Minnesota Hist.*, 15 (1934); *HG*, 113–15, for bibls.
133 *HG*, 48–9; Carman and Thompson (1962), 275–8.

View of the Central or Middle United States (Philadelphia, 1841) is an example. The writings of visitors, especially from overseas, are another source.[134]

Visual records, in particular pictures and photographs, are sources which may be both published and unpublished, but for convenience are treated in this section. Such materials can provide an extra dimension to the study of many aspects of the social and economic history of past communities.[135] They may not only record unique events in the history of particular places and the physical nature of local townscapes and landscapes at different times,[136] but also provide evidence of living and working conditions, industrial, commercial, and agricultural processes, urbanization, educational facilities, and so on.[137] Like all historical sources, however, they need to be used with care.[138] In particular, it is helpful to know who took the photograph or made the picture, for what purpose, and on what occasion. It is important, too, to realize that what is portrayed may not, in the case of a print of a drawing or painting, be entirely factually accurate, and that photographs may not be representative of the norm and may also be posed. In one way or another what is portrayed may reflect contemporary cultural presumptions.[139] Again there may be unconscious bias in the researcher. Caution should, therefore, be exercised in drawing conclusions from such evidence, and

---

[134] See, e.g., Ivan D. Steen, "Philadelphia in the 1850's as described by British travelers," *Pennsylvania Hist.*, 33 (1966).

[135] Schlereth, *Artifacts*, ch. 1; Kyvig and Marty, *Nearby History*, ch. 7 (q.v. for bibl.); Norman McCord, "Photographs as historical evidence," *Local Historian*, 13 (1978); Walter Rundell, "Photographs as historical evidence," *AA*, 44 (1978); Michael Thomason, "The magic image revisited," *Alabama Rev.*, 30 (1978); Brock, 213–14, 225; Robert A. Weinstein and Larry Booth, *Collection, Use, and Care of Historical Photographs* (1977).

[136] See, e.g., Peter B. Hales, *The Photography of American Urbanization, 1839–1915* (1984); Jane Sugden (ed.), *New England Past: Photographs, 1880–1915* (1981).

[137] See, e.g., James Borchert, *Alley Life in Washington . . . 1850–1870* (1980), app. B; Ronald E. Butchart, *Local Schools* (1986), 99–100; and works cited in them.

[138] Mick Gidley, *American Photographs* (British Assoc. for American Studies, 1983), 15–16 (bibl., 42–4); Marsha Peters and Bernard Mergen, "'Doing the best': the use of photographs in American Studies," *American Q.*, 29 (1977), 283 (bibl., 300–3).

[139] John Berger, *Ways of Seeing* (1972), 8.

wherever possible it should be linked with information drawn from other sources.[140]

Many state and local historical societies, libraries, and museums have files of prints, other pictures, and photographs.[141] In particular the Library of Congress[142] and the National Archives[143] have extensive collections of pictorial and photographic evidence covering many parts of the country. Some specific photographic collections are noted in later chapters. The large number of photographs and prints relating to the Civil War includes many that incidentally provide evidence on aspects of the life of communities other than those connected with the war.[144]

The writings of travelers, migrants, and explorers are very extensive, and these contain much local information, especially with reference to frontier and pioneer life, but also to more settled urban and rural communities. Reuben G. Thwaite's *Early Western Travels, 1748–1846* (32 vols., 1904–7), for instance, is one of the best of these sources.[145] There are many guides and bibliographies for such works,[146] some relating to particular regions and places.[147] The reports and records

[140] W. B. Stephens and R. W. Unwin, *Materials for the Local and Regional Study of Schooling, 1800–1900* (1987), 32–3.

[141] See *HG*, 50–2, 341–2; Makower; *NUCMC*; James McQuaid (ed.), *An Index of American Photographic Collections* (1982); Mick Gidley and Ian Craven, *Audio-Visual Materials for American Studies* (1983); Elizabeth Winroth, *Union Guide to Photographic Collections in the Pacific Northwest* (1978); Celestine G. Frankenberg (ed.), *Picture Sources* (1964 edn.); *Directory of Archives and Manuscript Repositories in the United States* (1988).

[142] Paul Vanderbilt (comp.), *Guide to the Special Collections of Prints & Photographs in the Library of Congress* (1955).

[143] See, e.g., NA, *The American Image: Photographs from the National Archives, 1860–1960* (1979) (q.v. for RGs likely to contain such records); NA, *Photographs of the American City* (n.d.); Mayfield S. Bray, *Still Pictures in the Audiovisual Archives Division of the National Archives* (1972); J. Eric Maddox (comp.), *Preliminary Inventory of Audio–Visual Records made by the National Archives and for It by Federal Agencies* (NC–121, 1965). And see n. 225 below.

[144] See, e.g., *HG*, 865–6; Brock, 143; Bray, *Still Pictures*; Dale E. Floyd, *The Southeast During the Civil War* (RIP 69, 1973).

[145] See also Hakluyt Soc. publics.

[146] *HG*, 137–8, 312 (Pierce); Prucha, 219–21.

[147] Gerald N. Grob, *American Social History Before 1860* (1970), sec. 2; Carman and Thompson (1962); Rodman W. Paul and Richard W. Etulian, *The Frontier and the American West* (1977), esp. secs. VIII, XVIII; John H. Franklin, *A Southern Odyssey; Travelers in the Antebellum North* (1976), 287–94. Works in Clark and in Wagoner and Camp (see Prucha, 220) are publ. in microform by Lost Cause Press. And see pp. 232–3.

of official exploration and surveying are noted in the section on cartographic sources below.

UNPUBLISHED SOURCES

A community history of any depth will usually need to draw on unpublished as well as published sources. These are to be found in record and archive depositories, county court houses, and libraries of many kinds, as well as in private and institutional hands. Some collections will be available in microform.[148] American depositories are rich in collections of private papers and the archives of businesses and institutions. The uniqueness of such items renders individual treatment here impossible, but for all the topics of later chapters the researcher should check for the possible existence of such records. One of the largest collections of material of this kind is that of the Manuscript Division of the Library of Congress, which contains the papers of presidents, politicians, reformers, labor leaders, feminists, explorers, businessmen, and many other individuals, as well as those of a multitude of institutions, societies, and movements, among which must be data on many American communities.[149] The most comprehensive guide to manuscript collections throughout the United States, but excluding for the most part official records, is the Library of Congress, *National Union Catalog of Manuscript Collections* (from 1962, in progress). This contains subject indexes which include place-names, and there is a personal names' index, too.[150] There are, of course,

---

[148] *Guide to Microforms in Print* (current edn.).

[149] A microfiche edn. of the publ. and unpubl. registers (finding aids) (with index) exists: *National Inventory of Documentary Sources in the United States: Manuscript Division, Library of Congress: Index* (Chadwyck-Healey, 1983: to be updated periodically). See also *Library of Congress Acquisitions, Manuscript Division* (from 1981).

[150] See also Philip M. Hamer (ed.), *A Guide to Archives and Manuscripts in the United States* (1961); Makower. Chadwyck-Healey's *Anglo-American Historical Names Data Base, Supplement 1* (1986) is a microfiche and computer tape covering personal names. There is an *Index to Personal Names in the National Union Catalog of Manuscript Collections, 1959–1984* (Chadwyck-Healey, 2 vols., 1988).

many other guides to particular collections and library holdings,[151] varying in detail. Many locally useful materials will naturally tend to be found in the state or region to which they pertain. The papers of important public figures are often found in larger libraries.

Some institutions have become centers for the collection of records pertaining to particular regions. Thus the University of North Carolina has built up a collection on the South; Cornell University has a collection relating to its region; and the Bancroft Library of the University of California, Berkeley and the University of Missouri are among those with large Western collections.[152] Likewise Indiana State University houses a collection on the Midwest.[153] State and other large historical societies, especially in the Midwest, often have large collections of manuscripts relating to the history of their regions.[154] Libraries in New York, particularly the New York Public Library, have extensive collections containing many items relevant to places throughout the country.[155] There is a useful microfiche edition (with published index) of guides and finding lists to archives and manuscript collections in many university and other important libraries and research centers.[156] Records held in some foreign libraries may sometimes

---

[151] See National Historical Publications and Records Commission, *Directory of Archives and Manuscript Repositories in the United States* (1988); Hamer, *Guide to Archives*, xix–xxi; *HG*, 38–40; Prucha, 47–51; *Writings on American History* (see p. 18 above); Ray A. Billington, *Guides to American History Manuscript Collections in the United States* (1952) (also in *MVHR*, 38 (1951)). See also Burnette, *Beneath the Footnote*, 193–264 (and, for a directory of state-level manuscript collecting agencies, 173–6).

[152] Prucha, 50 [G37]; Edith M. Fox, "The genesis of Cornell University's collection of regional history," *AA*, 14 (1951); Dale P. Morgan and George P. Hammond (eds.), *A Guide to the Manuscript Collections of the Bancroft Library*, vol. 1 (1963); Lewis E. Atherton, "Western historical manuscripts collection," *AA*, 26 (1963).

[153] Thomas P. Martin, "A manuscripts collecting venture in the middle west," *AA*, 17 (1954).

[154] Ernst Posner, *American State Archives* (1964), 21–2.

[155] Carman and Thompson (1960).

[156] *National Inventory of Documentary Sources in the United States: Academic Libraries and Other Depositories: An Index* (Chadwyck-Healey, 1984– , in progress; by names and subjects).

be relevant;[157] parts of the West were, of course, ruled by Mexico well into the nineteenth century.[158] Collections of the correspondence of immigrants may be found in their native country.[159]

Private papers embrace especially correspondence, business materials, and diaries. For diaries, some of which may have been published later, there are some useful bibliographies.[160] Such material can provide intimate detail not available in other sources. This is so, for instance, in the case of the many diaries kept by women on the frontier.[161]

Unpublished material of an official kind forms another great mine of information, and this includes both federal and state as well as more obviously local government records. Few local studies of any depth will be able to rely entirely on material available in the immediate locality. In particular the archives of the federal government, too often ignored by historians dealing with local themes, provide much evidence on the history of many communities.

The National Archives and Records Administration (henceforth referred to as the National Archives) exists to conserve the archives of the legislative, judicial, and executive branches of the U.S. government. Its vast collection, organized by provenance in numbered Record Groups, is briefly described in the *Guide to the National Archives of the United States* (1974,

---

[157] *HG*, 100–5, and, e.g., Grace G. Griffin, *Guide to Manuscripts Relating to American History in British Depositories . . .* (1946); John W. Raimo (ed.), *Guide to Manuscripts Relating to America in Great Britain and Ireland* (1979); Scottish Record Office, *List of American Documents* (1976); *Guide des Sources de L'Histoire des Etats-Unis dans les Archives Françaises* (Paris, 1976); Marian D. Learned, *Guide to the Manuscript Materials Relating to American History in the German State Archives* (1912, repr. 1965).

[158] See *HG*, 104 (Bolton). But it is not the purpose of this volume to cover sources for communities before they became part of the U.S.

[159] E.g., A. Eames, L. Lloyd, and B. Parry (eds.), *Letters from America: Captain David Evans of Talsarnau, 1817–1895* (Gwynedd Archives Service, Wales, 1975).

[160] See Prucha, 51 [G48], 75.

[161] E.g., Sandra L. Myers (ed.), *Ho for California! Women's Overland Diaries from the Huntington Library* (1980); Kenneth L. Holmes (ed.), *Covered Wagon Women: Diaries and Letters from the Western Trails* (7 vols., 1983–8); Lillian Schlissel, *Women's Diaries of the Westward Journey* (1983); Lillian Schlissel, "Women's diaries on the western frontier," *Am. Studies*, 18 (1977).

repr. 1987).[162] The bulk of the records noted in the *GNA* are in the National Archives building in Washington, DC,[163] and its ancillary depot, the Washington National Records Center, Suitland, MD,[164] but some, of a particularly regional nature, are held in the eleven regional branches of the National Archives (see below).

The entries in the *GNA* provide a general description of the organizational units and of the scope, nature, and chronological coverage of the records in each Record Group. They also at times note the existence of indexes, registers, and other research aids relevant to the particular Group, but this is done only selectively, as are indications that certain records have appeared in print. The *GNA* has an index but it is not intended as a general subject or place guide. It provides only entries of organizational units, very broad subjects, and important place-names. The information given on access and restrictions to access to certain records should be noted.

It has been claimed that "As sources of local history, federal records provide an incredible storehouse of community experience," and pointed out that the National Archives "holds millions of items that document the lives of ordinary citizens in local communities."[165] Some surveys of records in the National Archives on particular topics and particular localities exist,[166] but while worth consulting they are often out of date as regards materials more recently deposited by government departments and as regards the distribution of records in the various National Archives depositories.

---

[162] See also accession lists in *Prologue* (1969–); *List of Record Groups of the National Archives and Records Administration* (NA, 1986). Note, too, University of Illinois Library, *The Merenec Calendar of Federal Documents on the Upper Mississippi Valley, 1780–1890* (13 vols., 1971).

[163] Constitution Ave. at 7th and 9th Sts., Washington DC 20408, where a search card is obtainable.

[164] 4205 Suitland Rd., Suitland, MD 20409. There is a shuttle bus service to and from the downtown Washington building.

[165] Walch, *Our Family, Our Town*, iii, xvi.

[166] Frank B. Evans, "The National Archives and Records Service and its research resources – a select bibliography," *Prologue*, 3 (1971), q.v. for articles, etc. on particular agencies; and see, e.g., Ann M. Campbell, "In nineteenth-century Nevada: federal records as sources for local history," *Nevada Hist. Soc. Q.*, 17 (1974).

Serious students who visit the National Archives building in Washington, DC, may seek guidance there from "research consultants," on the material available for their chosen research, but it is as well to have a general idea of likely types of sources and pertinent Record Groups before arriving.[167] A library attached to the Central Research Room contains many (but not all) National Archives finding aids and catalogs. Among these are inventories, resource papers, and other lists which are generally available only at the Washington building. Some of these are particularly significant for community history and have been noted in later chapters.[168] Many of the National Archives finding aids and catalogs, however, have been published and may be available in large libraries throughout the country or through the Inter–Library Loan scheme.[169] They consist of series variously called Preliminary Inventories, Special Lists, Reference Information Papers, and Pamphlets Accompanying (or Describing) Microfilms (now called Descriptive Pamphlets), and references will be found in later pages to those of particular value for the study of certain topics at the local level.

The form taken by the Reference Information Papers (originally Circulars) varies, but they are all concerned with providing a description of records relating to a particular subject. Many provide excellent introductions to records useful for the study of local communities. The Preliminary Inventories are concerned with the deposited records of various government departments and agencies, and act both as indicators of content and finding aids. Many are substantial publications and not a few are invaluable for certain topics. The Special Lists go beyond the general descriptions found in the Preliminary Inventories and describe particular collections in terms of individual record items. In addition the National Archives has

---

[167] *A Researcher's Guide to the National Archives* (NA, current edn.); Constance Potter, "Research at the National Archives," *Perspectives*, 25, 3 (1987).

[168] Most unpubl. preliminary inventories bear the prefix NM (compiled by the Military Division) or NC (Civil Division).

[169] Many are available free or by purchase from the NA: see *Select List of Publications of the National Archives and Records Administration* (current edn.).

published a few comprehensive Guides relating to very broad topics.[170] A boon to researchers is the recent commercially published microfiche edition of the National Archives finding aids[171] (including Special Lists, published and unpublished Preliminary Inventories).[172]

Large numbers of the actual records in National Archives depositories have been microfilmed and they are available for purchase or consultation in libraries which have bought them. They are accompanied by pamphlets briefly listing their content (PAMs, PDMs, DPs). The microfilming policy of the National Archives is very significant for the future study of local communities, for it makes it increasingly feasible to make good use of evidence from unpublished federal sources. A number of catalogs of these microfilms relating to particular subjects has been published,[173] and there is also a comprehensive catalog which is periodically updated.[174]

Another help to researchers is the establishment in recent years of the regional branches of the National Archives, mentioned above. Many federal records indigenous to states and territories are deposited in one of these eleven regional repositories.[175] Of these records, perhaps those of greatest interest to community historians are the records of the U.S. district and circuit courts (RG 21) (see below). Others include customs records, Indian affairs records, and records of the Army Corps of Engineers on waterways (RGs, 36, 75, 77). Some of the regional branches publish guides to their collections, and usually a detailed inventory is available in their search rooms. Copies of such finding aids should be available in microfiche at

---

[170] E.g., Debra Newman (comp.), *Black History: A Guide to Civilian Records in the National Archives* (1984).

[171] *National Inventory of Documentary Sources in the United States: Federal Records: Index* (Chadwyck-Healey, 1985; updated versions in microfiche). The NA has produced its finding aids, publ. 1935–68, in microfilm (M248).

[172] And recently (1990) PAMs, PDMs (now DPs).

[173] See *Select List of Publications of the National Archives*.

[174] *MRR* (see abbreviations). *Prologue* carries details of recently produced microfilms.

[175] Listed with addresses and states covered in *Regional Branches of the National Archives* (NA, 1985); *Prologue* 19 (1987), 196–7; *HG*, 96; *Directory of Historical Societies and Agencies in the United States and Canada* (AASLH, current edn.).

the National Archives building in Washington, DC. Some collections have been the subject of articles.[176]

In addition each regional branch possesses a similar set of microform publications of certain federal records held at Washington, DC. These do not include all the microfilms published by the National Archives, but the set is being added to continually. Those records covered in the set which are specially useful for historians interested in particular areas include internal revenue assessment schedules for the 1860s (RG 58), and, where appropriate, certain records of the Bureau of Refugees, Freedmen, and Abandoned Lands (RG 105), the records of the Southern Claims Commission (RG 56), and the original manuscript returns of the decennial censuses, 1790–1880 and 1900 (RG 29), as well as various selections of "territorial papers." Except for a selection on the territory of Wisconsin, regarded as a supplement to the published *Territorial Papers* mentioned above,[177] these are distinct collections, all arranged by territories.[178]

Territorial papers of various kinds contain information on a number of topics discussed in later chapters,[179] as do the census population schedules. Some other collections of the National Archives and its branches which have a wide reference may be noted here. They include petitions and memorials to Congress and its committees and other Congressional committee records, such as hearings.[180] Unfortunately, however,

---

[176] E.g., Norman E. Tutorow, "Source materials for historical research in the Los Angeles Federal Records Center," *Southern California Q.*, 53 (1971); Norman E. Tutorow and Arthur R. Abel, "Western and territorial research opportunities in Trans-Mississippi federal records centers," *Pacific Hist. Rev.*, 40 (1971).

[177] See p. 19.

[178] All listed in *MRR*.

[179] For those in the Dept. of the Interior records (RG 48), see *Records of the Office of the Secretary of the Interior, 1833–1964*, pt. 1 (NA, NNF–48, 1984, T/S), 92–107; W. Turrentine Jackson, "Dakota territorial papers in the Department of the Interior archives," *North Dakota Hist. Q.*, 9 (1944); W. Turrentine Jackson, "Territorial papers in the Department of the Interior archives, 1873–1890: Washington, Idaho, and Montana," *Pacific Northwest Q.*, 35 (1944).

[180] *GNA*, 49–52, 54–5, 134 (RGs 46, 59, 128, 233). For RG 233, see Buford Rowland *et al.* (comps.), *Preliminary Inventory of the Records of the House of Representatives, 1789–1946* (PI 113, 1969). For RG 46, see Harold E. Hufford and Watson G. Caudill (comps.), *Preliminary Inventory of the Records of the United States Senate* (PI 23, 1950). See also Don W. Wilson, "The right to petition," *Prologue*, 20 (1988), 224–5; Ira Berlin *et al.*, "'To Canvass the Nation,'" ibid.

numerous committee records were erratically filed and preserved and the location of many is uncertain.[181] The records of
various federal courts also contain much evidence on many
topics. Those of the federal territorial, district, and circuit
courts (RG 21; mostly in regional branches) embrace bankruptcy, civil, criminal, equity, and admiralty (maritime)
cases,[182] as well as petitions and papers, on, for instance, taxes
and Civil War matters. There are a number of guides to these
court records,[183] and many of the records are available in
microfilm.[184] The records of the U.S. Court of Claims
(RG 123) cover claims against the federal government and
include reports[185] and records relating to Indian tribal rights,
Indian depredations, postal services, and land grants to railroads.[186] The records of the U.S. Supreme Court (RG 267)
contain both original jurisdiction and appellate case files, the
latter containing transcripts of lower court records.[187] A card
index provides names of parties in appellate cases.[188] There is
also a published index of opinions.[189]

[181] Brock, 116. For hearings, see Charles E. South and James C. Brown (comps.),
Hearings in the Records of the U.S. Senate and Joint Committees of Congress (SL 32,
1972), arranged by Congress and subject (e.g., immigration, Indian affairs, agriculture and forestry, education and labor, post offices, public land): despite title,
includes some hearings of House committees; Buford Rowland et al., (comps.),
*Printed Hearings of the House of Representatives ... in the National Archives ...
1824–1958* (SL 35, 1974; also arranged by Congress and subject).
[182] District courts dealt mainly with criminal, admiralty, and bankruptcy cases;
circuit courts mainly with civil cases.
[183] R. Michael McReynolds (comp.), *List of Pre-1840 Federal District and Circuit Court
Records* (SL 31, 1972) (app. II lists NA depositories with post-1840 federal courts
records; and app. III pre-1840 records not in NA depositories); PIs cited *GNA*, 90
(for Eastern PA, Southern NY), and unpubl. PIs NC-2(1962) (DC), NC-15(1962)
(Eastern VA), NC-21(1963) (NC, IL, ME, NJ, RI, and pts. of IA, LA, NY, NC,
OH, WA); Marion M. Johnson and Elaine Everly (comps.), *Preliminary Inventory
of the United States Court for the District of Wisconsin* (NA, Chicago Branch, 1968).
[184] *MRR*; NA, *Federal Court Records: A Select Catalog of National Archives Microfilm
Publications* (1987).
[185] See *Cases Decided in the Court of Claims of the United States* (many vols., 1963–).
For indexes and a digest: Schmeckebier and Eastin, 283–4.
[186] Gaiselle Kerner (comp.), *Records of the U.S. Court of Claims, 1783–1947* (PI 58,
1953).
[187] Marion Johnson (comp.), *Preliminary Inventory of Records of the Supreme Court of the
United States* (PI 139, 1973); James R. Browning and Bess Glenn, "The Supreme
Court collection at the National Archives," *Am. Jnl. Legal Hist.*, 4 (1960).
[188] Available in M408. Appellate case files in M214.
[189] Marion M. Johnson (comp.), *Index to the Manuscript and Printed Opinions of the
Supreme Court of the United States in the National Archives, 1808–73* (SL 21, 1965).

Court records, both of the federal and the state courts, may be important to community historians where decisions affected local affairs or when a county or city government was involved. Judicial records are, however, often less important for the actual cases and decisions than for the incidental information on particular aspects of the social and economic life of the community provided in testimony, ancillary records, and so forth.[190] Admittedly court records are often difficult to use. The arrangement of cases and reference to them are not by names of places but by case titles embracing the names of the parties involved, so that the searcher either needs to be able to recognize names as, for example, being those of local people or to have prior knowledge of the existence of a case and its approximate date. As for the types of court records, those pertaining to criminal trials are described in chapter 11; records in civil cases are similar in nature. Among civil case records attorneys' briefs, which outline the cases often in considerable detail as seen by the attorneys, are of great use.[191]

Not all federal archives are in the hands of the National Archives. Certain non-population census schedule records, for instance, have been dispersed to various universities and historical societies.[192] Some other records were dispersed much earlier. The Historical Records Survey of the Works Progress Administration published in 1939–40 a large number of volumes of an *Inventory of Federal Archives in the States*.[193] This is arranged in Series and within each Series by states. Series I provides a general discussion of the location, organization, and content of the records. The Series most likely to

---

[190] See, e.g., David R. Kepley, "An untapped treasure: research opportunities in Pennsylvania Federal District Court records," *Pennsylvania Mag. Hist. and Biography*, 105 (1981); Mary K. B. Tachau, *Federal Courts of the Early Republic: Kentucky, 1789–1816* (1978).

[191] Seymour V. Connor, "Legal material as sources of history," *AA*, 23 (1960), 159–60.

[192] See pp. 81–2.

[193] Sargent B. Child and Dorothy P. Holmes (comps.), *Bibliography of Research Projects Reports: Check List of Historical Records Survey Publications* (1943, repr. 1969). Some remain unpubl.: Loretta F. Hefner, *The W.P.A. Historical Records Survey: A Guide to the Unpublished Inventories, Indexes and Transcripts* (1980), 5–6.

interest community historians are those covering Federal Courts (Series II), the Treasury Department (including customs and internal revenue records) (III), the Justice Department (V), the Interior Department (including some General Land Office records) (VIII), and the Department of Agriculture (IX). Many of these records pertain to the twentieth century but some concern the nineteenth. The present whereabouts of the records may well be different from that indicated in the *Inventory*, and some may have been disposed of. As noted above, federal court records are now mostly in regional branches of the National Archives, and inquiry over records in other Series might well be made in the first instance to such branches.

Unfortunately the records of the governments of individual states, counties, townships, and cities have often been less well preserved and organized than have the National Archives.[194] Yet they are likely to provide the main sources for many aspects of local community history, and will be dealt with in later chapters as appropriate. State records of general interest include state census records and the records of state courts (which differed from state to state but included supreme courts, appeal courts, district, and county courts).

Some state historical societies have published older state records, but there is no comprehensive guide to state archives,[195] although there are many guides to the collections of individual states and local governments. These will be known to local librarians. In addition a microfiche edition (with published index) of finding aids, card catalogs, and indexes to collections in state archives, state libraries, and state historical

194 Posner, *American State Archives*; Jason Horn, "Municipal Archives and Records Center of the City of New York," *AA*, 16 (1953), 311–20; *HG*, 97–100 (addresses of state archives).
195 But see Posner, *American State Archives*; Hamer, *Guide to Archives; Directory of Archives and Manuscript Repositories in the United States*; John M. Kinney (comp.), *Directory of State and Provincial Archives* (1975); Carman and Thompson (1960). For some state and local government records in microfilm, see Library of Congress, *Records of the States of the United States: A Microfilm Compilation* (1949); Library of Congress, *A Guide to the Microfilm Collection of Early State Records* (1950) and *Supplement* (1951); see also *Guide to Microforms in Print*.

societies is in progress.[196] There are, too, 28 published volumes of inventories of state archives, 180 volumes of inventories of municipal and town archives and 628 volumes of inventories of county archives, prepared by the WPA Historical Records Survey.[197] It may be noted, too, that much unpublished material, the result of fieldwork undertaken by the Survey, has now been cataloged.[198] Useful material collected by the WPA Federal Writers' Project and the Writers' Program, now in the Library of Congress and various state depositories, is also available.[199] It includes data gathered for state and local guide books on many topics, and transcripts of first-person "narratives" on such topics as sharecropping, working-class life, urbanization, and slavery.

County records, much underused by historians, are yet said to "constitute the most important historical documentation of America's past."[200] Guidance to these is provided not only by the Historical Records Survey volumes, mentioned above, but by an increasing (but still insufficient) number of more recent surveys. Later chapters will draw attention to such records.

CARTOGRAPHIC AND ASSOCIATED SOURCES

Maps and plans are particularly useful for the study of many of the topics discussed in later chapters. The cartographic record of local topographical change is not only a topic of investigation in its own right, but an essential factor in the understanding of such topics as settlement, land use, communications and transportation, housing conditions, local government and politics, population growth, and the physical distribution of differing social, occupational, and ethnic

---

[196] *National Inventory of Documentary Sources in the United States: State Archives, Libraries and Historical Societies: Index* (Chadwyck-Healey, from 1984, in progress; by names and subjects).

[197] Child and Holmes, *Check List of Hist. Records Survey Publications*.

[198] Hefner, *W.P.A. Historical Records Survey*.

[199] Ann Banks and Robert Carter, *Survey of Federal Writers' Project Holdings in State Depositories* (1985).

[200] Jones, 109.

groups, and of local amenities (such as parks, hospitals, schools, and churches). Maps and plans will also demonstrate the existence and whereabouts of industrial firms, mines, farms, plantations, and factories. By comparing maps and plans of different dates, and by using maps in conjunction with other sources discussed elsewhere (like census materials, voting records, contemporary descriptions, and so forth) the historian can build up a good picture of local communities and changes over time. Indeed maps are often best used in conjunction with other evidence which in turn they will often clarify or supplement.[201] At times, however, maps and plans may provide the only evidence.[202]

There must be few localities in the United States for which there are not maps and plans of some sort and for many places there will be a great number. The initial difficulty is not usually the location of *some* cartographic sources but the discovery of the variety of maps and plans which exist and which best suit a particular purpose. Fortunately there are many guides to published and unpublished cartographic material.[203] One of the best places to begin is the bibliography published by the Library of Congress.[204]

One of the main sources of map making has been the federal government, and its publications include maps of potential use to historians in different parts of the country.[205] For parts of the West the earliest maps available were made in the course of official expeditions of exploration or of surveys for specific purposes (like the canalization of rivers, railroad construction, and other internal improvements) and are often embedded in the published and unpublished reports on those undertakings, reports which are themselves sources for early topographical,

[201] See, e.g., work of Joseph Schafer described in *Prologue*, 1 (1969).
[202] Cf. J. B. Harley, "The evaluation of early maps," *Imago Mundi*, 22 (1968).
[203] See Prucha, 121–30; Makower.
[204] *The Bibliography of Cartography* (5 vols., 1973) with supplements (2 vols., 1980): incl. bibls. and lists of maps.
[205] Water Thiele, *Official Map Publications* (1938), ch. 11; Schmeckebier and Eastin, ch. 16; Martin Claussen and Herman R. Friis, *Descriptive Catalog of Maps Published by Congress, 1817–1843* (1941). For maps in the US Serial Set, see n. 206.

geological, and other information.[206] The postbellum reports of the Hayden, King, Powell, and Wheeler surveys of the West are well known. They cover the territories, the 40th parallel, the Rocky Mountain region, and west of the 100th meridian respectively, and include both descriptive and cartographic material.[207]

Of more general use to the community historian are the topographical maps published in numerous editions and revisions by the U.S. Geological Survey (formed in 1879).[208] The individual maps of this series represent not political divisions but quadrangle units bounded by parallels of latitude and meridians of longitude. Each quadrangle map is designated by the name of a prominent city or physical feature, and this must be known to identify the map concerned.[209] These maps have been produced on different scales but most commonly about 2,000 ft., half-mile (for some specific areas, especially in mining districts), and more often 1 mile and 2 miles to the inch, with other scales (frequently 4 miles to the

---

[206] Reps. listed in Adelaide R. Hasse (comp.), *Report of Explorations Printed in Documents of the United States* (1899); *Checklist* usually indicates vols. consisting entirely of maps, but maps are found in many other vols. See also *HG*, 46 (Ladd), 325–6; Thiele, *Official Map Publications*, 108–15; Prucha, 124; Herman R. Friis, "Highlights of the first hundred years of surveying and mapping the United States by the federal government, 1775–1880," *Surveying and Mapping*, 18 (1958); Herman R. Friis, "A brief review of the development and status of geographical and cartographic activities of the United States government, 1776–1818," *Imago Mundi*, 9 (1965), 77–8; Herman R. Friis, "The documents and reports of the United States Congress: a primary source of information on travel in the west, 1783–1861," in John F. McDermott (ed.), *Travelers on the Western Frontier* (1970); NA, *Geographical Exploration and Topographic Mapping by the United States Government, 1777–1952* (1952, repr. 1966, 1971); W. Turrentine Jackson, *Wagon Roads West ... 1846–1869* (1952), 382–8.

[207] See Laurence F. Schmeckebier, *Catalogue and Index of the Publications of the Hayden, King, Powell, and Wheeler Surveys (Geological Survey Bull.* 222, 1904); Friis, *Survey and Mapping*, 204–5; Ralph E. Ehrenberg, "Taking the measure of the land," *Prologue*, 9 (1977), 139–40; Ralph E. Ehrenberg, *Geographical Exploration and Mapping in the 19th Century: A Survey of the Records in the National Archives* (RIP 66, 1973), 12.

[208] *Checklist*, 483; Morris M. Thompson, *Maps for America: Cartographic Products of the U.S. Geological Survey* (1982 edn.). For early mapping of some areas, see Friis, *Surveying and Mapping*; Ehrenberg, "Taking the measure," 135–8.

[209] An index to the topographic maps for any state may be obtained from the Survey. All non-current topographic maps published by the Survey (the "Historical File") are available in microfilm on a state basis – contact National Cartographic Information Center, U.S. Geological Survey, 507 National Center, Reston, VA 22092. Some early maps are still in print.

inch) for desert and mountainous regions. They include contours and show a great variety of other features, such as settlements, schools, churches, communications, mining sites, and political boundaries.[210] Not all areas were covered in the nineteenth century but some were covered more than once. In such cases historians can gain evidence of topographical and other changes over time, by comparing the different editions and revisions.[211] In some parts maps made before the First World War represent a landscape relatively unchanged since early settlement. Maps of approximately 8 miles and 16 miles to the inch have also been produced for all states except Alaska and Hawaii, showing communications, places, waterways, and contours. The Geological Survey publishes periodically an index (or status) map, *Status of Topographic Mapping in the United States*, showing the state of coverage of the country by the Survey and the Office of the Chief of Engineers.

As well as the historical data obtainable from topographic maps, purely geological information can often contribute to an understanding of the past, aside from its obvious importance in mining areas. It can, for example, explain certain topographical developments and how environmental influences have affected settlement, types of farming, urban building development, transportation patterns, and land use generally.[212] In addition to its topographic maps the Geological Survey has published numbers of geological maps, and here the local historian will wish to secure the most recent. It has also produced series of bulletins and monographs. These often consist of surveys and reports on specific districts and on larger areas or states, regions, and territories, with an emphasis on geological information. They frequently

[210] Rollin D. Salisbury and Wallace W. Atwood, *The Interpretation of Topographic Maps* (1908), preface.
[211] See Thomas G. Manning, *Government in Science: The U.S. Geological Survey, 1867–1894* (1967), esp. ch. 5.
[212] See, e.g., Richard De Bruin and W. Hilton Johnson, *100 Topographic Maps Illustrating Physiographic Features* (1975); Peirce F. Lewis, *New Orleans: The Making of an Urban Landscape* (1976).

contain maps or have accompanying atlases and the data they contain may be of general use to the historian of local communities.[213]

The published volumes of the federal census are another official source of maps of various kinds, and relevant ones are noted in later chapters. The *Statistical Atlas of the United States* which was published as part of the 1870 census is chiefly important for its geological maps and for maps showing political divisions.[214] The 1880 census has detailed maps of most of the 222 large cities covered in its "Social Statistics of Cities" volumes.[215] Further statistical atlases were published for the 1890 and 1900 censuses.[216] Another important federal publication, little used by historians, is the *Atlas to Accompany the Official Records of the Union and Confederate Armies, 1861–1865,*[217] which contains not only battlefield maps but also detailed maps of some towns (including Richmond, VA and Knoxville, TN).

The historian of any particular locality will, of course, find many maps useful for his purposes in local libraries and depositories. Cartographic evidence of potential value may also be found among the records of the National Archives, which has large collections of maps and plans, published and unpublished.[218] In the Cartographic Archives Division alone there

---

213 *Checklist*, 471–8, 483; Baker, *Finding List*, 111–13; *Publications of the United States Geological Survey (not including topographical maps)* (Geological Survey, 1938). See also John M. Nickles, *Geologic Literature on North America, 1785–1918* (*Geological Survey Bulls.*, 746, 747, 1923, 1924); John M. Nickles, *Bibliography of North American Geology, 1919–1928* (*Geological Survey Bull.*, 823, 1931); and later bibls. issued by the Survey; Ehrenberg, "Taking the measure," 149–50; Robert M. and Margaret H. Hazen, *American Geological Literature, 1669 to 1850* (1980). N.B. *Catalog of the United States Geological Survey Library* (25 vols., 1964) and *Supplements* (21 vols., 1972–6).

214 Dubester (1950), 12–13; Schulze (1983), 139

215 Vols. XVIII, XIX. For Census Bureau maps in the NA, see below.

216 Dubester (1950), 24, 31.

217 HMD 261 (52–1), ser. 2998 (2 vols., 1891–2, reissued 1903).

218 Charlotte M. Ashby *et al.*, *Guide to the Cartographic Records in the National Archives* (1971): a detailed catalog for all RGs. The following account mentions only those important for community historians. See also Richard A. Bartlett, *Great Surveys of the American West* (1966), bibl.; Herman R. Friis, "Highlights of the geographical and cartographical activities of the federal government in the southeastern United States, 1776–1864," *Southeastern Geographer*, 6 (1966).

are some 1,800,000 maps and plans and three million aerial photographs.

In particular the records of the Office of the Chief of Engineers and of the former Corps of Topographical Engineers (RG 77) have been described as "the most valuable and historically significant group of maps ever deposited in the National Archives."[219] The maps and plans concerned, covering the period from 1804, vary in scale, but there are many large-scale maps of regions and local areas. They derive from the western explorations, military operations, and civil improvement works in which the Engineers were involved. The so-called Published Record Set of the Office of the Chief of Engineers for the period 1804 to c.1850 consists mainly of surveys for internal improvements in the eastern states, though some maps relate to the Ohio–Michigan boundary, the Northwest Territory, lands assigned to the Indians west of the Mississippi, the states of Texas and Florida, New Mexico Territory, the campaigns of the Mexican War, the Fort Smith–Sante Fé route, and the Oregon trail. Maps for the decade 1850–60 are concerned mainly with the territories west of the Mississippi, including general topographic maps, maps from explorations and surveys of particular areas, some river and harbor surveys, and a map of the state of Florida.[220] For the Civil War period the maps are mainly of military departments in Central and Southern states, parts of Virginia and Maryland (showing topographical details and often farm boundaries with names of residents, and of battlefields and campaigns).[221] For the period 1866–90 there are large numbers of maps of civil works, western exploration, and Civil War battlefields, many of which were published. From 1890 through 1960 most of the

[219] A. Philip Muntz, "Federal cartographic archives," *Prologue*, 1 (1969), 4. The following draws on this and on Ashby *et al.*, *Guide*. See also Patrick D. McLaughlin (comp.), *Transportation in Nineteenth-Century America: A Survey of the Cartographic Records in the National Archives* (RIP 65, 1973); Ehrenberg, "Taking the measure," 138–9; Ehrenberg, *Geographical Exploration*, 4–10 and esp. nn. 14, 19; Friis, *Surveying and Mapping*.
[220] See *Office of the Chief of Engineers Records, Pt. I* (NM–19, 1963–4) and *Supplement* (NM–78, 1967); *Pt. II* (NM–45, 1966) and *Supplement* (NM–79, 1967).
[221] For details, see William H. Cunliffe *et al.*, *A Guide to Civil War Maps in the National Archives* (1986).

maps (usually in several editions) relate to administrative matters and communications. Manuscript material in this Record Group includes many maps and plans deriving from explorations and surveys, military maps (including those relating to Indian and Mexican wars and the Civil War), and surveys for internal improvements (including cartographic records of the Mississippi River Commission, 1876–1954 and the Missouri River Commission, 1889–96). Catalogs exist for these collections. Record Group 77 also includes over 300 city plans dated before 1890, the majority of which have never been published.[222]

Senate records (RG 46) include many published and unpublished maps to do with a variety of matters, including the improvement of transportation and communications, 1825–40, which, for some areas, were the first accurate surveys.[223]

The records of the Post Office Department (RG 28) include state, county, city, and local center maps giving postal information, but incidentally other topographical data. The series of published postal route state maps, revised from time to time, dates from 1839. The city and local center (for rural areas) maps are unpublished and the county maps photoprocessed.[224] Postal route maps of 1839 for Mississippi, Louisiana, Missouri, and Arkansas, annotated (probably during the Civil War) to show the population of each county, distinguished by race and indicating free and slave blacks, crop yields and numbers of livestock, are among the records of the Geological Survey (RG 57). The Survey's records also include series of manuscript maps of states showing drainage and topography, and original drawings and surveys of certain urban areas, farm projects, rivers, lakes, forests, national parks and forests,

---

[222] Ralph E. Ehrenberg, *Cartographic Records in the National Archives Useful for Urban Studies* (RIP 68, 1973), 3–6. Records of engineer districts are held in regional branches of the NA: *GNA*, 239.

[223] *GNA*, 50; Ehrenberg, *Geographical Exploration*, 8; W. L. Joerg, "The internal improvement maps (1825–1835) in the National Archives," *Annals Assoc. Am. Geographers*, 28 (1938); RIP 65, 4; Ashby *et al.*, *Guide*, 6–8; and see p. 426.

[224] See p. 434 for details.

mining districts, and so forth.[225] They also contain some maps from the Hayden and Powell surveys.

The records of the Department of the Interior (RG 48) include manuscript, published, and photoprocessed maps of the United States, and parts of the United States, particularly the West and the South, indicating among other things the status of the public domain, Indian tribal locations and reservations, judicial districts, mining districts and claims, railroads, wagon roads, and natural resources.[226] Of particular interest are maps and other material relating to Pacific railroad surveys, 1849–58, not only giving information on routes but also showing topographical features, Indian locations, settlements, roads, and trails.[227]

Record Group 75, comprising the records of the Bureau of Indian Affairs, provides another collection of published and unpublished cartographic materials. These relate to exploration, boundary surveys, and topographical information on Indian cessions and reservations, including townships and townsites in Indian lands and reservations, rights of way across Indian land, and many other like topics.[228]

The records of the General Land Office (GLO) (RG 49) contain an enormous amount of cartographic and related material for the public-domain states deriving from the surveying, managing, and disposing of public lands. There is an

[225] Ashby, *Guide*, 141, 143; RIP 68, 8. Many of these form the basis for publ. maps: see above. For photographic records of the Geological Survey in NA, see Geological Survey, *Descriptive Catalogue of the Photographs* . . . *1869 to 1875* (1875) and its key, *Correlation List of New and Old Numbers* (1951).

[226] Laura E. Kelsay (comp.), *Cartographic Records of the Office of the Secretary of the Interior* (PI 81, 1955); *Records of the Office of the Secretary of the Interior, 1863–1964* (NA, NNF–48, 1984, T/S), pt. I, 204–8. N.B., too, Geological Survey Library, Dept. of the Interior, 345 Middlefield Rd., MS 955, Menlo Park, CA 94025: details, Makower, 26. And see pp. 426–7.

[227] RIP 65, 6–7. Many were used in *Reps. of Explorations and Surveys . . . for a Railroad from the Mississippi River to the Pacific Ocean . . . 1853–1856* (13 vols., 1861).

[228] Ashby, *Guide*, 146–8; RIP 68, 7–8; Muntz, "Federal cartographic archives," 5; Laura E. Kelsay (comp.), *List of Cartographic Records in the Bureau of Indian Affairs* (SL 13, 1954). See also Laura E. Kelsay (comp.), *Cartographic Records in the National Archives Relating to Indians in the United States* (RIP 71, 1974) (describes records in RG 49 [GLO] and other RGs).

excellent catalog of the collection.[229] It includes manuscript and annotated maps, boundary maps and plans, field notes, and published maps. All these are of potential use to the historian and topographer, particularly of the West, for, as has been claimed, "no mapping ever so profoundly affected the appearance of the land as did the township surveying method," visibly dividing the land "into endlessly repeated squares, reflecting the pattern of survey and sale." Road building and farming generally follow the original patterns marked out by the GLO.[230] The maps and plans include many of specific areas, regions, states, and territories, and in particular a large number of manuscript township and other plats of varying scales (but often of 2 inches to the mile). These, together with the accompanying surveyors' notes, topographic sketches, photographs, and other materials, provide much information. They include named natural features, township and section lines, roads and trails, drainage patterns, Indian villages, reserves, and cessions, boundaries of private land claims, other man-made features, mines, and mining plans. Larger scale township plats showing greater detail of settlement are described in chapter 4.

The GLO records also include manuscript and annotated plats showing early land claims for areas previously ruled by foreign powers,[231] and there are files relating to land-grant railroads and wagon roads which include maps.[232] The published maps in the GLO collection include standard maps of various dates covering whole states and territories, and special maps for the nineteenth century and later, among them maps, diagrams, and plats indicating the extent of public surveys,

---

[229] Laura E. Kelsay (comp.), *List of Cartographic Records of the General Land Office* (SL 19, 1964) (not all GLO maps and plans are incl. in this). See also Ashby, *Guide*, 148–57; Ehrenberg, *Geographical Exploration*, 1–4; RIP 65, 5–6; Robert W. Harrison, "Public land records of the federal government," *MVHR*, 41 (1954), 278–80; Donald B. Clements, "Public land surveys," *Surveying and Mapping*, 18 (1958); Ehrenberg, "Taking the measure," 130–2; pp. 174–5 below.

[230] See Robert W. Baughman, *Kansas in Maps* (1961), 51.

[231] William J. Heynen, *Pre-1930 Agricultural and Related Maps in the National Archives* (1971), 16; Gary L. Morgan, "Notes on genealogy," *Prologue*, 9 (1977), 179–80 for details.

[232] Jane F. Smith, "Settlement on the public domain as reflected in federal records," in Ralph E. Ehrenberg, *Patterns and Process* (1975), 301.

land district boundaries, Indian reservations, and lands designated under the homestead acts.[233] Manuscript and annotated
plats of townships and parts of townships compiled for one
purpose or another (especially initial disposal of public lands)
exist for various dates from the late eighteenth century for
more than twenty states. For parts of Louisiana plats are in the
records of the Office of the Chief of Engineers (RG 77).[234]
Such maps are to be found not only in the National Archives.
Public land survey plats have been and still are of use to local
administrative officers and the courts, so that versions may
well be on deposit at state and county levels. Except for
Oklahoma (the state records for which are in Washington,
DC), plats are available in each of the public-land states in the
offices of a state official or a local office of the Bureau of Land
Management, Department of the Interior.[235]

The records of the Bureau of the Census (RG 29) include a
few enumeration district maps, published and unpublished,
for censuses from 1880.[236] Also in the National Archives
(mainly in RGs 77, 92, 94, 98, 108, 393) are some 8,000
manuscript and annotated maps published by both sides in the
Civil War. These show communications and general topography and sometimes name individual landowners.[237] The
records of the Southern Claims Commission (in RG 56) also
include some maps.[238] Maps and surveys of areas near U.S.

[233] SL 19, 131.   [234] See p. 186.
[235] William D. Pattison, "Use of the U.S. public land survey plats and notes as descriptive sources," *Professional Geographer*, 8 (1956), 11. For location, see *Manual of Instructions for the Survey of Public Lands in the United States* (Bureau of Land Management, 1947), 13–17.
[236] James B. Rhoads and Charlotte M. Ashby (comps.), *Cartographic Records of the Bureau of the Census* (PI 103, 1958) lists maps by states. In 1921 the Dept. of Agriculture published a series of maps showing the boundaries of each county at the time of the censuses, 1840–1920. For county boundaries, see also p. 299.
[237] Cunliffe, *Guide to Civil War Maps*. And see Richard W. Stephenson, *Civil War Maps – An Annotated List* (1989); Clara E. LeGear (comp.), *The Hotchkiss Map Collection* (1951) for refs. to other Civil War maps; Dale E. Floyd, *The Southeast During the Civil War: Selected War Department Records in the National Archives* (RIP 69, 1972), 3–6.
[238] Sarah Larson, "Records of the Southern Claims Commission," *Prologue*, 12 (1980), 215.

boundaries are to be found in RG 76.[239] Maps in various Record Groups for a number of states and territories are the subject of a useful list and there are guides to maps for Iowa and Wisconsin territories.[240]

Aside from the cartographic activities of the federal government, enormous numbers of other maps and plans exist. Many emanate from the administrative activities of state and local governments.[241] The records of county registers of deeds, for example, may contain maps and plans of landed properties, often bound in plat books. County surveyors made many plats for judicial and administrative purposes (as for school and road districts), and these, too, are to be found among state and county records.[242] Commercially initiated cartographic materials also proliferated in the nineteenth century.

Many large collections of American maps and plans exist, and it should be realized that for the early nineteenth century evidence from maps made before 1800 may well still be significant. In particular the existence of maps of cities, counties, and larger areas, as well as townsite plats and estate surveys for the late colonial period, may be useful. Some of these are in foreign depositories.[243] There are some good guides to the main collections of cartographic materials.[244] The Library of Congress has large collections of maps, plans, and views, for

---

[239] See Daniel T. Goggin (comp.), *Preliminary Inventory of the Records Relating to International Boundaries* (PI 170, 1968).

[240] Janet L. Hargett (comp.), *List of Selected Maps of States and Territories* (SL 29, 1971); Laura E. Kelsay and Frederick W. Pernell (comps.), *Cartographic Records Relating to the Territory of Iowa, 1834–1846* (SL 27, 1971); Laura E. Kelsay and Charlotte M. Ashby (comps.), *Cartographic Records Relating to the Territory of Wisconsin* (SL 23, 1970).

[241] Herman R. Friis, "Cartographic and related records," AA, 13 (1950), 137.

[242] Charles C. Crittenden and Dan Lacy (eds.), *The Historical Records of North Carolina*, 1 (1938), 34; WPA, HRS, *Inventory of the County Records of Virginia. No. 60, Middlesex County* (1939), 116–18.

[243] Friis, "Cartographic and related records," 136–7. See also, e.g., Patrick D. McLaughlin (comp.), *Pre-Federal Maps in the National Archives: An Annotated List* (SL 26, 1971); John Sellers and Patricia M. Van Ee (eds.), *Maps and Charts of North America and the West Indies, 1750–1789* [in Library of Congress] (1981); Public Record Office, *Maps and Plans in the Public Record Office, 2: America and the West Indies* (London, 1974); John A. Wolter *et al.*, *World Directory of Map Collections* (Munich, 1986).

[244] See Prucha, 127–9; HG, 46–7.

which there are a number of general and specific guides and catalogs. These should be available in large reference libraries.[245]

One Library of Congress collection of great potential value for community historians in many parts of the country is its county land-ownership maps.[246] Such maps were produced in small numbers in the first decade of the nineteenth century by commercial firms, and later were often officially promoted by state governments. Very large numbers were published, particularly after 1850, while others remained in manuscript. By the middle of the century they usually showed administrative and political boundaries, physical features, communications, townsites, farms, mills, factories, churches, schools, and houses (with names of residents). Plans of towns and larger villages were often inset together with views of public buildings, factories, and farms. Atlases, comprising sets of these maps, with plans of towns, began to be published in the 1860s. The Library of Congress's collection of county land-ownership maps numbers some 1,450, largely dating from about 1840, pertaining to over 1,000 counties (about one-third of all American counties) with concentrations in the Northeastern and North Central states, Virginia, California, and Texas.[247] Since the maps (and atlases) may well in some cases predate the better-known plat books and the topographical surveys of the Geological Survey they are a source well worth searching.[248] Their importance for land use, residential patterns, and many other aspects of community history is clear.

The Library of Congress also has a large collection of maps and plans of cities. These vary from topographical to thematic

---

[245] See Prucha, 124, 128–9 [Q34, 62–4, 67, 69, 71]; Richard W. Stephenson (comp.), *Land Ownership Maps: A Checklist of Nineteenth Century County Maps in the Library of Congress* (1967); Michael H. Shelley (comp.), *Ward Maps of United States Cities: A Selected Checklist of Pre-1900 Maps in the Library of Congress* (1975); Richard S. Ladd (ed.), *Maps Showing Explorers' Routes* (1962). See also Library of Congress, *Bibliography of Cartography* (5 vols., 1973) and *Supplements* (2 vols., 1980).

[246] The following is based on Stephenson, *Land Ownership Maps*, q.v. for a list.

[247] Norman J. W. Thrower, "The county atlases of the United States," *Surveying and Mapping*, 21 (1961) indicates areas for which these exist.

[248] Available for purchase in microfiche from Library of Congress, Photoduplication Service, Dept. C, Washington, DC 20540.

maps dealing with such subjects as population, transportation, utilities, and public administration. Those showing city wards may be useful for urban historians, especially when used in conjunction with evidence from censuses and electoral records.[249]

Many of the published maps in the Library of Congress are to be found elsewhere, too, together with numerous other maps. For many regions, states, and large cities, catalogs and lists of local cartographic materials have been published.[250] State libraries and libraries of historical societies and large cities have often published guides to their collections.[251] Especially significant are the collections of the New York Public Library,[252] and of the American Geographical Society, which is a depository for maps issued by federal agencies.[253] The British Library (formerly the library of the British Museum) has large collections of American maps.[254]

As well as land-ownership maps (see above) large numbers of other maps of towns, counties, states, and regions were produced by unofficial bodies and for commercial purposes.[255] Immigration societies, for instance, published maps of some areas to encourage immigration and many maps are to be found in periodicals and books, especially guide books and books of travel.[256] A large number of canal, turnpike, and

[249] Shelley, *Ward Maps*, preface. Lists maps for thirty-five cities in 1880. Copies available from address in previous note.
[250] The Library of Congress, *Bibliography of Cartography* provides the best list. See also Prucha, 123–5, 127–30.
[251] The best guide is Library of Congress, *Bibliography of Cartography*.
[252] *Dictionary Catalog of the Map Division* [New York Public Library] (10 vols., 1971), with annual supplements, *Bibliographic Guide to Maps and Atlases*.
[253] Eva L. Yonge, "The map department of the American Geographical Society," *Professional Geographer*, 7 (1955). This library is now at Golda Meir Library, University of Wisconsin, PO Box 413, Milwaukee, WI 53201.
[254] British Museum, *Catalogue of Manuscript Maps, Charts and Plans, and of Topographical Drawings in the British Museum*, vol. 3 (1861); British Museum, *Catalogue of Printed Maps, Charts and Plans* (15 vols., 1967; Am. refs. arranged topographically).
[255] Walter W. Ristow, *Maps for an Emerging Nation: Commercial Cartography in Nineteenth-Century America* (1977).
[256] See Am. Geographical Soc., *Index to Maps in Books and Periodicals* (10 vols., 1968; and Supplements, 2 vols., 1976); Harold M. Otness, *Index to Early 20th Century Plans Appearing in Guide Books* (1978), marginally useful for U.S.; George H. Knoles, "Baedeker's United States," *Pacific Hist. Rev.* (March, 1944); Walter W. Ristow, "American road maps and guides," *Scientific Monthly*, 62 (1946).

railroad maps were published from before the middle of the century,[257] while the expansion of mining stimulated the production of geological and specifically mining district maps. There were also maps for immigrants about railroad and other routes to the mining and farming areas.[258] The Union Pacific Railroad in 1875, for example, published a map of central Kansas exhibiting lands for sale and showing many colonies of foreign-born immigrants.[259] *Cram's Standard American Railway System Atlas of the World* (various edns., 1890s) not only has railroad maps but street maps for some thirty U.S. cities.

Like the county maps described above, town and city maps also proliferated from 1850 providing detailed information on topographical matters and property ownership. Barrett Cushing, for example, had by 1858 published plans for all the towns in Massachusetts and maps of every county in the state. In urban areas many types of maps were produced for sale, like, for instance, R. W. Dobson's railroad maps of Chicago.[260]

Urban historians will find of particular value the commercial maps of cities using the panoramic or "bird's-eye" format which developed after the Civil War and was particularly in vogue from about 1870 to 1920.[261] Though not always accurate nor usually strictly to scale, they give a much better conception of the physical make-up of towns than conventional plans and show clearly street patterns, building profiles, and the pattern of the townscape viewed from an oblique angle. John W. Reps has reproduced in his books many of these bird's-eye plans of towns and cities, as well as other urban maps and plans, indicating the whereabouts of the originals.[262]

---

[257] Andrew M. Modelski (comp.), *Railroad Maps of the United States* (1976); Andrew M. Modelski (comp.), *Railroad Maps of North America: the First Hundred Years* (1984).

[258] E.g., Illinois Central Railroad, *Sectional Maps, Showing Location of over 2,500,000 Acres Select Farming and Wood Lands in the State of Illinois* (1867).

[259] Repr. in Baughman, *Maps in Kansas*, 84–5.

[260] Schlereth, *Artifacts*, 80–1.

[261] Library of Congress, *Panoramic Maps of Cities in the United States* (1984); I. N. Phelps Stokes and Daniel C. Haskell, *American Historical Prints: Early Views of American Cities, Etc.* (1932). Copies of some of such views may be purchased.

[262] *The Making of Urban America* (1965); *Town Planning in Frontier America* (1969); *Cities of the American West* (1979); *Cities on Stone* (1976). See also introductions to these works.

Introduction

After the Civil War increasing numbers of county atlases with separate town plats were produced, some providing attached directories of inhabitants with dates of settlement. In this period, too, official surveyors prepared plans for urban centers for fiscal purposes (tax-assessment maps), and commercial firms provided similarly detailed plans and bird's-eye views for real estate and insurance firms. Such plans were on a large scale, and by means of colors and symbols provide much detailed information. They give, for example, block and lot numbers from which property owners can be identified in the official city record books, and show the materials of which houses, factories, shops, churches, and other buildings were constructed. They also show architectural features such as lofts, skylights, and water tanks. Closely related are "land-use atlases" compiled from the plans but generally less detailed.

Fire-insurance maps are of considerable potential for urban historians.[263] The Sanborn Map and Publishing Company has produced fire-insurance maps for some 12,000 U.S. cities and towns from the second half of the nineteenth century. For most of the larger towns and all major cities, many editions of these appeared from the 1880s to the 1950s, and are purchasable from the Sanborn Company.[264] There is a large collection in the Library of Congress, and many exist in other libraries.[265] Other insurance company surveys and maps also exist, such as

---

[263] Walter W. Ristow, "United States fire insurance and underwriters' maps, 1852–1968," Q. Jnl. Library of Congress, 25 (1968) (repr. in Surveying and Mapping, 30 (1970)). See also Sanborn Map Co., Description and Utilization of the Sanborn Map (1953).

[264] 629 Fifth Ave., Pelham, New York, NY 10803.

[265] Walter W. Ristow, Fire Insurance Maps in the Library of Congress (1981); R. Philip Hoehn, Union List of Fire Insurance Maps Held in Institutions in the United States and Canada, vol. 1 (Alabama to Missouri) (1976); William S. Peterson-Hunt and Evelyn Woodruff, Union List of Fire Insurance Maps Held in Institutions in the United States and Canada, vol. 2 (Montana to Wyoming; Canada and Mexico, with Supplement and Corrigenda to vol. 1) (1977); Gary W. Rees and Mary Hoeber, Catalogue of Sanborn Atlases at California State University, Northridge (1973). See also R. Philip Hoehn, "Fire insurance maps in the Bancroft Library," Information Bull., 3 (1972); Makower. Many are available in microform: Chadwyck-Healey Inc.: 623,000 maps of 10,000 towns and cities arranged as in Fire Insurance Maps in the Library of Congress (but in black and white).

those of Ernest Hexamer and Nelson Barlow,[266] and local and national underwriters' associations also made surveys and plats. Some of these plans may be found in insurance-company files, among collections of business records, and in registries of deeds, local government offices, and so on.[267]

Yet other commercial maps include road maps issued for cyclists, as, for example, Charles G. Huntington's *Cyclist's Road Book of Connecticut* (1888). Many cyclists' maps were published by the League of American Wheelmen. Rand McNally began publishing road maps and guides for cyclists from 1894, and the annual *Rand McNally and Company Business* (later *Commercial*) *Atlas*, presenting maps of states with information on business, population, and transportation,[268] remains a standard reference. Early editions often locate tiny communities and railroad stops which are no longer in existence.

---

[266] For details and whereabouts, see Helena Wright, "Insurance mapping and industrial archaeology," *Jnl. Soc. Industrial Archaeology*, 9, 1 (1983), 6–13, 16; Hoehn, *Union List*; Peterson-Hunt and Woodruff, *Union List*. And see William Perris, *Maps of the City of New York Surveyed under the Direction of the Insurance Companies of the Said City* (34 vols., 1852–81).

[267] Wright, "Insurance mapping," 15.

[268] Ristow, "American road maps," 399.

CHAPTER 2

Demography

Reconstruction of the social composition and assessment of the changing size of past communities are basic tasks for the historian of local communities. Not only is the demographic pattern of a community of central significance in analysis of the characteristics and nature of the population of a city, county, or other locality, but without at least an outline of facts about population the necessary framework for investigating and comprehending many other aspects of local life will be lacking.

Aside from determination of the beginning of a settlement and the actual size of its population over time, analysis of the composition of that population in terms of age, sex, ethnicity (and before 1865 freedom and slavery), and occupations will help to recreate the character of the community. In an area of any size – a county perhaps, or a large city – the spatial distribution and density of population, too, may call for investigation, bearing in mind that the social ingredients of population may vary within the territorial boundaries of the area being studied, and that, in particular, there are likely to be differences between rural and urban parts and between the nature of one part of a city and another.

The residential experience of different groups in large towns is also of interest. Did occupational, ethnic, or immigrant groups cluster together, and, if so, how did this affect the characteristics of a neighborhood?[1] The whole topic of migration is significant, too. To what extent did in- and out-migration take place in a particular area? Who were those who came into a locality and where did they come from? Did the

---

[1] Theodore Hershberg, "The historical study of urban space," *HMN*, 9 (1976), 99.

characteristics of those who stayed (persisters) differ from those who left a town or district?

Another area of possible research lies in the distribution of wealth and social class within a community and its relationship to occupation, length of residence, place of domicile, age, ethnicity, race, education, and other factors, including perhaps study of political or social leadership (elite) groups within a community (see ch. 7). The consideration of the characteristics and fortunes of ethnic groups within local communities opens up another wide field. Embraced within it may be the resilience of ethnic characteristics and outlooks, inter-ethnic marriages, and the relationship between ethnicity and religion, politics, and other aspects of life, such as crime, prostitution, and so on, and the whole area of black life, slave and free, including the development of black areas in the large cities.[2]

Such research is likely to involve consideration of the typology of the constituent parts of communities, particularly households and families.[3] Included here are the distribution of different types of families (as nuclear, extended, or multi-generational) and the related make-up of households, and also the presence of sub-families, distinct families, and of distant kin, servants, boarders, and so on. The average size and age structure of families, the proportions of men and women, and boys and girls, the general age at marriage, fertility and illegitimacy rates, and mortality rates (related to age, causes of death, seasonality, and so on) can all be investigated. So, too, can the variations within a community of family patterns according to ethnicity, race, wealth, social class, occupation, religious adherence, ownership or otherwise of farms and other real property, population density of the neighborhood, length of residence, and like matters. Consideration of family and household structures may also take into account

---

[2] Stephanie W. Greenberg, "Neighborhood change, racial tension, and work location . . . Philadelphia, 1880–1930," *JUH*, 7 (1981); and see ch. 3.

[3] The family as a local and extra-local network is not considered here, but see Tamara K. Hareven and Maris S. Vinovskis (eds.), *Family and Population in Nineteenth Century America* (1978), 15; ABC-Clio, *American Family History: A Historical Bibliography* (1984).

differences of urban and rural characteristics in a locality. Family structures, of course, were not always static, but may well have altered over time, so that, for example, the life-cycle of an individual family might include a nucleated stage, but later an extended or multi-generational one, changing again perhaps as old age became an ingredient.[4]

The historian of the community will also generally wish to study all these topics over a period of time rather than just in particular years, seeking a dynamic rather than merely a static picture. Structures at one period may be compared with those at a later one, the nature of the change assessed, and reasons for it sought. This opens up the large related fields of social mobility (both inter- and intra-generational) and of spatial or geographic mobility within the area or locality, both of which can be pursued, taking into account many variables. Of particular interest may be the effects of transportation improvements, urbanization, and industrialization, and of large-scale population growth consequent on immigration. The relationship of the elements of social structure, especially occupation, class, ethnicity, and residential persistence, to political and agricultural matters is dealt with in chapters 4, 5, and 7.

The sources for the study of the topics just outlined are numerous. Newspapers, guide books, gazetteers, older county histories, diaries, biographies and autobiographies, reminiscences, letters and private papers, records of charitable, political, and social associations, church records – all these and others can contribute information on individuals, groups, and places, some of which may provide quantifiable data, some more subjective evidence.[5] All these types of

---

[4] See, e.g., Glen H. Elder, Jr., "Family history and the life course," *JFH*, 2 (1977); Howard P. Chudacoff and Tamara K. Hareven, "From the empty nest to family dissolution," *JFH*, 4 (1979); Tamara K. Hareven, "The family as process," *JSH*, 7 (1974); Robert V. Wells, "American demographic change and the life cycle of American families," *JIH*, 2 (1971); Hareven and Vinovskis, *Family and Population*, 15–16.

[5] For assocs., see, e.g., Hershberg, *Philadelphia*, 508; Walter S. Glazer, "Participation and power," *HMN*, 5 (1972). For church records used for occupational and residential mobility, see P. Johnson, *A Shopkeeper's Millennium* (publ. Ph.D. diss., Univ. of California, Los Angeles, 1975).

Sources for U.S. History

source are treated elsewhere in this volume. Central, however, to demographic studies are censuses, directories, vital records, voting records, probate records, and financial records of various kinds. It is these that are considered in this chapter.

CENSUS MATERIALS

Basic evidence for the demographic analysis of nineteenth-century American communities is found in the published and unpublished records of official censuses. A great deal of statistical data is provided in the published volumes of the decennial federal census, available in some large libraries in the original volumes or more often on microfilm.[6] For all these censuses some important data at state and county levels, extracted by the Inter-University Consortium for Political and Social Research, may be purchased.[7] From the first census of 1790, the federal censuses expanded in geographical coverage as the Union grew.[8]

The federal census volumes provide statistics of population and non-population data gathered from individuals, institutions, business firms, and local governments. Aggregates provided are fullest for the Union as a whole and for states and territories, but many statistics are given, too, for counties, townships, and the larger cities (sometimes at ward level), and not infrequently for towns and smaller cities. The following account concentrates mainly on the data provided at the levels below that of the state or territory, giving, where helpful, exact references to the census volumes.

The first published census, that of 1790, provides the actual names of heads of households (the only time individual names appear in the published volumes) and totals of free white males

---

[6] Essential guides are Dubester (1950), Schulze (1983), Schulze (1985); and see pp. 22–3, 41. Also useful are U.S. Bureau of the Census, *Twenty Censuses: Population and Housing Questions, 1790–1980* (1978); *Checklist*.

[7] For details see ICPSR, *Historical Demographic, Economic and Social Data: The United States, 1790–1970* (n.d.); *Guide to Resources and Services of the Inter-University Consortium for Political Research, 1974–5* (n.d.).

[8] See Schulze (1983), 420–4 for states and territories as they appear in the census vols. Schulze (1983), Schulze (1985) indicate for each census what areas are incl.

64

under the age of sixteen and of sixteen upwards, and of free white females (not differentiated by age), as well as totals of all other free persons, and numbers of slaves. Such information is given by counties but with a few exceptions not for smaller units. The 1800 and 1810 censuses give for counties, towns, and cities, numbers of free whites (differentiated by sex) in age groups, and totals of all other free persons (except untaxed Indians), of slaves, and of free white male and female heads of households.[9]

The 1820 census volumes present similar data but include also age groups for free blacks and the numbers of un-naturalized foreigners, as well as rudimentary figures for occupations (numbers engaged in agriculture, in commerce, and in manufacturing)[10] and for manufacturing establishments (numbers of men, boys, women, and girls employed in them).[11] The 1830 census volumes contain no occupational statistics but additional information includes, for counties, towns, and cities, a more detailed classification by age for whites (by sex) and for free blacks and slaves.[12]

In the published 1840 census the population is distinguished by age, race, and condition (slave or free) as in 1830, for counties, towns, townships, precincts, etc.,[13] and fuller details than before are provided for occupations.[14] Employed persons are classified as working in the following categories: mining, agriculture, commerce, manufactures and trade, sea and inland navigation, and as engineers or in the learned professions. And the numbers of military pensioners are given.[15] No such information on veterans occurs again until the 1890 census. A separate volume (Statistics) and the Compendium

---

[9] For 1810, vol. I.   [10] Vol. I.   [11] Vol. II (Digest).

[12] Vol. I, pt. II. Two Abstract vols. (one publ. by F. P. Blair, one by Duff Green) incl. the main data at county level. For handicapped and paupers in this and later census vols., see ch. 11.

[13] See also *Aggregate Amount of Each Description of Persons Within the Several Districts of the United States*, HED 76 (27–2), ser. 402 (1842) (males and females in each county by sex, race, condition).

[14] Vols. I, III (Compendium), 370–5, includes population totals by counties and principal towns for each previous census year.

[15] Names, ages, residences of pensioners, and names of heads of families they resided with, by counties and smaller units, are in vol. IV.

volume present, at county and minor division levels, the number of persons (mostly men) employed in various selected branches of mining, agriculture, horticulture, commerce, fisheries, forest products, and manufacturing.[16]

From 1850 the published censuses become increasingly complex. Volume I of the 1850 census contains most of the demographic statistics, including (for counties, cities, towns, townships, parishes, precincts, wards, hundreds, etc.) aggregate population figures. For counties these are classed by race, age, sex, quinquennial age groups, and whether free or slave. For counties there are also data on births, deaths, and marriages, numbers of dwellings, and numbers of families.[17] Additionally there is a useful table, alphabetically arranged, of all places named in the census, giving aggregate populations,[18] and another similar list for a number of large named cities.[19] The Compendium volume also has an alphabetical list of cities, towns, townships, hundreds, etc., with total populations,[20] and in an appendix tables of population by age and sex of the white and free-black populations of the leading cities in the North and Northwest. For the slaveholding states the same information is given together with that for slaves. In addition statistics relating to the nativity of the inhabitants of counties and leading U.S. cities are given.[21] Occupational information in the 1850 census is not provided below the state and territory level. Data on religious and educational matters in this and later censuses are noted in chapters 6 and 10.

The volumes of the 1860 census include totals by counties of population (by age groups, sex, race, condition) distinguishing free persons as native or foreign.[22] Where provided, the

16 Vol. II (Statistics); Compendium.
17 Pp. xcv–cii; State tables I, II, IV. For inf. on housing in this and other censuses, see ch. 11.
18 Pp. ciii–cxxxvi.
19 National tables XXXIV, XXXV (with retrospective data). See also vol. II, tables XXIII (29 leading cities; incl. details of nativity), XXIV, XXV (incl. details of age and sex in a few leading cities).
20 Compendium, 338–93.
21 Ibid., 395–8; 194–377, 399.
22 Vol. I, tables 1, 2, 4; Preliminary Rep., tables 3, 41.

population figures for cities, towns, and other units sub-ordinate to counties are classified by race, sex, and condition.[23] Data on the nativity of the population of forty-four large towns and cities,[24] distinguishing sex and race, and of eight large cities are also given.[25] Information on slavery is given for the last time: the number of slaveholders in each county categorized according to the number of slaves held.[26] For Indians the number (by age groups and sex) is given by counties in Indian territory with an estimate at state level of the number living tribally.[27] Other information in the 1860 volumes includes the number of families by county,[28] and occupational statistics which embrace numbers of adult males and females employed in the chief industries of each county.[29] The numbers employed in manufacturing are given for 102 cities of over 10,000 inhabitants.[30]

The 1870 published census provides, for counties and smaller civil divisions, the numbers of males and females by race, together with aggregated figures for earlier census years.[31] This census is, however, notorious for having omitted over a million former slaves in the Southern states. At county level and for some minor civil divisions children aged 5–18 (school age, distinguishing sex) are enumerated, as are males aged 18–45 (militia age), males aged 21 and over (voting age) and male citizens.[32] The populations of counties and of the fifty principal cities, are broken down by race, with classifications for native born (by state) and foreign born (by country), while statistics are also provided of those native born with foreign-born fathers or mothers or both. Numbers of foreign born are given, too, for smaller units than counties.[33]

---

[23] Vol. I, table 3. For populations of 126 principal cities, 1850 and 1860: Preliminary Rep., table 40.
[24] Vol. I, pp. xxi–xxxii.
[25] Vol. I, 608–15.   [26] Vol. II, 223–46. And see p. 135.
[27] Vol. I, table I; ibid., 605.   [28] Vol. IV, 340–51.
[29] Vol. III, tables I, II.   [30] Vol. IV, pp. xviii–xix.
[31] Vol. I, table III; Compendium, tables VIII, IX.
[32] Vol. I, tables XXIV, XXV; Compendium, table LVII.
[33] Vol. I, tables III, V, VII, VIII; Compendium, tables XIX, XX.

Occupational data for counties include numbers of male and female hands (distinguishing males over sixteen and females over fifteen) employed in manufacturing and mechanical industries and in specific industries,[34] and by specific occupation in thirty major cities.[35] For the fifty largest cities the numbers employed in all classes of occupation and four groups of occupation,[36] distinguished by age and selected nativity, are provided.[37]

The volumes of the 1880 census provide much more extensive information than exists for any previous census. Items concerned with economic matters are discussed elsewhere. Population totals are provided for counties,[38] and townships, and minor civil divisions,[39] and separately for cities of 4,000 people upwards,[40] for the hundred largest cities,[41] and for the fifty largest.[42] Sometimes retrospective totals for earlier census years are also given, and information on race is provided for counties and places of 4,000 upwards, and on nativity (native and foreign born, and place of birth by state or foreign country) for counties and places of 4,000 and more, as well as for the fifty principal cities.[43] For counties, the total male and female populations are provided and also the numbers of each sex of school age (5–17), of males of militia age (18–44) and of males of voting age (21 upwards).[44]

Occupation statistics (distinguishing age and nativity) are presented for the fifty largest cities in the same four categories

[34] Vol. III, tables IXA, IXB, XI. Table XV: numbers engaged in mining by county.
[35] Vol. I, table XXXII.
[36] Agriculture; personal and professional; trade and transportation; manufactures, mechanical, and mining industries.
[37] Vol. I, table XXXI. See also Compendium, tables LXVI–LXXI.
[38] Vol. I, table VIII; Compendium, table XVIII. Density of population by counties is also given. An Extra Census Bulletin provides the areas of states and territories by counties: Henry Gannett, *The Area of the United States and Territories and their Counties* (1881).
[39] Vol. I, table III; Compendium, table XIX.
[40] Vol. I, table IX.
[41] Vol. I, table XXV; Compendium, table CIX.
[42] Vol. I, tables XV, XVI.
[43] Vol. I, tables III, V, VI, VIII, IX, XIV, XV, XVI, and p. 471; Compendium, tables XXIII, XXIV, XXV, XXVI, XXXII, XXXIII. For general nativity figures in 100 principal cities, see Compendium, table CIX.
[44] Vol. I, table XXIII; Compendium, table XLI.

as for 1870, with totals for seventy-five occupations.[45] In addition, for each county and for the hundred largest cities, the number of male hands (aged over sixteen), female hands (over fifteen) and child employees in selected manufacturing industries, and aggregate numbers per type of industry, are given.[46] The numbers of hands in manufacturing, mechanical, and mining industries are also presented for the fifty cities, broken down by sex, age, and specific nativity.[47]

The 1880 census also includes two volumes (XVIII, XIX) on the "Social Statistics of Cities." These present contemporary and earlier data on 222 separate cities,[48] though the coverage is patchy in quality and quantity. For each city, aggregate population figures (from as early as 1790) are provided, distinguished by sex, race, and general nativity. These are followed by a brief historical account of the place, and indication of geographical location with details of railroad communications, tributary counties, topography, and climate. There are data on streets, public buildings, places of amusement, many public services and amenities, and economic matters (as markets, commerce and navigation, manufactures) – though not all these items are covered for each city.[49] Other local social data in the 1880 volumes include the value of real and personal estate per capita for counties and cities of 7,500 population upwards,[50] and information on newspapers and stone buildings in cities.[51]

The volumes, reports, and bulletins of the 1890 census have a particular importance in that almost all the original returns on which they were based have been destroyed. Population data, some embracing nativity, race, and sex, are presented for counties, cities of 25,000 population upwards, places of 2,500 and of 1,000 upwards, and for other towns, cities, and smaller territorial units, sometimes with retrospective statistics for

---

[45] Vol. I, table XXXVI.
[46] Vol. II, tables V, VI. Compendium, tables LIII, CV give similar evidence for the twenty and fifty largest cities.
[47] Vol. II, p. xxxiii.   [48] Listed Schulze (1983), 220, 224–5.
[49] See ibid., 221. And see pp. 311–12.   [50] Vol. VII, table IVa, 217–33.
[51] Vol. VIII, apps. B, C; vol. X, 100, 280–363.

previous census years.[52] Numbers are given, too, by counties and places of 2,500 and more, and of 25,000 and more, of all male citizens over twenty-one, males and females of school age (classified 5–17, 18–20, 5–20), and of males of militia age (18–44), by race.[53] Ages in quinquennial groups are provided for cities of 25,000 upwards.[54] For counties and for cities of 25,000 and more, the numbers are given of foreign born, distinguished by country of origin, and for those cities the numbers of foreign-born males classified as aliens and naturalized.[55]

Occupational data for 124 cities of 50,000 population and above is presented for those of age ten and over in selected occupations, classified by sex, general nativity, country of birth, race, age groups, illiteracy, and inability to speak English.[56] For counties and for 165 cities of 20,000 upwards,[57] the average number of employees is given divided by sex and age (males over sixteen, females over fifteen, children). Volume x of the 1890 census represents the most detailed census investigation of American Indians up to that time.[58]

The volumes of the 1900 census present a great deal of demographic data for counties and for cities of population 25,000 upwards, together with some information for minor civil divisions.[59] Sometimes retrospective information is provided for earlier census years. Total populations are given for counties,[60] for some 160 cities of 25,000 upwards (and by wards),[61] for townships, and for unincorporated cities, towns,

[52] Vol. I, pt. I, tables 4–6, 8, 15–19, 22–3, 29–31, 33–4, 50–62. See also Compendium pt. I, population tables 3, 4a, 5, 6, 13–16, 19–20; Abstract (2nd edn.), tables 1–3.
[53] Vol. I, pt. I, tables 72–4, 76, 78–80 (and p. clxxiv); Compendium pt. I, population tables, 22a, 22b, 22c, 24, 26–8. Some of these embrace distinction by nativity and parental nativity.
[54] Vol. I, pt. 2, table 8.
[55] Compendium pt. 2, foreign-born population, tables 2, 3, 5, 7. See also table 9 (distribution by years in U.S.).
[56] Vol. I, pt. 2, table 118.
[57] Vol. VI, pt. I, table 6; pt. 2, table 3.
[58] For fuller description, see pp. 160–1.
[59] Vol. I, 51–3, for divisions used in each state.
[60] Vol. I, table xv, 4; Abstract, table 92 (gives areas). For density: vol. I, pp. xxxviii–lvii.
[61] Vol. I, tables XXII, XXVI, 6, 7; Abstract, table 80.

Demography

villages, and boroughs.[62] There is much evidence, too, on race and nativity. For counties and places of 2,500 upwards the population is classified by nativity, race, and sex.[63] For counties, numbers of Indians, Chinese, and Japanese, as well as of whites and blacks are given (and for 1880 and 1890).[64] Much greater detail is provided for cities of 25,000 population and more. As well as numbers by race and nativity, this includes numbers and percentages of persons born in the same state as the particular city, of other U.S. born (by state or territory), of foreign born, and of U.S. born of foreign parentage (by state or territory). For this last category there is a breakdown according to the specific countries of which the parents were native.[65] Figures are also provided for these cities on the length of U.S. residence of foreign-born males and females.[66]

A series of tables provides data on citizenship of males of twenty-one upwards: they are classified by counties according to general nativity, race, and literacy,[67] and for cities of 25,000 upwards in more detail – as, for example, for foreign-born according to country of origin and ability to speak English.[68]

For cities of 25,000 upwards, the populations are also classified by age groups, according to sex, general nativity,[69] for those of school age (5–20) by sex, race, general nativity, and for males of militia and voting age, by race and general nativity.[70] For counties and places of 2,500 and over, numbers within school, militia, and voting-age groups are similarly classified.[71] For the largest cities (at least 100,000 population) the conjugal condition of the population is analyzed, classified by sex, general nativity, race, and age groups.[72] For cities of

---

[62] Vol. I, table 5. Abstract, table 91: population of places of 2,500+.
[63] Vol. I, tables 18, 19, 22, 24, 34.
[64] Vol. I, tables 20, 21. See also Special Census Bull. 3, 12th Census, *Distribution of Chinese and Japanese in the Western States and Territories.*
[65] Vol. I, tables 30–2, 35, 57–66, L, LVII, LXXVIII, LXXXVII; Abstract, table 82.
[66] Vol. I, tables 86–90.
[67] Vol. I, table 92.
[68] Vol. I, tables 80–5, 91; Abstract, table 86.
[69] Vol. II, table 9; Abstract, table 83.
[70] Vol. I, tables 80–5; vol. II, tables 19–21, 23, 25; Abstract, table 84.
[71] Vol. II, tables 26, 27 – broken down into wards for some places.
[72] Vol. II, table 32.

25,000 upwards the conjugal condition is classified only by sex.[73]

Occupational data in the 1900 published census includes the total numbers at work of males and females of ten years of age upwards in cities of 25,000 and more, classified by specific occupations.[74] For these cities, for counties, and for 1,341 cities and towns of under 20,000 inhabitants, the average numbers of men and women of sixteen and over, and children under sixteen employed in manufacturing and mechanical industries are given, together with data on average numbers and total wages.[75] Some of this information is provided also for earlier census years.

Not so far mentioned are the vital statistics contained in the published census volumes. Of these, details of births, especially below the state level, are comparatively rarely recorded.[76] Mortality statistics are much fuller, but even so of limited value.[77] The censuses of 1850 through 1900 report numbers dying in the year preceding the taking of the census. It has been alleged, however, that "in no department has the census failed more signally than in the statistics of mortality"[78] and they must, therefore, be used with extreme caution, and preferably in conjunction with other evidence. The great difficulty is that most of the information was collected at the time of the census and not from continuous records made at the time of death. And even if (as is unlikely) the census figures were accurate for the census year, that is no indication that that year was typical of the decade concerned.

[73] Vol. II, table 31; Abstract, table 87.
[74] Vol. II, table 94; Abstract, table 88. See also *Special Reps.: Occupations*, tables 42–3; *Special Reps.: Statistics of Women at Work*, tables 9–12, 23, 26–9.
[75] Vol. VIII, tables 3–6, 8, 9; Abstract, tables 174–5. But children working less than half time not incl.
[76] For details, see Schulze (1983), 149, 204–8, 229–301, 389–91. See also *A Discussion of the Vital Statistics of the Twelfth Census*, Bull. 15 (1904) (mortality data for eighty-three cities of 25,000+, for each year 1890–1900 – supplementary to inf. in the census); *Supplementary Analysis and Derivative Tables, Twelfth Census*, Special Rep., Bureau of the Census (1906) (includes discussion on vital statistics).
[77] But see pp. 82, 515n. For other sources for vital data: pp. 82, 93–6, 97, 258.
[78] *The Federal Census, Critical Essays*, American Economic Assoc., NS, 2 (1899), 121, q.v. for criticism of these statistics. Cf. Carmen R. Delle Donne, *Federal Census Schedules, 1850–80* (RIP 67, 1973), 22; Maris A. Vinovskis, "Recent trends in American historical demography," *Am. Rev. Sociology*, 4 (1978), 621.

With such caveats in mind, it may be noted that the 1850 and 1860 censuses classified deaths by cause, age, sex, race, free or slave, nativity, season and duration of sickness – for states and territories – and for some of those categories in 1850 for the largest cities. The 1870 census includes data on deaths only by states and territories. Only the censuses from 1880 are of much value for mortality statistics. For 1880 and 1890 the mortality schedules were not applied to areas where registration of deaths had been established. For those areas data were drawn from the records, printed and manuscript, collected continuously by the registration offices.[79] In non-registration areas the census mortality schedules were supplemented by voluntary returns from physicians.[80] In the 1900 census the registration records of some states and cities were accepted at face value. For others, where the accuracy of registration was suspect, such records were supplemented by enumerators' schedules, though often both were to some extent defective.[81]

The 1880 census provides, for cities and counties of 10,000 population upwards, statistics of deaths by age and sex, and also gives figures for deaths from certain specified causes.[82] For thirty-one large cities numbers of deaths are classified by sex, race, month of death, and in some cases by parentage.[83] A number of tables provide mortality data arranged by groups of counties.[84]

Despite its title, "Vital Statistics," volume IV of the 1890 census is largely confined to mortality statistics.[85] Part I gives deaths and death rates at certain ages and for certain causes, distinguished by race, nativity, and sex, for separate cities in the registration states, rural parts of the registration states, registration cities in non-registration states, and for particular

---

[79] Even so, great variations of accuracy existed: *Federal Census, Critical Essays*, 128–31. And see pp. 93–6.

[80] Carrol D. Wright and William C. Hunt, *The History and Growth of the United States Census* (1900), 98–9.

[81] Vol. III, pp. xi–xxix.

[82] Vol. XII, table XIII (A, B), also numbers of births and of those born or dying within the census year.

[83] Vol. XII, table XXII.

[84] For counties in each group, see vol. XI, pp. xlix–lxiii.

[85] See vol. IV, pt. I, 495–511 for topographical areas covered.

counties and groups of counties. For fifty-four cities information is provided by wards.[86] Part 2 is concerned with the
same sort of statistical data for twenty-eight cities of 10,000
population and over,[87] but in addition has detailed general
descriptions of the social and economic characteristics of the
cities and within them of their wards. Part 4 includes data by
groups of counties on male deaths in certain occupational
categories, distinguished by race and nativity.[88] Three separate
(unnumbered) volumes of the 1890 census cover the vital
statistics for the cities of New York and Brooklyn, Boston and
Philadelphia, and Baltimore and the District of Columbia,
broken down into wards and sanitary districts.[89]

For the 1900 census the "Vital Statistics" volumes provide
for each registration city the number of deaths in the census
year, according to race, general nativity, parental nativity, and
sex,[90] and by age groups and sex.[91] A table provides for each
city, group, and county in the registration states, the population, numbers of births and deaths, death rates at certain
ages, and deaths from certain causes, distinguished by race,
sex, general nativity, and parental nativity.[92] A series of unnumbered tables provides, for some 350 registration cities in
registration states and in non-registration states, numbers of
deaths, and for 1890 and 1900 death rates classed by sex, race
and nativity, and age.[93]

So far concentration has been on the published volumes
of the federal censuses, and for many purposes these will
suffice – especially to provide a basic demographic sketch or
background to detailed study of some other aspect of a

---

[86] Tables 1, 6. See also pt. 3, tables 6 (groups of counties in certain states), 18 (groups
of counties and registration cities).
[87] For a list of these, see vol. IV, pt. 1, 496.
[88] Vol. IV, pt. 4, table 5.
[89] Dubester (1950), nos. 232–4.
[90] Vol. IV, table 4; Abstract, tables 94–5.
[91] Vol. IV, table 5; Abstract, tables 96–7. Table 7 has figures for cities and groups by
particular cause of death (see also tables 98–9).
[92] Vol. III, table 19. And see table 22: death rates from certain causes in each county in
registration states.
[93] Vol. III, pp. lviii–lx, lxv–lxvii, lxxiv–lxxvii, lxxx–lxxxii. Table on p. lxi gives
deaths annually 1891–1900 and death rates 1890, 1900 for 22 principal cities.

community's history.[94] Where more advanced and detailed demographic analysis of communities is required, however, the researcher will usually need to use the manuscript schedules or returns from which the published census data were compiled. Indeed it has been claimed that the "manuscript Federal Population Census offers a combination of depth, breadth and continuity unmatched by any other American document."[95] Where they have survived,[96] the original population and other schedules of the census provide, by counties, parishes and townships, towns, cities, wards and precincts, most of the types of information detailed above for the published census volumes. In addition they give much data (particularly in the later censuses) on individual people and on specific family and household units. All the information sought by the census takers – the schedules of inquiry, together with instructions on how to interpret certain questions – is available in print with an indication of the sort of evidence the researcher may expect to find in the original returns.[97]

The schedules for the first federal census (1790), arranged by counties and sometimes minor divisions, present as well as the names of heads of households (available in print)[98] the number in each household of free white males of sixteen and over (including the head of the household) and the number below that age, the number of free white females (including heads of households), the number of all other free persons, and the number of slaves. The schedules for Delaware, Georgia, Kentucky, New Jersey, Tennessee, and Virginia are missing.

---

[94] E.g., William L. Bowen, "Crawford township, 1850–1870," *Iowa Jnl. Hist.*, 58 (1960).
[95] Keith R. Schlesinger, "An 'urban finding aid' for the Federal census," *Prologue*, 13 (1981), 251 (repr. Timothy Welch (comp.), *Our Family, Our Town* (1987)).
[96] See note 111 below.
[97] Wright and Hunt, *United States Census*. See also *Genealogical Research*, 20–6.
[98] *Heads of Families of the First Census of the United States Taken in the Year 1790* (1908) (separate vols. for individual states). See also Debra L. Newman, *List of Free Black Heads of Families in the First Census of the United States* (SL 34, rev. 1974), by states: does not give geographical location but page nos. of census vols. are provided.

Those for Delaware, Kentucky, and Virginia have been partially reconstructed from tax records.[99]

In the population schedules for the censuses of 1800 and 1810, which were identical in content, the entries are arranged by county, parish, township, town, or city, and for each household provide the name of the head and the numbers of white male and female members classified in five age groups. The remaining members of the household appear only as numerical totals as in 1790 – "other free" (except untaxed Indians) and slaves.

In the 1820 schedules numbers of slaves and free blacks are also classified by age and sex. In addition they provide the number of unnaturalized foreigners, and a rudimentary occupational classification indicates the numbers of those engaged in agriculture, in commerce, and in manufacturing. The 1830 census schedules are much the same as for 1820 but do not repeat the occupational data.[100] Age classifications are, however, more detailed, enabling the relationship of household members to heads to be guessed at with greater certainty. It may be noted here that in using microfilm copies of the 1830 schedules care should be taken in matching data on slaves to the household in which they belonged – since the slave data on the right-hand page of the schedule appear below the left-hand page in the microfilm rather than alongside it.[101] The 1840 schedules are in content similar to those for 1830. Data on occupations, however, are provided, and in the greater detail already noted for the published census volumes. Numbers of unnaturalized foreigners no longer appear.

A new phase was introduced with the 1850 census. In place of numbers of individuals in various categories appearing against the name of the head of household, each free individual was from then on named and data concerning him or her

---

99 Norman E. Wright, *Preserving Your American Heritage* (1981), 60–1.

100 See Carter G. Woodson (ed.), *Free Negro Owners of Slaves in the United States in 1830* . . . (1924, repr. 1968), arranged by state and county: provides names of owners and numbers of slaves classed by age. But N.B. slaves listed under a particular "owner" were not necessarily owned by him: Leonard P. Curry, *The Free Black in Urban America, 1800–1850* (1980), 270. For the handicapped, see ch. 11.

101 Wright, *Preserving Your American Heritage*, 68.

recorded personally. Households were enumerated together and families were numbered. From 1850 the census schedules thus acquire a much greater potential significance for the social investigator.

In 1850 each individual's age, sex, race, and, for males over fifteen, profession, occupation, or trade are given, together with a valuation of his or her real estate, place of birth (state, territory, or foreign country), whether married within the year past, whether at school, whether unable to read and write (if over twenty), and whether handicapped, pauper, or convict. From the 1850 census through that for 1880 and for the 1900 census,[102] the population schedules provide much the same basic information as just outlined. The significant differences and innovations may, however, be noted here.

Schedules of slaves in 1850 and 1860 were not as full as for free persons. They did not give names. Information was provided under the names of owners, typically listing male workers first, female workers second, and last the non-working (children and aged) males and females.[103] Nevertheless, it is possible to reconstruct the age and sex structure of slave communities in different sorts of plantations and other establishments.[104] Note that the census takers often gave less full addresses of slave owners in the slave schedules than in the free schedules, which may, therefore, need also to be consulted for study of slave distribution in a district.[105]

From 1880 no data on the value of property are given, but in the 1860 and 1870 returns the value of the personal property and real estate of individuals is recorded. Personal property here embraced all possessions not included under real estate,

---

[102] The 1890 schedules were almost entirely destroyed; for existing fragments see p. 80.

[103] RIP 67, 12 for details. Cf. Robert B. Watz, "Arkansas slaveholdings and slaveholders in 1850," *Arkansas Hist. Q.*, 12 (1953), tables 1, 2. Individual slaves enumerated in the schedules can sometimes be identified from probate records: see pp. 152–3.

[104] E.g., Sharman L. Richards and George M. Blackburn, "A demographic history of slavery: Georgetown County, South Carolina, 1850," *South Carolina Hist. Mag.*, 76 (1975), 224.

[105] Cf. Joseph A. Hazel, "Semimicrostudies of counties from the manuscripts of the census of 1860," *Professional Geographer*, 17 (1965), 16.

including money, bonds, livestock, jewelry, and furniture. Apart from enabling a rough categorization of the inhabitants of a place according to wealth, so recorded, the opportunity is given for comparing the wealth of one place in a district with that of others. It is possible, however, that the taxes during the Civil War may have made respondents to the 1870 census inquiries more wary over their statements of wealth than in 1860, and this must be kept in mind in any comparison of wealth in these two census years.[106]

Whether a parent was of foreign birth is indicated in the 1870 schedules and the 1900 schedules provide the place of birth (state, territory, foreign country) for each parent of all those included in the census. The 1900 schedules also give more details on immigrants: year of entry, whether naturalized, and whether able to speak English. The 1870 schedules also identified male citizens of twenty-one upwards, and those in that category whose right to vote had been denied or abridged.

From 1880 the schedules specifically state the relationship of each individual to the head of household (boarders, servants, and so on, as well as family relations).[107] Even so marital status is not indicated in 1880 except for wives of householders. The 1900 schedules do provide the conjugal state of individuals (as single, married, widowed, divorced),[108] and number of years married. Both the 1880 and 1900 schedules give the numbers of children born to each married woman and how many of them were still alive. They also provide details of tenure of home or dwelling: whether owned or rented, whether mortgaged, and whether a farm or a house.[109] The 1900 census returns indicate, too, where applicable, the street and street number of each house.

[106] See, e.g., David C. Klingamon, "Individual wealth in Ohio in 1860," in David C. Klingamon and Richard K. Vedder (eds.), *Essays in Nineteenth Century Economic History* (1975).
[107] Such relationship can, however, often be deduced in schedules for earlier censuses: J. Dennis Willigan and Katherine A. Lynch, *Sources and Methods of Historical Demography* (1982), 88–99.
[108] As do the surviving records of the 1890 census.
[109] For data on dwellings in the census, see ch. 11.

Details of the composition of ex-slave families after emancipation appear in the 1870 schedules and can provide clues as to the distribution of families in years before 1865, under slavery. The surnames of former slaves were often those of former owners.[110]

The 1870 schedules are also the first to give evidence on child labor. Occupations carried on by women and children under fifteen (restricted to those 10–15, 1880 and 1900) are shown. For children this meant regular, paid employment or activity contributing to the support of the family – not merely engagement in family chores.

To sum up: beginning in 1850, manuscript census returns enumerate each member of the household (except until 1870, slaves) separately, with his or her age, race, place of birth, school attendance, literacy, handicap, and, for males, occupation. In addition a number of other items were added, as, for instance, real property (1850, 1860, 1870), personal property (1860, 1870), female occupations (1860, 1870, 1880, 1900), parents' place of birth (1870: whether foreign born; 1880, 1900: actual U.S. state or foreign country of birth), relationship to head of household (1880, 1900), street address (1880, 1900), and whether owned (free or mortgaged) home or rented farm or house (1900).

The manuscript population schedules for the censuses of 1790 through 1870 are preserved in some 3,100 volumes in the National Archives (RG 29), arranged for each census by state or territory and then by county or parish. For the censuses of 1790 through 1820 there are no returns for some states and territories.[111] The 1860 schedules for Colorado and Washington territories are also missing.[112] Some federal population schedules not found in the National Archives are available

---

[110] Carole Merritt, "Slave family records," *Georgia Archive*, 6, 1 (1978), 17.

[111] For states and territories, counties and cities, with schedules in the NA, see Katherine H. Davidson and Charlotte M. Ashby, *Records of the Bureau of the Census* (PI 161, 1964), 128; Bureau of the Census, *Population Schedules, 1800–1870; Volume Index to Counties and Major Cities* (SL 8, 1951): vols. indexed before 1840 are photostat copies; those 1840–70 are original vols. Index distinguishes schedules for free and slave, 1850, 1860; and for a few large cities gives breakdown of wards.

[112] Joseph A. Hill, "The historical value of the census records," *AR Am. Hist. Assoc. ... 1908*, 1 (1909), 203.

elsewhere: duplicates for the censuses of 1800 through 1840 were deposited with federal district and superior courts: those for 1850 through 1870 with county courts, and these records have often been transferred to state libraries or state archives depositories.[113] The 1880 schedules have been transferred from the National Archives variously to state historical societies and other appropriate depositories.[114] All but a few of the 1890 schedules were destroyed by fire[115] and those for 1900 destroyed after being microfilmed. Indeed all the population schedules have been microfilmed and are available for private purchase. Many of those relating to particular states are also available in National Archives regional branches and in large libraries.[116] Some have been put into print in recent times.[117]

A large number of indexes to people named in the manuscript census returns exists.[118] In addition, for the 1880, 1900, and 1920 federal censuses, a finding aid for surnames, called Soundex, exists. This is arranged on cards by state or territory and then phonetically by surname of heads of households. Cards for the 1880 census give the names, ages, and

---

[113] PI 161, 129; *Genealogical Research*, 11, 16. Neil Franklin (comp.), *Federal Population and Mortality Census Schedules, 1790–1890, in the National Archives* (SL 24, 1971) lists population schedules by census, depository, and state.

[114] Listed PI 161, 130–1; *Genealogical Research*, 28–38; Franklin (see last note); NA, *Federal Population Censuses, 1790–1890: A Catalog of Microfilm Copies of the Schedules* (rev. 1979), 86.

[115] Fragments exist for AL, DC, GA, IL, MN, NJ, NY, NC, OH, SD, TX: for details see Wright, *Preserving Your American Heritage*, 79.

[116] See p. 41. For lists of microfilms, arranged by state, county, and city (and for large cities by wards), see NA, *Federal Population Censuses, 1790–1890*; NA, *1900 Federal Population Census: A Catalog of Microfilm Copies of the Schedules* (1978); *Genealogical Research*, 28–38. For borrowing, write Census Microfilm Rental Program, PO Box 2940, Hyattsville, MD 20784.

[117] E.g., Margaret C. Norton (ed.), *Illinois Census Returns, 1820* (Collections Illinois State Hist. Library, vol. 26, 1934).

[118] Indexes exist for most manuscript population schedules through 1850: see *Source*, 94–7; *Genealogical Research*, 18; *Directory of Census Information Sources* (current catalog of printed census publics., Summit Publications, PO Box 222, Monroe Falls, OH 45482); Mary M. Brewer, *Index to Censuses in Printed Form* (1969 and supplements; Century Enterprises, PO Box 607, Huntsville, AL 72740). For commercially produced "accelerated" indexes for censuses 1800–50, see current list from Accelerated Indexing Systems, Bountiful, UT. For censuses 1860, 1870, few indexes exist. For a method of locating individuals whose residence is known, see Keith Schlesinger and Peggy T. Sinko, "Urban finding aid for manuscript census searches," *National Genealogical Soc. Q.*, 69 (1981); Keith R. Schlesinger, "An 'urban finding aid' for the federal census," *Prologue*, 13 (1981).

birthplaces of all members of every household where there was a child aged ten or under. Separate cross-referenced cards exist for each of such children whose surname differs from that of the head of the household. For the 1900 census the Soundex covers all households and provides for each person the name, race, date of birth, age, citizenship, status, and place of residence. For urban dwellers the city, street, and house number are given. These indexes are available in microfilm from the National Archives.[119]

Worth noting is an ICPSR data collection for seven Southern cities compiled from samples of individuals in the manuscript population schedules for 1870 and 1880.[120] Variables for sampled persons include age, sex, marital status, school attendance, occupation, nationality, and real and personal wealth.[121]

In addition to the population schedules some of the nonpopulation schedules (from 1850) provide demographic data. Statistics based on these appear in the published census volumes, discussed above, where the sort of information they contain is indicated. Generally the manuscript returns on which the published material was based are arranged for the same territorial units as the population schedules. In 1870, however, the "social statistics" schedules were compiled from official documents, published reports, or manuscript records of institutions and presented by counties, except for cities of considerable size. The manufactures' schedules for 1880 were presented separately by special agents for cities of 8,000 and upwards.

The data available in the agriculture, manufactures' and mining, and religious and educational schedules are discussed in chapters 4, 6, 8, 9, and 10. The original returns are no longer

---

[119] For details, see *Federal Population Censuses, 1790–1890*, 75–90; *1900 Federal Population Census*, v, 83–4; PI 161, 113; Charles Stephenson, "Tracing those who left," *JUH*, 1 (1974); Charles Stephenson, "The methodology of census record linkage," *Prologue*, 12 (1980; repr. *JFH*, 5 (1980)).

[120] See p. 64.

[121] ICPSR, *Guide to Resources and Services, 1980–81* (n.d.), 57. The cities are Charleston, SC, Richmond, VA, Atlanta, GA, Savannah, GA, Mobile, AL, Norfolk, VA, New Orleans, LA.

with the National Archives,[122] and non-population schedules for 1890 and 1900 no longer exist. Colorado, Florida, Nebraska, and the territories of New Mexico and Dakota undertook mortality censuses in 1885, supported by the federal government.[123]

The defective nature of the mortality data in the censuses has been noted above. The original schedules may, nevertheless, contain usable information for the detailed study of small areas and the identification of named individuals. The returns give the names of those who had died in the year ending on June 1 immediately before the census. Deaths were grouped by town, city, district, or other subdivision, and were normally recorded in the place the family resided. Those for 1850 and 1860 indicate age, sex, race, condition (slave or free), married or widowed, place of birth (state, territory, or foreign country), month of death, profession, occupation or trade, disease or cause of death, and duration of terminal illness. The 1870 schedules are similar except that indication is given whether the father or mother of the deceased was foreign born. In that census and for 1880 the registration number of the deceased's family (in the population schedule) is also given and this aids identification. In 1880, where a death occurred in a census district which was not that of the deceased's family, an indication of the residence of the family is given. Further additional data in the 1880 mortality schedules include the length of residence in the United States of the deceased and the place of birth of both parents.[124]

As noted, the manuscript manufactures' schedules are dealt with in detail in chapter 8. They report, for larger firms, wage rates paid to skilled and unskilled workers and can thus give some idea of the income variation between those categories

[122] For locations, see RIP 67, app. For microfilms, PI 161; *MRR*. For mortality schedules, see E. Kay Kirkham, *The Counties of the United States, their Derivation and Census Schedules* (1961), pp. g, h.
[123] Dakota schedules are in State Hist. Soc., Bismarck, ND and South Dakota Hist. Soc., Pierre, SD. The others are in NA, Washington, DC.
[124] For location of surviving schedules, see above n. 122. Franklin, *Federal Population and Mortality Schedules* (also for copies and indexes). For microfilms, *MRR*; *Genealogical Research*, 14–16.

and between workers in different trades. This can be significant in any attempt to reconstruct the socio-economic
characteristics of a community, and also in assessing the effects
of industrialization on the standing of particular occupations.
Caution must, however, be urged, since the wage rates recorded have been judged the most difficult and unreliable
figures to work with in the censuses of manufactures (see
below).

There were other censuses than the federal ones. State and
territorial census material exists for some, but by no means all
states and territories. A number, like New York state, conducted decennial censuses midway between federal censuses,
but for some of the older states there is no record of any state
census for the nineteenth century.[125] Again, such censuses did
not always result in published reports and not all that did
appear in printed form did so as official publications or, if
officially produced, discrete volumes. The 1825 territorial
census for Florida, for instance, was never published, while
one for 1838 of that territory was published unofficially in
local newspapers. The 1855 state census for Florida was published in the state legislative journal.[126] Sometimes it was left to
later generations to carry out publication: the State Historical
Society of Idaho, for example, published the 1863 census of
Idaho territory in the 1930s.[127]

Many state censuses, particularly the earlier ones, were
poorly conducted. Sometimes the original manuscript schedules have survived, though often with gaps. Again the coverage of these censuses varied greatly. Quite often more detailed
information on individuals is given than in the early federal
censuses,[128] and, like the federal censuses, among them are

[125] For an overall survey of state censuses, see Dubester (1948). For NY see Marilyn
Douglas and Melinda Yates, *New York State Census Records, 1790–1925* (1981).
[126] Dorothy Dodd, "The Florida census of 1825," *Florida Hist. Q.*, 22 (1943); Clarence S. Brigham, "Ante-bellum census enumerations in Florida," *Florida Hist. Q.*,
6 (1927).
[127] *16th Rep. State Hist. Soc. Idaho, 1937–8* (n.d.), 60–4.
[128] E.g., the 1855 NY census records length of residence of each person: David D.
Davenport, "Duration of residence in the 1855 census of New York State," *HM*,
18 (1985); Michael B. Katz *et al.*, "Migration and the social order in Erie County,
New York: 1855," *JIH*, 8 (1978).

non-population as well as population schedules. There is a useful bibliography[129] listing those in print and those for which (so far as is ascertainable) original manuscript schedules have survived and their whereabouts and content.

Copies of a number of state censuses are in the National Archives in Washington, DC, and many of these are available in microfilm.[130] An analysis of the California state census for 1852 was produced in 1854 in the Compendium volume of the 1850 federal census, the federal census schedules for some Californian counties having been lost at sea. In 1885 a census was undertaken with federal funds in Colorado, Florida, Nebraska, and the territories of Dakota and New Mexico. Some of the schedules for this were published.[131] The originals were returned to Washington and are available in microfilm from the National Archives.[132] They are arranged by counties and enumeration districts, and include population, agriculture, manufactures (excluding mining), and (as noted above) mortality schedules. The demographic information is similar to that of the federal census of 1880. Other state censuses in 1885 were undertaken under the provisions of state laws and entirely at state expense.[133]

A few individual censuses of particular cities exist.[134] Most of these remain in manuscript unless published in recent times by historical societies – like the Los Angeles census of 1838. They vary in content but some were very full. The Boston census of 1845, for example, provided the pattern for the 1850 federal census. The census of Augusta, GA, taken in 1852, listed residents (with address, sex, and number of slaves owned), orphan children, free blacks, and transients.[135]

---

[129] Dubester (1948). A shortened list is in Schulze (1983), 431–6. See also *Source*, 113–18 (indicates if printed, indexed, or microformed).
[130] *MRR. Genealogical Research*, 23–38, indicates if publ. or in microform.
[131] Dubester (1948).
[132] See refs. n. 130 above.
[133] Detailed in Dubester (1948).
[134] *Source*, 120–1 lists extant city censuses.
[135] WPA, HRS, *Inventory of the County Archives of Georgia, No. 121, Richmond County (Augusta)* (1939), 79.

Other census-like records covering sections of communities may also exist and can be very useful.[136] These include listings of the numbers of children of school age or actually at school. Some of these provide parents' names, others only those of the children, usually with their ages. School enrollment and graduation records, too, may sometimes be useful for demographic purposes.[137] These and school listings may, however, underrepresent blacks, certain immigrant groups, and the poor generally, who did not school their children regularly.[138]

Other kinds of records, too, may provide demographic data. These include fiscal records. In Kentucky, for example, annual tax enumerations of adult males, 1873–1902, were published in state documents. Records of men of militia age, too, may be useful,[139] and jury lists are another possible source. The jury lists for 1816 and 1819 for New York City are in effect a census of male inhabitants over twenty-five years of age. They include, for each household, the ages of the males, and the number of children, women, servants, and slaves; the location of each dwelling; and the number of inhabitants (including their trade and whether journeymen), racial categories, and general wealth and property-holding qualifications.[140]

A unique census was the "Statements of Settlers" taken in 1806 by the Holland Land Company assessing the resources of settlers in its lands in central and western New York state.[141] For Philadelphia censuses of the free black population were undertaken by abolitionist and Quaker groups in 1838, 1847, and 1856. These include not only the usual federal-census-type data, but also information on membership of churches and

---

[136] See, e.g., John "D." Stemmons (comp.), *The United States Census Compendium: A Directory of Census Records, Tax Lists, Poll Lists, Petitions, Directories, Etc., Which Can be Used As A Census* (1973); *Source*, 121–8.

[137] See pp. 466, 468, 470.

[138] John M. Allswang, *A Home for All Peoples* (1971), 215–17. For censuses of freedmen, see p. 144.

[139] *Source*, 115, 121.

[140] Howard B. Rock, *Artisans of the New Republic* (1979), 328.

[141] Cornell Univ. Library: see *Source*, 123, 126.

societies, income, educational levels, school attendance, rent paid, property brought to Pennsylvania, and for those born slaves, how freedom was attained. For thirteen Ohio counties in 1863 there are lists of blacks who had entered the state since 1861.[142] Some counties and cities in the South maintained registers of "free persons of color."[143]

USING CENSUS EVIDENCE

Both the published censuses and the manuscript schedules present problems for the researcher, some of which have been touched on in the last section. The following comments are written primarily with the federal census in mind, but much that is said applies, too, to state and other censuses.

Census districts were subdivided into smaller districts (subdivisions, or enumeration districts) embracing whole towns, townships, wards, and so on. This means that census data refer to topographically identifiable areas for which evidence from other sources, like local government material, exists for a wide variety of topics. The linkage of census with other data thus provides considerable opportunities for the historian. The possibilities of such linkage are mentioned at various points in this section, but are explored in greater depth later in the chapter.[144] Difficulties associated with mortality statistics in the censuses have been noted above, those connected with occupations are dealt with below, and those relating to the poor and handicapped in chapter 11.

Some difficulties arise from the shortcomings of the censuses themselves. Demographic statistics drawn from the manufactures' schedules in the published reports may well contain errors arising from various causes; even in the manuscript schedules mistakes were made by the compilers. Thus in reporting the "average number of hands employed" marshals sometimes failed to distinguish part-time workers employed

[142] *Source*, 123–4; Theodore Hershberg, "Free blacks in antebellum Philadelphia," in Hershberg, *Philadelphia*, and see ibid., 506–7.
[143] James C. Bonner, *Milledgeville* (1978), 294.
[144] RIP 67, 1–2. For linkage, see section on social structure and social mobility, below.

over the year and seasonal workers, or to indicate whether or not they had adjusted figures to take seasonal working into account.[145]

Another drawback lies in underenumeration which occurred as a result of oversight by marshals, and because some individuals died or left the district after the census period began but before they were counted. Others were missed as they moved from one part of a census district to another, or when they came in from elsewhere. In towns some of the working class and some of those of racial and ethnic minorities tended to go uncounted.[146] In the 1880 census, for instance, Boston blacks were probably underenumerated by about one-third, and in the Southern states the number of blacks was considerably underestimated in the 1870 census.[147] Overenumeration might also occur.[148] In such cases it is not often very easy for the researcher to redress the situation.[149]

As for personal and real property data in the censuses, it is clear that there was deliberate as well as inadvertent misreporting.[150] In certain Southern states, for example, some people in 1870 judiciously underreported property values and livestock owned. Nevertheless data on wealth are more frequently and comprehensibly available from the censuses than from other sources, such as the tax returns. And for statistical measurement for comparative purposes, error is unlikely to be distributed in such a way as to introduce bias to an extent that would invalidate the exercise. Where possible, however, linkage with other sources should be sought.[151]

[145] Margaret Walsh, "The value of mid-nineteenth century manufacturing returns," *HMN*, 4 (1971), 45, q.v. for details.
[146] James Borchert, *Alley Life in Washington* (1980), 304–6.
[147] Elizabeth H. Pleck, *Black Migration and Poverty: Boston, 1865–1900* (1979), 215; Margo J. Anderson, *The American Census: A Social History* (1988), 89–90.
[148] Peter R. Decker, *Fortunes and Failures* (1978), 265.
[149] But see Peter R. Knights, "A method for estimating census under-enumeration," *HMN*, 3 (1970); Peter R. Knights, *The Plain People of Boston, 1830–1860* (1971), app. C; Robert G. Barrow, "The manuscript federal census," *Indiana Mag. Hist.*, 69 (1973), 189–90; John B. Sharpless and Ray M. Shortridge, "Biased underenumeration in census manuscripts," *JUH*, 1 (1975).
[150] Cf. Paul J. Lammermeier, "The urban black family of the nineteenth century," *Jnl. of Marriage and the Family*, 35 (1973), 444.
[151] See pp. 100–3, 377–8.

The reporting in the censuses of ages of individuals, and therefore of age-group totals, also contains inaccuracies. Because of the vagaries of census procedures the age recorded might be a year out, while other errors arose from incorrect responses by individuals. In particular, ages were rounded off to the nearest tenth anniversary. The reporting of the ages of the very young and the elderly is most likely to contain mistakes.[152] A possible way of alleviating the problem lies in the linkage of names in the census with other records which contain evidence of age and birth (as state marriage, birth, and death records).[153] Such discrepancies in age reporting must be borne in mind when using census data to trace individuals from decade to decade. There are other problems, too, in the linking of information on distinct persons, or of data on fathers and sons, in sequential censuses, and since such a process is a necessary ingredient in social mobility studies these problems must be recognized.[154]

Other problems derive from discrepancies in the censuses themselves. In the published volumes errors sometimes occurred when data were transcribed from the manuscript schedules, as happened with specific occupational information on free blacks in New York and New Orleans in 1850.[155] In the manuscript schedules illegible handwriting, careless entries, and outright omissions occurred. The names of individuals, both surnames and given names, may be wrongly spelled, spelled phonetically, Anglicized, spelled differently in different returns, and so on. Reporting of nativity can often lack precision: "Britain," for instance, may be used for Canada as well as England, Wales, Scotland, and Ireland; "Bavaria" may be attached to a particular person in one census and

---

[152] Cf. Peter R. Knights, "Accuracy of age reporting in the manuscript federal censuses of 1850 and 1860," *HMN*, 4 (1970); Dennis Kelly, "Linking nineteenth-century manuscript census records," *HMN*, 7 (1974), 73–4; Merle Curti *et al.*, *The Making of an American Community* (1959), app. I; Richard G. del Castillo, *The Los Angeles Barrio, 1850–1890* (1979), 179.

[153] See, e.g., Knights, *Plain People*, app. B.

[154] Useful here is Christian Pouyez *et al.*, "The linkage of census name data," *JIH*, 14 (1983). And see Hershberg, *Philadelphia*, 16.

[155] Curry, *The Free Black in Urban America*, 259.

"Germany" to the same person in another, and so on. Similar discrepancies occur with reference to birth in states of the Union.[156]

Some of these difficulties may be alleviated by searching not only for surnames with appropriate given names, but also by paying attention to occupation and age and to personal details of kin. Linking evidence from the federal censuses with data from other sources, like state censuses and directories, may be helpful.[157] And since the manuscript federal censuses yield names of persons other than householders only for the censuses of 1850–1880 and 1900, for periods outside those dates recourse to other sources is often essential. This may be so, too, for determining relationships between household members in the 1850–1870 schedules.[158]

Again, while the extent of residential persistence,[159] and the characteristics of those who tended to stay in a place, may be assessed from records of sequential censuses, the absence of individuals in one census who were present in the previous one gives no clue as to whether they had migrated or died (unless widowhood is indicated). Moreover, the apparent disappearance of a female often merely disguises the assumption of a new surname on marriage. And those who moved in and out of a district between censuses are not recorded at all in the census records. In such cases the use of ancillary data, especially from directories and marriage records, may again be of help.[160]

Other difficulties are connected with ethnicity. Conclusions on the impact of foreign-born groups in a locality are complicated by the fact that, for instance, children of Swedish-born parents appear in the census statistics as American born though to all intents and purposes they formed part of a Scandinavian culture group. Where the census returns provide

[156] Curti and Kelly as cited n. 152 above.
[157] See, e.g., Peter R. Knights, "Population turnover, persistence and mobility in Boston, 1830–60," in Stephan Thernstrom and Richard Sennett (eds.), *Nineteenth Century Cities* (1969).
[158] Willigan and Lynch, *Sources and Methods*, 98–9.
[159] For calculation of persistence rates (crude and adjusted for deaths), see Hal S. Baron, *Those Who Stayed Behind* (1984), ch. 5, pp. 152–4, and works cited.
[160] Cf. Robert V. Wells, *Uncle Sam's Family* (1985), 113–16.

evidence on parental nativity this may, therefore, need to be taken into account.[161] Note, too, that although indication of place of birth of husbands and wives gives a clue as to their origin (abroad or in a particular state) no evidence is given of their residence just before they came to settle in the community being studied. Where there are children, however, some indication of the family movements may be adduced from their birthplaces: though since these were recorded by state only, short-distance migration is often not ascertainable.

Attention to the geographic area for which the census evidence is available is usually essential. Thus when making comparisons from one census year to another it should be remembered that boundaries of census and enumeration districts did not always remain constant, nor is it always easy to ascertain where such boundaries ran. Frontier counties pose special problems in this respect.[162] Boundary descriptions of enumeration districts (with area sizes) exist in the National Archives (RG 29) from 1850 (available on microfilms T1210, 1224),[163] though several states and territories are not covered for the 1880 census, and while some pre-1900 contemporary census maps exist they are few.[164]

When gathering data on cities it is as well to note that growth of population and concentrations of non-rural occupations just outside the official city boundary will not be reflected in the reported census statistics for that place.[165] Again, the published censuses often lack discrete data on small towns. In New England and some Northern states, in particular, returns for "towns" often embraced large rural districts.

---

[161] Cf. George Boeck, "A historical note on the use of the census returns," *Mid-America*, 44 (1962), 46–50. And see pp. 133, 200.

[162] Cf. Jack E. Eblen, "An analysis of nineteenth-century frontier populations," *Demography*, 2 (1965), 400.

[163] RIP 67, 2; *MRR*. Listed in James B. Rhoades and Charlotte M. Ashby (comps.), *Preliminary Inventory of the Cartographic Records of the Bureau of the Census* (PI 103, 1958).

[164] *GNA*, 468. But see William Thorndale and William Dollarhide, *Map Guide to the U.S. Federal Censuses, 1790–1920* (1987) (county boundary maps for each census). For county boundaries, see pp. 54, 299.

[165] Adna F. Weber, *The Growth of Cities in the Nineteenth Century* (1899), 36–9.

Worse, the completeness of the published record of populations in the early censuses may vary within states from county to county and from township to township. Even as late as the 1860 census, for example, in Ohio and Indiana the published total populations of some townships embrace those of towns which are not separately reported, while in the same county other township totals exclude some town populations which are reported separately – but without indication as to which situation applies. Yet for other counties in the same states all subdivisions down to small hamlets are clearly distinguished.[166]

In such cases, and indeed generally for specific areas within counties, townships, and cities, recourse to the manuscript census schedules may be needed. Careful scrutiny of these will often enable more exact geographical plotting of entries. Some census takers recorded addresses at the top of sheets and some indication of when a beat, a precinct, or an area covered by a particular post office had been completed. Correlation with postal route maps, directories, church records, and so on, can shed further light.[167] Again the existence of towns not separately reported in the census can be inferred from concentrations of non-agricultural occupations and by linkage with other data from, for example, directories, gazetteers, plat books, nineteenth-century county histories, and county atlases. Indeed the boundaries of many towns are often described in county histories.

Linkage of the manuscript census schedules with other sources may also be fruitful in the study of certain other topics. This is so, for instance, where particular ethnic concentrations in large cities, or areas with certain physical or social attributes, did not conform to census or other official boundaries.[168]

The use of the census for studying mortality rates has been noted above. Census evidence can also be used for calculating

[166] Edward K. Muller, "Town populations in the early United States censuses," *HMN*, 3 (1970).
[167] See, e.g., Hazel, "Semimicrostudies," 15–19; Laurence A. Glasco, "Computerizing the manuscript census," *HMN*, 3 (1969), 3–5.
[168] Cf. RIP 67, 23; Schlesinger, "An 'urban finding aid'," 352.

Sources for U.S. History

fertility rates. The analysis of mortality and fertility rates is, however, a specialized field fraught with difficulties for the uninitiated. Those seeking to investigate these topics would do well to acquaint themselves with current work, paying particular attention to the techniques used.[169] Suffice it to say here that fertility rates can be estimated by calculating the ratio of children of, say, under ten per woman of child-bearing age (say 15–45).[170] When comparing black and white fertility rates the underenumeration of blacks and a likely higher infant mortality among them will need to be taken into account.[171]

The relationship between fertility rates in a locality and other variables, including, for instance, population density, urbanization, industrialization, age of the county, land values, availability of land, value of dwellings, proportions of foreign born, education, and religion, can also be deduced from census data, used in conjunction with other sources, like directories.[172] Where it is sought to relate fertility to particular small areas, individual plantations, or types of plantations (as according to size or crop raised), the manuscript schedules will need to be used, in conjunction with such sources as plantation and probate records.[173]

[169] E.g., Maris A. Vinovskis (ed.), *Studies in American Demography* (1979), and refs. in next note.
[170] Donald J. Bogue and James A. Palmore, "Some empirical and analytical relations among demographic fertility measures," *Demography*, 1 (1964); Sherman L. Richards and George M. Blackburn, "A demographic history of slavery," *South Carolina Hist. Mag.*, 76 (1975), 221–4; Yasukichi Yasuba, *Birth Rates of the White Population in the United States, 1800–1860* (1962), 29–35; Vinovskis, "Recent trends in American historical demography," 614; Eblen, "An analysis of frontier populations," 407; Tamara K. Hareven and Maris A. Vinovskis, "Marital fertility, ethnicity, and occupation," in Vinovskis, *Studies in American Demography*, 481–2; Wells, *Uncle Sam's Family*, 34–6.
[171] Stanley L. Engerman, "Changes in black fertility, 1880–1940," in Hareven and Vinovskis, *Family and Population*, 131.
[172] See, e.g., Wendall A. Bash, "Changing birth rates in developing America," *Milbank Memorial Fund Q.*, 41 (1963); Maris A. Vinovskis, "A multivariate regression analysis of fertility differentials among Massachusetts townships and regions in 1860," in Charles Tilly (ed.), *Historical Studies of Changing Fertility* (1978); Don R. Leet, "Human fertility and agricultural opportunities in Ohio counties ... 1810–60," in Klingaman and Vedder, *Essays in Nineteenth Century Economic History*.
[173] Richard H. Steckel, "The fertility of American slaves," *Explorations in Economic Hist.*, 7 (1982). And see pp. 152–3, 154–5.

VITAL RECORDS AND FAMILY RECONSTITUTION

Vital records, that is those recording the birth, marriage, and death of individuals, are extensively used by genealogists and works of reference exist to assist in tracing such records in the original and in printed and microform copies.[174] Such finding aids can, of course, be useful for wider purposes. The value of vital records is, however, less than might be expected for the nineteenth century and often evidence taken from the census records has been preferred for calculating such matters as birth and death rates and their relationship to such social factors, as age, race, ethnicity, neighborhood, and occupation.

The limited value of vital records is due largely to the incompleteness of registration. There was no national system of registration and the matter was left to the states and to individual cities. Civil registration of births and deaths, it is true, began as early as 1841 in Massachusetts, but most states did not institute state-wide registration until after 1900, though in many states county, town, or city civil registration preceded state registration. Of those records of the process that survive many are available in print or microform and some are indexed.[175] Nevertheless registration records are often incomplete and the level of accuracy varied greatly. Data are perhaps least trustworthy for the first years of registration. Deaths, aside from those of infants, were probably more efficiently recorded than births.[176]

Birth registration records usually provide the name of the individual and the date and place of birth, names of parents and occupation of the father, and sometimes the ages, places of residence or birth of the parents, and the number of other

---

[174] U.S. Public Health Service, *Where to Write for Birth and Death Records* (Public. No. 630 A–1, 1968) and *Where to Write for Marriage Records* (No. 630 B, 1968); Val D. Greenwood, *The Researcher's Guide to American Genealogy* (1973), ch. 9.

[175] For details, see Wright, *Preserving Your American Heritage*, 33–6; and 40–3 for addresses of state offices for vital statistics registration (with dates such registration began, distinguishing births, deaths, marriages). See 1st edn. of this book, publ. as *Building an American Pedigree* (1974) for survey of 100+ cities which recorded vital statistics before state registration.

[176] *The Federal Census, Critical Essays*, 128–31. And see p. 515n.

live births to the parents.[177] Death registration records provide the deceased's name, address, cause of death, age at death, date and place of birth, and names of parents and their state or country of birth. Sometimes local officials published details of deaths weekly in local newspapers.

Civil registration of marriages has always been a county or town responsibility and records usually date from the time of organization of the place concerned.[178] Marriage records include licenses and applications for licenses, consent notices or decrees, marriage intentions, bonds, certificates, returns, and, most importantly, marriage registers. The last contain the names of the bride and groom and the place and date of the marriage. Some provide race and place of birth of each partner. It should be noted that some who married in cities were not really part of the city community, while some licenses were issued to residents who got married elsewhere.[179]

In addition to the actual vital registration records there are contemporary compilations of statistical data derived from them. These are found in the annual reports of registers of boards (departments, bureaus) of public health and of health officers, and in annual mayoral messages, sanitary surveys, and bills of mortality.[180] Some states issued monthly bulletins of vital statistics. Sometimes such records distinguish deaths by race and by season and perhaps relate them to age and cause of death. In larger cities different wards may be distinguished.[181] Hoffman has provided in print death

[177] For owners' slave birth registers, see p. 155.
[178] Exceptions were NY, PA, SC, UT, which did not require such registration until the 1880s.
[179] Cf. Richard S. Alcorn and Peter R. Knights, "Most uncommon Bostonians," HMN, 8 (1975), 102, 113n.
[180] For work based on these, see Ira Rosenwaike, Population History of New York City (1972).
[181] See, e.g., Clayton R. Koppes and William P. Norris, "Ethnicity, class, and mortality in the industrial city," JUH, 11 (1985); Rose A. Cheney, "Seasonal aspects of infant and childhood mortality," JIH, 14 (1984), 561–85; Condrun Cheney and Rose Cheney, "Mortality trends in Philadelphia," Demography, 19 (1982), 98–123. For approaches to identifying and correcting fluctuations in registration totals deriving from administrative changes, see Robert Gutman, "The birth statistics of Massachusetts during the nineteenth century," Population Studies, 10 (1956). See also publics. of the Am. Public Health Assoc. and of the Am. Statistical Assoc.

registration data for thirty-nine cities of over 100,000 inhabitants in 1900, eighteen of them continuously from 1871.[182]

As noted above, mortality statistics published in the federal censuses for 1880, 1890, and 1900, embraced, for areas where vital registration existed, statistics derived from state and local registration. For other areas in those years and for all areas in the censuses of 1850 through 1870, details for the census year were taken from the original schedules, which give the names of the individuals concerned.

Despite the incompleteness of vital registration records (except for certain areas, notably Massachusetts),[183] historians could make more use of them than they have. Registration records can be used as ancillary sources for linking with census data. If, for instance, a sample group of individuals has been selected from the manuscript census schedules, vital records can give additional information about them. Thus the data in vital records on occupation, age, and place of birth may be more exactly stated than in the census returns, and addresses, lacking from other sources, may be provided. Marriage records can certainly yield information not in the census records: the maiden name of the bride, for example. Marriage records offer, too, a possible source for studying the influence of women and particularly of intermarriage patterns among ethnic groups and socio-economic groups, age at marriage, and so on, and of upward social mobility resulting from marriage rather than change of occupation – an aspect of social mobility largely neglected by historians.[184] One study used data from marriage registers, directories, and census records to study the living patterns of newly married couples in the

---

[182] Frederick L. Hoffman, "The general death rate of large American cities, 1871–1904," *Q. Publics. Am. Statistical Assoc.*, 10 (1906). See also Robert Higgs, "Cycles and trends of mortality in 18 large American cities, 1871–1900," *Explorations in Economic Hist.*, 16 (1979).

[183] Even here they leave much to be desired: Maris A. Vinovskis, *Fertility in Massachusetts from the Revolution to the Civil War* (1981), app. B.

[184] Mark Friedberger and Janice R. Webster, "Social structure and state and local history," *Western Hist. Q.*, 9 (1978), 310; Alcorn and Knights, "Most uncommon Bostonians," 14n. Social mobility is discussed more fully below.

1860s and 1870s.[185] Death registration records linked with census data can also shed light on mortality differentiated by disease, age, ethnicity, residence, and neighborhood.[186]

In addition to civil registration records, church records of births (or baptisms, christenings), marriages, and deaths (or burials) may be available, and many of these predate civil registration. A large number of such records has been microfilmed by the Genealogical Society of Utah.[187] Evidence regarding mortality may be obtained, too, from cemetery tombstones and sexton's records. Cemetery sextons' records at Jefferson, LA, for instance, provide name, date and cause of death, age, nativity and sex, together with additional remarks.[188] Sometimes such records also give details of parentage. Records of these kinds may be found in denominational or local depositories or still with the churches concerned. They are most useful for details of particular individuals and families, but are often not sufficiently comprehensive to form a basis for the statistical measurement of trends.

Used with the manuscript census schedules from the 1850 census onwards and with church records and other genealogical material, vital records may, however, if sufficiently complete, contribute to family reconstitution, a technique so far used more by students of English and European demographic history than American historians.[189] This method consists of reconstituting a random sample of families in a community – that is building up a picture of the genealogical structure of each family – from which can be derived "such key variables as

---

[185] Howard P. Chudacoff, "Newlyweds and family extension," in Hareven and Vinovskis, *Family and Population*.

[186] Hershberg, *Philadelphia*, 509; Richard A. Meckel, "Immigration, mortality, and population growth in Boston, 1840–1880," *JIH*, 15 (1985), 393–417.

[187] Family History Library, 35 N West Temple St., Salt Lake City, UT 84150. And see p. 258.

[188] Colin B. Hamer, Jr., "Records of the city of Jefferson, 1850–1970," *Louisiana Hist.*, 17 (1976), 63.

[189] See Wells, *Uncle Sam's Family*, 34, 36, 150; Willigan and Lynch, *Sources and Methods*, ch. 8; E. A. Wrigley (ed.), *An Introduction to English Historical Demography* (1966), 96–159; René Leboutte *et al.*, "Analysis of reconstituted families," *HM*, 20 (1987); Darnell S. Scott and Michael S. Hindus, "Premarital pregnancy in America, 1640–1971," *JIH*, 5 (1975), and studies cited therein.

age at marriage, infant mortality, pre-nuptial conception rates, average intervals between births, age-specific fertility, average duration of marriage,"[190] and so on. Existing genealogies may also be utilized.[191]

Family reconstitution is, however, very time consuming and is naturally biased towards the characteristics of families who stayed long enough in a community for family profiles over time to be constructed. In view of the high degree of geographic mobility in the nineteenth century, this is a serious drawback.[192] Again, genealogies are often biased towards the better-off and the important and those who had offspring, and do not necessarily provide a representative sample. Even when it is not possible to produce reliable statistics from such exercises, however, a general impression may be obtained, and, of course, if particular families (as those of city elites) are being studied this technique has considerable potential.

For black families the weakness of birth and death records is a difficulty, particularly in the case of slaves.[193] It may be possible to reconstruct the antebellum family structure of slave communities[194] from slave marriage registers (compiled in 1866 and in many places with retrospective information), plantation lists of slaves, the manuscript census schedules of 1860 and 1870, slave narratives, planters' diaries, Freedmen's Bureau records, and so on (see ch. 3). The 1870, 1880, and 1900 census schedules may provide data connecting the antebellum and postbellum periods. Nevertheless, even supposing relevant data are available, such exercises are by no means easy.

[190] E. A. Wrigley, "Parish registers in population history," *Amateur Historian*, 6 (1963–5), 149.
[191] Vinovskis, *Fertility in Massachusetts*, 172.
[192] Warren S. Thompson and P. K. Whelpton, *Population Trends in the United States* (1933, repr. 1969), 228.
[193] Ibid.
[194] See, e.g., Herbert G. Gutman, *The Black Family in Slavery and Freedom, 1750–1925* (1976).

DIRECTORIES, TAX RECORDS, AND OTHER SOURCES

The value of directories as a general source and their availability has already been noted.[195] For local demographic and
social analysis they are especially valuable, particularly when
used in conjunction with other evidence, such as that available
in the census and tax records. Directories were commercially
produced and being subject to no overall regulation tended to
differ somewhat in content, and the following observations
must be considered in that light. Some county directories were
compiled embracing within them cities and smaller units. For
almost all United States cities, however, discrete city directories began to be published regularly before their populations
reached 30,000 or so.[196] City directories of a general nature are,
therefore, very common, and some of these had business
sections. For the larger cities, distinct mercantile and business
directories were also published. General directories often
listed all males of employable age or male (and occasionally
female) heads of households, with their occupations, home
addresses, and occupational addresses.[197] Where only a home
address is provided it may be inferred that the individual was
retired, followed a calling that had no fixed place of work
(and, therefore perhaps of a casual nature), or that his occupation was in some way menial. Absence of occupational data
has been found in some places to have denoted clerical or other
salaried work.

Sometimes other information, like birthplace, was included.
A general tally of in- and out-migration was provided in
some directories in the form of tables giving the number of
names from the previous year's directory no longer included,
and occasionally also noting the number of additional names.
The researcher could, where tables like this are lacking,
deduce this information himself, though its rudimentary

---

[195] See pp. 31–2, and below pp. 121, 321–2.
[196] Stephan Thernstrom and Peter R. Knights, "Men in motion: . . . urban population
mobility in nineteenth-century America," *JIH*, 1 (1970), 13.
[197] See, e.g., Knights, *Plain People*, app. A; Peter R. Knights, "City directories as aids
to antebellum urban studies," *HMN*, 2 (1969).

nature must be recognized. Some omissions were the result of death or of failure in business (resulting in a single entry where there had been a double one). Additions again included already resident youngsters who had reached the age for inclusion.[198]

In some ways directories constitute a more useful source than the census returns. This is particularly so when they exist annually over periods of time, providing year to year data as against the five- or ten-year intervals of the census. They are especially important for detailed occupational information, since even the manuscript census schedules before 1850 either give no details of employment or report it very imprecisely.[199] And sometimes directories exist where manuscript census returns are missing. Directories also represent an excellent source for pinpointing the exact residence of individuals by linking listed addresses with the street maps they usually carried. They are thus of value in the study of occupational and residential mobility (including persistence) and for plotting the geographic distribution and concentration of, for example, racial and ethnic groups, trades and industries.[200]

They are useful, too, for identifying the rich and powerful and indicating their prominence in business and in political, social, religious, and administrative affairs.[201] Some compilations, like *Voters and Tax-Payers of DeKalb County, Illinois* (1876) and *The People's Guide: A Business, Political and Religious Directory of Hendricks County, Iowa* (1874), were more comprehensive than the elite directories described below, but nevertheless underreported the less well-off. At the other end of the

---

[198] Thernstrom and Knights, "Men in motion," 13–15, 18; Sidney Goldstein, "City directories as sources of migration data," *Am. Jnl. Sociology*, 60 (1954).

[199] Cf. Sam B. Warner, *The Private City* (1968), 227; Decker, *Fortunes and Failures*, 265–6.

[200] Cf. Stuart Blumin, "The historical study of vertical mobility," *HMN*, 1 (1968), 9, 11; Schlesinger, "An 'urban finding aid'," 253–62; Thernstrom and Knights, "Men in motion," 13–14; Wells, *Uncle Sam's Family*, 115; Kathleen N. Conzen, "Patterns of residence in early Milwaukee," in Leo F. Schnore (ed.), *The New Urban History* (1975), 152–3.

[201] Cf. Edward Pessen, *Riches, Class, and Power before the Civil War* (1973), 348.

scale, some Southern directories distinguished blacks by a "c," "col.," or an asterisk, or listed them separately.[202]

Despite their advantages, directories need to be used with caution. They were not, and never claimed to be, censuses, and their coverage was not comprehensive. Certainly women and youths (and their occupations) were often ignored. The foreign-born, very recent immigrants, and transients were frequently underreported,[203] as were small shopkeepers, the semi-skilled and unskilled, particularly laborers, and female heads of households. Laborers of long residence were much more likely to be entered than those more recently settled. The same was so of blacks. On the other hand owners of factories and businesses, those owning a certain amount of property, and the generally well-off and socially significant were almost always listed.

In tracing individuals it should be noted that differences in surname may occur in successive directories, maybe as a result of spelling changes or Anglicization. Again suburbs outside city boundaries may be ignored, posing difficulties in assessing residential mobility.[204]

The most readily available source for the distribution of wealth, other than the self-reporting of property in the censuses of 1850–1870 (see above) are tax assessments and receipts. Federal fiscal records include tax lists for the direct tax of 1798, mainly for Pennsylvania, Maryland, and Massachusetts. These are topographically arranged and comprise particular lists for dwelling houses of over $100 value on lots of two acres or less (giving details of buildings, and names of owners and occupants), for all other lands, lots, buildings, and wharves (with details of those over a certain value, and names of occupiers or owners and value), and for slaves (with totals, numbers aged 12–50, numbers exempt from tax, names of superintendents or owners). Also useful for comparative purposes are general lists and summary abstracts which conflate

---

[202] Howard N. Rabinowitz, *Race Relations in the Urban South, 1865–1890* (1978), 425–6.

[203] But see John W. Blassingame, "Before the ghetto," *JSH*, 6 (1972–3), 467.

[204] Thernstrom, *Other Bostonians*, 280–2. Suburban directories may exist.

the data in the particular lists and present totals by township and district.[205]

The National Archives holds records of other taxes. There are fragmentary assessment lists for 1815–16 (RG 217), arranged by state, collection district, and taxpayer, which provide descriptions of land, buildings, slaves, and furniture, details of families, and amounts of tax paid. In the same record group (RG 217) there are records of assessments and tax receipt books, 1865–6, for a direct federal tax in the Confederate states (except Florida). The assessment lists, arranged by state and county, generally include a description of the land, numbers of acres and lots, valuation, amount of tax, and name of owner. The receipt books, similarly arranged, also provide the name of the owner, amount of tax paid, and a description of the land.[206]

Other federal tax records include assessment lists falling within the years 1862–73 (RG 58).[207] Originally they concerned taxes levied on income and certain possessions (like carriages, yachts, watches, silver plate), on receipts from canals, railroads, steamboats, and ferries, on banks, savings institutions, and insurance companies, and on stamp duties and licenses for pursuing certain trades. But the basis of taxation altered greatly over the period so that the value of these records for the relative prosperity of a community over time is limited.[208] They comprise annual, monthly, and special lists for most states (except some in the South) and territories, and

---

[205] For location and details, see Forrest R. Holdcamper (comp.), *Preliminary Inventory of the Records of the Internal Revenue Service* (NC 151, 1967), 4; Hope K. Holdcamper, *Statistical Data on the National Wealth and Money Supply to be Derived from Internal Revenue Records* (RIP 55, 1973), 1–2; *Genealogical Research*, 247. And see, e.g., Record Commissioners of the City of Boston, *The Statistics of the United States Direct Tax of 1798; as Assessed on Boston* (1890). Records of federal taxes, 1804–40, for NY are in the state archives: New York State Education Dept., *Guide to the Records in the New York State Archives* (1981), 61.

[206] NC 151, 6; RIP 55, 3–4.

[207] Some (for 1862–6) available in microfilm: *MRR*. Some originals are in NA regional branches: *Genealogical Research*, 250.

[208] For details, see RIP 55, 3–4; *GNA*, 178–9; *Genealogical Research*, 247, 250; Cynthia G. Fox, "Income tax records of the Civil War years," *Prologue*, 18 (1986) (repr. in Walch, *Our Family, Our Town*).

are arranged by county. Under each individual's name they record the value, assessment, or enumeration of taxable income or items, and the payment due. Embraced within the series are returns for a federal tax on incomes over $600, a level excluding most people.[209] From 1874 records of more limited direct federal taxes exist, arranged by state and collection district, and many originals are available in the regional branches of the National Archives. Those relating to individuals rather than corporations are, however, limited in number.[210]

As well as records of federal taxes there are those of state, city, and county taxes levied on real and personal property and for specific purposes, like the upkeep of schools. Many of these survive, often arranged by township,[211] and are very important for the community historian: those of North Carolina have been described as a "Domesday Book far more detailed than William's."[212] The nature and content of these records, however, vary.[213] The county tax records of Illinois, for example, include road and school tax lists (giving names of payers and details of property), assessment and collection books for taxes on personal property (showing, for individuals, town lots, stock in trade, horses, cattle, and watches) and on real estate (including owner's name, description and acreage of the land, value, and amounts of other taxes), and general county summaries.[214]

Like directories and census schedules, tax records list individuals by name and can, therefore, contribute to the study of social structure and social and geographic mobility. They are

[209] Clyde Griffen, "Occupational mobility in nineteenth-century America," *JSH*, 5 (1972), 329n.
[210] NC 151, 13–25; *Genealogical Research*, 250, for details of states, dates covered, and location.
[211] See pp. 214–15.
[212] Charles C. Crittenden and Don Lacy (eds.), *The Historical Records of North Carolina*, 1 (WPA, HRS, 1938), 44.
[213] See Harry L. Watson, *Jacksonian Politics and Community Conflict* (1981), 325–8; Hamer, "Records of Jefferson," 51–67.
[214] Theodore C. Pease, *The County Archives of the State of Illinois* (1915), pp. cii–cvii, cix, cx.

useful for tracing individuals and linking with occupational data to categorize members of a community for the reconstruction of its social make-up. They can be used, too, to trace the economic growth of a community (as inferred from its aggregated fiscal liability) and to indicate the relative wealth of individuals, families, and particular occupational or ethnic groups, and to demonstrate changes in their fortunes. Since property taxes indicate the whereabouts of real estate they can be linked with evidence in directories, local histories, newspapers, and so on to pinpoint locations and define the boundaries and levels of prosperity of various city neighborhoods.[215] They can, of course, be linked, too, to the data on real and personal property in the census records. Among county records there may also be appraisals of property in connection with tax suits.

In some places annual lists were published of those inhabitants taxed above a certain level. These give the assessed value of their real and personal estate. Thus we have *Lists of Persons ... Who Were Taxed Twenty-five Dollars and Upwards in the City of Boston* published by the city's assessor's office in 1836.[216] Such records are at least useful for indicating some of the wealthiest persons in a community.[217]

Fiscal records do, however, have limitations. For example, many forms of wealth were not taxable, tangible assets, like real estate, were often undervalued, underassessment generally was common, and not all inhabitants declared all they should have. Again, errors were made by the assessors, particularly with regard to the spelling of names. In some cities taxes on real estate were levied on occupiers rather than on owners, but this is not necessarily obvious from the records. Finally, property or investments in another city or county do not appear in the tax lists of the city or county being

215 Cf. Blumin, "Vertical mobility," 9.
216 Frederic C. Jaher, "Nineteenth-century elites in Boston and New York," *JSH*, 6 (1972–3), 36, 73.
217 Pessen, *Riches, Class, and Power*, 11–12, 347–8.

103

considered, though the wealth of individuals may well have been dispersed over more than one tax district.[218]

Other types of record which can be utilized in reconstructing the levels of wealth of individuals, groups, or parts of a city or county, include those relating to ownership of personal property (like bills of sale, chattel mortgages, conditional contracts of sale, and liens), from which entrepreneurial activity, too, may be identified, and real property records such as deeds, mortgages, leases and releases, and so on. Plats can be used to estimate the extent of real-estate ownership among occupational or ethnic groups.[219] Such records are often found among those of courts or of city officials, such as the receiver or register of deeds. They may be augmented by ward maps and real-estate and fire-insurance atlases, which, with photographs, if they exist, can provide further indication of the nature of the properties.[220] Wage records and business accounts[221] can add extra insight – as into the occupational hierarchy and evidence of upward mobility.[222]

Credit-reporting agency records may be of great value for providing detailed information on the economic standing and assets of local businessmen and farmers. The records of R. G. Dun and Company are the most important and information on them is given in chapter 8. Possibly access may be obtained to the savings-bank accounts of individuals in the nineteenth century though confidentiality may dictate that published information derived from them may not mention names.[223]

The records of life-insurance companies can provide useful

[218] Watson, *Jacksonian Politics*, 326–7; Griffen, "Occupational mobility," 316, 329n; Blumin, "Vertical mobility," 5–6; Kathleen N. Conzen, "Mapping manuscript census data for nineteenth-century cities," *Hist. Geography Newsletter*, 4 (1974), 1; Edward Pessen, "The egalitarian myth and the American social reality," *AHR*, 76 (1971), esp. 994–1,000; Pessen, *Riches, Class, and Power*, 11–19, 34, 38, 85–6, and ibid., 19, 22 for conversion of assessed values into actual wealth. But see Whitman Ridgway, "Measuring wealth and power in ante-bellum America," *HMN*, 8 (1975), 75.
[219] See pp. 56, 212.   [220] See pp. 33, 57–9, 332.   [221] See pp. 375–6.
[222] See, e.g., Thomas Dublin, "Women workers and the study of social mobility," *JIH*, 9 (1979), 653.
[223] Knights, *Plain People*, p. xii.

data on individual businessmen, as well as on the activities of the insurance companies themselves, and postal records can be used to identify the relative size and prosperity of towns in an area.[224] Indeed it has been suggested that postal records are particularly valuable in "analyzing settlement patterns of townships on the public domain," and the development of the postal service was "an integral part of such pioneer history."[225]

Though often existing in insufficient numbers for very widespread statistical analysis, probate records can add another dimension to the study of social structure. In particular, wills, inventories (moveables, etc.) and appraisals (of real estate), and executors' reports of division and distribution,[226] can provide at least an impression of status, life styles, and standards of living of individual persons and families. If sufficient of these sources exist for the same period, for occupational or ethnic groups, they may act as additional evidence to data from other sources. Names and personal details of children and kin, details of outstanding credits and debts owed, and information on real and personal estate (including possession of slaves), may all be derived from these records. They can throw light on family structure and family relationships, and be used to study inter-generational social mobility.[227] On the other hand it must be realized that wills indicate only property and standards of life at the time of making the will – property may have been dispersed after that. Again, wills frequently attached no values to the items which they mentioned, and assessors perhaps tended to undervalue large holdings.[228]

A unique source for Tennessee exists in the replies to questionnaires sent to 1,650 Tennessee Civil War veterans (*c.* 1914–22). These shed some light on relationships between slave

---

[224] Harold F. Larkin, "Retention of life insurance records," *AA*, 3 (1972). For postal records, see pp. 434–6.

[225] Jane F. Smith, "Settlement of the Public Domain as reflected in federal records," in Ralph E. Ehrenberg (ed.), *Pattern and Process* (1975), 298.

[226] Cf. Pessen, *Riches, Class, and Power*, 27 n.10. The Family History Library, Salt Lake City (n. 187 above) has a large collection of microformed probate records. For fuller discussion, see pp. 215–16.

[227] Blumin, "Vertical mobility," 4.

[228] Cf. Robert W. Doherty, *Five New England Towns, 1800–1860* (1977), 104.

holders and non slave holders, economic and educational opportunities for whites (including the propertyless and poor in the area), wealth related to occupation, and so on. They are, of course, subjective and open to the usual criticisms of the recollections of old men.[229]

Voting records, such as election returns, registers of voters or poll books, and voting abstracts, make it possible to add another dimension to any analysis of social structure by relating social characteristics to political activity. This topic is dealt with in chapter 7. Similarly analysis of secondary-school enrollment and graduation records may be linked with other data to determine whether, for example, attendance at such schools was an ingredient of upward social mobility, what social or occupational groups sent their offspring to secondary school, and whether there were differences in the treatment of sons and daughters in this respect.[230]

Special surveys of particular places prepared for various purposes may sometimes be found in state documents. Thus an annual report of the New Jersey Board of Health contains a table of the population of each dwelling in Paterson in 1883, and another (in 1887) statistics of the age structure of the population of Newark, 1883–6. An Ohio document for 1869 contains an estimate of the population of Toledo.[231]

SOCIAL STRUCTURE AND SOCIAL MOBILITY

Some comments on the value of various types of records for the purpose of studying the social structure of communities and the social mobility of their inhabitants have already been made. These subjects, however, deserve further consideration. The nature of census data, as well as that of certain other types of record, like directories, dictates that in an age of computers and increasing familiarity with statistical

---

[229] Publ. as Colleen M. Elliott and Louise A. Moxley (eds.), *The Tennessee Civil War Veterans Questionnaires* (5 vols., comp. Gustavus W. Dyer and John T. Moore, 1985). Cf. *AHR*, 91 (1986), 740–1.

[230] Cf. Reed Ueda, "The high school and social mobility in a streetcar suburb," *JIH*, 14 (1984).

[231] 7th and 11th *ARs, New Jersey Board of Health* (1883, 1887); *AR Secretary of State, Ohio* (1869).

techniques, quantitative methods will play a significant part in the study of social structure and allied topics. Given the wide range of variables provided in the published and manuscript census records at the level of counties and smaller units, the potential number of correlation exercises that can be undertaken is enormous.[232] Statistical analysis can, of course, be practiced at varying levels of sophistication, and the various methods cannot be dealt with here.[233] Researchers coming fresh to such work should look at the writings of others and manuals on statistical techniques, paying particular attention to factor and regression analysis,[234] and methods of systematic, random, and cluster sampling. Sampling is often essential where a large city or densely populated area is being studied, but approaches are controversial.[235]

The linkage of evidence from various types of contemporaneous sources giving details of a person, group, or topic at a particular point in time,[236] and the linkage of data in records of different dates (as in two sequential decennial censuses), may

---

[232] Cf. Barnes E. Lathrop, "History from the census returns," *Southwestern Hist. Q.*, 51 (1948), 307; Ralph Mann, *After the Gold Rush* (1982).

[233] For analysis of census data see Curti, *Making of An American Community*, app. A; Glasco, "Computerizing the manuscript census"; del Castillo, *Los Angeles Barrio*, 177–8.

[234] For factor and regression analysis, see Willigan and Lynch, *Sources and Methods*, chs. 11, 13.

[235] For guidance, see Hubert M. Blalock, Jr., *Social Statistics* (1972 edn.), ch. 21; Willigan and Lynch, *Sources and Methods*, 193–201; Bill Williams, *A Sampler on Sampling* (1978); Roger S. Schofield, "Sampling in historical research," in E. A. Wrigley (ed.), *Nineteenth-Century Society* (1972), 146–90; A. Stuart, *Basic Ideas of Scientific Sampling* (1962); William G. Cochran, *Sampling Techniques* (1977). For examples and discussions of sampling, see Thernstrom, *Other Bostonians*, esp. app. A; Kathleen N. Conzen, *Immigrant Milwaukee, 1836–1860* (1976), 232–3; Alcorn and Knights, "Most uncommon Bostonians," 98–114; Stephan Thernstrom, "Rejoinder to Alcorn and Knights," *HMN*, 8 (1975), 115–20; R. Christian Johnson, "A procedure for sampling the manuscript census schedules," *JIH*, 8 (1978), 515–31; Joel Perlman, "Using census districts in analysis, record linkage and sampling," *JIH*, 10 (1979); Olivier Zunz et al., "Sampling for a study of population and land use of Detroit in 1880–1885," *Social Science Hist.*, 1 (1977), 307–22; Alwyn Barr, "Occupational and geographic mobility in San Antonio, 1870–1900," *Social Science Q.*, 51 (1970). For spin samples, see Lee Soltow, *Men and Wealth in the United States, 1850–1870* (1975), 4–6; Edward Bubnys, "Nativity and the distribution of wealth: Chicago, 1870," *Explorations in Economic Hist.*, 19 (1982), 102–4.

[236] E.g., Gretchen A. Condron and Jeff Seaman, "Linkage of the 1880–81 Philadelphia death register to the 1880 manuscript census," *HM*, 14 (1981).

often be useful in the study of social structure, socio-economic mobility, residential persistence, and like topics. In such exercises attention to difficulties, some of which have been noted elsewhere, is needed. In particular, careful consideration should be paid to composition of the geographical unit being studied and possible variations in its boundaries over time or as recorded in different types of record, and also to ways of identifying the same people in different sources.[237]

A general impression of the societal characteristics of a community, and chronological changes in those characteristics, may be obtained by analyzing at various points in time the economic structure of the place concerned: the spread of its inhabitants' occupations among various trades, industries, and other callings, and the general prosperity or otherwise of those economic activities.[238] In this sort of study a functional analysis of the inhabitants is commonly chosen – as, for instance, a division into primary occupations (extractive: agriculture, fishing, mining), secondary (manufacturing, construction), and tertiary (commerce, transportation, public service, professions), with a subdivision of the secondary into types of industrial activity. In large places the investigation of spatial distribution of people, housing, industries, business, and so on, and the physical characteristics of residential and other districts and the occupational and other social attributes of their inhabitants, can illuminate the socio-economic nature of different parts of a town.[239] As has been pointed out, "From the population and dwelling statistics one can prepare density

[237] See Pouyez, "The linkage of census name data"; Dennis Kelly, "Linking nineteenth-century manuscript census records," *HMN*, 7 (1974); Perlman, "Using census districts"; Theodore Hershberg *et al.*, "Record linkage," *HMN*, 9, 2 and 3 (1976); Michael B. Katz *et al.*, "Migration and the social order in Erie County, New York: 1855," *JIH*, 8 (1978); Michael Katz and John Tiller, "Record linkage for everyman," *HMN*, 5 (1972); Hershberg, *Philadelphia*, app. II; Ian Winchester, "The linkage of historical records by man and computer," *JIH*, 1 (1970); Ian Winchester, "On referring to ordinary persons," in E. A. Wrigley (ed.), *Identifying People in the Past* (1973) (q.v. for detailed bibl.).
[238] Willigan and Lynch, *Sources and Methods*, 99–101. And see chs. 4, 5, 8, 9.
[239] Cf. Thomas Smith, "Reconstructing occupational structures," *HMN*, 8 (1975), 134; Theodore Hershberg *et al.*, "Occupation and ethnicity in five nineteenth-century cities," *HMN*, 7 (1973), 179; Margo A. Conk, *The United States Census and the New Jersey Urban Occupational Structure, 1870–1940* (1980).

lists: the number of people per house, per acre, per ward and so forth . . . If these density lists are compared to similar lists of occupations and ethnic origin, a rough outline of the social and class patterns of the community will emerge."[240]

Often historians will, however, wish to investigate in greater depth the social stratification of particular communities, by analyzing the hierarchical groupings of people by class, status, and wealth. This may be undertaken both for whole communities and for different districts within large towns. The chief ingredient of such characteristics is again considered to be occupation: "occupation may be only one variable in a comprehensive theory of class, but it is the variable which includes more, which sets more limits on the other variables than any other criterion of status."[241] Occupation is often linked with prestige, wealth and income, educational standards, working conditions, standards of living, and career opportunities.

Data on occupation are primarily derived from sources outlined above: censuses, directories, fiscal records, and so forth. Statistical analysis of such evidence can shed light on the economic (and therefore also social) structure of a community at a particular time and changes over the years. Various schemes of occupational classification have been used for such analysis of class and status, and the historian seeking to undertake an exercise of this kind for a community would do well to examine what others have done and comments made on their methods.

Occupational classification may be based either on economic criteria or according to status or prestige.[242] In the first method, occupations are placed in several categories according to wealth or income – based perhaps on the average wealth or income of the members of the group, or maybe on the

---

[240] Sam B. Warner, *Streetcar Suburbs* (1962), 176.
[241] Stephan Thernstrom, *Poverty and Progress* (1964), 84. Cf. Theodore Hershberg and Robert Dockhorn, "Occupational classification," *HMN*, 9 (1976), 59; Margo A. Conk, "Occupational classification in the United States census: 1870–1940," *JIH*, 9 (1978), 117–18.
[242] Smith, "Reconstructing occupational structures."

proportions of well-off to poor persons.[243] The second method divides persons into manual and non-manual workers, subdividing each of these groups to make five to seven hierarchical categories. Thus, for instance, we may have professional people, those in commercial occupations, skilled artisans, semi-skilled workers, and laborers (or unskilled workers).[244]

In practice the use of occupational classification to depict social structure presents problems.[245] Many of these stem from the nature of the source material – particularly the census returns in which occupational descriptions were often vague. Some persons were returned by trade (as "baker," for instance) without indication whether they were employer or employee, skilled or unskilled. Titles like "clerk" and "artisan" were also used imprecisely, disguising levels of function, skill, income, class,[246] and status. One clerk might in effect be a manager, another a menial unit in a counting house. Again, similarly described manual workers included both those in casual employment and those in permanent jobs. Over time, too, the same person pursuing the same occupation may be found described differently in the returns of successive censuses. And, of course, the same occupational description may disguise changes over the decades in the nature and status of the job concerned – especially where a community underwent industrialization. Again, changes in the relative position of different occupations in the social hierarchy may have

---

[243] Michael B. Katz, "Occupational classification in history," *JIH*, 3 (1972–3), 84.

[244] See, e.g., Alba M. Edwards, "A social economic grouping of the gainful workers of the United States," *Jnl. Am. Statistical Assoc.*, 27 (1933); Thernstrom, *Other Bostonians*, app. B; Decker, *Fortunes and Failures*, app. B; Thernstrom, *Poverty and Progress*, 91–3; Knights, *Plain People*, app. E; Howard P. Chudacoff, *Mobile Americans* (1972), 85–6; Michael B. Katz, *The People of Hamilton, Canada West* (1975), chs. 2, 3, pp. 343–8.

[245] For the following discussion, see esp. Smith, "Reconstructing occupational structures," 135–6; Conk, "Occupational classification," 119–20, 123; Griffen, "Occupational mobility," 312–13; Hershberg and Dockhorn, "Occupational classification," 60–1; Thernstrom, *Other Bostonians*, 293–302, 336–7; Katz, "Occupational classification"; Hershberg et al., "Occupation and ethnicity."

[246] Michael B. Katz, "Social class in North American urban history," *JIH*, 11 (1981), q.v. for discussion of a method of distinguishing by class rather than merely by occupation.

occurred over time. Certain skilled craftsmen, for instance, may have overtaken low-grade clerks in social prestige.

The linkage of census records to other sources where individuals are identified by occupation can help. Proprietors and employers are, for instance, more likely to appear in directories than are employed workers. Property data again may provide a means of differentiation. The need remains, however, for careful consideration in the allocation of individuals and occupational groups to particular social categories, and for avoidance of too-confident assertions based on such exercises. In the 1850 census returns, for instance, female occupations were not recorded, nor in the 1860 census were those for married women, so that reporting in those years was male biased.[247]

It should be realized, too, that, especially within a numerous occupational group, considerable variations of wealth and income often existed – related perhaps to age, levels of skill, success in business, and so on. Thus the impression of homogeneity must at times be avoided and the extent of the deviation from the mean considered. Moreover, it was family income rather than individual income that sometimes determined living standards. And if the investigator is engaged in a comparative work – for instance, contrasting the structure of one community in a district with that of another – the likelihood that occupational categories necessarily equated socially or economically in different places should not be assumed automatically.

To avoid some of the difficulties of reliance totally on occupations as a measure of social stratification some historians have devised classifications in which, while occupation remains the main criterion, categorization is adjusted in some cases according to the evidence of levels of income or property ownership.[248]

[247] Cf. Stuart M. Blumin, *The Urban Threshold* (1976), 89. For sources for female occupations, see Clyde and Sally Griffen, *Natives and Newcomers* (1978), 228–42.
[248] Knights, *Plain People*. ch. 5 and app. E; Thernstrom, *Other Bostonians*, esp. app. B; Conzen, *Immigrant Milwaukee*, 234–8.

It would be wise, anyway, to attempt for the community being studied some assessment of other criteria of social status for linkage with occupational data. Here evidence of wealth, using data on real and personal property, numbers of servants and of slaves, relative wage rates, ownership or otherwise of shops, businesses, dwelling houses, residence in multi-household dwellings, and credit ratings,[249] may be taken into account. So may the locality of residence, particularly in larger towns where places of residence may be as good an indication of social status as declared occupation. Average levels of tax assessment can give a clue to the socio-economic character of different residential areas. Ethnicity and race, and participation in local affairs, including political activity, may also reflect social standing. So, too, may educational factors: whether children were sent to work at an early age or kept at school, and the levels of literacy in an occupational group. These are matters for which evidence is discussed elsewhere.[250]

As for distinction between those similarly described (by occupation) in the census returns, particularly the critical distinction between masters and journeymen, recourse to city directories, which usually confine entries to the employers, may help. Division of such occupational groups by age or wealth, using census, fiscal, or other evidence, may also assist in avoiding lumping together those whose social position varied greatly.[251] More ambitiously the construction of a detailed sample of identified masters and journeymen from a variety of sources[252] may enable the researcher to identify distinguishing characteristics, such as the ratios of the two groups within particular trades, for possible extrapolation to the community at large.[253]

Household and family structures are, of course, important

---

[249] See pp. 377–8, 379–80.   [250] See chs. 3, 7, 10.
[251] Smith, "Reconstructing occupational structures," 135.
[252] E.g., for masters: membership lists of employer assocs., business records, directories; for journeymen: benefit and employee assoc. membership rolls, payrolls, trade-union records.
[253] Smith, "Reconstructing occupational structures," 136–8 for details.

Demography

ingredients of the general social structures of local communities and may be related to many of the variables discussed here – such as occupation, social standing, wealth, ethnicity, race, and so forth, though the topic is perhaps too large a one to be dealt with here, except briefly.[254] Suffice it to say that many of the types of record outlined above can be used for the study of family and household structure in the local setting. Vital records and directories are particularly important, but the manuscript census records from 1850 provide the best source.[255] The linkage of information from several censuses over time may be quite revealing. Thus Elizabeth Pleck's study of a single census year stressed the existence of two-parent black families in Boston, but in tracing the same families longitudinally over several censuses she found a great deal of marital instability.[256] Census material can, of course, also be linked to other evidence. The technique of family reconstitution has been noted above. It is true that not until 1880 do the federal census schedules indicate specifically the relationship of individuals to the head of household. Nevertheless, every individual was named in the censuses from 1850 onwards and relationships can often be deduced in the census schedules of 1850, 1860, and 1870.[257]

The structure of households, as distinct from family groups, cannot be revealed by vital records, and here the census returns are essential, particularly for such matters as

[254] Useful are articles in such jnls. as *Jnl. Marriage and the Family*; *JFH*; *JIH*. See also ABC-Clio, *American Family History: A Historical Bibliography* (1985).

[255] E.g., Edward T. Pryor, Jr., "Rhode Island family structure: 1875 and 1960," in Peter Laslett and Richard Wall (eds.), *Household and Family in Past Time* (1972); Edmund L. Drago, "The black household," *Prologue*, 14 (1982), 81–8; B. F. Angresti, "The first decade of freedom," *Jnl. Marriage and the Family*, 40 (1978); Barbara Laslett, "Household structures on the American frontier," *Am. Jnl. Sociology*, 81 (1975); Barbara Laslett, "Social change and the family," *Am. Sociological Rev.*, 42 (1977).

[256] Elizabeth H. Pleck, "The two-parent household," *JSH*, 6 (1972); Pleck, *Black Migration*. And see Elliott Rudwick, "Black history in the doldrums," *JUH*, 9 (1983), 255–6.

[257] See, e.g., Richard A. Easterlin *et al.*, "Farms and farm families in old and new areas," in Hareven and Vinovskis, *Family and Population*, app. A; Willigan and Lynch, *Sources and Methods*, 97–9.

multi-family households, and the presence of servants and distant relations, and of lodgers.[258]

The study of urban elites has been undertaken largely with reference to their political affiliations and outlook (see ch. 7), but it may also be considered an aspect of the investigation of social structure. Where large numbers are involved, as in a big city, quantitative methods may be applied to biographical materials to shed light on the characteristics of such people, but at all events evidence on individuals can contribute to general impressions. For this purpose fiscal, probate, and census data on wealth, affiliations and kinship networks, and a whole host of other sorts of sources can also be utilized. These include gazetteers, directories, *Who's Who*s, social registers, and so on, some of which were specifically compiled to publicize local leading figures. Such, for instance, was the *Elite Directory for San Francisco and Oakland* (1879) which listed 2,340 persons (1.2 percent of the population) and included membership lists of private clubs. Likewise the *Portrait and Biographical Album of Rock Island County, Illinois* (1885) provides, for prominent inhabitants, information on place of birth, age, education, occupation, church affiliation, family details, clubs and societies, and sometimes political affiliation – though not always with accuracy. Biographical dictionaries, biographies, autobiographies, memoirs, diaries and journals, genealogies, private and business papers, political party and church records, and membership lists of clubs, philanthropic, literary, and artistic organizations, associations, and institutions, as well as local newspapers, can all be searched for evidence on such people.[259]

And while unofficial published assessments of the wealth of leading citizens, like those compiled by Moses Beach,[260] must be regarded as unreliable in detail and often in the level of

[258] See, e.g., John Modell and Tamara K. Hareven, "Urbanization and the malleable household," *Jnl. Marriage and the Family*, 35 (1973).
[259] See esp. bibl. inf. in Pessen, *Riches, Class, and Power*, 82–4, 336–41; and, e.g., Jaher, "Nineteenth-century elites"; Miller, *Jacksonian Democracy*; Frederic C. Jaher, *The Urban Establishment* (1982).
[260] E.g., *The Wealthy Citizens of the City of New York* (1855).

wealth recorded,[261] they remain a source for identifying the better-off. Contemporary opinions, expressed or implied in local newspapers about the social standing of groups, families, and individuals, though subjective, may also be useful.

Related to social structure is social mobility.[262] For the historian of local communities, social mobility includes relative changes in the socio-economic standing of particular occupational, ethnic, or other groups, the rise or fall in the standing of individuals within the society being studied, and also the extent to which such changes occurred and the characteristics of the persons involved.[263]

Since the community historian is not concerned with the fate of individuals or families once they leave the place with which he is concerned, his study of social mobility will relate largely to "persisters" – those who stayed within the community – though, of course, he may wish to investigate whether out-migration was in any way related to social mobility.[264] Were those who left failures or on the upgrade? Generally, however, it is not practicable to investigate the fortunes of those who left a community, though random sampling techniques may offer some returns.[265]

If a large city or an extensive district or region is being studied, the historian may wish to see if geographic, or spatial, mobility (for example, changes in a person's district of

[261] Ridgway, "Measuring wealth," 75; Pessen, *Riches, Class, and Power*, 347.
[262] For the concept, see Willigan and Lynch, *Sources and Methods*, 413–18.
[263] See Chudacoff, *Mobile Americans*; Decker, *Fortunes and Failures*; Clyde Griffen, "Making it in America," *New York Hist.*, 51 (1970); Michael P. Weber, *Social Change in an Industrial Town* (1976); Thernstrom, *Other Bostonians*; Thernstrom, *Poverty and Progress*; Knights, *Plain People*. See also Blumin, "Mobility and change"; Paul B. Worthman, "Working class mobility in Birmingham, Alabama, 1880–1914," in Tamara K. Hareven (ed.), *Anonymous Americans* (1971).
[264] Persistence and emigration rates among occupational groups are also of interest to community historians. Cf. Thernstrom, "Rejoinder to Alcorn and Knights"; Knights, *Plain People*, ch. 6; David W. Galenson and Daniel S. Levy, "A note on biases in the measurement of geographic persistence rates," *HM*, 19 (1986); Decker, *Fortunes and Failures*, 74, 266–7.
[265] Charles Stephenson, "Tracing those who left," *JUH*, 1 (1974); Michael D. Ornstein and A. Gordon Darroch, "National mobility studies in past time," *HM*, 14 (1978), 152–3.

residence, or moves from country to town) was associated with social mobility.[266] It should be noted, however, that because of transport considerations, geographic mobility in towns was more limited in the nineteenth century than it is today. There was often a need to live near one's work, so that residential districts characterized entirely by income were less common than now, and a simplistic correlation should not be assumed.[267]

The measurement of the social mobility of individuals and families assumes the use of an identifiable hierarchical classification valid over the necessary time span, to which career patterns can be referred. As we have seen the construction of such classification for social structure is not easy, and it is, therefore, not to be wondered at that the chronological measurement of changes in social standing is even more difficult. It has been suggested, for instance, that a classification based on occupational status (as unskilled, semi-skilled, low white-collar, high white-collar), suitable for measuring the hierarchy of occupational status, is not necessarily a proper classification for measuring social mobility. It has been argued that three systems of classification are needed – by personal wealth, by occupation ranked as mean wealth, and by occupation ranked by imputed prestige.[268]

The nature of the available evidence determines, however, that, as with social structure, occupation is the most likely basis for measuring social mobility. There are, of course, difficulties here. Too-ready inference that change in occupation resulted in change in economic circumstances must be avoided.[269] After all, many occupational moves were horizontal ones to jobs different but not more or less remunerative or

[266] E.g., Richard J. Hopkins, "Occupational and geographic mobility in Atlanta, 1870–1896," *JSoH*, 34 (1968).

[267] Cf. Alan N. Burnstein, "Immigrants and residential mobility," in Hershberg, *Philadelphia*; Stephanie W. Greenberg, "Industrial location and ethnic residential patterns in an industrializing city," in ibid.

[268] Roberta B. Miller, "The historical study of social mobility," *HMN*, 8 (1975), 94; Katz, "Occupational classification," 64–70. See also Willigan and Lynch, *Sources and Methods*, 14–15.

[269] Blumin, "Vertical mobility," 1–13, q.v. for discussion.

of different social standing.[270] Again, within each occupational group levels of wealth varied according to such factors as age, length of experience, personality, degree of success, district in which the trade was plied, inherited capital, family involvement in business, and so forth. In the case of merchants, for instance, an individual could move from a very modest income to great affluence without changing his occupational status. And the wages earned by men in the same job might vary greatly from firm to firm in the same community. Nor did the skilled necessarily always earn more than the unskilled.

In statistical analyses age, for example, can be controlled but it is unlikely that information on all variables will be available. If possible, linkage of occupational data with data on wealth should be attempted in order to obtain at least an impression of the general levels of income and property holding within an occupational group compared with those for other callings. As noted above, however, evidence on wealth is limited in scope and validity.[271] Again, it must be recognized that much social mobility occurred *within* a particular occupation, so that there may be a need for a hierarchic classification of jobs within particular trades. And as far as individuals are concerned, upward and downward social mobility might result from factors other than those so far mentioned: by marriage, by inherited property, or by successful or unsuccessful legal or financial ventures unconnected with occupation.

Prestige, besides, as a factor of standing and mobility, was not always related directly to occupation or earnings: it might, for instance, be based on marital or family connections, future prospects, or educational attainments. Residential mobility may be pertinent here, in the case of town dwellers, since social standing was so often connected with place of abode. The significant movement from membership of the "floating, unstable, propertyless" sector of the working class to the settled, respectable, property-owning sector of the community, may well be discerned from patterns of home owner-

[270] Stephan Thernstrom, "Notes on the historical study of social mobility," *Comparative Studies in Society and History*, 10 (1967–8), 168.
[271] See above. Cf. Howard M. Gitelman, *Working Men of Waltham* (1974), 182–7.

ship, savings, and residential continuity. Place of residence may, however, also be affected by ethnic considerations.[272]

As for the study of inter-generational social mobility, this poses all the difficulties associated with linking individuals over time, and is hard enough in the case of fathers and sons; for females, who changed names on marriage, it is even more difficult.[273]

Given the likely lack of evidence on many of the matters considered in this section, and considering the other difficulties discussed before, the complexity of work in this area is only too obvious. Conclusions based solely or mainly on statistical analysis, however sophisticated, of the sort of evidence outlined above, should be regarded as tentative.[274] Indeed, although the fruitfulness of such techniques cannot be denied and quantifiable evidence for demographic history is particularly rich for the nineteenth century, the historian attempting to reconstruct a past society would be wise not to confine his attention to the statistical analysis of quantifiable material. After all, although such exercises can provide valuable new evidence, they can often give only partial answers to crucial questions. Too often they do not answer the questions why? or how? The answers to these will usually have to be sought in traditional qualitative sources. The section on the ethnic dimension in the next chapter to some extent illustrates this.

---

[272] Thernstrom, "Historical study of mobility," 171; Burnstein, "Immigrants and social mobility."

[273] Cf. Harmut Kaelble, *Historical Research on Social Mobility* (1981), 14.

[274] Ibid., 12; Kathleen N. Conzen, rev., *JSH*, 6 (1972–3), 358–64.

CHAPTER 3

Ethnicity and race

THE ETHNIC DIMENSION

Until fairly recently there was a surprising dearth of ethnic historical studies, and although that is no longer the case,[1] there is still much scope for investigation of ethnic aspects of community history – especially in the ethnic dimension of the social structure of communities and the experience of immigrant and ethnic groups in work, politics, religion, family life, and social matters like housing and poverty. Some reference to source material for the ethnic element in politics, religion, economic matters, and welfare may be found in chapters 4, 6, 7, 8, and 11.

A considerable body of recent secondary work is available to provide background material on, for example, federal immigration policies, and on the history of specific ethnic groups, and some work has been undertaken on local aspects of ethnicity and on immigrants in cities generally and in certain large cities in particular.[2] In addition, various institutions have acquired important collections of material relating to immigrants and ethnic matters. Among these are research

---

[1] Rudolph J. Vecoli, "The resurgence of American immigration history," in Kellogg and Walker.

[2] For bibl. refs. etc., see citations *HG*, 450–9; Prucha, 166–73, 178 [Y34], 188 [AA6]; Vecoli (as n. 1 above), 188–91; A. William Hogland, *Immigrants and their Children in the United States: A Bibliography of Doctoral Dissertations, 1885–1982* (1984); Francesco Cordasco and David N. Alloway (comps.), *American Ethnic Groups . . . A Bibliography of Doctoral Dissertations . . .* (1981). Bibls. of urban history are also useful. For some areas special bibls. exist. The following encyclopedic works are also useful: Stephanie Bernardo, *The Ethnic Almanac* (1981); Stephan Thernstrom (ed.), *Harvard Encyclopaedia of American Ethnic Groups* (1980).

centers and historical societies devoted to the study of such topics.[3]

Some of the records described in the last chapter are particularly useful for investigating the size and characteristics of ethnic groups in local communities. Fiscal and business records, in particular, shed light on levels of prosperity, while from census materials statistical evidence on the numerical strength of different groups may be obtained, together with data on family and household structures, relative age–structures, property-holding, and on occupational and residential concentrations, and so on.[4] Aside from the references indicated in the discussion of censuses in chapter 2, some published Special Reports of the Federal Bureau of the Census are particularly valuable for large cities. Thus, for instance, the Special Report on occupations in the 1900 census provides, for 161 cities of 25,000 and over and for 78 of 50,000 and over, statistics of numbers in specific occupations by nationality (native or foreign born or of foreign parentage, by country).[5] Since statistics provided on a ward basis can distort the reality of ethnic residential patterns,[6] detailed city censuses, such as a Boston city census of 1850 which provides a street-by-street

3   They include Western Reserve Hist. Soc., Ohio State Hist. Soc., Balch Institute for Ethnic Studies, Philadelphia, univs. of Michigan, Utah, Southern Illinois at Edwardsville. See also Rudolph J. Vecoli, "The Immigration Studies Collection of the University of Minnesota," AA, 32 (1969); Immigration History Research Center (Univ. of Minnesota), Guide to Holdings (1976); Vecoli, "The resurgence of American immigration history," 191–2; Robert M. Warner and Francis X. Blouin, "Documenting the great migrations and a century of ethnicity in America," AA, 39 (1976); John G. Svoboda and David G. Dunning (comps.), Preliminary Guide to Ethnic Materials in Great Plains Repositories (1948); Francis X. Blouin, Jr. and Robert M. Warner, Sources for the Study of Migration and Ethnicity: A Guide to Manuscripts in Finland, Ireland, Poland, the Netherlands, and the State of Michigan (1979), esp. 16, 18; and see Markower, index under "ethnic groups," "immigrants and immigration"; Prucha, 18 [B81]. For refs. to ethnic historical societies and their publics. and to research centers, see Marjorie K. Joramo (comp.), A Directory of Ethnic Publishers and Resource Organizations (1979); Lubomyr R. Wynar (comp.), Encyclopedic Directory of Ethnic Organizations in the United States (1975).
4   See, e.g., Donald B. Cole, Immigrant City (1963), 226–7; Dean R. Esslinger, Immigrants and the City (1975); Robert A. Burchell, The San Francisco Irish, 1848–1880 (1979), 189; Stuart M. Bluin, The Urban Threshold (1976), 81, 88, 91, 93–4.
5   Occupations of the Twelfth Census (1904). Cf. Statistics of Women at Work . . . Twelfth Census (Special Rep. 1907).
6   Cf. Theodore Hershberg, "The historical study of urban space," HMN, 9 (1976), 100.

tabulation of the nativity of residents, may be of particular value.

General impressions of ethnic clustering may often be deduced from a study of surnames in census schedules, and census data can be supplemented by older county and other local histories which often provide much biographical information on individuals and their backgrounds. Local directories and similar publications, like almanacs, can also help to identify concentrations of ethnic groups and the dominant occupations followed in such concentrations. Directories are not as comprehensive as the later manuscript census records, however, and caution must be observed in conclusions drawn from them. Thus the fact that directories list only heads of households led one historian to assert that the Newburyport Irish rarely found employment in factories, whereas it has been shown that Irish youths (who did not appear in the directories) were so employed in large numbers.[7] Some directories provide information on the ethnicity of voters, so assisting investigation of the ethnic factor in political matters.

As well as directories, immigrant guides, like *The German in America, or Advice and Instruction for German Emigrants in the United States* (1851), can give both specific information on and general impressions of the nature and concentration of immigrant groups. So, too, may travelers' descriptions. The most useful of such guides and accounts are those which see the state of affairs through the eyes of an outside observer and treat such topics as the status of various occupations and the hierarchy of local organizations, which resident Americans might have taken for granted.[8]

And where ethnic newspapers existed, they will, of course, be very useful, shedding light on many aspects of the life of particular ethnic groups. For Boston, for instance, they reported arrivals and departures of individuals and families, meetings of societies, and the activities of leading members of the communities, and reflected and influenced the views of the

---

[7] Stephan Thernstrom, *Poverty and Progress* (1964), 282n.
[8] Cf. Kathleen N. Conzen, *Immigrant Milwaukee, 1836–1860* (1976).

immigrant on the urban society in which he found himself.[9] In larger towns these newspapers were numerous. By the later nineteenth century a very large number of foreign language periodicals and newspapers was being published in the United States as well as English-language publications relating to particular ethnic groups. Their files are prime sources for the historian, and there are a number of finding aids.[10]

As well as the immigrant press, ordinary local newspapers may contain evidence, including correspondence and comment, which can provide different viewpoints on ethnic groups within an area. Thus Chicago's English-language newspapers carried contemporary articles on the local Italians.[11] Again local newspapers may contain data which can be utilized to build up a detailed picture of crime patterns, involving among other things the members of ethnic communities.[12]

Likewise newspapers and journals attached to religious denominations representative of particular ethnic groups may be especially useful for the history of such groups and for such topics as inter-ethnic rivalry (see ch. 6). The religious press must, however, be used with caution and in conjunction with other evidence. The Jewish press of Columbus, OH, for example, represented the activities and reflected the life of only a minority of the town's Jewish community: particularly those from eastern Europe.[13] It should be remembered, too, that Jews were not merely Jews, but might also be Germans, Poles, and so on, so that information on them may be found in newspapers and other records relating to those groups, too.

---

[9] Oscar Handlin, *Boston's Immigrants* (1979 edn.), 267–8.

[10] Citations Prucha, 168–9; Anita C. Milner, *Newspaper Indexes* (3 vols., 1977–82). Note *The Newspaper and Serial Holdings of the Immigration History Research Center, University of Minnesota, Pt. I: Ukrainian American Periodicals* (Bremen, W. Germany, 1984) (this center – 826 Berry St., St. Paul, MN 55114 – has a large collection of ethnic newspapers). The WPA, HRS has calendared and listed some ethnic newspapers. For immigrant labor press, see p. 346n. For black press, see p. 30.

[11] Cf. Michael F. Funchion, *Chicago's Irish Nationalists, 1881–1890* (1976), 151; Cole, *Immigrant City*, 234.

[12] David R. Johnson, "Crime patterns in Philadelphia, 1840–70," in Allen F. Davis and Mark H. Haller (eds.), *The Peoples of Philadelphia* (1973).

[13] Marc L. Raphael, *Jews and Judaism in a Midwestern Community* (1980), 1.

Ethnicity and race

The relationship between ethnicity and political outlooks, rivalries, and other activity may be studied in the sources described in chapter 7, particularly those concerned with elections and those which enable analysis of voting patterns and their link with wards with ethnic concentrations. Aside from censuses, other public documents – federal, state, county, and municipal – as well as associated unpublished materials, are likely to yield statistical and other evidence on ethnic communities and immigrants generally.[14] State records, particularly for states where immigrants arrived from overseas and other states which attracted large inflows of immigrants, are particularly worth searching. Thus a Massachusetts document records for the years 1855–65 numbers and percentages of the foreign-born population by counties, and for 1880–4 statistics of nativity also by counties. The published reports of the overseers of the poor of that state also contain much statistical data on alien paupers. Again a Pennsylvania state document of 1808 records a request for the incorporation of a community of German immigrants in Butler county, and in 1827 there is a report relating to a German community at Economy, Beaver county, giving a history of that community.

In the second half of the nineteenth century most states and territories set up boards or commissions of immigration and the reports and unpublished records of these bodies may be valuable for local research.[15] The Wisconsin state archives, for instance, include in the Executive Department files on immigration, 1852–1905, manuscript reports and letters of the state agents and commissioners on immigration.[16] These boards often produced their own guides for prospective immigrants, like the *Emigrants' Guide to the State of Michigan* (New York, 1849) published in English, Dutch, and German.

[14] See, e.g., Robert Ernst, *Immigrant Life in New York City, 1825–1863* (1949), 297–9; John Bodnar, *Immigration and Industrialization* (1977), 202–3.
[15] Cf. Valerie G. Browne and David J. Johnson, *A Guide to the State Archives of Michigan: State Records* (1977), 19; Val D. Greenwood, *The Researcher's Guide to American Genealogy* (1974), 406–7. And see Friedrick Kapp, *Immigration and the Commissioners of Emigration of the State of New York* (1870, repr. 1969), 85–104.
[16] Conzen, *Immigrant Milwaukee*; Frederick C. Luebke, "Ethnic group settlement on the Great Plains," *Western Hist. Q.*, 8 (1977), 411.

Official immigration and naturalization records relating to individuals may also be of some use to community historians, since the social characteristics of certain port towns and communities in their hinterlands were significantly affected by the fact that large numbers of immigrants entered the United States through them, though many stayed only for a short time. Numerous other towns, particularly in the Midwest, were characterized by ethnic homogeneity.

Passenger lists for ships bringing immigrants are a source which has attracted much attention from genealogists so that useful lists and indexes exist.[17] Prior to 1820 ships were not required to file passenger lists, though some such lists have survived. Consequent on an Act of 1819 requiring such a procedure, however, many passenger lists from then to the end of the century survive, particularly for the east coast and Gulf ports (those for San Francisco being destroyed in 1906). Some of these have been published.[18] Originals exist mainly in the National Archives, Washington, DC,[19] and at Temple University.[20] There are, however, indexes, and both lists and modern indexes are available in microform.[21]

These passenger lists comprise customs passenger lists for 1820–1905 in the records of the Customs Bureau (RG 36) embracing original lists, copies, and abstracts.[22] The originals, of which only a small proportion survive, confined to seven

[17] P. William Filby, *Passenger and Immigration Lists Bibliography, 1538–1900* (with *Supplement and Index*) (1981; index useful for places and types of immigrant. Replaces Harold Lancour, *A Bibliography of Ship Passenger Lists, 1538–1825* (3rd edn., 1963)). See also Olga K. Miller, *Migration, Emigration, Immigration* (1974) (for bibl. of works using these records).

[18] E.g., Michael H. Tepper (ed.), *Passenger Arrivals at the Port of Baltimore, 1820–1834* (1982). And see last note.

[19] *GNA*, 168–70, 345–6.

[20] Philadelphia, PA 19122.

[21] See P. W. Filby and Mary K. Meyer (eds.), *Passenger and Immigration Lists Index. A Guide to Published Arrival Records of about 500,000 Passengers to U.S. and Canada in the 17th–19th Centuries* (3 vols., 1981); *Genealogical Research*, 47–57; *Immigrant and Passenger Arrivals: A Select Catalog of National Archive Microfilm Publications* (1983); *MRR*.

[22] The following draws on *Genealogical Research*, 41–57; Frank H. Serene, "American immigrant genealogy; ships' passenger lists," *Prologue*, 17 (1985); William E. Lind, "A general view of urban population research possibilities in the National Archives," in Jerome Finster (ed.), *The National Archives and Urban Research* (1974), 34.

ports, provide for each ship the name of each immigrant, tourist, or returning American citizen, with age, sex, occupation, name of country of origin, and country of intended settlement. The copies record, with dates of arrival, the names of immigrants and the ports of emigration and arrival of the vessel. The abstracts allot immigrants to the quarter of the year of arrival, and to the port of arrival, with sometimes an indication of port of embarkation. Copies and abstracts of customs passenger lists exist in large number but are by no means complete.

In addition there are so-termed transcripts compiled from the copies and abstracts, found in bound volumes in the "General Records" of the Department of State (RG 59). These provide, by quarter and year of arrival and by vessels, names of passengers with their age, sex, occupation, country of origin, and country of intended settlement.[23] They are not available in microform.

From 1883 for Philadelphia, and somewhat later for eight other ports,[24] there are, among the records of the Immigration and Naturalization Service (RG 85), immigration passenger lists or manifests. These derive from Acts of 1882 and 1893 which established and refined a system of registration of immigrants through state boards or commissions. The immigration passenger lists provide similar information to those of the Customs but may include more details on place of birth and final destination of immigrants into the United States, together with data on resident relatives with whom the immigrants intended to stay.

Such records naturally contain many inaccuracies and omissions.[25] For historians of those ports which received the immigrants they may nevertheless provide data on an important aspect of local life. Those interested in their use to shed light on ethnic groups in other places may, however, find them time-consuming and fraught with difficulties. Yet it may be

---

[23] See also *List of Passengers . . . 1819, to . . . 1820*, SD 118 (16–2), ser. 45, which includes part of these and some from a missing vol. For indexes to these vols. see *Genealogical Research*, 43.

[24] For ports and dates, see Greenwood, *Researcher's Guide*, 404–5.

[25] Robert V. Wells, *Uncle Sam's Family* (1985), 107.

possible by linkage with census and other evidence, particularly data deriving from research into particular families, to use them fruitfully, and, if not to compile statistical data, to gain impressionistic insight. In searching for particular individuals or groups of immigrants the task is eased if the port, vessel, and approximate date of arrival are known. Sometimes, too, foreign emigration records (see below) can provide additional information.

Perhaps easier to utilize and of more potential relevance to the community historian, are naturalization records, which are more likely to pertain to the area of settlement than do the passenger lists. They include declarations of intent to become citizens, petitions for grant of citizenship, depositions, and orders granting citizenship. Such records often provide the researcher with the name, address, occupation, and the country and date of birth of the applicant, together with an indication of the place of emigration, and the date and place of arrival in the United States, the number of years resident in America, and names, ages, and birthplaces of spouse and children. They are to be found among local, state, and federal court records. The pertinent federal records are those of U.S. district courts at the National Archives, Washington, DC and its regional branches.[26]

Data based on such records were sometimes published in state documents. For example, an Ohio document of 1904 provides statistics of naturalized persons (with nativities) for the counties of the state for the years 1857–8 through 1903–4. It may be noted, too, that the schedules of the 1870 federal census indicate whether males of twenty-one were citizens.

Since many immigrants and blacks were poor and ill-housed, federal, state, and city documents and archives concerned with living standards, housing, education, health, sanitation, fire risks, welfare, pauperism, and the like (see chs. 10, 11), often contain information on the social life of ethnic

---

[26] *Genealogical Research*, 63–9 lists location of federal naturalization records by states; and see *GNA*, 72–90. For local court records, see Jones, 163, and, e.g., Richard J. Cox and Patricia M. Vanorney, "The records of a city," *Maryland Hist. Mag.*, 70 (1975), 300–30; Greenwood, *Researcher's Guide*, 349–56.

groups in towns and cities. Indeed, where sizeable communities are concerned it is likely that reports of municipal officers and bureaus generally will contain information on ethnic groups. Reports of state bureaus of labor statistics often provided such data in relation to occupations, wages, housing conditions, and so on. Thus, the reports of the Michigan Bureau of Labor and Industrial Statistics contain evidence on nativity in the Detroit population and on the views of native and foreign-born labor towards immigration.[27] And the first report of the Tenement House Commission of New York City (1902) contains compiled data on the number of families in each block in Manhattan in 1902, and the ethnic composition of the residents of each street can be deduced from this source.[28]

Federal documents which may be worth searching include those on labor and on pauper immigrants, as well as general statistical reports.[29] The Commissioner of Labor, for example, published a detailed study of Chicago's Italians in 1897 embracing demographic, general social, educational, occupational, and health statistics,[30] and in two earlier reports gave information by states on workers' costs of living (distinguishing ethnic groups) in the iron, steel, coal, textile, and glass industries.[31]

Annual reports on immigration[32] provide little information for the local historian except statistics of emigrants (by country of origin) arriving in each customs district. The testimony in a *Report on the Importation of Contract Labor* may be worth searching. It contains much miscellaneous evidence on individual firms bringing in immigrants, with details of country of origin of these people, their working conditions, wages, and so on:

---

[27] Melvin G. Holli, *Reform in Detroit* (1969), 261.

[28] Gilbert Ofosky, *Harlem: The Making of a Ghetto . . . 1890–1930* (1968 edn.), 190–1.

[29] E.g., State Dept., Bureau of Statistics, *European Emigration: Studies in Europe of Emigration Moving out of Europe . . .* (1890).

[30] 9th Special Rep., *The Italians in Chicago* (1897), SD 138 (55–1), ser. 3564.

[31] *6th* and *7th ARs* (1890, 1891): HED 265 (51–2), ser. 2867: HED 232 (52–1), ser. 2958.

[32] In ARs Secretary of State, 1820–70; Bureau of the Treasury, ARs on Foreign Commerce, 1869–95; ARs Superintendent (later Commissioner) of Immigration, 1892–1903 (there is some overlap).

the indexes include the names of individual firms and employers.[33]

The numerous volumes of the *Report of the United States Immigration Commission* (1910–11)[34] are a mine of information on foreign immigrants, but much of it is not relevant to the historian of particular communities. Some may, however, be of potential use. The statistics in volume 3 are mainly at national and state level, but some data for cities are taken from the 1890 census.[35] Volumes 6–25, a subset of twenty-five parts, are arranged by industries and much of the data is conflated.[36] Some information at state level, and for some particular places, is, however, to be found, as, for example, on the ethnic origin of workers in Bayonne, NJ. Volumes 26–27 cover immigrants in selected districts in New York, Chicago, Philadelphia, Buffalo, Cleveland, and Milwaukee, providing much statistical information.[37] Volumes 29–33 comprise a subset of five volumes giving details on the schooling of the children of immigrants. Volumes 30–33 contain very detailed data for a number of cities.[38]

Similarly local evidence on ethnicity in the *Report of the Industrial Commission* (1900–2)[39] is limited. Volume xv, however, has a useful section on the distribution of certain ethnic groups in agriculture, which provides details of individual counties and places.[40] Volume v contains information

[33] See, e.g., HMD 572 (50–1), ser. 2579. Cf. Rep. Committee on Manufactures of the Sweating System, HR 2309 (52–2), ser. 3140 (1892); *Investigation . . . [into] Causes of the General Depression in Labor and Business*, HMD 29 (45–3), ser. 1863, HMD 5 (46–2), ser. 1928 (both 1879); and testimony to Committee on Education and Labor upon Relations between Labor and Capital, on immigrant labor: 4 vols. publ. 1885 as rep. of the committee, but the actual rep. never publ. (not in US Serial Set).

[34] 42 vols. (1910–11): SDs, various nos. (61–2, 3), ser. 5865–82. Vol. 42 is an index. See Laurence F. Schmeckebier, *The Statistical Work of the National Government* (1925), 95–103.

[35] Pt. 1: *Statistical Review of Immigrants, 1820–1910*, pt. 2: *Distribution of Immigrants, 1850–1900*, SD 756 (61–3), ser. 5878.

[36] *Immigrants in Industry*, SD 633 (61–2), ser. 5667–84.

[37] *Immigrants in Cities*, SD 338 (61–2), ser. 5665–6.

[38] *Children of Immigrants in Schools*, SD various nos. (61–3), ser. 5871–5.

[39] 19 vols. (1900–2), HD 476 (56–1), 494–5 (56–2), 71–82 (57–1), ser. 3990–2, 4168–9, 4338–49.

[40] *Immigration and Education*, HD 184 (57–1), ser. 4345, pp. 495–646.

on state legislation on hours of work, child and female labor, wages and contracts, and so on, which may provide useful background evidence.[41]

Since poverty was often connected with crime, information on the socio-economic conditions and outlook of poor groups (including ethnic and black concentrations) and the extent to which they came into conflict with society can be found in records relating to crime and punishment, detailed in chapter 11, including newspapers, police and other state and local government department records and reports, and court and prison records.

Records in the National Archives, aside from those already mentioned,[42] which may be of use in the study of ethnic groups in different parts of the country include tax records, discussed in the last chapter, and consular records. The published reports of United States consuls in foreign cities[43] provide details of the background of immigrants but usually no local American information. Their correspondence (NA, RG 59) may, however, throw light on the life of immigrants in America.[44]

The records of foreign governments, like British consular correspondence and reports,[45] may also be useful. Letters of British consuls in Boston, for instance, provide information on the condition of Irish immigrants (still technically British subjects).[46] Danish police registers record contacts between prospective emigrants and emigration agents.[47]

Where it is known that certain immigrant groups tended to work in particular trades or industries, any source material relating to those enterprises may well yield useful data. Thus,

---

[41] *Labor Legislation*, HD 476 (pt. 5) (56–1), ser. 3992.

[42] N.B. Nathan Reingold, "Resources on American Jewish history in the National Archives," *Publics. Jewish Hist. Soc.*, 47 (1958).

[43] See *Checklist*, 921–2, 932–8 for refs. and indexes. And see p. 404.

[44] *GNA*, 132. Cf. Ernst, *Immigrant Life*, 299.

[45] See pp. 414–15 for refs.

[46] Handlin, *Boston's Immigrants*, 274. Cf. Blouin and Warner, *Sources for the Study of Migration*.

[47] Kristian Hvidt, *Flight to America: The Social Background of 300,000 Danish Emigrants* (1975). Cf. Gordon W. Kirk, Jr., *The Promise of American Life* (1978), 13 (uses Dutch records).

a study of San Francisco Italians made use of accounts in official and other records of the fishing industry and of the *Pacific Wine and Spirit Review*, and much evidence on Italians in Chicago is in the official records of those employed in the municipal service.[48] Personnel records, like payrolls, of large business enterprises, may also yield information.[49] For businessmen and the bigger farmers, the records of R. G. Dun may provide evidence on ethnic background and connections.[50]

Further evidence on the life of ethnic communities may be found in contemporary writings, and in biographies, reminiscences, and private papers of individuals and families. The Chicago Historical Society, for instance, holds the private papers of many eminent Irish residents, and much material of this sort is in the Library of Congress.[51] This kind of source tends, of course, to be biased in favor of the more successful. Diaries, too, though very useful, were often kept by unrepresentative people.[52] A broader spectrum may be represented in the hundreds of humdrum family histories and scrapbooks which exist and in surviving private correspondence.[53] The Northern Ireland Public Record Office, Belfast, the libraries of Trinity College, Dublin, and other Irish libraries, for instance, house very many letters from Irish immigrants in America, and Irish correspondence may be found, among other places, in the Bancroft Library, University of California, Berkeley. It may be, too, that oral history collections cover the later nineteenth century – like those held by the Ohio

---

[48] Deanna P. Gumina, *The Italians of San Francisco, 1850–1930* (1970), 212, 215.
[49] Warner and Blouin, "Documenting the great migrations," 320; Richard N. Juliani, "The use of archives in the study of immigration and ethnicity," *AA*, 39 (1976), 476.
[50] See pp. 377–8.
[51] Cf. Gary J. Kohn, *The Jewish Experience: A Guide to Manuscript Sources in the Library of Congress* (1986).
[52] John F. McClymer, "The study of community and the 'New' social history," *JUH*, 7 (1980), 106.
[53] See, e.g., William I. Thomas and Florian Znaniechi, *The Polish Peasant in Europe and America* (5 vols., 1918–20); Alan Conway (ed.), *The Welsh in America* (1961); Theodore C. Blegen (ed.), *Land of their Choice* (1955) (Norwegians); Henry S. Lucas, *Dutch Immigrant Memoirs and Related Writings* (2 vols., 1955); Charlotte Erickson, *Invisible Immigrants* (1972).

Historical Society and made use of in a study of Jews in Columbus.[54]

Reports and other records of philanthropic and charitable organizations (see ch. 11) can often provide information on the structure of ethnic groups in individual places and on their standards of living. Thus the annual reports of the New York Association for Improving the Condition of the Poor are a rich source for economic and social conditions of immigrants,[55] and contemporary social reformers in Chicago produced in 1895 a detailed analysis of conditions in that city in which ethnic dimensions are considered.[56] The records of private organizations like chambers of commerce, and those of all sorts of church benevolent societies and missions are also worth searching for they are likely to be useful for the history of concentrations of poor ethnic groups. Any existing records of the Salvation Army in particular will probably yield evidence on slum areas. Similarly the records of interdenominational bodies (including the Y.M.C.A. and the Y.W.C.A.) can often be tapped. The Benevolent Fraternity of Churches in Boston, for instance, was in close contact with immigrant communities in that city as its annual reports for the years 1835 to 1866 show.[57]

Many ethnic communities, especially in larger cities, possessed their own societies – political, cultural, social, professional, mutual, and charitable – and their records and publications provide much evidence.[58] The New York German Society (Deutsche Gesellschaft der Stadt New-York), for example, has left annual reports (1846–65) full of information on aid to German immigrants, including valuable statistics.[59] Apart from reports, there may also be minutes of meetings and membership lists, and other useful records. Pamphlet literature, both produced by ethnic organizations

[54] Raphael, *Jews and Judaism*, 452–3.
[55] Ernst, *Immigrant Life*, 300.
[56] Jane Addems *et al.*, *Hull-House Maps and Papers* ... (1895).
[57] Handlin, *Boston's Immigrants*, 276.
[58] See Wynar, *Encyclopedic Directory*; Blouin and Warner, *Sources for the Study of Migration*, 14–16; Rudolph J. Vecoli, "For mutual, moral and material assistance," *Spectrum*, 2 (1976).
[59] Jay F. Dolan, *The Immigrant Church* (1975), 172; Ernst, *Immigrant Life*, 300.

and others, on topics pertinent to immigrant or racial groups, is likely to be available for many towns and will often shed light on specific issues and general conditions.

Much group colonization was organized by ethnic organizations in conjunction with state boards and the railroads, so that railroad company records may be useful, too,[60] and often ethnic groups had particular connections with certain religious sects. Indeed it has been said that "no institution was more pervasive in the early lives of immigrants than the churches."[61] Local denominational and church records (see ch. 6) are thus likely to be invaluable for ethnic studies (particularly when used in conjunction with other sources, like the censuses). For example, Catholic archdiocesan, diocesan, and parochial records have been used for the study of ethnicity in several cities where significant racial groups traditionally attached to that church lived: like the Irish, Italians, Poles, and Germans.[62] A study of Chicago Italians used parish records, parish histories, the archdiocesan newspaper, anniversary booklets, and the like. These together provided information on individual members of the community and their families, church attendance, community services, and charities provided by the local churches, and on relations between the ethnic groups and their fellow citizens and local government. The parish registers include addresses of individuals and provide the basis of the study of geographic mobility.[63] Registers may also provide evidence on family structures, and so on. Denominational histories, especially if regionally orientated, can sometimes also be useful. For immigrant communities from Germany and northern Europe the local Lutheran Church records may be useful. In some cities Jewish communities left a great variety of religious and religiously related records including the papers of rabbis.

Information on ethnic communities is also to be found in records concerning education (see ch. 10), since schools and

---

60 Cf. Luebke, "Ethnic group settlement," 410–11. And see pp. 223–4.
61 Warner and Blouin, "Documenting the great migrations," 322.
62 E.g., Funchion, *Chicago's Irish Nationalists*, 151.
63 Nelli, *Italians in Chicago*, 284. Cf. Richard Juliani, "Church records as social data," *Records of the American Catholic Hist. Soc. of Philadelphia* (1975).

other educational establishments were often particularly connected with ethnic groups. Some denominations, the Catholics in particular, provided their own schools. School records
themselves can give an indication, therefore, of ethnic concentrations, and of social conditions within ethnic groups. Censuses of schoolchildren arranged by the country of origin of
their parents are also sometimes available and school record
books may provide similar evidence.

BLACK AMERICANS

In many respects sources for the study of black Americans in
the local community do not differ from those for the study of
other people. Free blacks bought and sold property, made
wills, paid taxes, belonged to churches, and were involved in
court cases like other members of the community. Nevertheless the institution of slavery, the experience of Civil War and
Reconstruction, and subsequent discriminatory treatment of
blacks does mean that their history in a community was often
different from that of whites, and some types of record provide information specific to the black experience. There is
indeed much scope for the study of blacks, slave and free,
within particular communities.[64] Topics inviting attention are
wide reaching. The institution of slavery in the Southern states
stands out, and here there is certainly need for local studies,
since regional generalizations are not necessarily valid for
particular places, and conditions in large plantations may have
been very different from those on smaller farms in the same
county.[65] Again more attention has been given to slavery in
large cities than in small towns.

Aspects of slavery worth investigating include: the
economics of the institution, embracing the extent to which it
was profitable in agricultural holdings of different sizes and
in industrial and other enterprises (a matter of considerable

---

[64] Cf. Elinor Miller and Eugene D. Genovese (eds.), *Plantation, Town, and County:
Essays in Local History of American Slave Society* (1974).
[65] David D. Bellamy, "Slavery in microcosm," *JNH*, 62 (1977), 339; Ruben F.
Kugler, "U. B. Phillips' use of sources," *JNH*, 47 (1962); George Frederickson and
Christopher Lasch, "Resistance to slavery," *Civil War Hist.*, 13 (1967).

controversy);[66] the nature and geographical ramifications of the domestic slave trade; the extent and nature of ownership by large plantation holders, smaller men, poor whites, other blacks, and maybe Indians, and in towns as well as rural areas; the conditions of slave life – including diet, housing, clothing, punishment, medical attention, recreation, attitudes to the slave family, inter-slave relations; slave religion, education, and culture; demographic aspects of slave communities and slave families; slave resistance; and local government regulation of slavery. Another field of study comprises the identification of local abolitionists, their views as individuals and as members of abolitionist societies, together with those of their opponents.

Then there is the experience of the Civil War and emancipation. The economic and social conditions created by the war and the period of military government in the South are large areas of study. They include the effectiveness of the work of the Bureau of Refugees, Freedmen, and Abandoned Lands (henceforth referred to as the Freedmen's Bureau) in looking after the ex-slaves, and supervising the change to the position of free laborers and farmers; the relationship of the Bureau's local agents to the civil government and to the defeated whites generally, and whether or not these officials really promoted black interests or sided with planters and local politicians.[67]

Other important topics include the institution of schooling for ex-slaves in the South, and the effects of emancipation and desegregation generally on race relationships, on politics, and on Southern agriculture and industry. Again community historians in the non-slave states may want to look at the condition of free blacks before and after the Civil War, the extent of black concentrations, and the effect of migration from the

[66] See Alfred H. Conrad and John R. Meyer, *The Economics of Slavery and Other Studies in Econometric History* (1964); Robert W. Fogel and Stanley L. Engerman, *Time on the Cross* (1974); Herbert G. Gutman, "The world two cliometricians made," *JNH*, 60 (1975).
[67] See George D. Humphreys, "The failure of the Mississippi Freedmen's Bureau in black labor relations, 1865–1867," *JMH*, 45 (1983) and works cited; J. Thomas May, "The Freedmen's Bureau at the local level," *Louisiana Hist.*, 9 (1968).

South on living conditions of blacks and others and on the labor market.[68] Race relations in the North and the general position of blacks in Northern society as to wealth, occupation, political and religious affiliation, family and social structure, and racial differences in occupational patterns are all worth investigation.[69] Source material for the study of some of these topics is discussed in other parts of this volume, particularly in chapters 4, 5, 6, and 10. Demographic and occupational matters, too, are dealt with in chapter 2 where the basic evidence available in such records as censuses and directories in particular is detailed.[70]

An enormous library of secondary work on the American black exists[71] and the community historian will need to acquaint himself with what has already been written for his chosen area. Lenwood G. Davis has compiled a series of bibliographies of works concerning blacks in different parts of the United States.[72]

Many libraries and archives departments have substantial collections relating to black Americans;[73] the Library of

[68] Cf. Elizabeth H. Pleck, *Black Migration and Poverty* (1980); John E. Daniels, *In Freedom's Birthplace* (1914), 463–8.
[69] Other topics may be suggested by articles in *Trends in Hist.*, 3 (1982).
[70] But note Bureau of the Census, *Negro Population of the United States, 1790–1915* (1918) (county totals 1880, 1890, 1900); Peter D. McClelland and Richard J. Zeckhauser, *Demographic Dimensions of the New Republic . . . 1800–1860* (1982) (table B4: estimated black population in territories for which there was no census; table D1: estimated regional migration of blacks).
[71] See citations *HG*, 470–82, and section 44; Prucha, 180–6; *Directory of Afro-American Studies in the United States* (African Studies Assoc., 1976); Dwight L. Smith (ed.), *Afro-American History: A Bibliography* (2 vols., 1974, 1981); Joseph Wilson and Thomas Weissinger (eds.), *Black Labor in America, 1865–1983: A Select and Annotated Bibliography* (1986); Harry L. Watson, "Conflict and collaboration," *Social Hist.*, 10 (1985); Randall M. Miller and John D. Smith (eds.), *Dictionary of Afro-American Slavery* (1989); Louise V. Kennedy and Frank Ross, *Bibliography of Negro Migration* (1934); for biography and autobiography, see below p. 157. And see note 174 below. The jnl. *Slavery and Abolition* has annual bibls.
[72] E.g., *Blacks in the State of Ohio, 1800–1976* (1976).
[73] See citations, Prucha, 181–2; *NUCMC*; Makower; and Xavier Univ., *Guide to the Heartman Manuscripts on Slavery* (1982); Richard C. Davis and Linda A. Miller (eds.), *Guide to the Cataloged Collection in the . . . William R. Perkins Library, Duke University* (1980; refs. to many plantation account books). The black culture collection of the Trevor Arnett Library, Atlanta University, is available in microform. The papers of O. O. Howard (head of the Freedmen's Bureau) are in the library of Bowdoin College, Brunswick, ME.

Congress has a particularly large number.[74] Many federal records are of value in studying the history of blacks at the local level. Those that record the debates in and proceedings of Congress[75] contain much miscellaneous information and give some idea of the attitudes and tactics of representatives from various parts of the country with regard to slavery and the treatment of free blacks.[76] Many other federal documents contain local information especially relating to slavery and the Reconstruction period. Some of the more important may be mentioned here.

The most significant of such documents are for the period of the Civil War and its aftermath. Prior to the establishment of the Freedmen's Bureau, reports on freed slaves include a *Report on the Condition of Freedmen in the Department of the Gulf* (1864) and *The Freedmen of Louisiana: Final Report of the Bureau of Free Labor, Department of the Gulf* (1865).[77] Then there are annual reports (1867–70) of the commanders of the five military districts covering the Southern states (appended to the annual reports of the Secretary of War) which are full of information on the social and political scene and Ku Klux Klan activities in particular localities. For example, the 1868 report contains reports of arrests of Klan members in Memphis, a letter reporting alleged whippings and hangings and a general reign of terror in Maxville, Washington county, KY, and death threats and attacks on colored teachers at Spring Hill and Smyrna, TN. Some data are provided on affairs concerning blacks in communications from Freedmen's Bureau agents – as, for instance, on outrages and murders in Kentucky.[78]

---

74 John McDonough, "Manuscript resources for the study of negro life and history," *Q. Jnl. Library of Congress*, 26 (1969): see esp. the so-called Slave Papers, and the collections of abolitionists like Matthew Simpson; John L. Sellers (comp.), *Civil War Manuscripts: A Guide to Collections in the Manuscript Division of the Library of Congress* (1986): index includes places.

75 See pp. 23–4.

76 Debra L. Newman (comp.), *Black History: A Guide to Civilian Records in the National Archives* (1984), 67–72.

77 Both comp. Thomas W. Conway as publs. of the U.S. Army, Dept. of the Gulf, Bureau of Free Labor. Not in the US Serial Set.

78 HED 1 (40–3), ser. 1868, pp. 145, 156, 161, 190–2.

The *Report of the Joint Select Committee to Inquire into the Condition of Affairs in the Late Insurrectionary States* (1872),[79] with testimonies, is a multi-volume source concerned with Ku Klux Klan activity and the illegal mistreatment of blacks generally. The evidence is very detailed and contains much incidental information about the political outlooks of blacks, attitudes of whites to black education, the state of black schooling, the social and economic conditions of blacks, and so on. The report is arranged by states.[80] The *Report of the Joint Committee on Reconstruction* (1866)[81] relating to Tennessee, Virginia, North and South Carolina, Georgia, Alabama, Mississippi, Florida, Louisiana, and Texas, contains in the testimony much evidence on Southern attitudes towards freedmen and the operations of the Freedmen's Bureau. Evidence taken by the similarly named *Report of the Select Committee on Reconstruction* (1869)[82] contains the results of an investigation into pressures on freedmen to vote Democrat and other voting irregularities in Georgia and Mississippi. Indexes draw attention to evidence relating to each county and for many witnesses an indication of place of residence is given. Many other documents relate to the denial of voting rights to blacks.[83] The *Report of the Select Committee to Investigate the Causes of the Removal of Negroes from Southern States to the Northern States* (1880),[84] and accompanying testimony, contains much information on the treatment of blacks in Southern states (especially Louisiana) and on race relations generally. Since most of the blacks concerned settled in Kansas and Indiana the document is important for those states, too. Indexes of witnesses indicate clearly their place of residence.

There may also be special reports on outbreaks of racial

---

[79] SR 41 (42–2), ser. 1484–96; HR 22 (42–2), ser. 1529–41.

[80] Pt. 1: rep. and minority view; pt. 2: NC; pts. 3, 4, 5: SC; pts. 6, 7: GA; pts. 8–10: AL; pts. 11–12: MS; pt. 13: FL.

[81] HR 29, 30 (39–1), ser. 1272–3.

[82] HMD 52, 53 (40–3), ser. 1385. For the records of the committee, see Munden and Beers, 76.

[83] See pp. 324–5.

[84] SR 693 (46–2), pts. 1, 2, ser. 1899, pt. 3, ser. 1900. For extracts, see Benjamin Franklin *et al.*, "Documents," *JNH*, 4 (1919).

violence in particular places. There are, for instance, reports in 1866 on riots sparked in New Orleans by attacks on black troops, which are extremely detailed and accompanied by testimony.[85] The *Report of the Select Committee on Outrages in the Southern States* (1871) with testimony, relates mainly to the political and social conditions in North Carolina at the close of the war and immediately after.[86]

The official *War of the Rebellion: A Compilation of the Official Records of the Union and Confederate Armies*[87] is a mine of information on military affairs during the war and sometimes contains local information relevant to studies of blacks and slave plantations. Documents relating to the Court of Claims and the Southern Claims Commission are noted in chapter 4 and those relating to the Freedmen's Bureau later in this chapter. These, however, represent only the more obvious documents useful as sources for black social history. Investigators would do well to search the index to the US Serial Set.[88] Information appears sometimes in apparently obscure places. For instance a *Statement of Absconded Slaves in the Hands of Seminole Indians ... 1839* provides, for the slaves, data on family relationships and their owners' names.[89] Some federal documents not in the Serial Set may also be useful. Thus a Bulletin of the Bureau of Labor: *The Negroes of Farmville, Virginia – A Social Study* (1898), provides a demographic study of blacks embracing age, sex, and birthplace of individuals, the age-structure of the black population, conjugal conduct, data on births and deaths, and on schooling and illiteracy, occupational structure, wages and family economy, and value of real estate owned.[90]

Much unpublished federal material on blacks is to be found

---

[85] HED 68 (39–2), ser. 1292; HR 16 (39–2), ser. 1304. Cf. HR 101 (39–1), ser. 1274 (Memphis riots).

[86] SR 1 (42–2), ser. 1468. Original testimonies in NA: Munden and Beers, 39.

[87] 130 "serials," 70 vols., 1880–1901; additions and corrections inserted in each vol. 1902; available in NA microfilm. For the original records, see Munden and Beers, 281–2.

[88] See p. 22.

[89] HD 225 (25–3), ser. 348, pp. 83–9, 95–6.

[90] No. 14. See also testimony to the Committee on Education and Labor, cited n. 33 above.

in Record Groups of the National Archives.[91] This relates particularly to aspects of slavery, and to the Civil War and Reconstruction periods in the South.

Information on the position of slaves and their treatment during the war, found in correspondence, proclamations, petitions, and the like, is to be found in the Confederate War Department records (RG 109),[92] and in various Union military and naval records, not all of which can be detailed here.[93] The records of the Attorney General (RG 60) contain material on the slave trade and fugitive slaves, and on black rights during Reconstruction and later.[94]

The most significant collection of records in the National Archives relevant to black history is that of the Freedmen's Bureau (RG 105),[95] which acted as ward for ex-slaves in the Southern states after the defeat of the Confederacy. The Bureau was active in providing food, clothes, and medical attention to destitute freedmen and refugees, and transportation to their homes (or relocating them elsewhere), in acting as a sort of employment agency in supervising the drawing up of labor contracts, terms of indenture and child apprenticeship,[96] in registering ex-slave marriages and assisting black servicemen. It supervised the leasing of abandoned and confiscated buildings and land, and the maintenance of camps and lodgings for the homeless. It cooperated with voluntary philanthropic bodies to bring relief and schooling to the blacks,[97]

[91] Robert L. Clarke (ed.), *Afro-American History: Sources for Research* (1981); Newman, *Black History*; and, for examples, Ira Berlin *et al.*, *Freedom: A Documentary History of Emancipation, 1861–67 . . .* Series 1, vol. 1, *The Destruction of Slavery* (1985).

[92] Elizabeth Bethel (comp.), *Preliminary Inventory of the War Department Collection of Confederate Records* (PI 101, 1957).

[93] See, e.g., naval records (RG 45) and records of the Quartermaster General (RG 92), Secretary of War (RG 107), Headquarters of the Army (RG 108), Provost Marshal General (RG 110), Judge Advocate General (RG 153). Berlin, *Freedom*, vol. 1 gives examples. Other military records are dealt with below.

[94] *GNA*, 336; Paul Lewinson, *A Guide to Documents in the National Archives for Negro Studies* (1947), 4, 7.

[95] Many (not all) are available in microfilm: NA, *Black Studies: A Select Catalog of the National Archives Microfilm Publications* (1984), 19–81; *MRR*. PAMs and PDMs provide useful introductions. These microfilms are available in NA regional branches.

[96] Rebecca Scott, "Battle over the child," *Prologue*, 10 (1978).

[97] For the Bureau's educational records, see ch. 10.

and it sought to investigate racial outrages and murders. Its records are a prime source for the social and economic condition of blacks in the formerly disaffected states, border states and the District of Columbia during the period 1865–72 and indeed for the general history of the South in the period of Reconstruction. They consist of two groups: headquarters' records and those relating to field operations in the states.[98] They are too extensive to treat in detail here, but the more important records for historians of local communities may be noted.

Very important are the periodic reports made by officials of the Bureau. The annual, quarterly, and monthly reports of assistant commissioners summarized the work of the Bureau in particular states. These provide information on the political and economic situation, together with much statistical data compiled from the reports of subordinates, as, for example, on the numbers of refugees and freedmen provided by named local stations with food, clothing, and medical aid, distinguishing dependents and categorizing by type recipients of aid. In addition these officials made reports on abandoned and confiscated land, and superintendents of schools reported on freedmen's schools.[99]

It may be noted here that the reports of assistant commissioners for some years are available in published form.[100] Additionally the annual reports of the Commissioner (from 1865) providing evidence for each state, presumably based on information supplied by assistant commissioners and inspectors, were published in the reports of the Secretary of War

---

[98] See *GNA*, 263–4; Elaine Everly (comp.), *Preliminary Inventory of the Records of the Bureau of Refugees, Freedmen, and Abandoned Lands: Washington Headquarters* (PI 174, 1973) (there is also an unpublished NA inventory: "Records of the Bureau of Refugees, Freedmen, and Abandoned Lands, 1856 [*recte* 1865]–1880," July 1984, covering the same records); Elaine Everly and Willna Pacheli (comps.), *Inventory of the Field Offices of the Bureau of Refugees, Freedmen, and Abandoned Lands* (3 pts. and records of the Adjutant General's Office, 1872–8, NM–95, 1973–4); Elaine Everly, *Statistical Records of the Bureau of Refugees, Freedmen, and Abandoned Lands* (RIP 48, 1973); *Black Studies*, 19–81; Munden and Beers, 355–79. The following account draws on these.

[99] See pp. 481–4. For availability of these manuscript records, see below.

[100] *Reps. Assistant Commissioners for the Freedmen's Bureau since 1865*, SED 27 (39–1), ser. 1238.

(1866–71) and separately.[101] Individual places, counties, and towns, are often mentioned in these reports, and there are synopses of laws affecting blacks in the former slave states. The Louisiana report for 1865–6, for instance, includes a table of numbers of employed freedmen, by parishes.[102] For the historian of local communities the records of field offices are very important[103] – especially the reports of officers below the level of assistant commissioner. These records were arranged differently in different states but the work of such officers was everywhere similar. Superintendents, sub-assistant commissioners, agents, and others, issued rations, witnessed labor contracts and terms of indenture, registered marriages, heard freedmen's complaints, settled disputes, and were concerned with freedmen's education. Their numerous reports to the assistant commissioners pertained to subdistricts, such as individual cities and counties. Some reports were regular monthly returns, but there were other miscellaneous reports on particular topics (as racial outrages), and there were also statistical returns.

For some topics these records contain the same information as do the assistant commissioners' reports, but often with additional comments and in greater detail. Louisiana subordinate officers, for instance, provided personal details of freedmen and poor whites given assistance, including for ex-slaves the names of former owners. Generally these extensive records provide a wealth of local details on the administration of relief, employment of freedmen, labor conditions in agriculture, race relationships, and numbers helped with food, employment, and transportation. They give details of the Bureau's protection of freedmen's legal rights, its supervision of abandoned lands and houses, and its work with philanthropic societies which helped with schooling and other matters.[104]

---

[101] See *Checklist* for refs.
[102] In *Reps. Assistant Commissioners*, SED 6 (39–2), ser. 1276, LA.
[103] See, e.g., Barry Crouch, "Hidden sources of black history," *Southwestern Hist. Q.*, 83 (1980); Catherine Silverman, "Trends in black Reconstruction history," *Trends in Hist.*, 3 (1982), 67–8.
[104] RIP 48, 1–3, 6; *Black Studies*, 21 and under state entries. And see pp. 482–4.

The manuscript monthly and annual reports of the assistant commissioners are to be found among headquarters' records, together with correspondence. Some of this material is identified not only by state but by district.[105] The various reports and returns made by subordinate officers to assistant commissioners, likely to be especially significant for particular communities, are among the official records of the Bureau, filed by state and by officers; much of this material is identifiable by locality.[106] The records of local agents, perhaps the most fruitful for local detail, include correspondence, daily journals, account books, and memoranda books, but unfortunately are not, like many of the assistant commissioners' records, available in microform and must be consulted at the National Archives.[107]

Much correspondence between the Washington headquarters, assistant commissioners in the states, and local subordinate officers has survived, together with correspondence with outside bodies and individuals. Among the headquarters' records series of "letters received" and "synopses of letters and reports received" are letters and reports on the condition of the freedmen from assistant commissioners (as already noted) and societies, members of Congress and private persons. These sometimes include enclosures of manuscripts, newspaper clippings, and printed matter.[108] Field office collections of letters received by assistant commissioners also exist, often with registers which summarize the correspondence. Such material is of particular interest for local affairs since it contains letters on specific incidents as well as routine affairs, petitions, and letters and reports from the civilian agents and other subordinate officers working in individual counties.[109] There may be indexes of persons and subjects.

[105] Series 15, 20; PI 174, 8–9.
[106] Detailed NM–95; *Black Studies*, 29–82 (indicating which in microform).
[107] Listed in NM–95. Cf. Barry A. Crouch and Larry Madaras, "Reconstructing black families," *Prologue*, 18 (1986), 119; J. Thomas May, "Study of a Louisiana agent," *Louisiana Hist.*, 9 (1968).
[108] There are some registers of letters and indexes: *Black Studies*, 25–6; PI 174, 8–9, q.v. for details.
[109] Cf. Barry A. Crouch, "View from within," *Chronicles of Smith County, Texas*, 12 (1973).

Headquarters' out-correspondence includes copies of letters and replies endorsed on returned in-letters. Files of the correspondence of assistant commissioners to the Commissioner may include copies of annual and monthly reports, as well as letters to subordinates and civilians. Much of such correspondence is about routine matters, but some letters relate to specific matters, like court cases, and there is correspondence with, and reports to, philanthropic societies.

The variety and bulk of field-office records for individual states is very great and cannot be fully detailed here,[110] but among them are registers of black orphans, and registers of freedmen's applications for relief or land, and of records relating to freedmen's labor contracts and indentures.[111] Labor contracts between employers (usually farmers) and freedmen indicate the period of service, wage rates, and type of work. There are also many records concerning outrages against blacks. Indeed many agents kept records of crimes by whites against blacks and by blacks against blacks, and on the state of law and order generally.

The coverage provided by the records varies chronologically and topically for the individual states, and for some there are records not paralleled elsewhere. For Louisiana, for instance, there are reports on the condition of freedmen arranged by plantation, and inspection reports for individual plantations. Together these may include the name of the parish and plantation, the agent's name, the name of the owner or lessee, the number of freedmen (by sex), the type of contract and average wages, the numbers of schools and pupils, and the acreages under cultivation and types of crops.

For all the states, operations reports by subordinate officers in narrative form are very useful. They provide evidence of the economic and social conditions of the locality where the officer was stationed, with particular stress on race relations and freedmen's education. Ration reports list quantities of food,

---

[110] See NM-95.
[111] Cf. Barry A. Crouch, "Freedmen's Bureau records," in Clarke, *Afro-American History*, 79–84, 87.

clothing, and medicine issued to freedmen and other refugees, indicating the extent of their destitution, and registers relating to help with transportation also exist. Land reports list abandoned or confiscated land held by the Bureau.[112]

There are many demographic surveys providing local information. For Alabama, for example, there are census returns for blacks and whites for 1866 numbering males and females in decennial age groups for each county.[113] A survey of Houston, TX, in 1866 indicates where blacks lived and their occupations, what property they owned, and whether they owned or rented their homes.[114] For Virginia, censuses of freedmen made by counties in 1865 and 1866 are very detailed and may be used to study household structure.[115]

Particularly interesting for black family relations and family structures are records relating to the marriages of freedmen. In the Bureau's headquarters' records are freedmen's marriage certificates and similar records for 1861–9, arranged alphabetically by state.[116] More useful for the community historian are the registers of marriages among the field office records. These were kept by subordinate officers and most give the names of the couple and the date of the marriage. Some may provide the ages of the spouses, their color, and the color of their parents. Many also give information on pre-1865 unions, with data on the length of those unions, age of the parties at marriage, and details of offspring.[117]

Complaints books or registers kept by subordinate officers usually list the names of freedmen, and the nature of the

[112] For details, see pp. 186–7.
[113] NM–95, pt. I, 12. Publ. in *Reps. Assistant Commissioners*, cited above.
[114] Cited Crouch, "Hidden sources," 217.
[115] Munden and Beers, 379; Herbert G. Gutman, "Persistent myths about the Afro-American family," *JIH*, 6 (1973).
[116] PI 174, 12.
[117] NM–95, pt. I, 248 and *passim*; Elaine C. Everly, "Marriage registers of freedmen," *Prologue*, 5 (1973); Andrew Billingsley and Marilyn C. Greene, "The other side of slavery," in Clarke, *Afro-American History*, 130–7. Not all such records are in the NA; some are with state archives and in county court houses: cf. James D. Walker, "Black family history resources in U.S. military records," *World Conference on Records, 1980*, 4, 2 (1980), no. 339, pp. 6–7. And see Herbert G. Gutman, *The Black Family in Slavery and Freedom, 1750–1929* (1976), 18, 550; Gutman, "Persistent myths," 192.

complaint, and sometimes give a summary of the case.[118] Other field office records include court papers for cases in which freedmen were involved. For Georgia, for example, there is a series of such papers arranged by case for 1866, mostly tried in civil courts, including copies of trial proceedings, Bureau officers' reports and affidavits.[119] Some cases were investigated in the short-lived freedmen's courts.[120] For Virginia there are weekly reports of the proceedings of these courts. For North Carolina there are records of cases tried in various courts 1865–8, which include statements and depositions, and monthly reports on such cases by subordinate officers.[121] Field office records also include much on freedmen's education (see ch. 10).

For the period before the establishment of the Freedmen's Bureau, the records of the Civil War Special Agencies of the Treasury Department (RG 366) include evidence on the regulation of the employment and welfare of freedmen.[122] Some field records of Treasury agents, mainly registers and leases of abandoned lands, are found in RG 105, as are some relevant War Department records. These latter pertain to the work of the Army in providing relief and employment for freedmen during the Civil War, and include the records of freedmen's home colonies and those of the officers in charge of the various "freedmen's departments" established during the war – including the Bureau of Free Labor in Louisiana, the Superintendency of Freedmen in the Mississippi Valley, and the Department of Negro Affairs in Virginia.[123]

The records of the Freedmen's Branch of the Adjutant General's Office, which took over from the disbanded Freedmen's Bureau in 1872, include records of field officers

---

[118] RIP 48, 6; NM–95, pt. 1, 248 and *passim*. Cf. W. A. Low, "The Freedmen's Bureau and civil rights in Maryland," *JNH*, 37 (1952), 238; Gutman, *Black Family*, 167–8, 573.

[119] NM–95, pt. 1, 99.

[120] Cf. James Oakes, "A failure of vision: the collapse of the Freedmen's Bureau courts," *Civil War Hist.*, 25 (1978).

[121] *Black Studies*, 57, 78.

[122] *GNA*, 179–80; PI 174, 3; Newman, *Black History*, 340.

[123] Listed NM–95, apps. For publ. reps. of "freedmen's departments," see above, p. 136.

stationed in the Southern and border states,[124] and much correspondence and other records relating to claimants for relief. They are found both with the Freedmen's Bureau records (RG 105) and those of the Adjutant General (RG 94).[125] Most of the correspondence concerns military affairs but some letters from private persons and business firms include complaints about obstructions to emancipation and reports on the condition of freedmen and destitute whites, and on economic conditions generally in the conquered areas. There are also reports on lawlessness, riots, and racial violence in various parts of the South and on political corruption. For the period 1871–80 there are detailed reports on the activities of the Ku Klux Klan and troubles over the election campaigns of 1874–5.[126] RG 94 also includes the papers of the American Freedmen's Inquiry Commission of the 1860s,[127] which consist largely of evidence of freedmen and others grouped geographically. There is an index of witnesses' names.

The records of the five military districts into which the South was organized, 1867–70, among the records of the Army Continental Commands (formerly in RG 98, but now in RG 393),[128] are useful for the period of Reconstruction. They supplement the records of the Freedmen's Bureau, since there was close liaison between the Army and the Bureau. They contain data on fugitive slaves, the status of blacks, race relations, freedmen's rights, the position of blacks in the courts, black labor contracts, outrages and the maintenance of order, the registration of black voters, and election returns, and are particularly valuable for Florida, Texas, and Louisiana.[129]

[124] Detailed NM–95, pt. 3, 538–48.
[125] Lucille H. Pendell and Elizabeth Bethel, *Preliminary Inventory of the Records of the Adjutant General's Office* (PI 17, 1949), 83–7; PI 174, 37–41.
[126] Munden and Beers, 253–6, 266; *Black Studies*, 13–14 (q.v. for microfilms).
[127] Munden and Beers, 390–1.
[128] Elaine Everly et al. (comps.), *Preliminary Inventory of the Records of the United States Army Continental Commands, 1821–1920* (PI 172, 5 vols., 1973), esp. vol. 1.
[129] Munden and Beers, 411–17, for details of records for each district; *Black Studies*, 82 (q.v. for microfilms).

Other relevant federal archives[130] include the records of the Bureau of Indian Affairs (RG 75) which contain much evidence on blacks living with Indians, including those held as slaves. The enrollment (or "census") cards of the Five Civilized Tribes, 1898–1914, and ancillary records, distinguish former slaves and new-born freedmen.[131] Among the records of the General Accounting Office (RG 217) are the papers of the Board of Commissioners for the Emancipation of Slaves in the District of Columbia, 1862–3. These contain, among the petitions of former slave owners, details of the number, names, and value of the former slaves for whom compensation was claimed (indexed by name of petitioner).[132]

U.S. district and circuit court records (RG 21: in NA regional branches) include material on the slave trade for southern New York state and eastern Pennsylvania to 1843, on slavery in North Carolina, and on manumission, emancipation, and fugitive slaves for the District of Columbia, eastern North Carolina, and southern New York state. Some claimants seeking redress in the Court of Claims (RG 123) were blacks and plantation owners, so that papers ancillary to claims (like wills, contracts, titles to real estate, and testimony) contain data on slavery and the place of blacks in the plantation economy. Similar are the records of the Southern Claims Commission (RG 217) detailed in chapter 4.

Among Senate records (RG 46), petitions and memorials from private citizens and state legislatures on matters concerning the freedmen and Reconstruction generally may be of use for the community historian. This Record Group also contains reports and records of Senate committees to which the Senate journals can be used as indexes to locate information on blacks.

The records of the Bureau of the Comptroller of the Currency (RG 101) embrace those of the Freedmen's Savings and

---

[130] The following draws on Lewinson, *Guide to Documents*; Newman, *Black History and Black Studies* (q.v. for microfilms) without further citation and these should be referred to.
[131] These cards are at NA, Fort Worth regional branch. See also RG 217, annuity rolls: *Genealogical Research*, 184.
[132] Ukon E. Uya, "Using federal archives," in Clarke, *Afro-American History*, 20.

Trust Company, 1865–74, which had branches in cities in the states of New York and Pennsylvania, and various Southern states. These include the journal of the board of trustees, minutes of committees and inspectors, correspondence, depositor signature books, records of dividends paid, and loan and real-estate ledgers and journals. Registers of depositors provide biographical details of ex-slaves including age, birthplace, previous and current residence, occupation, name of former owner, name of employer, and data on spouses, children, parents, and other relations.[133] The registers for each state are arranged by city of the bank branch; indexes to now-lost deposit ledgers serve as indexes to the registers and dividend payment records, 1882–9.[134]

In RG 36, among the records of the Customs Service, are slave manifests for some Southern ports providing details of imported slaves including names of the shipper and the person or company the slaves were destined for. Up to 1808 these include slaves from overseas.[135]

Some correspondence received by the National Board of Health, 1879–84 (in RG 90), grouped by state, contains demographic information, data on mortality rates of blacks, and details of their state of health. A register of the letters provides addresses of the senders with some indication of the content and serves as an index.[136] There is, for instance, a report on black mortality and health of blacks in various wards of Norfolk, VA in 1878–9.

The data on blacks in the manuscript federal censuses (RG 29) have been noted in chapter 2,[137] but may be summarized briefly here. The censuses of 1790 through 1840 provide the names of free black heads of households, with the numbers of those in their households. In addition they give the numbers of

---

133 *GNA*, 161; Meyer H. Fishbein, "Business history resources in the National Archives," *Business Hist. Rev.*, 38 (1964), 241; *Genealogical Research*, 180–1; Carole Merritt, "Slave family history records," *Georgia Archive*, 6, 1 (Spring, 1978), 18–19.
134 Available in microfilm: *Black Studies*, 10–11.
135 *Genealogical Research*, 185.
136 All in microfilm: *Black Studies*, 93–4.
137 See pp. 75–9; Newman, *Black History*, 38–44.

slaves, listed under the names of owners.[138] The returns for the censuses of 1850 and 1860 were arranged (again by state and county) into free and slave schedules. All members of free black households were distinguished by name and the same data provided as for whites. In the slave schedules individual slaves were rarely named; normally they were listed under their owner's name as numbers in sex and age categories.[139]

From 1870 blacks and whites appear in the same schedules and the same data are provided for them, though they are conveniently distinguished by race.[140] Thus the 1870 schedules can be utilized to identify ex-slave families in the South and elsewhere. And the census schedules generally provide opportunities for the study of black migration and all the demographic and occupational features discussed fully in chapter 2. In conjunction with other records they can be used to illustrate relationships between black residence and social and economic factors.[141] It has been suggested that comparison of the same group of slaves in sequential censuses is more reliable for estimating slave mortality than using the mortality schedules, because of the underreporting of slave deaths.[142]

Another body of evidence on blacks at the local level is provided by the public records of the various states. Many state censuses present statistics of slaves and free people of color.[143] State constitutions, statutes, and legal codes record the official status of slaves and free blacks and the obligations and rights of slave owners, though revelation of the actual

---

[138] Debra L. Newman, *List of Free Black Heads of Families in the First Census ... 1790* (SL 34, rev. 1974), lists alphabetically by state (not smaller divisions) with page refs. to census vols. Not all black heads were named. For interpretation of "owners," see p. 76n.

[139] For data on free Northern blacks, comp. from 1850, 1860 censuses etc., by National Museum of American History, see Makower, 57.

[140] As are other races, like Chinese, Indians, mulattoes. The difficulties of mulatto registration are not considered here: see Hershberg, *Philadelphia*, 396–8.

[141] See, e.g., Henry Taylor, "The use of maps in the study of the black ghetto-formation process," *HM*, 17 (1984).

[142] Maris A. Vinovskis, "The demography of the slave population in antebellum America," *JIH*, 5 (1975), 463–4; Reynolds Farley, *Growth of the Black Population* (1970), 58–75. For the other sources useful for slave mortality estimates, see Richard H. Steckel, "Slave mortality," *Social Science Hist.*, 3 (1979).

[143] See Dubester (1948), for details.

position will require recourse to other sources.[144] The papers of Southern state governors during Reconstruction and after are often useful generally for the background of race relations, but contain little specific to particular communities.[145] Attitudes of Northern and Western whites to slavery and blacks generally may be illustrated in the records of debates of state constitutional conventions – as in California in 1849 and Michigan in 1835–6. Journals and records of debates in state legislatures and the reports of committees and state officials (especially those concerned with education, health, labor, agriculture, crime, and the poor) provide similar general information but are more likely also to contain evidence relating to particular places. Indexes to state documents should therefore be searched.

Some examples may be cited. A Pennsylvania state document of 1858 contains petitions from two counties over the influx of fugitive slaves and manumitted blacks. The records of the Land Commission of South Carolina, the only Southern state to establish such a body, provide evidence on the redistribution of land to ex-slaves.[146] The Annual Report of the Massachusetts Bureau of Labor for 1904 contains a detailed investigation into the social and industrial condition of blacks in Boston and seven other cities in the state in 1900.

County records, particularly in the South, represent a significant source for black local history. These records may include, aside from court records of judicial cases, "freedom papers" (manumission records, proofs, and affidavits of freedom), permits for slaves to leave the state temporarily, tax records (giving names of owners and numbers of slaves), cohabitation records (records legalizing former slave marriages), apprenticeship records, reports and records of superintendents of public instruction and of the overseers of the poor, marriage records, election returns, and so on. There

[144] Cf. T. Laprade, "Some problems in writing the history of American slavery," *South Atlantic Q.*, 10 (1911).
[145] Cf. Howard N. Rabinowitz, *Race Relations in the Urban South, 1865–1890* (1978), 422.
[146] Gilbert Ofosky, *Harlem* (1968 edn.), 190; Carol K. R. Blesser, *The Promised Land* (1969), p. xiv.

may well also be registers of free blacks. Thus in Fairfax county, VA, registers (1822–6) record whether those registered were born of free parents or, if manumitted, by whom and whether by will.[147] Such registers are not, however, always comprehensive.[148] There may also be county records of sales of slaves (providing prices and occupations)[149] and registers of slaves entering the state (as kept in Georgia from 1817).[150] Deeds, jail records, and records relating to mortgages may also provide information on slaves.[151] Land-entry books and deed books can indicate the purchase of land by free blacks and the transfer of land to them, and can be used in conjunction with other evidence, such as that of the censuses and tax records, to measure the extent of black landownership.[152]

Municipal records, particularly those of the larger cities in the South, are likely to contain much evidence relating to the treatment and status of blacks. The city ordinances of Little Rock, AR, for example, regulated the hiring of slaves, laid down punishments for offences by slaves, imposed slave curfews, and so on.[153] Council minutes, tax records, registers of free blacks, and other records similar to those of counties can provide more information. Nearly half the Heartman Collection on slavery in New Orleans (at Xavier University), for example, consists of municipal records, including some relating to free blacks. Among these are business contracts, shipmasters' bonds for bringing blacks into port, police reports, tax records, and reports from the city workshop.[154] City, county, and state governments and agencies often used slaves and jailed blacks for garbage collection, road repairs, drainage works, street cleaning, and so on, so that police records and

---

[147] Donald Sweig (ed.), *Registrations of Free Negroes* (1977).

[148] See Ira Berlin, *Slaves Without Masters* (1974), 327–30.

[149] Cf. U. B. Phillips, *American Negro Slavery* (1918, repr. 1966), 368–70 (prices based on bills of sale in four major markets). But probate records (see below) may give better data on values.

[150] Merritt, "Slave family history records," 18.

[151] See, e.g., Cox and Vanorney, "The records of a city," 296.

[152] Edward H. Bonekemper, "Negro ownership of real property," *JNH*, 55 (1970).

[153] Paul D. Lack, "An urban slave community," *Arkansas Hist. Q.*, 41 (1982).

[154] *Guide to the Heartman Manuscripts on Slavery*. Many are in French; some available in microfilm.

the labor records of local government departments and appropriate state records may also contain data on black workers.[155]

The records of judicial cases in county and other courts[156] provide another important source for the position of blacks in local communities. Aside from recording disputes over slaves and slavery, and detailing offences committed by free blacks and slaves, and the nature of penalties inflicted, they provide much incidental evidence on the lives of slaves and other blacks, on race relations and attitudes, and on social and economic conditions. The testimony of witnesses may be particularly informative. Sometimes court records relating to slave cases were kept separately from other cases.[157]

A most useful work of reference for cases in the higher courts is that of Helen T. Catterall,[158] which records all cases involving slaves, slavery, and blacks in the highest court in each state to 1875, together with the opinions of the U.S. Supreme Court on cases referred to it. Subjects of cases covered include suits for freedom, fugitive slaves, and acts of violence and resistance.[159] Much evidence on individual cases is provided in Catterall. Unfortunately place-names are not included in the index and the sections on each state may have to be searched. The names of those involved, particularly important planters, may, however, be recognized by the researcher. References to the full law reports of cases are given. These, it may be noted, contain information on many cases not included in Catterall and can, of course, be searched.[160]

Probate court records are valuable for evidence on the

[155] Cf. Robert S. Starobin, *Industrial Slavery in the Old South* (1970), 31.
[156] See pp. 42–3, 537–8, and, e.g., Edward L. Ayers, *Vengeance and Justice* (1984); Robert G. McPherson (ed.), "Georgia slave-trials, 1837–1849," *American Jnl. Legal Hist.*, 4 (1967), 257–83, 364–77; Edward M. Steel, Jr., "Black Monongalians," *West Virginia Hist.*, 34 (1973).
[157] Cf. John C. Edwards, "Slave justice in four middle Georgia counties," *Georgia Hist. Q.*, 57 (1973), 265–6.
[158] *Judicial Cases Concerning American Slavery and the Negro* (5 vols., 1926–37, repr. 1968).
[159] Cf. Marion J. Russell, "American slave discontent in the records of the high courts," *JNH*, 31 (1946): Paul Finkelman, *Slavery in the Court Room: An Annotated Bibliography of American Cases* (1985; useful for secondary sources, but no topographical index).
[160] See pp. 25–6.

composition of slave families, size of slave holdings, and attitudes of owners to slaves, and for valuation of slaves. Wills show to whom slaves were left and why, attitudes to particular slaves or to type of slave (as house or field), and indicate if freedom is to be granted, or slaves to be hired out to pay debts, and so on. Estate settlements (accounts of how instructions in wills were carried out) may show hiring contracts and indicate whether grants of freedom were honored and whether the integrity of slave families was considered.[161] Appraisals and inventories often list slaves indicating sex and money value and may also give age and physical condition, and may provide a better indication of slave prices than bills of sale which give for groups only a lump sum and lack personal details.[162]

Throughout the century newspapers are an important source for black history at the community level, providing much data in news reports, editorials, correspondence, advertisements, obituaries, and so on.[163] They are particularly valuable for conditions and attitudes in the years preceding the Civil War, the war years, and the period of Reconstruction. Many city and small-town newspapers in the South run by whites were dominated by racial themes. They included, as well as reports of specific incidents, trials, and so on, advertisements for the sale and hiring of slaves, and reports on the use of slaves in particular factories. There were also many newspapers and periodicals run by or largely benevolently inclined towards blacks. Among these were antebellum publications. After 1865 there were many black periodicals in the South. Numerous guides to the black press exist.[164]

Northern abolitionist newspapers and periodicals often

[161] Cf. James W. McGettigan, Jr., "Boone County slaves," *Missouri Hist. Rev.*, 72 (1978); Randolph Campbell, "Human property," *Southwestern Hist. Q.*, 76 (1973).

[162] Randolph Campbell, "Local archives as a source of slave prices," *Historian*, 36 (1974); Fogel and Engerman, *Time on the Cross*, vol. 2, 21, 24–6, 79–87.

[163] See, e.g., Philip S. Foner and Ronald L. Lewis (eds.), *The Black Worker*, vol. 1 (1869), *passim*; Martin E. Dann (ed.), *The Black Press, 1827–1890* (1971); Henry L. Suggs (ed.), *The Black Press in the South, 1865–1979* (1983); Penelope L. Bullock, *The Afro-American Periodical Press, 1838–1909* (1981).

[164] Citations Prucha, 182–3; Donald M. Jacobs et al. (eds.), *Antebellum Black Newspapers, Indices to New York Freedom's Journal (1827–1829), The Weekly Advocate (1837), and Colored America (1837–1841)* (1976).

contained information about slave conditions in places in the South.[165] The monthly journals of Northern missionary societies, like the *American Freedman* (1866–7) and the *Freedmen's Record* (1865–71) are valuable for the Reconstruction period. The *Freedman* of Indianapolis, an illustrated weekly established in 1888, for example, contained a great deal on places in the South. In 1893 it published 178 despatches by correspondents in 32 Arkansas towns and villages, plus letters to the editor, covering many topics – including racial discrimination, black education, the economic condition of blacks, blacks and the land, relevant political and legislative affairs, religious matters, and, indeed on every aspect of black life.[166] During Reconstruction local newspapers in the South carried directives and orders from the Freedmen's Bureau, some of which are not among the Bureau's own records,[167] and in this period some papers were concerned mainly with providing advice for freedmen farmers.[168]

Other sources of information at the community level include older local and county histories which often contain information on plantations, including references to slaves and other blacks, which is no longer available elsewhere. The numerous observations and travel accounts of foreign and American visitors and soldiers on the state of affairs in the South, before, during, and after the Civil War,[169] may also contain useful data relating to the condition of blacks in particular localities.[170]

The private records of plantation and other slave owners are another important source for local study. They include

---

165 See John W. Blassingame and Mae G. Henderson (eds.), *Antislavery Newspapers and Periodicals* (3 vols., 3rd edn. with Jessica M. Dunn, 1980–1); J. Cutler Andrew, *The North Reports on the Civil War* (1955). For serials available in microform, see Hoornstra, 233, 254–5.

166 William B. Gatewood (ed.), "Arkansas negroes in the 1890s," *Arkansas Hist. Q.*, 33 (1974).

167 Martin Abbot, *The Freedmen's Bureau in South Carolina, 1865–1872* (1967), 147.

168 Cf. Allen W. Jones, "Voices for improving rural life," *AH*, 58 (1984).

169 See Thomas D. Clark (ed.), *Travels in the Old South: A Bibliography* (1956), and, e.g., John W. Blassingame, *The Slave Community* (1972), 244–8.

170 E.g., James S. Buckingham, *The Slave States of America* (3 vols., London, 1842); Frederick L. Olmstead, *A Journey in the Seaboard Slave States . . .* (1859).

plantation diaries and journals (essentially business records but often including personal data),[171] financial accounts, correspondence, records of hirings of slaves, records of work done by slaves, deeds of gift of slaves,[172] inventories of slaves, and slave birth registers.[173] There are numerous collections of such records, including many in the Library of Congress.[174] For the postbellum period there may be share-cropping contracts or wage records and other financial accounts which may shed light on the economic status of blacks and relations of white employers with their black workers.[175] Autobiographies and memoirs of slave owners and other white Southerners are more suspect, but may yet be useful for attitudes and certain factual information.[176]

For slaves and free blacks not engaged in agriculture the records of manufacturing and mining establishments and other businesses can be useful. For slaves owned by transportation and mining companies, gas companies, and so on, there is evidence in unpublished records and in published reports, such as railroad reports to state boards of internal improvement.[177]

Contemporary pamphlets and books on the topic of slavery and the rights of blacks abound.[178] Many are polemical and general in nature, but some contain details of individual

---

[171] E.g., Edwin A. Davis (ed.), *Plantation Life in the Florida Parishes of Louisiana, 1836–1846* (1943). And see pp. 219–20.

[172] E.g., "Documents relating to slavery," *Procs. Massachusetts Hist. Soc.*, 2nd ser. 20 (1907), 512–21.

[173] See Gutman, *Black Family*, facing p. 86.

[174] McDonough, "Manuscript resources," Kenneth M. Stampp (general ed.), *Records of Ante-Bellum Southern Plantations from the Revolution through the Civil War* is a microfilm edn. of holdings in the Library of Congress and other libraries (for details, see Univ. Publics. of America, *Record Collections* (1987), 10–11); and see Henry Barnard, *Slavery, Part I: A Bibliography and Union List of the Microform Collection* (Microfilming Corp. of America, 1980).

[175] Cf. Edward K. Eckert, "Contract labor in Florida during Reconstruction," *Florida Hist. Q.*, 47 (1968).

[176] See Blassingame, *Slave Community*, 242–4, for list of publ. autobiographies and memoirs.

[177] See also pp. 151–2, 153.

[178] Lawrence S. Thompson, *The Southern Black, Slave and Free: A Bibliography of Anti- and Pro-Slavery Books and Pamphlets . . . to 1950* (1970).

places, and may also be used to identify the local adherents of different viewpoints and their particular attitudes.

The records and publications of Northern abolitionist societies, found in state and local archive depositories, libraries, and historical societies, often contain data on the South as well as on the position of blacks in particular Northern states.[179] Such evidence may include opinions expressed by individual whites and blacks, and correspondence about particular cases and places. Many of the societies published monthly journals and annual reports. The official reports of the American Anti-Slavery Society (in the Library of Congress), and of other abolitionist societies contain much on the social and legal position of blacks. The records of state societies of this kind are particularly valuable for the condition of blacks in places in their states. The Ohio Anti-Slavery Society, for example, published a report on the condition of "the people of color" in that state, and the extensive records of the Pennsylvania State Society for Promoting the Abolition of Slavery[180] provide much information on blacks in antebellum Philadelphia. The archives of the American Colonization Society, in the Library of Congress, founded to send ex-slaves to Liberia, include records relating to slaves in particular places in the South.[181] Such records, together with other data, such as private papers and records of religious bodies, also provide evidence for the study of abolitionist movements within particular communities and areas.

The records and publications of the various churches and religious groups and associations comprise an extensive source for the effects of opposing views on slavery in the churches of the South, and the activities of black churches and of missionaries. They are particularly fruitful of information on the attitudes of Northern and Southern Christians towards the education and religious and social life of blacks, and on charitable relief and assistance. The *Sociological Canvases*

[179] Dwight L. Dumond, *A Bibliography of Antislavery in America* (1965); Louis Fuller, *The Crusade Against Slavery* (1960), bibl.; and see bibls. cited above.
[180] At Hist. Soc. Pennsylvania, 1300 Locust St., Philadelphia, PA 19107.
[181] James M. Gifford, "Anti-black bias in antebellum source materials," *Louisiana Studies*, 14 (1975).

(1896–9) conducted by the Federation of Churches and Christian Workers of New York City, for instance, give statistics of black populations, wage rates, rents, and the cost of living generally.[182] Charitable and religiously orientated organizations varied in nature. They included, for example, antebellum Southern enterprises at the local level, like the Association for the Religious Instruction of Negroes in Liberty county, GA, which published annual reports, through to the larger postbellum freedmen's aid societies, whose publications were more extensive. If they exist, records of self-help societies, cooperative insurance groups, and the like, found among Northern blacks, especially among urban ex-slaves, may shed light on the communities into which they settled and their life there.[183]

In recent years historians have made increasing use of evidence emanating from the black communities, including slave communities, themselves: in particular fugitive slaves' testimonies, slave narratives, letters, diaries, and autobiographies.[184] Black autobiographies and memoirs[185] are likely to be biased or exaggerated. Moreover, large numbers of early publications of this kind were ghost-written or heavily edited by whites. Nevertheless they may contain some useful information and cannot be ignored.

Another extensive body of material, also needing circumspection in use, consists of the many interviews with ex-slaves recorded in the early twentieth century.[186] Ex-slaves interviewed in the 1920s and 1930s were then old and had been children at the time of emancipation, so that all the difficulties

---

[182] Ofosky, *Harlem*, 190–1. For missionary jnls., see pp. 282–3.

[183] Cf. Theodore Hershberg, "Free blacks in antebellum Philadelphia," in Hershberg, *Philadelphia*, 379–80. And see pp. 281–9, 486–7, 507.

[184] See esp. John W. Blassingame, "Status and social structure in the slave community," in Harry P. Owens (ed.), *Perspectives and Irony in American Slavery* (1976); John W. Blassingame, *Slave Testimony* (1977).

[185] See Prucha, 184 [Z38]; Stephen Butterfield, *Black Autobiography in America* (1974); Sidonie Smith, *Where I Was Bound* (1974); Blassingame, *The Slave Community*, 240–2. For biographies and autobiographies, see citations Prucha, 183–4; *Black Biographical Dictionaries, 1790–1950* (microfiche, Chadwyck-Healey, 1989; there is a printed index, ed. Nancy K. Burkett *et al.*). And see Willie L. Rose, *A Documentary History of Slavery in America* (1976), 458–9.

[186] See Charles H. Nichols, *Many Thousand Gone* (Leiden, Neth. 1963).

of defective memory, exaggeration, repetition of hearsay as fact, deliberate bias, and so on, apply. Moreover, it is necessary to take account of the possible influence of unskilled and perhaps biased white interviewers who couched questions in such a way as to encourage replies in accord with their own prejudices, and also of fear of offending whites in the period of the 1930s depression. Again female ex-slaves were underrepresented. Nevertheless this enormous body of evidence cannot be ignored any more than biased and less than accurate evidence found in written sources.[187] The narratives provide a great deal of detail on the social structure of slave communities, the relations of slaves with their owners, the relationship between house and field slaves, and the everyday workings of the plantation economy, and also give information on emancipation and on the period of Reconstruction.[188]

There are a number of published collections of slave narratives, of which the most extensive is that edited by George P. Rawick.[189] This comprises transcripts of interviews with ex-slaves conducted by the Works Projects Administration in 1936–8,[190] and similar transcripts collected by Fisk University in the late 1920s.[191] Though unindexed, the volumes are arranged by states.[192] Only a few of the WPA narratives for Virginia are included in this publication, but many are

---

[187] Cf. C. Vann Woodward, "History from slave sources," *AHR*, 79 (1974); John W. Blassingame, "Using the testimony of ex-slaves," *JSoH*, 41 (1975); Paul D. Escott, *Slavery Remembered* (1979), 4–8.

[188] Leon F. Litwack, *North of Slavery: The Negro in the Free States, 1790–1860* (1961); Leon Litwack, "The emancipation of the negro abolitionist," in Martin Duberman (ed.), *The Anti-Slavery Vanguard* (1965).

[189] George P. Rawick, *The American Slave Narratives: A Composite Autobiography* (19 vols., 1972). For works based on these narratives, see Escott, *Slavery Remembered*; Stanley Feldstein, *Once a Slave; The Slave's View of Slavery* (1971); Blassingame, *The Slave Community*; George P. Rawick, *From Sundown to Sunup* (1972); Eugene D. Genovese, *Roll Jordan Roll* (1974); Gutman, *The Black Family*; Ann Banks, *First-Person America* (1980, repr. 1981).

[190] Vols. 2–17 previously available in typescript, 1941. Available in microfiche:' W. P. A., *Slave Narrative Collection* (Univ. Kentucky Press, 1972). See also Norman R. Yetman, "Life under the 'peculiar institution'," *Selections from the Slave Narratives* (1970).

[191] Vols. 18–19, comprising two collections (one by A. P. Watson, the other by Ophelia S. Egypt) previously in mimeograph, 1945. For a description of the Fisk collections, see Escott, *Slavery Remembered*, 4–5.

[192] Vol. 1 has bibl.

Ethnicity and race

separately published.[193] A supplement to Rawick's publication comprises twelve volumes of additional slave narratives recorded by the WPA.[194]

A NOTE ON AMERICAN INDIANS

Something has been said elsewhere on the sources for treaties with Indians, Indian agriculture and land use, on education for Indians, on trade with Indians, and on missionary activity addressed to Indians.[195] The study of Indian tribal communities is, however, a highly specialized subject and the amount of secondary and primary material too extensive to be dealt with in this book.[196] A prodigious amount of unpublished material is in the National Archives,[197] and there is much in other depositories, too.[198] All that is offered

[193] Charles L. Perdue, Jr., et al. (eds.), Weevils in the Wheat (1976).
[194] Jan Hillegas and Ken Lawrence (eds.), The American Slave: A Composite Autobiography Supplement, Series I (12 vols., 1978).
[195] See pp. 234–8, 281–7, 289, 436–8, 489–93.
[196] But see HG, 462–4; Prucha, 187–94; Henry P. Beers, Bibliographies in American History, 1942–1978 (1982), 254–61; Francis P. Prucha, A Bibliographical Guide to the History of Indian-White Relations in the United States (1977) and Supplement (1982); Barry Klein, Reference Encyclopedia of the American Indian (1986 edn.); U.S. Dept. of the Interior, Biographical and Historical Index of Americans and Persons Involved in Indian Affairs (8 vols., 1982); Dictionary Catalog of the Edward E. Ayer Collection of Americana and American Indians in the Newberry Library (16 vols., 1961, and supplements, 1970, 1980). For federal documents, see works cited pp. 20–2, and Steven L. Johnson, Guide to American Indian Documents in the Congressional Serial Set, 1817–1899 (1977). For Indian newspapers and periodicals, see p. 30.
[197] See GNA, index; works cited in ch. 5, esp. those comp. Edward E. Hill and Laura E. Kelsay; Prucha, Bibliographical Guide (also for federal documents); Oliver W. Holmes, "Indian-related records in the National Archives," in Jane F. Smith and Robert M. Kvasnicka (eds.), Indian–White Relations (1976) (and other essays in this book); E. Kay Kirkham, Our Native Americans: Their Records of Genealogical Value (1980); Mary S. Schusky and Ernest L. Schusky, "A center of primary sources for plains Indian history," Plains Anthropologist; Journal of the Plains Conference (1970); Gaiselle Kerner (comp.), Records of the U.S. Court of Claims, 1783–1947 (PI 58, 1953), 13–16, 21–2, 30–1; Records of the Office of the Secretary of the Interior, 1833–1964 (NA, NNF–48, 1984), pt. I, T/S, passim. N.B. Cynthia G. Fox (comp.), American Indians: A Select Catalog of National Archives Microfilm Publications (1984).
[198] See Prucha, 190–1, and, e.g., Angie Debo, "Major Indian record collections in Oklahoma," in Smith and Kvasnicka, Indian–White Relations; Joseph G. Svoboda, A Guide to American Indian Resource Materials in Great Plains Depositories (1983); John A. Fleckner, Native American Archives (1984); Dictionary Catalog . . . Newberry Library (cited above); and see guides cited pp. 35–7.

here is a brief note, largely on demographic evidence.[199]

For Indian population history the chief sources are the federal census volumes and manuscript population schedules (see ch. 2) and the enumerations undertaken by the Bureau of Indian Affairs.[200] Indians living in or near white settlements were recorded in the regular census population schedules, though the census of 1860 was the first to distinguish Indians as a separate race. The 1860 and 1870 censuses did not cover Indians on reservations but only (and often inaccurately) those living in non-Indian households. The 1880 census included a special enumeration of Indians living near military reservations. It provides the tribal name, the reservation, the agency, the nearest post office, as well as the number in each household, the Indian name (with English translation) of each person in the family, relationship to the head of the family, marital and tribal status, and data on occupation, education, ownership of property, and sources of subsistence.[201] The 1890 census included a special schedule covering all reservations, and resulted in a significant published volume – volume x of that census (on Indians taxed and non taxed) which is very full.[202] For each state and territory the total Indian population (by sex) is presented together with aggregates of Indians in prison, those on reservations (not numerated in the general census), and those off reservations (also counted in the general census). Totals for individual agencies and reservations are also given. There are, too, statistical data on social characteristics and economic matters (most fully at state and territory level) together with general descriptive accounts of matters like education, occupations and

---

[199] See Henry F. Dobyns, *Native American Historical Demography: A Critical Bibliography* (1976); Paul Stuart, *Nations within a Nation: Historical Statistics of American Indians* (1987).

[200] The following draws on Carmelita S. Ryan, *Vital Statistics in the National Archives Relating to the American Indians* (RIP 61, 1973).

[201] Available in NA (RG 29) in 4 vols.: Katherine H. Davidson and Charlotte M. Ashby (comps.), *Preliminary Inventory of the Records of the Bureau of the Census* (PI 161, 1964), 101.

[202] See also p. 235. Four Extra Census Bulletins for this census relate to Indian tribes: see Schulze (1983), 267–8. And see Compendium, pt. 1, Population table 16 (civilized Indians by counties).

employment, language, housing, and religion, and there are many illustrations, including photographs of villages.

More important for Indian tribal communities are enumerations undertaken by the Bureau of Indian Affairs and held in the National Archives (RG 75). Early enrolled enumerations and other investigations of various tribes date from 1817. They are most complete for Cherokee, Creek, Choctaw, and Seminole Indians. Annual "censuses" began in 1885. These included the name of each Indian, with age, sex, birth date, and relationship to head of family.[203] Ancillary records which may be used in conjunction with the census include annuity rolls and registers of Indian families compiled in preparation for allotments on reservations. These provide much detail on individual families and are particularly useful for the study of family structure. The annuity rolls date from the early 1840s and since they predate the annual "censuses" are especially useful for the period before the 1880s.[204] There are also other census-type records for individual tribes in particular districts.[205] The so-called final rolls of the Five Civilized Tribes compiled by the Dawes Commission (1893–1905)[206] are of more use to genealogists than to local historians.

To such largely statistical data may be added information from other federal records, particularly the correspondence between the Bureau of Indian Affairs and its various local superintendencies and agencies, which embrace many reports, as well as agency and superintendency records themselves[207] and the records of Christian missions and missionaries (see ch. 6).

---

[203] Available in microfilm: *MRR*. There is an index of tribes with their reservation or agency in *Source*, 110. See also Robert Svenningsen (comp.), *Preliminary Inventory of the Pueblo Records Created by Field Offices of the Bureau of Indian Affairs* (PI 192, 1980), 13–14.

[204] Details: RIP 61, 5–6; *Genealogical Research*, 162.

[205] For list, see *Source*, 110–12.

[206] *Source*, 118; *Genealogical Research*, 160, 162; NNF–48, pt. I, 202; PAM 1186, *Enrollment Cards for the Five Civilized Tribes, 1898–1914* (1982).

[207] See chs. 5, 10 for details of these and other useful records.

CHAPTER 4

The land, settlement, and farming: I

The lives of a high proportion of nineteenth-century Americans were connected with farming and the land. At the beginning of the century the Eastern states were to varying degrees settled and the character of their communities reflected to some extent earlier developments. Much of the rest of the country, however, remained to be peopled and exploited so that as the frontier rolled westwards the settlements and communities that emerged were essentially creations of the nineteenth century. For the historian the study of both change in the rural and farming history of older communities and of communities and farming areas from their beginnings is a considerable challenge.

The general themes of frontier development and settlement, the disposal of the public domain and the nature of early and later land use are connected and suggest many other topics for investigation. The disposal of the public domain was a complex matter affecting the history of many parts of the country.[1] The effect of the land laws on the timing of settlement and its character and the subsequent economic and social consequences of later land sales and leases between individuals embrace topics worthy of local study. These include the part played by speculation in the development of the new lands and its social and economic effects, who the speculators were, the relationship between the development of tenancy and speculation, and the part played in land development by land companies, railroads, other institutions, and individuals.

[1] See Benjamin H. Hibbard, *History of Public Land Policies* (1924); Roy M. Robbins, *Our Landed Heritage. The Public Domain, 1776–1936* (1942); Paul W. Gates, *History of Public Land Law Development* (1968) and its bibl.; and works cited below, p. 165n.

The financial and contractual aspects of farming are also worthwhile research topics. These include the significance of credit and the characteristics of tenancy and ownership. How was credit obtained and why? Was tenancy an indication of exploitation associated with rural poverty or was it economically beneficial in the extension of agriculture, and a natural stage by which a credit-lacking farmer gradually moved up the ladder to ownership? How did local people view it? To what extent was tenancy an attribute of ethnic background or of age? And how far was it reflected in types of farming pursued, kinds, numbers, and proportions of livestock, attitudes to conservation of fertility, and so on?

From the human point of view the personal characteristics of the settlers and their successors provide another area of study.[2] The ethnic and religious background, the age and social standing of settlers and how these may have affected the types of settlement founded and the kind of farming pursued, and land transmission practices,[3] are important. Did ethnic or religious homogeneity make for a community more socially integrated and topographically concentrated than where there were settlers of diverse backgrounds?[4] Did settlers come in groups or singly? What part was played by family and hired labor? Did families stay in an area or were they highly mobile? Who were the farm laborers and did they become farmers? What were the relationships between the cattlemen and homesteaders, Indians and whites, squatters and new landowners, and between farmers and miners, railroad companies and settlers?

Again in many areas it may be interesting to look at the changes in farming that occurred as the frontier moved further away, as railroads and other forms of transportation developed, and as large centers of consumption or smaller urban

---

[2] Cf. Hal S. Barron, "Rediscovering the majority: the new rural history of the nineteenth-century North," *HM*, 19 (1986).

[3] Cf. Robert C. Ostergren, "Land and family in rural immigrant communities," *Annals Assoc. Am. Geographers*, 71 (1981), and works cited.

[4] Cf. Allan G. Bogue, "Social theory and the pioneer," *AH*, 34 (1960); Harold D. Woodman, "The state of agricultural history," in Herbert J. Bass (ed.), *The State of American History* (1970), 230–1.

centers grew up in formerly rural areas. The impact of agricultural and other machinery, the effect of irrigation projects, the history of lumber companies and forestry, and the development of marketing and distribution of agricultural produce, and of the supply of seeds and fertilizers, all invite research.

Central to all this is the nature of the agricultural enterprise. Of what size and value were the farms in a district? Were they largely subsistence enterprises or were they market orientated? Did they specialize in certain types of crops or livestock, or were their efforts diversified? How productive, how profitable, were they? What were the constraints of geography and climate? These are all interesting avenues to explore, bearing in mind that changes over time in all these areas of investigation also need consideration.

In the South, the economic and social aspects of plantation agriculture serviced by slaves present a distinct topic for study,[5] and to that may be added others peculiar to that region, in particular the impact of the Civil War and Reconstruction, and the emergence of free black farmers and laborers on a large scale, the fortunes of the small non-slave-owning farmer before and after the war, and the effects of particular systems of land tenure and property relations on the exploitation of estates. Were sharecropping and lien systems the natural outcome of the market economy? Were they part of a repressive labor system imposed by the old planter class? Were they sought by the freedmen as a positive choice? How far can these systems explain continuing poverty, lack of mechanization, and so on? To what extent was gang labor used and with what effects?

All these and others, like the intricacies of forestry and lumbering, are items for investigation which the sources discussed below should help to elucidate.[6] Many historians have,

[5] See Gerald D. Nash, "Research opportunities in economic history of the South after 1800," *JSoH*, 32 (1966).
[6] For other research topics, see Fred Bateman, "Research developments in American agricultural history since 1960," *AgHR*, 31 (1983), 146–8.

of course, given attention to these and related matters,[7] and there are some regional guides.[8] Nevertheless, there is almost unlimited scope for further research particularly at the county and sub-county level.

The types of source suitable for local research into public land disposal, settlement, and agricultural structure, are often the same and are, therefore, discussed together in the following pages.[9] Some comment is made on their particular use to the historian and some attention given to the linkage of different types. For many topics the best use will be made by drawing together evidence from different kinds of sources. The same records can, of course, shed light on many other topics of interest to community historians – as far ranging as the development of transportation, mining activities, Indians,

[7] See *HG*, 387–92; Douglas E. Bowers (comp.), *A List of References for the History of Agriculture in the United States, 1790–1840* (1969); George R. Taylor, *American Economic History before 1860* (1969), 20–1; Thomas Orsage, *The Economic History of the United States Prior to 1860: An Annotated Bibliography* (1971), 23–36; Edward C. Kirkland, *American Economic History Since 1860* (1971), 9–15; John T. Schlebecker, *Bibliography of Books and Pamphlets on the History of Agriculture in the United States, 1607–1967* (1969); Everett E. Edwards, *A Bibliography of the History of Agriculture in the United States* (U.S. Dept. of Agric., 1930); Paul W. Gates, "Research in the history of American land tenure," *AH*, 28 (1954), 121–6; Louise O. Bercaw *et al.*, *Bibliography on Land Settlement* (U.S. Dept. of Agric., 1934); Joel Schor (comp.), *A List of References for the History of Black Americans in Agriculture, 1619–1980* (1981); Vivian B. Whitehead (comp.), *"Agricultural History": An Index, 1927–1976* (1977); Vivian B. Whitehead (comp.), *A List of References for the History of Agricultural Technology* (1979). And N.B. Wayne D. Rasmussen, "The F. Hal Higgins Library of Agricultural Technology," *Technology and Culture*, 5 (1964), 575–7. Paul W. Gates, *The Farmer's Age* (1960) and Fred A. Shannon, *The Farmer's Last Frontier* (1961 edn.) contain bibls. on settlement and agriculture. For dissertations, see Dennis C. Nordin, "Graduate studies in American agricultural history," *AH*, 41 (1967). Note the National Agricultural Library (U.S. Dept. of Agric.) for which see *Dictionary Catalog of the National Agricultural Library, 1862–1965* (73 vols., 1965–70); *National Agricultural Library Catalog* (1967/70–   ). See also the monthly *Bibliography of Agriculture* (1975–   ). Edward L. and Frederic H. Schapsmeier, *Encyclopedia of American Agricultural History* (1975) is also useful.

[8] See Bateman, "Research developments"; Allan G. Bogue, "Farming in North American grasslands: a survey of publications, 1947–80," *AgHR*, 30 (1982) (also in *Great Plains Q.*, 1 (1981)); *HG*, 390–1. The Agricultural History Center, Univ. of California, Davis, CA 95616 has publ. a series of bibls. of works on different regions, each title beginning *A List of References for the History of Agriculture in . . .*

[9] For a selection of types of sources, see Wayne D. Rasmussen (ed.), *Agriculture in the United States: A Documentary History* (vols. 1, 2, 1975). For sources on forestry, see Cloudaugh M. Neiderheimer (comp.), *Forest History Sources of the United States and Canada* (1956) (lists some 300 collections).

education, relations between federal and state governments, local political history and social movements, family history and structures, and social and spatial mobility, as well as aspects of ethnicity, many of which topics are the subject of other chapters in this book.

Moreover, some of the records described below lend themselves to the application of quantitative techniques and so to exercises in assessing possible relationships between different social and economic variables. Thus, to give a single example, the relationship of farm size to tenancy or ownership might be looked at. Worthwhile statistical work has been undertaken,[10] and more could be done in this field so long as it is realized that statistical evidence can illuminate only certain aspects of the history of agriculture and rural life and that local communities contained people who did not conform to norms, averages, and tendencies, but who are just as much part of the history of that place as those who formed majorities.

For all topics bearing on land and settlement the evidence derivable from maps and plans may be important. Many of the items discussed in the section on cartographic sources (ch. 1) may be useful here. Some attention to particular types of plats and maps is also given below.

Basic to research into settlement and the land market and into local agriculture and land use is an understanding of the public land system and the distinction between public domain states and other states. This may be briefly summarized here. In all the states, aside from the thirteen original ones, together with Kentucky, Maine, Tennessee, Texas, Vermont, and West Virginia, the title to public land (the public domain) was vested in the federal government, consequent on cession from the former colonial powers, various purchases, treaties made, and conquest. It was federal government policy to transfer much of this land by grant or sale into private ownership, and this was carried out under the terms of various Acts. Prior to disposal the lands were surveyed and recorded and divided

---

[10] See Robert P. Swierenga, "Towards the 'new rural history'," *HMN*, 6 (1973); Robert P. Swierenga, "Quantitative methods in rural landholding," *JIH*, 13 (1983); and works cited in these articles.

into townships, sections, and further subdivisions. Certain land was set aside specifically for communal purposes, particularly education, and granted to the states. Other land, assigned to individual states to assist in the development of communications, draining of swamps, and the encouragement of education, was sold off by the states to raise money for those purposes. Federal land grants were also made to canal companies, wagon roads, and railroads. For the passage of federal land direct to individuals, local land offices were established. These disposed of the lands, mainly by sale or in return for military bounty warrants and scrip, but in some cases freely (as under the Homesteads Act of 1862 and also to encourage settlement in Florida, Oregon, and Washington state). The offices also considered private land claims from those with title of some kind from former colonial powers (in parts of Alabama, Arizona, Arkansas, California, Colorado, Florida, Illinois, Indiana, Iowa, Louisiana, Michigan, Mississippi, Missouri, New Mexico, and Wisconsin) or on other grounds of prior settlement. In the thirteen colonial states and the six others listed with them above, there was no public-domain land, and lands not already granted to individuals at Independence were in the hands of the states themselves, and state governments, like the federal government, followed a policy of passing these lands on to individuals, corporations, and institutions. It has been said that the "disposal of the public domain was perhaps the most important single factor in the political as well as the economic life of the United States."[11] This was certainly so of the pioneer history of most townships and communities in the public-domain states, and the records that derive from the disposal of public lands are crucial for the investigation of many of the topics outlined above.

FEDERAL SOURCES GENERALLY

For the territories, from the late eighteenth century many relevant letters and other official records are reproduced in print in the *Territorial Papers of the United States* and in *American*

[11] Marion Clawson, *The Land System of the United States* (1968), 54.

State Papers.[12] These contain much detailed local data on private land claims, on the disposal of public land, and on settlement, together with a great deal of local information. The *Territorial Papers*, a selected compendium of National Archives records, contains lists of individuals issued with land patents (that is, title to land) and many memorials and petitions concerning land, settlement, and problems such as squatters' rights. Other National Archives collections of "Territorial Papers," (from RG 48: Dept. of the Interior) also contain information on agriculture, the cattle industry, and public lands. In the *American State Papers* the volumes entitled *Public Lands* and *Claims* covering 1789 to 1837 pertain to the trans-Appalachian and trans-Mississippi regions. In this collection are petitions and memorials concerning land and related matters, surveys, and Supreme Court decisions. Among these is much evidence on private land claims (based on British, French, and Spanish grants) in areas ceded to the United States, frequently in the form of reports by land commissioners to Congress, giving the names of many individuals. There is now a published nominal index to the nearly 80,000 claimants to land mentioned in these volumes.[13] A number of other works may be useful for any investigation of the jungle of claims and counterclaims to lands that were inherited by the federal government.[14]

An enormous amount of evidence for the history of settlement, land acquisition, and agriculture exists in the published documents and unpublished records of Congress and of the

---

[12] See pp. 19, 21–2 for refs.

[13] Phillip W. McMullin, *Grassroots of America: A Computerized Index to American State Papers: Land Grants and Claims (1789–1837)* (1972), includes rejected claims.

[14] Joseph M. White, *A New Collection of Laws [etc.] . . . of Great Britain, France and Spain, Relating to the Concession of Land in their . . . Colonies* (2 vols., 1839); WPA, HRS, *Spanish Land Grants in Florida* (5 vols., 1940–1); Ralph E. Twitchell, *The Spanish Archives of New Mexico*, vol. 1 (1914); Albert J. Diaz (comp.), *A Guide to the Microfilm of Papers Relating to New Mexico Land Grants* (1958); J. N. Bowman, "History of the provincial archives of California," *Southern Q.*, 64 (1982); Munden and Beers, 525; Henry P. Beers, *Spanish and Mexican Records of the American Southwest* (1979); *Source*, 229–30 and works cited; Paul W. Gates, "Private land claims in the South," *JSoH*, 22 (1956); David Lighter, "Private land claims in Alabama," *Alabama Rev.*, 20 (1967); R. S. Cotterill, "The national land system in the South, 1803–1812," *MVHR*, 16 (1930); Robert V. Haynes, "The disposal of lands in the Mississippi Territory," *JMH*, 24 (1962); and below, pp. 170, 179, 211.

various departments, bureaus, and agencies of the federal government – indeed so much that it would be impossible to list it all here. Attention is, therefore, given to some of the more important federal sources with reference to other works which may be of assistance. In particular the various guides to federal documents noted above should be consulted.[15]

The chronology of public land disposal and its character was determined by federal legislation, and knowledge of the laws relating to public lands is necessary for the local or regional researcher. There are a number of aids.[16] Published Congressional debates, reports of committees, and hearings, may be worth searching around the times relevant to local developments.

There are a multitude of Congressional committee, commission, and departmental reports concerning the land and its use, and related topics. Thus significant evidence of contests between farmers and cattlemen is contained in a report of the Public Land Commission of 1880, and a report on prices, wages, and transportation of 1892–3 and the *Report of the Industrial Commission* of 1900–2 are full of evidence bearing on the history of agriculture and trade in agricultural products.[17] A *Report of a Committee on Agriculture and Forestry on the Condition of Cotton Growers in the United States* (2 vols., 1895),[18] contains in the first volume a valuable index indicating the names of cotton planters giving evidence, with their state and county, and listing reports on the production of cotton with names and residences of the individual farmers who made them. These reports were responses to a request for data on

---

[15] See pp. 20–2. Federal records on immigration (some cited ch. 3) may throw light on agriculture and settlement.

[16] E.g., *Laws of the United States of a Local or Temporary Character . . . upon which the Public Land Titles in Each State and Territory Have Depended . . .* (2nd edn., 1884, 2 vols.; mentions many persons and places); Thomas Donaldson, *The Public Domain* (1880, rev. 1881, 1884). W. W. Lester, *Decisions of the Interior Department in Public Land Cases . . .* (1860) summarizes legislation, administrative instructions, and legal decisions. See also Daniel M. Green (comp.), *Public Land Statutes of the United States* (1931); Francis W. Lauren, *A Compilation of the Most Important Congressional Acts [etc.] to do with Water Resources* (1938) (for irrigation).

[17] HED 46, 48–51 (46–2), ser. 1923; SR 1394 (52–2), ser. 3074; HD 179, 180 (57–1), ser. 4340, 4341 (*Rep. Industrial Commission*, vols. X, XI).

[18] SR 986 (53–3), ser. 3290–1.

production costs and provide details of various costs for the season 1891–2 (including labor for named types of work, seeds, ginning, bagging, fertilizers, interest, rent, depreciation), together with yield per acre and cost per pound weight. There is also much data on the trade in raw cotton and many statistics of cotton sales and production.

Unpublished federal records (in the National Archives) which may be of use include petitions and memorials to the Senate (RG 46) and to the House (RG 233). These contain information on private land claims,[19] and petitions and correspondence from early settlers and land speculators about a variety of matters.[20] There are, for example, in RG 233, claims for recompense for damage to settlers' property by Indians in the War of 1812, which contain data on the social and economic activities of frontier farmers, often including lists of livestock and details of crops.[21]

Of particular value are the records of federal district and circuit courts (RG 21).[22] These include criminal, civil, equity, and bankruptcy litigation files, and may well contain material throwing light on the public domain, land claims, land speculation, water rights, agriculture, settlement, slavery, and so on. Some for the District of Columbia, for example, contain records relating to slaves and reports of appraisers on goods, chattels, and personal estates.[23] Again the New Hampshire court records contain lists of tracts sold to satisfy the unpaid taxes of non-residents in 1811, providing names of owners (possibly speculators), acreages involved, and cost of the land.[24] The case records of the U.S. Court of Claims (RG 123) contain evidence relating to the General Land Office and

[19] For documents on private land claims, see *CIS US Serial Set Index*.
[20] *GNA*, 50, 52.
[21] Richard S. Lackey (comp.), *Claims in the Lower South* (1977).
[22] See p. 42 for location, etc.
[23] Janet Weinert (comp.), *Preliminary Inventory of the Records of the United States District Courts for the District of Columbia* (NC–2, 1962). And see Thomas E. Wiltsey, "Court records and local history," in Timothy Walch (comp.), *Our Family, Our Town* (1987); Beverly Watkins, "'To Surrender All His Estate'," *Prologue*, 21 (1989).
[24] James K. Owens, "Federal court records of New Hampshire," *Historical New Hampshire*, 25 (1970), 39–40.

railroad companies,[25] and in Senate records (RG 46) there is a series of some 160 internal improvements maps, 1825–35, prepared for proposed routes of roads and canals east of the Mississippi River, some of which show cultivated fields, and which are for certain areas the first accurate surveys.[26]

The most significant federal records for the topics being discussed here, at least for the public domain states, are, however, those of the General Land Office. From 1812 the GLO supervised the district land offices and indeed all aspects of public domain administration.

The published annual reports of the Commissioner of the General Land Office are central to any investigation of settlement in the public land states. From 1817 to 1848 they are contained within the annual reports of the Secretary of the Treasury, and from 1849 within the annual reports of the Secretary of the Department of the Interior. Their contents include statistics of public land disposed of by each land office and many detailed reports, often including maps, from each of the (local) surveyors general. There are also many other federal documents emanating from the GLO. In 1852, for example, a large volume is devoted to an extremely detailed report by the register and receiver of the land office of Monroe, LA, on private land cases. Other GLO documents are also specific to certain places. There is, for example, a report on lands in Knox county, IN, in 1869–70, and a statement of sales of land at Augusta, KS, in 1871–2.

For detailed research at the local level, however, the vast body of unpublished records spawned by the GLO (RG 49) provides a mine of information on agriculture and settlement, and indeed on other aspects of local life.[27] Large numbers of these records are in the National Archives building in

[25] Gaiselle Kerner (comp.), *Preliminary Inventory of the U.S. Court of Claims, 1783–1947* (PI 58, 1953), 18.

[26] Ralph E. Ehrenberg, *Geographical Exploration and Mapping in the Nineteenth Century* (RIP 66, 1973), 8.

[27] *GNA*, 371–7; Harry P. Yopshe and Philip P. Brower (comps.), *Preliminary Inventory of the Land Entry Papers of the General Land Office* (PI 22, 1949); Jane F. Smith, "Settlement on the public domain as reflected in federal records," in Ralph E. Ehrenberg (ed.), *Patterns and Process* (1975), 290–1.

Washington, DC, and the Washington National Records Center,[28] but many are dispersed elsewhere – in regional branches of the National Archives,[29] in local offices, and in state[30] and other historical societies' collections, as well as in other depositories.[31] To track down the available sources for the initial sale of public lands in a particular area is a necessary preliminary to investigation, but is not always easy. Indeed the current disposition of these records has been called "an archivist's nightmare."[32] Some land records have disappeared and those extant may be difficult to use effectively without some prior knowledge of their history and nature.[33]

It is particularly important in a local study to understand the survey system in the public domain states,[34] and to ascertain what local land office was concerned with the disposal of public lands in the area being investigated, since most land records are filed with reference to particular offices. Land office jurisdictions did not, moreover, follow state or county boundaries, and jurisdictional areas covered by individual offices might alter over time. Information on this topic is best sought from the officers now in charge of the collections of land records. There is no comprehensive catalog of the whereabouts of federal land records, but a start has been made recently towards the compilation of a systematic index and

[28] Some are microfilmed: *MRR*.
[29] *GNA*, 371–7. For a list, see *Genealogical Research*, 222, 225.
[30] Ronald E. Grim, "Mapping Kansas and Nebraska," *Great Plains Q.* (Summer, 1985), 179, 181, 195–6n; Victoria Irons and Patricia C. Brennan, *Descriptive Inventory of the Archives of the State of Illinois* (1978), 552–644. For a computerized record of public land sales in IL comp. from GLO records handed over to the state, see *For the Record: Newsletter of the Illinois State Records*, 3, 2 (1979), 5, 1 (1982).
[31] See, e.g., Munden and Beers, 527–9; "U.S. Public Land Office records at the University of Alabama Library," *Mississippi Genealogical Exchange* (1975). For locations for each state, see *Source*, 238–52.
[32] Grim, "Mapping Kansas," 195n.
[33] The following account draws on *GNA*, 371–7; PI 22; Smith, "Settlement"; Robbins, *Our Landed Heritage*; Gates, *Public Land Law Development*; Robert W. Harrison, "Public land records of the federal government," *MVHR*, 41 (1954) (also publ. in Vernon Carstensen (ed.), *The Public Lands* (1963), q.v.); Richard S. Lackey, "The genealogist's first look at federal land records," *Prologue*, 9 (1977); L. Waffen, "Federal land records," *Prologue*, 5 (1973); *Genealogical Research*, 207, 225.
[34] See, *inter alia*, C. Albert White, *A History of the Rectangular Survey System* (1983); Lola Cazier, *Surveys and Surveying of the Public Domain, 1785–1975* (1976); Lowell O. Stewart, *Public Land Surveys* (1935, repr. 1976).

calendar to cover materials in the National Archives at Washington and elsewhere. The first volumes of this *Federal Land Series* have been published.[35] Of these, Volumes 1 and 3 are perhaps of most general interest, but Volume 2 includes some of the records of land syndicates issuing deed titles to lands within their grants.[36]

For the community historian, general information on the time and nature of the disposal of public lands in the areas being investigated will be of prime interest. For that purpose the correspondence and survey data will be important. The general correspondence of the GLO in the National Archives at Washington, DC, (RG 49) includes "out" letters, 1796–1939, and "in" letters, 1796–1908. They relate to surveys, claims and warrants, grants to railroads, agricultural college scrip, school lands, forest reserves, timber trespasses, illegal fencing of public domain by cattlemen, irrigation rights, mining matters, railroad rights of way, and so on.[37] Those received from the general public, of which there are many, are of great potential value for local study. Unfortunately both "in" and "out" letters are not topographically arranged. "Out" letter copies are chronologically ordered while "in" letters are arranged alphabetically by name of sender. Letters sent by the Division of Forestry concerning timber and forestry matters are filed with the general correspondence.[38] In addition, in the records of the Division of Surveys, are reports, memoranda and letters from surveyors general of public-land states including records relating, among other matters, to surveys of townsites, private land claims, military reservations, transportation, Indian troubles, and climatic

---

[35] Clifford N. Smith, *Federal Land Series: A Calendar of Archival Materials on the Land Patents ... with Subject, Tract, and Name Indexes* (vol. 1, *1788–1810*, 1972; vol. 2, *1799–1835*, 1973; vol. 3, *1810–1814*, 1980; vol. 4 (2 pts.), *Virginia Military District of Ohio*, 1982, 1986). See Clifford N. Smith, "Federal land records," *National Genealogical Soc. Q.*, 60 (1972); rev. in *Indiana Mag. Hist.*, 69 (1973), 73–5.

[36] Vols. so far publ. incl. material from RGs 49, 56, microfilmed in M25, M27, M733, and records concerning Ohio (for which vols. 2, 4 (1) are also significant). For full details see introd. to the vols.

[37] Some is indexed and calendared in Smith, *Federal Land Series*. Smith suggests (vol. 1, p. xii) that officers' personal papers may also be useful.

[38] Neiderheiser, *Forest History Sources*, 14.

conditions. Some of these letters are available in microfilm.[39] For some of the Western states there is in regional branches of the National Archives in Los Angeles, Seattle, and Denver, correspondence sent and received by surveyors general and their officers, including letters from the GLO Commissioner, other government officials, business firms, and members of the public.[40]

The large collection of GLO maps and plats has been described in chapter 1. Together with their accompanying field survey notes, of which there are thousands of volumes, the township plats[41] provide a rich source. The plats and field notes are arranged by states in a headquarter office series and in a local land office series. The notes are often more informative than the plats, but together they provide identification of particular lands and general information on the physical characteristics of the area, vegetation, roads, Indian and pioneer trails, drainage patterns, Indian villages, and Indian cessions and reserves, and in some cases the names and plots of pre-survey settlers with, occasionally, sketches of their dwellings. The copies of the plats that were originally sent to local land offices were annotated in those offices to show the initial disposition of the land within section subdivisions, or of individual tracts in a township. Sometimes they show the purchaser's name.[42]

Large numbers of plats were published or utilized in the commercial and official published atlases and land-ownership maps;[43] many survey and other maps showing townships and location of named landowners' claims in the various National

[39] MRR.
[40] GNA, 375; Gilbert Dorame (comp.), Records of the Bureau of Land Management (FRC, Los Angeles, 1960); Victor Wesphall, The Public Domain in New Mexico, 1854–1891 (1965), bibl.
[41] Some duplicates may be with state records: see below.
[42] Gary L. Morgan, "Notes on genealogy," Prologue, 9 (1977), 179–80; Smith, "Settlement," 291–2; Harrison, "Public land records," 489–91; William D. Pattison, "Use of the U.S. public land survey maps and notes as descriptive sources," Professional Geographer, 8 (1956); RIP 66, 2–4 (q.v. for details of states for which local office plats exist in NA, Washington, DC).
[43] See p. 56. N.B., too, Richardson W. Stephenson, Landownership Maps . . . in the Library of Congress (1967).

Archives record groups have been listed,[44] and there is also a description of maps relating to early agriculture.[45] Used in conjunction with other cartographic material[46] and other land records, plats and survey notes can shed much light on early topography and settlement patterns, in particular the relationship between settlement and cultural and physical factors.[47] They can suggest reasons for certain lands being chosen by early settlers before others, and so on.

The GLO records also contain some townsite plats, on a large scale, generally 200 feet to the inch, most of which were never published. They vary greatly but are usually very detailed, showing streets, block and lot boundaries, location of buildings, railroad rights of way, and sometimes names of lot owners and information on land use. It should be noted, however, that many townsite plats in the 1830s represent pious hopes rather than reality: towns projected by speculators that never materialized. "Scores of paper towns," it is said, "lined interior rivers."[48]

Other GLO records concerning the public domain include tract books, land entry papers, patent files, and "monthly abstracts." The status of each section of the public domain is recorded in tract books which are kept up to date. These are ledgers, arranged by township and range, which provide a most useful record of the initial claimants to the land and a topographical index of the conveyance of title from the federal government to the first private owner. Information contained in them includes the date of the transaction, the name of the local land office, the entry number, the acreage of the land conveyed, the total cost, and the price per acre, together with the type of entry and the name of the entryman.

A set of tract books once maintained at the headquarters

[44] See citations on pp. 49–55.
[45] William J. Heynen, *Pre-1830 Agricultural and Related Maps in the National Archives* (1971).
[46] GLO records include map files containing maps of canals, railroad rights of way, etc.: PI 22, 6; and see p. 428.
[47] Michael P. Conzen, "Spatial data from nineteenth century manuscript censuses," *Professional Geographer*, 21 (1969).
[48] Ralph E. Ehrenberg, "Taking the measure of the land," *Prologue*, 9 (1977), 131–2; Malcolm J. Rohrbough, *The Land Office Business* (1968), 240.

office of the Bureau of Land Management is now distributed in two places.[49] The Bureau maintains, in its Eastern Estates Office,[50] the books for the public-domain states east of the Mississippi River and for Minnesota, Iowa, Missouri, Arkansas, and Louisiana west of the river. The tract books for all the Western states are held at the NA, Washington National Records Center, Suitland, MD.[51] All these tract books have, however, been microfilmed and so are available for searchers in many centers. The sets of tract books originally maintained at district land offices remained there while the offices operated, but were deposited elsewhere after those offices closed on completion of public-land sales. They are to be found with other public-land records in state offices of the Bureau,[52] regional branches of the National Archives, and in state archives or agencies, particularly the depositories of state historical societies.

Tract books complement the plats and survey notes, providing additional evidence for early settlement patterns. They again show the types of land settled in relation to existing features, like streams and forests, and point to the connection between settlement and later influences, like railroads. Used in conjunction with other data they can be very useful. For instance, census population schedules can provide biographical data on those of the entrymen who actually settled. And both census data and the evidence from tract books are convenient for statistical approaches to the initial settlement of an area.[53]

The tract books serve also as indexes to another important type of record, the land entry papers. Mostly case files, these represent the legal acquisition by an individual or company of

[49] *Genealogical Research*, 209, 215.
[50] 350 S. Pickett St., Alexandria, VA 22304.
[51] The basic documentation for land entry in the Western states is now concentrated in one depository: *Prologue*, 3 (1971), 48, 120.
[52] For Western state offices holding tract books and microfilms, see *Source*, 239–52.
[53] Cf. Jane F. Smith, "Commentary," in Meyer H. Fishbein (ed.), *The National Archives and Statistical Research* (1973), 174; Joseph Schafer, "The Wisconsin Domesday Book," *Wisconsin Mag. Hist.*, 4 (1921–2), 63; Joseph Schafer, "The microscopic method applied to history," *Minnesota Hist. Bull.*, 4 (1921–2); Jane F. Smith, "The use of federal records in writing local history," *Prologue*, 1 (1969), 29–33; Gates, *Farmer's Age*, 183.

a tract of public land. The files were forwarded to Washington by district land offices for the issue of patents, and are housed in the Washington National Records Center at Suitland.[54] For the period before 1908 they are arranged by type of entry, state, and land office. The main types of entry were credit, cash, donation,[55] military bounty, and homestead. In addition there were private land-claim entries.

Many of the files are sparse in content, containing merely the name of the entryman, his application to purchase a specific and described piece of land, and a final certificate of entitlement. But others hold many miscellaneous papers, including plats. From these it may be possible to derive such information as the address of the entryman at the time of application, descriptions of houses, barns, fences, walls, and other improvements, dates of initial residence, data on types of crops and the areas under cultivation, and personal details such as the age, place of birth, and citizenship of the entryman, and details of his household and family.[56]

Aside from the actual agricultural information they contain, the land entry papers can thus add to our knowledge of the pattern of settlement and the characteristics of land purchasers in an area. Used collectively they can indicate the relative shares of large and small purchasers in the land market, the financial details of settlement, and, again, the locations preferred. They can also provide information on how many completed the requirements for a homestead claim, and evidence of speculation.

It may be noted here that case files for townsites were not at first differentiated from other land entry files and were often included with them.[57] But special land entry case files exist for the reservation or purchase of townsites from about 1844 and more generally from 1880, when the GLO created a separate

---

[54] Listed PI 22.
[55] N.B. PAMs 145, 203 which relate to registers which serve as indexes to the files.
[56] For details, see *Genealogical Research*, 215–17; Val D. Greenwood, *The Researcher's Guide to American Genealogy* (1974), ch. 15; Richard S. Maxwell, *Public Land Records of the Federal Government, 1800–1950, and Their Statistical Significance* (RIP 57, 1973).
[57] Ralph E. Ehrenberg, *Exploration, Surveying, and Mapping Records in the National Archives* (1971), 4.

category for such applications (Townsite Case Files, Division "K": RG 49). These files include descriptions of sites, maps and plats,[58] and photographs, and represent a greatly under-used source for the history of early towns, especially in the trans-Mississippi region.[59] The growth of such centers might, of course, have had a considerable effect on the agriculture of the region.

Where the land entry file documentation was found valid, a patent, or deed, was issued providing legal title of ownership. Most copies of the patents issued to 1908 are in volumes in series parallel with those in the land entry files, arranged chronologically by state and land office. They provide the name of the patentee, location of the land, land entry identification, and the date of issue. Being standardized, such data again lend themselves to quantitative analysis. Not all claims resulted in the issue of a patent, and canceled case files (traceable through the tract books) may be consulted and may provide information on why claims were not completed.[60]

The land entry papers can be used as indexes to the patent copy volumes. For the period before 1908 there is no comprehensive index of entrymen found in the land entry papers, but incomplete indexes exist in the National Archives, Washington, DC, for certain types of entry, and there are name indexes by land office in certain Western states. Otherwise use may be made of the tract books, or the "monthly abstracts" of entries sent forward by district land office registers and receivers and available in Washington.[61]

Apart from their value as indexes the monthly abstracts are themselves valuable sources. They contain names of

58 See also pp. 53–4.
59 Smith, "Settlement," 296, 302; PI 22, 3n. Arthur Hecht, *Index to the Records of the GLO in the National Archives Relating to Town Sites . . . 1855–1925* (1945) is a list available only in NA, Washington, DC.
60 RIP 57, 7; *Genealogical Research*, 215. For whereabouts for various states, see *Source*, 227–52. Patents deriving from military bounty land warrants are not arranged by state and are kept by the Bureau.
61 For details of formal indexes and other means of marrying tract, land entry, and patent records for the same entryman, see PI 22, 4; Harrison, "Public land records," 493–4; Smith, "Settlement," 293–4; *Genealogical Research*, 215–16. And see p. 204.

entrymen, location of tracts, acreages, types of entry, and, for cash entries, the price per acre and the total sum paid. They can thus be used like tract books to assess the chronological progress of settlement in a particular area, the general size of holdings, and how much land was taken by non-residents and by settlers.

Other GLO records of likely value for local study[62] include case files on military reservations, and canal and reservoir grants which may be linked to the relevant letters, orders and proclamations, and surveys and cartographic materials noted above. Special files for the period 1829–1935 relating to about eighty individual land-grant rail or wagon roads exist. These include correspondence, maps, and field notes, and details of contests between railroads and individual settlers over conflicting land claims. There are also files concerned with contests over mineral lands, surveys and investigative reports of special agents, and records of special boards, as for townsites and private claims. Townsite board records embrace financial accounts, records of sales of lots, block diagrams, and minutes of meetings. As well as private claim board records there are case files connected with such claims in parts of fifteen present-day states, areas originally under British, Spanish, Mexican, and French jurisdiction. They include petitions, plats, deeds, reports, and correspondence.[63]

The published documents of the Treasury Department (apart from GLO reports), particularly its Bureau of Statistics, can also yield information on farming and farm marketing, which may help to connect local economic activity with the wider economic network of which it became part. This bureau, for example, published from 1876 to 1891 a series of annual *Reports on the Internal Commerce of the United States*[64] which includes information related to the marketing of agricultural produce. Thus in the 1881 report there are data on the

---

[62] The following draws on Smith, "Settlement," 300–1; PI 22, 5–6; RIP 66, 4.

[63] *Genealogical Research*, 222, q.v. for indexes and microfilms of private land claims in CA; John P. Heard, "Records of the Bureau of Land Management in California and Nevada," *Forest Hist.*, 12 (1968), 26, n.26; Bowman, "Provincial Archives of California," 73–6. And see pp. 53–4, 168, 171, 173, 182, 211.

[64] See p. 422.

overland movement of cotton and on the movement of grain and flour from the Western and Northwestern states to the seaboard states, with prices of freight by water and rail, and information on freight wars. The report for 1888 provides statistics of the amount of tobacco received at New Orleans from 1821–2 to 1856–7. And another Treasury document (of 1894) gives statistics of sheep by states and territories, 1840–90, and prices of wool in New York, 1824–93, and Philadelphia, 1865–84.[65]

A *Special Report on Immigration; Accompanying Information for Immigrants*,[66] produced by the Treasury Bureau of Statistics in 1871, is very important. It provides, by states and territories, information on land prices and rentals, staple products, facilities of access to markets, costs of farm stock, and kinds of labor in demand. There is much very detailed information on the state of affairs in many counties. Thus for Manitowoc county, WI, to cite only one, the following data are provided: price per acre of small improved farms, price of unimproved land, yearly rent and the kinds of agreements for share cropping, the chief crops grown and their sale price, and the price of various types of stock. It is noted, too, that the village of Manitowoc had a large harbor on Lake Michigan and was the market and port for the county. The railroad was about forty miles away. The quality of land was good in the western and southern parts of the county, and, where timbered, oak, beech, and maple were the main trees. The demand for labor was confined mainly to farm work but there was a woolen mill, four factories producing timber products, and several saw mills. Most of the foreign-born laborers were German. Much land was unoccupied.

Among the unpublished records of the Treasury in the National Archives (RG 56) there is correspondence relating to public land,[67] which includes information on pre-emption rights, land grants for canals, plans of townships, monthly

[65] HMD 94 (52–2), ser. 3110. See p. 401.
[66] See *Checklist*, 1,170; *NUC*, vol. 612, p. 233.
[67] Carmelita S. Ryan and Hope K. Holdcamper (comps.), *Preliminary Inventory of the General Records of the Department of the Treasury* (PI 187, 1977), 13, 30–1. Some is microfilmed: *MRR*.

accounts of registers and receivers, letters from individuals, and issuances of final certificates. There is also a series of a dozen maps compiled just after the end of the Civil War showing for an area adjacent to the lower Mississippi Valley, plantations, abandoned plantations, and those in the latter category that were leased, as well as government farms for freedmen in parts of Virginia and North Carolina.[68] The records of the special agencies of the Treasury, established to supervise trade in occupied areas of the Confederacy during the war, contain data on seizures of cotton.[69] The records of the Bureau of the Customs (RG 36) contain much on the smuggling of cattle over the Mexican border, a significant matter in the history of the range-cattle industry.[70] Some federal tax records can also be of value in identifying land-owners and providing particulars of their lands and buildings, ownership of slaves, and their financial situation.[71]

The published annual reports of the Secretary of the Interior contain information submitted by territorial governors on the state of agriculture and land use. The report of the Governor of Arizona Territory, for instance, in 1895 includes an appendix of statistical data by counties on numbers of different kinds of stock and amounts of land cultivated, reclaimed in the year, and still reclaimable, together with more general information.[72] For the political activity of cattlemen in the range-cattle industry, the personal papers of territorial governors and correspondence relating to their appointments have been found informative. They contain much on the leading people in the areas concerned, most of whom were connected with the industry. The so-called "cattle wars" in the Western states (especially Wyoming) in the 1880s and 1890s are documented in the correspondence of the U.S. Attorney General (RG 60), as is the matter of trespass by cattlemen on Indian lands.[73]

[68] *GNA*, 156; PI 187, 131–2.
[69] Munden and Beers, 223–40; and see ibid., 240–1 for records of cotton purchases by the U.S. government.
[70] Herman Khan, "Records in the National Archives relating to the range cattle industry, 1865–1895," *AH*, 20 (1946).
[71] For details see pp. 100–1. For non-federal taxes, see below.
[72] HD 5 (54–1), ser. 3383, esp. p. 405.
[73] Khan, "Range cattle industry," 189.

The Department of the Interior's unpublished archives include records relating to bounty lands, 1842–83, and to forest reserves, 1891–1902.[74]

Since much public land was granted directly or indirectly to railroad and canal companies, documents connected with internal improvements may contain information of significance (see ch. 9). A useful summary of land granted to individual states for the purpose of supporting improved communications, and from 1857 of land granted direct to railroads, based on the GLO records, was published in 1908.[75]

The Lands and Railroads Division of the Department of the Interior, which functioned from 1849 (though not so named until 1870) was concerned with land-grant railroads and wagon roads. The annual reports of the federal Commissioner of Railroads are, therefore, important. Moreover, for some railroad companies government-appointed directors issued their own reports, published as federal documents. Those for the Union Pacific Railway provide an example.

The unpublished records of the Lands and Railroads Division are very extensive. They include, in particular, correspondence with other government departments, especially the GLO, and with land officers and others in the field. The subjects to which this correspondence relates include land surveys, the disposal of the public domain, railroad and canal grants, wagon roads and rights of way, land grants to the states, Indian lands, Indian depredations, private land claims, reclamation and irrigation, military and other reservations, illegal fencing by cattlemen after the Act of 1884, and records concerning the settlement of Oklahoma, 1889–92.[76]

For a proper understanding of the settlement aspects of railroad land grants it is necessary to use both the GLO records and those of the Lands and Railroads Division. Valuable, too,

[74] *Records of the Office of the Secretary of the Interior* (NA, NNF–48, 1984), pt. I, pp. 53, 70–1.
[75] *Statement Showing Land Grants ... to Aid in the Construction of Railroads, Wagon Roads, and Internal Improvements...* (1908). Cf. W. J. Donald, "Land grants for internal improvements in the United States," *Jnl. Political Economy*, 19 (1911).
[76] NA, NNF–48, pt. I, pp. 145–74; *GNA*, 366. The correspondence and its indexes are available in microfilm (PAM 620, 1966): *MRR*.

are the records of the Office of the Commissioner of Railroads (as it was called from 1881) (RG 193). These include annual and other reports from forty government and state-aided railroads, which contain, among other materials, evidence on the amount of land sold to actual settlers.[77] The records of the Interstate Commerce Commission (RG 134), particularly its case files, contain details of railroads and immigrants and of the relationship between farmers and the rail companies.[78]

Naturally the records of those federal agencies specifically established to deal with aspects of agriculture are important.[79] Unhappily the Department of Agriculture's unpublished records (RG 16) are very incomplete and for the nineteenth century comparatively scanty. Potentially most useful among them, for local purposes, is the correspondence from 1879 of the Commissioner and Secretary of Agriculture. This includes, for instance, petitions from constituents, and correspondence with black farmers and black land-grant colleges. There are some nominal and subject indexes.[80] Despite the sparseness of its unpublished material the Department published many documents and other items which may be worth searching.[81] Its annual reports were published between 1837 and 1848 as part of the annual reports of the Commissioner of Patents. From 1849 to 1861 they appear as separate volumes, though still as part of the Patent Office reports, but from 1862 they appear as distinct reports of the Department

[77] Smith, "Settlement," 300–1; Marion M. Johnson (comp.), *Preliminary Inventory of the Records of the Commissioner of Railroads* (PI 158, 1964); *GNA*, 411.

[78] Leonard Rapport, "Interstate Commerce Commission case files," in Walch, *Our Family, Our Town.*

[79] See Harold T. Pinkett, "Early records of the U.S. Department of Agriculture," *AA*, 25 (1962), drawn on in the following account.

[80] *GNA*, 423–4; Guy A. Lee, "The general records of the U.S. Department of Agriculture in the National Archives," *AH*, 19 (1945); Guy A. Lee et al., *Preliminary Checklist of the Records of the Office of the Secretary of Agriculture, 1939–1941* (1945); Helen F. Ulibarri (comp.), *Preliminary Inventory of the Records of the Office of the Secretary of Agriculture* (PI 191, 1979); Roland C. McConnell, "Importance of records in the National Archives on the history of the negro," *JNH*, 34 (1949), 149. Some available in microfilm: *MRR.*

[81] Useful are R. B. Handy and Minna A. Cannon, *List by Titles of Publications of the . . . Department of Agriculture . . . 1840 to . . . 1901* (1902); George F. Thompson, *Index to Authors . . . in Documents of the U.S. Department of Agriculture, 1841 to 1897* (1898). See also the library catalog of the Dept., cited above, n. 7.

of Agriculture. These reports are indexed so can readily be utilized by researchers.[82]

The index entry for Ohio may give some idea of the sort of information to be found in the annual reports: agricultural statistics; company for importing English cattle; culture of brown corn; fruits; mustard crops and seed sales; premium crops; small crops; state reports of agriculture; vintage; and wheat crops. It is true that much of the content is of a generally informative kind, often exhorting certain practices and so on, but some of the information is very detailed at the local level. The report for 1851, for example, relates that farmers in Muskingum county, OH, were selling butter in Philadelphia. The report for the following year gives a lengthy account of butter production in Stark county, OH.[83] Localized information is found in the annual reports in special reports of different subjects. The report for 1885, for example, deals with the distribution of Southern cattle fever by states, but often mentioning individual counties. Some reports also print letters or summaries of letters from correspondents, including, for instance, information on experiments in stock rearing and crop production carried out in particular places. There are data, too, on the wages paid for farm labor.

From 1895 some of the data formerly found in the annual reports was published separately in the *Yearbook of the United States Department of Agriculture* (1894–). Included in the yearbook were the largely hortatory but still informative reports and articles which sometimes contain local information (as, for example, on frost damage in Florida in 1894–5 in the 1895 edition) but also statistics of wholesale prices of agricultural produce in certain important U.S. cities, farm prices of the same produce (with information back to 1890), and statistics of the chief crops and livestock for certain geographical areas.

The Commissioner of Agriculture also published, from 1863 to 1876, *Monthly Reports* which contain extracts from

[82] *Index to the ARs U.S. Dept. of Agriculture . . . 1837 to 1893* (1896). There was no AR for 1846.
[83] Robert L. Jones, "The dairy industry in Ohio prior to the Civil War," *Ohio Archaeological and Hist. Q.*, 56 (1947), 65.

letters on farming matters, arranged topically, with the geographical origin of the writer usually (and the name sometimes) given, and other information, including special reports. In 1867, for example, there is a report on grasshoppers in Kansas. Many circulars were also produced by the Department of Agriculture. These were mailed to thousands of crop correspondents and regularly provided information of a statistical kind on the acreages of growing crops and their condition, the yield and the price obtainable. Such figures were also summarized in the annual and monthly reports. In addition the Department produced many special publications, among them *Albums* published by the office of the statistician, providing agricultural data at the state level.

From 1884 there are the annual reports of the Department of Agriculture's Bureau of Animal Industry,[84] which contain, for instance, excerpts from correspondents concerning stock, as well as articles and other reports. Thus the first of these annual reports includes information on an outbreak of cow disease in Richmond county, NY, and on Southern cattle fever in Virginia.[85]

The unpublished records of the Agricultural Section of the Patent Office (RG 16) include for the period 1839–60 letters from farmers on crop prospects and agricultural practices, essays, and completed questionnaires (from individual farmers, agricultural societies, and others) concerned with the distribution of seeds and plants from abroad. RG 16 also contains correspondence and a large collection of photographs on those aspects of agriculture in which the federal authorities interested themselves (arranged alphabetically by subject).[86]

Among the records of the Bureau of Agricultural Economics (RG 83) are a number of rough manuscript maps for 1898 providing data on acreage statistics for each truck (green

---

[84] *Checklist*, 206–7. See also Harold T. Pinkett (comp.), *Preliminary Inventory of the Records of the Bureau of Animal Industry* (RG 17) (PI 106, 1958).

[85] HMD 25 (48–2), ser. 2311, pp. 461–7, 469–70.

[86] *GNA*, 423; Lee, "General records . . . Department of Agriculture"; PI 191, 7, 8, 45; Meyer H. Fishbein, *Early Business Statistical Operations of the Federal Government* (RIP 54, 1973), 14–18; Harold T. Pinkett, "Records of the first century of interest of the United States government in plant industries," *AH*, 29 (1955).

vegetable) crop by states and indicating in which counties the particular crop was grown commercially.[87] In the same Record Group is a collection of photographs relating to farm operations from 1896, and some 200 unpublished county-outline crop and stock maps for the period 1839–1919. For the Civil War period there are some maps in the records of the Office of the Chief of Engineers (RG 77) which contain data on land use and agriculture.[88]

For land and agriculture in the South after the Civil War the records of the Bureau of Refugees, Freedmen, and Abandoned Lands (1865–72) are invaluable. They are fully described in chapter 3, but some remarks may be made here. The annual reports of the Commissioner provide much general information and a great number of aggregated statistics. Local researchers will, however, often need to examine the unpublished records on which the reports are based.[89] These (RG 105) contain a mass of evidence, the most relevant being in the records of the Commissioner and in those of the Bureau's land division. They include papers of or emanating from each of the assistant commissioners of the various Southern states, and records of field officers (superintendents, sub-assistant commissioners, agents), and registers of claimants and letters received. Most useful among these are the various reports made by assistant commissioners and other officers. There are narrative reports of operations, while various monthly reports (including land reports) provide intimate details of confiscated and abandoned lands and such lands restored to former owners. These may indicate the location of the land, numbers of buildings, names of former owners and of tenants, and statistics of acreages cultivated, cleared, and wooded.

Registers of applications by freedmen for land include details of the applicants' families and their resources for

[87] William J. Heynen, *Cartographic Records of the Bureau of Agricultural Economics* (1971), 5.
[88] *GNA*, 457; Heynen, *Pre-1930 Agricultural . . . Maps*, 4 (indicates, in app. I, p. 21, chronological coverage for each crop and gives details of other maps relating to crops and farms in RGs 83, 95, incl. some based on censuses). See ibid., app. II, pp. 2–3, for the RG 77 maps.
[89] See RIP 48; PI 174; *Black Studies* (q.v., too, for microfilms of records in RG 105): cited ch. 3, nn. 95, 98.

working a farm. There are also "applications for leasing" files, registers of leased plantations, and applications for restoration of property (pertinent to planters' efforts to dislodge black squatters).[90] "Book records" are particularly useful for the local scene. They consist of the papers produced by individual land agents, such as correspondence, journals, memoranda books, and monthly and quarterly reports. The agents were concerned to promote agricultural recovery and their reports contain a great deal on the condition of freedmen, and on labor relations between the larger farmers and planters and their freedmen workers. They supply details of new tenurial arrangements for working the land and the difficulties involved, though it has been suggested that some of this evidence is highly suspect.[91] Sometimes they provide information on the general economic condition of their districts. Other records of the assistant commissioners and their officers include labor contracts between planters and freedmen, giving details of terms of engagement. In addition there are records of apprentice indentures, some of which provide details of individuals. For Louisiana there may be payrolls for plantation laborers.

Claims against the federal government arising from the Civil War resulted in large numbers of records many of which contain information on farmers and planters and other agricultural matters, including much on the depredations of the war and its aftermath on Southern estates, and generally on the sort and scale of farming being conducted in various localities.[92] Among the records of the Treasury (RG 56) are letters relating to such matters as the leasing of plantations, permits to purchase cotton, and case files for claims for cotton and abandoned property from 1861.[93] The Treasury records also embrace the main records of the Commissioners of Claims (known as the Southern Claims Commission),

[90] See, e.g., Lawrence N. Powell, *New Masters* (1980), 235.
[91] Brock, 211. See also Ralph Shlomowitz, "Planters' combinations and black labor in the American South," *Slavery and Abolition*, 9 (1988), and works cited.
[92] Cf. Frank W. Klinberg, "Operation and reconstruction," *North Carolina Hist. Rev.*, 25 (1948); Michael K. Honey, "The war within the Confederacy," *Prologue*, 18 (1986).
[93] PI 187, 79–80; *GNA*, 154–5.

1871–80.[94] Among these are registers of claims which include claims from farmers, for which there is an incomplete geographical list.[95] These and other papers of the Commission are available in microfilm.[96]

The files of allowed claims are among the records of the Third Auditor of the Treasury Department (RG 217). These, often extensive, are arranged by state and county and are especially useful for the community historian generally as well as the historian of local agricultural matters. They may include petitions, depositions of witnesses, and reports of special agents on the claims and summary reports.[97] Files on disallowed claims and claims barred are among the records of the House of Representatives Committee on War Claims (RG 233) and for consultation require the consent of the Clerk of the House.[98] The collections of case files, however, are by no means complete, and the identification of useful extant files is difficult.[99] Nor should the *Consolidated Index* be regarded as a complete list of Southern Unionists who suffered depredations.[100]

Records of other war claims are among those of the Court of Claims (RG 123).[101] They include petitions, depositions, opinions, titles to real estate, and so on, relating to plantation owners and others whose land had been abandoned or seized, and provide information on the plantation economy and other

94 See Frank W. Klinberg, *The Southern Claims Commission* (1955); *GNA*, 154. An index to the Commissioner's jnl. and a register of property owners is in RG 39.

95 The *AR*s of the Commission are in the US Serial Set (see pp. 21–2) and contain lists of claimants by states. The last *AR* (HMD 30 (46–2), ser. 1929) contains a complete list of claims barred, withdrawn or dismissed (and see n. 98 below). N.B., too, U.S. Commissioner of Claims, *Consolidated Index of Claims Reported ... 1871 to 1880* (1892) and the various lists and indexes of private claims among federal documents: see Sarah Larson, "Records of the Southern Claims Commission," *Prologue*, 12 (1980), 218.

96 NA, M87: includes in roll 14 the *Consolidated Index*.

97 *GNA*, 59–60; Debra L. Newman, *Black History* (1984), 275; Munden and Beers, 193–6.

98 For some data on disallowed cases, see U.S. Commissioner of Claims, *Summary Rep. on all Cases ... Disallowed Under the Act of ... 1871* (4 vols., 1876–81).

99 Munden and Beers, 596.

100 Larson, "Records of the Southern Claims Commission," q.v. for assistance with the case files.

101 See William A. Richardson, *History, Jurisdiction, and Practice of the Court of Claims* (1885). Some records have been retained by the court.

agricultural matters. There are also files on Indian depredations, largely for the period of the 1860s through 1890–1.[102] The Court of Claims section of the Justice Department has amongst its records (RG 205),[103] miscellaneous items relating to claims pertaining to the Civil War and later which may be useful. They include records concerning the wartime seizure of cotton and Indian depredations later in the century.[104] Often such records, which include affidavits, briefs, depositions, and so on, contain much general evidence on life in frontier communities and on farms.

From such sources the state of agriculture in the South during the Civil War, Reconstruction, and later can be studied in depth. In conjunction with other evidence they can shed light, in particular, on the state of plantations and estates. The effect of federal policies at the local level on the freedmen can also be assessed and insight given into the nature and extent of share cropping, gang labor, and so on in postbellum local economies.[105]

Some other federal records important for agricultural history may be mentioned. The *Report of the Industrial Commission* (1900–2) contains in one volume a digest of evidence on matters relating to many aspects of farming, trade in agricultural products, and labor matters.[106] Another volume has a report on the agricultural distribution of certain ethnic groups of immigrants (as, for instance, Italian agricultural colonies in Vineland, NJ and Bryan, TX), and a table showing the condition of agricultural labor and demand for immigrants arranged by states, counties, and localities.[107] A volume on the

[102] PI 58, esp. 16–17, 21–2; Munden and Beers, 128–31.
[103] Some duplicate records in RG 123 noted above. For details, see Gaiselle Kerner and Ira N. Kellogg, Jr. (comps.), *Preliminary Inventory of the Records of the Court of Claims Section of the Department of Justice* (PI 47, 1952); Munden and Beers, 424; *GNA*, 351–2. See also details of claims records, 1839–1914, in RG 92 (Quartermaster General's Office) in *Genealogical Research*, 230–1; Munden and Beers, 290–1.
[104] For Indian depredations there are related records in RG 75.
[105] See, e.g., James Smallwood, "Perpetuation of caste," *Mid-America*, 61 (1979).
[106] Vol. x: HD 179 (57–1), ser. 4340 (indexes incl. places). And see *Materials in the National Archives Relating to Labor and Labor Problems* (RIC 10, 1942), 7.
[107] Vol. xv: HD 184 (57–1), ser. 4345.

distribution of farm produce has data on the distribution of cereals, including information on the relations of individual railroads with county elevators. It also contains details of the milk trade in nine large and forty-seven smaller cities and towns, and of the hay trade in various large centers (with county details for Virginia), as well as statistics of the fruit and vegetable trade in nine markets. An appendix gives details of grain facilities on the Northern Pacific lands, by station, owner, type of building (as elevator, warehouse, or mill), and capacity.[108] Yet another volume includes special reports on the tobacco trade and farm labor, and a digest of laws and court decisions (by states) relating to grain inspection, elevators, and warehouses, and information on boards and departments of agriculture.[109]

Two reports on forestry (by Franklin B. Hough) in 1878 and 1882 may provide significant information.[110] The earlier one, for instance, includes data on the lumber trade of Chicago, a great deal on the export of timber in various forms (by customs districts), and individual reports on some states, with much miscellaneous evidence on particular localities. There is, for example, a table of acreages of timber by counties in Wisconsin.

For the Western states, in particular, the records of the Forest Service, which originated in 1880 as the Division of Forestry in the Department of Agriculture, may provide some local information on forestry and the lumber industry.[111] The annual reports of the Division (published with those of the Department) only occasionally provide data below the level of states or regions. Unpublished material (RG 95) includes correspondence from 1886, covering the work of the Division in timber testing and cooperation with state authorities and private agencies. Among these are many survey maps of forest

[108] Vol. VI: HD 494 (56–2), ser. 4168.
[109] Vol. XI: HD 180 (57–1), ser. 4341.
[110] See *NUC*, vol. 256, pp. 75, 78 for refs.
[111] From 1881 the GLO administered forest reserves.

sale areas.[112] There are also letters and reports of supervisors for parts of Montana, Colorado, and New Mexico (1898–1904), and photographs of 1898–1900 of reserves in various Western states.[113]

The correspondence of the Bureau of Indian Affairs (RG 75) and the records of its land division include information on permission to drive cattle across Indian lands, logging operations, and timber trespasses and illegal grazing on Indian lands. The journals, correspondence, and reports of the Office of Naval Records (RG 45) contain forest maps and information on the acquisition of timber for naval purposes.[114] The records of the Soil Conservation Service (RG 114) contain maps of Indian Territory and Oklahoma, giving information, mainly from the mid 1880s, of land cultivation and of crops and livestock produced.[115] For many parts of the country settlement was established at the expense of the Indians and there is a large literature of public documents and a mountain of federal records concerned with Indian–white relations, among which is a great deal about early white settlement (see ch. 5).

FEDERAL CENSUS EVIDENCE

The records of censuses of one kind or another are a source for the history of local agriculture and landholding that cannot be ignored. Being quantitative in nature they lend themselves to statistical analysis, but useful work can be done not only by those able to use, for example, sophisticated correlation

[112] For other maps, drawings, and other inf. for forests, woodlands, and the lumber industry, see Heynen, *Pre-1930 Agricultural . . . Maps*, 1–2, 9–10. See also certain vols. of *Reps. of Explorations and Surveys to Ascertain . . . a Route for a Railroad from the Mississippi River to the Pacific . . .* (12 vols., 1857), SED 78 (33–2), ser. 758–68; SED 46 (35–2), ser. 992.
[113] GNA 427, 430; Harold T. Pinkett (comp.), *Preliminary Inventory of the Records of the Forest Service* (PI 18, rev. 1969); See also Neiderheiser (comp.), *Forest History Sources*, 17–19 (q.v. for other RGs useful for forest hist.); Richard C. Davis, *A Guide to North American Forest History: Archives and Manuscripts in the United States and Canada* (1977); Gerald Ogden (comp.), *The U.S. Forest Service: A Historical Bibliography, 1876–1972* (1976); Richard C. Davis, *Encyclopedia of American Forest and Conservation History* (2 vols., 1983).
[114] Khan, "Range cattle industry"; Neiderheiser, *Forest History Sources*, 13, 21.
[115] Heynen, *Pre-1930 Agricultural . . . Maps*, 14.

techniques perhaps aided by computers, but also by those who confine themselves to using figures in a more modest fashion. It should, anyway, be appreciated that data on agriculture and the numbers of people engaged in it given in the federal censuses are of dubious accuracy for 1840, while for 1850, and to some extent for later census years, they can by no means be regarded as entirely accurate.[116] For that reason census evidence should wherever possible be used in conjunction with evidence from other sources. That said, the federal censuses remain important sources, and the published volumes contain not only statistics but descriptive material. Agricultural data in the published volumes of the census are often at the level of states, but increasingly from the middle of the century, statistics for smaller units, especially for the county, are given. In the following account it is information below state level that has been stressed.[117] The ICPSR collection of historical data based on the published volumes of the federal census, described fully elsewhere,[118] includes agricultural evidence. The nature of this is summarized here with reference to the census volumes on which it is based, and in addition local statistics not covered by the ICPSR set are also indicated.

Data on farms and the state of the land in the ICPSR set includes for states and counties: numbers of farms (censuses of 1850, 1870, 1880, 1890, 1900), of farms in categories of size (1860, 1870, 1880, 1890, 1900), of acres in farms (1880, 1890, 1900), of farms with buildings (1900), of acres in improved and unimproved farms (1850, 1860),[119] of acres of improved

---

116 Brock, 49–51; Gavin Wright, "Note on the manuscript census samples," *AH*, 44 (1970), 95–9; *Memorial of the American Statistical Assoc.* (1844), SD 5 (28–2), ser. 449, 4–5.

117 Basic agricultural data are found in the following vols.: 1850: Compendium, Statistical View (Dubester (1950) no. 33), counties, cols. 23–57; 1860: vol. II, counties, pp. 2–183, 193–219; 1870: vol. III, tables IV, V, VII; 1880: vol. III, tables V, VII; 1890: vol. V, tables 5, 6, 8, 10, 12, 14, 18, 20, 22, 24; 1900: vol. II, table 106; vol. V, tables 10, 19, 35, 40, 44, 47.

118 See p. 64.

119 "Improved": cleared land used for grazing, orchards, vineyards or tillage or fallow; "unimproved": other land used in connection with the farm, etc. (1860 census). But definitions changed and this should be taken into account: John D. Black, *The Rural Economy of New England* (1950), 137–61; Hal S. Barron, *Those Who Stayed Behind* (1984), 28, 143: *U.S. Census of Agriculture, 1964*, vol. II (1967), ch. I, 10–11.

and unimproved land (1870) (in farms, 1880, 1890, 1900), of acres of tilled improved land in farms (1890), of acres of improved meadows, pastures, etc. in farms (1890), of acres of unimproved woodland (1870), of acres of unimproved woodland and forests in farms (1880), and numbers of acres of other unimproved land in farms (1880).[120] Information on the value of farms and other assets and on various types of expenses includes: the value of farms (censuses of 1850, 1870), of farm land, fences, buildings (1880, 1890), of farming implements and machinery (1850, 1860, 1870, 1880, 1890, 1900), of livestock (1850, 1860, 1870, 1880, 1890, 1900), of animals slaughtered (1850, 1860, 1870), of orchard products (1850, 1860, 1870), of produce of market gardens (1850, 1860, 1870), of all farm products (1870, 1880, 1890), of farm products not fed to livestock (1900), and value of forest products (1870); the cost of building and repairing fences (1880), and cost of fertilizers (1890); and the expenditure on farm labor (1900).

For statistics of crops and yields the ICPSR data is much less full than the published volumes, both in chronological coverage and in the numbers of types of crops covered, giving information only on the number of bushels of barley, buckwheat, Indian corn, oats, rye, wheat (1880, 1890), and numbers of acres planted of each of these (1890). The census volumes also provide quantitative data, mostly from 1850 through 1900, on Irish and sweet potatoes, rice, tobacco, cotton, hay, clover and grass seed, hops, hemp, flax and flax seed, silk, wool, peas and beans, dairy products, maple sugar, molasses, beeswax, and some other products, as well as numbers of various kinds of livestock. Data on poultry and milk are not given until 1870.

Statistics of the agricultural workforce reproduced in the ICPSR base include: the numbers of persons engaged in agriculture (1820, 1840),[121] and for the antebellum South the numbers of slaves (categorized by age and sex in each census

---

[120] Nos. of farms and acreages may be somewhat overstated in the published censuses: Black, *Rural Economy*, 54–60; Paul G. Munyon, *A Reassessment of New England Agriculture in the Last Thirty Years of the Nineteenth Century* (1978 edn.), 10, 71–2.

[121] Census vols.: 1820: vol. I, table 1; 1840: vol. I, unnumbered table.

1800 through 1860), the numbers of persons holding specified numbers of slaves (1860),[122] and the total numbers of slave owners (1860).

Useful, too, is the inclusion in the ICPSR set of information on ownership and tenantship: numbers of farm owners, part owners, owners and tenants, managers, cash tenants, and share tenants (1880, 1890, 1900).[123] Additionally the ICPSR collection includes a "farm-land data set" drawn from the compilation of Pressly and Scofield, itself based on the agricultural censuses.[124] This provides average market values of farmland, fences, and buildings per acre for the census years 1850 through 1900 (and for later dates) for every county in the Union. These evaluations do not, however, include stock, implements, machinery, or crops, though, as noted above this information is available for certain census years. Again note that the market value was not the same as the assessed value for tax purposes. Nevertheless this source provides a standard measure of land values for the whole of the second half of the century and beyond.

Researchers without access to the ICPSR collection can, of course, obtain the information, if more onerously, from the census volumes themselves. But it must be emphasized that, in addition to the extra information on crops noted above, the original volumes do contain a great deal of other data not reproduced in the ICPSR set.

The agricultural information in volume III of the 1880 published census is particularly exhaustive, including not only statistical data but detailed reports on a number of topics. These reports were also published separately.[125] Those on cereal production and flour milling provide information on certain states, though not very detailed local data. The report

122 Slaves were returned as "belonging" to the person in whose family or plantation they worked, regardless of the legal position
123 Distinguished 1900 by race. The 1890 census vol. also does this.
124 Thomas J. Pressly and William H. Scofield (eds.), *Farm Real Estate Values in the United States by Counties, 1850–1959* (1965) (all counties from 1850 or the census date following constitution).
125 See Dubester (1950); Schulze (1983), 181. Census Bureau records (NA, RG 29) contain lists of Louisiana sugar planters by counties, and records of agents investigating meat products, 1869–80: *GNA*, 466.

on the culture and curing of tobacco, however, deals with production in each tobacco state with much localized information. It covers not only processes but costs, wages, and so on. It can also be linked with another report on the manufacture of tobacco which covers prices, commercial distribution, exports, and information on individual cities engaged in such activity. The report on cattle, sheep, and swine provides state-by-state information including a great deal about the cattle-range industry, including organization and marketing.

Volumes v and vi of the 1880 census comprise a report on cotton production which includes production details for each county in the cotton states,[126] its population (white and black), the area of tilled land, the area in cotton, corn, oats, and wheat, and the total cotton production and average per acre. There may be a description of the terrain and the soil in different parts of each county and remarks on the crops and the relation of county to total state production. There are also abstracts of returns by correspondents (usually one per county) covering similar topics and much incidental detail. Indeed there is an enormous amount of local information both statistical and descriptive to be culled from these volumes, which have indexes covering county names.

Volume ix of the same census covers forests and includes detailed maps showing the distribution of different types of forests and the density of afforestation. Descriptive accounts contain references to many localities and sometimes statistical data on a county basis.[127] Extra Census Bulletins for the 1880 census include one providing cotton production by counties and another giving cereal production for counties.[128]

The 1890 census, in volume v, includes evidence on a number of horticultural and agricultural activities mainly at state level and on viticulture at county level, as well as a report on irrigation in the West. This report contains details

---

[126] All state sections also publ. separately; LA rep. repr. also as Extra Census Bull. (1881) (Dubester (1950), no. 163).
[127] Summarized in *Forestry Bull.*, 1–25 (1881–3): see Dubester (1950), no. 161.
[128] See Dubester (1950), nos. 166, 167; Schulze (1983), 262–3.

of irrigation at county level with statistical data on irrigated acres and farms, and crop data. It also contains descriptive information on individual counties. Volume XII of that census covers real-estate mortgages and includes maps of all states showing by county the average value of encumbrance and the average value per farm acre. There is also a table, by counties, of the number and amount of real-estate mortgages made and the number of acres and lots covered for the decade 1880–9. A detailed investigation of 102 counties is also included.[129]

Volume XIII of the 1890 census, on the proprietorship and indebtedness of farms (and homes), presents for individual counties statistics of owned and hired farms in 1880 and families owning and hiring farms in 1890, as well as families occupying owned, hired and free, and unencumbered homes.[130] Many Census Bulletins based on preliminary results of the 1890 census were also published.[131]

The agricultural information in the 1900 census is presented in volumes V and VI and includes reports on the production of cereals, cotton, tobacco, vegetables, and sugar, with very detailed county-level statistics.

The Census Bureau produced in published cartographic form data derived from the censuses of 1870, 1890, 1900, 1910, and 1920, in sets of a *Statistical Atlas of the United States*. Included are demographic data but also the distribution of woodland and of the cultivation of various crops, of dairy produce and livestock, and the amount of land in farms.[132] For the 1890 census there are also maps giving information on irrigation.[133] Also based on the census are maps of the

---

129 Vol. XII, 154–295. Cf. William G. Murray, *An Economic Analysis of Farm Mortgages in Story County, Iowa, from 1854 to 1931* (1933), 412. And see pp. 212–14.

130 Tables 96, 98.

131 Schulze (1983), 366; Dubester (1950), nos. 227–8, 237. There was also an Extra Census Bull. on tobacco production: Schulze (1983), 376.

132 For details, see Heynen, *Pre-1930 Agricultural . . . Maps*, 1–2; Katherine H. Davidson and Charlotte M. Ashby (comps.), *Preliminary Inventory of the Records of the Bureau of the Census* (PI 161, 1964), 55. See also U.S. Dept. of Agriculture, *Atlas of American Agriculture* (1918); Charles O. Paullin, *Atlas of the Historical Geography of the United States* (1932, repr. 1975); Sam B. Hilliard, *Atlas of Antebellum Southern Agriculture* (1984).

133 See index, and Heynen, *Pre-1930 Agricultural . . . Maps*, 2, 12, for other sources on irrigation.

Southern states and Virginia for 1860 showing the distribution of the slave population by counties, and a map of Missouri indicating the number of slaves, free blacks, and whites in each county in the north of the state.[134]

Using statistical and other information derived from the published census reports (including perhaps the ICPSR collection and the Pressly and Scofield volume) it is possible for the community historian to write a sound account of farming in a county or larger area, which will be especially detailed from the middle of the century onwards.[135] He can, for example, demonstrate the extension of landholding in a locality from decade to decade, the farm density and the relative proportions of establishments in different size categories, and thus the relative importance of large farms or smaller ones in an area. Of course "farm" is a crude unit of measurement. In comparing numbers of farms from one decade to another it should be remembered that at the lowest level the extent of the inclusion of very small holdings varied from census to census and this affects the comparability of totals unless taken into account. Moreover, it is not necessarily to be assumed that a "farm" represented a consolidated holding. Widely separated tracts operated by one person constituted, as far as the census takers were concerned, a single farm. So long as these facts are kept in mind such census data remain important.

From the published censuses the historian can also trace the extent of actual exploitation of the land aside from its mere acquisition. From 1850 he can ascertain what crops were being grown in his area and in what quantities, and their relative significance, as well as the importance of livestock farming, fruit growing, market gardening, and so on in an area. Thus the essential characteristics of local agriculture can be judged and changes (as, for example, from initial subsistence farming, to single crop specialization, to diversification, and to broader regional specialization)[136] can be noted.

---

[134] Heynen, *Pre-1930 Agricultural . . . Maps*, 1. Cf. Hilliard, *Antebellum Southern Agriculture*, 28–38.
[135] E.g., Michael P. Conzen, *Frontier Farming in an Urban Shadow* (1971), 22–5.
[136] Cf. ibid., 3 and ch. v.

Data in the census volumes on the valuation of farms are, as noted, extensive, and can be used, together with data on values of farm products, to assess levels of prosperity, and changes and fluctuations over time. Light may be shed on, for instance, the effect on farm values, and therefore on the prosperity of a locality, of external factors, such as the building of a railroad, the growth of a city in the neighborhood, the Civil War in the South, Indian troubles, general economic recessions and booms, and so on.

Certain caveats may, however, be given here over treating changes in average values of farms in a county.[137] For example, there was a tendency for the best land to be the first settled, so that average values for the county concerned may drop as other lands were acquired, though in fact no fall in the level of local prosperity had really occurred. There is something to be said, therefore, for using, as well as average values of farms, their total value per county. Again counties were large and not always homogeneous in physical and other characteristics; average valuations may well disguise considerable variations within a county. Land around large cities was often enhanced in value for reasons other than the intrinsic worth of the farmland, or was used for certain types of farming, such as dairying or truck farming, not typical of the surrounding areas as a whole.

Aside from the valuation of land and buildings, a proper assessment of values must also take into account other assets, particularly the value of farm machinery, and, in the South, the numbers of slaves. And consideration of these factors can lead to the posing and answering of other pertinent questions. Since the growth or otherwise of capital equipment in the form of implements and machinery is available in terms of value, it may be possible (by combining such data with other evidence) to assess the impact of mechanization on output and on the amount of land improved. For areas where slave labor was used, the levels of that kind of capital investment can be plotted from the beginning of the century to the census before

[137] Cf. Pressly and Scofield, *Farm Real Estate Values*, 9.

the outbreak of the Civil War (though returns were probably not always accurate) and in 1860 we can see whether the slaves in a county were held largely by a few owners, whether there were many owners of a small number of slaves, or whether there was a mixture. At the end of the century the extent to which black Americans had become owners or tenants of farms in a county can also be seen.

From 1880 it is possible to ascertain the extent (in terms at least of numbers of farmers) of ownership and tenancy, and more exactly the relative numbers of cash tenants and share-croppers, and the extent to which some were owners of some land but rented other land, too. Moreover, the distinction between blacks and whites in this respect can also be seen. Again the movement from tenancy to ownership may be deduced by comparing one census with another, and the published censuses can indicate the number of persons (farmers, planters, laborers, and so on) engaged in agriculture and the proportions of total populations they represent.

Not only is it possible to construct a detailed picture of the economic structure of agriculture in counties and larger areas from the published census volumes, but the population censuses can also yield other evidence which, combined with the agricultural data, can further illuminate the social conditions within which farming operated. For example, the process of settlement and the turnover of settlers can be determined.[138] Again the number of aliens (unnaturalized foreigners) for each county is given, and the number of foreign born is provided by counties for 1860, and for 1870, 1880, and 1900 this information is classified into numbers born in different states of the Union and different countries or world regions. In the 1900 census numbers are subdivided into whites, blacks, and Indians. For 1900, too, the figures are classified by age and sex, and for 1880, 1890, and 1900 evidence is provided of numbers of native born with foreign-born parents. For the decadal years 1850 and 1860 categorization by place of birth is given only at the state level, but this is still valuable for purposes of

---

[138] See. e.g., James C. Malin, *The Grasslands of North America* (1947).

regional comparison. Since some historians believe that ethnic and religious homogeneity or concentration could lead to more stable and better integrated communities this may well be useful information. Some circumspection in deducing the likely importance of ethnic groups merely from the total numbers of foreign born must, however, be exercised. Children of immigrants may well have been born in America yet socially were as much part of ethnic groups as their parents. Using census totals of foreign born in assessing the ethnic characteristics of agricultural (or other) communities may, therefore, exaggerate the significance of the American born. For that reason the information on the native born with foreign parents should be taken into account, and for 1900 age and sex groups can also be considered. The same remarks apply in the analysis of persons born in different states of the Union.

Published census data also include detailed information, usually by counties, of the incidence of membership of different church groups, and on the educational levels of the adult inhabitants, data on school attendance, and so on (chs. 6, 10), all of which can fill out the profile of county agricultural communities. Again it has been suggested that speculative activities by farmers can be deduced from the size of farms. Thus the average Iowa farm in 1850 was 185 acres, in 1860 165 acres, too large for the average farmer to handle, and the fall in the average to 134 acres by 1870 indicates the likelihood that many settlers had sold off their surplus land.[139]

All this evidence is useful both to the historian of the single county and to those dealing with larger areas. It is valuable, too, for the historian interested in comparing districts within a certain area. Counties may thus be ranked or grouped according to average value of farms, or the type of crops grown, whether grazing or arable, or the extent of ownership and tenantship and other criteria, and differences in prosperity between one area and another and fluctuating relationships over time can be deduced. In areas which were not wholly or

---

[139] Robert P. Swierenga, *Pioneers and Profits* (1968), 35n.

overwhelmingly agricultural and rural, however, categorization of counties by wealth will need to embrace not only farming valuations but the comparative incidence of other wealth. Useful here are the data provided in the censuses (and the ICPSR collection) of the value of real and personal property (not distinguished) in 1850 (by states only), of the "true" (not the tax assessed) value of personal and real estate in 1860 and 1870, and of the assessed value of real and personal estate in 1870 and 1880.[140]

Historians have long been aware that the richness of the U.S. census data makes possible valuable investigations of related social characteristics. It is clear that all this quantitative data can be used for quite sophisticated exercises in correlations between many variables.[141] The possible relationship of such variables as ethnicity, color, religion, ownership and tenancy, farm size, and elaborations of these, may be worth investigating. Less complicated aggregative methods applied to this material may also provide worthwhile information. It need not be felt that sound and significant findings are impossible without advanced mathematical skills.

Unpublished material deriving from the federal censuses and relating to agriculture includes among the National Archives, manuscript maps of 1861 (1 inch to 10 miles), based on the 1860 census, for eight Southern states (including Virginia and West Virginia) showing the acreages of improved land, numbers of certain kinds of livestock and horses, amounts of wheat, corn, oats, tobacco, hay, ginned cotton, and rice, all by counties. Additionally, they depict numbers of whites, free blacks, and slaves, and of males available for military service. A map of the Southern states in 1880 portrays areas of cotton cultivation. There are also census enumerators' maps, large-scale maps of counties and other small administrative areas,[142] which have detailed accompanying notes on crops, soil, and climate.[143]

---

[140] Assessed value of real and personal property is given in 1860 by states only.
[141] Cf. Conzen, *Frontier Farming, passim.*
[142] Heynen, *Pre-1930 Agricultural . . . Maps*, 1–2, 18–19; GNA, 468–9.
[143] There is much inf. on climate, 1871–94 in NA, some providing evidence on state of crops: Heynen, *Pre-1930 Agricultural . . . Maps*, 6–8.

Sources for U.S. History

More generally important census material, however, exists from 1850 in unpublished agricultural schedules organized by counties and townships from which the statistical information in the published volumes was compiled,[144] not always, it is alleged, entirely accurately.[145] These schedules enable the researcher to bring his investigation down to the level of smaller units than the county and indeed to the individual farmer.[146]

Non-population schedules, of which the agricultural schedules are a part, exist for the censuses of 1850 through 1880.[147] The agricultural schedules include returns relating to each farm operator – a farm being a managerial unit, not necessarily consisting of topographically contiguous territory. Only farms with produce valued at $100 or more annually were included and in 1870 and 1880 farms of less than three acres were omitted, too, unless they sold $500-worth of produce in the year. The data available for each farm returned are those detailed above for the statistical content of the published censuses,[148] covering (for the years indicated) details of crops, livestock, land use and acreages, machinery, implements, ownership and tenantship, valuations, wages and employment, and so on.[149] It was intended to exclude from the agricultural schedules of 1880 ranch cattle kept "beyond the frontier of close and continuous settlement," these being the subject of a special report in the published volumes. In fact the agricultural schedules do contain useful data on such range stock.[150]

[144] Carmen R. Delle Donne, *Federal Census Schedules, 1850–80* (RIP 67, 1973); Barnes F. Lathrop, "History from the census returns," *Southwestern Hist. Q.*, 51 (1948).
[145] Cf. Fred Bateman and Jeremy Atack, "Profitability of Northern agriculture in 1860," *Research in Economic Hist.*, 4 (1979), 92 and works cited.
[146] There are also schedules for 1840, arranged in rough geographical order by state, including nos. employed in agriculture and the kind, quantity, and value of agricultural, horticultural, and forest products: PI 161, 109–10. But too much reliance on these statistics is unwise: Carroll D. Wright and William C. Hunt, *History and Growth of the United States Census* (1900, repr. 1966), 76–90.
[147] For refs. to location and microfilms, see pp. 81–2.
[148] The items incl. in each census are listed in Jane L. Davidson, "Agricultural census schedules, 1850–1880," *Genealogy*, 75 (1983); Wright and Hunt, *United States Census*.
[149] The social statistics schedules incl. farm wage inf. for each district.
[150] Lathrop, "History from the census returns," 302n.

Clearly the agricultural schedules can be used to illuminate in greater detail all the matters covered by the published censuses. Since the schedules are arranged by townships they can, for instance, be used to distinguish different types of farming in different parts of the same county, the extent and location of farm settlement in a county[151] (perhaps restricting the extent of former open-range cattle raising), and so on, over the years. In addition, since they identify individuals, they lend themselves to linkage with other personalized data to show a great deal about individual farmers and different types of farmers in the same area. Thus comparison of acreages from original-entry land records with farm acreages in the censuses may shed some light on the amount of land held by speculators.[152]

The linking of agricultural schedules with the population census schedules is particularly fruitful. It can reveal individual farmers' ages, their place or country of birth, the value of their real estate (1850 through 1880) and of their personal property (1860, 1870 only), as well as other sociological information (such as the sex, age, relationship, and occupation of all members of the farm household, and their literacy levels). Such comparison may also give some idea as to which kinds of farmer were likely to stay in a particular area and which were likely to be more mobile. It can be seen whether farmers sharing particular social characteristics (as of age, ethnicity, family size, and so on) also shared economic attributes (as size of farm, whether owner or tenant, type of farming pursued, value of capital, and use of machinery). And changes over time in the structure and social characteristics of the local farming community can be deduced by comparing the information from census year to census year.

Again, judicious linkage of data in the agricultural and population schedules can help in the problem of distinguishing tenants and owners among farm operators. The agricultural schedules do not do this until 1880, with consequent difficulties

[151] Cf. Michael P. Conzen, "Spatial data from nineteenth century manuscript censuses," *Professional Geographer*, 21 (1969).
[152] Swierenga, *Pioneers and Profits*, 25–46. But see Seddie Cogswell, Jr., *Tenure, Nativity and Age as Factors in Iowa Agriculture, 1850–1880* (1975), 10.

in establishing the extent of tenancy before that. Thus, for example, postbellum plantations are often not discernible in the agricultural schedules, the number of recorded farms in the postbellum South bearing no relation to the number of land-owners.[153] Operators without valued property recorded in the population schedules for 1850, 1860, and 1870, however, may be tenants rather than owners: though identification in this way is by no means simple.[154] Linkage of census evidence and records of land ownership and taxation should be attempted, too, where possible.[155] Comparison of population and agricultural census material can also help to identify those listed as "farmers" in the population schedules who do not appear as farm occupiers in the agricultural schedules and who are therefore likely to have been landless laborers, retired farmers, or new farmers of insufficient standing to be able to report harvest data.[156]

The detailed information in the manuscript population and agricultural censuses makes possible more sophisticated and extensive correlation exercises than can be undertaken with the published census data. Thus explorations may be made of the relationships between such factors as age, ethnicity, family size, farm size, type of crops grown or livestock reared, ownership or tenancy, and use of family or hired labor. All these can be tested in varying degrees of mathematical sophistication according to the inclinations and facilities of the researcher. It is possible to build up a static picture of a community or locality at a particular census year or to show changes in these relationships from one decade to another. Thus it has been shown how the number of farming families

---

[153] Cf. Enoch M. Banks, *The Economics of Land Tenure in Georgia* (1905), 33; Kenneth S. Greenberg, "The Civil War and the redistribution of land," *AH*, 52 (1978), 301–2.

[154] See Frederick A. Bode and Donald E. Ginter, *Farm Tenancy and the Census in Antebellum Georgia* (1986), esp. ch. 2.

[155] See John T. Houdek and Charles F. Heller, Jr., "Searching for nineteenth-century farm tenants," *HM*, 19 (1986).

[156] Cogswell, *Tenure, Nativity and Age*; Donald L. Winters, *Farmers Without Farms* (1978); Allan G. Bogue, *From Prairie to Cornbelt* (1968 edn.), 64–5; Merle Curti *et al.*, *The Making of an American Community* (1959), 59–60, 140–56 and app. I; Robert P. Swierenga, "Quantitative methods in rural landholding," *JIH*, 13 (1983), 796–9; Randolph B. Campbell, "Planters and plain folk," *JSoH*, 40 (1974), 373.

without children in three Massachusetts' townships almost doubled between 1870 and 1880, family labor being replaced by hired hands, and the average age of farmers rose as youngsters drifted to the towns.[157]

It is possible, too, to show what the common characteristics of successful or unsuccessful farmers in an area were,[158] and to attempt answers to significant questions. Was success related to farm size, location in the county, type of crops grown, or other activity followed? Was it relevant if the man was an owner or a tenant, how old he was, how large his family, whether he belonged to a particular ethnic group, or whether he was near a railroad, or to particular combinations of these factors? Similarly the characteristics of those farmers or laborers who settled and stayed for long periods as opposed to those who were mobile, and of tenants as opposed to owners, may profitably be investigated.

Of course, record linkage and correlation exercises need not be confined to the evidence from the censuses. Information from, for example, directories may fill in details between census years, and much general information may be culled from newspapers, and from the records concerning land ownership (dealt with above), tax records, court records, title deeds, private papers, and indeed from many of the types of records described elsewhere in this volume.

A number of data samples on agriculture drawn from the manuscript census schedules exists.[159] They include a random sampling from those for 1860, covering over 21,000 rural households (among them some 12,000 farms) in 102 rural counties in twenty Northern states, available for researchers on computer data tapes.[160] A somewhat smaller data collection

[157] Jonathan Prude, *The Coming of Industrial Order* (1983), 194.
[158] For assessment of farm profitability, see Bateman and Atack, "Profitability of Northern agriculture."
[159] See Swierenga, "Quantitative methods," 792–5.
[160] *Agricultural and Demographic Records of 21,118 Rural Households Selected from the 1860 Manuscript Censuses* (data tapes, 1973). For availability and comment, see Fred Bateman and James D. Foust, "A sample of rural households," *AH*, 48 (1974). See also Donghyu Yang, "Notes on wealth distribution of farm households," *Explorations in Economic Hist.*, 21 (1984); and works of Richard Easterlin cited *AgHR*, 31 (1983), n. 22.

exists for a sample of some 5,000 farms and of free and slave populations in 409 counties in the South.[161]

Other federal sources are discussed in the section on Indian lands and agriculture in the next chapter.

[161] Yang, "Notes on wealth"; articles in *AH*, 44 (1970); Donald Schaefer and Mark Schmitz, "The Parker–Gallman sample and wealth distribution for the antebellum South," *Explorations in Economic Hist.*, 22 (1985); Donghyu Yang, in ibid., reply; Mark D. Schmitz and Donald F. Schaefer, "Using manuscript samples to interpret antebellum Southern agriculture," *JIH*, 17 (1986).

CHAPTER 5

The land, settlement, and farming: II

There are many records, other than those of the federal government, which illuminate the study of land settlement and its use.

STATE AND LOCAL GOVERNMENT RECORDS

In addition to the federal agricultural census records, some published and unpublished records of similar state censuses may survive.[1] A census of Iowa for 1856, for instance, resulted in a printed volume summarizing by township manuscript-schedule data on farm acreages and improved and unimproved farm land. The New York state decennial censuses from 1825 through 1875 contain information on agriculture and land-ownership.[2] In 1885 censuses which embraced agricultural information were taken in the states of Nebraska, Colorado, and Florida and the territories of New Mexico and Dakota. Copies of the manuscript schedules are available in the National Archives (RG 29) and on microfilm, for all but Dakota for which the schedules are missing. Since these censuses provide similar information to that found in the federal census returns of 1880 and are for a period five years after the last available federal schedules, they are likely to be very valuable for localities in the areas concerned. They contain names of farm owners, information on tenure, acreages, and farm values, details of costs, estimated values of various farm products, and numbers of different types of livestock.[3]

[1] See Dubester (1948).
[2] Robert P. Swierenga, *Pioneers and Profits* (1968), 41; Merilyn Douglas and Melinda Yates, *New York State Census Records, 1790–1925* (1981), 48–50.
[3] Katherine H. Davidson and Charlotte M. Ashby (comps.), *Preliminary Inventory of the Records of the Bureau of the Census* (PI 161, 1964), 109–11.

It is not possible to deal here with other relevant records of each state. They are likely, however, to be equally as important as federal records for the community historian. In state-land states the often considerable areas of ungranted public lands at the time of Independence were vested in state governments which continued to dispose of them to individuals in much the same way as in colonial times. The New York state archives, for instance, include large numbers of records relating to bonds and mortgages for sale of state lands, lists of purchasers of state lands, and so on.[4] Some of the records of these initial grants for certain of these states are to be found with those of later land transfer between individuals – that is with county records (see below). In others, such as Georgia, Maryland, Massachusetts, Pennsylvania, Tennessee, Virginia, and also Texas, they are kept in state land offices. Such records may include the entry or application for a grant from an individual, plats or surveys (with descriptions of the bounds of the land), registers of licenses to applicants (again describing the land), and copies of patents.[5]

As for the public-domain states, Congress from the early nineteenth century made over public land to them to fund public education, drain swamps, and support internal improvements, like making rivers navigable and establishing railroads. The disposal of this land is covered in Acts of state legislatures. The control and dispersal of it generated records both published and unpublished. So, too, did state governmental concern with agricultural matters generally.

The unpublished records of state land officers, found with other state records, were similar in nature to federal land records, discussed in the last chapter,[6] and should be taken into account in any investigation of local land settlement and land

[4] NY State Education Dept., *Guide to Records in the New York State Archives* (1981), 59–60.
[5] Val D. Greenwood, *The Researcher's Guide to American Genealogy* (1974), 268–70, 282–3. For guides, indexes, etc., for state land-office holdings and location of land grants, titles, etc., in these states generally, see *Source*, 240–52.
[6] Cf. Swierenga, *Pioneers and Profits*, ch. 3; John P. Heard, "Resources for historians; records of the Bureau of Land Management in California and Nevada," *Forest Hist.*, 12 (1968), 25.

disposal.[7] And it may be noted here that some federal land-office records (of district land offices) were transferred to state authorities from the late 1870s.[8]

The legislatures of the individual states, of course, debated agricultural and land matters and legislated on them, so that state records of debates and the content of statutes, as well as the records of legal cases,[9] are important both for purely agricultural topics and for land affairs. State laws, for example, regulated agreements between landlords and tenants and reports of state courts can shed light on the legal situation.[10] It may be suspected, however, that views expressed in debate and policies pursued by legislatures reflected the interests of the larger and more powerful farmers rather than those of smaller men.

State documents important in the study of the disposal of land and the extent of speculation, and of ownership and tenantship, include reports of supreme courts, registers of state land offices, state land office commissioners, treasurers, auditors, surveyors general, commissioners of public works, school commissioners (concerned with the disposal of school lands), and secretaries of agriculture. The Iowa State Auditor, for example, reported annually from 1847 the total acreage of land assessed for tax in each organized county. The Kansas and Nebraska auditors chronicled receipt and disposition of lands and data, by counties, on acres cultivated and yield of crops. The annual reports of the Comptroller-General of Georgia (1865–1919) provide yearly statistics of property values, of improved and wild lands, and so on, for each county, and from 1874 information on the lands of whites and blacks is distinguished.[11] The Commissioner of Statistics for Wisconsin's annual reports provide numbers of trees planted and

---

[7] Cf. Robert P. Swierenga, "The Iowa land records collection," *Books at Iowa*, 13 (1970), 30.
[8] See p. 176.
[9] See pp. 25–7, 42–3.
[10] See, e.g., Donald L. Winters, *Farmers Without Farms* (1978), 73, 140.
[11] Swierenga, *Pioneers and Profits*, 25; Leslie E. Decker, *Railroads, Lands and Politics* (1964), 402–3; Robert P. Brooks, *The Agrarian Revolution in Georgia, 1865–1912* (1914); Enoch M. Banks, *The Economics of Land Tenure in Georgia* (1905), 34, 63–4.

growing in each county in 1876 and 1877, and the report of the State Engineer of California in 1880 has much on irrigation and water policy in that state.

Indeed, when the whole field of agriculture is considered the documents published by the states are extremely numerous and difficult to do justice to here. The researcher should consult catalogs of state documents. For New York state (1789–1904), for example, Hasse (see List of abbreviations) has sixteen pages of references under "Agricultural" and "Agriculture," while for Ohio for the same period there are nearly 200 pages of references in these categories. The significance of many of these documents, particularly those that survey the condition of agriculture in the state concerned, is difficult to exaggerate, though clearly they cannot be detailed here. The Ohio entries in Hasse may, however, be taken as an example. The items include the Ohio *Agricultural Statistics* which provide annually, 1858–90, returns of acreages and yields as submitted by township assessors, and numbers of horses, cattle, sheep, and hogs, as well as quantities of wool; and for the period 1896–1904 data by counties. The annual reports of the bureau of statistics of labor for 1857 through 1886 provide each year a table indicating the general condition of agriculture in each county in the state. Additionally there are the annual reports of the board of agriculture, 1846–1904,[12] and many other publications of that board – including, for example, reports on various matters pertaining to individual counties, and crop bulletins. For 1881 there are stock and crop reports from about a thousand township correspondents. Very many other publications and reports on a host of topics are listed, including, for instance, the annual reports of farmers' institutes. The reports of county agricultural societies in Ohio are published as state documents, as is the case in other states.

In many other states, too, the reports of state boards of agriculture provide very detailed information, including data collected from surveys of farmers,[13] and often they embrace,

---

[12] For work on these, see Robert L. Jones, "The dairy industry in Ohio prior to the Civil War," *Ohio Arch. and Hist. Q.*, 56 (1974).

[13] Richard Bardolph, *Agricultural Literature and the Early Illinois Farmer* (1948), 75–6.

or even largely consist of, reports from county, local, or state agricultural societies. They form an important body of source material for agriculture and rural life generally, particularly from the 1840s, often containing very detailed localized information. Territorial and state immigration commissioners' reports, too, often contain evidence on the general state of agriculture and opportunities for reclamation of land. In Illinois there was a state entomologist whose reports are particularly important for the types of diseases and pests faced by farmers in the region.[14]

Unpublished state archives on agricultural matters cannot be detailed here, but the researcher should seek the records of the state officials and departments for which published documents have been found useful. In the South for the Reconstruction era the official correspondence of state governors, which includes letters from planters, may be valuable.[15] The state archives of California at Sacramento include copies, translations, and indexes (made 1866–7) of Spanish and Mexican land records. The principal records relating to private land claims in Louisiana, Missouri, and Florida are in the possession of those states.

For detailed work at the local level the historian will need to consult local government records, particularly those concerning land transactions between individuals, tax assessments, and probate records. Where available WPA, HRS inventories of county records or more recent catalogs of such records should be consulted.

Original land entry books, usually kept by county registers of deeds, duplicate the information on first owners of formerly public domain found in the federal records of patents issued, though not all patents were so recorded.[16] The recording of all land transfers subsequent to the original grant of public domain was usually the responsibility of the county (or

---

[14] Bardolph, *Agricultural Literature*, 84–8.
[15] Cf. Lawrence N. Powell, *New Masters* (1980); Paul W. Gates, *Agriculture and the Civil War* (1965), 382.
[16] Swierenga, "Iowa land records," 26–7; Swierenga, *Pioneers and Profits*, 25; *Source*, 226; Clifford N. Smith, "Federal land records," *National Genealogical Soc. Q.*, 60 (1972), 251.

occasionally of another local government unit),[17] and records of this are found amongst the archives of the county (or other unit) existing at the time of the transaction. These often voluminous archives include copies of conveyances or deeds (the documents recording the transfer of real estate), embracing warranty deeds, deeds of gift, deeds of partition, mortgage deeds, and so on.[18] Thus the records of the Clerk of the Monroe, WV, county court include ninety-two volumes of deed registers dating from 1797.[19] The deed usually contained the names of the grantor and the grantee, the date, and a legal description of the land. Entry books often provide an index to the deed files, though there may also be specially compiled indexes.[20] With the deeds may be plats, or these may be in plat books or files. Where files exist, they provide maps showing the property, and may be accompanied by other papers such as surveyors' notes. Abstracts of title, including a summary of each conveyance of a property, may be obtained from official and commercial abstractors who exist in most localities, and these abstracts may serve as indexes to the original records, or, where those are missing, as an alternative source of information.[21]

Records of mortgages (including liens and trust deeds) provide the names of the parties involved, a legal description of the property, the amount of the loan, and the terms of the mortgage. The files of these may also contain copies of related records. There may also be records of leases, providing such information as the arrangements for rent, the duration period of the lease, the size of the farm or land leased, the residence of the landlord, and contractual obligations. Where no register

[17] Except in territories prior to becoming states. For custodians of such records in the states, see Greenwood, *Researcher's Guide*, 309–10.
[18] See ibid., 286–90 for these and other legal terms connected with land.
[19] WPA, HRS, *Inventory of the County Archives of Virginia, No. 31, Monroe County (Union)* (1938).
[20] Jones, 149. Cf. Theodore C. Pease, *The County Records of Illinois* (1915), lxvii–lxxiii.
[21] Donald D. Parker, *Local History* (rev. Bertha E. Josephson, 1944, repr. 1979), 51–2; Greenwood, *Researcher's Guide*, 286; Donald W. Meinig, "Railroad archives and the historical geographer," *Professional Geographer*, 7 (1955), 8; O. Lawrence Burnette, Jr., *Beneath the Footnote* (1969), 69–70.

was kept, however, the contracts may have been returned to the landlord on expiry of the lease, so that the evidence will have disappeared.[22]

Where they have survived, such records can throw light on the physical pattern of landholding in an area, on land speculation (by identifying purchasers of large amounts of land and what they did with it), on the extent and nature of tenancy (through leases), and on the operation of land-credit markets (through mortgages).[23] If they are compared with the land entry tract books and abstracts of entries to public, railroad, and state lands, they can indicate to what extent early entrymen and settlers, by selling parts of their holdings, indulged in speculation. Dummy entrymen, used by cattle, timber, and mining companies, speculators, cotton planters, lumbermen, and settlement promoters to build up large holdings, may be revealed. There is, therefore, considerable scope for work at the county and sub-county level.[24]

Used collectively, county mortgage records can indicate the extent of mortgage lending, the rates involved, the identity of investors and middlemen, and the economic effect of credit of this type on the local agricultural community. Additionally they can contribute to the history of individual farms.[25] County records of mortgages and deeds can also be used to reveal the establishment of large estates based on

[22] Winters, *Farmers Without Farms*, 116, 139–40. For refs. to terms of sharecropping contracts arranged by Southern states, see Stephen J. DeCanio, *Agriculture in the Postbellum South* (1974), 278–86.

[23] Cf. Paul W. Gates, *Landlords and Tenants on the Prairie Frontier* (1973), 122–7, 202–37; Robert P. Swierenga, "Quantitative methods in rural landholding," *JIH*, 13 (1983), 801–2, 805–6; Robert P. Swierenga, "Land speculation 'profits' reconsidered," *JEH*, 26 (1966); Robert P. Swierenga, "The equity effects of public land speculation in Iowa," *JEH*, 34 (1974). For a survey of writings on mortgage and credit, see Allan G. Bogue, "Land credit for northern farmers, 1789–1940," *AH*, 50 (1976). For census data on mortgages, see p. 196.

[24] Cf. Paul W. Gates, "Research in the history of the public lands," *AH*, 48 (1974), 34–6, 40; Yasuo Okada, *Public Lands and Pioneer Farmers* (Tokyo, 1971).

[25] See, e.g., William G. Murray, *An Economic Analysis of Farm Mortgages in Story County, Iowa, 1854–1931* (1933), a seminal study of mortgage records; and other works cited Swierenga, "Quantitative methods"; Bogue, "Land credit." Robert F. Severson, Jr. *et al.*, "Mortgage borrowing as a frontier development," *JEH*, 26 (1966) provides an example of methodology.

pre-Independence land titles.[26] Foreclosures on farm mortgages, for example by banks,[27] can also be studied from county land records and give an impression of the general prosperity or otherwise of farming in an area at particular times. They can also identify the farmers who failed and those who continued, perhaps building prosperity on credit arrangements. Other sources can help to suggest the characteristics of the kind of farmer who failed and the kind who succeeded.

Tax records on real and personal property (usually arranged by townships) have survived in large quantities in county archives and contain much information.[28] Whereas the census schedules give data of this kind only for each tenth year, tax returns may exist for runs of sequential years. Real-estate tax records (assessments, lists of taxable goods, collectors' books, and so on) provide varying amounts of information. Apart from the name of the payer and the amount of tax, they may also indicate the value of improved and unimproved lands, acreages and values per acre, numbers of slaves, the name of the previous owner, the date of purchase or entry, the owner's place of residence, and the location of the tract or tracts, with a description. Where comparison is being made of the land in frontier areas held by residents and non-residents (possibly speculators) it should be noted that non-residents' land may have been assessed more severely.[29]

Personal property-tax records may contain, for each individual, at various times in the nineteenth century, the numbers and value of horses, mares, colts, mules, cattle, sheep, hogs, stock in trade, money and credit, and tools and machinery. Before abolition the numbers of slaves, sometimes categorized by age, are also included. Taxable items, of course, varied from state to state,[30] and over time, and categories of taxable

[26] Paul W. Gates, "Private land claims in the South," *JSoH*, 22 (1956); Lawrence B. Lee, "American public land history," *AH*, 55 (1981), 289.
[27] E.g., Paul W. Gates, "The role of the land speculator in Western development," *Pennsylvania Mag. Hist. and Biog.*, 66 (1942), 61.
[28] See pp. 102–4.
[29] Robert P. Swierenga, "Land speculation and frontier tax assessments," *AH*, 44 (1970).
[30] For federal tax records, see pp. 100–2.

property tended to become increasingly complex as the century progressed. Annual county abstracts may exist, summing up this data. It has been suggested that tax rolls can indicate the area in a locality actually in private hands more accurately than can land entry records. In 1850 about half the land recorded in tax rolls in central Iowa did not appear as being in either the improved or the non-improved portions of local farms nor in town lots and was probably in the hands of speculators.[31]

Ancillary local tax records may include lists of delinquents, again with details of the property and its valuation, and records of the sale of delinquents' property. Records of tax liens may shed light on aspects of speculation and on the credit market.[32]

Much of this tax data can be utilized for the same purpose as the information in census schedules, particularly to identify the numbers and proportions of large as opposed to small farmers and planters. It can also be used in conjunction with and to supplement census-schedule evidence.[33] Since individuals' names appear in both the tax and the census records, prosperous, not-so-prosperous, and poor farmers and farming families can be identified and residents distinguished from non-resident landowners.[34] The proportions of the various categories can give an idea of the economic state of the locality. Fortunes of individual farmers over the years can be plotted and the possible connection with other ascertainable factors discussed. Extension of farm boundaries and the erection or improvement of buildings can be noted.

Probate records represent another important set of sources for the history of rural communities.[35] These are generally

[31] Swierenga, *Pioneers and Profits*, 43–4.
[32] For this topic, see Swierenga, "Quantitative methods," 806–7; Swierenga, "Land speculation"; Robert P. Swierenga, *Acres for Cents* (1976).
[33] Cf. Frank L. Owsley, *Plain Folk of the South* (1949); Frank L. and Harriet Owsley, "The economic basis of society in the late ante-bellum South," *JSoH*, 6 (1940).
[34] Cf. Harry L. Watson, *Jacksonian Politics and Community Conflict* (1981), 28–9n.
[35] For types see Norman E. Wright, *Preserving Your American Heritage* (1981), 97–106; Greenwood, *Researcher's Guide*, 12–14, 17; *Source*, 177–85 (q.v. for details of the probate process). And see p. 105.

located among court records – usually those of county courts or sometimes of courts otherwise named, as, for example, probate courts.[36] Some have been microfilmed, especially by the Genealogical Society of Utah, and for some there are published indexes. Wills and administrators' reports (sometimes copied into indexed books) may provide details of farmers' stock, crops, machinery, and tools. They may mention real estate, slaves, tenanted property farmed by others, family members involved in the farm (or not), as well as debts and loans. Sometimes black landowners can be distinguished. And wills can give clues as to inheritance practices.[37]

Inventories and appraisers' valuations list more exactly the dead person's property at the time of death. They may contain valuations of such property, embracing standing as well as harvested crops, stock, implements and machinery, and cash in hand, credits, and debts.[38] Probate records provide evidence for the history of individual farms and ranches and of the families who ran them, and for the extent of their activities. They can show, for example, the scale of operations of individual cattle ranchers from the value and numbers of their stock.[39] If they exist in sufficient quantity they can be used collectively to provide evidence of the nature of farming in a particular area (bearing in mind that farming is a seasonal affair, and that they will reflect conditions at the time of the agricultural year at which death occurred).

Other official material of use includes the records, published and unpublished, of those larger cities (and of the counties in which they were situated) which were railroad centers and centers for the marketing of agricultural produce. They may be worth searching for information relating to hinterland farming and their own marketing activities.

---

[36] For types of court in each state, see Greenwood, *Researcher's Guide*, 234–8.
[37] Mark W. Friedberger, "Probate and land records in rural areas," *AH*, 58 (1984); Jones, 142–4; Luther P. Jackson, "The Virginia free negro farmer, 1830–1860," *JNH*, 24 (1939), 406–7.
[38] G. M. Gates, "Some sources for Northwestern history: probate records," *Minnesota Hist.*, 17 (1936); Jones, 144–5.
[39] John D. Guice, "Turner, Webb and cattle-raisers in the old Southwest," *Western Hist. Q.*, 8 (1977).

The land, settlement, and farming: II

BUSINESS, PERSONAL, AND RELATED RECORDS

The records of individual farmers and their business contacts can, if available, enable the historian of rural areas to deepen his study considerably. Such material may still be in private hands, but the libraries of universities, historical societies, and other institutions, as well as state and local libraries, may hold collections.[40] Some have appeared in print.[41]

Farmers' diaries and account books (often the two were combined) vary in detail and in the nature of the topics covered.[42] It may be possible to use them to show the daily and seasonal activities of local farms. There is likely to be much on the weather and its impact on farm fortunes, and there may be comment on crops, and information on the purchase and replacement of tools and machinery, changes in methods and types of farming, and on prices paid for produce, supplies, and labor. Some account books can reveal an almost non-cash economy, and occasionally the diaries and letters of farmhands have survived to provide a different viewpoint.[43]

It would be easy to produce narrative of an antiquarian kind from isolated evidence of this kind. Used judiciously and in the context of general and statistical evidence of other types, however, farmers' records can add greatly to a serious study of a local agricultural community. If accounts, even of a single farmer, have survived for a period of years in sufficient detail they can give some idea of whether the farm was largely of a subsistence kind or was market orientated, and may add to the evidence on the profitability or otherwise of farming in the

---

[40] See, e.g., "Agricultural records in the Baker Library [Harvard Univ.]," *Business Hist. Soc. Bull.*, 9 (1935).

[41] E.g., Wayne E. Kiefer, *Rush County, Indiana* (1969), app. 1; Clarence S. Pain (ed.), "The diaries of a Nebraska farmer, 1876–1877," *AH*, 22 (1948); Rodney C. Loehr (ed.), *Minnesota Farmers' Diaries* (1939).

[42] Everett E. Edwards, "Agricultural records," *AH*, 13 (1939); R. C. Loehr, "Farmers' diaries," *AH*, 12 (1938); "The importance of farm and general store account books in business history," *Business Hist. Soc. Bull.*, 5 (1931); G.M.G., "Some sources for Northwest history: account books," *Minnesota Hist.*, 16 (1935); Winifred B. Rothenberg, "Farm account books," *AH*, 58 (1984).

[43] David E. Schob, *Hired Hands and Plowboys . . . 1815–1860* (1973), 273. For farm labor see also *AgHR*, 31 (1983), 145, and works cited.

area, and the effect of war, economic depressions, and so on. Sometimes the methods of trading – through middlemen, on credit, for example – can be deduced. Payments on loans may be recorded in the accounts, as well as information on mortgages and foreclosures.

Again, the extent to which family and hired labor was used, permanently or seasonally, whether hired labor was likely to be kin, and so on, may sometimes emerge from a study of diaries and accounts.[44] There will also often be much data on the social life of the farm family and incidentally of the neighborhood in such records: school, church, leisure activities, and social customs generally may have been recorded. So, too, occasionally, may a farmer's views on other matters that concerned him particularly, like the various farm protest movements and other political activities, or his attitude to middlemen. Sometimes comments on elections are recorded. One historian has used a record book in conjunction with a land-office tract book to illustrate one Nebraska farmer's experiences in setting up a homestead, the subsequent production and profits, how he brought the land into cultivation, rebuilt his own house, fenced the land, and later rented it out and fell into debt.[45] Clearly linkage with the other types of record dealt with in this chapter and the last will often be essential.

Farmers' correspondence, too, may be useful,[46] particularly for frontier and pioneer settlement. Letters from emigrants to the home country and letters to the Eastern states from those who were establishing new farms in the West may depict contemporary conditions, difficulties, and hopes. The correspondence of more established farmers, especially of a business nature and covering a number of years, may illuminate all sorts of farming activity, mortgaging, marketing, and so on, as well as providing information on local rural life generally. Collections of letters which have since been printed

[44] For inf. in farm accounts, see Clarence H. Danhof, "The farm enterprise," *Research in Economic Hist.*, 4 (1979).
[45] Homer E. Socolofsky, "Land disposal in Nebraska, 1854–1906," *Nebraska Hist. Mag.*, 48 (1967).
[46] William F. Baron and Anne F. Bridges, "Making hay," *AH*, 57 (1983).

demonstrate the potential value of this type of evidence.[47] Farm records may also include rental contracts which will illustrate types of land tenure.[48]

Plantation records and the papers of planter families, where they have survived, are often very detailed and diverse, containing a wealth of business information, data on management practices (including the supervision of labor), profitability or otherwise, and the general state of trade. They embrace diaries, memoranda books, journals, financial accounts,[49] correspondence, instructions, lists of slaves, records of slave births and deaths, accounts of food and clothing provided for slaves, and so on, as well as legal papers.[50] Where the planters were absentees there is likely to be much correspondence with overseers and managers. Such sources are very important for the study of localities in the Southern states where cotton, rice, sugar, and tobacco production was significant, and for insight into the social and economic condition of places in those states. In drawing conclusions about plantations in a locality, however, care should be taken not to generalize from too few examples, or at least to do so with caution. The common factor of slavery in the antebellum period should not be allowed to erode the distinctions to be made between raisers of different kinds of crops, plantations of different sizes, and so on.

Important collections of plantation records exist at the Alabama Department of Archives and History, Montgomery, at the Mississippi Department of Archives and History, Jackson, at the Southern Historical Collection at the University of California, Chapel Hill, at Louisiana University Department of Archives, Baton Rouge, at Duke University, at Tulane

---

[47] E.g., Joseph Schafer, "Immigrant letters," *Wisconsin Mag. Hist.*, 16 (1932); Charlotte Erickson, *Invisible Immigrants* (1972); Edwards, "Agricultural records"; Wayne D. Rasmussen (ed.), *Agriculture in the United States*, vol. 2 (1975).

[48] See Rosser H. Taylor, "Post-bellum Southern rental contracts," *AH*, 17 (1943); John M. Faragher, *Sugar Creek* (1986), 186; and p. 187.

[49] To be used with caution: Brock, 206–7.

[50] For examples, see John R. Commons *et al.* (eds.), *A Documentary History of American Industrial Society* (1958 edn.), vol. 1; Lincoln Griffith (ed.), "The plantation record book of Brookdale farm, Amite County, 1856–1857," *JMH*, 7 (1945).

University, New Orleans, and at North Carolina State University, to name some depositories.[51] Many plantation records and planter family papers and memoirs have appeared in print.[52]

More generally in the country as a whole the reminiscences of old-timers, published as books or in local journals and newspapers in the early twentieth century or before, or reproduced by historians, can also fill out otherwise impersonal evidence. For certain purposes contemporary photographs and artifacts, such as farm implements, found, for example, in local and specialized museums, may add to the historian's knowledge of aspects of the farming he is investigating.[53]

Details of local farming communities should, of course, be set in the context of what is known of the general fabric of the agricultural economic structure of the particular region, the background to which will be ascertainable from secondary sources. More detailed research on the records pertaining to the activities of land companies, railroads, county stores, tobacco and cotton dealers, elevator companies, packing and processing firms, stockyards, and so on, can, if they are available, further illuminate matters. They should provide information on prices received by the farmer for his produce, and on prices he had to pay for supplies, machinery, fertilizers, seed, and so on. They may throw light on the mechanics of operations – systems of credit, the part played by banks and middlemen, and the lien system in the South. Credit-reporting agency records, like those of R. G. Dun, include details of farmers as well as of other businessmen. Bank records can also provide evidence on loans and mortgages.[54]

Certain specialized collections are sometimes of value. These include the records of farming corporations which owned and worked land on a large scale.[55] And the

[51] See also *NUCMC*. The locations of some planters' papers are listed in William K. Scarborough, *The Overseer* (1966), 229–35. See also Powell, *New Masters*; Edgar T. Thompson, *The Plantation: A Bibliography* (1957).
[52] Scarborough, *Overseer*, 236–7; Powell, *New Masters*, 236–8.
[53] For agricultural museums, see Gates, *Farmer's Age*, 425.
[54] See pp. 377–8, 379–80, 380–3.
[55] Cf. Gates, "Research in the history of the public lands," 48–9.

McCormick manuscripts, the business papers of the famous reaper manufacturing company,[56] include an enormous body of correspondence with farmers from 1856. The records of mail order houses and of seed merchants, of which several collections exist, may also be of interest.[57] Business papers of lumber companies and saw mills can be useful for forest history and the timber trade.[58]

In the larger cities that were centers of agricultural marketing and farm supply, traders' organizations may have left vital evidence on the history of agriculture in dependent localities. The Chicago Board of Trade, for example, from 1859 published its *Annual Statistics of Trade and Commerce of Chicago*, which is packed with information relevant to the economic development of Illinois, and its archives include daily price quotations for farm produce for futures trading from 1881 onwards.[59] Reports of city boards of trade and chambers of commerce can also provide details of prices paid to farmers for their produce.

The records of county stores can give some indication of the standards of life in local agricultural communities, and reflect the prosperity or otherwise of the district, detailing what prices farmers paid for groceries, clothes, and household goods. Some stores were established and stocked by "furnishing merchants" who were able to supply goods and cash on credit to farmers, so becoming intermediaries between them and the meat packers, grain, seed, and cotton speculators, wholesale mercantile houses, fertilizer firms, and the like. The financial records of such stores can reveal the nature and extent of this business in a locality, how far they were acting as

[56] McCormick Collection at the State Hist. Soc. of Wisconsin, 816 State St., Madison, WI 53706 (formerly in Chicago).
[57] See C. R. Barnett, "Horticultural trade catalogues," *Agricultural Library Notes*, 1 (1926), 76–7; D. St. J. Manks, "Trade Catalogues in the library of the Massachusetts Horticultural Society," *Agricultural Library Notes*, 3 (1928), 295–6; A. M. S. Pridham, "Collections of horticultural catalogues in Cornell University Library," *Agricultural Library Notes*, 4 (1929).
[58] See lists in Cloudaugh M. Neiderheiser, *Forest History Sources of the United States and Canada* (1956).
[59] Owen Gregory, "The Chicago Board of Trade archives," *AH*, 56 (1982).

petty bankers, and how far local farmers were under their control.[60]

Information on land sales and speculation may be culled from advertisements (in newspapers and broadsheets) and from the business papers of speculators and land agencies and companies. Usually such business records consist of "in" correspondence and copies of "out" letters, memoranda of articles of association, prospectuses, annual reports, and, less frequently, of financial accounts. Several collections of such material exist.[61] Some speculators were, of course, resident far from where the land was situated. The records of one important land agency in Iowa include many letters from potential purchasers in the East indicating the kind of land they wanted.[62] Such records need to be studied in conjunction with the land entry records and deed registers described earlier.[63] Records in Amsterdam (Netherlands) of the Holland Land Company, which owned over five million acres of land mainly in New York and Pennsylvania and sold it directly to settlers in small amounts, are available in microfilm.[64] They include financial reports, records of court actions, maps, deeds, investment records, land-purchase records, and a great deal of correspondence.

Mention may be made, too, of registers and other records of so-called "claim clubs," ostensibly associations aiming to uphold pre-emptive rights to land against later homesteading sales, but which were often a front for land speculation. These

[60] Thomas D. Clark, "The furnishing and supply system in Southern agriculture since 1865," *JSoH*, 12 (1946).
[61] E.g. those cited in Gates, "The role of the land speculator"; Swierenga, *Pioneers and Profits*.
[62] Swierenga, *Pioneers and Profits*, 249.
[63] For use of land, business, and other records together to assess profitability of further land speculation, see Allan and Margaret Bogue, "'Profits' and the frontier land speculator," *JEH*, 17 (1957); Swierenga, "Land speculator 'profits' reconsidered."
[64] Publ. 1985, available Reed Library, SUNY-Fredonia, NY 14063. See also Robert W. Bingham (ed.), *Holland Land Company Papers* . . . (Buffalo Hist. Soc. Publics., 32–3, 1937, 1941). Cf. William Wyckoff, "Land subdivisions on the Holland Purchase in Western New York State, 1797–1820," *Jnl. Hist. Geography*, 12 (1986); William Wyckoff, *The Developer's Frontier* (1988) (q.v., p. 231, for depositories in the U.S. containing material).

were numerous in Iowa, Minnesota, and contiguous states westwards.[65]

Many railroads played an important role in promoting land settlement.[66] They were in some respects land companies, concerned with selling the land at their disposal to settlers both for immediate profit and for their own long-term prosperity. Indeed Paul Gates has said of the Illinois Central Railroad that at first it "was primarily a land company and secondarily a railroad company." Railroad and canal companies maintained land and agricultural agents in the field as well as emigration officers in the Eastern states and even abroad.[67] Large companies variously possessed land, agricultural, and colonization departments, with land offices. They maintained continuous contact with the departments of federal, state, and city governments, and particularly with the General Land Office and the state land offices. They advertised land for sale, arranged for potential purchasers to visit the area, and so on. The companies were also engaged in the transportation of farm products, cattle, and lumber, so that their other records, if in existence, can be used to study general output and marketing.

All this activity produced masses of published and unpublished material relevant to the study of local and regional settlement and land development, and incidentally these data often shed light on many aspects of social life in the new farming communities which emerged as a result of it.

It would, however, be difficult to generalize about what sort of records may have survived, since this varies from company to company. Those surviving the nineteenth century are most likely to be deposited in university, historical society, or public libraries or archive depositories. The published annual reports of the company will usually embrace reports of the company's land commissioner or secretary, and

[65] Swierenga, *Pioneers and Profits*, 15; Allan G. Bogue, "The Iowa claim clubs," *MVHR*, 45 (1958). See, e.g., Benjamin F. Shambaugh (ed.), *Constitution and Records of the Claim Association of Johnson County, Iowa* (1984).

[66] Paul W. Gates, *The Illinois Central Railroad and its Colonization Work* (1934); Richard C. Overton, *Burlington West* (1941).

[67] Cf. James B. Hedges, "The colonisation work of the Northern Pacific Railroad," *MVHR*, 13 (1926); John D. Unruh, Jr., "The Burlington and Missouri Railroad brings the Mennonites to Nebraska, 1873–1878," *Nebraska Hist.*, 45 (1964).

of the president and the treasurer. The Land Commissioner of the Illinois Central Railroad in such reports, for instance, provided each year much detailed information on the amount of land sold, its location, and its price, on the agricultural and business conditions of particular localities, the prospects for immigration, the methods of advertising, and a great deal of financial data.[68]

Unpublished railroad-company material likely to be of value if available includes the minutes of meetings of directors, correspondence of the president, correspondence between headquarters and branch offices, digests of law cases, and, perhaps, scrapbooks of newspaper clippings, photographs, and the like. Pamphlets and other advertising material produced by or for the company and its agents may exist. Again the private papers of important company officials or even of the local land agents and emigration officers may also possibly exist.

The most significant railroad- and canal-company records for the researcher into land settlement and early agriculture are likely to be those of company land departments. These, aside from correspondence (itself likely to be of great interest), should include ledgers and account books, providing information on the location of the land concerned, cancellations, and other data. And in the archives of the colonization bureau of the Chicago, Burlington, and Quincy Railroad, at Omaha, for instance, are extensive records of the various agricultural experiments sponsored by the company.[69]

If railroad- and canal-company records are not available, much about the disposal of their lands in the localities through which their permanent way passed can be culled from county and other records. If company records are available they can be linked to the related records of federal, state, and city administrations and to other sources discussed elsewhere in this and the previous chapter. Since railroad land policies and other activities were often the object of critical attention by political

[68] Gates, *Illinois Central*, 340 (details in bibl. indicate extent of evidence existing for some companies).
[69] Overton, *Burlington West*, 541.

groups representing farming interests, linkage with the records of such groups (see below) and with information in local newspapers may also be fruitful.

As well as the railroads, societies of an ethno-religious nature also promoted colonization and these may have left records. They tended to work in conjunction with the railroad companies and with state boards of immigration, so that the details of their efforts may also be tracked down in state and railroad records, as well as in the records of denominational groups.[70]

RECORDS RELATING TO FARMERS AND POLITICS

The records of orthodox political activity involving elections do not differ in rural areas from elsewhere and are dealt with in chapter 7. The way farmers voted at various federal and local elections may well be worth study and these records may, therefore, need to be used. Here, however, mention may be made of the sort of source material which pertains to those political movements from after the period of Reconstruction which were particularly associated with farming interests and communities. These include the Granger Movement, the National Farmers' Alliance, and the People's Party.[71]

Since these groups were active in seeking federal and state legislation and regulation, especially of the railroads, in the interests of farmers (especially small farmers), federal and particularly state documents, such as Senate, House, and Assembly journals, records of debates, reports of committees, and court records, reports of railroad, transportation, and agricultural boards and commissioners, and of attorneys general, as well as other departmental reports (like those of labor boards), laws, and official statistics, should all be searched. In

---

[70] See works cited Frederick C. Luebke, "Ethnic group settlement on the Great Plains," *Western Hist. Q.*, 8 (1977), 410–11.

[71] For Granger sources see bibls. in Solon J. Buck, *The Granger Movement* (1933); John D. Hicks, *Populist Revolt* (1931). See also Dennis S. Nordin, *A Preliminary List of References for the History of the Granger Movement* (1967); Henry C. Dethloff (comp.), *A List of References for the History of the Farmers' Alliance and the Populist Party* (1973); HG, 393–4.

those states where Populism was strong (especially Colorado, Kansas, Minnesota, Nebraska, and North Carolina) state documents are particularly important for that movement. The *Report of the Board of Railway Commissioners of the State of Nebraska, 1886* (1887) contains evidence of many typical complaints. North Carolina *Public Documents* for 1889 through 1893 have much on the political situation resulting from Alliance and Populist activities.

Bearing in mind likely partisanship and exaggeration, the daily and weekly press is, however, probably the most fruitful source for this sort of activity, and indeed for rural politics throughout the century. Local and out-of-state newspapers reported all significant developments, views and counter-views, and so on. Some newspapers and journals associated themselves particularly with or against certain of these movements, while some, like the *People's Party Paper* were directly sponsored.[72] The *National Economist* was the official journal in the South of the National Farmers' Alliance and Industrial Union, while in Virginia the weekly *Virginia Sun* was an Alliance and Populist journal carrying all important news of activity in the state, reporting meetings very fully. The Colored Farmers' National Alliance and other rival black farmers' associations published their own newspapers.[73] There was, too, a burst of contemporary monographs and magazine articles, as well as the sort of pamphlet literature associated with political activity.

Leading figures involved in these political activities have sometimes left personal papers and published memoirs or autobiographies. Biographical information on such people may be discovered in the usual sort of sources. If they were involved in elections for office, election results can be consulted.[74] The Donnelly papers at the Minnesota Historical Society constitute an extensive collection of Populist material,

[72] For relevant newspapers, see Buck, *Granger Movement*, 321–9; Hicks, *Populist Revolt*, 456–8.

[73] William F. Holmes, "The demise of the Colored Farmers' Alliance," *JSoH*, 41 (1975), refs.

[74] See pp. 329–32, and, for the use of election results and platforms in handbooks, Solon J. Buck, *The Agrarian Crusade* (1920).

and other collections useful for the study of Populism include
the Waller, Allen, and Maxwell papers.[75] The national organizations of these movements produced their proceedings and
other publications. The National Grange issued reports, too,
of national congresses, and reports of its officers. There may
also be published or manuscript proceedings, and minutes of
meetings of state and county organizations, correspondence,
and other unpublished local materials.[76]

Such sources should provide information on these movements in many parts of the country and may be combined with
other evidence. Those sources which provide biographical
information about members and leaders may, for example,
indicate their socio-economic characteristics. Records of votes
for the People's Party can be linked with census and directory
evidence to demonstrate the spatial, ethnic, wealth, and occupational bases of support.[77] Both the Farmers' Alliance and the
Granger Movement carried on educational and social activities
and cooperative ventures, and the same sources will throw
light on these activities. Agricultural education is covered in
chapter 10.

OTHER SOURCES

Commercially produced maps (see ch. 1) are another useful
source for settlement and land use, and many are located in
larger libraries. A particularly good collection of county land-
ownership maps is in the Library of Congress.[78] Maps in this
collection date mainly from 1840, with some earlier ones,
chiefly for Pennsylvania and Virginia. For the period 1840
through 1860 many counties in the New England states and
parts of Ohio are represented, as well as some counties in

[75] For details and locations, see Hicks, *Populist Revolt,* 447.
[76] See, e.g., James S. Ferguson, "The Grange and farmer education in Mississippi," *JSoH,* 8 (1942); Roy V. Scott, "Grangerism in Champaign County, Illinois, 1873–1877," *Mid-America,* 43 (1961). Cornell Univ. has a collection of National Grange material.
[77] Stanley B. Parsons, "Who were the Nebraska Populists?," *Nebraska Hist.,* 44 (1963), 93–5.
[78] Richard W. Stephenson, *Land Ownership Maps ... in the Library of Congress* (1967). Cf. Michael P. Conzen, "Landownership maps and county atlases," *AH,* 58 (1984).

Indiana, Illinois, Wisconsin, and Iowa. For the South there are
maps showing plantations in counties along the Mississippi
River. For the 1860s and 1870s New England is not well
represented, the maps in the collection being mainly of counties in Virginia, Pennsylvania, Texas, and the North Central
states, while for the last two decades of the century there is a
heavy concentration of maps of counties in Texas, with others
of widely dispersed counties (California and eastern South
Dakota being represented more than most). Maps for the
Western states, aside from Texas, are relatively few. Most of
the maps in the Congressional collection are commercial in
origin, but some are of official provenance. The non-commer-
cial maps derive mainly from the activities of the Confederate
Army Engineers and the Texas General Land Office. The
commercial publications were sometimes based on land-office
plats.

A great deal of useful evidence exists, too, in the records of
agricultural societies,[79] which flourished from about the
middle of the century. State, county, and other local agricultural societies produced pamphlets and essays on agricultural
matters, and their transactions were usually published in
agricultural periodicals or noted in reports published as state
documents. The *Transactions of the State Agricultural Society of
New York* for 1864, published as a state document, for instance, includes a map of grape lands in Urbana and Pulteney,
Steuben county, while the *Transactions of the Connecticut Agricultural Society* (1865) contains a detailed account of the
marketing in Boston, New York, and Baltimore of cheese
from Litchfield county. Indeed the local agricultural societies,
apart from providing much useful data, are themselves
worthy of study for their likely influence on local farming
activities and practice.[80] Sometimes unpublished records such
as minutes of meetings survive.[81] Such material may well

[79] HG, 393–4.
[80] Cf. Robert L. Jones, "A history of local agricultural societies in Ohio to 1865," *Ohio State Arch. and Hist. Q.*, 52 (1943); Rodney H. True, "The early development of agricultural societies," *AR Am. Hist. Assoc., 1920* (1925).
[81] Cf. R. H. True (ed.), "Minute book of the Agricultural Society of Albemarle," *AR Am. Hist. Assoc., 1918* (1921), vol. 1, 263–349.

identify the professionally active and wealthier farmers of the district,[82] and give some indication of their views, as well as throw light on the general interests, practices, and problems of local agriculture.

For historians interested in fruit-producing areas, the published transactions of the horticultural societies, which grew up distinctly from agricultural societies as fruit growing became increasingly differentiated from farming generally in the second decade of the century, may be important. They contain minutes of annual meetings of fruit growers, and "fruit lists," usually compiled at the level of counties, showing the varieties of different fruit grown. And, of course, there is an enormous quantity of contemporary work which lack of space prevents being described here.[83]

Newspapers provide a central source for agricultural history. Local newspapers in a rural area are likely to contain references to the ongoing scene – the state of the crops, the effect of the weather, market conditions, the activities of particular farmers, and current matters of interest or controversy, such as rail freight or the establishment of grain elevators, and information on prices. Many newspapers published weekly market reports summarizing the statistics of animals auctioned and their prices.[84]

As far as other items are concerned, there was usually a tendency in the local press to stress the unusual rather than normal activities. But published correspondence reflected public opinion on farming issues, and the advertisements of stock dealers and of farmers for labor and workers for jobs, are as important or perhaps more so than the news items. Additionally there will be announcements of county and other fairs, meetings of agricultural societies, and so on. Anniversary issues may well contain significant historical

[82] Cf. Brock, 204.
[83] See *AR U.S. Commissioner of Agriculture* (1868), HED (unnumbered) (40–3), ser. 1383, for a list.
[84] Cf. Arthur G. Peterson, *Historical Study of Prices Received by Producers of Farm Products in Virginia, 1801–1927* (1929); Daniel C. Smith and Anne E. Bridges, "The Brighton market: feeding nineteenth-century Boston," *AH*, 56 (1982).

information about the community and the agricultural development of the area. Biographical data on local farmers and speculators are commonly found in local newspapers and can be linked with evidence from directories, census material, county histories, and the like.

Editorials, news reports, and advertisements often contain a great deal on investment and speculation in land, and some idea of the extent of speculation can be deduced from this sort of evidence. Land companies indulged in much advertising in the press as well as through pamphlets and broadsheets. Southern antebellum newspapers contain advertisements for slaves and other evidence of local plantation conditions. Urban papers will often contain information useful to the agrarian historian, particularly on land sales, market conditions, prices and the like, and on general conditions in neighboring rural areas. And after the Civil War there was a black agricultural press.[85] The *Southern Workman* (1872–86), for example, carried a column devoted to agricultural advice to freedmen farmers.

National journals of a general kind, particularly those with an interest in economic affairs, are also important sources of local agricultural information – especially those of long standing like *Hunt's Merchants' Magazine and Commercial Review* (1849–70), *De Bow's Review* (from 1846) and *Niles' Weekly* (later *National*) *Register* (1811–49).[86] *De Bow's Review*, for example in the late 1850s published statistics of tobacco received at New Orleans from the interior.[87] The *Banker and Tradesman* (from 1873, title varies) contains information by counties and smaller areas in certain states on particular real-estate conveyances and mortgages. Other contemporary publications of factual data can also be valuable. The publications of Champonier and the Bouchereaus, for instance, contain the

[85] Allen W. Jones, "Voices for improving rural life," *AH*, 58 (1984).
[86] All in microfilm. See also Norval N. Luxon, *Niles' Weekly Register* (1947). For other agricultural serials in microform, see Hoornstra, 233.
[87] Gray, *History of Agriculture*, vol. 2, 1,037.

names, location, and production of Louisiana sugar plantations.[88]

In addition to these, periodicals and magazines devoted to agriculture were very numerous in the nineteenth century.[89] Apart from the *Agricultural Museum* (1810–12) and the *American Farmer* (1819–97) (both available in microfilm)[90] they are most common from the later 1820s. Something like a hundred started before the Civil War and though some were short lived others published many volumes. Some, like the *Farmer's Register* (1833–43), the *Southern Planter* (1841–), and the *Southern Cultivator* (1843–1935; all available in microfilm) were concerned mainly with Southern interests; others, like the *Cultivator* (1834–65; also in microfilm), were Northern journals, though often containing articles, travelers' accounts and correspondence concerning Southern agriculture and slavery. Some publications were more specifically regional, like the *New England Farmer* (1822–90), the *Maine Farmer* (1833–1924; title varies), the *Prairie Farmer* (1841– ; title varies), all three of which are available in microfilm, the *Minnesota Farmer and Gardener* (1860–2), the *Pennsylvania Farm Journal* (1851–7), and *Moore's Rural New Yorker* (1849–). There was a whole series of journals devoted to dairy farming,[91] but in general these journals spread their wings wide, covering all aspects of agriculture and of rural life. Much of the material they contain is very localized and many of the journals printed a great deal of correspondence. The *Cultivator* in 1850, for instance, carried a detailed description by a Massillon, OH, correspondent of the preparation of flax for paper mills by farmers in Summit county. The *Aratora*, a North

[88] P. A. Champonier, *Statement of the Sugar Crop in Louisiana* (1844 and later edns.); Louis and Alcée Bouchereau, *Statement of the Sugar and Rice Crops Made in Louisiana* (1868–9 and later edns.). See J. D. B. De Bow, *Industrial Resources of the Southern and Western States* (3 or 4 vols., 1852–3), for slavery.

[89] Albert L. Demaree, *The American Agricultural Press, 1819–1860* (1941); Gilbert M. Tucker, *American Agricultural Periodicals* (1909); Edwards, "Agricultural records," 12–13; Gates, *Farmer's Age*, 426–7; Bardolph, *Agricultural Literature*. See also Stephen C. Stuntz, *List of Agricultural Periodicals of the United States . . . 1810 to . . . 1910* (U.S. Dept. of Agric., 1941); Fred A. Shannon, *The Farmer's Last Frontier* (1961), 383–4; *HG*, 395.

[90] Claribell R. Barnett, "The *Agricultural Museum*," *AH*, 2 (1928); Harold T. Pinkett, "The *American Farmer*," *AH*, 24 (1950).

[91] John T. Schlebecker, "Dairy journalism," *AH*, 31 (1957).

Carolina farming journal, filled many of its columns with contributions from local working farmers and with replies to editorial inquiries.[92] The *Minnesota Farmer and Gardener* provides descriptions of agricultural conditions in parts of the state which were already well settled, and the editor recorded his observations on the farming of different areas as he made tours around the state along the lines of Arthur Young's agricultural tours in England.[93]

These journals give a good idea of how people perceived certain matters, such as the role of tenancy in agricultural development, the pressures being put on local farmers, what farmers were being advised to do, and what they read. News items provide information on the various steps by which virgin land was turned into productive farms, and information on the types of crops grown, changes in these, and similar data for livestock. The rise and decline of cooperatives may find mention, and there will be a great deal on prices and on the local marketing of farm produce.

Observations on local agricultural conditions by travelers and others in their published accounts can sometimes yield important evidence, though they naturally vary in accuracy a great deal and should be used with caution.[94] Examples of such descriptions giving agricultural information include James Flint's *Letters from America . . . on the Agriculture of the Western States . . .* (1822), Robert Barclay's *Agricultural Tour in the United States and Upper Canada* (1842), and Robert Russell's *North America, its Agriculture and Climate* (1857). *Thwaite's Early Western Travels, 1748–1846*, in thirty-two volumes, is a valuable source for travelers' first impressions of the daily workings of public-land disposal: surveys, purchases, grants, land companies, public sales, private claims – all receive attention and comment. Travelers in the Southern states from the

[92] Richard Bardolph, "A North Carolina farm journal in the middle fifties," *North Carolina Hist. Rev.*, 25 (1948), 65–6.
[93] Everitt E. Edwards, "Some sources for Northwestern history," *Minnesota Hist.*, 18 (1937), 408.
[94] Citations *HG*, 137–52; Prucha, 219–21; Gates, *Farmer's Age*, 428–30; Clarence H. Danhof, *Change in Agriculture* (1967), 301–4, and for contemporary manuals, etc., 304–7.

North and from Britain were often highly critical from a moral point of view of what they saw. Some accounts such as those of James Caird and Finlay Dun are particularly good.[95]

Emigrants' guides and gazetteers were designed to provide information for would-be farmers and are therefore useful to the historian, though naturally such literature was intended to entice, and conditions were portrayed optimistically. The same must be said of the broadsheets and other materials in addition to open advertisements produced by land companies, railroads, and others seeking to sell or lease land. Indeed speculators were responsible for a flood of pamphlets, booklets, travel books, and emigrant guides openly or otherwise advertising their projects. So long as it is realized or suspected that these accounts are really advertisements, such works can still be of use. And anyway this activity was all part of the history of emerging communities.

Finally it may be noted that foreign sources may be useful. British governments, for instance, took a keen interest in American agriculture and U.S. trade in agricultural products, and there are many British Parliamentary Papers (the equivalent of federal documents) devoted to these topics. There are, to cite but a few at random, reports on the prospects of farmers in California in 1897 and on the agriculture of Maine about the same year and a collection of correspondence of 1884 on the manufacture of butter and cheese in New York state.[96] British business firms, like the Prairie Cattle Company, Ltd., registered in Edinburgh, Scotland, also had interests in America, and evidence of their activities may be available in British sources,[97] some of which are on microfilm at the Bancroft Library, University of California, Berkeley.[98]

---

[95] James P. Caird, *Prairie Farming in America* (1859); Finlay Dun, *American Farming and Food* (1881); Raymond G. Taylor, "Some sources for Mississippi Valley agricultural history," *MVHR*, 7 (1920–1).

[96] BPP 1897 LXXXVIII; 1899 XCVII; 1884 LXXII. BPPs on America are repr. in Irish Universities Press, *Area Studies, United States of America* (60 vols., 1971): agricultural papers are in a single vol. but many vols. of commercial reps. may also be relevant.

[97] E.g., *Stock Exchange Yearbooks*, and company registration offices in London, Cardiff and Edinburgh. See p. 388.

[98] W. Turrentine Jackson, *The Enterprising Scot* (1968), 370–1.

INDIAN LANDS AND AGRICULTURE

The advance of settlement westwards involved white pressure on native Americans. It is not intended to deal here in any great detail with records relating to Indian settlements and land use either before the arrival of white settlers or on the reservations. The U.S. government inherited and continued British policy towards the Indians based on the principle that the Indians had a right to use and occupy their lands which could be extinguished only by consent. The tribesmen were, therefore, over the years, deprived of their lands, settled in reservations, given individual allotments, and so on, all within a framework of legality. This process resulted in a vast body of official records, published and unpublished, as well as much other contemporary evidence from a variety of sources. The history of the American Indian has, moreover, inspired a great library of secondary works.[99]

For those historians who wish to extend their interests in this direction certain works may, however, be referred to. For example, for laws, treaties, and land cessions, the works of Kappler and Royce will be of assistance.[100] Swanton provides a key to the different tribes in each state with an indication of where their land was, cessions made, and where they moved to, indicating often quite exact locations of villages in present-day counties.[101]

Many federal documents relate to Indians. Aside from Acts, ordinances, and proclamations, there are the reports of Congressional debates and many Congressional documents.[102] Central are the annual reports of the Commissioner of Indian

---

[99] See pp. 159–60.

[100] Charles J. Kappler, *Indian Affairs, Laws and Treaties* (5 vols., 1903–41); Charles C. Royce, *Indian Land Cessions in the United States* (digest covering 1784–1894, publ. in *18th Rep. U.S. Bureau of American Ethnology, 1896–7*, 1899). See also *Statutes at Large*, vol. 7 (treaties to 1850); John H. Martin (comp.), *List of Documents Concerning the Negotiation of Ratified Indian Treaties, 1801–1869* (SL 6, 1949), for records in NA, RG 75.

[101] John R. Swanton, *The Indian Tribes of North America* (1952, repr. 1968).

[102] See Steven L. Johnson, *Guide to American Indian Documents in the Congressional Serial Set, 1812–1899* (1977). N.B. *American State Papers: Indian Affairs* (see pp. 21–2).

Affairs,[103] published up to 1849 as part of the annual reports of the Secretary of War and thereafter in the annual reports of the Secretary of the Interior (and from 1833 also in departmental editions). These, which draw on information from agents and superintendents in the field, include details of pre-allotment Indian agriculture in the reservations and acreages under cultivation.[104] Details by states of supervised Indian land holdings, 1881–1933, are provided in the statistical supplement to the Commissioner's report for 1940.[105] The Department of Agriculture published in 1932–3 a useful volume of references to Indian agriculture.[106] Volume x of the 1880 federal census, devoted to American Indians, includes information on Indian lands and agriculture, with detailed maps of some reservations. The census of 1900 (vol. v) provides by states data on land values for Indian farms, and on agriculture in Indian reservations.

The greatest collection of unpublished material on Indians is in the National Archives and its branches. The records of the Indian and Swamp Land Division of the General Land Office (RG 49) are important for Indian land matters,[107] and should be used in conjunction with the records of the Bureau of Indian Affairs (RG 75) for which there are excellent guides.[108] Especially useful among the records in RG 75, because related to specific areas, is the correspondence between the Bureau

---

[103] Extracts are in Welcomb E. Washburn, *The American Indian and the United States* (4 vols., 1973; also includes treaties to 1868); index does not include all places mentioned. For exact refs. see Johnson, *Guide; Checklist*, 481–2.

[104] Data on selected reservations are repr. in Leonard Carlson, *Indians, Bureaucrats, and the Land* (1981), app. A. 6.

[105] Also in ibid., app. A. 1.

[106] *Agriculture of the American Indians: A Classified List of Annotated Historical References* ... (1932–3). These refs. are embraced in Everitt E. Edwards and Wayne D. Rasmussen (eds.), *A Bibliography on the Agriculture of American Indians* (1942). See also citations Prucha, 192–3 [AA68, 78]; R. Douglas Hurt, *Indian Agriculture in America* (1988).

[107] Oliver W. Holmes, "Indian-related records in the National Archives," in Jane F. Smith and Robert M. Kvasnicka (eds.), *Indian-White Relations* (1976), 21; and see above p. 174.

[108] Edward E. Hill (comp.), *Preliminary Inventory of the Records of the Bureau of Indian Affairs* (PI 163, 1965); Edward E. Hill (comp.), *Guide to the Records in the National Archives of the United States relating to American Indians* (1982); and see GNA, 377–89 and *passim*.

and the individual Indian superintendencies and agencies established to oversee Indians in their districts.[109] These, including detailed reports, are full of information. The National Archives has produced a valuable index to the geographical jurisdictions of the particular superintendencies and agencies, with historical sketches of each, and file references to letters received from them, 1824–80, together with a tribal index showing by which agency each tribe was covered.[110] Some agency and superintendency records are in the National Archives, Washington, DC; many are now deposited in regional branches of the National Archives. They include not only correspondence and reports, but some tract books and land plats. Many agency and superintendency records are available in microfilm.[111]

Also among the Bureau's records are many maps relating to Indian lands. The central map files (early 1800s to c.1938) include maps variously showing tribal lands and reservations, land bought from the Indians, townships and townsites on Indian lands, irrigated, cultivated, and uncultivated lands, grazing, mineral and timber lands, allotments to individuals, and rights of way of railroads, canals, and so on across Indian land. There are other maps, too, showing cultivated land, timber land, and irrigation facilities on Indian reserves. In the records of the Bureau's land division are not only maps from 1872, many of reserves, but also field notes and surveys of Indian lands and reservations (1832–1919), plat books, mainly connected with reservations, and most showing individual allotments (1858–1923), and records of allotments to tribes. There are records, too, relating to land sales and leases, including, for the period 1844 to 1922, appraisals – schedules of valuations of reserved lands, trust lands, and townsites. All the appraisals give the location of the land concerned, and indeed

[109] See *GNA*, 386–7; PI 163, vol. 2; Robert Svenningsen (comp.), *Preliminary Inventory of the Pueblo Records Created by Field Offices of the Bureau of Indian Affairs* (PI 192, 1980).
[110] Edward E. Hill, *Historical Sketches from . . . Letters Received by the Office of Indian Affairs, 1824–80* (1967). PI 163, vol. 2 lists the records of each superintendency and agency. Cf. Hill, *Guide*, 129–94.
[111] *GNA*, 386–7; *MRR*.

are arranged by reservation, tribe, or state. Some provide indications of land use. From the 1860s records relating to Indian trust lands in individual states include some tract books and evidence of use for agriculture.[112]

The Bureau's records, of course, also contain much information on conflicts between settlers, ranchers, and the Indians involving lands, boundaries, and depredations by Indian attackers. The Army had a great deal to do with the Indians on the frontier and in reservations. The published annual reports of the Secretary of War are thus worth consulting.[113] The unpublished records of the Military Archives Division of the National Archives also contain much on relations with the Indians.[114] The most important are those of the Adjutant General's Office (RG 94) (particularly incoming and outgoing correspondence, reports from military posts and regular army regiments,[115] and reservation files), and the records of Army Continental Commands (RG 393) which were organized geographically.[116] In these and other military records are details of wars, campaigns, expeditions, Indian tribes, removal of intruders from Indian lands, and illicit trading with the Indians. Also among the War Department's records is a mass of material relating to the removal of the Five Civilized Tribes.[117]

Finally, Indian depredation case records, which contain

[112] See PI 163, esp. 58–60, 98–100, 119–36; Laura E. Kelsay (comp.), *List of Cartographic Records of the Bureau of Indian Affairs* (1977 edn., repr. 1981); William J. Heynen, *Pre-1930 Agricultural and Related Maps in the National Archives* (1971), app. III; Carmelita S. Ryan, *Vital Statistics in the National Archives Relating to the American Indians* (RIP 61, 1973), 2n. For relevant cartographic records in other NA RGs, see Hill, *Guide*; Laura E. Kelsay (comp.), *Cartographic Records in the National Archives of the United States Relating to American Indians* (1974); GNA, 388–9.

[113] *Checklist*, 1,201–10. For the Civil War years see also War Dept., *The War of the Rebellion: A Compilation of the Official Records of the Union and Confederate Armies* (130 series, 70 vols., 1880–1910), available in NA microfilm.

[114] See Hill, *Guide*; GNA, passim; L. Marie Bouknight et al., *Guide to the Records of the Military Archives Division Pertaining to Indian–White Relations* (1972); Gaston Litton, "The resources of the National Archives for the study of the American Indian," *Ethnohistory*, 2 (1955), 199–200.

[115] Most are on microfilm: *MRR*; Bouknight, *Guide*, app. I.

[116] Bouknight, *Guide*, 66–83 lists the records of each district.

[117] See, e.g., Grant Foreman, *Indian Removal* (1932), esp. 399–404. And see *Indian Removals* (5 vols., 1834), SD 512 (23–1), ser. 243.

much on relations with Indian tribes in various places, are among the records of the U.S. Court of Claims (RG 123), and the records of the Soil Conservation Service (RG 114) contain evidence on agriculture in Indian lands.[118]

[118] Gaiselle Kerner (comp.), *Records of the U.S. Court of Claims, 1783–1947* (PI 158, 1953), 21–2, 30–1; *GNA*, 90–2; Heynen, *Pre-1930 Agricultural . . . Maps*, 14.

CHAPTER 6

Religion

Although religion may not have played a central part in national history during the nineteenth century, its impact on everyday life was considerable. Churchgoing, proselytizing, the Bible and its teachings, activities deriving from church societies and the like, all loomed large in the lives of many Americans. The extent of all this activity is demonstrated in the mass of published and unpublished material relating to religious matters that has survived in libraries, record offices, and elsewhere.

There are many aspects of local religious history to which community historians may with profit turn their attention. At the most local level they may wish to investigate the history of an individual church, congregation, or parish,[1] and this need not be a mere antiquarian exercise. Such a study could well embrace an account of the foundation of a church or the establishment of a parish, presbytery, and so on. It could include such topics as the size of the congregation and its social and ethnic composition, and the administrative and organizational structure of the local unit and its relationship with superior echelons of the denomination to which it belonged, or perhaps with a supervising missionary society. Examination could be undertaken of who the leading lay members and lay preachers were, their occupations, political outlook, racial attributes, and so forth; on how the church financed its buildings and activities and paid its minister or priest; what church societies, charities, schools, and so on existed and the part they played in the local community; relationships with the congregations of other denominations within the locality; and the

---

[1] See L. C. Rudolph, "Writing a history of your church," *JPH*, 53 (1975); Peter Guilday, "The writing of parish histories," *ER*, 93 (1935).

biographical details of the clergy who served the church, their theological, moral, and social outlook, their preaching style, their relationship with their flock, their general influence in the community, and the extent of their success or failure. The significance of individual ministers, preachers, and missionaries in frontier and backwoods areas and in large cities may well be worth studying in depth, and not only for the purely religious history of a community. In the South the part played by black and white ministers in abolition campaigns might be investigated. Again, the styles of worship within congregations, as demonstrated by the kinds of services and sermons they enjoyed and the number and length of services on Sundays and at other times, are worth considering, as is the existence or otherwise of Sunday schools and attitudes to children in the church.

None of these aspects of religious life is likely to have remained static through succeeding decades and it is an important task for the community historian to tackle the movie as well as the snapshot. The nature and reasons for change need investigation. Periods of disagreement within the congregation or between pastor and laymen may require explanation, and reasons may be found to be internal or part of wider disputes within denominations or churches in an area. The same topics could, of course, be investigated for all churches in a town, county, or region. Here the general collective influence of clergy, churches, and their members on the life-style of the community and of the family, the part played in "social gospel" work – charitable and philanthropic – and in education (see ch. 10) might be pursued.

Again, the history of a particular missionary society or denomination in a city, county, or wider area, or ecclesiastical unit like a diocese, might be studied. The growth of regional administrative structures and the relationship with other societies and denominations, and changes over time, may be considered. Often denominations collaborated or at least lived in peace; sometimes they were locked in struggle (as were the Baptists and Presbyterians in the 1830s). The activities in the South of Northern denominational churches during

Reconstruction may have been significant in some places. In certain areas or cities it may be interesting to investigate attitudes towards the influx of Catholics,[2] or Jews, or the establishment of churches by controversial sects, like the Mormons, or of Utopian communities, or the difficulties that arose when the same denomination catered for different ethnic groups, as, for example, Irish and German Catholics.[3]

Indeed the relationship between ethnicity and religion, particularly in places where there were high proportions of immigrants, is a topic with many facets. What churches did European immigrants join when faced by the absence of the denominations they favored in their parent country? How far were ethnically orientated churches more than mere religious institutions in the part they played in the lives of their congregations? To what extent was adherence a matter of ethnicity rather than of theological conviction? The part played in the social orientation of immigrants and of urban blacks and their settlement may in some areas be an important topic. So, too, may the social and economic functions of black churches in the South.

For some places and for some periods there may be evidence for investigating the influence and significance of camp meetings, revivalism, evangelicalism, and the impact of such controversial matters as evolution and the textual criticism of the Bible on the churches in a locality and their congregations. Disputes over the morality of slavery and segregation, and over the place of the black, free or bond, in the churches of the South, are special issues for historians of that region.[4] An

[2] E.g., Arthur M. Schlesinger, "A critical period in American religion, 1875–1900," *Procs. Massachusetts Hist. Soc.*, 64 (1932), 545–6. For sources for the American Protective Assoc., see Donald L. Kinzer, *An Episode in Anti-Catholicism* (1964), 323–34.

[3] Jay P. Dolan, *The Immigrant Church* (1975); Henry B. Leonard, "Ethnic conflict and episcopal power," *CHR*, 62 (1976).

[4] E.g., Donald G. Mathews, *Religion in the Old South* (1977); Albert J. Raboteau, *Slave Religion* (1978); H. Shelton Smith, *In His Image But...* (1972); Richard R. Miller, *Slavery and Catholicism* (1957); *HG*, 835; Erskine Clark, "An experiment in paternalism," *JPH*, 53 (1975); Daniel W. Harrison, "Southern Protestantism and the negro," *North Carolina Hist. Rev.*, 41 (1975); Irving S. Kull, "Presbyterian attitudes towards slavery," *CH*, 7 (1938); Kenneth K. Bailey, "Protestantism and Afro-Americans in the old South," *JSoH*, 41 (1975). And see Burr, 683–93.

important topic, too, is the effect of the Civil War and Reconstruction both on Northern and on Southern churches and on religious practices and organization in the South. The emergence of black churches and the distinctiveness of black Christianity is a topic of wide interest,[5] to which community history should be able to contribute significantly. The work of missionary societies also needs to be taken into account in the South, as it does on the moving frontier and in rural areas generally among white settlers and among Indians,[6] and in the poorer areas of towns. Though briefly noted here, these are large and significant areas for research.

In the populous cities and the frontier regions the difficulty of maintaining churches among continually changing populations is another theme for investigation. And in manufacturing areas it will often be fruitful to consider the reaction of the churches to the social conditions created by industrialization and urbanization – especially in direct social action, or indirectly in support of city missions and charitable and philanthropic organizations. Church attitudes to drunkenness,[7] prostitution, child labor, sweat-shop labor, and racial discrimination, and the impact which these attitudes had on the community, is another large area for research.[8] In the large towns, particularly, the attitude of the churches to social reform movements, organized labor, socialism, and so forth, may be of interest.[9] Again, it may sometimes be worth considering how far the motives for the foundation of churches and the promotion of religious activity, as well as for church social work in communities, particularly industrial communities, may be explicable in terms of social control rather than

[5] Robert T. Handy, "Negro Christianity and American church historiography," in Jerald C. Brauer (ed.), *Reinterpretations in American Church History* (1968). See also *HG*, 481; bibl. in Edwin S. Gaustad, *Historical Atlas of Religion in America* (1976), 158.
[6] Henry W. Bowden, *American Indians and Christian Missions* (1981), bibl., 234–44.
[7] Mark E. Lender, *Dictionary of American Temperance Biography* (1984).
[8] E.g., Paul R. Lucas, "The church and the city," *Minnesota Hist.*, 44 (1974).
[9] See works cited in Charles H. Hopkins, *The Rise of the Social Gospel in American Protestantism, 1868–1915* (1940); Aaron I. Abell, *The Urban Impact on Protestantism, 1865–1900* (1943); Gregory H. Singleton, *Religion in the City of Angels* (1979).

religion.[10] Another possible topic lies in the investigation of the possibility of the emergence of a social hierarchy of churches of the same denomination in a single city, differentiated by the social background of members in various residential areas.[11]

Statistical data can be linked with other evidence to demonstrate the relative strength (measured by numbers of members and churches) of different denominations in an area, and their geographical or spatial distribution. Such analyses would seem essential for any historian treating religion generally at the local level. The part played by individual clergymen and their followers in organized political movements, like Grangerism and Populism, and in the larger political parties, is also a theme worth studying, as well as the possible link between the religious preferences of local populations and the incidence of particular political outlooks.

The relationship of religious affiliation to other personal and group characteristics in communities and localities is a topic that lends itself to the techniques of quantification and statistical analysis.[12] Sources discussed below make it possible, in some circumstances, to group individuals according to religious preference and to demonstrate the extent to which that preference appears to relate to voting habits in political elections,[13] to the wealth or occupations of the persons considered, and to their ethnic background, geographical concentration, and so on. The relationship of membership of a particular denomination or congregation to leadership in business, local government, and in politics, and to social mobility can also be tested.[14]

[10] E.g., Jonathan Prude, *The Coming of Industrial Order* (1983), 125; Ralph E. Luker, "Religion and social control in the nineteenth-century American city," *JUH*, 2 (1976).
[11] See, e.g., Michael S. Franch, "The Congregational community in the changing city, 1840–70," *Maryland Hist. Mag.*, 71 (1976).
[12] E.g., Kevin J. Christiano, *Religious Diversity and Social Change* (1987).
[13] Lee Benson, *The Concept of Jacksonian Democracy* (1961), 192.
[14] E.g., Stephan Thernstrom, "Religion and occupational mobility in Boston, 1880–1963," in William Aydelotte *et al.* (eds.), *The Dimensions of Quantitative Research in History* (1972); Kathleen S. Kutolowski, "Identifying the religious affiliations of nineteenth-century local elites," *HMN*, 9 (1975).

In such studies some historians, faced with a multiplicity of denominations, especially in populous cities, have found it useful not only to distinguish groups of Protestants and Catholics, but to categorize populations according to their theological outlooks – as, for example, into evangelical, and non-evangelical Protestants and Catholics, or into the liturgical and the pietistic.[15] Such work opens up areas of great potential interest, though it would be unfortunate if all local studies of religion ranged themselves around such matters alone. Finally, it may be that some historians will be interested in studying the history of church architecture and buildings in a city or larger area.

While accepting the likelihood of regional variations in religious history and the possibility of local diversity, the community historian coming fresh to the topic of religion should be aware of the general structure of national development as perceived by historians of religion. Certain recent interpretations in particular should be of interest,[16] while general historiographical surveys and debates can also assist him by providing a general framework so that he can judge how far his own researches can support generalized theories of development and change in American religious life.[17]

All in all there is no lack of topics to interest the historian of religion at the community and regional levels, and it may well

---

[15] Stephan Thernstrom and Richard Sennett (eds.), *Nineteenth-Century Cities* (1969).

[16] See *HG*, 512–21; and, e.g., Robert T. Handy, *A Christian America* (1971); Sydney E. Ahlstrom, *A Religious History of the American People* (1972), and works cited p. 1,105; Edwin S. Gaustad, *Dissent in American Religion* (1973).

[17] See Edwin S. Gaustad, *American Religious History* (1966), and works cited pp. 8–13; Sydney E. Mead, "Prof. Sweet's religion and culture in America," *CH*, 22 (1953); Sydney E. Mead, "Denominationalism," *CH*, 23 (1954); Elwyn A. Smith, "The forming of a modern American denomination," *CH*, 31 (1962); Ernest R. Sandeen, "The lively experiment," *Jnl. of Religion*, 44 (1964); Henry F. May, "The recovery of American religious history," *AHR*, 70 (1964–5); Paul A. Carter, "Recent historiography of the Protestant churches in America," *CH*, 37 (1968); Sydney E. Ahlstrom, "The moral and theological revolution of the 1960's and its implications for American religious history," in Herbert J. Bass (ed.), *The State of American History* (1970); Sydney E. Ahlstrom, "The problem of religion in America," *CH*, 39 (1970); Martin E. Marty, "Religious behavior," *Social Research*, 41 (1974); Glenn R. Bucher, "Options for American religious history," *Theology Today*, 33 (1976); Nathan O. Hatch, "The Christian movement and a demand for a theology of the people," *JAH*, 67 (1980).

be that the multiplication of detailed and well-based local studies in this field will contribute significantly to current debate on the part played by religion generally in the history of nineteenth-century America, as well as to the histories of different denominations. Thus Cyrus Adler's view that "we shall never be able to write a history of the Jews in America until the history of each community has been separately examined,"[18] could be echoed for other religious groups.

Local research may, of course, reveal that, as in some other aspects of life, regional differences were too great to be forced by historians into a single mold. Certainly local studies of religion will throw light not only on religious matters, but also on other aspects of local life, as, for example, migration patterns, social conditions, political behavior, and ethnic history.

GENERAL SOURCES, SECONDARY AND PRIMARY

Secondary material on religious history is extensive, though if used judiciously it need not overwhelm, and it is essential for the community historian to have a sound general background. Gaustad's historical atlas of religion (cited above) provides not only cartographic and tabular data on the various denominations over a long period but also a convenient summary of the general history of the different denominations. Older works of the same kind contain many statistics and other details at state and local level about the activities, institutions, publications, and membership of different denominations and congregations.[19] Certain guides to the nature and beliefs of the various denominations, with brief histories of their development, are also useful.[20]

---

[18] Quot. Isodore S. Meyer, "The American Jewish Historical Society," *Jnl. Jewish Bibliography*, 4 (1943), 22.

[19] E.g., Joseph Belcher, *The Religious Denominations of the United States* (Philadelphia, 1855), based on almanacs, etc.

[20] See citations Prucha, 198–9, 204–5; Lee Rosten, *A Guide to the Religions of America* (1955); Benson Y. Landis, *Religion in the United States* (1965); E. T. Clark, *The Small Sects of America* (1936, 1949); Julian Pettee, *List of Churches* (1948); Samuel S. Hill (ed.), *Encyclopedia of Religion in the South* (1984).

The secondary literature, of course, contains much that pertains to the religious history of particular regions, states, and localities, and to specific aspects of religious history. The researcher will need to know what work has been undertaken before. There is no lack of bibliographical assistance, both for books and articles.[21] For more recent work such journals as *Church History* can be consulted, along with periodicals connected with individual denominations or geographical areas.[22] When denominations or congregations in an area were especially connected with certain ethnic groups, bibliographies relating to the history of such groups may well be useful.[23]

For most denominations there are both recent and older general histories, which often contain references to particular places and communities as well as providing necessary background information. Most will contain bibliographical references, and specialized bibliographies of the history of individual denominations also exist.[24] William W. Sweet's *Religion on the American Frontier* publishes many original source materials.[25] There are also books and articles on the history of individual denominations in particular states or regions, of which older ones may be regarded as primary

---

[21] *HG*, section 24; Burr; Nelson R. Burr, *Religion in American Life* (1971); Peter G. Mode, *Source Book and Bibliographical Guide for American Church History* (1912, repr. 1964); American Theological Library Assoc., *Religion Index One: Periodicals* (1949/52–), *Religion Index Two: Multi-Author Works* (1976–); Robert deV. Brunkow (ed.), *Religion and Society in North America: A Bibliography* (1983); Charles H. Lilly, *Bibliography of Religion in the South* (1984); Ernest R. Sandeen and Frederick Hale, *American Religion and Philosophy: A Guide to Informational Sources* (1978); *Catholic Periodicals Index* (later *Catholic Periodicals and Literature Index*) (1930–); Dewey D. Wallace, Jr., "Recent publications on American religious history," in Kellogg and Walker. And see bibls. in Gaustad, *Historical Atlas*; Ahlstrom, *Religious History*; sources cited n. 17 above; and articles in *Library Trends*, 9, 2 (1960). For dissertations, see Burr, 13–14; and above p. 18.

[22] E.g., L. C. Rudolph and Judith E. Endelman, *Religion in Indiana: A Guide to Historical Resources* (1986).

[23] E.g., Silvano M. Tomasi and Edward E. Stabili (comps.), *Italian Americans and Religion: An Annotated Bibliography* (1978). And see ch. 3.

[24] See citations Prucha, 199–202.

[25] Vols. 1, *Baptists* (1926); 2, *Presbyterians* (1936); 3, *Congregationalists* (1939); 4, *Methodists* (1946). All repr. 1964.

sources.[26] The publications of denominational historical societies, like the *Historical Magazine of the Protestant Episcopal Church* and the *Catholic Historical Review*, may be mentioned. Some denominational journals relating to particular states have from time to time existed – like the *Illinois Catholic Historical Review* (1918–29).

Information on church buildings will be found in many of the sources described below. In addition, there are collections of photographs, pictures, and measured drawings of many churches in the Library of Congress and in many other repositories. The Historic American Buildings Survey and the *National Register of Historic Places* deserve special note (see ch. 1).[27] For Congregational churches the records of the Congregational Church Building Society (1833–1928) at the Chicago Theology Seminary may be worth searching.

The geographical distribution of church buildings may be recorded in maps and plans (ch. 1) and in local directories. Thus a *Business Advertiser and General Directory of the City of Chicago for the Year 1845–6* produces detailed prints of church buildings in that city. The destruction of churches in the South during the Civil War may be studied in the records of the particular denominations, and especially in reports of special investigations, like that on South Carolina by the Protestant Episcopal Church.[28]

Church and parish histories, published and unpublished, are legion, and though many are superficial and hagiographical, some are sound and all may contain evidence not available elsewhere. Older histories of the activities of individual denominational associations, or other bodies, in particular states

---

[26] E.g., James Leaton, *History of Methodism in Illinois, from 1793 to 1832* (1883); W. T. Stott, *Indiana Baptist History, 1798–1908* (1908); D. Burt, "Congregationalism in Minnesota," *Congregational Q.*, 2 (1860); Robert Davidson, *History of the Presbyterian Church in . . . Kentucky* (1847). Charles C. Goss, *Statistical History of American Methodism* (1866) and Herbert C. Weber, *Presbyterian Statistics . . . 1826–1926* (1927) have useful data.

[27] And see Nelson R. Burr, "Sources for the study of American church history in the Library of Congress," *CH*, 22 (1953), 236, q.v. for other refs. to sources for church architecture, incl. Detroit Photographic Co.'s collection.

[28] Cited Daniel W. Harrison, "The effects of the Civil War on Southern protestantism," *Maryland Hist. Mag.*, 69 (1975).

or regions, may likewise contain much data on individual places and churches. These are to be found not only in local libraries, but among collections of denominational and church archives. Catholic diocesan records frequently have collections of parish histories.[29] Older state, town, and county histories, too, usually contain information on the progress of religion in their areas, recording the foundation of churches and the names of those involved. They often give data on the size of congregations, and information about church organization, ministers, buildings, societies, activities, and so forth. Indian tribal histories sometimes contain references to missionary activity.[30]

For many parts of the country, descriptions of the state of religion are to be found in the published accounts of travelers from overseas or from other parts of America.[31] These are usually subjective but nevertheless may provide useful evidence. Some, like James Dixon's *Personal Narrative of a Tour Through a Part of the United States and Canada with Notice of Methodism in America* (1849), were especially interested in religious matters. Travelers in the South often remarked on church practices with reference to slaves and other black Americans.

Indeed travel literature, reminiscences of everyday life, preachers' diaries or journals, and autobiographies and memoirs of active laity, form an enormous body of potentially valuable material. They are especially significant sources for frontier areas, but are also important for the religious history of many parts of the country. For the South, slave and ex-slave narratives and autobiographies, some of which are published,[32] may contain intimate details of the religious life of unfree blacks, and information on plantation missions.[33]

[29] See, e.g., James M. O'Toole, *Guide to the Archives of the Archdiocese of Boston* (1982), 51.
[30] For tribal histories, see Robert F. Berkhofer, *Salvation and the Savage* (1965, repr. 1972), 179–80.
[31] See, e.g., Burr, 561–71; Joseph P. Ryan, "Travel literature as source material for American Catholic history," *Illinois Catholic Hist. Rev.*, 10 (1928), 2 pts.; and p. 34 above.
[32] See pp. 157–9.
[33] See Milton C. Sernett, *Black Religion and American Evangelicalism* (1975).

Family records, like diaries,[34] scrapbooks, letters, and photographs, and other miscellaneous items, may also throw light on the religious flavor of life in individual communities or areas.[35] Since the work of individual clergy, priests, ministers, pastors, rabbis, and so on, was so important in the history of individual congregations and communities, biographical data on these men may well be significant. Many biographies, memoirs, and autobiographies of ministers and preachers have appeared in print,[36] and those pertaining to local characters may well be in large libraries in the state, city, or region in which they were active. Older as well as more recent directories of clergy, denominational encyclopedias, and the like, as well as more general guides to biography may also be searched for biographical and other information.[37]

The unending activity of a multitude of denominations and sects and of auxiliary or related societies, in both religious and philanthropic fields, has produced a plethora of contemporary published material in the form of books, booklets, pamphlets,[38] broadsheets, reports, catalogs, anniversary programs, and so forth. It is, therefore, difficult to give very specific references here – but the subject catalogs of local libraries should be searched.

Sermons can in certain circumstances be of use for community history. If the content of collections of sermons known to have been delivered in a particular church are

---

[34] See, e.g., Edwin S. Gaustad (ed.), *A Documentary History of Religion in America* (1982–3), vol. 1, 397–400.

[35] Cf. Martin E. Marty, "Religious behavior," *Social Research*, 41 (1974), 245–6, 258.

[36] See Prucha, 203–4; Ahlstrom, *Religious History*, 1,126–8; Henry W. Bowden (ed.), *Dictionary of American Religious Biography* (1980); Davis Bitton, *Guide to Mormon Diaries and Autobiographies* (1977).

[37] E.g., William B. Sprague, *Annals of the American Pulpit; or Commemorative Notices of . . . American Clergymen . . .* (9 vols., 1857–69); E. C. Scott, *Ministerial Directory of the Presbyterian Church, U.S., 1861–1941* (1942); Henry A. White, *Southern Presbyterian Leaders* (1911); Alfred Levine, *Encyclopedia of the Presbyterian Church in the United States of America* (1884); William Cathcard, *The Baptist Encyclopedia* (2 vols., 1883); A. A. Benton, *The Church Cyclopedia* (1883); Matthew Simpson, *Cyclopedia of Methodism* (1880); *Catholic Encyclopedia* (15 vols., 1967); John T. Ellis and Robert Trisco, *A Guide to American Catholic History* (1982 edn.), 55–126; Peter Guilday, "Guide to the bibliographical sources of the American hierarchy," *CHR*, 5 (1919), 6 (1921) (names A–N); and see Burr, 44–6; and p. 18.

[38] See *Pamphlets in American History: A Bibliographic Guide to the Microform Collection* (Microforming Corp. of America, 1979–83), Group v.

analyzed, the moral and religious pressures (as, for example, on temperance, renewal of vows, duties of parents) can be hazarded with reference to a congregation whose membership is known. Some idea of the preaching style and the moral and theological outlooks of particular ministers can be ascertained. Collections of sermons, published and manuscript, exist in some denominational collections. The Library of Congress has a huge collection of sermons and theological pamphlets and many other libraries also have important collections.[39]

Denominational directories, variously called also handbooks, registers, almanacs, yearbooks, annuals, and the like, exist for many denominations.[40] Though not all were in fact published each year, they nevertheless exist in large numbers and are valuable both for details at a particular point in time and for comparison of the same matters over a period of years. They often contain data on the organizational and geographical structure of the denominations concerned, with lists of clergy and lay office holders, and details of individual churches. Some contain statistics of church membership.[41] In addition some contemporary religious handbooks or surveys exist which seek to cover all the main denominations at a particular time, and can provide useful statistical and general information. One of the more reliable of these is Joseph Belcher's *The Religious Denominations in the United States, their History, Doctrine, Government, and Statistics* (1855).[42] The works of Robert Baird in the 1840s and 1850s also provide statistical and other information, some of which is valuable for regional and local studies.[43] Municipal and other local directories generally listed churches and their ministers, sometimes with other data about them.

Religious and other newspapers and periodicals are a prime source for many aspects of religious history. The local press

---

[39] Burr, "Sources . . . in the Library of Congress"; Burr, 948–9.

[40] See Burr, 29–30. N.B. Joseph H. Meier, "The official Catholic Directory," *CHR*, 1 (1915): title varies; complete set at Catholic Univ. of America.

[41] Paul Goodman, "A guide to American church membership data before the Civil War," *HMN*, 10 (1977).

[42] For others, see Timothy L. Smith, *Revivalism and Social Reform in Mid-Nineteenth Century America* (1957), 240.

[43] See Gaustad, *Historical Atlas*, 173 for details of these and similar works.

will provide evidence of the existence of particular churches with information on ministers and leading laity, and religious controversies will be aired there.[44] Obituaries and reminiscences will provide retrospective evidence. Of course, the usual caveats about newspaper evidence apply, and indeed some newspapers had definite religious biases, particularly against Catholicism.[45] Northern newspapers were often strongly abolitionist and antagonistic to the ambivalence of Southern churches towards slavery.

Alongside the regular press, religious newspapers and periodicals[46] proliferated in the United States in the nineteenth century.[47] Some, like the *Chicago Pulpit* (1871–3), were non-denominational, but many, like the *Kansas Catholic* were attached to a particular denomination. Some had a wide circulation, but, even when published outside a particular area, may contain local information. The *Presbyterian* (from 1831, available in microfilm), for instance, published reports on far-flung Presbyterian congregations. Such periodicals also published extracts of proceedings of synods and presbyteries. Some were published in foreign languages.[48] Others with a broad base and geographical coverage were organs for particular points of view. Thus *Colored America* (1837–41) and the *Christian Recorder* (1852–62), journals useful for the history of

---

[44] For value for identification purposes, see Paul J. Kleppner, "Lincoln and the immigrant vote," *Mid-America*, 48 (1966), 183–5.
[45] E.g., Thomas M. Keefe, "The Catholic issue in the Chicago Tribune before the Civil War," *Mid-America*, 57 (1975).
[46] For data on these in the federal censuses, see pp. 290–1.
[47] For finding lists, see pp. 29–31. For indexes to some church newspapers, see Anita C. Milner, *Newspaper Indexes* (3 vols., 1977–82). For indexes and guides to periodicals, see Burr, 119–21; *Union List of Baptist Periodicals* (1960); Claude E. Spencer, *Periodicals of the Disciples of Christ and Other Related Groups* (1943); Eugene P. Willging and Herta Hatzfeld, *Catholic Serials of the Nineteenth Century in the United States* (17 vols., 1959–68, *Statistical Analysis*, 1 vol., 1968); Gerald Albough, "American Presbyterian periodicals and newspapers, 1752–1830," *JPH*, 41, 42 (1963, 1964); Robert Singerman, "The American Jewish press, 1823–1983," *American Jewish Hist.*, 73 (1984); Paul F. White, *Index to the "American Jewish Archives", Vols. 1–24* (1979). For periodicals in microform, see Hoornstra; American Jewish Periodical Center, Hebrew Union College, Cincinnati, *Jewish Newspapers and Periodicals on Microfilm* (1984).
[48] E.g., Eugene Willging and Herta Hatzfeld, "Nineteenth-century Polish Catholic periodical publications in the United States," *Polish American Studies*, 12 (1955), 13 (1956). And see p. 122.

black Christianity in the South, held an antagonistic attitude towards slavery. Many religious newspapers and periodicals circulated in specific localities or regions.[49] There were, for instance, over sixty Baptist newspapers and periodicals in the South Atlantic states in the period 1802–65.[50] *Der Lutheraner* was the organ of the Lutheran Missouri synod in the middle of the century, and there were specific Catholic diocesan and city newspapers. Missionary periodicals are noted below.

Some religious newspapers and periodicals provide more general information on certain communities than the strictly religious. Jewish publications, for example, represent Judaism as a religion but also provide much data on the broader interests and activities of Jewish communities. Again, most Catholic publications were connected with particular ethnic groups, so that "there was frequently cause to wonder whether a given publication was first Catholic, or first Irish, German, French, and so on."[51] The opinions expressed in denominational newspapers can, therefore, provide an insight into the views not only of certain churches on political, moral, and social matters, but into the general history of local ethnic groups, too.[52] In some places the existence of atheism, free-thinking, and elements hostile to religion can be demonstrated by the existence of anti-religious newspapers, like the *Western Examiner*, published in St. Louis, MO, 1834–5.[53]

Many of the more serious religious periodicals were concerned mainly with general theological and moral issues, matters of social concern, and book reviewing, and may thus contain little of direct use for the historian of a particular community. Denominational weekly newspapers are more likely to contain relevant articles, comments, letters of local

[49] See, e.g., Wesley Norton, *Religious Newspapers in the Old Northwest to 1861* (1977); Sweet, relevant sections; Francis J. Weber, *A Selected Bibliographical Guide to California Catholic Periodical Literature, 1844–1973* (1973); Willging and Hatzfeld, *Catholic Periodicals.*
[50] Martin E. Marty *et al.*, *The Religious Press in America* (1963, repr. 1972), 40; Henry Stroupe, *The Religious Press in the South Atlantic States, 1802–1865* (1956).
[51] Marty, *Religious Press*, 69.
[52] Cf. Jasper W. Cross, "The St Louis Catholic press and political issues, 1845–1861," *Records of the Am. Catholic Hist. Soc. of Philadelphia*, 80 (1969).
[53] Dale K. Doepke, "The Western Examiner," *Missouri Hist. Soc. Bull.*, 30 (1973).

interest, and reports of, for example, particular philanthropic ventures and accounts of revivals. Philanthropic activity, especially in the larger towns, may also be documented in specialist publications (see ch. 11).

TYPES OF DENOMINATIONAL RECORDS

The archives of most Protestant denominations in America usually embrace both the records of individual congregations or churches, and those of assemblies (variously named) of representatives of churches in a certain geographical area. Often there was a hierarchy of assemblies with a national or regional one at the top. Thus, for example, Presbyterians were organized in sessions (the individual congregations), presbyteries (consisting of session representatives for a large area), synods (often coinciding geographically with states), and a general assembly for a larger area (nation or region). Methodist congregations were arranged in circuits, district conferences, jurisdictional conferences, and general conferences. Lutheran congregations were loosely organized in synods, the Moravian churches in provinces, the Baptists in district associations, and so on.[54] The Protestant Episcopal Church and the Catholics had the traditional hierarchy of parishes, dioceses, and archdioceses. The national disputes which culminated in the Civil War resulted in some denominations, like the Baptists, being split, with separate organizations in the South. Such divisions persisted after the war, so that distinct collections of records for particular denominations multiplied.

The community historian will need to search both the records of the individual congregation and those of higher structures. The records of the meetings of congresses, conventions, conferences, councils, presbyteries, synods, assemblies, and associations at their various levels often consist mainly of minutes of proceedings or journals. For the more important bodies, and certainly for the central or national ones, these will often have been published. They tend to contain information

[54] For maps showing locations of Baptist assocs., Methodist circuits, and presbyteries in the West in 1800, see Gaustad, *Historical Atlas*, 55, 76, 89.

on current issues, debates, and decisions,[55] and may illuminate church strategy, the extent of lay or clerical control, and internal differences and dissensions – as, for example, over slavery and the segregation of black worshipers. Indeed, for the South there is much evidence on the black religious experience in such minutes – as, for instance, the status, rights, and representation of black members, congregations, and ministers. They can reveal such matters as whether black churches were regarded as a separate "branch" or "arm" of the denomination in particular areas.[56]

The part played in these assemblies by delegates or clergy from particular churches or localities, their attitudes, and the views they expressed as revealed in records of proceedings, can provide interesting evidence for community history. Such proceedings may also provide other information on individual churches or on the churches of an area. Thus removal of rural churches to neighboring towns as population patterns changed may be recorded.[57] Details of mission, revival, and camp meetings may be noted, as well as reports from itinerant preachers and evangelists on their work, reports on auxiliary church societies, on Sunday schools, on the fortunes of the denomination in particular places, and indeed on many other topics concerning individual churches and their members and relations with the larger organization.[58] The records of the Massachusetts General Congregational Association include, for example, reports from district associations on the state of religion in 1823–9, 1831, and 1862.[59]

From the early years of the nineteenth century statistical and other factual data on individual congregations are often found in the proceedings of assemblies and conferences and may

---

[55] See William W. Sweet, *Rise of Methodism in the West* (1920); William W. Sweet (ed.), *Circuit-Rider Days along the Ohio* (1923).

[56] Clifton H. Johnson, "Some archival sources on negro history in Tennessee," *Tennessee Hist. Q.*, 28–9 (1969), 402; Sweet, vol. 3, 216–17; and works cited nn. 4, 5 above.

[57] Cf. Glenn N. Sisk, "Churches in the Alabama black belt, 1875–1917," *CH*, 23 (1954), 162, 172.

[58] E.g., Sweet, vol. 3, ch. 6; vol. 4, ch. 12.

[59] William H. Allison, *Inventory of Unpublished Material for American Religious History in Protestant Church Archives and Other Repositories* (1910).

represent the only evidence on some congregations.[60] Sometimes they include tables listing individual churches, with dates of foundation, names of ministers, and numbers of attenders (sometimes distingushing males and females, adults and children, probationers and new members, communicants, and so forth), as well as numbers of baptisms, deaths, expulsions and leavers, and financial details. If there was a Sunday school, numbers of attenders, officers, teachers, books in the library, and other information may be given. Compendia of the details were also sometimes published in yearbooks and the like. Often such statistical evidence predates census information on numbers of churches and their accommodation, and so is valuable for assessing the strength of denominations in particular areas.[61]

Another topic on which information may be found in such records is the moral and social outlook of various denominations in an area, and even of individual congregations. Matters of church discipline are often documented and it may be seen whether, for example, the same standards and sanctions were applied to whites and blacks, free and slave. Evidence on disciplinary matters may also be found in the minutes of local associations and individual congregations.[62]

As well as general annual conferences there were also sometimes special conferences like the Baptist Convention for Missionary Purposes held in Philadelphia in 1814.[63] Again, where black sections had their own organizations, the records of these will shed light on black religious life.[64] There are also records of some organizations of black clergy.[65]

[60] Richard N. Côté, "South Carolina Methodist records," *South Carolina Hist. Mag.*, 85 (1984), 53.
[61] Goodman, "Guide to American church membership," 184–7 (and 188–90 for available membership data by denominations).
[62] See, e.g., Bailey, "Protestantism and Afro-Americans," 456–7. Sometimes case files of church trials exist: Robert H. Williams, "Methodist church trials in Illinois," *Methodist Hist.* (1962); Sweet, vol. 2, ch. 11. Cf. J. Glen Clayton, "South Carolina Baptist records," *South Carolina Hist. Mag.*, 85 (1984), 323.
[63] Sweet, vol. 1, 632.
[64] E.g., *Minutes Annual Conference African Methodist Episcopal Church for the Baltimore District*, many vols.
[65] E.g., *Minutes of the Third Presbyterian and Congregational Convention, Together with the Organization of Evangelical Assocs. of Clergymen of Color...* (1858).

The records of individual congregations are naturally most important for local studies. Many of these are likely to be available, some still with the church itself, others in repositories. They are multifarious in nature[66] but the main types may be noticed here. Records of church membership, like church rolls, class lists, registers of communicants, and so on, were in some cases compiled annually. Where they exist (and many are lost or destroyed) they provide evidence not only on the size of congregations, but (if used with other data on individuals, like census records, tax lists, directories) also on their social, ethnic, and perhaps political composition. Such evidence can also give insight into the influence of members of certain denominations or churches in local political or business activity, and shed light on the relationship between local religious characteristics and voting patterns and on the social and economic structure of particular church communities. In smaller places or areas of dispersed rural settlement, however, some worshipers may have attended a particular church because it was accessible rather than through convinced adherence to the denomination to which it belonged. Such a likelihood should be taken into account. So, too, should the possibility of changes of religious allegiance, which may have been quite frequent.[67] Evidence of switches of allegiance especially by groups rather than individuals may point to conflict within local congregations or denominations.

In the South, church rolls and church minutes may show whether or under what conditions free blacks and slaves were members of congregations: whether they were distinguished from whites in the rolls, whether they were regarded as full members, whether they worshiped in separate pews or buildings, whether they were admitted to the ministry or to other positions of prominence, and how often they attended. These records may indicate, too, what happened after emancipation – whether, for example, separate black churches were created. Where there were distinct black congregations these may have kept their own rolls and minutes.

[66] Cf. Anne A. Hage, *Church Records in Minnesota* (1983).
[67] Cf. Kutolowski, "Identifying the religious affiliations," q.v. for other caveats.

Other church records providing names of members include rate rolls, collection lists, subscription lists, and lists of the excommunicated. Most churches kept records of the arrival or removal of members and issued documents of introduction: variously called, for example, certificates of transfer (Friends), letters of transfer (Protestant Episcopal), letters of admission (Baptist), dismissions (Congregationalists), and certificates of membership (Mormons).[68]

Such transfer records as well as admission registers and the minutes or proceedings of church meetings (including vestries, sessions, and business committees), can, like conference registers, be used to identify trustees, officers, lay preachers, and committee members – that is the active leaders of congregations. Cemetery and burial records, church plaques, and so on, may do the same. Pew rental or sale records and charts can supplement membership rolls in giving a clue to the relative wealth, social standing, or aspirations of lay members.[69] Methodist circuit plans not only provide lists of local preachers, class leaders, and other officials, but record the places and buildings in which preaching took place and when services were held. The journals of circuit riders are, incidentally, also useful for insight into the state of affairs in frontier and other remote rural areas.[70]

As well as church and vestry minutes and the like, which should shed much light on the ongoing business and activities of the congregation or church,[71] there may also be records of reports to higher bodies and other correspondence, perhaps with associations, conferences, and so on. The records of the Second Baptist Church in Holyoke, MA, for instance, include copies of annual letters giving detailed accounts of the progress of religion in the local community.[72] Financial accounts,

[68] Val D. Greenwood, *The Researcher's Guide to American Genealogy* (1973), 358–9.
[69] Kutolowski, "Identifying the religious affiliations," 9, 12; P. Johnson, *A Shopkeeper's Millennium* (publ. Ph.D. diss., Univ. of California, Los Angeles, 1975), 259–62.
[70] See, e.g., Sweet, vol. 4, Jnl. of Benjamin Lakin.
[71] E.g., William E. Friff, "Minutes of the vestry, St. Bartholomew's parish, 1822–1840," *South Carolina Hist. and Genealogical Mag.*, 51 (1950); Sweet, vol. 1, ch. XI.; vol. 2, ch. IX.
[72] Constance M. Green, *Holyoke, Massachusetts* (1939), 394.

minutes of women's and youth groups, and legal papers, church bulletins, newsletters, programs of events, anniversary souvenirs, and so on, can in aggregate provide much important evidence.

The individual congregations of most denominations kept registers or other records of births, baptisms or christenings, marriages, and deaths or burials. These are sources important for demographic purposes and also for compiling social profiles of congregations:[73] size, age structure, and sometimes social or ethnic characteristics (deduced from the names of the subjects and of other identifiable persons mentioned – spouses, parents, witnesses). Names of officiating ministers may also appear. It should be remembered, however, that baptisms were not always of infants, and for Baptists never.[74]

Since such records are a prime source for genealogical research much effort has gone into recording their existence and making them available. The activities of the Church of Jesus Christ of Latter-day Saints (Mormons) in microfilming and indexing vital records (and other records giving names of individuals) should be noted. An extensive collection of microfilmed material is available freely for researchers visiting the Family History Library in Salt Lake City, and copies may be acquired through the branch libraries of the church.[75] For searching out individuals the Mormon "International Genealogical Index" is of great use.[76]

Roman Catholic and Quaker records are in some ways rather different from those of many other denominations. Catholic archives consist basically of archdiocesan (metropolitan) and diocesan records, parish records, and corporate and institutional records (like those of church societies and

[73] Thomas W. Kremm, "Measuring religious preferences in nineteenth-century urban areas," *HMN*, 8 (1975), 138, suggests a multiplier of 15 per baptism for total size of a congregation. See also Dolan, *Immigrant Church*, 73.

[74] Baptist records of birth are rare; deaths were recorded.

[75] For topographical spread of records filmed and other inf., see Larry R. Gerlach and Michael L. Nicholls, "The Mormon Genealogical Society and research opportunities in early American history," *William and Mary Q.*, 32 (1975).

[76] At Family History Library (see n. 113 below), church branch libraries, and some other large libraries.

religious orders).[77] Episcopal registers may include formal data on such matters as the dedication of churches and statistical summaries of diocesan activity. Diocesan journals are official diaries or chronicles of events in the diocese.[78] Diocesan council or consultors' minute books, dating from the later nineteenth century, contain information, for example, on the formation of new parishes, including ethnic parishes. There may also be deeds and deed registers, and so on.

There are likely also to be large collections of letters received from priests, petitions and protests of the laity, and copies of episcopal "out" letters and of general pastoral letters, as well as legal and financial records and data on baptisms and marriages and on individual churches. There will probably be many records relating to clergy and perhaps to some laymen, and observations on the local social and political scene as it affected Catholics.[79] There may be, too, annual spiritual and financial reports on individual parishes.[80] Some of these may not be in English and these and some others will often throw light on the general state of ethnic communities as well as on their relationship to the Catholic Church.[81] In addition there may be reports to European missionary societies by American bishops, seeking financial aid and providing general information on the state of affairs in their dioceses and particularly in large cities.[82] Records of charitable and philanthropic organizations connected with the church, and of its schools and orphanages,

[77] Thomas F. O'Connor, "Historical and archival activities of the Roman Catholic Church in the United States," *Bull.AASLH*, 1 (1946); Thomas F. O'Connor, "Catholic archives of the United States," *CHR*, 31 (1946); Ellis and Trisco, *Guide to American Catholic History*; Evangeline Thomas (ed.), *Women Religious History Sources: A Guide to Repositories in the United States* (1983) (covers also non-Catholic orders); M. A. Healey, "Archives of Roman Catholic orders and congregations of women," *AA*, 33 (1970).

[78] Cf. James M. O'Toole, *Guide to the Archives of the Archdiocese of Boston* (1982), 3–4.

[79] E.g., Patrick Cunningham, "Irish Catholics in a Yankee town," *Vermont Hist.*, 44 (1976).

[80] Willliam F. Louin, *Diocesan Archives* (1941); Frances J. Weber, "Chancery archives," *AA*, 28 (1965); O'Toole, *Guide*, 20–1; James O'Toole, "Catholic diocesan archives," *AA*, 43 (1980), 287–8.

[81] See, e.g., Silvano M. Tomasi, *Piety and Power* (1975), 11.

[82] Dolan, *Immigrant Church*, 173 (some microfilm copies are at Notre Dame Univ.).

are also likely to be found.[83] If such collections are at all full for
the period being studied there should be plenty of evidence to
provide the basis for diocesan histories, and to contribute
much to parish and church histories.

The archives of Catholic parishes embrace records concerning the foundation and history of individual churches, correspondence with bishops, and summaries of reports on the
spiritual state of the parish (the *status animarum*) and its general
condition. Catholic baptisms and marriages are recorded in
parish registers and records were also kept of first communion
and confirmation, and of deaths and burials.[84] Pulpit announce-
ment books report notices read out at services, including
banns, news of activities of parochial societies (among them
charitable societies), and information on schools and on a
multitude of topics likely to give an insight into the life of the
parish. Priests' diaries record the daily events in their lives, and
records of boards of lay trustees (usually persons of property
and social standing) will give an idea of the leading members
and families in the congregation and the part they played.

The provincial archives of the Catholic religious orders in
the United States may contain copies of sermons and contemporary "chronicles" of the history of individual parishes and
missions. These latter are often full of detailed information.
The Pauline mission chronicles, for example, contain dates of
duration of missions, statistics of attenders (distinguishing
males, females, and children), numbers of those taking temperance pledges, and so forth.[85] Useful for Redemptorist activities in parish missions or revival meetings are the published
annals of that order.[86] Some *Acta et Decreta* (acts and decrees) of
Catholic synods and councils (for example, *Acta et Decreta
Concilii Plenarii Baltimorensis*) have been published and provide

[83] James O'Toole, "Catholic church records," *New England Hist. and Genealogical
Register*, 132 (1978), 257. And see pp. 286–7, 509.
[84] James O'Toole, "The Roman Catholic family in North America," *Procs. World
Conference on Records, 1980*, vol. 3 (1980).
[85] Cf. Dolan, *Immigrant Church*, 174–5, q.v. for refs. relevant to many parts of the
country. See also Jay P. Dolan, *Catholic Revivalism* (1978). For histories of religious
communities, see Ellis and Trisco, *Guide to American Catholic History*, 127–47.
[86] J. Wuest, *Annales Congregationis SS Redemptoris Provinciae Americae* (5 vols.,
1888–99, 1914–24).

information on matters of current concern and on organizational plans.

Some foreign records may be useful for the study of Roman Catholicism in certain parts of the United States. Most important, both for the Hispanic Southwest and for communities containing Italian, Irish, and certain other ethnic immigrants, is the collection of letters and reports sent by the hierarchy, clergy, and laity in America to the Congregation de Propaganda Fide in Rome,[87] for which there is a published guide and a calendar.[88] Other collections in Rome include correspondence from Italian parishes in the United States as well as memoirs of Italian priests who served in America.[89]

Other foreign records containing material on Catholics in America include the archdiocesan archives of Westminster, Dublin, Havana, and Quebec, and materials in the national archive repositories of Mexico, Spain, Canada, and France, and in various colleges and universities in Canada.[90] The published reports of the Leopoldine Association (or Foundation) of Vienna, Austria, founded in 1829 to help the Catholic missions of North America, contain digests of correspondence between priests and prelates in the United States and the Association's headquarters in Vienna.[91] An analysis of bishops' reports in the first twelve volumes (1831–9) was published in 1933.[92] A financial account accompanies each report. The sixth report contains supplements which list Catholic and

---

[87] John B. McGloin, "The Roman Propaganda Fide archives," *CH*, 33 (1964); Francis J. Weber, "Roman archives of Propaganda Fide," *Records*, 76 (Am. Catholic Hist. Soc., 1965), 245–8.

[88] Carl R. Fish, *Guide to the Materials for American History in Roman and Other Italian Archives* (1911), 119–95: still useful but superseded by Anton Debevec (comp.), Finbar Kenneally (ed.), *United States Documents in the Propaganda Fide Archives: A Calendar* (1st ser., 7 vols., 1966–77, index vol., 1981; 2nd ser., 3 vols., 1980–3). Some microfilms of this material are at Notre Dame Univ.

[89] Tomasi, *Piety and Power*, 11. See also John W. Manigaulte, "Sources for American history in three Italian archives," *AA*, 27 (1964), 60–1.

[90] O'Connor, "Historical and archival activities," 301n.

[91] *Berichte der Leopoldinen-Stiftung im Kaisertume Osterreich* (Nos. 1–84, 1831–1913) (copies at Catholic Univ. of America; microfilm at Notre Dame Univ.).

[92] In Theodore Roemer, *The Leopoldine Foundation and the Church in the United States (1829–1839)* (1933). Synopsis of the first 31 reps. is in *CHR*, 1 (1915), 56–63, 175–91.

non-Catholic seminaries, colleges, and universities in the United States with dates of establishment and numbers of students. Non-Catholic religious societies are also listed with foundation dates, and there is a comprehensive survey of all Catholic dioceses in the United States for the year 1832. The Leopoldine Association also has a collection of unpublished letters and reports on German Catholic communities in the United States.[93]

Yet other foreign sources include a collection of some 2,300 letters in the archives of the Ludwig-Missionverein in Munich, Germany, written by bishops, priests, nuns, and laymen in the United States,[94] and diocesan reports and letters of missionaries in America to the Society for the Propagation of the Faith in Paris and Lyons, France.[95]

Quaker archives are usually well preserved. They reflect the organization of the Society of Friends by "meetings": preparation (preparative or particular), weekly, monthly, quarterly, yearly, and sometimes three yearly.[96] The monthly meeting[97] (separate ones for men and women) was the organization of the individual congregation and dealt with business presented by preparation and weekly meetings. Few records of preparation or weekly meetings survive and it is the records of the monthly meetings that are most valuable for community history. In them, the bulk of the business of local Friends is recorded: consideration of requests for membership, noting of birthright membership, detailing of removing members (sometimes in a removal certificate

[93] Dolan, *Immigrant Church*, 173. Microfilms and English translations are at Notre Dame Univ.
[94] See Dolan, *Immigrant Church*, 173 for these. Cf. Theodore Roemer, *The Ludwig-Missionverein and the Church in the United States (1838–1918)* (1933), which (p. 153) refers also to 300 such letters publ. Munich *Annalen*, 1848 to 1918, most of which have not survived in the original.
[95] Microfilms at Notre Dame Univ.
[96] Willard C. Heiss, "Guide to research in Quaker records in the midwest," *Indiana Hist. Bull.*, 39 (1962); Willard C. Heiss, "American Quaker records and family history," *Procs. World Conference on Records, 1980*, vol. 4 (1980); Greenwood, *Researcher's Guide*, 377–81.
[97] See, e.g., Willard Heiss (comp.), *Milford Monthly Meeting, Wayne County – Indiana: Indiana Quaker Records*, vol. 6 (1960).

book), records of complaints of undesirable behavior, and registers of disownment. In addition, appointments of elders and lists of marriages, births, and deaths were recorded.

The quarterly meeting records include summaries of the reports from the various monthly meetings and note of the resolution of problems or decisions to refer matters to the yearly meeting. Yearly meeting minutes may exist both in published and manuscript form. They may include reports from committees, as for example, on temperance, education, Indians, and so on (committees which may also have left other records), information on the deaths of prominent members, and statistics of membership of the various monthly meetings. In addition there may be records of meetings for Sufferings, a regular body functioning when the yearly meeting was not in existence. And there are often among Quaker records many journals, manuscript and printed, diaries, correspondence, account books, and the like.

A SURVEY OF DENOMINATIONAL COLLECTIONS

It has been said that denominational archival materials "are to be found in every section of the country, in every city and town, hamlet and open country where churches have been established,"[98] and that every denomination and almost every congregation has its own records. These are scattered in a multitude of places: in church buildings, banks, libraries,[99] record repositories, universities, museums, and state and other historical societies,[100] as well as in the homes of clergy and lay officers and of private individuals. Some of the collections of religious records may have calendars or catalogs,

[98] William W. Sweet, "Church archives in the United States," *CH*, 8 (1939), 44–5.
[99] See Dorothy Rodda, *Directory of Church Libraries* (1967); George M. Ruoss, *World Directory of Theological Libraries* (1968).
[100] Roscoe M. Pierson, "Denominational collections in theological, seminary and church historical libraries," *Library Trends*, 9 (1960–1), lists major denominational hist. socs. noting publ. and unpubl. archive collections. See also James V. Geisendorfer (comp.), *Religion in America: A Directory* (1983); Makower.

published or unpublished, or have been the subject of detailed articles.[101]

It is not practical to list here all the very many institutions holding records of potential interest to the historian. Attention may, however, be drawn to a number of surveys and guides to the more significant of such collections,[102] and some of the major repositories are noticed in the following pages – especially those holding materials significant for churches, in widely spread parts of the country. Indication of the whereabouts of specific collections, in the ensuing pages and in the guides cited, should, however, be checked by users of this book.[103] Religious records are more likely to have been moved about than is the case for many other kinds of records, and despite considerable effort to secure accuracy there is no guarantee that the information given below is up to date.

Special mention should be made of the WPA, HRS

---

101 E.g. Burr, "Sources for the study of American church history"; Joseph B. Turner, "A catalogue of manuscript records in ... the Presbyterian Historical Society," *JPH*, 8 (1915) (not confined to Presbyterian records); Clifton H. Jones, "Manuscript sources in religious history at the Historical Resource Center," *South Dakota Hist.*, 7 (1977); and refs. in following pp.

102 August Suelflow, *Preliminary Guide to Church Records Depositories* (1969): for all denominations. Allison, *Inventory* is still useful. These and the following have been drawn on in the ensuing pp. with only occasional further ref.: Sweet, "Church records" (revised in *Yearbook of American and Canadian Churches*, various edns.); Greenwood, *Researcher's Guide*, 390–9; William W. Sweet, "Church archives in the United States," *AA*, 14 (1951); Pierson, "Denominational collections"; Lawrence O. Burnette, *Beneath the Footnote* (1969), 77–103; *Source*, 137–48; E. Kay Kirkham, *A Survey of American Church Records ... before 1880–1890* (1978 edn.; useful for local collections); Mabel E. Deutrich, "American church archives," *AA*, 24 (1961); "Church archives and history" (series of articles on Mormon, Catholic and Presbyterian records), *Bull. AASLH*, 1, 10 (1946); Sweet; Binsfield, "Church archives." And see general guides to manuscript collections (pp. 35–6), esp. *Directory of Archive and Manuscript Repositories in the United States* (1988 edn.), and *NUCMC* (covers some but certainly not all religious collections). Recent inf. on collections, additions, locations, etc., may be noted in *CH*, *AA*, *Yearbook of American and Canadian Churches*. Edmund L. Binsfield, "Church archives in the United States and Canada," *AA*, 21 (1958) is a list of publ. refs., updated in Soc. American Archivists, *Religious Archives in the United States and Canada: A Bibliography* (1984).

103 See recent edns. of *American Library Directory*; *Directory of Special Libraries and Information Centers*; AASLH, *Directory of Historical Societies and Agencies in the United States and Canada*.

"Inventory of Church Records" (or "Archives"), published 1937–41. This provides many detailed lists of church records, by denominations, in various states, counties, and cities.[104] Many of the records listed by the Survey are, however, not now where they were when the inventories were compiled and not all are easy to trace. In the following descriptions of denominational records the WPA inventories are not in every case noted. Editions and calendars of religious records have sometimes been published by various bodies.[105]

Baptists The chief repositories for Baptist records are at Rochester, Louisville, and Nashville, but there are also official depositories for different states.[106] The various collections based at the American Baptist Historical Society, at Rochester,[107] are important particularly for the Northern Baptist Convention (now the American Baptist Convention). They include almost complete files of Baptist state convention reports, minutes of many associations, collections of the correspondence of clergy and laity, and church record books – as well as many files of religious periodicals.

At the Southern Baptist Theological Seminary, Louisville,[108] are the records of many individual Southern Baptist churches and the minutes of Southern associations.[109] Also useful for Southern Baptists is the growing collection of original and microfilmed local church records, correspondence, pastors' papers, and annual reports at the E. C. Dargan

---

[104] See p. 45 and guides cited there; John G. Barrow, *A Bibliography of Bibliographies in Religion* (1955), 185–98 (lists inventories by states); Binsfield, "Church archives" (lists them by denomination).

[105] E.g., the North Carolina Hist. Commission publ. the records of the Moravians in that state (11 vols., 1922–69).

[106] Listed F. Wilbur Helmbold, "Baptist records for genealogy and history," *National Genealogical Q.*, 61 (1973), 175–7.

[107] 1106 South Goodman St., Rochester, NY 14620; with Colgate Rochester/Bexley Hall Crozer Theological Seminaries, Ambrose Swasey Library, 1100 South Goodman St.

[108] 2825 Lexington Rd., Louisville, KY 40280–0294.

[109] See Sweet, vol. 1, bibl., ix, 629.

Library, Historical Commission of the Southern Baptist Convention, at Nashville.[110]

Other Baptist collections are largely connected with the area of the college repositories in which they are housed and tend to be strong on papers of clergy who taught at those institutions. They include Furman University (Greenville, SC 29613), Baylor University (Waco, TX 76798), Franklin College of Indiana (Franklin, IN 46131, for manuscript collections for Indiana), the University of Richmond (Richmond, VA 23173), Bethel College (Saint Paul, MN 55112, for the records of the Historical Committee of the Baptist General Conference), and Andover-Newton Theological School, Massachusetts[111] (which includes the papers of the Baptist historian, Isaac Backus).[112]

Church of Jesus Christ of Latter-day Saints Mormon church records are highly centralized in the Church Archives and, for family and vital records, in the Family History Library of the Church.[113] The church has an outstandingly full archive which includes regular reports from wards (individual congregations), stakes (groups of wards), and missions, as well as large collections of diaries, letters, manuscript histories, and published materials. There are well-preserved vital records, all of which are also on microfilm. The all-embracing nature of record-collecting by the Mormons makes their Salt Lake City repositories unique mines of information on the life and

[110] 127 9th Ave. North, Nashville, TN 37234. See most recent microfilm catalogs, and lists in *Baptist Hist. and Heritage*. See also Lynn E. May, Jr., "Baptist information retrieval system," ibid., 10 (1975); Bill Sumners, "Selected guide to archival and manuscript collections in the Dargon-Carver Library," ibid., 19 (1984); Johnson, "Some archival sources on negro history," 406–9; Clayton, "South Carolina Baptist records."

[111] 169 Herrick Rd., Newton Center, MA 02159.

[112] See Allison, *Inventory*, 34–56, for this collection (formerly at Boston). For other repositories, see *Source*, 141; Jones, "Manuscript sources."

[113] Church of Jesus Christ of Latter-day Saints, Historical Dept., Church Library Archives, 50 E North Temple St., Salt Lake City, UT 84150; Family History Library of the same church, 35 N West Temple St., Salt Lake City, UT 84150. See also Hyram L. Andrus and Richard E. Bennett, *Mormon Manuscripts to 1846: A Guide to the Holdings of the Harold B. Lee Library* [Brigham Young Univ.] (1977). And see Makower, 205. N.B., too, Susan L. Fales and Chad J. Flake, *Mormons and Mormonism in U.S. Government Documents: A Bibliography* (1989).

Religion

activities, secular and religious, of the communities within which church members lived, and in particular on their commercial activities. The Salt Lake City collections include also complete files of the main Utah local newspapers which naturally contain much on church affairs. A large collection of Mormon archival material is also at the New York Public Library,[114] and the Historical Records Survey volumes include an extensive listing of Mormon pioneer reminiscences.[115]

Congregationalists The American Congregational Association's collection at Boston consists mainly of missionary records (and since the church's activities were so bound up with missionary work, this is a prime source)[116] and of records of Congregationalism in New England. The New England records embrace minutes of the General Associations of Congregational Churches and state associations, records of individual churches, correspondence and sermons of leading ministers, collections of personal papers, and much pamphlet literature. The Chicago Theological Seminary[117] has records of the Congregational Church Building Society and of the Chicago Congregational Association, together with histories and records of various churches, private journals and diaries, and files of Congregational periodicals. Other collections of Congregational materials are at the Hartford Seminary Library,[118] Grinnell College,[119] Dartmouth College,[120] Oberlin College,[121] the Andover-Harvard Theological Library,[122]

---

[114] Fifth Ave. and 42nd St., New York, NY 10018.
[115] Virgil Peterson, "Behold there shall be a record kept among you," *Bull. AASLH*, 1 (1946); Church of Jesus Christ of Latter-day Saints, *LDS Records and Research Aids* (1978); *Source*, 142; Max J. Evans and Ronald G. Watt, "Sources for Western history of the Church of Jesus Christ of Latter-day Saints," *Western Hist. Q.*, 8 (1977). For the Reorganised Church of Jesus Christ of Latter-day Saints, write to History Commission of that church, Auditorium, River and Walnut, Independence, MO 64051.
[116] Congregational Christian Hist. Soc., 14 Beacon St., Boston, MA 02108.
[117] Chicago Theological Seminary, 1164 East 58th St., Chicago, IL 60637.
[118] 77 Sherman St., Hartford. IL 06105.
[119] Burling Library, PO Box 805, Grinnell, IA 50112–0811.
[120] Hanover, NH 03755.
[121] Oberlin, OH 44074
[122] 45 Francis Ave., Cambridge, MA 02138.

and at the Evangelical and Reformed Historical Society of the United Church of Christ.[123]

Disciples of Christ (Christian Church)   The policy of the Disciples of Christ is for archives to be kept by individual congregations, but collections of records do exist at their historical society,[124] at Transylvania University, Lexington, KY, at the Disciples Divinity House, Chicago,[125] and at Culver-Stockton College, Canton, MO 63435. Among these are records of individual churches which include correspondence, diaries, sermons, and ministers' papers.[126]

Jews   Jewish records are not only religious but embrace many aspects of the life of American Jewish families and communities.[127] The collections of the American Jewish Historical Society include books, periodicals, and manuscript records relating to Jewish congregations, communities, and organizations in America and elsewhere.[128] At the Hebrew Union College,[129] the American Jewish Archives consist largely of photographic and other copies of records, but also have some originals. This collection includes congregation (synagogue and temple) records embracing, for example, byelaws and constitutions, minute books, membership lists, records of births, marriages and deaths, records of fraternities, legal and financial papers, correspondence, trustees' minutes, cemetery records, and records of associated social organizations. There are also published and unpublished histories of congregations, and vast collections of papers relating to individuals including

---

[123] 555 West James St., Lancaster, PA 17603. For others, see *Source*, 147–8 (and 142 for the Evangelical Congregational Church); Jones, "Manuscript sources."

[124] 1101 19th Ave. South, Nashville, TN 37212.

[125] 1156 57th St., Chicago, IL 60637.

[126] See also addresses in *Source*, 142.

[127] Philip P. Mason, *Directory of Jewish Archival Institutions* (1975); Aryeh Segall (ed.), *Guide to Jewish Archives* (1981); ABC-Clio, *The Jewish Experience in America: A Historical Bibliography* (1983). For HRS vols. referring to Jewish records, see Binsfield, "Church archives."

[128] 2 Thornton Rd., Waltham, MA 02154. See Mason, *Directory*, 20–8; Segall, *Guide*, 39–40; Isadore S. Meyer, "The American Jewish Historical Society," *Jnl. Jewish Bibliography*, 4 (1943), and separately publ. 1943.

[129] 3101 Clifton Ave., Cincinnati, OH 45220–2489. For periodicals at this college, see p. 251n.

rabbis (such as diaries, lectures, sermons, biographies, and memoirs) as well as extensive files of periodicals. There are some guides.[130]

Other records of possible use to historians of particular localities are at the Spertus College of Judaica (Chicago records),[131] the Jewish Archives Center,[132] and in various state and other local Jewish historical society collections.[133] The Yivo Institute for Jewish research[134] possesses material for the study of Jewish life, but most of its collection pertains to Jews outside America.[135]

Lutherans The archives of the various Lutheran organizations of America, many of which have united over the years in successive mergers,[136] are not always easy to track down. They are distributed in a variety of depositories including individual synods and congregations.[137] Some collections may, however, be mentioned here. The records of the American (Danish) Evangelical Lutheran Church (AELC), the Finnish Evangelical Lutheran Church, and the United Lutheran Church in America (ULCA) – all of which merged as the Lutheran Church in America in 1962,[138] one of the bodies which in 1988 became the Evangelical Lutheran Church in

---

[130] Segall, *Guide*, 37–8; Jacob R. Marcus, "The American Jewish Archives," *AA*, 23 (1960); Selma Stern-Taeubler, "Survey of the Jewish Archives in America," *Archivum*, 4 (1954); Stanley F. Cheyet, *The American Jewish Archives* (1972); James W. Clasper and M. Carolyn Dellenbach, *Guide to the Holdings of the American Jewish Archives* (1979); Mason, *Directory*, 11–19; *Manuscript Catalog of the American Jewish Archives* (4 vols., G. K. Hall, 1971). Cf. sources used in articles in Jack Wertheimer (ed.), *The American Synagogue* (1987).

[131] 618 South Michigan Ave., Chicago, IL 60605; Segall, *Guide*, 44.

[132] Balch Institute Library, 18 South 7th St., Philadelphia, PA 19106.

[133] See Segall, *Guide*, 46–69.

[134] 1048 Fifth Ave., New York, NY 10028.

[135] Mason, *Directory*, 60–9.

[136] Julius Bodensieck (ed.), *Encyclopedia of the Lutheran Church* (3 vols., 1965). The Lutheran Church in America, the American Lutheran Church, and the Assoc. of Evangelical Lutheran Churches united to form in 1988 the Evangelical Lutheran Church in America.

[137] Helen M. Knubel (ed.), *An Introductory Guide to Lutheran Archives and Collections* (1981). See also Mabel Deutrich, "Archival development in the Lutheran churches in the United States," *AA*, 15 (1952); Alice M. Kendrick and Helen M. Knubel, *The Oral History Collection of the Archives of Cooperative Lutheranism* (1984). For up-to-date inf. on the archives of the churches named in the last note, see *1989 Yearbook of the Evangelical Lutheran Church in America*.

[138] *Source*, 143–4.

America – are in a number of depositories.[139] At Chicago are, among others, records of the AELC, ULCA, and the Augustana Synod.[140] At Augustana College are manuscript collections of various churches, clergy, and others, and a large number of congregational histories from 1850.[141] The Swenson Swedish Immigration Center at the college has microfilms of Swedish Lutheran congregational records.[142] The collection at the Wentz Memorial Library[143] includes records of the Pennsylvania, Allegheny, and Susquehanna synods and material on congregations in central Pennsylvania. It is particularly useful for German Lutheran congregations. The Krauth Memorial Library[144] contains collections useful for the history of Lutherans in eastern Pennsylvania and New England, New Jersey, and upstate New York. Records relating to the southern states are at Columbia and Salisbury,[145] and include manuscript records of congregations. Among other collections are those at Allentown (which embrace numbers of church histories),[146] at Greenville (for records of western Pennsylvania and West Virginia),[147] at New York (for the predecessors of the New York Synod)[148] and at St. Peter (for the former Augustana Synod, Minnesota and Red River Valley conferences, and Northwest Synod of the United Lutheran Church in America, including original congregational records).[149]

139 Guidance may be obtained from the Chief Archivist, Evangelical Lutheran Church in America, 8765 West Higgins Rd., Chicago, IL 60631–4198. I am grateful to Elisabeth Wittman, the present Chief Archivist, for much help in preparing this section.
140 Seek through address in last note.
141 Augustana College, Box 175, Rock Island, II 61201–2210.
142 And of Swedish Baptist, Methodist, and Evangelical Free Church congregations.
143 Lutheran Theological Seminary, 66 West Confederate Ave., Gettysburg, PA 17325.
144 Lutheran Theological Seminary, 7301 Germantown Ave., Philadelphia, PA 19119–1794.
145 Lutheran Theological Southern Seminary, 4201 North Main St., Columbia, SC 29203; North Carolina Synod Archives, 1988 Lutheran Synod Dr., Salisbury, NC 28144. See Richard N. Côté, "South Carolina religious records: other denominations," *South Carolina Hist. Mag.*, 86 (1985), 57–9.
146 Muhlenberg College, Allentown, PA 18104–5586. See Heinrich P. Kelz (comp.), *The Pennsylvania German Collection* (1969).
147 Thiel College, College Ave., Greenville, PA 16125–2183.
148 Metropolitan New York Synod, ELCA, 360 Park Ave. South, New York, NY 10010.
149 Gustavus Adolphus College, St. Peter, MN 56087.

Another group of Lutheran churches in America, of Scandinavian and German origin (namely the Evangelical Lutheran Church (Norwegian), the American Lutheran Church (German), and the United (Danish) Evangelical Lutheran Church), after successive mergers resolved into the American Lutheran Church in 1960, which itself was one of the bodies merging to form the Evangelical Lutheran Church in America in 1988. The records of the antecedent bodies of the American Lutheran Church are now at Chicago, St. Paul, Dubuque, and Northfield.[150] They include records of synods, conferences, and congregations, and private papers. The Concordia Historical Institute[151] contains the voluminous collection of printed and manuscript records of the Lutheran Church – Missouri Synod, including many nineteenth-century private papers.[152] The Institute publishes a journal and will give advice on the location of church records. The Wisconsin Lutheran Seminary Library archives at Mequon[153] include, from the middle of the century, district and synod reports and correspondence, which embrace information on individual congregations of the Wisconsin Evangelical Lutheran Synod and their members.[154]

Other depositories holding nineteenth-century Lutheran records include Duke University, NC. The Bentley Historical Library, University of Michigan, Ann Arbor, has microfilms of some Finnish-Lutheran congregational records, and other Finnish-Lutheran material includes the Suomi Synod records of the Finnish Evangelical Lutheran Church at Suomi College.[155] The annual *Lutheran Church Directory for the United States* is useful for determining to which synod a Lutheran church belonged.[156]

---

[150] Luther Northwestern Seminary, 2481 Como Ave. West, St. Paul, MN 55108; Wartburg Theological Seminary, 333 Wartburg Place, Dubuque, IA 52001; St. Olaf's College, Northfield, MN 55057. For Chicago seek through address in n. 139 above.

[151] 801 De Mun Ave., St. Louis, MO 63105–3199.

[152] See August R. Suelflow, *The Heart of Missouri* (1954).

[153] 6633 W. Wartburg Circle, 117N, Mequon, WI 53092.

[154] Information from Martin O. Wesherhaus, Archivist, Jan. 1985.

[155] Hancock, MI 49930: see Suelflow, *Preliminary Guide*, for details.

[156] Now publ. ELCA Publishing House, 4265, 5th St., Minneapolis, MN 55440.

Mennonites The archives of the Mennonite Church[157] are mainly at Goshen College, Goshen, IN 46526. They include papers of officers, committees, and organizations of the denomination and some archives of district conferences and individual congregations. There are smaller collections at various Mennonite colleges in the Midwest, as, for example, Bethel College,[158] Bluffton College, Bluffton, OH 45817, and Eastern Mennonite College.[159]

Methodists In the nineteenth century the Methodists were divided into a number of bodies, the chief being the Methodist Episcopal Church, the Methodist Episcopal Church South, and the Methodist Protestant Church. There is no single central archive for American Methodism and in the past the records, apart from those of general conferences, were laxly kept and many have been lost. Local church records are now often to be found in collections made by the Methodist historical societies, and in other centers.[160]

One of the most important depositories is the United Methodist Center.[161] Here the General Commission on Archives and History has one of the most extensive collections of annual conference minutes of the Methodist Episcopal Church and the Methodist Episcopal Church South, together with an enormous body of general published material relating to Methodism.[162] Other significant collections are at the Garrett-Evangelical Seabury Western Seminaries United Library[163]

157 N.B., Mennonite Brethren Publishing House, *The Mennonite Encyclopedia* (4 vols., 1955–9).
158 300 East 27th St., North Newton, KS 67117: Anabaptist-Mennonite records. See John F. Schmidt, "The story of a library," *Mennonite Life*, 9 (1954).
159 Harrisonburg, VA 22801–2462. N.B. also Center for Mennonite Brethren Studies, 4824 East Butler, Fresno, CA 93727; Center for Mennonite Brethren Studies, Tabor College, 400 South Jefferson, Hillsboro, KS 67063; locations, Makower, 323, 324.
160 For HRS vols., see Binsfield, "Church archives"; and see Sweet, vol. 4, 733–45.
161 Drew Univ., Madison, NJ 07940. Previously at Lake Junaluska, NC.
162 William E. Lind, "Methodist archives in the United States," *AA*, 24 (1961), 437–8 (drawn on in the following account); Goodman, "Guide to American church membership," 190.
163 2121 Sheridan, Evanston, IL 60201.

(which has important manuscript holdings and runs of Methodist periodicals), at the Library of the Southern New England Conference,[164] at Emory University, Atlanta, GA 30322 (which has long runs of minutes of particular and annual conferences and of journals of the two Methodist Episcopal churches), at Ohio Wesleyan University,[165] and at Duke University. The Duke University collection is especially valuable for records relating to North Carolina Methodism and to the Methodist Episcopal Church South generally. It includes annual conference journals and board reports, correspondence, diaries, circuit riders' journals, district conference records, and church histories.

Southern Methodist material is also to be found in collections at the Perkins School of Theology, Southern Methodist University, Dallas, TX 75275, at Wofford College, Spartanburg, SC 29302, and at the Methodist Publishing House, Nashville, TN. De Pauw University, Greencastle, IN 46135, has sets of minutes of the general conference of the Methodist Episcopal Church South and of the former Southern Conference, and much more Methodist material, with special reference to Indiana.[166] Collections relating to the Evangelical United Brethren Church (now merged with the United Methodist Church) are at the church's historical society in Dayton, OH.[167] Records of some of the individual Wesleyan Methodist and Pilgrim Holiness churches across the country are at the library of the Wesleyan Church (formed from these two denominations in 1968) in Indianapolis.[168]

Moravians　The Moravian Church has collections of material for its two provinces, Bethlehem, PA, and (for the southern region) Winston-Salem, NC, for each of which there are

[164] Boston Univ., MA 02215.
[165] 43 University Ave., Delaware, OH 43105.
[166] See also Edwin Schell, "Methodist records . . . in north Virginia," *AA*, 27 (1964); Côté, "South Carolina Methodist records."
[167] 1810 Harvard Building, Dayton, OH 45406. For other Methodist repositories, see *Source*, 144–5; Suelflow, *Preliminary Guide*, 85–107.
[168] Ex inf. Daniel L. Burnett, Director, Archives and Hist. Library, Wesleyan Church, 8050 Castleway Dr., Indianapolis, IN 46250–0434.

repositories.[169] The collections are very extensive and detailed. They include church diaries, daily diaries of congregations, personal diaries of ministers and laymen, some vital records, membership lists, financial accounts and minutes of church boards and of many church and provincial organizations. Among the archives are voluminous records of "town and country" congregations (in which Moravians lived among non-Moravians) as well as records of "exclusive congregations" in which only church members could own property or conduct business.[170] Much general social information of life in the communities is contained in these records, and there are also records relating to missionary activity including that among German settlers and Indians. Until 1850 Moravian records are in German, after that in English.

Presbyterians   There are numerous collections of Presbyterian records.[171] The Presbyterian Church has a central depository in the offices of its General Assembly in Philadelphia. There, in the holdings of the Presbyterian Historical Society,[172] are runs of the minutes of the General Assembly, and of the general assemblies of the Old and New schools (reflecting the split of 1839), and quantities of pamphlets and sermons, files of religious newspapers, large manuscript collections, and extensive collections of missionary records.[173] The Historical

[169] 41 Locust St., Bethlehem, PA 18018; Moravian College, Main and Elizabeth Ave., Bethlehem, PA 18108; Archives, Moravian Church in N. America, S. Province, 4 East Bank St., Winston-Salem, NC 27101-5307. See also Publics. NC Hist. Commission, *Records of the Moravians in North Carolina* (1922–54).

[170] Kenneth G. Hamilton, "The resources of the Moravian church archives," *Pennsylvania Hist.*, 27 (1960); Kenneth G. Hamilton, "The Moravian archives at Bethlehem, Pennsylvania," *AA*, 24 (1961); Paul A. W. Wallace, "The Moravian records," *Indiana Mag. Hist.*, 48 (1952); Robert B. Downs, *Resources of Southern Libraries* (1938), 53.

[171] Presbyterian Library Assoc., *Union Catalog of Presbyterian Manuscripts* (1964); Binsfield, "Church archives," 327–8, for HRS; Sweet, vol. 2, 888–9. For the various bodies, see Russell E. Hall, "American Presbyterian churches," *JPH*, 60 (1982).

[172] 425 Lombard St., Philadelphia, PA 19147.

[173] Charles A. Anderson, *Special Collections in the Presbyterian Historical Society* (1951); Edward B. Shaw, "Calendar of the Shane papers," *JPH*, 19 (1940); Gerald W. Gillette, "Piety, papers and print: the Presbyterian Historical Society," *Drexel Library Q.*, 6, 1 (1970).

Foundation of the Presbyterian and Reformed Churches, at Montreat,[174] has hundreds of volumes of published minutes and a substantial collection of records of individual churches, sessions, presbyteries, synods, and general assemblies for the various Southern Presbyterian and Reformed churches. There are also large collections of papers of ministers, missionaries and prominent laymen, pamphlets, church periodicals, and histories of individual churches. Records relating to the Associated Reformed Presbyterian Church are also at this repository.[175]

Regional depositories which have records including manuscript materials are at various Presbyterian seminaries and the like: San Francisco Theological Seminary (containing the official records of the church in that area and papers pertaining to ministers and missionaries),[176] Auburn Theological Seminary (for New York presbytery and synod records),[177] Jesuit-Krauss-McCormick Library,[178] the Reformed Presbyterian Theological Seminary (for the records of the United Presbyterian Church and its predecessors, the Associate and Associate-Reformed Presbyterians),[179] and Princeton Theological Seminary.[180] For the Southern body there are records at the Union Theological Seminary, Richmond, VA 23227, Louisville Presbyterian Theological Seminary,[181] and Mayville College.[182] In addition, Wisconsin State Historical Society[183] has

---

[174] Assembly Dr., Box 847, Montreat, NC 28757.
[175] Thomas H. Spence, Jr., "The Historical Foundation of the Presbyterian and Reformed churches," *Bull. AASLH*, 1, 10 (1946); Thomas H. Spence, Jr. (comp.), *Survey of Records and Minutes in the Historical Foundation of the Presbyterian and Reformed Churches* (1943); Thomas H. Spence, Jr., *Catalogues of the Presbyterian and Reformed Institutions* (1952); Thomas H. Spence, Jr., *The Historical Foundation and its Treasures* (1960); *A Great Collection of Presbyterian and Reformed Literature* (Hist. Foundation . . . 1944); Richard N. Côté, "South Carolina Presbyterian records," *South Carolina Hist. Mag.*, 85 (1984), 149–50.
[176] Write Graduate Theological Union Library, 2400 Ridge Rd., Berkeley, CA 94709.
[177] 3041 Broadway, New York, NY 10027.
[178] 1100 East 55th St., Chicago, IL 60615.
[179] 7418 Peru Ave., Pittsburgh, PA 15208–2594.
[180] Speer Library, Mercer St. and Library Pl., Princeton, NJ 08540.
[181] 1044 Alta Vista Rd., Louisville, KY 40205.
[182] Mayville, TN 37801.
[183] 816 State St., Madison, WI 53706.

material relating to Kentucky, and the University of Chicago holds a great deal (in the Durrett collection) on Presbyterians in the West, including journals, diaries, memoirs, and sermons.

Protestant Episcopal Church   Records of the Protestant Episcopal Church may be with individual churches or in the offices of individual dioceses, in bishops' residences, or in other libraries and depositories geographically relevant to particular dioceses.[184] Some, for example, are at Trinity College, [185] Maryland Historical Society,[186] Berkeley Divinity School,[187] Massachusetts Diocesan Library,[188] and Virginia Diocesan Library.[189] They are likely to contain, as do the Missouri diocesan records at St. Louis,[190] records of individual churches, convention journals, minutes of diocesan councils, bishops' papers, and records of philanthropic and social societies and agencies connected with the diocese.[191]

The main repository for the archives of the church, however, is the library of the Episcopal Theological Seminary of the Southwest.[192] Here is the collection of the church's historical society, which includes the archives of the General Convention of the Church,[193] state convention journals, and diocesan periodicals. Most important for community historians in many parts of the country is the extensive run of diocesan journals, full for most dioceses and complete for many. There is also a large number of parish histories from many parts of America, biographies of ministers and

---

[184] Suelflow, *Preliminary Guide*, 37–51; and for HRS vols., Binsfield, "Church archives," 329–31.

[185] 300 Summit St., Hartford, CT 06106.

[186] 201 West Monument St., Baltimore, MD 21201.

[187] 140 Prospect St., New Haven, CT 06511.

[188] 1 Joy St., Boston, MA 02108.

[189] 110 West Franklin St., Richmond, VA 23220.

[190] 1210 Locust St., St. Louis, MO 63103–2322.

[191] Charles F. Rehkopf, "The archives and historical collections of the diocese of Missouri," *Hist. Mag. Protestant Episcopal Church*, 51 (1982). Cf. Alan M. Schwarz, "Church archives of South Dakota," ibid.

[192] 606 Rathervue Pl., PO Box 2247, Austin, TX 78768.

[193] John M. Kinney, "Archives of the General Convention of the Episcopal Church," *AA*, 32 (1969).

important laymen, the correspondence, diaries, and sermons
of particular bishops, and a large collection of pamphlet
material.[194] Data on early nineteenth-century town-level
membership is very full.[195] Also in this collection are the
archives of the Domestic and Foreign Mission Society (from
the 1820s) which embrace correspondence and reports from
missionaries. There are, too, significant collections relating to
the church at the General Theological Library, New York
City,[196] and at the Sterling Memorial Library, Yale
University.

Roman Catholics   Some Catholic collections have been noted
in the previous section. In general, Catholic records in the
United States have not always been well preserved, and access
to those that exist is not always straightforward.[197] Many
records remain in the hands of individual parishes and inquiries should first be made there. Depositories, however, are
legion.[198] For records in individual states *Studies in American
Church History* [199] should be consulted. The main depositories
are largely organized by archdiocese and diocese.[200]

The most extensive collection is that of the archdiocese of
Baltimore,[201] which was the sole metropolitan see in the
United States until 1846, and which assumed jurisdiction over
Louisiana from the time of the Purchase.[202] At Notre Dame
University, Notre Dame, IN 46556, are the Catholic

[194] Dorman H. Winfrey, "Protestant Episcopal Church archives," *AA*, 24 (1961).
[195] Goodman, "Guide to American church membership," 188.
[196] 175 North Ave., New York, NY 10011.
[197] Henry J. Browne, "The American Catholic archives tradition," *AA*, 14 (1951).
[198] See Ellis and Trisco, *Guide to American Catholic History*, xi–xii; Suelflow, *Preliminary Guide*, 8–33.
[199] Catholic Univ. Press, many vols.
[200] Thomas McAvoy, "Catholic archives and manuscript collections," *AA*, 24
(1961); Francis J. Weber, "Printed guides to archival centers for American Catholic history," *AA*, 32 (1969); Thomas F. O'Connor, "Historical and archival
activities of the Roman Catholic Church in the United States," *Bull. AASLH*, 1
(1946) (and similar article in *CHR*, 31 (1946)). Paul P. Ciangetti, "A diocesan
chronology of the Catholic Church in the United States," *CHR*, 28 (1942), lists
ecclesiastical jurisdictions with refs. to official documents. Gaustad, *Historical
Atlas*, 103, maps diocesan boundaries in 1822.
[201] Catholic Center, 320 Cathedral St., Baltimore, MD 21201.
[202] John T. Ellis, "Guide to the Baltimore Cathedral archives," *CHR*, 32 (1946).

Archives of America, which consist of the extant records of the archdioceses of Detroit, Cincinnati, New Orleans, and Vincennes (of particular interest for Catholicism in the West), as well as certain personal papers of clergy and laymen. There are important though less extensive collections of the archdioceses of New York, Boston, Portland, San Francisco, and Santa Fé, mostly found in the respective metropolitan chanceries.[203] St. Louis University[204] has the records for the archdiocese of St. Louis[205] and the western Jesuit archives (some on microfilm), many of which pertain to missionary work in the Midwest and elsewhere.[206]

Records relating to Jesuit missionary[207] and educational activity are also to be found at Gonzaga University,[208] St. Mary's College,[209] Woodstock College,[210] Fordham University,[211] the Institute of Jesuit History, Loyola University (which has many photographs and microfilms),[212] and at Georgetown University.[213] Georgetown University also has other Catholic materials including the papers of J. G. Shea, the Catholic historian. There are also depositories for collections relating to the religious orders – Vincentian Fathers, Franciscans, and

203 Francis J. Weber, "Sources for Catholic history of California," *Southern California Q.*, 57 (1975); Francis J. Weber, *A Select Guide to California Catholic History* (1966), 157–62; Francis J. Weber, "The San Francisco Chancery archives," *The Americas*, 20 (1964); Francis J. Weber, "Printed guides," 355; Fray A Chanez (ed.), *Archives of the Archdiocese of Santa Fé, 1678–1900* (1957) (much on Franciscan missions). N.B. M. Claude Lane, *The Catholic Archives of Texas* (1961); Paul J. Foik, "Survey of source materials for the Catholic history of the Southwest," *CHR*, 15 (1929).
204 221 North Grand Boulevard, St. Louis, MO 63103.
205 Frederick G. Holweck, "The historical archives of the Archdiocese of St. Louis," *St. Louis Catholic Hist. Rev.*, 1 (1918).
206 John F. Bannon, "The Saint Louis University collection of Jesuitica Americana," *Hispanic American Hist. Rev.*, 37 (1957).
207 For other missionary papers, see Deutrich, "American church archives," 397; William N. Bischoff, "Tracing manuscript sources," *Bull. AASLH*, 2 (1950), 108–9. For missionary activity, see below.
208 E 502 Bone Ave., Spokane, WA 99258.
209 Kansas City, KS 66536.
210 Woodstock, MD 21163. The MD provincial archives at Woodstock are listed in Thomas Hughes, *The History of the Society of Jesus in North America*, vol. 1 (1908), 25–7, and see 1–31 for American Jesuit sources generally. Cf. the *Woodstock Letters* (1872–) which reprints records from this collection.
211 Leon Lowenstein Building, 60th St. and Columbus Ave., New York, NY 10023.
212 5430 University Ave., Chicago, IL 60615.
213 Joseph Mark Lauinger Library, Box 37445, Washington, DC 20013.

Religion

Dominicans.[214] Yet other collections of note are at St. Mary's Seminary and University,[215] St. Charles Borromeo Seminary (which has a great deal of published and unpublished material including personal papers),[216] and the Catholic University of America, Washington, DC (for papers of important Catholics).[217]

Salvation Army The main sources of the army's activities are the *War Cry* (1881–) and the *Conqueror* (1892–7).[218] Records of organizations, institutions, posts, corps, and citadels should be sought locally.[219] The army has a central depository.[220]

Shakers Records relating to the Shakers are in the Western Reserve Historical Society,[221] and the Ohio Archaeological and Historical Society.[222] Manuscript materials include covenants, laws, legal and land records, financial accounts, membership records, diaries and journals, testimonies and biographies, sermons, and collections of photographs.[223] Shaker items at the Library of Congress include official and personal diaries and papers relating to Shaker lands.[224]

Society of Friends Original Quaker manuscript records[225] may reside with the regular yearly meetings.[226] Philadelphia yearly

214 McAvoy, "Catholic archives," 413–14; O'Connor, "Historical and archival activities," 298–9. For female orders, see Thomas, *Women Religious History Sources*.
215 Roland Pk., Baltimore, MD 21210–1994.
216 Overbrook, Philadelphia, PA 19151–1518.
217 See Francis J. Weber, "The Catholic University of America archives," *Records*, 77 (Am. Catholic Hist. Soc., 1966), 50–9.
218 Herbert A. Wishey, Jr., *Soldiers without Swords* (1955), 229. For other publ. primary and secondary material, see Abell, *Urban Impact*, 263.
219 Those for MI and NJ are listed by HRS: Binsfield, "Church archives," 332.
220 Planned to move to Verona, NJ, in 1990.
221 10825 East Boulevard, Cleveland, OH 44106.
222 I–71 and 17th Ave., Columbus, OH 43211.
223 Kermit J. Pike, *A Guide to Shaker Manuscripts in the Library of the Western Reserve Historical Society* (1974; indexes items pertaining to particular communities).
224 Largely relating to CT, OH, KY, NY, NH, arranged by communities. N.B. also Shaker Community Inc., US Rt. 2D, Hancock, MA 01201, for publ. records; and Makower, index "Shakers."
225 For nature of Quaker records, see pp. 262–3, above.
226 Lyman W. Riley and Frederick B. Tolles (comps.), "A guide to the location of American Quaker meeting records," *Bull. Friends' Hist. Soc.*, 40 (1951). For HRS inventories, see Binsfield, "Church archives," 323.

meeting records[227] are divided and deposited at Haverford College and Swarthmore College.[228] These depositories hold other Quaker records, too, and there are important collections elsewhere. In particular in New York City are records for New York yearly meetings,[229] and for subordinate meetings scattered through northern New Jersey, all of New York state, west Connecticut, and Vermont. They include records of births, deaths, and marriages.[230] Among other collections are those at Guilford College,[231] and Rhode Island Historical Society,[232] and there are many more depositories, usually serving particular topographical areas.[233]

Unitarians and Universalists   Unitarian and Universalist repositories include the library of the Meadville Theological School, Lombard College,[234] the Rhode Island Historical Society,[235] and the Crane Theological School, Tufts University.[236] Particularly important are the collections at the Andover-Harvard Theological Library,[237] which include records of some individual Unitarian and Universalist churches, regional Universalist records, and those of the Unitarian Sunday School Society.[238] Much material is, however,

---

[227] See Friends Hist. Soc., *Inventory of Church Archives: Society of Friends in Pennsylvania* (1941), to be superseded by new guide, 1989. Many of these records are microfilmed. See also Thomas E. Drake, *The Quaker Collection at Haverford* (1956); *Guide to the Manuscript Collection of Friends' Historical Library of Swarthmore College* (1981).

[228] Haverford, PA 19041; Swarthmore, PA 19081.

[229] Quarterly Meeting House, 15 Rutherford Pl., New York, NY 10003.

[230] Richard S. Bowman, "Records of Quaker ancestry," *Connecticut Ancestry*, 14 (1971–2).

[231] Guilford College Library, 5800 Friendly Ave., Greensboro, NC 27410.

[232] 121 Hope St., Providence, RI 02906.

[233] Barbara Curtis, "Archival information: depositories of Quaker records in the Middle West," *Quaker Hist.*, 72 (1983); Heiss, "American Quaker records," 11–12.

[234] 5701 South Woodland Ave., Chicago, IL 60637.

[235] See n. 232 above.

[236] Medford, MA 02155.

[237] 45 Francis St., Cambridge, MA 02138.

[238] Alan Seaburg, "Some Unitarian manuscripts at Andover-Harvard," *Harvard Library Bull.*, 26 (1978); Alan Seaburg, "The Universalist collection at Andover-Harvard," *Harvard Library Bull.*, 28 (1980).

scattered in a large number of depositories, including state historical societies.

Others There are, of course, many other denominations, among them the Brethren of Christ Church, the Pentecostals, Reformed bodies, and various Adventist sects, which space does not allow to be treated here.[239]

SOURCES FOR MISSIONARY WORK

In addition to the records of the denominations and their churches there are also records relating to the missionary work undertaken by mission societies, some of which were connected with particular churches,[240] and, in the case of Catholics, by religious orders. This embraced proselytizing on the frontier and remote areas and in the poorer parts of populated cities, and was at times significant in the religious history of many localities. The societies and their local auxiliaries were concerned with the establishment of churches, the organization of worship, revivalist activity and conversion among white settlers and European immigrants, and the social and moral state of these people. They were also concerned with the spiritual and general condition of black slaves and freedmen, but much of the activity of many missionary societies was directed towards Indians.

The societies and the Catholic and other religious orders generated an enormous amount of source material both published and unpublished, and it is impossible to treat it comprehensively here.[241] Published histories of mission societies and their work, both those written in the nineteenth and early twentieth centuries by contemporaries or near-

---

[239] For the records of these, and others, see refs. cited above n. 102. Note also Côté, "South Carolina religious records: other denominations"; Jason Horn, "Seventh Day Adventist archives," *AA*, 17 (1954); Vern Carner *et al.*, "Bibliographical essay," in Edwin S. Gaustad (ed.), *The Rise of Adventism* (1974).

[240] Some have been touched on in the last section; and see Sweet.

[241] But see Thomas, *Women Religious History Sources*. For foreign Catholic missions to U.S., see also above.

contemporaries,[242] as well as more recent works,[243] may well contain data of interest to historians of particular areas as well as giving clues to the existence of other source material. Some of the older histories, like Isaac McCoy's *History of Baptist Indian Missions* . . . (1840), consist largely of the authors' experiences as missionaries. Large numbers of contemporary biographies, autobiographies, and reminiscences were published in the nineteenth century and are available for the researcher. Again, some historical societies have published materials emanating from missionaries,[244] and there is a plethora of secondary literature on particular areas, territories, states, and individual missions.[245]

Most of the missionary societies published annual reports and there may also be reports of bodies serving particular areas.[246] This type of record contains vast amounts of official data, like treasurers' reports, progress reports, correspondence, reports of meetings and speeches, lists of members, and so forth. Together with the mass of other reports, pamphlets, and divers other published material, these reports form a potentially important (if biased) body of sources for the historian of particular localities.

So, too, do magazines and newspapers issued by or in association with the societies or their parent denominations.

---

[242] E.g., John O. Charles and Thomas Smith, *The Origin and History of Missions* . . . (2 vols., 1837); William Gammell, *History of American Baptist Missions* . . . (1840 and later edns.); Ashbel Green, *Historical Sketch . . . of the . . . Missions of the Presbyterian Church of the United States* (1838); Nathan Bangs, *History of the Missions . . . of the Methodist Episcopal Church* (1832); Joseph Tracy, *History of American Missions to the Heathen* (1840) (available in microfiche).

[243] E.g., Robert G. Torbet, *Venture of Faith . . . 1814–1954* (1954) (Baptists); Julia C. Emory, *A Century of Endeavor, 1821–1921* (1921) (Protestant Episcopal); Sweet, *passim*; Wade C. Barclay, *History of Methodist Missions* (3 vols., 1949–57). Some inf. on work with Indians is in these, but for Indians see also, e.g., Berkhofer, *Salvation and the Savage*, esp. bibl.; James P. Ronda and James Axtell, *Indian Missions* (1978); Henry W. Bowden, *American Indians and Christian Missions* (1981), 234–44; *HG*, 467. See also C. O. Paullin, *Atlas of the Historical Geography of the United States* (1932). Ron Chepesiuk and Arnold Shankman, *American Indian Archival Material* (1982) lists unpubl. material for 11 states, incl. records of missionary work and Indian churches.

[244] E.g., Charles Anderson, "Frontier Mackinac Island, 1823–1834," *JPH*, 25 (1947).

[245] See, e.g., citations Berkhofer, *Salvation and the Savage*, 167–78.

[246] Cf. Nash K. Burger, "The Society for the Advancement of Christianity in Mississippi," *Hist. Mag. Protestant Episcopal Church*, 14 (1955).

Many of these contain local information including letters from missionaries in the field (though often abridged and edited) and other information, as, for instance, on schools. Such publications were legion, some short lived, many undergoing successive changes of name. They include, to cite a few from very many, the *Missionary Record . . . Of the Protestant Episcopal Church* (1833–5), the *American Missionary Register* (1820–5), the *Home Missionary Monthly* (1878–1909), the *Baptist Missionary Magazine* (title varies; 1817–1909), and the *Spirit of Missions* (from 1836).[247] Some like the *Massachusetts Missionary Magazine* (1803–8), served a particular state or locality, others were produced for Indian readers, sometimes with English summaries or translations. General denominational and religious periodicals are also likely to contain information on missionary activity: the Methodist Episcopal Church's *Christian Advocate* (title varies; from 1826, available in microfilm) is an example. Journals published by Northern missionary societies are important for the religious and general conditions of blacks in the South during Reconstruction. Examples are the *American Missionary* (1865–90) published by the American Missionary Association, the *American Freedman* (1866–9), the *Freedmen's Record* (1865–73) published by the New England Freedmen's Aid Society, and the *National Freedman* (1865–6).

Some of the depositories and collections of denominational archives detailed in the last section hold records relating to the activities of missionaries and mission societies and reference should be made to the information given there. Again, the minutes and proceedings of denominational congresses, conferences, councils, conventions, and the like contain information on mission work, as may much denominational literature, including periodicals.

For the chief missionary societies there are usually significant collections of published and unpublished records, and for certain periods of the religious history of many areas these

---

[247] For periodicals relating to missions on microfilm, see Hoornstra, 248. There is an index to *Spirit of Missions*, vols. 1–65, 1836–1900 (1902). See also Nash K. Burger, "An overlooked source for Mississippi local history: the Spirit of Missions, 1836–1954," *JMH*, 7 (1954).

may be important. Unpublished materials often consist of letters and reports, diaries, notes, photographs, and so forth, pertaining to missionaries and their work, to churches, congregations, Sunday schools, Bible societies, and the like. Such material is also to be found among collections of personal and family papers and among diocesan and other denominational collections. It is not possible here to detail the records of all the many denominational missionary societies (whose history is made more complicated by changes of name, often consequent on splits or amalgamations).[248] A few, however, may be mentioned.

The records of the American Home Missionary Society,[249] supported by the Congregationalists and Presbyterians and the Dutch Reformed and Associated Reformed churches, cover most of the century. They have been described as "an unequaled source of firsthand historical data,"[250] both on religious matters, including early congregations, and on general social conditions. They consist[251] of vast numbers of letters and of detailed and often frequent reports from missionaries in the field to the secretary of the society in New York, together with copies of letters from the officials to the missionaries.[252] The minutes of the executive committee have not, however, survived.

Congregational and Presbyterian mission work with the Indians was undertaken also under the auspices of the American Board of Commissioners for Foreign Missions, whose records[253] include a large collection of unpublished

---

[248] See Berkhofer, *Salvation and the Savage*, bibl.

[249] Previously United Domestic Mission Soc., later Congregational Home Missionary Soc.

[250] L. C. Rudolph, *Hoosier Zion* (1963), 195.

[251] Colin B. Goodykoontz, *Home Missions on the American Frontier* (1939), 429, q.v. for a survey of home missions and bibl. of other records and publ. works.

[252] At Chicago Theological Seminary, 5757 South University Ave., Chicago, IL 60637. Available in microfilm: David G. Horvath (ed.), *A Guide to the Microfilm Edition of the American Home Missionary Society* (1975). And see, e.g., Sweet, vol. 3, ch. 9.

[253] Mainly at Houghton Library, Harvard Univ., Cambridge, MA 02138. See Mary Walker, "The archives of the American Board," *Harvard Library Bull.*, 6 (1952); Berkhofer, *Salvation and the Savage*, 167–8, q.v. for records of the Western Missionary Soc.

correspondence with missionaries (available in microform), journals, diaries, and reports, and must be regarded as a prime source for religious endeavor among the Indians. With these records are those of the United Foreign Missionary Society which was absorbed in 1826. The published annual reports of the American Board should also be consulted.[254]

The records of the Society for Propagating the Gospel among the Indians and Others in North America, a Congregationalist society, are at the Massachusetts Historical Society.[255] Annual reports of the American Baptist Home Mission Society are available, among other places, at Rochester, NY.[256] Unpublished records of the Baptist Home Mission Society and the Baptist Board for Foreign Missions are useful for work among the emancipated slaves and the Indians.[257] A few records of the Home Mission Board of the Southern Baptist Convention exist, including lists of missionary appointments, 1857–83.[258] Much information is to be found, too, in the collected papers of individual missionaries.[259]

The archives of the American Missionary Association, a Northern abolitionist society founded in 1846 by Methodist and other Northern churches, contain a great deal of correspondence, reports, maps, pamphlets, and photographs to do with evangelical work.[260] Some of this collection relates to missions to the Indians, but most concerns the society's

---

[254] Publ. in *Missionary Herald* with "view of other Benevolent Institutions." For dates, titles, and microfilms of the *Missionary Herald*, see Hoornstra, 142.

[255] 1154 Boylston St., Boston, MA 02215-3695. See also *NUC*, vol. 554, 406–7 for publs. of and about this soc.

[256] Colgate-Rochester/Bexley Hall/Crozer Theological Seminaries, Ambrose Swasey Library, 1100 South Goodman St., Rochester, NY 14620.

[257] At American Baptist Archives Center, PO Box 851, Valley Forge, PA 19482–0851. Also available in microfilm at American Baptist Hist. Soc.

[258] At Southern Baptist Home Mission Board, 1350 Spring St. NW, Atlanta, GA 30367–5601.

[259] E.g., at Kansas State Hist. Soc., 120 West 10th St., Topeka, KS 66612. For details, see Berkhofer, *Salvation and the Savage*, 173–4.

[260] Amistad Research Center, Tulane Univ., New Orleans, LA. Some purchasable in microfilm: Amistad Research Center, *Author and Added Entry Catalog of the American Missionary Association Archives...* (3 vols., n.d.).

abolitionist activities and its educational work with Southern blacks during the Civil War and Reconstruction.[261]

Other missionary materials include collections of societies associated with the Old School Presbyterians,[262] and the Domestic and Foreign Missionary Society of the Protestant Episcopal Church. The latter's records include minutes, correspondence, and other materials.[263] The Methodists, too, have extensive collections,[264] and specialized collections are also, among other places, at the Union Theological Seminary[265] (which has records of early work among the Indians, records of conferences, and many periodicals and other publications), and the Moody Bible Institute, Chicago, IL 60610.

Information on early Catholic missions may be found in published records like *Annales de la Propagation de la Foi* (from 1822) and those reproduced by the American Catholic Historical Society and other historical societies.[266] Collections of archives of the Jesuits, who were active in missionary activities, have been detailed above. The California Mission Documents (1769–1853) and the Archive of the Apostolic College of Our Lady of Sorrows of Santa Barbara (1853–85) are at the Santa Barbara mission.[267] The records of the Bureau of Catholic Indian Missions, consisting of correspondence, scrapbooks, and photographs, are at Marquette University, Milwaukee.

Materials relating to the activities of the local mission societies serving the evangelical and social needs of the poor of the larger cities are likely to be found with the records of

---

261 Chepesiuk and Shankman, *American Indian Archival Material*, 69–70.

262 For details, see Berkhofer, *Salvation and the Savage*, 171–2; Charles A. Anderson, "Index of American Indian correspondence," *JPH*, 31 (1953). See also Sweet, vol. 2, ch. 13.

263 At address in n. 192 above, whence a list is available. Cf. Sam L. Botkin, "Indian missions of the Episcopal Church in Oklahoma," *Chronicles of Oklahoma*, 36 (1958).

264 Esp. at Drew Univ., Madison, NJ 07940. See Lind, "Methodist archives," 38–9.

265 Burke Library, Broadway at Reinhold Nieburh Pl., New York, NY 10027. See Frank W. Price, "Specialist research libraries in missions," *Library Trends*, 9 (1960).

266 E.g., Grace L. Nute, *Documents Relating to Northwest Missions, 1815–1827* (Minnesota Hist. Soc., 1942).

267 Maynard J. Geiger, *Calendar of Documents in the Santa Barbara Mission Archives* (1947). See also Francis J. Weber, *A Select Bibliography: The Californian Missions, 1765–1972* (1972); Weber, *Select Guide to California Catholic Literature*.

church congregations and in city libraries and other local depositories. Such societies often produced much pamphlet literature.

Bible and tract societies may be considered to have been missionary endeavors of a sort.[268] The library of the American Bible Society (founded 1816) contains correspondence and other records as well as much published material.[269] This society and other more localized Bible societies, like the Kentucky Auxiliary Bible Society and the Philadelphia Bible Society, published their own annual reports, as indeed did some county Bible societies.[270] In the same way there are published annual reports for the American Tract Society[271] and local tract societies, such as the New York City Tract Society. The activities of Bible and tract societies are noticed, too, in newspapers and religious journals, and in the reports of missionary societies and denominations.

Similar sorts of evidence are likely to exist for church and other temperance societies, Sunday school unions,[272] and the like. For example, the Episcopal Church Temperance Society and the Presbyterian Committee on Temperance have left annual reports and minutes. The American Sunday School Union and its state and city auxiliaries published annual reports. There are also unpublished records of local unions, like those of the Philadelphia City Sunday School Union, and of individual schools, some very detailed. The proselytizing activities of such organizations were part and parcel of the religious scene, and can hardly be ignored by those investigating the religious history of those local communities where they existed.

Especially for the early nineteenth century, the records of British religious societies working in North America may be

[268] J. Orin Oliphant, "The American missionary spirit, 1828–1835," *CH*, 7 (1938).
[269] 1865 Broadway, New York, NY 10027. Records are microfilmed.
[270] See John W. Kuykendall, *Southern Enterprise* (1982), 171–2.
[271] Records destroyed. But see *Publications of the American Tract Society* (12 vols., New York, n.d.) for copies of tracts.
[272] The American Sunday School Union's records are at Presbyterian Hist. Soc., 425 Lombard St., Philadelphia, PA 19147. They incl. records for Sunday schools all over the U.S. See Anne M. Boylan, *Sunday School* (1988), 213–15; Clifford S. Griffin, *Their Brothers' Keepers* (1960), 307–8.

of use.[273] Those of the London Missionary Society (material for the period 1799–1840),[274] the Catholic Colonial Missions (correspondence, 1803–27),[275] and the Wesleyan Methodist Missionary Society (minutes and correspondence, 1791–1868)[276] are available in microform.[277] The published annual reports of the last named of these societies are available in some American libraries.

The annual reports and other published and, where available, unpublished material relating to other religious, quasi-religious, and philanthropic societies may also throw light on general social, moral, and spiritual conditions in towns and other localities. Among such organizations may be local Y.M.C.A.s and Y.W.C.A.s.[278] The Chicago Y.W.C.A., for example, published its annual reports, while for the Chicago Y.M.C.A. there are also unpublished minutes for the nineteenth century. Indeed, for the larger cities, material of all sorts of locally active societies in direct or indirect association with the churches is likely to exist in libraries and elsewhere.

More particularly religious societies may include state, city, and other local religious and theological discussion and study groups, sacred musical societies, and so on. Many of these will have left some traces in published, and maybe unpublished, material to provide added evidence of the religious life and activity in a locality. Local records pertaining to such societies have in some cases been listed in WPA, Historical Records Survey inventories, sometimes with church records. State

---

273 Oliphant, "American missionary spirit," 128. For Catholic missions from continental Europe, see above pp. 261–2.

274 In Archives of the Council for World Missions, School of Oriental and African Studies, Univ. of London, London WC1E 7HP.

275 In Westminster Cathedral Archives, Westminster, London SW1.

276 In Archives of the Methodist Church, Overseas Division, at address in n.274 above.

277 Catholic Colonial Mission: Microform Academic Publishers, East Ardsley, W. Yorks, England. Others: Inter Documentation Co. A.G., Postrasse 14, 6300 Zug, Switzerland.

278 Charles H. Hopkins, History of the Y.M.C.A. in North America (1951), note on sources; Burr, 577–8. And see p. 131. YMCA of the USA Archives, Univ. of Minnesota Library, 2642 University Ave., St. Paul, MN 55114 has many publics. and some records.

documents (see next section) may also shed light on this sort of activity.

For the South similar records for societies established to ameliorate the condition of emancipated blacks, like the Freedmen's Aid Society (1866–80), may be of interest.[279] In frontier regions records of religious societies devoted to settling groups of immigrants on the land are important for ethno-religious culture in some places. Since such societies often worked with railroad companies and state boards of immigration, the records of those bodies may provide ancillary evidence.[280] And the records of the Congregational Church Building Society have information on building projects on Indian reserves.[281]

GOVERNMENT RECORDS

The federal censuses contain data on local religious matters. The published volumes of the censuses of 1850 and 1860 provide by counties the number of churches of each main denomination, and an aggregate for "minor sects," accommodation figures, and the value of church property. It is not, however, always clear whether under churches "church buildings" or "church organizations" (congregations without buildings) were returned. In the 1870 published census this anomaly was rectified by providing the numbers of church buildings and church organizations, as well as the information on seating and property.[282] For some territories for 1850 and 1860 there are no returns, and for a few counties in several states they are also lacking.

No religious data is included in the volumes of the 1880 census, except in those on the "Social Statistics of Cities,"[283] where churches in individual cities are occasionally mentioned.

[279] See pp. 156–7.
[280] See pp. 123, 132, 223–4, 419; Francis C. Luebke, "Ethnic group settlement on the Great Plains," *Western Hist. Q.*, 8 (1977), 410–11, and works cited.
[281] Chepesiuk and Shankman, *American Indian Archival Materials*, 69–70, q.v. for locations.
[282] 1850: vol. I, states and territories, table XIV (and Compendium vol. for twelve cities); 1860: vol. IV, 332–496; 1870: vol. I, table XVII.
[283] Vols. XVIII, XIX.

The 1890 census provides, for counties and some 120 cities with over 25,000 inhabitants, aggregate numbers of religious organizations and of church edifices with total seating and data on property values. In addition the numbers of communicants or members are given. The same details are given for Lutherans by synods and for Catholics and Episcopalians by archdioceses, dioceses, and so on, and for Presbyterians by presbyteries. Information is also provided on Sunday schooling.[284] Volume x of that census has some information on Indian religion.

The 1900 census volumes contain no religious data, but in 1906 a special investigation of religious bodies was reported by the census authorities. This provides, for states, territories, some cities, and various denominational areas, such information on religious organizations as numbers of communicants or members (by sex), numbers of church edifices and seating capacity, and value of church property and parsonages. For ministers it gives the number, ratio to church membership, and average salaries. It also provides dates of establishment of organizations, languages used in church services, information on domestic mission work, and statistics of black organizations.[285]

Maps showing by counties the distribution of the various main denominations based on the census volumes are available in some modern historical atlases,[286] and some of the census volumes themselves also reproduce some of the statistical data on religion in cartographic form.

Other information, too, relating to religion is to be found in the published census volumes. For the 1850 census the number of religious newspapers in each state is given, with data on numbers of copies and circulation.[287] For 1860 the numbers of monthly, quarterly, and annual publications are

---

[284] Vol. ix (Statistics of Churches), 51–87, 89–115, 119–808. For summaries by sects, states, church districts, see H. K. Carroll, *The Religious Forces of the United States* (1893).

[285] *Special Rep.: Religious Bodies: 1906* (2 vols., 1910) pt. 1 (pt. 2: data by denominations).

[286] E.g., Gaustad, *Historical Atlas*. Much of the statistical data on religion in the census vols. is incl. in the ICPSR set: see p. 64.

[287] Vol. i, states, table xii.

distinguished.[288] For 1850 the numbers of Sunday-school and church libraries with the number of books is shown by county and state,[289] and in 1860 by state only.[290] The 1870 census provides data on Sunday and church libraries and on religious newspapers and periodicals in more detail than before, but only at state level.[291] In 1880, however, such publications are listed by counties with dates of origin.[292]

The manuscript social statistics schedules of the federal censuses of 1850, 1860, and 1870 provide the data on individual churches noted above for units smaller than the county. These form part of the "non-population" schedules distributed to various depositories in 1918.[293] The records of the Bureau of the Census in the National Archives (RG 29) include statistics of congregations of Lutheran synods in 1890, giving the name of each church, its county, the number of its buildings with seating capacity, the number of members, and the value of its property.[294]

Some state censuses embraced religious data,[295] like the special schedules for New York state for each decadal year 1835 through 1875.[296] Aside from these, more purely local religious censuses may have been taken. If this was so, they are likely to have been reported in the local press. Such a census was taken at Newburyport, MA, in 1850.[297]

Census data can provide an important framework for the history of religion in a region, giving an indication of the relative size of different denominations, topographical concentrations, and changes over time. Used in conjunction with data on actual members and the characteristics of memberships (occupational, ethnic, political), census information can

[288] Vol. IV, 321-2.   [289] Vol. I, states, table XIII.
[290] Vol. IV, 505.   [291] Vol. I, tables XIVA, XV, p. 492.
[292] Vol. VII, 199-355.
[293] Listed in Carmen R. Delle Donne, *Federal Census Schedules, 1850-80* (RIP 67, 1973), app.; *Source*, 108-9.
[294] Katherine B. Davidson and Charlotte M. Ashby (comps.), *Preliminary Inventory of the Records of the Bureau of the Census* (PI 161, 1964), 38; *GNA*, 466.
[295] See Dubester (1948).
[296] Marilyn Douglas and Melinda Yates, *New York State Census Records, 1790-1925* (1981). Cf. Kutolowski, 'Identifying the religious affiliations," 13n.
[297] Stephan Thernstrom, *Poverty and Progress* (1964), 268.

contribute to a general picture of the social structure of a community. The quality of the statistical data provided in the federal, and probably other, censuses is, however, uneven. Difficulties derive from inadequate coverage by census takers, and, for example, differing definitions of membership between denominations. Some caution is, therefore, needed in interpreting and perhaps adjusting the data. Numbers of attenders at particular churches were not necessarily strong adherents of that denomination. Baptists, for example, might attend Methodist churches if there were none of their own or if it were more convenient. Moreover, as has been pointed out, the census schedules list "many 'clergymen' in towns without churches, and county histories often tell of 'societies,' classes, or organizations lacking buildings." A religious index based on seating in church buildings may, therefore, be defective.[298] Nevertheless with care census evidence on religious matters can be used to good effect.[299]

Among other federal records, the archives of the War Records Division of the Bureau of Refugees, Freedmen, and Abandoned Lands (NA, RG 105) may contain evidence on the effect of the Civil War on churches in the South and the religious state of blacks.[300] The various reports on Reconstruction (among federal documents)[301] might also be searched. The archives of the Bureau of Indian Affairs (NA, RG 75) include letters from missionaries and the papers of Indian agents which also contain evidence of missionary activity.[302] The published reports of the Bureau and the *Territorial Papers*[303] also contain information on mission work including schools. Petitions by abolitionists to Congress (NA, RGs 46 and 233)[304] offer the opportunity of relating the localities of origin of petitioners to the religious flavor of those localities.[305]

[298] Ronald P. Formisano, *The Birth of Mass Political Parties* (1971), 137–9.
[299] E.g., Christiano, *Religious Diversity*, 26–41, q.v. for analysis of religious data in federal censuses 1890, 1906.
[300] See pp. 139–45.
[301] See p. 136–8.   [302] See p. 161.   [303] See p. 19.   [304] *GNA*, 50, 52.
[305] E.g., Judith Wellman, "Women and radical reform in antebellum upstate New York," in Mabel E. Deutrich and Virginia C. Purdy (eds.), *Clio was a Woman* (1980).

State and municipal documents are likely to include those recording the incorporation of particular churches and of religious and kindred societies. Other documents may provide detailed evidence of divers kinds. The documents of the state of Pennsylvania, for example, contain the managers' reports and treasurers' accounts of the Bible Society of Philadelphia for 1835–6, while those of Ohio include annual statements on church buildings by state inspectors for 1893–4 through 1903–4. Indexes to state publications should, therefore, be consulted. State and municipal reports on charities, almshouses, the unemployed, poor relief, labor problems, and the like, may be of particular value for evidence on the social and philanthropic work of local churches and their ancillary societies.[306] When social statistics have been collected by state labor bureaus their reports may be useful. The Indiana Bureau of Statistics' biennial report for 1883, for instance, provides statistics by counties of numbers of churches and church members and value of church property.

The county records likely to be of most use in religious studies of local communities are vital and ancillary records and records of probate. Records of marriages, marriage licenses, and marriage and land transfer records may provide (as well as spouses' names) the name and denomination of the officiating minister. Similarly, death certificates may provide ethnic information on the deceased and details of the clergyman who officiated at the funeral service. Probate records, particularly wills, sometimes mention religious affiliation or suggest it through the bequests. Such records may not only provide some evidence on the churches in existence and the ministers working in a particular area, but, used in conjunction with census population returns, directories, and tax lists, can give a clue as to the size of particular denominations in a locality, and their social characteristics, such as ethnic background.[307] They

---

[306] See pp. 344–5, 502–7. Cf. Nathan I. Huggins, *Protestants against Poverty* (1971); Green, *Holyoke*; Timothy Walch, "Catholic social institutions . . . Chicago and Milwaukee," *CHR*, 64 (1978). And see Smith, *Revivalism and Social Reform*, essay on sources.

[307] See n. 14 above.

Sources for U.S. History

can be used, too, to trace the occupational mobility within a community of members of religious groups.[308] When local religious bodies were initially organized, their acts of incorporation and charter officers were often recorded by county clerks.[309]

[308] Cf. Olivier Zung, *The Changing Face of Inequality* (1982).
[309] Kutolowski, "Identifying the religious affiliations," 12.

CHAPTER 7

Local government, politics, and organized labor

LOCAL GOVERNMENT

Local government institutions in the nineteenth century possessed judicial, administrative, legislative, and executive functions, so that they embraced many aspects of community activity and affected the ordinary American much more in his daily life than did the activities of federal and state governments. Often they operated, too, within a grassroots political context. The records of local government, where they survive, are, therefore, a prime source for the community historian not only for investigation of the organization and workings of local government itself, but for insight into local politics and into other topics. Similarly records other than those *of* local government may provide evidence *about* local government.

There are many topics worth researching, including the changing nature of local government structures, the administrative functions of different offices, boards, committees, and so on, the relationship between city and county and the state, as well as between the county and the township and the county and the city, the sources of local government income and how it was spent, the relationship between local government and commerce, industry, and business (including investment in canals, railroads, and other enterprises), and the provision of local services and amenities (education, welfare, utilities, fire prevention, public-health facilities, policing, and the administration of justice – some of which are discussed in other chapters). In the South local government during Reconstruction is an important topic. The characteristics of the personnel involved and the political dimension of local government matters is another and is explored in the second section of this chapter.

Because of the great diversity of local government organization in the United States, both geographically and chronologically within the nineteenth century, it is difficult to be very specific, and impossible here to be comprehensive about its records and other records that may shed light on its activities.[1] Nevertheless some guidance is attempted here,[2] with the caveat that generalizations disguise variations and often ignore much divergence. The forms of local government with which this chapter is concerned are principally the incorporated municipality existing in all states and called by a variety of names (as city, borough, village, town), the New England town, the township, and the county (or, in Louisiana and Tidewater South Carolina, the civil parish). The basic unit of local government was the county (or in New England, town) covering areas larger than that of individual settlements and designed originally for what was primarily a rural nation, and with roots in the British colonial past, and indeed in medieval England.

In New England the town (a largish area embracing country districts as well as nucleated settlements) was the significant unit, its basis being the annual and special town meetings which chose selectmen as an executive. Counties existed in New England but were comparatively weak organizations, used mainly as electoral and judicial units. In New York, Michigan, Illinois, and Wisconsin, counties were divided into townships (sometimes also called towns) to form two layers of local government with township representatives (administrators of their own townships) comprising a usually large board of county supervisors or commissioners. A variation of this system evolved in a triangular region marked roughly by New Jersey, Oklahoma, and the Dakotas. In the states in this region there was both township and county government, but township representation on county boards was generally lacking, small boards being directly elected. In the South, and later the far West, the obverse of the New

[1] For greater detail, see Jones.
[2] Some local government records (as tax, land, vital, probate, and school) are described elsewhere: see index.

England system pertained, with the county the dominant local government unit, divided into districts to assist in the administration of elections, justice, roads, and schools. Where there were "townships," these were administrative districts of the county. The county court and, later, boards going under various names, formed the effective government. In the Midwest it was the practice to incorporate villages or minor cities as separate and distinct administrative entities from the township. Generally, however, with the particular exception of Virginia,[3] counties or New England towns enjoyed jurisdiction of some degree within the boundaries of the incorporated municipalities. Such an outline, however, is certainly oversimplified and in many states and parts of states the situation did not exactly fit this description.

Generally county (and New England town) government was concerned with the conduct and administration of elections, the establishment and maintenance of roads and bridges, the establishment of ferries, relief of the poor and control of vagabonds, the maintenance of bastards, the probate of wills, the administration of estates and the protection of widows and orphans, the apprenticeship of indigent children, the collection of taxes (state and county levies), the administration of justice, police and jails, and in some states educational duties. In the South it was also concerned with matters concerning slaves, such as emancipation and punishment and the organization of slave patrols.[4] It might, too, have the right to fix the county seat and to establish townships, and to incorporate ferries, toll roads, toll-bridge companies, and literary and benevolent societies. The records of the ruling bodies, courts, and officers of counties reflect their roles.[5] The practice whereby justices who comprised the county courts were appointed by state governors or were self-perpetuating

[3] But in VA the jurisdiction of incorporated towns (as opposed to cities) and counties overlapped.
[4] See, e.g., Robert M. Ireland, *The County Courts of Antebellum Kentucky* (1972); Ralph A. Wooster, *People in Power* (1969), ch. 4; Raymond A. Winslow, Jr., "The North Carolina county court," *Genealogy*, 73 (1982), 4–10.
[5] Merle Curti *et al.*, *The Making of an American Community* (1959), 262–5.

through co-option, usually gave way during the century to an elective process. When county courts were displaced as the ruling body of the county, and administrative and judicial functions were separated, county commissioners assumed the one and courts and judges the other.

The powers of counties and New England towns were delegated by state legislatures and subject to revision and withdrawal by those bodies. The creation within county boundaries of corporate cities, turnpike companies, and the like by state governments also affected their powers. From the judicial point of view the various county courts were certainly part and parcel of the state system of justice, their decisions subject to review by circuit and other courts. Nevertheless, to regard counties as merely the state government writ small would give a very wrong impression. In practice they often had the characteristics of and some legal claim to quasi-self government. In Kentucky, for instance, "once created they refused to be abolished, fought with neighboring counties over boundaries, resisted encroachment on their own territories, engaged in internecine struggles over county seats, and besieged the legislature with requests that their own particular problems be ameliorated by special legislation [which] ... contributed to [the state's] ... prevailing condition of localism."[6]

Through such special legislation individual county governments might extend their powers and the privileges of their members or officers considerably. Moreover, since the legislation was often specific to a certain county, differences in county organization and activities could evolve in the same state. Indeed, in Louisiana there was so much special legislation that each civil parish (the equivalent of a county elsewhere) operated almost to a code of its own.[7] Again, county governments often drafted bills which because of influence or pressure of business were passed by the legislature without change. And, additionally, counties normally had the right to

[6] Robert M. Ireland, *Little Kingdoms: The Counties of Kentucky, 1850–1891* (1971).
[7] Robert D. Calhoun, "The origin and early development of county-parish government in Louisiana," *Louisiana Hist. Q.*, 18 (1935), 90–1, 153–4.

execute their own minor laws, ordinances, and regulations, and to raise their own local taxes.

As for incorporated municipalities, it has been said that no American system of city government had evolved even by the late nineteenth century. "It is true that all cities had an independently elected mayor; they had a council. At this point, the unity ended."[8] Moreover, a multitude of changes in organization and powers occurred for particular municipalities during the century. In larger towns, city government had duties and responsibilities similar to those of counties, embracing education, welfare, sanitation, policing, street and public-building maintenance, control of markets, and so on. The historian of communities and local areas needs, therefore, to be aware of the diversity of forms of local government even within the confines of a single state and to make himself as aware as possible of the situation in the places whose local government and politics he wishes to investigate.

The structures of county government in particular states, often extremely complex, have, of course, often been the subject of modern analysis. The introductions to those WPA Historical Records Survey volumes for the various states which list the records of individual counties provide summaries of county government structure. They also comment on the duties and powers of county officials and institutions as well as giving information on the nature of the records pertaining to them. During the nineteenth century many new counties were formed out of other counties, so that topographical boundaries could suffer successive changes and counties changes of name. Some counties disappeared.[9]

The first place to seek primary sources is in state or territorial records. State "blue books" and legislative manuals

---

[8] Ernest S. Griffith, *A History of American City Government* (1974), 235.

[9] For the establishment and descent of particular counties, see Joseph N. Kane, *The American Counties* (1983 edn.) (incl. independent cities); E. Kay Kirkham, *The Counties of the United States* (1961); Jones, 169. Also useful are publ. state and federal censuses, Acts of state legislatures. For civil division maps in NA (Dept. of Agric. and WPA) see Gary L. Morgan, "Notes on genealogy," *Prologue*, 9 (1977), 181. And see Thomas D. Rabenhorst, *Historical U.S. County Outline Map Collection, 1840–1980* (1984); John H. Long, *Historical Atlas and Chronology of County Boundaries, 1788–1980* (5 vols., 1984); above p. 54n.

issued periodically by state governments give information on government agencies and the executive and judicial branches of state government and their functions and personnel, and may also include the names of county office holders and other data on local government units.[10] The structures of county government and the duties of its ruling bodies, courts, and officers are to be found in the various state and territorial constitutions – and for most states there was more than one constitution during the course of the nineteenth century. The texts of the constitutions are usually available as successive codes published by state governments.[11] In addition there will be general Acts and Acts specific to certain counties (the special legislation mentioned above) among the (usually published) statutes of the state concerned. Indeed, as the years from the inauguration of the constitution passed, the duties and powers of county government increasingly derived from legislation. Further elucidation may be found in the published journals of state legislatures, in the debates and proceedings of constitutional conventions, in reports, resolutions, and documents printed by the legislatures, and perhaps in reports of legislative committees.[12]

For the most part, incorporated municipalities derived their civic rights and privileges from charters granted by the state or territorial government. Like counties, they were subordinate to state government and not independent of it, but in nature were said to differ from counties, whose existence was dictated from above, by originating in the expressed wish of their inhabitants to be incorporated. Details of their original charters are to be found in the Acts of the state or territorial legislature. Thus, to take a single example, the Acts of Louisiana record the incorporation of the city of Jefferson in 1850, delineating its topographical bounds, setting out the structure

---

[10] See David W. Parish (ed.), *State Government Publications: An Annotated Bibliography* (1981 edn.), 25–61. Commercial publics. may also provide such inf.

[11] And see Francis N. Thorpe (ed.), *The Federal and State Constitutions* . . . (7 vols., 1909); William F. Swindler (ed.), *Sources and Documents of United States Constitutions* (10 vols., 1973–9; 2nd ser. 1982–). For constitutional conventions, see p. 27.

[12] N.B. Robert U. Goehlert and Frederic W. Musto, *State Legislatures; A Bibliography* (1985).

of its elected government (a council of mayor, aldermen, freemen, comptroller, harbor master, commissary of streets and landings, and a collector of taxes) and indicating such further officers to be appointed by the council.[13] Fresh charters and amendments, which might often alter the structure considerably – as, for example, making the mayoralty a quasi-independent organ of city government elected directly by the citizens – are also to be found in the state statutes.[14] Such changes had political implications, separate elections of mayors and other officials, and of boards (especially in the area of finance) giving those concerned a power base of their own. Municipal charters and amendments to them may also be found among city archives, and sometimes they have been collected together in print. Studied in sequence they will give details of the changing nature and powers of the municipality and its officers and officials and changes in the topographical area of the city.[15]

In addition to granting charters, state legislatures passed many special Acts pertaining to the affairs of individual cities. These often derived from pressure from special interests within a city or from when one political party controlled the state legislature and another the government of a particular city. Thus, for instance, there are over 400 special laws of Massachusetts relating to Boston alone.

Other published and unpublished state records may also be useful for the student of local government. State documents contain the reports of those state agencies operating within city and county limits. The Massachusetts legislature, for example, established a state commission to supervise railroads and street railways throughout Massachusetts and every street railway company, even within chartered cities, was

[13] Collin B. Hamer, "Records of the city of Jefferson, 1850–1870," *Louisiana Hist.*, 17 (1976).
[14] Cf. William B. Munro, *The Government of American Cities* (1916 edn.), 10–11, and see (pp. 62–3) for the "home-rule" charter system in MO, CA, WA, MN by 1900, enabling larger cities to frame own charters. Cf. WPA, HRS, *Inventory of the County Archives of California, No. 29, Napa County* (1941), 40–2.
[15] See, e.g., W. Earl Weller, "The expanding charter life of Rochester," in Edward R. Foreman (ed.), *Centennial History of Rochester, New York*, vol. 3 (1933). Cf. Melvin G. Holli, *Reform in Detroit* (1969), 260.

incorporated by special Act of the state legislature. Some cities were covered by state police boards, and a number of miscellaneous state boards performed many local government functions in New York City and Brooklyn as late as 1870. The reports of special committees established to investigate particular aspects of city and county government may also be published as state documents. A Kentucky document of 1814–15 reports on charges against a J.P. in Estill county, and another of 1888 concerns alleged corruption at elections in a particular county.[16] Various committees of New York state reported on many aspects of life within New York City in the nineteenth century. State governments had special interests in state capital cities, where they owned buildings and employed many staff. Thus the Georgia legislature set up a special committee in 1868 to examine the public buildings in the incorporated city of Milledgeville.[17]

Correspondence between county and municipal and state (or territorial) officials about matters requiring cooperation (as the collection of state taxes, reports to state superintendents of health) or over disputes, often provides useful evidence. It may be available in the records of the governments concerned – but is most likely to have survived in state archives. Among unpublished state records, too, will be many memorials, petitions, and letters from individuals, firms, and groups of one kind or another pertaining to local government administration, some urging, some complaining and recommending state action on local government affairs. There may well also be lists of county officials and justices.

For detailed investigation of local government affairs, and particularly of day-to-day administration, the records of the city, county, or New England town must be a prime source, if they have survived.[18] They will reflect the judicial, administrative, legislative, and executive functions of the government concerned. Such records vary in nature greatly, though most

---

[16] *House Jnl., Kentucky, 1814–15*, 113–15; Ireland, *Little Kingdoms*, 51, 157.
[17] James C. Bonner, *Milledgeville* (1978), 294.
[18] For some guides to local government records, see Palic, 146–9; and see p. 27.

are likely to be unpublished.[19] The most important to the student of local government are usually the minutes or pro-ceedings of the body in which the corporate powers of the county resided – boards of commissioners, supervisors, police commissioners, chosen freemen, selectmen, or by whatever name they went, or where the county court was that body, the records of the court, particularly its order book, which pro-vides a synopsis of the court's business.[20] Connected are likely to be the working papers of cases, records of general sessions of the peace, petitions on various topics (particularly roads and licenses to keep taverns, ferries, and so on), lists of juries, records of elections or appointments of J.P.s, constables, school trustees, boards and inspectors, and reports from over-seers of the poor, supervisors of roads, records of apprentice-ship, evidences of freedom of blacks, manumissions, details of guardianship of orphans and minors, and naturalization records.[21] Also important (where all authority was not vested in the county courts) are the judicial records of the various courts, and the records of the clerk to the circuit courts. The court records included court files (criminal and common law) and probate records (including inventories and appraise-ments): see last section of this chapter.

Financial records of county government may also be fruit-ful. They are miscellaneous in nature, the most generally important being treasurers' annual reports, account books, audited accounts, and correspondence. From a detailed exam-ination of such records much can be learned of the workings of local government and of the financial links between county and state (county treasurers were, for example, responsible for the transmission of state taxes and the proper distribution of moneys allotted by the state), and between counties and ancil-lary units like school districts.

[19] The WPA, HRS, has publ. transcripts of county records for various states (e.g., TN). And see J. G. Hodgson, *The Official Publications of American Counties: A Union List* (1937).
[20] Cf. Curti, *Making of an American Community*, ch. 10; Ireland, *County Courts*, 181.
[21] Cf. Jones, 122–7; Theodore C. Pease, *The County Archives of the State of Illinois* (1915), lxxxvii–lxxxviii; John W. Durel, "New Hampshire county court records," *Historical New Hampshire*, 31 (1976).

The records of Bond county, IL, may serve as an example.[22] They embrace the records of the county clerk, the county clerk-probate, the clerk to the circuit court, and those of the recorder of the circuit court. The county clerk's records included those of the county commissioners, county court records, taxation records, records of vital statistics, rating records, and other miscellaneous records. The county commissioners' (later supervisors') records contained tavern and ferry licenses, tax rates, registers of blacks, marriage licenses and certificates, various reports, surveys of roads, boundaries of road districts, and lists of juries and appointed officers. County court records included the common law record, common law and criminal court files, the naturalization records, judgment and execution dockets, fee books (criminal and common law), and records concerning the handicapped and public health. Among the fiscal records of the court were tax schedules and assessment and collection records. Vital statistics records included marriage licenses and registers, and registers of births and deaths. There were also registers of physicians and veterinary surgeons. The county court records also embraced poll books and abstracts of rates, registers of county and township officers and commissioners (showing name, office, date of election, and term held), reports of the county clerk, circuit court, sheriff, and treasurer of fees and emoluments, and records of sales of school lands. The records of the county clerk-probate included the probate record embracing all documents, probate files, dockets and fee books, and a record of wills. The records of the clerk to the circuit court included the chancery, criminal and common law files, naturalization records, judgment and execution dockets, and J.P.s' transcripts, coroners' records, and other items. The records of the recorder of the circuit court consisted mainly of deed and mortgage records, the surveyor's records, township plats, original land entry records, and certificates of levy, sale, and redemption.

---

[22] Pease, *County Archives of Illinois*, 52–9.

Where county governments devolved powers and duties to townships – most importantly in matters of tax collection, road maintenance, responsibility for the poor, and elementary schooling – the township (or "town") records may be sought. These are likely to consist of the record of the annual town meeting, the records of the town clerk, executive trustee, or board, and those of the township officers, perhaps including those of the treasurer. In Indiana, for instance, town records might include for each township those of a trustee, an advisory board, an assessor, J.P.s, and constables, all elected officers. Sometimes there may also be records of separate officers or boards for districts – as school boards, road overseers, and so on.[23]

Records of the corporated communities have not always been well looked after and are sometimes difficult of access.[24] Where they exist their nature and extent will vary according to the size and significance of the place. Municipal charters have been noted above. The most significant records are the minutes or proceedings of the meetings of the governing body – city council, borough commission, board of aldermen, board of directors, or whatever name was given. Thus the journal of the proceedings of the Baltimore city council, dating from 1801, records the actions on proposed legislation, nominations for city offices, communications from the mayor and reports of committees of the council and of city agencies.[25] Reports like these are likely also to exist in detail separately. Such records shed light on many aspects of public life touched by the activities of the council and its committees and agencies.

Legislative decisions taken by local governing bodies are usually recorded in the laws and ordinances of the city or place concerned, and these will illuminate many aspects of local history apart from the activities of the local council itself.

---

[23] Clyde F. Snider, *Township Government in Indiana* (1932), 5–7.
[24] Richard J. Cox, "A reappraisal of municipal records," *Public Historian*, 3 (1981).
[25] Richard J. Cox and Patricia Vanorney, "The records of a city," *Maryland Hist. Mag.*, 70 (1975), 294.

The Ordinances and Resolutions of Baltimore City Council from 1797 consists of 200 volumes, a considerable body of historical evidence in itself.[26] Corporations of large cities often issued periodic publications indicating the laws then in force, and sometimes other information. The *Memphis Digest*, for example, extant for various years, published the city's charter and amendments to it as well as the local ordinances.[27] Official city manuals may include not only names of and biographical data on council members or at least lists of office holders, but also statistical data of various kinds. Holyoke, MA, for instance, published a *Municipal Register* which provides data on taxation and valuations of property.[28]

The more populous the place the more extensive would its provision of services have been, and the various municipal and county officers and administrative departments are likely to have generated evidence of their activities. The reports, often annual, of boards, committees, departments, and agencies dealing with, for instance, education, health, public safety, fire services, policing, urban amenities and transportation, harbors, and so on, and those of treasurers, auditors, engineers, inspectors, and superintendents of various kinds, may be found in different forms. Sometimes they were printed with corporation minutes, sometimes as individual city or municipal documents, or as free-standing papers, and sometimes as compilations of reports often combined with a mayoral message. Such reports are likely to contain, especially for large places, a great deal of statistical data, but they usually go much further than that, giving explanatory comments on the facts, indications of policy, and so on. In certain circumstances special reports on particular matters were published by municipalities, as, for example, in the 1860s a joint report by the city councils of Boston and Roxbury, MA, concerning the annexation of Roxbury to Boston. Chicago published a report

[26] Cox and Vanorney, "The records of a city," 294
[27] Gerald M. Capers, Jr., *The Biography of a River Town* (1939), 272.
[28] Constance M. Green, *Holyoke, Massachusetts* (1938), 398. Cf. Bayard Still, *Milwaukee* (1965), 608.

on common schools in 1838, New Orleans one on sewerage in 1879 and one on the city's debts in 1882.[29]

In the second half of the nineteenth century the dominant position of the city council was often, but not always, eroded, as state legislatures took the administration of various municipal departments away from council committees and gave them to newly established officials or to popularly elected boards. Again in some places the administrative functions of the mayor were expanded at the expense of those of the council. Such developments will be reflected in the records.

For large cities, as for populous counties, there are likely to be unpublished records. These may include the working records of the various municipal departments and officials, together with the ancillary papers of the city council itself and of committees and boards. Among these there may be fiscal records, records relating to real property, electoral registers and voting records, and perhaps vital statistics. At Baltimore, for example, the "City Papers" contain among other matters, market house licenses and rents, petitions, correspondence, committee reports and messages of the city council, proceedings of the city commissioners and department of public works (on paving streets, establishing grades, maintaining bridges, building sewers, etc.), correspondence of the city register and of the board of health and the health commissioner, legal opinions of the city solicitor, details of appointment of officials, contracts and correspondence of the water board, insurance policies, bounty applications and awards, enlistment certificates, muster rolls and discharges from the Civil War period, correspondence of the mayor, and oath books for city office holders. Many of these collections date from 1797, the year after the granting of the city's charter, and others from early in the nineteenth century. There are records, too, of the incorporation by the city of religious, social, and business institutions and alterations to those

---

[29] Sam B. Warner, *Streetcar Suburbs* (1962), 203n; Bessie L. Pierce, *A History of Chicago*, vol. 1 (1937), 442; Joy J. Jackson, *New Orleans in the Gilded Age* (1969), 331.

charters. In addition there are about a thousand volumes of poll books (records of voters) and election returns for city officials and the state senators and representatives, judges, state attorneys, sheriffs, and clerks of court. The port records include bonds for licenses of vessels, and financial records of duties and fees. There are also large collections of real property records embracing deeds, mortgages, releases, leases, assignments, rights of way, commissions to re-establish boundaries, surveys, and plats.[30]

Smaller places, and places incorporated at a later date, are unlikely to have such a wealth of material; nevertheless they may yet have substantial collections of certain types. Jefferson, LA, not incorporated until 1850, for example, possesses among other materials very full records of its treasurer's department, surveyors' records relating to public works, and police records. Tax lists name payers with the amounts due and paid, and the records of assessors of property list the lands, buildings, and other property (including slaves) subject to tax.[31] In New England some places which were small but of long standing, however, possess numerous records. Thus Newington in Hartford county, CT, which even in 1900 boasted of a population of only just over one thousand, nevertheless has, for the nineteenth century, records of the town clerk, the town treasurer, the registrar of vital statistics, auditors' records, selectmen's records, and records of highway surveyors, game wardens, haywards and pound keepers, fence viewers, surveyors of weights and measures, constables, and health officers. There are board of education records, records of town meetings, electoral and voting records, and many tax records.[32]

For many places, petitions and memorials from citizens to be found in municipal archives are likely to fill out the information on public policies and services, as, too, are the local

---

[30] Cox and Vanorney, "The records of a city."
[31] Hamer, "Records of the city of Jefferson."
[32] WPA, HRS, *Inventory of the Town and City Archives of Connecticut: No. 2. Hartford County, Vol. XVII, Newington* (1939).

newspapers and directories. Public meetings, sometimes used in cities for the purpose of proposing charter changes and civic improvements, may be recorded both in city archives and in the press.

Since county governments had duties and performed certain functions within the bounds of chartered cities, particularly over, for example, the care of the poor, and since county and city governments were anyway often brought in contact with each other, the records of one may well throw light on the administrative history of the other – and similarly with contiguous counties.

The most likely places in which to find published city and county records are city, state, university, and historical society libraries. Such institutions may also have collections of published pamphlets issued by local governments. Unpublished materials may be in state archives, historical society collections, public libraries, city halls, and county court houses. Continuing division of older counties over the years means that evidence for earlier periods may sometimes need to be sought in the records of parent counties. Some local government archives will have been cataloged, many have been inventoried by the WPA, and some have been published for the use of historians.[33] For larger cities there is likely to be a corpus of modern secondary works, and for cities and counties generally older local histories must be regarded as an important source for factual data. To these may be added the memoirs, diaries, and correspondence of those engaged in local government.

When local government services and utilities are being considered, it is as well to note that sometimes they began as privately run institutions or businesses and for their pre-official history investigation of their early records is needed, if they exist. The trustees of the Philadelphia Gas Works, for instance, produced annual reports, the Birmingham (Alabama) Water Works Company left papers and letterbooks, and the Deluge Fire Engine Company of Germanstown, CT,

---

[33] E.g., reps. on Boston, MA, town records: publ. as city documents.

left its minutes.[34] Much information on such enterprises, however, is likely to be found in directories and newspapers and in local political and administrative records, broadsheets and pamphlets, especially for the time when municipalization was being considered.

Although the control of local government, both county and municipal, was the prerogative of individual states, nevertheless the records of the federal government may sometimes provide valuable data. Federal policy was, for instance, concerned over much of the Union, with surveys of rivers, harbors, and so on. The military was involved in this work and subsequent improvements and with military installations, while the federal government gave permission for railroads to be laid, bridges to be built, and so on, in the public domain. These, and such matters as federal buildings in cities and federal interest in elections locally held, brought local and federal governments into contact. Thus among federal documents, to cite a few of very many, are to be found a memorial of the city council of Philadelphia requesting Congress to make appropriation for improvement of navigation of the Delaware River, a grant to the corporation of Council Bluffs, for public uses, of a certain lake situated near that place, a resolution authorizing the mayor and council of Baltimore to occupy a lot owned by the U.S. government, and a memorial of the authorities of Paris, TX, for ratification by Congress of an Act of the Choctaw Nation granting a right of way to the Saint Louis and San Francisco Railroad Company. Another document relates the claim of the city of Baltimore for money expended in the war of 1812.[35]

Civil War and Reconstruction saw military rule imposed on counties and cities in certain states and the normal pattern of local government interfered with. Thus the Army assumed responsibility for law and order, for supervising elections, for land redistribution, and for educational reform. Federal

---

[34] Frederick M. Bender, "Gas light, 1816–1860," *Pennsylvania Hist.*, 22 (1955); Carl V. Harris, *Political Power in Birmingham, 1871–1921* (1977), 299; Carl M. Becker, *The Village* (1981), 205.

[35] HMD 48 (42–3), ser. 1572; SR 657 (46–2), ser. 1898; SR 825 (53–3), ser. 3346; SMD 18 (47–2), ser. 1993; HED 519 (49–1), ser. 2436.

documents shed light on the state of local affairs during these years.[36] One, for instance, records the removal of the city councils of Jefferson City and New Orleans by the military commander of the area for infringement of his orders, another the suspension of the functions of the board of police of the city of Baltimore. Another records the inability in 1867 of a judge to hold court in Lavaca county, TX, because of the impossibility of obtaining jurors.[37]

Further evidence on relationships between the U.S. Army and local governments in the South during the period of military government can be found in the records of the Army Continental Commands in the National Archives (RG 393 – formerly in RG 98).[38] The Freedmen's Bureau published records and its unpublished records in the National Archives (RG 105) throw light on friction between local government officials and the Bureau over the treatment of blacks.[39] Indeed it might be considered that the field offices and subordinate field offices of the Bureau represented a kind of imposed local government (especially in regard to official relief of the needy and the education of blacks). Their records and related federal records are described in chapter 3. Information on counties and cities in this period may also sometimes be found in the *War of the Rebellion: A Compilation of the Official Records of the Union and Confederate Armies.*[40]

Data on local government, particularly that of larger cities, are also contained in the published volumes of the federal censuses, though the quality of evidence on municipal finance has been criticized.[41] The 1880 census includes a very detailed report on the "Social Statistics of Cities," arranged by states with tabulated indexes of cities and subjects.[42] Data on local government matters include (though not for every city

[36] Some cited pp. 136–8.
[37] HED 15 (40–2), ser. 1341; HMD 22 (37–1), ser. 1115; SED 14 (40–1), ser. 1308, p. 217.
[38] See p. 146.
[39] See pp. 139–46. Cf. Ireland, *Little Kingdoms*, 63–70, 174.
[40] 130 "serials," 70 vols., 1880–1901. Available NA, M262.
[41] Lance E. Davies and John Legler, "The government in the American economy, 1815–1902," *JEH*, 26 (1966).
[42] Vols. XVIII, XIX.

covered) information on finance, municipal cleansing, drainage, garbage disposal, sanitary authorities, cemeteries, parks, fire departments, gas supplies, waterworks, schools and libraries, public buildings, police, and penal, reformatory and charitable institutions and hospitals. The amount of detail varies considerably and is extensive for some very large cities like New Orleans. Although there are references to governing bodies, however, as for example details of its control of the police, usually the structure of local government is not discussed, though this may be described in sections on "history." Nevertheless for a few places, like Salt Lake City, there is a detailed account of local government organization.

A report on wealth, debt, and taxation in the 1890 census[43] provides much statistical data on the financial situation of counties, municipalities, and school districts. Part 1 gives details of public debt for 1880 and 1890 by counties and municipalities, and occasionally "villages."[44] The bonded debt for counties and municipalities of 4,000 inhabitants upwards is further broken down into debt relating to bridges, cemeteries, fire departments, funding floating debt; improvement of harbors, rivers, wharves, canals, and water power; parks and public places, public building; railroad and other debt; refunding of old debt; schools, libraries, sewers, streets, war expenses, and waterworks – indicating rates of interest and dates of maturity.[45] Part 2 gives in great detail by counties (1880, 1890) data on true valuation of real estate, and for counties, cities, and minor divisions (1890) data on assessed valuation of taxed property and *ad valorem* taxation.[46] For municipalities of 4,000 and over in 1890 details of finances for 1880 and 1890 are provided: assessed value of property taxed, *ad valorem* taxation, and debt; and for 1890 true and assessed valuations of real estate.[47] There are also detailed statistics of

[43] Vol. xv (2 pts., 1892, 1895).
[44] Counties, 288–326; municipalities, 329–534. Not all municipalities named: some combined as "places having no debt," "places not named."
[45] Pp. 562–851.
[46] Pp. 62–99, 103–373. Details of places prefaced by accounts of nature of assessed valuation in the state and methods of accounting, etc.
[47] Pp. 376–403.

receipts and expenditures for county governments and for governments of cities of 4,000 and over. Information on receipts includes balance at the start and finish of the year and monies from investments, loans, state governments, minor divisions, non-state taxation, fees, fines, licenses, sales of property, and so on. Details of expenditure cover repayment of loans, payments on buildings, works, charities, street maintenance, sewerage, fire control, health, education, libraries, salaries, and such like. In addition there are details of receipts and expenditure by counties on public schools.

At the end of the century the Department of Labor's *Statistics of Cities* (1902) provides data on municipal finances of certain cities. Law reports provide another source of information on local government affairs. Counties and cities were frequently involved in litigation – often over their legal powers – with other local governments, with the state government, with companies and corporations, and with individuals. Appeals from county courts were heard in appellate courts of one kind or another. For that reason the published series of law reports[48] may be worth searching, particularly if there is prior knowledge of the existence and some idea of the date of a particular case. Usually these publications do not index the names of cities or counties. However, it may be fruitful to look in the indexes under such headings as "counties," "municipal corporations," "towns," "incorporated townships," and so on. The *Pacific Recorder* reported a decision of 1883 that power of appointment of the police commissioners of the city and county of San Francisco did not lie with the judge of the San Francisco superior court.[49] Two years later the *Atlantic Reporter* recorded the details of a case between the state of New Jersey and the mayor and city of New Brunswick over the city council's power to dismiss its chief of police.[50]

Finally the importance of newspapers as a significant source for the history of local government must be stressed. Many decisions and reports of rural local governments were

---

[48] See pp. 25–6; and, e.g., Ireland, *Little Kingdoms*.
[49] Vol. 1 (1884), 158.   [50] Vol. 1 (1886), 496.

officially placed in local newspapers. In other circumstances, when the minutes of the governing bodies of counties and cities have not survived, local newspapers may provide a record of important decisions, and even when original minutes do still exist press reports may contain more explanatory detail than the official record. Again editorials, reports, letters from newspapers may all shed light on the day-to-day activities of local government and local feelings about such matters, as well as providing information on leading individuals, election results, appointment of officers, and so on. Above all the local press will provide, for the activities of local government, the political context in which it operated, but on which official records so often give little information. Local government was, indeed, at the center of local political life, with which the next section is concerned.

POLITICS

Investigation of political aspects of the past has been one of the main thrusts of American historians,[51] and has often taken the form of detailed studies of state and local politics. There is, however, still plenty of scope for further work at the local level. As has been said, "Patterns of political structure and political process inevitably develop in a local setting; the struggle for control and power is carried out within the context of community institutions where the concerns of people concentrate."[52]

The student of the history of local politics has in fact a dual task. On the one hand he needs to examine local aspects of national politics, particularly the local response to national issues as indicated in presidential and congressional elections, and to some extent in elections to state legislatures. On the other he needs to investigate the specifically community

---

[51] See citations, HG, 377–80; Prucha, 143–6; ABC-Clio, The American Electorate: A Historical Bibliography (1984). For political movements associated with farming see ch. 5.

[52] Samuel P. Hays, "Archival sources for American political history," AA, 28 (1965), 19.

politics: the activities of local political leaders and parties, their control of local administration, the peculiarly local issues which divided communities, and so on. In practice the two will overlap (as will the types of sources). Those active in county government, for instance, were sometimes also members of state legislatures, so that county government became part and parcel of the wider political scene. The political significance of the county was enhanced as a result of the development, in the 1820s and 1830s, of national and state conventions for selecting party candidates. Counties became electoral districts in many states and emerged as units for party political activities, and bases for policy making and the spoils system.

Moreover, the actual process of government of counties, towns, and especially large cities was in nineteenth-century America often essentially political in one sense or another. For that reason many historians will seek to treat local administrative history along with political: the source material certainly overlaps. For that reason many of the records noted in the last section will be essential for the study of community politics. This is particularly the case for those records concerned with executive decisions, legislation, and long-term policies, though less so for the records of day-to-day routine on the part of officials.

Two significant aspects of local politics are worth particular attention: first, the basis of local political power and the views and policies of the political leaders and their followers, and of the political parties and factions they represented as manifested locally; and second, the opinions and voting history of the electorate as a whole, the man in the street.

Political power may sometimes have reflected economic strength, but it was not necessarily always equated with office holding. The possibility of an underlying power of economically well-off elites in influencing important political decisions in a community must also be considered, as must the possibility that local political power was fragmented with different groups, led by men of diverse social standing, exercising influence in different fields.[53] These and other hypotheses may be borne in mind, but they should not be allowed to influence the analysis of the evidence in advance. And these are not the only topics worthy of investigation. In places in the South, for example, the relationship between antebellum and postbellum political leadership may be of interest, as well as the impact on local politics of defeat in war and the imposition of military rule. Analysis of the social, ethnic, religious, occupational, and economic backgrounds of political leaders (not merely those who achieved office) and investigation of who initiated political decisions and who benefited from the decisions, may give indications of who controlled political change.[54] The support given to the various policies or viewpoints by differing groups in the community may be deduced from the evidence of records of voting at elections, while other records exist for studying the relationship between voter behavior and socio-economic characteristics.[55]

Leaders and leadership groups   Information on the background, and general activities of individual politicians and groups of politicians, as well as the characteristics of political leaders such as Congressmen, members of state legislatures, city mayors, county judges, other city and county officials, and members of local government councils, important committees, and the like may be derived from a variety of sources, many of which have been detailed in other parts of this volume.[56] And the same applies to evidence on the politically active who did not hold formal office, in particular extra-official "bosses."

Many state records include lists or rosters of county officers (as sheriffs, circuit court judges, probate judges, county clerks, tax receivers and collectors, coroners, surveyors,

---

[53] E.g., Floyd Hunter, *Community Power Structure* (1953); Robert A. Dahl, *Who Governs?* (1961).

[54] Whitman H. Ridgway, *Community Leadership in Maryland, 1790–1840* (1979), 204–7, suggests a quantitative method of differentiating degrees of influence in decision making, etc.

[55] Cf. Samuel P. Hays, "History and genealogy," *Prologue*, 7 (1975).

[56] See esp. last section, and ch. 2. For a survey of research: Samuel P. Hays, "The changing political structure of the city in industrial America," *JUH*, 1 (1974).

rangers, J.P.s, police court members, constables, and possibly mayors). County court minutes and order books, and other records, as well as municipal records of the same kind, and state and local government manuals can provide names of officials appointed by the local governments. Most important for further biographical data on these people are census schedules, directories, and gazetteers. These can give individuals' occupations, and where they lived, while tax records can provide some indication of wealth. Materials collected by genealogists and family historians may also in some cases yield much data on family background.

There is also likely to be a good deal of published biographical information on many local leaders.[57] Local compilations of important citizens published in the nineteenth and early twentieth centuries abound. Sometimes there are diaries, memoirs, or autobiographies, which, while useful, will need to be used cautiously. The autobiography of Boss Ruef of San Francisco, published serially in the San Francisco *Bulletin* in 1912, is an example.[58] Older county and other local histories, souvenir publications, and histories of local institutions, such as business firms, societies, and church congregations, abound in biographical accounts and incidental data on people publicly active. Outstanding political figures may have been the subject of modern published biographies or dissertations, or have had their important speeches published. Local newspapers will contain not only information on the activities of local leaders, but eventually obituaries, which, however hagiographical, may contain useful factual information.

It is fairly simple to find biographical data on state governors,[59] and for Congressmen a modern reference work provides details of all those elected in each Congress for every district.[60] Another work provides, by Congresses to 1841,

[57] *HG*, sec. 10:3; Melvin G. Holli and Peter d'A. Jones, *Biographical Dictionary of American Mayors, 1820–1980: Big City Mayors* (1981). And see p. 18.

[58] See Walton Bean, *Boss Ruef's San Francisco* (1952).

[59] Citations, Prucha, 114–15; Roy R. Glashen, *American Governors and Gubernatorial Elections, 1775–1978* (1979).

[60] Kenneth C. Martis, *The Historical Atlas of the United States Congressional Districts, 1789–1983*, vol. 1 (1982).

details for each Congressional district which include the names of the counties it embraced and the names of the representatives, together with their local county, post office, and party affiliation.[61] Further biographical data on Congressmen is available both in print[62] and in machine-readable form. The ICPSR has compiled machine-readable data on candidates contesting at county-level elections for the offices of President, Governor and Representatives in Congress from 1788.[63] Even more important for community history are the numerous biographical directories for state legislatures.[64]

The unpublished papers of local politicians and other local notables may well exist, and many collections are to be found in various libraries and other depositories.[65] Although not all such collections provide as much information as historians might wish, they cannot be ignored and are sometimes invaluable. A study of New York politics, for instance, found the papers of leading politicians vital in giving "an intimate portrait of the decisive political moves of the time along with the calculations of the movers."[66] Correspondence of Congressmen,[67] too, may be full of information on local political issues. Thus the papers of Congressman Nils P. Haugen throw light on the part played by the Bennett law issue in Wisconsin communities in the election of 1890.[68] It is unfortunate that for the later nineteenth century the advent of the telephone has in some instances rendered such collections sparser than was

[61] Stanley B. Parsons et al., United States Congressional Districts, 1788–1841 (1978). Vol. for 1842–1942 planned.

[62] Lawrence F. Kennedy et al. (comps.), Biographical Directory of the American Congress, 1774–1971 (1971). Congressional Directory (from 1809) contains biographical inf. See also Thomas B. Alexander and Richard E. Beringer, The Anatomy of the Confederate Congress (1972); and for the Confederacy, citations, Prucha, 150.

[63] For ICPSR, see p. 64. Largely based on Kennedy, Biographical Directory. See ICPSR, Guide to Resources and Services, 1980–1981 (n.d.), 212–13. And see p. 320n.

[64] Prucha, 115–16.

[65] See pp. 35–7.

[66] Alvin Kass, Politics in New York State, 1800–1830 (1965), 209.

[67] See John J. McDonough and Marilyn Parr (comps.), Members of Congress: A Checklist of their Papers in . . . the Library of Congress (1980); Kathryn A. Jacob and Elizabeth A. Hornyack, Guide to Research Collections of Former United States Senators, 1789–1982 (1982). Correspondence of some Congressmen has been publ.: see Brock, 129.

[68] Roger E. Wyman, "Wisconsin ethnic groups and the election of 1890," Wisconsin Mag. Hist., 51 (1968).

previously the case.[69] Again, the possibility, or even likelihood, that materials unflattering to the reputation of the subject have been weeded out, is something to take account of. But these drawbacks should not detract too much from the value of such evidence for local political history.

The official records of Congress and of state legislatures[70] contain, as noted above, many references to matters of local political significance. The activities of members in these assemblies were to some degree extensions of community politics and may reflect local political attitudes. The way that these political leaders spoke and voted in their assemblies may, therefore, be very important for the community historian. The records of debates (found in the journals of the legislative assembly concerned) can thus shed light on the views and policies of these men and perhaps on local pressures on them. Reports of important speeches can be found, too, in newspapers, and may even have been published as pamphlets.

Perhaps even more important sources than speeches are the records of voting in the legislatures. Roll-calls, found in the transactions of Congress,[71] and in the journals of state legislatures and constitutional conventions, indicate the way legislators voted on main issues, bills, second and third readings, and on procedural motions. Analysis of these can reveal a great deal about the outlook of individual politicians themselves, and give a clue as to influences on them emanating from the localities they represented. Since roll-calls cover all those who voted, and not only those who spoke in debates or those always in the limelight and reported in the newspapers, they can be particularly valuable. Such evidence of voting in city councils is not so readily available, though some record is to be found in newspapers, municipal reports, and municipal archives. Where they exist they offer great scope for research.[72]

The technique known as scalogram analysis, Guttman scaling, or legislative roll-call analysis, which involves arranging

[69] James B. Crooks, *Politics and Progress* (1968), 237.
[70] See pp. 23–4, 26–7.   [71] See pp. 23–4.
[72] Cf. Hays, "Archival sources," 22; Ruth A. Rowles and Kenneth C. Martis, "Mapping Congress," *Prologue*, 16 (1984).

legislators' responses on an ascending scale, can be useful for composing a profile of the outlook and attitudes of political representatives as indicated by the way they voted, for providing a measure of comparison with the views of other legislators, and for determining membership of a group likely to vote similarly on particular types of issue. Over time variations and shifts in attitudes of individuals and groups can be detected. Such analysis does not, of course, explain the patterns it reveals, though it may suggest inferences to be pursued through investigation of other kinds of evidence. And, naturally, knowledge of the procedures and customs of legislative chambers is needed, or voting at particular stages of bills, for instance, may be misinterpreted.[73]

For Congress there is a valuable machine-readable data collection which records the responses (for each Congress, the Continental Congresses, and the Congress of the Confederation) of members on all issues that reached a recorded vote. These are coded and organized in a form suitable for analysis. The collection embraces, too, descriptions of the issues concerned and other relevant material. Use of this collection, in conjunction with data on individual Congressmen from sources such as those outlined above, can illuminate the relationship between the policy of legislators and the characteristics and politics of their constituency areas.[74]

Records listing delegates to city, county, state, and national party conventions, members of city and county party

---

[73] For methods, see Louis Guttman, "The basis for scalogram analysis," in Samuel A. Stoffer et al., Measurement and Prediction (1950); Patrick L. McLaughlin et al., "A computer program for Guttman scaling of roll calls," HM, 18 (1985); Duncan McRae, Jr., "A method for identifying issues and factions from legislative votes," Am. Political Science Rev., 59 (1966); Lee F. Anderson et al., Legislative Roll-Call Analysis (1966); Richard J. Jensen, Historians' Guide to Statistics (1971), 116–21, 198–205; Joel H. Silbey, The Shrine of Party (1967), 13–16, app. II; George M. Belknap, "A method of analysing legislative behavior," Midwest Jnl. Political Science, 2 (1958). For examples, see Rodney O. Davies, "Partisanship in Jacksonian state politics," in Robert P. Swierenga (ed.), Quantification in American History (1970); Thomas B. Alexander, Sectional Stress and Party Strength (1967).

[74] An ICPSR (see p. 64) holding: ICPSR 4, "US Congressional roll call voting record, 1789–1976." ICPSR also has a collection on the partisan composition of each state legislature. See Michael W. Traugott et al., "Computer-readable data sources," in Jerome M. Clubb et al. (eds.), Analyzing Electoral History (1981), 29–30.

executive committees, and officials of local party clubs, can be used to identify political leaders not of the first rank who might rarely be reported in the press and did not run for Congress, for state legislatures, or local councils or offices.

As well as investigating individual leaders, the community historian may well seek to identify "leadership groups" which may have been depositories of political power or the nuclei of political pressure groups, and to reveal the common characteristics of their members and changes over time. The analysis of collective biographical material (political prosopography),[75] linked to the kind of sources used for the analysis of social structure (such as censuses, directories, and tax records: ch. 2) can be used to provide data on occupations, wealth, residence, age, sex, marital connections, religion, place of origin, ethnicity, and so on,[76] and to determine the characteristics of parties, factions within parties, and leadership or elite groups generally.

In more populous places, analysis of the membership of professional societies, benevolent agencies, cultural organizations, charitable institutions, social clubs, and prestigious church congregations, taken in conjunction with consideration of members' business associates, whether they resided in the same neighborhood, intermarriage, and so on, may prove useful for the understanding of the seats of power and influence.[77] Investigation of the socio-economic characteristics of city officers at New Haven, CT, 1784–1897, for instance, demonstrated that whereas mayors were for many years largely drawn from the professional classes, from about 1842 they were mainly persons engaged in business and industry. Aside from identifying social class and economic characteristics of political leaders, it is possible to approach the topic also by identifying from the same kind of sources those

---

[75] Lawrence Stone, "Prosopography," *Daedalus*, 100 (1971); Samuel P. Hays, "The social analysis of American political history," *Political Science Q.*, 80 (1965), 377–81.

[76] Cf. Richard Jensen, "Quantitative collective biography," in Swierenga, *Quantification*; Jean Barman *et al.*, "Prosopography by computer," *HMN*, 10 (1977); William G. Roy, "Collecting data on American business officials ... ," *HM*, 15 (1982).

[77] Cf. Frederic C. Jaher, *The Urban Establishment* (1982).

Sources for U.S. History

citizens in potentially significant categories (ethnic, religious, socio-economic) and then determining the extent of their participation in local politics and government.[78] Membership lists of clubs and societies and information on members found in directories, guide books, newspapers, and so on, used in conjunction with census evidence, are useful for defining possibly influential social groups, and perhaps those of particular ethnic backgrounds. Investigation of such societies may also indicate the extent to which they may have formed a web of socio-political influence in local communities.[79] Thus, for instance, the commercial elite of a city or county may be deduced from lists of officers and directors of banks, insurance companies, and the like, from house publications, directories, and so forth, and compared with the membership of active political groupings.

Another approach providing information of the political views of those active in local politics, though perhaps not holding office or official positions, is to analyze the socio-economic characteristics of numbers of individual voters identified from newspaper accounts of local or state political meetings, political petitions, or other open and reported political activity.[80]

Political events and activities As to tracing actual political events, it should not be too difficult to find detailed evidence for most places on the evolution of policy, opposition and public debate, compromise, failure or success, and on campaigns, electioneering, and the various issues emerging from time to time which made up the maelstrom of local politics. Biographical sources, personal papers, and newspapers have already been mentioned. In addition many of the official records described in the section on local government above,

---

[78] Dahl, *Who Governs?*, 12–13, 330. Cf. Donald S. Bradley and Mayer Zald, "From commercial elite to political administrator," *Am. Jnl. Sociology*, 71 (1965).
[79] Don H. Doyle, "The social functions of voluntary associations in a nineteenth-century town," *Social Science Hist.*, 1 (1977); Walter S. Glazer, "Participation and power," *HMN*, 5 (1972); and below.
[80] Cf. Thomas B. Alexander *et al.*, "The basis of Alabama's two-party system," in Joel H. Silbey and Samuel T. McSeveney, *Voters, Parties, and Elections* (1972).

will also be useful, particularly where they give clues to the
political reasons for decisions and legislation. Thus the
municipal records of Birmingham, AL, linked with newspaper and pamphlet evidence, illuminate the systematic
deprivation of blacks' access to the electoral process after
1890.[81] And the minutes of town meetings, meetings of
county and city governments, and of important local government committees may be particularly valuable – especially
where they indicate reasons for decisions. The Town Clerk of
Concord, MA, for instance, kept very detailed minutes of
town meetings, recording the debates as well as the matters
voted on.[82]

Useful, too, may be correspondence between local government officials and officers and private individuals, business
organizations, and so on, where it exists. Petitions, to state
legislatures and to city and county governments, of citizens
and organized groups seeking to secure particular privileges,
supporting or opposing appointments of individuals to office
or proposed legislation, or complaining against existing situ-
ations or policies, may throw light on aspects of public
opinion and public pressure, in the context of which the
politicians worked, and by which they may have been
influenced.

In the National Archives, the correspondence files of Congressional committees and of many of the federal agencies can
provide evidence on the views of individuals, groups, and
organizations on many political issues of varying significance
in places all over the country. Perhaps easier of access and
providing similar sorts of information are petitions and memorials to Congress which exist in hundreds of thousands
among the records of the House and Senate (RGs 46, 233).[83]
Carefully used, they can provide the key to the composition
of aspects of public opinion on many political and other
issues. Since they were signed, the authors may be identified

---

[81] Harris, *Political Power in Birmingham*, 282.
[82] Townsend Scudder, *Concord* (1947), 391.
[83] *GNA*, 50, 52; Philip Muntz, "Sources in the National Archives relating to vital
statistics, public opinion, and population data," in Meyer H. Fishbein (ed.), *The
National Archives and Statistical Research* (1973), 91.

from such sources as city directories and census records, thus enabling the historian to assess the types of people supporting or opposing particular measures.[84] Petitions may also be found in the transactions of Congress and in published federal documents. Congress, for example, published seventeen messages received from Carolina communities in 1834 over the Bank War of that time.[85]

For Southern communities, many federal documents and unpublished materials in the National Archives contain data on racial aspects of politics, particularly on illegal attempts to prevent blacks exercising their right to vote during the Reconstruction period.[86] Among the records of the Adjutant General (RG 94) are details, including local information, of the Army's intervention in political affairs in the South. His published annual reports (in the reports of the Secretary of War) sometimes also give brief indication of such activity. In his report of 1874, for instance, he noted that troops were requested by the civil authorities of Coffee county, TN, to maintain the law and assisted in the arrest of perpetrators of outrages in various Southern states.[87]

In the annual reports of the commanders of the five military districts covering the South, 1867–70 (which are also published in the reports of the Secretary of War),[88] there is a great deal on political insurrection. For instance, it is recorded that the municipal authorities of Augusta, GA, felt that they were about to be resisted by "a combination."[89] Other evidence is also in the Secretary of War's reports: the Governor of California, for instance, in 1868 sought military assistance to prevent riots on election day in San Francisco.[90] A great deal of evidence on the supervision of Congressional elections and the enforcement of voting rights is in the unpublished records of

[84] Constance M. Green, *Washington* (1962), 406; Ira Berlin *et al.*, "'To Canvass the Nation'," *Prologue*, 20 (1988), for examples.
[85] Cited Harry L. Watson, *Jacksonian Politics and Community Conflict* (1981), 160–1. See below for petitions on elections.
[86] E.g., Papers committee to investigate state of affairs in Maryland, 1867 (in RG 233). See Buford Rowland *et al.* (comps.), *Records of the United States House of Representatives, 1789–1946* (PI 113, 1959), vol. 1, 170, 177.
[87] HED 1 (pt. 2) (43–2), ser. 1635.   [88] See p. 136.
[89] HED 1 (40–3), ser. 1367, p. 115.   [90] Ibid., p. xxxix.

the Attorney General (Justice Department) (RG 60). The "source-chronological files" (1870–84) and the "year files" (1884–1909) of correspondence are particularly valuable for the South and border states in the postbellum period and later.[91] The published annual reports of the Attorney General are less useful for local evidence.

Congressional debates and petitions to Congress, noted above, and federal documents of various dates and kinds provide much information on alleged frauds in Congressional elections and on contested elections and suchlike topics.[92] Examples of such federal documents include a report on the 1876 election in Louisiana which provides much local evidence, including tables by parish of votes cast and rejected with details of reasons for rejection (though there is no index).[93] Again, the *Report of a Senate Committee to Inquire into Alleged Frauds and Violence in the Elections of 1878* includes, for Louisiana, South Carolina, and Mississippi, evidence of witnesses (arranged by county and Louisiana parish) with a very detailed synoptical index.[94] There are similar reports for elections in other Southern states in the 1870s,[95] and some of the federal documents relating generally to Reconstruction and in particular to the activities of the Army, the Freedmen's Bureau, and the Southern Claims Commission, detailed elsewhere in this volume,[96] may also contain evidence on the political situation in Southern localities. Case records relating to election frauds may be found in records of United States Attorneys (RG 118).[97]

[91] *GNA*, 338. And see p. 139. Cf. Richard O. Curry (ed.), *Radicalism, Racism, and Party Realignment* (1969), 316.

[92] See *A Historical and Legal Digest of All the Contested Election Cases in the House of Representatives ... 1789–1901* (HD 510 (56–2), ser. 4172, 1913): contents page indicates persons with their state, and text may give considerable local data. See also *Checklist*, 1653, and *CIS, US Serial Set Index* (see p. 22) under key words; Schmeckebier and Eastin, 174–5.

[93] Rep. Sub-committee of Committee of Privileges and Elections: SR 701 (44–2), ser. 1735–7, 3 vols.

[94] SR 855 (45–3), ser. 1840. Cf. HR 140 (45–3), ser. 1866 (FL and LA).

[95] See *CIS, US Serial Set Index* under key words.

[96] See pp. 136–8, 140–1, 187–8, and for material in the Library of Congress, refs. p. 136n. HED 30 (44–2), ser. 1755, Use of the Army in ... Southern States (1877), includes *inter alia* extracts from local newspapers.

[97] *GNA*, 344.

Where significant policies, decisions, or controversies involved relations with the governing bodies or officials of neighboring cities or counties, their records may need to be searched. State archives, including the correspondence of governors, may throw light on relationships between local and state governments. For that purpose it is often worth while for the community historian to consult secondary works on general state history, and, for any particular place, on the histories of neighboring communities. State documents, too, may yield information on political matters, especially on corrupt practices at elections. A Kentucky document of 1883–4, for instance, contains the report of a committee that investigated bribery and corruption at recent elections for various offices.[98]

Sources for railroad history (see chs. 5, 9), such as the annual reports of railroad companies and their publications, including pamphlets, can shed light on the political activities of railroad companies and their relationships with local groups or individuals.

Pamphlets, addresses, and broadsheets issued by individuals, political parties, and other organized interested groups, often found collected in large libraries, will illustrate more directly the declared attitudes and intentions of political leaders and parties and the views of pressure groups on current issues. Analysis of the coverage of different topics in such publications and in newspaper editorials and the like can reveal the outlooks and priorities of different political parties or politicians, their changes over time, and how far they differed from the standpoint of the parties concerned at national level.[99] Such material, together with politicians' correspondence and private papers, where they exist, may illuminate how party organizations worked at the local level.[100]

Some district and party conventions left printed and manuscript records,[101] and sometimes the archives of local pressure

[98] House Jnl., Kentucky (1883–4), 1,319.
[99] Cf. Michael F. Holt, *Forging a Majority* (1969), 371–2: but the approach described is a rough and ready measure.
[100] See use made of a pamphlet collection in Watson, *Jacksonian Politics*.
[101] Cf. Brock, 166–9.

and interest groups may exist to fill out the picture of the nature of varying political viewpoints and of the types of persons who belonged to such organizations. Thus in Chicago the papers of the Citizens' Association of Chicago and of the Municipal Voters' League provide material on middle-class reformers and their political efforts around the turn of the century.[102] Newspapers sometimes reported meetings of such societies, and these and directories can be used to discover who their officers and other adherents were. Such information can then be used in conjunction with other evidence to determine the socio-economic, residential, ethnic, and other character-istics of such groups.

As with many aspects of community history, prime sources for political history are the daily and weekly newspaper and the periodical press. A study of the politics of the cities of the Midwest in the later nineteenth century found that the major daily papers "not only recorded the comings, goings, and utterances of the politicians, but ably described the operation of party organizations, gave incisive summaries of public opinion, reported polls," and so on.[103] Such sources also list names of delegates to state political conventions, indicating perhaps politically active members of county courts and the like. The obvious fact that much reporting of political matters was not disinterested and often frankly partisan, is not necess-arily a disadvantage so long as it is recognized by the re-searcher. In most towns of any size there was more than one newspaper, and different papers often represented different political affiliations or preferences, with specific prejudices for or against local personalities or matters of controversy. The historian is thus given considerable insight into different pol-itical, ethnic, religious, and factional viewpoints on the same matters, and can also probably deduce the basic facts about actual events and follow the varying attempts to manipulate public opinion one way or another.[104] Some labor newspapers

[102] Cf. Humbert S. Nelli, *Italians in Chicago, 1880–1930* (1970), 285; Crooks, *Politics and Progress*, 238.

[103] Richard Jensen, *The Winning of the Midwest* (1971), 317.

[104] Cf. Thomas M. Keefe, "The Catholic issue in the Chicago Tribune before the Civil War," *Mid-America*, 57 (1975).

contain local political information, while professional journals, like *Municipal Affairs* (1887–1902/3) carried articles on local political leaders and urban politics.

In perusing newspaper files, particular attention should be paid to the reporting of party and group meetings, district and state party conventions, and political campaigns, as well as of important council meetings, debates, legislative decisions, and so on. But editorial commentaries on those events and on the policies of personalities and parties should also be noticed. In addition some papers carried such features as investigative reports, informative background essays, "chatty behind-the-scenes gossip," lists of association office holders, and interviews with prominent figures.[105] Letters to the press may also be informative of the differing views of members of the general public, some of whom may be identifiable from other sources, such as directories. In New York, to quote one instance, even correspondence, to, from, and between city officials found its way into the press.[106] On the matter of black suffrage, referenda were held in most Northern states, often repeatedly, during the Reconstruction era. Voting results at a county and township level may be available in newspapers or state archives.[107] Finding aids, bibliographies of newspapers and periodicals, and the like, are noted above.[108] Newspapers were often numerous in the larger towns. In smaller towns and rural areas, where newspapers from the past may not have survived in such quantities, the files of newspapers of neighboring communities and cities may be of value.

Many national periodicals, like the *Political Science Quarterly* (from 1886), the *Quarterly Journal of Economics* (from 1886), and *Forum* (from 1886), sometimes carried informed articles on political affairs in the larger towns and cities; and for some areas and for certain issues religious periodicals, like the

105 Harris, *Political Power in Birmingham*, 295–8.
106 Seymour J. Mendelbaum, *Boss Tweed's New York* (1965), 187–8.
107 See Robert R. Dykstra and Harlan Hahn, "Northern voters and negro suffrage," in Swierenga, *Quantification*, 230.
108 See pp. 28–31; and note Joseph R. Conlin, *The American Radical Press* (2 vols., 1974); William Miles (comp.), *The People's Voice: An Annotated Bibliography of American Presidential Campaign Newspapers, 1828–1984* (1987).

American Catholic Quarterly (from 1876), may be of use.[109]
There were also periodicals connected with or published by
political parties or groups and purveying their views and news.[110]

Elections and voters   Sources for the investigation of disputed
and corrupt elections have been noted in the previous section.
The pamphlets, addresses, and broadsheets issued by political
parties and pressure groups, the speeches of political leaders
and others, and correspondence and editorials in the press, all
noted above, may by inference give some idea of why people
voted as they did. The political outlook of ethnic and ethno-
cultural (or religio-ethnic) groups was quite often discussed
openly in contemporary newspapers.[111] Yet, however useful
such source materials may be, conclusions about elections and
voting patterns drawn solely from them can be misleading.[112]
Certainly research in recent decades shows that close attention
to the study of voting returns can add greatly to an understanding of past public opinion,[113] and of the local political
scene.[114]

To know who voted for whom may not be as important as
knowing why people voted as they did, but it is a necessary
preliminary to that more significant problem. And records of
voting may suggest the likelihood of certain connections
between political outlook and affiliation and factors like
ethnicity, religious attachment, social and occupational
groupings, and residential location. Such relationships can be
examined at a particular point in time, but it is also of interest
sometimes to attempt to assess changes over a period.[115] Voting records, it has been said, "have at least one unique advantage: they are the only documents left by the American

---

[109] Those named here are available in microfilm. For fuller lists, see Jensen, *Winning of
the Midwest*, 318–19; Holli, *Reform in Detroit*, 260. Cf. Kass, *Politics in New York
State*, 209–10.

[110] See Walter Goldwater, *Radical Periodicals in America, 1890–1950* (1966).

[111] See, e.g., Lee Benson, *The Concept of Jacksonian Democracy* (1970 edn.), chs. 8, 9.

[112] Angus Campbell *et al.*, *The American Voter* (1960), 12.

[113] Lee Benson, "An approach to the scientific study of past public opinion," *Public
Opinion Q.*, 31 (1967–8), 562–6.

[114] ABC-Clio, *The American Electorate: A Historical Bibliography* (1984).

[115] J. Rogers Hollingsworth and Ellen J. Hollingsworth, *Dimensions in Urban History*
(1979), 121–5, and sources cited.

public from which inferences can *directly* be drawn about mass opinions concerning public policies. "[116] Indeed, for such purposes, records of voting on all sorts of matters are useful. These include voting on special issues, like the secession conventions in the South,[117] as well as voting in the regular presidential and gubernatorial elections, in elections for party conventions, for Congress, and for state legislatures, and in urban, county, and other local elections.

Voting records are extensive, though not always easy to track down. Recent compilations, mostly for the more important elections, may be consulted first.[118] Here we may note the ICPSR computer-readable data file known as "Candidate and constituency statistics of elections in the United States, 1798–1978," embracing voting returns for the offices of President, governors, and Congressional representatives. The returns are organized by states, Congressional districts, and counties, with counties being the basic unit. Small units (like wards) are not distinguished.[119] Those making use of this data file should remember that comparability over time is affected by boundary changes and by changes in the type of data collected, differences in the basis of classification, and so forth. And useful as such aids to research are, there are no compilations of voting statistics for state and other local elections, analysis of which is often desirable in the study of local politics.[120] Nor do such data bases often provide voting figures for units smaller than the county as a whole – which for certain kinds of socio-political analysis (as for heavily populated urban areas) may be too large and heterogeneous a unit.

[116] Lee Benson, *Towards the Scientific Study of History* (1972), 152.
[117] See Lewy Dorman, *Party Politics in Alabama from 1850 through 1860* (1935); Percy L. Rainwater, *Mississippi ... 1856–1861* (1938); Charles B. Dew, "The long lost returns," *Louisiana Hist.*, 10 (1969).
[118] See citations, Prucha, 146 [T34, 35, 37, 39]. Some previously unpubl. county election returns are in J. R. Pole, *Political Representation in England and the Origins of the American Republic* (1966), app. II. *Congressional Quarterly's Guide to U.S. Elections* (1975) covers at state and district levels, 1824–1974, presidential, gubernatorial, Congressional elections.
[119] See p. 64n; Jerome M. Clubb, "The Inter-University Consortium for political research," *HMN*, 2 (1969), 2–3.
[120] But for certain states some are listed in Walter D. Burnham, "Printed sources," in Clubb, *Analyzing Electoral History*, 45–70.

Some election results were certainly reported in the local press. Indeed, for some places, particularly before the 1860s, newspaper data may be the only evidence available. For Atlanta, GA, for instance, newspapers provide the only complete source for the names of all candidates for local office and for officers' votes on committees in the later nineteenth century.[121]

Apart from in the press, voting records may be found in a variety of other published sources,[122] including, particularly from the 1860s, the journals of state legislatures, and in official state, county, and city publications, like registers, manuals, and handbooks.[123] State manuals for Connecticut, Pennsylvania, Ohio, Michigan, and Iowa, for example, provide returns for statewide contests at the level of minor civil divisions, like townships and urban wards and precincts.[124] Commercially produced almanacs are also a valuable source. The *Tribune Almanac* (from 1834; to 1854 called the *Whig Almanac and Politicians' Register*),[125] for instance, provides information on presidential and other elections at county level. The *Chicago Daily News Almanac*, in the later nineteenth century, actually contains precinct returns for all the major Chicago elections (with ethnic breakdowns of the electorate by precincts for some years) as well as biennial ward and township election returns for Wisconsin, Michigan, and Illinois. City returns by wards are sometimes to be found in directories.

The voting returns for many small units, however, rarely if ever found their way into print and the originals may be difficult of access. Yet such records often exist in large quantities in county court houses, city archives, state libraries, and suchlike depositories. For Massachusetts, Connecticut, Maryland, and Virginia, for instance, there are extensive voting files covering long periods of time.[126] The city of Baltimore has a

---

[121] Eugene J. Watts, *Social Bases of City Politics* (1978), 178–9.

[122] Many cited in Burnham, "Printed sources," 44–70.

[123] Charles Peers and Oliver Williams, *State Manuals, Blue Books, and Election Results* (1962), mainly twentieth century.

[124] Hays, "Archival sources," 20–1.

[125] 1838–1914. For 1858, 1860, 1864 only, gives town and ward returns.

[126] Burnham, "Printed sources," 42. Cf. J. R. Pole, "Suffrage and representation in Maryland from 1760 to 1810," *JSoH*, 24 (1958).

large number of files of election returns for many state and local issues and offices.

Often voting returns in county and city archives are to be found among the records of the local election boards established in the nineteenth century. Most researchers make use of voting returns or abstracts of election returns listing at county or town level votes for each candidate for each office, though such records do not usually give details at precinct level. Precinct returns have, however, sometimes survived and when available are, of course, valuable.[127]

Comparison over time, as already noted, must take into account changes in the boundaries of electoral units, and sometimes historians will need to reconstitute data along the lines of former counties or other units which have at some time been subdivided or had their boundaries altered.[128] And researchers will need anyway to be aware of the exact territorial extent of the units they are studying – for example, to facilitate the correlation of demographic data with voting evidence.[129] Maps of electoral units are often published and available in public libraries. Several nineteenth-century atlases show county and township boundaries and those of wards in larger cities. City and state official registers and manuals, as well as commercial almanacs, will often contain ward maps.[130] The statistical atlas which comprised part of the 1870 census has maps of political divisions.[131]

Having acquired voting statistics the community historian may, by linkage with other sources, analyze voting behavior in such a way as to illuminate greatly the political actions and outlooks of the mass of the local population, and so add a

[127] Jones, 158. Many listed in WPA, HRS inventories.
[128] See, e.g., J. Morgan Kousser, *The Shaping of Southern Politics* (1974), 271–2; Phyllis F. Field, *The Politics of Race in New York* (1982).
[129] Watson, *Jacksonian Politics* advises caution: NC antebellum voters could vote in any precinct in their county and were not confined to that in which they lived.
[130] Martis, *Historical Atlas of United States Congressional Districts* (maps districts, defines boundary changes, lists representatives). N.B., too, Parsons, *United States Congressional Districts*; Michael H. Shelley, *Ward Maps of U.S. Cities* (1975) (25 largest cities, 1880, and 10 others). For county boundaries, see pp. 54n, 299.
[131] Dubester (1950), 12–13.

further dimension to the history of local politics. What sort of
voters seem to have voted for what party or what candidate?
Who actually were the individuals who voted or refrained
from voting? How were allegiances affected by particular local
or national issues? Was it likely that pressure was brought to
bear on the voter? Did voting patterns bear a relationship to
the ethnic, religious, or wealth characteristics of the populations of the counties, cities, precincts, or wards concerned?
Was voting perhaps related to the extent of commercializa-
tion, rurality, urbanity, or suburbanity of districts? Are cycles
of voting discernible? How did support for the various political parties vary over time? How did third-party activity affect
the previously established pattern? And to what extent did
voters change party allegiances from one election to
another?[132] Questions like these are all worth while considering.

A good deal of work along these lines has already been
undertaken – mainly for major elections in large cities and at
state or county level – in order to assess possible correlations
between voting patterns in different wards or counties and
the social characteristics of voters in those places. Thus the
political outlook of the dominant socio-economic, religious,
and ethnic elements within them can be determined. Such
study of aggregate groups has been very fruitful but cannot
be undertaken without some knowledge of statistical
techniques.[133]

Correlation of voting patterns with other quantifiable
socio-economic data (as ethnicity,[134] religion, occupation,

[132] For a methodology in this case, see Kleppner, *Evolution of American Electoral
Systems*, 129–30.
[133] See p. 8; works cited in Allan G. Bogue, "United States: The 'New' political
history," *JCH*, 3 (1968); Melvyn Hammarburg, "An analysis of American electoral data," *JIH*, 13 (1982–3); Allan G. Bogue, "Quantification in the 1980s," *JIH*,
12 (1981–2). Cf. Samuel P. Hays, "The use of archives for historical statistical
inquiry," in Fishbein, *National Archives and Statistical Research*, 66; Samuel T.
McSeveney, "Ethnic groups, ethnic conflicts, and recent quantitative research in
American political history," *International Migration Rev.*, NS 7 (1973).
[134] See p. 123. Cf. Lawrence H. Fuchs (ed.), *American Ethnic Politics* (1968), bibl.;
Raymond E. Wolfinger, "The development and persistence of ethnic voting,"
Am. Political Science Rev., 59 (1966); Thomas W. Kremm, "Cleveland and the first
Lincoln election," *JIH*, 8 (1977).

wealth) can be undertaken by combining voting return evidence with that from such sources as directories, tax records, and the published volumes and manuscript schedules of federal and other censuses. The ICPSR data files (see above) include not only voting statistics, but also, for the same territorial units, data drawn largely, but not solely, from the published federal censuses, such as total population, distribution by age, race and sex, occupation, and information on income and property ownership, with some evidence of religious affiliations, schooling, and literacy.

Methods of analyzing the socio-economic and ethno-religious structure of local communities have been described elsewhere.[135] Classification of people into broad religious groups[136] may make correlation between religious and voting patterns easier than attempting to make use of a multitude of denominational distinctions. Broad categories often coincided with particular outlooks on life, with political overtones – as, for instance, attitudes to temperance and prohibition. That said, care must be taken to avoid amalgamating groups with very different social and economic backgrounds because they seem religiously akin. Even within denominations there were differences – as, for instance, between Catholics of different ethnic origins. Nor were all Germans or Irishmen Catholics – and these groups tended in Pittsburgh, for instance, to vote according to religion rather than ethnic origin.[137]

It should, too, be borne in mind in such studies that the socio-economic composition of the electorate of wards, precincts, townships, or other electoral areas did not necessarily reflect the characteristics of the total population of those places.[138] Property, residential, educational, racial, and tax-

---

[135] See pp. 106–15, 120–3, 243–4. Cf. Ronald P. Formisano, "Analyzing American voting, 1830–60," *HMN*, 2 (1969).

[136] Cf. Richard Jensen, "The religious and occupational roots of party identification," *Civil War Hist.*, 16 (1970); Ronald P. Formisano, *The Birth of Mass Political Parties* (1971), ch. 8.

[137] Paul Kleppner, "Lincoln and the immigrant vote," *Mid-America*, 48 (1966).

[138] George H. Daniels, "Immigrant vote in the 1860 election," in Silbey and McSeveney, *Voters, Parties, and Elections*.

paying qualifications often restricted the franchise.[139] More-over relationship to other variables may be affected by the actual proportion of voter "turn-out." Taking this into ac-count is likely to be a task of considerable complication. In undertaking it, consideration may need to be taken of voting by those not legally enfranchised and other frauds.[140] This aside, however, if the actual number of enfranchised persons is known, the rate of participation of voters in the political process may be ascertained by comparison with the number of votes cast and the relationship of such participation to particu-lar issues can also be deduced.[141] Since some directories, and other sources, indicate the political affiliations of voters, varying participation of different groups and political parties may be assessed. The identity of those eligible to vote can more generally be ascertained from registers of electors, which list – for voting districts – voters by name, giving such information as addresses, places of birth, occupations, and whether taxes were paid. Reasons for removal from the regis-ter may also be noted.[142] A few states (including New York, Ohio, Louisiana, Kentucky, and Tennessee) conducted periodic censuses of electors.[143]

For many places there may be sources which identify indi-viduals who voted, and considerable scope exists for such research at the community level. It has been pointed out that "as a practical matter the secret ballot did not exist in the United States for nearly the entire nineteenth century."[144] In

---

[139] See state constitutions. Also useful: Kirk H. Porter, *A History of Suffrage in the United States* (1918), though has inaccuracies; Charles O. Paullin, *Atlas of the Historical Geography of the United States* (1932, repr. 1975). For female suffrage, see *Commission on Data for the Massachusetts Constitutional Convention, Bull. No. 33* (1914).

[140] Ray M. Shortridge, "Estimating voter participation," in Clubb, *Analyzing Electoral History*, and works cited; Gerald Ginsburg, "Computing turnout," *JIH*, 16 (1986), 588–602.

[141] Cf. Samuel T. McSeveney, "Voting in the Northeastern states during the late nineteenth century," in Silbey and McSeveney, *Voters, Parties, and Elections*, 197–202.

[142] Jones, 157. Many listed in WPA, HRS inventories.

[143] Richard P. McCormick, "Suffrage, classes and party alignments," *Public Opinion Q.*, 46 (1959–60), 397.

[144] Philip Converse, "Change in the American electorate," in Angus Campbell and Philip Converse (eds.), *The Human Meaning of Social Change* (1972), 277.

those states where there was viva voce voting or where the recording of individual voting preferences was required, poll books, where they survive, provide an invaluable source. These recorded the names of those who actually voted in elections and their vote choice and should be sought in record depositories. Collectively they can be extensive. At Baltimore, for example, about a thousand volumes exist for the period 1800–89.[145]

Even in states where voting was ostensibly covert, it is sometimes possible to find out the way individuals voted. Parties and political leaders kept lists of supporters and unofficial "poll books" were sometimes kept by corrupt election officials.[146] Anyway, since voting laws differed from state to state and, moreover, some states changed their practices more than once during the nineteenth century, the investigator will need to determine the actual regulations for the period under review. In this way the significance of poll-book and electoral-register evidence can be properly assessed. Incidentally, the running controversies over the ballot and voting procedures are themselves a worthwhile topic for local study.

Once individual voters have been identified and the way they cast their votes determined, they may be further brought to life by linkage with biographical information from census schedules, directories, tax lists, and so on. In this way the researcher can "associate general patterns of voting behavior directly with other characteristics of individual voters. The result is, in effect, a partial collective biography of the entire electorate."[147]

It is worth stressing, however, that a real understanding of electoral and other politics cannot be obtained solely from statistical evidence. Correlation coefficients cannot, for example, show *why* certain groups tended to vote in certain

[145] Cox and Vanorney, "The records of a city," 300. Many listed in WPA, HRS inventories.
[146] See refs. in Paul F. Bourke and Donald A. Debats, "Identifying voting in nineteenth-century America," *Perspectives in American Hist.*, 11 (1978), 288: this is drawn on here and should be consulted. See also Paul F. Bourke and Donald A. Debats, "Individuals and aggregates," *Social Science Hist.*, 4 (1980).
[147] Kenneth J. Winkler, "A social analysis of voter turnout in Ohio, 1850–1860," *JIH*, 13 (1983).

ways.[148] The general knowledge obtained from more traditional sources – biographies, journals, letters, newspapers, and so forth – perhaps used in conjunction with quantitative material, is most likely to give a rounded picture. Thus statistical evidence on the voting behavior of individuals and groups, linked with literary evidence about political leaders, may well shed light on the power bases of such leaders and may be particularly relevant to the study of the "boss" system and machine politics.[149] Such linkage of evidence may also illuminate the activities of middle-class reformers and the extent to which ethnicity and poverty forwarded machine politics or to which party political allegiances were undercut by ward interests in significant local issues.[150]

Finally, although social science theories of group behavior may suggest to the historian possible reasons which might not otherwise have occurred to him,[151] the investigator of community history, as of all history, should be aware of the dangers of ahistorical approaches.[152]

ORGANIZED LABOR AND LABOR TROUBLES

It is fashionable to interpret labor history broadly to embrace working-class working and living conditions and working-class attitudes and way of life generally, rather than concentrating solely on the history of the labor movement, working-class institutions, and worker–employer relations. Topics like social structure and social mobility, public health and housing are, however, discussed in other chapters of this book. So,

[148] For more sophisticated techniques for voter behavior research, see Peyton McCrory *et al.*, "Class and party in the secession crisis," *JIH*, 8 (1978), esp. 431–2n.

[149] Cf. Zane L. Miller, *Boss Cox's Cincinnati* (1968), ix; Kass, *Politics in New York State*, ix; John D. Buenker and Nicholas C. Burckel, *Progressive Reform: A Guide to Information Sources* (1980), "Urban reform."

[150] Cf. Elmer Cornwell, "Bosses, machines, and ethnic groups," *Annals Am. Academy of Political and Social Sciences*, 353 (1964); John M. Allswang, *Bosses, Machines and Urban Voters* (1977); Martin Schefter, "The electoral foundations of the political machine," in Joel H. Silbey *et al.* (eds.), *The History of American Electoral Behavior* (1978).

[151] See, e.g., Benson, *Concept of Jacksonian Democracy*, 270–87 for a classification system for possible determinants of voting behavior.

[152] Cf. Stephen L. Hansen, "The illusion of objectivism," *HM*, 12 (1979).

Sources for U.S. History

too, is child and female labor, though some useful references may be found on this topic in the following pages. Stress in this section is on the sources relating to worker organizations and to events like strikes and lockouts which had political overtones. Some of the sources discussed in other chapters in relation to industrial and business history and ethnic groups may also be useful for labor unions and radical political activity.

Much secondary work has been published on labor history,[153] and many works concerned with economic aspects of local community history may also embrace organized labor. Trade unions occupied a minor place in national life before the twentieth century, but they existed from the early nineteenth century and often had a significance in local communities at particular points in time.

So many federal documents relating to labor, labor disputes, trade unions, and allied subjects were published that they cannot all be treated here. The index of the US Serial Set should be consulted.[154] Some of the more important documents may, however, be mentioned. The report of 1895 of the Strike Commission on the Chicago strike of the previous year is well known.[155] Others include a report of 1887 of a select committee on labor troubles in Missouri, Arkansas, Kansas, Texas, and Illinois, and another on such difficulties in the anthracite regions of Pennsylvania, 1887–8.[156] And a document of 1898 includes a list of organizations (national, state, city, and local branches and unions) affiliated to the American Federation of Labor, with addresses of local representatives.[157]

---

[153] Citations, *HG*, 427–34; Prucha, 209–10; Ralph E. McCoy and Donald Gsell, *History of Labor and Unionism in the United States: A Selected Bibliography* (1953); Gene S. Stroud and Gilbert E. Donahue (comps.), *Labor History in the United States: A General Bibliography* (1961); ABC-Clio, *Labor in North America: A Historical Bibliography* (1985); Fred D. Rose, *American Labor in Journals of History. A Bibliography* (1962); Mary R. Heslet, *The Labor Movement in the United States: An Annotated Bibliography* (1963). *Labor Hist.* publishes an annual bibl.

[154] See p. 22; and for reps. on depression in labor and business (1879) and on sweated trades (1892), pp. 363, 364.

[155] SED 7 (53–3), ser. 3276.

[156] HR 4174 (49–2) 2 pts., ser. 2502; HMD 4147 (50–2), ser. 2676.

[157] SD 318 (55–2), ser. 3615, pp. 44–55.

The nineteen volumes of the *Report of the Industrial Commission* (1900–2), created to investigate labor and industrial practices,[158] are a mine of information on conditions in the last years of the nineteenth century and are well indexed. Volume V includes digests of state laws relating to labor. Volume XVII is devoted to "Labor Organizations, Labor Disputes, and Arbitrations," with a special report on railroad labor. It includes (part I) information on state laws and court decisions. Part II of the volume contains details of national labor organizations (by trades), some of which had particular significance in certain localities. Part III provides data on collective bargaining agreements and arbitrations (by trades) and also details of arbitrations by state governments (including statutory provisions), and useful references to the records of strikes kept by state bureaus. Volumes VII and XIV, entitled "Relations and Conditions of Capital and Labor Employed in Manufactures and General Business," contain, especially in the testimony, much data relating to labor legislation and trade unions, disputes, and difficulties. Volume XII, consisting of a like report relating to the mining industry, provides similar evidence. Volume IV, on transportation, contains evidence on strikes and trade unions in the transportation industries (and has an index of places). Volume X, devoted to agricultural labor, has some information on labor organizations and the index of testimony may be worth searching. Volume VIII is concerned with the Chicago labor disputes of 1900.

The testimony given before the Committee on Education and Labor upon Relations between Labor and Capital, published in 1885,[159] presents a massive collection of evidence, from many parts of the country, on disputes, strikes, arbitrations, labor organizations and politics, conditions of work in different industries and trades, hours of work, wages, contracts, child and female labor, immigrant and black labor, and

---

[158] HD 476 (56–1), 494–5 (56–2), 177–87, 380 (57–1), sers. 3990–2, 4168–9, 4338–49; and see p. 364. The Commission's only extant records are its minutes (in NA, RG 240): see GNA, 464; *Materials in the National Archives Relating to Labor and Labor Problems* (RIC 10, 1942), 7.

[159] 4 vols., publ. as Rep. of the Committee, but actual rep. never publ. Not in US Serial Set.

on the general conditions of the working classes in industry, mining, and agriculture. Not all places mentioned in the text are in fact indexed, but a judicious use of the indexes may be worth while.

The annual reports of the U.S. Commissioner of Labor[160] are full of information on economic and social matters, some of it of a local nature, and though they begin in 1886 some contain retrospective data. A few of these reports in particular may be noted.[161] The first (1886) includes a synopsis of state labor laws.[162] The third (1887) provides details of strikes and lockouts, including data on individual cases (identifying localities), for the eighteenth century to 1881. It also gives, for 1881–6, statistical data on strikes, and similar data on lockouts with an indication of the locality and reasons for each lockout. In addition this report provides details of state labor legislation and of court decisions on individual strikes, combinations, conspiracies, boycotts, and so on. The tenth report (1896), also devoted to strikes and lockouts, gives similar data on them as does the third report,[163] but for 1887–94 (plus some omissions from the third report). Thus, to give an example of the amount of detail provided, it is recorded that a strike occurred from February 6 to 8, 1893, in a firm making knee pants in Brooklyn, NY. The union which called the strike for increased wages succeeded in closing the establishment for a while; the employees (ten men and one woman) were not replaced but lost $30 in wages and continued to work seventy-two hours a week for the same pay as before the strike.

Aside from these regular annual reports,[164] the Bureau of

[160] See *Checklist*, 616–17.
[161] See Paul K. Edwards, *Strikes in the United States, 1881–1974* (1981), for use of this material.
[162] For state laws on child labor, see *HG*, 426–7; William F. Ogburn, *Progress and Uniformity in Child Labor Legislation* (1912), esp. app.; John R. Commons *et al.*, *History of Labour in the United States* (4 vols., 1918–35), vol. 3, 403–4; Elizabeth H. Davidson, *Child Labor Legislation in the Southern Textile States* (1930). And see pp. 365–6.
[163] For difficulties in using 3rd and 10th reps. for local inf., see Sari Bennett and Carville Earle, "The geography of strikes in the United States, 1881–1894," *JIH*, 13 (1982–3). Cf. the more general 16th Rep. (1901), covering 1881–1901, and Bureau of Labor Statistics, *Strikes in the United States, 1880–1936* (1938).
[164] See also refs. in Commons, *History of Labour*, vol. 2, 579–80.

Labor produced other useful publications, including a bi-monthly bulletin,[165] a monograph on *Labor Disturbances in the State of Colorado from 1880 to 1904* (1905),[166] and a series of special reports. The tenth special report (1905) sets out the labor laws in force at the end of 1903 with court decisions relating to them. But perhaps the most important of these special reports is the third (1893).[167] This provides an abstract of each of the 174 reports relating to social and industrial topics issued by state bureaus or departments of labor in twenty-seven states, from the first issued by the Massachusetts Bureau of the Statistics of Labor in 1869. In addition an index to the contents of each of these reports is given. This publication is valuable both in itself and as a key to the more detailed original state reports, which are shown to be most fruitful sources. Among significant index entries to search are "arbitration and strikes," "strikes," and "trade unions." The fifteenth annual report of the Pennsylvania Bureau of Industrial Statistics (1887) is, for example, noted as providing an extensive account of the Knights of Labor organization in that state, while the first biennial report of the Illinois Bureau of Labor Statistics (1879, 1880) is recorded as having an account of trade societies and wages. Similarly the thirteenth annual report of the Massachusetts Bureau (1892) has a 233-page section analyzing the answer to the question "Why is it that the working people of Fall River are in a constant turmoil, while at Lowell and Lawrence they are quiet?," and providing much data on relationships between employers and employees. The second annual report of the Missouri Bureau of Labor Statistics and Inspection (1881) published a report on strikes and arbitration including extracts from returns of trade unions, detailing their numbers, wages, and so on, and from replies of manufacturers about arbitration procedures. The second annual report of the Rhode Island Bureau of Industrial Statistics (1888) published

---

[165] For titles, see *Subject Index of the U.S. Bureau of Labor Statistics ... [to] 1915.*
[166] SD 122 (58–3), ser. 4765.
[167] *3rd Special Rep. U.S. Bureau of Labor: Analysis and Index of all Reports Issued by Bureaus of Labor Statistics ... Prior to ... 1892* (1893).

descriptions of the various labor organizations, furnished by
their members. Such examples could be multiplied.

The published federal census volumes do not generally
provide data on labor disputes or unions. An exception is the
1880 census (vol. xx). This contains a report on trade societies
which includes a table giving the number in each state of local
unattached labor unions and the number of branches of
national unions, arranged by type of trade or industry. In the
same volume is a brief report enumerating strikes and lockouts
in 1880, again by state and trade and industry. The main
section of the volume, devoted to the statistics of wages,
presents reports by individual named firms (arranged by industries or trades) and these often provide information on
strikes and lockouts (or their absence) as reported by the firms.
Thus Bromley Brothers of Philadelphia, carpet manufacturers, reported only two strikes in the previous twelve years,
and gave details of one – an unsuccessful thirteen-week strike
by girl hand-loom weavers.

Certain record groups in the National Archives contain
information on disputes, strikes, lockouts, riots, and labor
problems generally. Records of the Bureau of Labor (later
Labor Statistics; RG 257) include correspondence, reports,
and other items, some of which pertain to strikes and unions –
but mainly from 1913.[168] Correspondence of the Secretary of
War's office (RG 107) may sometimes give details on the use of
the military to suppress riotous laborers. The Adjutant General's records (RG 94), 1803–1917, include material on labor
disputes in firms with War Office contracts and on the use of
troops in the railroad strikes of 1877 and 1894, while troubles
on the railroads, 1894–5, are documented in the records of the
Quartermaster General (RG 92).[169] The general correspondence of the Bureau of Engineering (Navy Department; RG
19), 1885–1940, contains files relating to strikes and trade
union matters, as does the general correspondence of the

[168] GNA, 493; O. L. Harvey, "Inventory of Department of Labor records," LH, 4
(1963), 196–8.
[169] RIC 10, pp. 1, 12; Elaine C. Everly, "State and local history sources in the Military
Archives Division," in Timothy Walch (comp.), Our Family, Our Town (1987),
31.

Yards and Docks Department (Navy Department; RG 71), from 1842.[170]

Among the Secretary of the Interior's records (RG 48) are mine inspectors' reports which cover strikes and disputes in coal mines in Utah (1885–96), New Mexico (1892–1907), and Indian territories (1893–1907).[171] Some of this data appears in the published annual reports of the Interior Department.[172] The published report on New Mexico for 1894–5, for example, prints a copy of a miner's annual agreement at Gallup Mine, Bernalillo county, which contains a clause against joining a strike or combination.[173] The National Mediation Board's records (RG 13) contain papers relating to rail labor mediation.[174] The papers of the Potomac Company (later the Chesapeake and Ohio Canal Company), 1785–1938 (now in RG 79: National Park Service), include details of strikes and labor unrest and violence – as in Allegany county, MD, in 1840.[175]

The central files of the Justice Department (RG 60) contain records from the 1880s relating to trade unions, disputes, labor relations generally and labor laws, including the activities of labor and radical organizations, among them the Knights of Labor.[176] Federal district court records (RG 21), now largely in regional branches of the National Archives, include records of cases concerning labor unions, conspiracies in restraint of trade, and so forth – as in New York state from the 1820s.[177]

Indeed, court records generally are an essential source for labor unionism and employer–labor relations. Prosecutions for criminal conspiracy, used as a weapon against unionism,

---

[170] RIC 10, 5, 16: *GNA*, 309.   [171] Ibid., 7–8.

[172] Not all were publ.: see *Checklist*.

[173] HD 5 (54–1), ser. 3383, pp. 70–1.

[174] Forrest R. Holdcamper (comp.), *Preliminary Inventory of the Records of the Bureau of Labor Statistics* (NC–62, 1964), 1; *GNA*, 559; Paul Lewinson, "The archives of labor," *AA*, 17 (1954), 21.

[175] *GNA*, 401–2; Meyer H. Fishbein, "Labor history resources in the National Archives," *LH*, 8 (1967), 340–1; Richard B. Morris, "American labor history prior to the Civil War," *LH*, 1 (1960), 315.

[176] RIC 10, 8; Fishbein as last n., 332; Cannon and Fine, "Repository of labor records," 29.

[177] *GNA*, 83.

are well documented in the law reports of the higher courts of record.[178] These were reported in the press and sometimes in separate private publications.[179] They illustrate the attitudes and activities of unions and their supporters and the reaction of employers, the courts, and non-union labor to labor unions, and the treatment of strikers and demonstrators generally. Records of city and county courts, findings of grand juries, police reports, and jail records may all throw light on these matters. The Baltimore city jail records, for instance, show that heavy prison sentences could be imposed for breaking labor contracts.[180]

Since state legislatures passed labor legislation, knowledge of state labor laws is necessary for the study of labor history at the local level. Sources summarizing these have been noted above. They are available in full in the published legal codes of the states. Petitions to state legislatures on labor matters are another important source and are usually available in state archive collections. Such records for South Carolina, for instance, indicate the existence of white bondage and peonage in the antebellum South.[181]

State documents generally are likely to provide a rich mine of information. The annual reports of the Ohio state Inspector of Mines, for instance, include information on strikes and arbitrations during the year. The report for 1887–8 provides a table indicating for each strike the name of the mine and its county, the dates of the strike, the numbers of men involved, the cause, and the outcome. There are also for Ohio many documents providing accounts of individual strikes in different industries, and, in the 1890s, annual reports of a state board of arbitration. Again, the annual reports of the Auditor General of Pennsylvania for 1875–6 and 1876–7 contain details of expenses incurred over riots in the anthracite coal regions.

[178] See pp. 26–7.
[179] Some are repr. in John R. Commons *et al.*, *A Documentary History of American Industrial Society* (1910–11), vols. 3, 4, *Labor Conspiracy Cases.*
[180] Morris, "American labor history," 311–13.
[181] Richard B. Morris, "White bondage in ante-bellum South Carolina," *South Carolina Hist. and Genealogical Mag.*, 49 (1948); Richard B. Morris, "The course of peonage in a slave state," *Political Science Q.*, 65 (1950).

Governors' proclamations and the annual reports of state adjutants general and their unpublished records may detail the use of the militia in quelling labor riots.[182]

A federal document summarizing periodic reports of state labor bureaus has been noted above.[183] The full reports published as state documents are a significant source containing more detailed and more specifically local evidence. The report of the New York Bureau of Statistics of Labor for 1895 (1896), for example, includes "comments of different union branches on the 8-hour question." The unpublished records of these state labor bureaus, if they exist, will be worth searching, but most appear not to have survived for the nineteenth century.[184]

County histories and other such works may mention labor disputes, but, though given little space here, local newspapers must be regarded as a prime, and often only, source for specific information on riots, strikes, lockouts, law cases, and such like manifestations of breakdowns in labor–employer relations. In their news reports, letters, and editorials, newspapers can provide insight into different contemporary viewpoints. A sample of Pennsylvania newspapers, 1799–1840, found reports on 135 strikes, while the Tredegar Iron Works strike of 1847 is largely undocumented except in the press.[185] Obituaries may give information on local labor leaders. The national press, too, like *Niles' Weekly* (later *National*) *Register* (1811–49; available in microform) carried reports on important labor disputes.

Radical, labor orientated, and union newspapers and journals, such as the *National Laborer* (1836–7), the *National Trades' Union* (1834–7), the *Mechanics' Free Press* (1828–35), the *Mechanic* (1844–5), and the *American Workman* (1868–72), may well contain information relevant to particular localities, especially on law cases, conferences, union constitutions, statements by

---

[182] Cf. Robert D. Ward and William W. Rogers, *Labor Revolt in Alabama* (1965), esp. ch. 4 nn.; *Rep. Labor Disturbances in . . . Colorado* (1905): SD 122 (58–3), ser. 4765, quoted records.

[183] P. 341.

[184] Paul Lewinson, "State labor agencies: where are their records?," *AA*, 19 (1956).

[185] W. A. Sullivan, *The Industrial Worker in Pennsylvania, 1800–1840* (1953), 217–30; Morris, "American labor history," 316–17.

unions, reports of union committees, cooperatives and radical organizations.[186] This is especially so for serials connected with certain regions – as with the *Labor Review* (1890–2) published in Kansas City, the Boston *Labor Leader* (1887–97), and the *Union* (1886–8) of Manchester, NH.[187] Papers like the *Mechanics' Free Press* (1828–35) and the *Democratic Press* (1829), as well as the local press are important sources for the local activity of organizations like the Working Men's Party, as well as for trade unions. Some papers connected with particular immigrant ethnic groups may be useful for certain places.[188]

Reminiscences and autobiographies of politicians, labor leaders, and businessmen may also on occasion be useful.[189] Works like Terence V. Powderly's *The Path I Trod*[190] and his *Thirty Years of Labor* (1889, 2nd edn. 1890),[191] and Samuel Gompers's *Seventy Years of Life and Labor* (1925), are well known, but the memoirs of less famous leaders, like Joseph Buchanan's *The Story of a Labor Agitator* (1903), especially if their activities were locally orientated, may be worth looking for.[192] The unpublished papers of such men should also be sought. Industrialists' letters and diaries, and the less commonly available papers of working men, can provide viewpoints on labor relations other than those openly expressed. Business records and the records of chambers of commerce and of employers' associations, where they exist, may also throw light on labor relations.

---

[186] See examples in Commons, *Documentary History*, vols. 5–8.

[187] See Walter Goldwater, *Radical Periodicals in America, 1890–1950* (1966); bibls. and citations in Leon Fink, *Workingmen's Democracy* (1983); Edward Pessen, "La première presse du travail," in Jacques Godechot (ed.), *La Presse Ouvrière, 1819–1850* (1966); Commons, *History of Labour*, vol. 2; Commons, *Documentary History*, vol. 10, 142–51 (with locations); Brock, 278n. For labor serials in microform, see Hoornstra.

[188] See Dirk Hoerder, *The Immigrant Labor Press in North America, 1840s–1970s: An Annotated Bibliography* (3 vols., 1987). For other ethnic newspapers, see pp. 121–2.

[189] See pp. 18, 317.

[190] Ed. Harry J. Carman *et al.* (1940).

[191] Q.v., 225–6, for records of national conventions of Knights of Labor at Philadelphia, 1876, Pittsburgh, 1877.

[192] See also Gary L. Fink (ed.), *Biographical Dictionary of American Labor* (1984) (1974 edn. was titled *Biographical Dictionary of American Labor Leaders*); Bernard Johnpoll and Harvey Klein, *Biographical Dictionary of the American Left* (1987).

Published labor-union material, especially for the later decades of the nineteenth century, is voluminous. It includes unions' constitutions, proceedings of their conventions, mountains of pamphlets, and an extensive array of minor publications. Many unions published their own journals, which have sometimes survived in long runs and often contain information on activities in different communities.[193]

A very useful aid is the *Guide to the Local Assemblies of the Knights of Labor*.[194] The Knights of Labor was the largest single labor union in the country, embracing craft and manual occupations and including as members blacks, women, and immigrants. It often acted militantly in organizing strikes and was active in local and political issues generally. Some local studies of the Knights have been undertaken,[195] but there is scope for further regional and local research.[196] The *Guide* surveys official publications of the Knights, such as the annual *Proceedings of the General Assembly* and the *Journal of United Labor* (1880–9),[197] and provides data on the 12,000 local assemblies from the first in 1869 down to 1890. This is arranged geographically by state and county, giving for each geographical unit the name of the community (and population, 1880, 1890) in which the local assembly was organized, with dates of existence, annual enrollment figures, and membership characteristics (as race, gender, ethnic composition). In addition the book notes more detailed original sources available for consultation. The proceedings of the annual sessions

---

[193] Lloyd G. Reynolds and Charles Killingworth, *Trade Union Publications* (3 vols., 1944–6). See also Bernard G. Naas and Carmelita S. Sakr (comps.), *Labor Union Periodicals: A Guide to their Location* (1956); Mark E. Woodbridge, *American Federation of Labor and Congress of Industrial Organizations Pamphlets, 1889–1955, A Bibliography* . . . (1977); *Pamphlets in American History: A Bibliographic Guide to the Microform Collection* (1979–83, Microfilming Corp. of America), Group II.

[194] Jonathan Garlock (comp.) (1982; updates ICPSR, *Knights of Labor Data Bank*: computer tape index, 1973).

[195] E.g., Fink, *Workingmen's Democracy*; Richard Oestreicher, "Socialism and the Knights of Labor in Detroit, 1877–1886," *LH*, 22 (1981); Paul Buhle, "The Knights of Labor in Rhode Island," *Radical Hist. Rev.*, 17 (1978).

[196] Cf. Garlock, *Guide*, xi–xii.

[197] But not its successor, *Jnl. Knights of Labor* (1890–3), which might be searched.

of some district assemblies and other local records may, for instance, survive – like the minute book of the Raleigh, NC, Local Assembly 3606 for 1886–90.

Though of limited value for the community historian there are also the publications of the Federation of Organized Trades and Labor Unions of the United States and Canada (1881–6) and its successor, the American Federation of Labor (from 1886), of which the reports of proceedings of annual sessions may be noted.

In recent decades much effort has gone into the establishment of special collections of published and unpublished materials on labor history, and though these are much thinner on data for the nineteenth century than for the twentieth some do contain valuable material for years before 1900. A useful compilation indicates the existence of particular labor unions and the nature and whereabouts of the records of individual unions (as contracts, correspondence, financial accounts, minutes, negotiations, and so on).[198]

Among specialist collections, those of the Wisconsin Historical Society are outstanding. They include records of the American Federation of Labor, 1881–1953 (embracing material on strikes and agreements from 1898, and papers of Samuel Gompers) and records of the Knights of Labor, 1884–98.[199] For the Working Men's Party and the Socialist Labor Party, the Society possesses large quantities of records including those of state committees and sections in Massachusetts, New Jersey, New York, Washington, and Texas. There are also records for Wisconsin concerning strikes and riots in various towns from the 1870s, and records of cooperative associations, 1862–96. The Society also holds the materials collected by John R. Commons and Richard T. Ely for their work on American industrial society. These include transcripts of early labor journals and rare labor

---

[198] Paul Lewinson and Morris Rieger, "Labor union records in the United States," *AA*, 25 (1962). Cf. Francis Gates, *Reference Guides for Labor Research* (1957) (directories, bibls., handbooks, guides to special collections relating to labor and employer assocs.).

[199] Henry J. Browne, *The Catholic Church and the Knights of Labor* (1949), 380.

pamphlets.[200] Other state historical societies, including those of Ohio, Idaho, Nevada, and North Dakota, as well as the Chicago Historical Society, also have significant collections of labor archives.[201]

Several universities, too, have important holdings. Among them are Wayne State University,[202] Pennsylvania State University,[203] the University of Maryland (including the cigar workers' union records from 1864 and those of the tobacco workers' union from 1896),[204] the University of Illinois (including union records and the papers of Thomas J. Morgan, President of the machinists' union in Chicago, 1874, and active in city politics),[205] Georgia State University,[206] Temple University,[207] the University of Texas (including the railroad brotherhood's records of the 1880s),[208] Cornell University (including much published material and microforms of labor-related newspapers),[209] the University of California at Berkeley (including records relating to unions and employers in the West from 1850, pamphlets and other printed sources),[210]

---

[200] Henry J. Browne, "Raiding labor's records," *AA*, 17 (1954); F. Gerald Ham and Margaret Hedstrom (eds.), *A Guide to the Labor Papers in the State Historical Society of Wisconsin* (1978) and articles on this collection and the "Wisconsin school" in *LH*, 7 (1966), 23 (1982), 25 (1984).

[201] Dennis East, "Labor resources in the Ohio Historical Society," *LH*, 23 (1982); Philip P. Mason, "Labor archives in the U.S.," *LH*, 23 (1982), 489.

[202] Warner W. Pflug, *A Guide to the Archives of Labor History and Urban Affairs, Wayne State University* (1974), and articles by Philip P. Mason in *LH*, 5 (1964), 23 (1982), *Archivaria*, 4 (1977).

[203] See articles in *LH*, 13 (1972), 23 (1982). Mostly post 1900.

[204] Mary Boccachio, "Labor resources at the University of Maryland at College Park," *LH*, 23 (1982).

[205] Patricia W. Onsi, "Labor history resources of the University of Illinois," *LH*, 7 (1966).

[206] Robert Dinwiddie and Leslie Hough, "An emerging archival institution: the Southern Labor Archives," *Georgia Archive*, 6 (1978); Robert Dinwiddie and Leslie Hough, "The Southern Labor Archives," *LH*, 23 (1982).

[207] Ken Fones-Wolf, "Sources for the study of labor history in the urban archives of Temple University," *LH*, 23 (1982); *JAH*, 72 (1985–6), 763.

[208] Robert A. Gambel and George Green, "Labor archives at the University of Texas at Arlington," *LH*, 23 (1982).

[209] J. C. Miller, "Labor resources in the Cornell University libraries," *LH*, 1 (1960); Richard Strassberg, "Labor resources in ... Cornell University," *LH*, 23 (1982); *Guide to the Records of the Labor Management Documentation Center* (T/S, n.d., Cornell Univ.).

[210] Francis Gates, "Labor history resources in the libraries of the University of California, Berkeley," *LH*, 1 (1960).

Harvard University,[211] and New York University.[212] The Immigration History Research Center at the University of Minnesota includes some labor materials among the files of radical non-English language newspapers and holdings relating to immigrant labor movements.[213]

The University of Michigan has the Joseph Labadie collection, important for the Detroit area, 1880–1920, and for Labadie's correspondence with other labor leaders, as well as papers of other labor activists, and a large collection of pamphlets and ephemera.[214] The Catholic University of America (Washington, DC) has the very important collections of Terence V. Powderly and John W. Hayes, relating to the Knights of Labor, in which they were prominent. These records include materials which have already proved to be of value for local evidence, among them much correspondence, diaries, and press cuttings.[215]

The collections of other specialist, state, and local public libraries should be searched for local material.[216] Bridgeport Public Library, for instance, has materials on the labor movement in Connecticut. The New York Public Library's large collections of labor records include items on strikes, lockouts, bargaining, and labor legislation, as well as relevant papers of individuals, families, and government agencies,[217] including

[211] Robert W. Lovett, "Labor history materials in the Harvard University Library," *LH*, 4 (1963).

[212] David Gracy, "History and reminiscence," *Archivaria*, 4 (1977), 152–3.

[213] Rudolph J. Vecoli, "Labor related collections in the Immigration History Research Center," *LH*, 23 (1982; to be updated in forthcoming issue of *LH*).

[214] Eleanor H. Scanlan, "The Labadie collection," *LH*, 6 (1965); R. C. Stewart, "The Labadie labor collection," *Univ. Michigan Alumni Q.*, 53 (1947); Philip P. Mason, "Labor archives in the U.S.," *Archivum*, 27 (1980), 170–1; Edward C. Weber, "The Labadie collection in the University of Michigan library," *LH*, 23 (1982). Chadwyck-Healey Inc. proposes (1989) to publ. a microfiche of "Anarchist pamphlets, 1830–1985" from this collection and the Library of Congress.

[215] Henry J. Browne, "The records of American labor," *Catholic Univ. of America Bull.*, 23 (1965).

[216] See *NUCMC*; *Directory of Archives and Manuscripts in the United States* (1988 edn.); Markower, index under "labor and labor unions"; Mason in *LH*, 23 (1982), 489: Philip P. Mason (ed.), *Directory of Jewish Archival Institutions* (1975), 43–4, 63–4.

[217] Mason in *LH*, 23, 489; Edward De Roma, "Notes on resources for research in labor history in . . . New York Public Library," *LH*, 4 (1963).

some papers of Samuel Gompers.[218] The Library of Congress has a large collection of primary sources on labor history, including thousands of pamphlets and broadsides, among them political campaign publications aimed at working-class voters.[219] The library's collection of trade-union records includes local membership lists and records of the American Federation of Labor (AFL).[220] AFL records are to be found also at Wisconsin and in a large number of other repositories, among them the Federation's own library.[221]

The library of the United States Department of Labor possesses an enormous collection of printed materials, including items on industrial relations, arbitration, conciliation and labor laws, as well as files of trade union publications, proceedings, constitutions, reports, journals, and so on. A detailed catalog enables easy reference to items connected with particular events – as, for example, the textile workers' strike at Fall River, MA, in 1875.[222]

Finally, mention may be made of reports, by German diplomats and other agents, on the American labor movement, radical European immigrants, and general economic conditions in half a dozen large U.S. cities, now in depositories in Potsdam (Germany) and Bonn (Germany).[223]

---

[218] Lewinson, "Archives of labor," 22. For Gompers, see also Stuart B. Kaufman (ed.), *The Samuel Gompers Papers* (2 vols., 1986, 1987).

[219] James Gilreath, "Labor history sources in the Library of Congress," *LH*, 25 (1984); Library of Congress, *The Catalog of Broadsides in the Rare Books and Special Collections Division of the Library of Congress* (1972). See n. 214 above.

[220] Paul T. Heffon, "Manuscript sources in the Library of Congress for a study of labor history," *LH*, 10 (1969).

[221] AFL and Congress of Industrial Organizations Library, 815 16th St. NW, Washington, DC 20006. See also Peter J. Albert and Harold L. Miller, *The American Federation of Labor Records* (1981): a guide to *American Federation of Labor Records: The Samuel Gompers Era, 1877–1937*, Series I, microform (Chadwyck-Healey, 1981) (Series II is (1989) forthcoming); American Federation of Labor: pt. I, Statutes and Agreements File, 1892–1953, microfilm: see Univ. Publics. of America, *Research Collection* (1987), 14 for details.

[222] Margaret E. Brickett, "Labor history resources in the U.S. Department of Labor library," *LH*, 2 (1961), 236–8; *Catalog of the U.S. Department of Labor Library* (1975).

[223] For details and examples, see Dirk Hoerder (ed.), *Plutocrats and Socialists: Reps. by German Diplomats and Agents on the American Labor Movement, 1878–1917* (1981), q.v. 397–400 for list of reps., by cities.

CHAPTER 8

Manufacturing, mining, and business activity

The economic structure of local communities and regions is a basic ingredient of community history. One aspect of this, agriculture, has been treated in chapters 4 and 5. This chapter and the next are concerned with source materials for the history of manufacturing, mining, commerce, and communications.

INDUSTRY AND BUSINESS

Topics which could be considered in the local history of manufacturing and business activity are legion.[1] Fundamental is the analysis of the economic characteristics of the community concerned – the main kinds of industries and businesses and changes in their relative importance over time, embracing the growth of specialization, diversification, decline, or disappearance of certain sectors, and so on. It may be pertinent here to take into account the impact of external influences – technological change, influx of population, transportation improvements, growth of centers of consumption, expansion of banking and credit facilities, and the general fortunes of the national or regional economy.

Aspects of the main industries and trades in a community which may need investigation include the numbers of firms involved, the types of goods produced or sold, methods of manufacture, processes and machinery, use of power, and the

---

[1] For secondary works, see Prucha, 206–9; *HG*, 397–8, 410–17, 424–6; George R. Taylor (comp.), *American Economic History before 1860* (1969); Edward C. Kirkland (comp.), *American Economic History since 1860* (1971); and citations pp. 16–18. Victor C. Clark, *History of Manufactures in the United States* (3 vols., 1929, repr. 1949), draws on many sources: indexes and notes provide refs. to original sources and places.

scale of production. In addition it may well be significant to look into the organization of establishments (single entrepreneurs, family businesses, partnerships, larger companies), including management techniques, sources of capital, relations with banks, use of credit, markets for produce, and sources of raw materials. The size of the labor force and its structure is another topic for research, embracing such aspects as the distribution of different sorts of occupations, female and child labor, black and slave labor, ethnic composition, and wages and working conditions.[2]

For retailers and small craftsmen, service and commercial firms, the numbers involved, the types of goods, sources of supply, profitability, changes in function over time, and so on, can be considered. And sometimes a community historian may wish to investigate individual firms, factories, or particular businessmen in detail. For a wider area than a single town or city, comparative analysis may be undertaken of the distribution of different industries and businesses, including differences in numbers and sizes of enterprises and of their workforces and output as well as variations in the extent of capital involved. Again, links may be sought between the economic structure of a community and its social structure, or study may be undertaken of the relationship between local politics and business and industrial interests.

There are many official sources which will assist in research into such topics. Basic, perhaps, is census material. Both federal and state censuses provide information on local economic matters that cannot be ignored. The data on occupations provided in the manuscript returns of the federal population censuses and the published census volumes have been discussed already in chapter 2. It will be obvious that the occupational structure of a community will give a general idea of the nature of its industries and trades, though census categories like "laborer," "clerk," and so on, will not indicate the nature of the enterprise in which such people worked.

Additional to this information, and capable in some cases of

2 See also chs. 2, 7, and 10 *passim* (child labor).

being used in conjunction with it,[3] are the data provided by the so-called censuses of manufactures which form part of some of the federal censuses. It must be admitted that these have long been regarded as "among the weakest in the whole range of census reports ... susceptible of more misleading interpretations than any other group," and even as "reservoirs of popular error."[4] Without knowledge of their defects and complexities it is often difficult to avoid deriving from them an incorrect picture of the past, particularly at the local level. Caution is thus advised[5] – but they *can* be used to advantage.[6]

The first of such surveys was that of 1810. A few of the manuscript schedules for this are to be found among the population schedules (NA, RG 29 – providing, for each manufacturing establishment, its type, its owner's name, the quantity and estimated value of the goods produced, and occasionally the quantity of raw materials used), but the vast majority of the original returns no longer exist.[7] A digest by Tench Coxe of the original schedules was, however, published,[8] and provides statistics (by industry and by states and territories, districts and counties) of the number of enterprises, and the product value, and, for some industries, quantities of goods produced. Despite the fact that original returns were incomplete and often inaccurate (particularly for areas containing large cities) and that often errors were introduced in the compilation of the digest, Coxe's compilation is the first detailed account of American manufacturing. Though crude and defective as a statistical source, it nevertheless contains

3 Theodore Hershberg, "The Philadelphia social history project," *HMN*, 9, 2–3 (1976), 51.
4 *Federal Census, Critical Essays*, Am. Economic Assoc. Publics., NS 2 (1899), 257.
5 Cf. Laurence F. Schmeckebier, *The Statistical Work of the National Government* (1925), 269–70; Brock, 55–6.
6 E.g., Philip Scranton, "Milling about," *JUH*, 10 (1984).
7 For list of extant schedules, see Katherine H. Davidson and Charlotte M. Ashby (comps.), *Preliminary Inventory of the Records of the Bureau of the Census* (PI 161, 1964), app. IX. They are available in M252. Cf. Meyer H. Fishbein, *Early Business Operations of the Federal Government* (RIP 54, 1973), 8–9.
8 1810 Census, vol. II: *A Statement of the Arts and Manufactures of the United States ... 1810* (1814); also publ. in *American State Papers: Finance*, vol. 2, 425–39. For microfilms of this and the other publ. censuses of manufactures, see Schulze (1983); Schulze (1985).

very useful information on manufacturing for community historians.[9]

A further census of manufacturing establishments was taken in 1820. The original returns, which are available in the National Archives (RG 29) though with many gaps, are now arranged by states and counties. They show the location of each establishment, its owner's name, the type and quantity of raw materials used, the number of employees (men, women, boys, girls), the kind and extent of machinery, and the amount of capital invested, paid annually in wages and needed for contingent expenses. They also indicate the sort of goods produced, and the value of the annual output, together with remarks on the conditions of the establishment, and the demand for its goods, and sales.[10]

There is also a published "Digest of Manufacturing Establishments in the United States, 1822." This presents details of materials, machinery, capital, employees, and general observations.[11] It was, however, probably even more defective than the 1810 survey. The original schedules were themselves imperfect, lacking much information that should have been included because of the unwillingness of manufacturers to supply it, and the "Digest" itself omitted data to be found in the schedules. Moreover the "Digest" does not give figures for individual firms. For that reason some researchers will need to consult the schedules in preference to the "Digest."

No such survey was attempted in 1830,[12] but manufacturing and commercial data were collected as part of the special schedules for the 1840 census. The original schedules do not indicate individual enterprises but contain statistics of capital invested, numbers of people employed, the kind, quantity, and value of products of mines, agriculture, horticulture, commerce, fisheries, forests, and factories, arranged roughly

[9] Meyer H. Fishbein, *The Censuses of Manufactures, 1810–1890* (RIP 50, 1973), 6–7. Cf. Paul F. Paskoff, *Industrial Evolution* (1983), xviii.

[10] PI 161, 104–5; available M279, with film of appropriate pp. of the "Digest" (see below). N.B. NA, *Indexes to Manufacturers' Census of 1820* (n.d., cited *Source*, 109).

[11] Publ. as vol. II, 1820 Census and in *American State Papers: Finance*, vol. 4, 28–223; with supplement in ibid., 291–9 (incl. note of districts and counties for which no returns). For repr. see Schulze (1983), 43.

[12] But see below, pp. 362–3.

geographically by states. They are in the National Archives (RG 29). Again, however, the returns were defective: data were often omitted, and were also inaccurate – the numbers of persons employed in mining, commerce, and manufactures did not, for example, equate with the figures given for occupations drawn from the enumeration schedules of the census.[13] The published report[14] was consequently also defective, with totals often much smaller than they should have been. The censuses of manufactures for 1850, 1860, and 1870 were much more professional and the results certainly more accurate. In 1850, for instance, it was made compulsory for manufacturers to supply information. Of the published reports for 1850 and 1860 only the latter, however, contains much localized information: statistics at county level, by industries and crafts, cost of raw materials, numbers of male and female employees, costs of labor, and the value of the product. Occasionally the county figures embracing large towns are broken down into wards.[15]

The reports for 1850 and 1860 were, nevertheless, defective in many particulars. Certain industries or parts of industries were ignored, some industries were underenumerated, and errors were made in transferring data from the manuscript schedules.[16] The original manuscript schedules were also not free from error,[17] but recent research shows beyond doubt that data in the manuscript schedules were much more accurate and informative than those in the published reports for 1850 and 1860. This was particularly so at the level of individual counties and cities.[18] Aside from this, the manuscript

---

[13] Memorial Am. Statistical Assoc., 1844: SD 5 (28–2), ser. 449, 6–8; RIP 50, 12–13; Margaret Walsh, "The census as an accurate source of information," *HMN*, 3 (1970), 3–4.

[14] 1840 Census, vol. II.

[15] 1860 Census, vol. III, state tables, 1, 2. 1850 Census, Compendium vol. (Dubester (1950), no. 33) gives county data on certain industries for only capital invested, employees, value of product.

[16] Walsh, "The census as an accurate source," 4–7; Margaret Walsh, "The value of mid-nineteenth century manufacturing returns," *HMN*, 4 (1971), 43.

[17] Cf. William D. Walsh, *The Diffusion of Technological Change in the Pennsylvania Pig Iron Industry, 1850–1870* (1975), 16–18; and see pp. 360–1.

[18] Walsh articles cited n. 16 above; RIP 50, 16–17; Ernest M. Lander, "Charleston: manufacturing center of the old South," *JSoH*, 26 (1960), 330.

schedules provide details on individual enterprises which cannot be expected to appear in the aggregate statistics of the published reports.[19] Items included are the name of owner or corporation, name of firm or product, amount of capital invested and materials used, data on motive power and machinery, male and female wage rates,[20] and quantities, kinds, and values of products.

The community historian would, therefore, be well advised to utilize where possible the manuscript schedules for these censuses. Even so, before being reprocessed in a systematic way the data in these schedules need to be subjected to careful examination to ascertain weaknesses and hazards. The researches of Margaret Walsh should be studied by any historian seeking to use these records at the regional, county, or town level.[21]

The 1870 published census provides county statistics for selected industries, giving the numbers of establishments and employees and the value of wages, materials, and products.[22] Although, again, not without defect,[23] this census was certainly more efficiently collected and compiled, and comparison of the published report with the manuscript returns suggests much greater accuracy than was the case with earlier censuses. As before, the original schedules provide information for the community historian not found in the published reports.

Though the same basic information was collected for 1880, a great deal of extra detailed evidence was gathered, especially on wages, machinery, and power.[24] For certain industries with large establishments (textile manufactures, iron and steel, coke, glass, mining, distilleries and brewing, shipbuilding,

---

[19] Cf. *Federal Census, Critical Essays*, 331–2.
[20] Much wage data in the censuses are said to be of doubtful value: Charles J. Bullock, "Wage statistics," in ibid.
[21] Cited above. Walsh treats difficulties and makes suggestions for processing returns.
[22] Vol. III, table XI.
[23] John B. Jentz, "A note on evaluating the error in the Gilded Age manufacturing census," *HM*, 15 (1982), 79.
[24] For details, see RIP 50, 19–27; Carmen R. Delle Donne, *Federal Census Schedules, 1850–80* (RIP 67, 1973), 14–18.

fisheries) special agents collected statistics throughout the United States and these were not noted by the regular enumerators. In addition special agents gathered industrial statistics for all cities of over 8,000 inhabitants. The published volumes of the 1880 census thus contain much detailed information. A general report of 1882 includes industrial data on twenty principal cities: number of establishments per industry, amount of capital, number of employees, and value of raw materials and finished goods.[25]

Volumes XVIII and XIX of this census, on the social statistics of cities, contain descriptive information on commerce, navigation, and manufactures for many individual cities. For some of the larger ones statistics on numbers employed in certain industries and values of raw materials and products are presented. Volume XX, on wages in manufacturing, provides, in the section on individual industries, the names and localities of particular manufactures with local data on wages and occupations. Volumes XVI and XVII, on water power, include (by counties) an indication of the products of mills situated on specific streams.

Most important of the 1880 volumes, however, is volume II, specifically devoted to manufactures.[26] This includes descriptive reports on certain industries and statistics of manufacture. Some statistics are at the level of counties and larger cities. There is, for instance, information on the iron and steel industry by counties, which includes the number of establishments, amount of capital, number of hands (male, female, juvenile) and data on wages, hours of work, number of operating months in the year, value of materials and produce, and weight of produce.[27] Similar evidence is provided for the most important industries (specified) and for the total manufactures in each county.[28] County data on glass manufacture are also given. There are, too, similar data for the large cities. The reports on specific industries (hardware, cutlery, and edge

[25] For details, see Schulze (1983), 251; Dubester (1950), no. 158.
[26] See also vol. XX, noted p. 342.
[27] Table VII of that section.   [28] Tables IV, V.

tools; iron and steel; silk; cotton; chemicals and salt; glass) contain some local information. State and some other place-names are included in the indexes to each of these reports, and an overall index to the whole volume has state entries and occasional entries for specific places.

Although there were certainly discrepancies between the 1880 manuscript schedules and the published volumes, a higher degree of accuracy than before is likely.[29] The community historian will, nevertheless, again find greater detail in the original schedules, if they are available.

A special census of 1885, covering Colorado, Florida, Nebraska, and the territory of New Mexico, the manuscript schedules for which are in the National Archives (RG 29),[30] contains data on the products of industry. The schedules list the name of each owner and of his business and product, the amount of capital invested, wages and hours of work, number of months operational, value of materials and products, and amount and type of power used.

For the 1890 census the Compendium volume provides similar information to that for 1880. In addition, volume VI, on manufacturing industries, contains, in part 1, statistics for states and industries.[31] Part 2 presents for the 165 principal cities (20,000 inhabitants and over) general statistics of manufacturing establishments,[32] and for the same cities statistics for fifty selected industries, together with data on employees and wages in those industries. Rather dubious comparative data for 1880 and 1890 for 100 cities are also given.

The four parts of the published 1900 census of manufactures comprise volumes VII to X of the census set.[33] Volume VII (part 1) is arranged basically by industries, with many statistics at state level. It includes, however, a section on the localization of industries,[34] which contains statistics on the value of

---

[29] Hershberg, *Philadelphia*, 511; RIP 50, 21, 26–7.
[30] Available in M158, 352, 845, 846.
[31] Table 6 has some data on nos. of employees and wages at county level.
[32] But in such a way as to make comparison with 1880 data almost impossible: *Federal Census, Critical Essays*, 334.
[33] See also 1900 Abstract vol. (1902 edn.), tables 171–6.
[34] Pp. CXC–CCXIV.

products in staple industries in certain cities with comparison of the total value of their industrial output. A section on urban manufactures contains statistics of the number of establishments, capital, wage earners, and value of products in 100 of the principal cities.[35] There are similar data for 209 cities of 20,000 population and above, with specific information on named hand trades.[36] Similar information is provided for individual counties and cities in volume VIII (part 2), urban data being broken down by specific industries. Volumes IX and X contain special reports on selected industries with much data at state level, but now and then some local information.

In sum, though the published reports of the later manufacturing censuses are likely to be much more accurate than those earlier in the century and will often meet the needs of community historians, the original unpublished schedules, where extant, may be preferred, as giving more information on individual firms and data for areas smaller than the units covered in the published reports. Extant manuscript manufacturing schedules for the censuses of 1850 through 1880 have been transferred from the National Archives to other depositories, where they may be consulted.[37] Microfilm copies of some are available through the National Archives. Schedules for 1890 and 1900 no longer exist.

Two final points may be made on the federal manufacturing censuses. In all those from 1850, information on enterprises producing less than $500-worth of goods was not collected, nor were trades not conducted in distinct establishments noted. Even allowing that many which did not fall into these categories were probably reckoned by hard-pressed census takers to do so, the absence of a record of such enterprises represents a serious gap in the evidence. There was probably a considerable underenumeration of certain handicraft trades (like the metal trades). To some extent the occupational data in the population schedules may help, though in them working women and children were undercounted, and the researcher

35 Table xv.
36 Tables xxi, xxiv (with some comparison with 164 cities in 1890).
37 See RIP 67, app.; *Source*, 108–9; PI 161, 109–11, app. A.

360

will need to cull information from other sources, like newspapers and directories. The 1870 manuscript schedules for
Chicago, for instance, give only eleven bakeries whereas 152
appear in a directory for that year.[38]

Again, with reference to child labor,[39] it should be noted
that comparison of the 1870 and the 1880 evidence with that
for 1890 is difficult because of variations in the age ranges
determined for child workers, and also that the 1900 census
omitted as workers children working less than half time.[40] The
likelihood of parental and employer evasion and mendacity
must also be admitted.[41] Moreover, the manuscript census
returns are often vague as to the exact nature of child employment. Large numbers of children were returned as "works in
store," "works for tailor," "works in mill," and so on.[42] Nor
is it usually possible to distinguish mere child laborers from
apprentices.[43]

As well as the reports of those state censuses of 1885 mentioned above, and the occupational data found in many state
censuses, the published reports of some state censuses contain
statistical data on local industry and mining. Perhaps the best-
known examples are the four industrial censuses taken for
Massachusetts in 1837, 1845, 1855, and 1865. In addition, the
1875 Massachusetts census (1877) contains a volume on manufactures and occupations, while the 1885 and 1895 ones (1888;
1898–9) have volumes on manufactures, fisheries, and commerce, and the 1905 Massachusetts census (1908) a volume on
trade and manufacture. The census publications for most
states, however, are neither so comprehensive nor do they
spread over such a long period of time. The Rhode Island
census publications include industrial evidence for 1865, 1875,
1885, and 1895; Michigan's have manufacturing, mining, and

[38] Jentz, "A note on evaluating the error," 78–81.
[39] For inf. on child labor in federal censuses, see also ch. 2.
[40] H. L. Bliss, "Census statistics of child labor," *Jnl. Political Economy*, 13 (1904–5), 246–8.
[41] Jeremy P. Felt, *Hostages of Fortune* (1965), 231; Paul H. Douglass, *American Appren-ticeship and Industrial Education* (1921), 57.
[42] See, e.g., Joel Perlmann, "After leaving school," in Ronald K. Goodenow and Diane Ravitch (eds.), *Schools in Cities* (1983), 5.
[43] Carl F. Kaestle, *Evolution of an Urban School System* (1973), 98.

fishery data for only 1884 and 1894; Oregon's for only 1875.[44] For most of such state censuses the original manuscript returns have not survived. Where they have, however, they are likely to contain more detailed information.[45] Occasionally industrial evidence may also be found in more purely local censuses of one kind or another – as in the town census of Newark, NJ, in 1826.[46]

There is, therefore, much evidence on local industry and commerce in censuses of various kinds. It should be linked, however, wherever possible, with evidence available from other sources. Many federal and state records other than the censuses contain much on local industry and trade. Indeed, so many are of potential value that they cannot all be listed here. For federal documents the researcher should search the US Serial Set index under, for example, the names of industries of known significance in his area of study and under such entries as "manufactures." Some of the documents noted in the section on labor in chapter 7 provide details of working conditions (including child labor) and incidentally on other aspects of manufacturing. A special report of 1875, on wages and conditions of the working classes, presents details of a few named firms and other local evidence – as, for instance, the wages paid in certain trades in some cities in the early 1870s.[47]

Some other federal documents may be noted. Of special significance is Louis McLane's *Documents Relative to the Manufactures of the United States* (1833)[48] which serves to fill the gap in the censuses of manufactures between 1820 and 1840. A most valuable compilation, it contains a great deal of evidence supplied by individual factory and works owners, and also for places, listing individual businesses with much greater detail about them than in directories. Thus, for example, for many places in New Hampshire it provides the type of each

[44] For others, see Dubester (1948).
[45] For extant originals, see ibid., app. Cf. Charles N. Glaab and Lawrence H. Larsen, *Factories in the Valley* (1969)
[46] In *The First Jubilee of American Independence* (Newark, NJ, 1826).
[47] HED 21 (44–1), ser. 1686.
[48] HED 308 (22–1), ser. 222, 223 (repr. 1969): vol. 1, ME, MA, NH, VT, RI, CT; vol. 2, NY, NJ, DE, PA, OH.

individual business (and sometimes the proprietor's name), the value of its real estate and fixtures, the kind of power used, the value of tools, machinery and apparatus, the number and value of horses and other animals, the value of stock, amounts and value of different kinds of materials used and much detail about them, details of goods produced and their disposal, numbers of various kinds of employees and their wages, rates of profit, expenses, and so on. Other details often provided include whether the company was private or joint-stock, the amount of capital invested in ground, buildings, and machinery, level of productivity, average wages, numbers of hours worked, marketing methods, and details of foreign competition.

Some memorials and petitions to Congress by groups of industrialists and merchants are published as federal documents and may shed light on local interests, outlooks, and particular difficulties: as, for instance, the petitions of New York journeymen hatters and coppermakers in 1807, and a petition of Philadelphia artisans, merchants, and industrialists in 1834. The Philadelphia petition was from over 10,000 persons and indicated their occupations. They included entire manufacturing enterprises with the owner's name followed by those of the workers, thus showing the pattern of employment.[49]

Documents concerned with periods of depression or crisis may also be of value. The report and testimony of an investigation into industrial and commercial depression, published in 1879,[50] for instance, has a great deal, especially in the evidence, on living conditions, wages, strikes, unemployment, child labor, hours of work, and transportation, and is as important for the attitudes of those giving evidence (employers, the self-employed, craftsmen, and so on) as for more factual information. Embedded in the testimony are detailed data on industries in particular places – as, for instance, statistics of boot and shoe production in fourteen Massachusetts cities and

[49] *American State Papers: Finance*, vol. 2, 257–8; HD 86 (23–1), ser. 256; Philip B. Scranton, *Proprietory Capitalism* (1983), 114.
[50] HMD 29 (45–3), ser. 1863; HMD 5 (46–2), ser. 1928.

towns showing also hours of work. The index is inadequate but does give some assistance in finding local evidence.

Again, a report on the conditions of the cotton industry published in 1895[51] includes (vol. 1) letters from New England cotton manufacturers giving their views on prices of raw material, sometimes providing details of their foreign markets and business methods (like dealing in futures on the New York and New Orleans exchanges). Volume 2 contains figures for annual sales of spot cotton in New York, New Orleans, Houston, Memphis, Savannah, Charleston, and St. Louis over the period 1842–94. A well-indexed report of 1892 on sweated trades, provides, in the testimony, details of working conditions in firms in New York City, Boston, Cincinnati and environs, Rochester (NY), Chicago, and Baltimore, embracing child and female labor, wages, hours, sanitary conditions, housing conditions, disease, immigrants, and trade unions.[52]

The extensive *Report of the Industrial Commission* (1900–2) has already been noted in connection with labor relations, and certain of its volumes provide a significant source of information on industry and trade.[53] In particular volume 1 (on trusts and industrial combinations) gives some data on individual institutions. Volumes VII and XIV include evidence on wages and hours, and child and black labor in various trades and industries, and volume VII contains special reports on certain industries (including iron and steel, glass, boots and shoes, clothing sweat shops, and textile milling). Judicious use of lists of witnesses, which show residence, and of the indexes to these and other volumes of the report, will help in finding local information.[54]

A report on immigration of 1871[55] includes, in some of its reports on individual places (see ch. 4) and opportunities for

---

[51] SR 986 (53–3), ser. 3290–1 (2 vols.).

[52] HR 2309 (52–2), ser. 3140.

[53] See *Checklist*, 1,515 for refs. The only extant original records are the Commission's minutes in RG 40: GNA, 464.

[54] A general index is in vol. XIX. Vol. VIII also has inf. on child labor. For other useful vols., see pp. 128–9, 339.

[55] Edward Young, *Special Rep. on Immigration* (U.S. Bureau of Statistics, 1871).

immigrants, details of local industries. In Manitowoc county, WI, for example, a woolen mill, two furniture factories, a tub-and-pail factory, a stove factory, and several saw and shingle mills were recorded. Forty years later the report of the Immigration Commission (1910–11) contains, in volumes 6–25,[56] accounts of immigrant workers in particular industries.

Very important, too, are certain reports of the Commissioner of Labor.[57] His 3rd and 10th annual reports (for 1887, 1894), on strikes and lockouts, noted in chapter 7, contain incidentally other useful information on individual firms. His 14th report (for 1899) covers working women in twenty-one large cities, with statistical data on various industries. The 6th and 7th reports (for 1890, 1891) are concerned with costs of production in the iron, steel, coal, textile, and glass industries. Like the 11th report (1895–6), on working conditions and wages, these include little information specific to particular communities but they do provide at regional and sometimes state level background information on production costs, wages, cost of living,[58] and child labor. The 3rd special report of the Commissioner (1893) published synopses of reports of state bureaus of labor statistics to 1892 and serves both as a source in itself and a key to such reports, where the researcher can find more local detail on aspects of industry, including child labor.[59]

Embedded in the multi-volume *Report on the Condition of Women and Child Wage Earners in the United States* (1910–13)[60] is much local evidence on child labor. Employment in various industries and trades is covered in volumes 1–5 and 18, which provide data for a number of individual cities. Volume 6 gives

---

[56] SD 633 (61–2), ser. 5667–88. For details of each vol., see Schmeckebier, *Statistical Work*, 95–6.
[57] For Dept. of Labor's library and its records, see p. 351.
[58] Cf. John Modell, "Patterns of consumption, acculturation, and family income strategies," in Tamara K. Hareven and Maris A. Vinovskis (eds.), *Family and Population in Nineteenth-Century America* (1978), and citations.
[59] Fully cited p. 341n. Has useful index. For such state reps. see below.
[60] SD 645 (61–2), ser. 5685–703, 19 vols. And see Walter B. Palmer, "Women and child workers in cotton mills," *Q. Publics. American Statistical Assoc.*, 12 (1912). For child labor legislation, see above, p. 340n.

summaries of child-labor legislation prior to 1860. Volume 7 covers conditions under which children left school for work in a number of places, and includes tabular data on the social, economic, and educational status of the 622 children studied. Volume 14 provides causes of death of women and child cotton-mill operators in three cities, 1905–7.

The annual reports of the Quartermaster General, published in the annual reports of the Secretary of War, give details of goods purchased by the Army under contract and include names of firms and their locations, dates of transactions, and quantities of goods and their prices. His unpublished records, in the National Archives (RG 92), and those of the Chief of Ordnance (RG 156) include correspondence, abstracts of contracts and bonds and agreements with firms supplying the Army.[61] Similar material is in the records of the treasury of the Confederacy for 1861–5 (RG 109).[62]

Record Group 241 (NA), contains the records of the Patent Office,[63] which may sometimes include useful information. For instance, they provide evidence on certain factories in Delaware: one, that of Joseph Bancroft at Rockford, in 1857 had 2,750 spindles and 80 looms working, served by 30 males paid $5 a week and 50 females at half that amount.[64] The published reports of the Commissioner of Patents appeared in various forms from 1837. The weekly *Official Gazette* (from 1872) lists patents and trade marks, and also records the decisions of the Commissioner and of the federal courts in patent cases. There are separately published annual indexes to

[61] See Meyer H. Fishbein, "Business history resources in the National Archives," *Business Hist. Rev.*, 38 (1964), q.v., 238–40, for other War and Navy dept. sources.

[62] *GNA*, 721; Henry P. Beers, *Guide to the Archives of the Government of the Confederate States of America* (1968) (index under "business firms"); Elizabeth Bethel (comp.), *Preliminary Inventory of the War Department Collection of Confederate Records* (PI 101, 1957), 220–5.

[63] *GNA*, 469–70. And see "Using patent records," *Prologue*, 19 (1987), 254; Joseph G. Jackson, "Records of research," *Patent Office Soc. Jnl.*, 35 (1953); Nathan Reingold, "U.S. Patent Office records as sources for the history of invention and technological property," *Technology and Culture*, 1 (1960); James A. Paulauskas (comp.), *Additional Improvement Patents, 1837–1861* (SL 39, 1977); James E. Primas (comp.), *List of Names of Inventors in the Case Files . . . Patent Rights, 1836–75* (NC-20, 1963).

[64] Harold B. Hancock, "Materials for company history in the National Archives," *AA*, 29 (1966), 30.

patents, patentees, and trade marks appearing in the *Gazette*,[65] and in some cases this information may be valuable to community historians.

Aside from state censuses, many other state records provide evidence on local economic matters. Not all these can be noted here and relevant catalogs of state documents and guides to state archives should be searched. Some useful state documents are noted in chapter 7 (last section) and in the next section of this chapter, and a few other types of state record may be mentioned here.

The published annual reports of state inspectors of various kinds, especially those of workshops and factories,[66] may shed much light on the industries concerned and on child and female labor. For New York state, for example, the inspector of lumber's reports provide data by counties and cities. Those of factory inspectors in Ohio date from 1884 and they also issued many circulars – as, for instance, in 1891 a description of a model factory in Columbus, and from 1891–2 to 1900–1 tables of factories and commercial buildings inspected, with names of owners or agents, locations, and purpose. The reports of the Wisconsin factory inspectors include data on the condition of each establishment inspected, with the numbers of male and female employees, and details of sources of power: for localities (and by industry) details of new factory building in the previous year are given. There may also be unpublished inspectors' papers and reports – like those of the Wisconsin lumber inspectors from 1864, which include weekly statistics of lumber scaled at logging camps, 1881–2.[67]

There are other useful state records, too, worth searching for. The annual report of the Rhode Island Board of

---

[65] See Baker, *Finding List*, 151–4; Anne M. Boyd and Rae E. Rips (eds.), *United States Government Publications* (1949 edn.), 363 for details and for the few reps. on patents before 1837. Useful are M. D. Leggett, *Subject Matter of Patents for Inventions, 1790–1873* (3 vols., 1974); Edmund Burke, *List of Patents . . . 1790 to 1847* (1847); "List of all patents granted . . . 1831," *New American State Papers, Science and Technology*, vol. 4, *Patents* (1973). For litigation, see *Brodix's American and English Patent Cases* (20 vols., 1887–92); James B. Robb (ed.), *A Collection of Patent Cases Decided in the Supreme and Circuit Courts of the United States* (2 vols., 1854).

[66] Sometimes incl. in reps. state bureaus of labor statistics: see below.

[67] David J. Delgado (ed.), *Guide to the Wisconsin State Archives* (1966), 123.

Agriculture for 1898 includes an account of the industrial features of Newport county, and in 1898 that state published a special report on the depression in the cotton industry. A New York state document of 1840 presents a report on the "peculiar advantages of the village of McIntyre and its vicinity for extensive manufacture of iron"; and another includes a table for Essex and Clinton counties showing for 1846–51 the number of forges, price of iron, amounts of charcoal used, costs of production, value of iron produced, wages, and so on. Not a few state documents include data on child and female labor, though in many no such indication is given in their titles.[68]

For the last three decades of the nineteenth century, however, the most fruitful single source among state documents is likely to be the annual or semi-annual reports of bureaus of statistics of labor or of industrial statistics, the first of which was that of Massachusetts (established in 1869).[69] Subjects covered in these reports include indentures, occupations, wages, workers' living and working conditions, apprenticeship practices, child and female labor, commodity prices, rents, and mechanization.

For industrial states the amount of local data embedded in these reports is prodigious. For example, those of the Massachusetts Bureau of Statistics of Labor contain enormous amounts of evidence on the various industrial towns in the state. The report of the Ohio bureau for 1877 includes evidence for furnaces, foundries, rolling mills, and machine shops. The Pennsylvania bureau's report for 1882–3 provides some 370 pages of statistics by counties of various manufactures and firms, with details of the labor force and production. The Indiana Bureau of Statistics in its fourth annual

[68] E.g., Massachusetts HD 98, 1866 (testimony on violation of child labor laws); docs. cited Robert H. Bremner *et al.* (eds.), *Children and Youth in America* (2 vols. in 3, 1970–1), vol. I, 597–9, 617–18.
[69] A list with dates estd. is in *3rd Special Rep. U.S. Bureau of Labor*, 5–6, which also provides a key to subjects in the reps. to 1892. See also U.S. Dept. of Labor, *Index to All Reps. Issued by Bureaus of Labor Statistics* (1902). The monthly *Bull. Dept. of Labor* summarizes the reps.

report (1882) provides data on manufactures, 1881–2, by industries and counties, showing the number of establishments, capital value of raw materials and of the product, number of employees, and costs including wages.

The administrative records of city and county governments have been dealt with in chapter 7, but it may be noted here that those of large municipalities, especially, provide much evidence on local economic activity. Particularly in the early decades of the century the licensing of certain trades, the enforcement of the economic privileges of freemen and the regulation of weights and measures were important, and city charters, council minutes and ordinances, as well as the records of officials, will provide information on these matters. Some of these regulatory practices died out but licensing and local government registration may have continued.[70] State and county archives often contain revealing material relating to the incorporation and dissolution of corporations. This can provide evidence of the purpose of the business (as manufacturing), its capital, stockholders, directors, property, and so on. From 1852 Baltimore required business organizations to file their charters and amendments to them with the clerk of the Superior Court, and an immense "Charter Record" consequently survives.[71] Filed copies of the annual reports of such corporations may also exist in local government archives. The records of Philadelphia, for instance, include annual statements from manufacturing corporations giving the establishment's name, amount of stock, stockholders' names and numbers of shares held, debts owed to and by the firm, cash in hand, and investments.[72] The direct involvement of local government in business activities, as in the supply of water, ownership of wharves, and so on, also generated records (ch. 7).

[70] Jones, 166.

[71] Richard J. Cox and Patricia M. Vanorney, "The records of a city," *Maryland Hist. Mag.*, 70 (1975), 294–5.

[72] John Daly, *Descriptive Inventory of the Archives of the City and County of Philadelphia* (1970), 19. Cf. *Guide to the Records of the New York State Archives* (SUNY, 1981), 131.

Federal, state, and local tax records provide information not only on banks, insurance companies, and individual businessmen,[73] but also on the number and types of business and industrial enterprises in counties, towns, and regions,[74] giving some idea of their significance in terms of the value of buildings, merchandise, trade stock, and money on loan and at hand. In addition they can give a rough measure of comparison of the extent of economic activity in various towns in a region, but it must be appreciated that they are by no means comprehensive in their coverage of financial assets. They are dealt with more fully in chapter 2.

Records of litigation involving business are among the archives of courts from the local courts upwards. Court records on bankruptcy provide not only the details of proceedings in particular cases but often include business records and generally provide information on the nature of the trade concerned in particular communities, including business methods and organization. They are to be found both in the county court records and those of federal district courts. The case files of bankruptcy in the Sangamon county court, Illinois, for example, include for the period 1878–97 such items as inventories of merchandise and stock, inventories of accounts, lists of creditors, and assignments of debtors for creditors. For the Baltimore county court there are insolvency papers, with indexes, from the 1840s onwards.[75]

The bankruptcy case files in the U.S. district court records include petitions of bankruptcies filed by creditors against debtors, creditors' bonds and affidavits, proofs of debts owed, schedules of bankrupts' assets and of debts owed to and by them, depositions, examinations, transcripts of commissioners' meetings, and certificates of bankruptcy. Account books and other material may be

[73] Cynthia G. Fox, "Income tax records of the Civil War years," *Prologue*, 18 (1966). Cf. Harold B. Hancock, "Materials for company history in the National Archives," *AA*, 29 (1966), 29.
[74] See Francis X. Blouin, *The Boston Region, 1810–1850* (1980), ch. 2.
[75] Roy C. Turnbaugh, Jr., *A Guide to the County Records, in the Illinois Regional Archives* (1984), 164; Cox and Vanorney, "The records of a city," 297–8.

included.[76] They are found in regional branches of the National Archives (RG 21).[77] Additional information may be in the volumes of *Federal Cases* and the *Federal Reporter*.[78] The *Bankruptcy Court Reporter* (1867–8) and the *National* (formerly *Weekly*) *Bankruptcy Register* (1868–82), periodicals reporting important cases and principal rulings in bankruptcy of the U.S. district judges, may also be consulted.[79]

The records of other types of court cases, both civil and criminal, may also provide interesting material.[80] Admiralty cases, for example, include, especially after 1851, details of litigation relating to navigable waterways. Probate records, described in chapter 2, may prove useful for the wills of businessmen and for inventories, appraisements and accounts, and sales of goods.

Non-governmental sources for the study of industry and trade are also extensive. Contemporary surveys of commerce and manufacturing are often local or regional in content. Examples are *Statistics of Lowell Manufactures, January, 1851* (Lowell, MA, 1851) and Lorin Blodget, *Census of Manufactures of Philadelphia* (1883), a very detailed work. A survey of Pennsylvania iron production in 1849 is more detailed than the 1850 federal census schedules.[81] Walter R. Bagnall, *The Textile Industries of the United States* (1893) quotes from many original sources, giving much detail about individual places and firms. It may be cited as an example of a contemporary work which is itself a primary source.

The papers of local businessmen and companies, from

---

[76] See *Act of 1800 Bankruptcy Case Files . . . Maryland, 1800–1803* (PDM 1031, 1979); David R. Kepley, "An untapped treasure," *Pennsylvania Mag. Hist. and Biography*, 105, 3 (1981); Thomas E. Wiltsey, "Court records and local history," in Timothy Walch (comp.), *Our Family, Our Town* (1987), 192–6; James K. Owens, "Documenting regional business history," *Prologue*, 21 (1989); Beverley Watkins, "'To Surrender All His Estate'," ibid.

[77] *GNA*, 73–905.

[78] See p. 26.

[79] See Charles C. Soull, *The Lawyer's Reference Manual of Law Books and Citations* (1984 edn.), 13, for details. *American Bankruptcy Reps.* starts 1899.

[80] See, e.g., Robert A. Silverman, *Law and Urban Growth . . . Boston Trial Courts, 1880–1900* (1981), esp. 151–8.

[81] Paskoff, *Industrial Evolution*, xix.

Sources for U.S. History

craftsmen and storekeepers to large manufacturing concerns, are of special value for the economic history of individual communities.[82] They abound in local depositories.[83] The collection of such papers at Baker Library, Harvard University, is perhaps the best known.[84] Other important collections of business records include those at the University of Virginia, Duke University, Cornell University, and the State Historical Society of Wisconsin. Many records, however, remain in private hands and with existing firms.

Purely personal papers, especially correspondence, may be fruitful of commercial information, perhaps indicating reasons for decisions, or elaborating in subjective terms details of business activity. Letters written to friends and relatives in other parts of the country or abroad sometimes touch on local economic conditions.[85] In addition, personal papers may embrace wills, tax records, inventories of property, memoranda, deeds, and records of personal investment – and thus shed light on business activity. Reminiscences of workers, including former child workers, may also exist.

Such material can fill out the information found in statistical sources, like the published federal censuses, and provide intimate detail on individual stores, firms, and industries.[86] They can suggest, for particular enterprises or groups of enterprises, reasons for emergence, success, decline, failure, and so forth. They can provide evidence on the scale of the enterprise, on

[82] Oliver W. Holmes, "The evaluation and preservation of business archives," AA, 1 (1938); Lewis E. Atherton, "Cataloging and use of the Western mercantile records," Library Q. (Chicago), 8 (1938); Donald D. Parker, Local History (rev. Bertha E. Josephson, 1944, repr. 1979), 72–6; Ralph M. Hower, "The preservation of business records," Bull. Business Hist. Soc., 11 (1937) (separately publ. 3rd edn. 1941); "The publication of business records," Archives, 1 (1951); Edie Hedlin, Business Archives (1978); Karen M. Benedict (comp.), A Select Bibliography on Business Archives and Business Management (1981).

[83] NUCMC; Directory of Archives and Manuscript Repositories in the United States (1988); Robert W. Lovett, Directory of Business Archives in the United States and Canada (1980) (very selective; mainly 20th century). See also citations, Prucha, 208; George H. Evans, Jr., Business Incorporations in the United States, 1800–1943 (1948).

[84] Robert W. Lovett and Eleanor C. Bishop, Manuscripts in Baker Library: A Guide to Sources to Business, Economic and Social History (1978 edn.); Robert W. Lovett, "The appraisal of older business records," AA, 15 (1952).

[85] See, e.g., Charlotte Erickson, Invisible Immigrants (1972).

[86] E.g., Clifton Paisley, "Tallahassee through the storebooks," Florida Hist. Q., 53 (1974).

methods of operation including sources of supply, markets and customers, relations with transportation firms, suppliers and sales outlets, credit policies, operating and production costs, use of machinery, and technical processes. For the workforce they can supply data on size and composition, wages and conditions of employment, and, for the owners, the nature of their involvement, their policies and priorities. And, of course, changes in size, organization, ownership, trading and manufacturing practices, and reaction to competition and changed conditions over time, can all hopefully be illustrated from good collections of business records. Such records can also provide much miscellaneous evidence on the general social and economic history of particular communities – including price levels, wage levels, and labor relations.

The basic financial accounts of small businesses may include books of original entry, cash books, and ledgers.[87] Books of original entry (often called day books or journals) recorded daily transactions, often as they occurred. Sales, purchases, consignments, movements of money, and so on, were noted. For larger firms there may be separate day books for credit sales, credit purchases, bills received, bills due, and goods returned. Waste books and blotters are terms given to rough-and-ready types of journal. In cash books were entered receipts and payments of money, balanced daily or at longer periods. Cash books may summarize more detailed records, such as wage and freight books and bank pass books, which themselves will provide more detail and are collectively useful if the cash books have not survived. Similar information to that in the cash books may be found in journals or ledgers (see below) under the heading "cash account."

Some day books, especially those of small businessmen in the early stages of their careers, were the only accounts kept, but usually books of original entry were summarized in ledgers. Sometimes there were both general and subsidiary ledgers. Subsidiary books might include debtor and creditor accounts, or departmental or branch-office account books,

[87] G.M.G., "Some sources for Northwest history: account books," *Minnesota Hist.*, 16 (1935); Christopher Clark, "The household economy," *JSH*, 13 (1979).

and embrace also distinct books for purchasing, manufacturing, sales, employees, and such like. Stock sheets, too, may exist to elaborate the information in the general ledgers. Customers' accounts ledgers, for instance, may indicate the extent of credit allowed and the existence, especially in the West, of barter. The more elaborate the accounting system, the more likely is it that there will be some kind of indexes.

Less likely to have survived, but of great value for certain purposes if they have, are the original records of transactions – like invoices, vouchers, receipts, orders, sales checks, shipping notices, and bills of lading, which will provide minute details of the goods and services concerned. Sometimes customers' invoices were copied into invoice books (a term also used for stock inventories) and orders into order books. Some order books recorded goods ordered from the trader concerned, others noted orders made by him to wholesalers, summarized in materials ledgers. Clearly such records are of immense value in reconstructing the organization of local business, especially the volume and sources of goods bought and the geographical extent of sales.

Labels printed on the front of account books do not always accord with the use to which they were actually put, so that it is always wise to look inside. Again in family businesses, private accounts and other matters may be included with the record of business affairs. The keeper of a Williamsburg, VA, general store, for instance, entered his household expenses in his business account book, while a tailor in the same town entered in his ledger not only details of work done for customers but a record of local marriages.[88]

Other financial records of businesses, particularly larger concerns, include tax records, treasurers', accountants', and auditors' reports, payroll summaries and analyses, and balance sheets summarizing the financial state of the firm and indicating assets, liabilities, and net worth. There may also be, for manufacturing establishments, records of the cost and inventory value of machinery, equipment, raw materials, and

---

[88] Colonial Williamsburg Foundation, Research Library, account bk. C. Tompkins, 1819–21; Sweeney papers, account ledger, 1830.

products. Semi-annual reports of accounts may have been drawn up. Annual statements summarizing a company's fortunes and financial state over the year are most important: some were published in local newspapers.

Administrative and organizational business records include the minute books of meetings of stockholders, directors, and executive committees, and those of departmental meetings. The value of these records to the historian varies according to the amount of detail included in them. Unfortunately many company minute books record only formal decisions without noting the discussions which went before. There may also be sales, production, departmental, and branch and other administrative reports. Files of letters received and books recording letters sent out (the use of carbon copies dates only from about 1897)[89] can be of interest. They are especially valuable for the activities of mercantile firms, since they enable the whole web of the business activity to be reconstructed: wholesale centers and houses used; routes and methods of transportation for goods; existence of partners; use of agents and correspondents; relations with customers and their geographical spread; and use of credit and barter. Correspondence for manufacturing firms was less extensive and less significant in content, but can provide similar information on policy matters, sources of raw materials and machinery, and identification of customers.

The legal records of businesses include partnership deeds and memoranda, charters or articles of incorporation and amendments to them, lists of stockholders, deeds and titles to property, leases, licenses, mortgages, contracts and agreements, records of patents, stock and bond ledgers, and litigation records.

Employment records of firms can also be useful, especially those of manufacturing, transportation, and mining concerns. They consist of personnel files and books, time books, payrolls, shop rules and regulations, and records relating to labor unions (such as agreements and minutes of negotiations). These can provide data on the numbers and categories of

---

[89] Letter-press copies date from *c*.1830, but are not common.

personnel, wages and hours of work, rates of attendance and turnover, and labor relations generally. They can also give evidence on social matters, such as the ethnic or racial make-up of the workforce.

Details of the nature, volume, and value of trade and production, and changes over time, can be deduced from inventories of stock and materials, stock ledgers, sales records, sales manuals, price lists, catalogs, pattern books, prospectuses, portfolios and trade circulars, and trade catalogs.[90] For manufacturing and mining enterprises there may also be maps, plans, charts, drawings and specifications, and reports of engineers and other technical reports. In addition house publications, scrapbooks of news clippings, and perhaps collections of photographs of plant processes, buildings, and personnel may exist.[91]

The records of associations of manufacturers and of chambers of commerce and boards of trade provide another useful source. The New England Cotton Manufacturers' Association, for example, published transactions which were continued as those of the National Association of Cotton Manufacturers. Such associations sometimes produced membership lists and other publications. The Boston Association of Master Tailors produced a price list in 1811, and in 1842 the proceedings of a convention of manufacturers and traders in the shoe and leather trade were published in Boston. The Chicago Board of Trade's archives[92] are of significance not only for the business activities of that city but also for the economic history of places whose farmers traded through Chicago. They include much correspondence, cash market prices (from 1863), statistics of imports, exports, and grain storage (from 1859), and daily price quotes for wheat, corn, oats, and other produce for futures trading (from 1881).[93] The Chicago Board had the right to arbitrate disputes among its members over contracts, and records relating to this function

[90] Lawrence B. Romaine, *A Guide to American Trade Catalogs, 1744–1900* (1960).
[91] Cf. Mildred Simpson, "Photographs in a business setting," *AA*, 45 (1982).
[92] Library of Univ. of Illinois at Chicago Circle, Chicago, IL 60680.
[93] Owen Gregory, "The Chicago Board of Trade's archives," *AH*, 56 (1982); *Directory of Business Archives in the United States and Canada*.

are very informative.[94] For port towns, chamber of commerce records (see ch. 9) may give information on shipping. Records of such organizations in smaller places may be less impressive but are nevertheless likely to be useful to the local economic historian. Runs of their annual reports, for example, can give a general impression of the fortunes of the local economy.

Credit-reporting agency records may also be valuable. Of them the most important are the credit reports of R. G. Dun and Company – the Dun and Bradstreet collection deposited at Baker Library, Harvard University.[95] These are reports by local correspondents or agents in almost every town and city in America, on local businessmen, regarding their suitability for receiving credit. They are contained in some 2,580 ledger volumes covering about three million individuals. Usually reports include details of the subject's occupation, length of time in business, amount of own capital in the firm, an estimate of his net worth, the value of his personal and real property, and his general business prospects. Many also contain personal details on his family, marital status, age, ethnicity, personal character, record in meeting financial obligations, and former residences and business experience. Where relevant, names of partners and of those whom he succeeded in business may appear. Reports were continually updated, so that career patterns may be observed. The records cover the period 1841–90, with a concentration of data in the 1850s to 1870s. Of course, such reports tend to be confined to firms and individuals in business likely to apply for credit and make purchases outside their own communities. They are thus biased towards merchants, manufacturers, brokers, bankers, and large farmers. For such individuals they are considered to possess a high degree of accuracy, being based on records many of which are perhaps no longer extant and some never openly available – including bank records,

---

[94] Information from Rena Schulz, Newberry Library, Chicago.
[95] James H. Madison, "The credit reports of R. G. Dun & Co. as historical sources," *HMN*, 8 (1975), 128–31; Peter R. Decker, *Fortunes and Failures* (1978), x, 90–100, 181, 267–70; Glaab and Larsen, *Factories in the Valley*, 213.

business accounts, and balance sheets, as well as tax assessments and the like.

The value of such records for the study of local economic activity and of business, political, and social elites in individual communities is clear. They can contribute, by linkage with many of the other types of sources treated in chapter 2, to the study of social structure and social mobility. They are, for example, considered more accurate than tax assessments and the real and personal property returns in the censuses. There are indexes, arranged by county, city, and individual or firm, though these sometimes present difficulties and are not always complete. Permission from the Dun and Bradstreet Company is needed to publish data from the reports, but this is invariably granted.

Local newspapers can provide much information on industry and business in the communities they served. They carry general reports of changes, labor troubles, trade crises, new enterprises, expansion and contraction of businesses, and so forth. They also publish obituaries of business leaders, advertisements for employees (including child workers), and, sometimes, the annual reports of large firms. Advertisements for products can form a useful basis for analysis of the sorts of goods made by different local firms, the extent of specialization, and so on.[96] Newspapers are an essential source for local commodity prices.[97] Naturally the larger and more successful local firms will get more mention and make most use of the press for advertising – a bias in the source to be taken into account.

In addition, periodicals with commercial and industrial leanings may contain information on local industry and provide general background. Well-known productions of this sort include the *Boston Commercial Gazette* (1795–1840), *Niles' Weekly* (later *National*) *Register* (1811–49, available in microform), the *Merchants' Magazine and Commercial Review* (New York, 1839–70, available in microform), the *Industrial South*

---

[96] Cf. Stuart M. Blumin, "Black coats to white collars," in Stuart W. Bruchey, *Small Business in American Life* (1980), 108–14.

[97] See Thomas S. Berry, *Richmond Commodity Prices, 1861–1865* (1985).

(1881?–7), and *De Bow's Review* (from 1846, available in microform).[98] Some carry information on child labor. Similarly, specialized trade journals may be important for certain industries, like the *Paper Trade Journal* (1872–1927, available in microform). Some journals are regionally orientated: the *Southern and Western Textile Excelsior* (Charlotte, NC, 1893–1907), the *Pacific Coast Wood and Iron* (1884–1900), and the *Pacific Lumber Trade Journal* (1895–1900) are examples.

Aside from the occupational information in local directories, noted in chapter 2, some have business sections, while there are also special local business directories and almanacs which can be most informative for industrial communities. They list not only large and some small businesses, but also the names of directors. They provide, together with the manufacturing censuses, some evidence for distinguishing craftsmen in the population census returns who were employers from those who were not. Some directories were national in coverage, but specific to particular industries – so may be useful for local research.[99] Data on some large firms may be found in stock market directories, like the *Manual of Statistics* (from 1896). Also useful is the *Rand McNally and Company Business* (later *Commercial*) *Atlas* (from 1876), which provides state maps with business, transportation, and demographic data. There may also be official directories devoted to business and industry: the state of Pennsylvania, for instance, published an industrial directory giving information on the output and workforce of the various industries of the state.[100]

Credit-reference books are another useful source. These were annual publications often produced by trade associations or trade journals and modeled on the best known, R. G. Dun's *Mercantile Agency Reference Books* and *Bradstreet's Book of Commercial Ratings*.[101] They listed names and addresses of business

---

[98] Originally *Commercial Rev. of the South and West . . .*

[99] E.g., J. P. Lesley, *The Iron Manufacturer's Guide to the Furnaces, Forges and Rolling Mills of the United States* (1859).

[100] Cf. Burton W. Folsom, Jr., *Urban Capitalists* (1981), 184.

[101] For Bradstreet and Dun's commercial publics., see *NUC*. Some pertained to individual states and cities.

firms, geographically arranged, with an index on size and credit rating,[102] and also contained information on other local business facilities, like banking. Contemporary city and county histories may well include descriptions of firms and businessmen, often hagiographical, but nevertheless containing useful factual data.

The records of some foreign countries may also contain valuable evidence. This is particularly so of reports of foreign consuls stationed in the United States.[103] There is, for instance, a British consular report of 1882 on Pittsburgh's coal and iron industry.[104]

Special kinds of business enterprises are banks and insurance companies, for their records not only illustrate their own activities and fortunes but also provide much evidence on those of others and on the local economy generally. The domestic records of banks include, like those of other companies, minutes of meetings of boards of directors, stockholders' records, financial reports and records, and correspondence.[105] Their correspondence may include communications with branches, and the annual reports of large banks may have been published. Other bank publications may include annual reports, reports of investigative committees and of committees of stockholders, reports to state legislatures, and their charters and rules.[106] Records relating to their customers shed light on other businesses in the community. The ledger of the Bank of Augusta, GA, for 1880–4, for example, provides a record of depositors and the amounts deposited and withdrawn.[107] There may also be

---

[102] William G. Roy, "Collecting data on American business officials in the late nineteenth and early twentieth century," *HM*, 15 (1982), 144, 151.

[103] For consular reps., see pp. 414–15. And see citations p. 28 n.112. For German agents' reps., see p. 351.

[104] BPP HC 1882, LXXII, 993.

[105] Hower, "The preservation of business records," 36. Factual details of some banks are publ. in J. Van Fernstermaker, *The Development of American Commercial Banking, 1782–1837* (1965).

[106] Cf. George D. Green, *Finance and Economic Development in the Old South: Louisiana Banking, 1804–1861* (1972), 239–42.

[107] WPA, HRS, *Inventory of the County Records of Georgia, No. 121, Richmond County (Augusta)* (1939), 58.

registers of applications for loans and discounts and of mortgages.[108]

Local newspapers may record evidence on banking issues, since these often divided local communities.[109] Local and commercial directories and county histories may also provide brief factual data on banks, perhaps giving names of directors. Commercial credit reference publications, like those of Dun and Bradstreet, cited above, include references to banks. Useful information may also be found in the annual reports of bankers' associations, court records, tax records, bankers' periodicals (like the *Bankers' Magazine* (1846–1943), available in microform; title varies) and other commercial publications, like *Hazard's United States Commercial and Statistical Register* (1839–42) and the *Commercial and Financial Chronicle and Hunt's Merchants' Magazine* (from 1865).

There are many state documents concerning banks, for the general economic significance of banking to local communities and the involvement of banks in local politics led to the official collection and promulgation of much factual information on them. Bank charters appear in state and territorial Acts and Statutes, as do general laws regulating banks. The background to these may be revealed, with political implications, in journals of state legislatures which will contain reports on debates. Reports of committees on banks and banking, including special investigating committees, may also have been published as state documents and find mention, too, in the journals. Thus there is record in the *Assembly Journal* for New York state, 1828, of a report on a petition for a bank at Ogdensburg. A Louisiana state document of 1838 provides important statistical data on most New Orleans banks, 1835–8, while another of 1840 contains the report of an investigative committee revealing details on the financial condition, debtors and creditors, and practices of the banks in the state during a financial crisis.[110] Among Connecticut

---

[108] For use of loan records, see Andrew A. Beveridge, "Studying community, credit and change by using 'running' records from historical sources," *HM*, 14 (1981).

[109] Cf. Milton S. Heath, *Constructive Liberalism* (1954), chs. 8, 9.

[110] Green, *Finance and Economic Development*, 248.

documents is a report of a committee of examination of the banks in the state in 1837. For Massachusetts, published abstracts of bank returns for various dates provide the numbers of banks in each town and their assets.

Annual reports of state commissioners or superintendents of banking are another source for information, summarizing the financial condition of banks and commenting on current banking issues. Those of the New York state banking department, for example, cover the years 1870 to 1885. The report for 1869–70 includes a tabulated list of banks, showing, for each, among other things, location, amount of capital, and amount of securities held. Some annual reports of state auditors, state treasurers and bureaus of labor statistics may also carry information on banks.

In the National Archives, the general records of the Department of the Treasury (RG 56) contain, among the correspondence (series "ZO"), a great volume of communications on banks and banking between government officials and the banks, as well as reports, statements, and accounts relating to the deposit of public money in individual deposit banks.[111] Among the records of the Comptroller of the Currency (RG 101) are reports on national banks and case files concerning insolvent banks, as well as the records of the Freedmen's Savings and Trust Company.[112]

A series of federal documents provide from 1833 evidence on the condition of banks throughout the United States.[113] These may include extracts from the reports of state bank commissioners and superintendents with a great deal of statistical data on individual banks. Included are historical sketches, auditors' reports, abstracts of reports of investigative committees, and much other information on capital, circulation, discounting, deposits, and general conditions. Some banks were engaged in activities other than pure banking, so that

[111] Hope K. Holdcamper and Carmelita S. Ryan (comps.), *Preliminary Inventory of the General Records of the Department of the Treasury* (PI 187, 1977), 19–20, 83–5; *GNA*, 152, 167.
[112] See pp. 147–8.
[113] *Checklist*, 1,010, 1,069–70; *US Serial Set Index* (p. 22 above), under "Condition": to 1863 on state banks; from 1863 on national banks in the states.

there is also evidence on, in particular, bank involvement in canal, railroad, and mining enterprises. There are, too, large numbers of other federal documents pertaining to banks and banking in different states, among them the annual reports of the Comptroller of the Currency.[114]

Isolated fire-insurance policies may survive among the papers of businesses or individuals. More important may be the records of insurance companies, especially those covering fire and marine matters, which can throw considerable light on local industry and trade.[115] Maps produced by fire-insurance companies, detailed in chapter 1, can provide an enormous amount of information on the buildings belonging to local firms and generally on the composition and commercial activities of local enterprises.[116] Very useful where they have survived are fire-insurance societies' registers of policies. These record the date of each policy, its number, the name of the policy holder and an inventory, and perhaps plan, of the property insured with its insurance valuation. Alone, or better in conjunction with other evidence, including fire-insurance companies' correspondence with agents and clients, such registers can contribute not only to many aspects of local economic history but also to the history of local topography and buildings. Register entries can be used to investigate the owners, lessees, and subtenants of individual industrial and commercial buildings, and, collectively, the distribution of ownership and tenantship, in, say, particular local industries at certain times. They indicate the site of the insured buildings, very often with reference to adjoining property, and are thus of interest to the local historical geographer. They provide for the historian interested in local building history an indication of the size of buildings, the dates of erection, and the materials of which they were constructed. Thus, to cite a rather simple

---

[114] See *US Serial Set Index*; and House of Representatives, *List of Publications ... by the Committee on Banking and Currency ... 39th–91st Congress* (1970); *Checklist*, 1,064–5.

[115] N.B., Humbert O. Nelli, *A Bibliography of Insurance History* (1976). For marine insurance, see pp. 384, 403, 413.

[116] See, e.g., Lay J. Gibson, "Tucson's evolving commercial base, 1883–1914: a map analysis," *Hist. Geography Newsletter*, 5 (1975); Scranton, *Proprietary Capitalism*, 142.

policy, the register of the Mutual Assurance Company of Richmond, VA, shows that in 1846 in Williamsburg, VA, one Robert McCandlish owned a store in the main street occupied by certain named merchants. The building was of brick covered with timber. A plan is provided of the store and its outbuildings, with an evaluation, and an indication of neighboring property is also given.[117]

Where substantial numbers of policies are recorded for an area in a particular period they will provide evidence of the topographical distribution of different industries in a community, and the extent and nature of partnerships, the occupational structure of specific industries, and so on. The registers are particularly valuable for the study of the scale of the business unit, measured in terms of fixed capital, in the form of buildings and plant. They can show the ownership of such fixed capital and its value, the types of machine and other plant used or newly introduced, and the different sorts of buildings and their industrial function. The adding of extra policies to cover additional buildings or plant may give an indication of the growth of an enterprise, and of times of prosperity and expansion in a local industry. Where businessmen owned property in different places a clue may be given to such matters as their channels of distribution of goods. Some information will be provided, too, on the type of stock kept. The calculation of total assets is, however, not possible, since trade credits, an important component of working capital, were not at risk by fire and so not insured.[118]

Insurance-company records may still be held by the companies themselves, but many for the nineteenth century are in libraries and other depositories. The Huntington Library, for instance, has a collection of one company covering almost a century. The Insurance Library Association, Boston, has fire, marine, and other insurance records covering 1684 to 1906. Such records can be very extensive. The records of the Mutual Assurance Company, Richmond, VA, include

---

[117] Virginia State Library, Richmond, policy 14398.
[118] Regina Reynolds and Mary E. Ruwell, "Fire insurance records," *AA*, 38 (1975). Cf. works cited W. B. Stephens, *Sources for English Local History* (1981 edn.), 136–8.

hundreds of volumes and thousands of other items, 1795–
1942, and are in the Virginia State Library.[119]

The existence of insurance companies is detailed in certain
tax returns, directories (some of which are devoted entirely to
such companies), and in official documents. For instance, for
New York state annual reports of the Comptroller, 1869–
1903, include tables of the various types of authorized insurance institutions and, from time to time, more detailed
information on individual companies.

MINING

There is much secondary literature on mining history in particular areas including histories of individual mines and
mining companies.[120] Community historians will, therefore,
need to search out what has already been written before taking
further steps. For California, for instance, Guddie's work
provides locations for and other details of some 4,000 mining
camps.[121]

Newspapers appeared quickly in mining communities and
contain an enormous amount of local evidence. Although not
given much space here, they must be regarded as an extremely
important source of information on rushes, mining activity,
and life in mining communities.[122] Some reflect their local
mining connections in their titles – like the *Mohave County
Miner* (Kingman, AZ), the *Butte Miner* (Montana), the *Daily
Central City Miners' Register* (Colorado; title varies), and the
Utah Mining Gazette. Non-local trade journals, too, like the
Mining Magazine (New York, 1853–7) and the *Engineering and
Mining Journal* (New York, from 1864) have data on individual
companies and mining districts. The San Francisco *Daily*

[119] Philip Hamer, *A Guide to Archives and Manuscripts in the United States* (1961), 36,
239; Canley L. Edwards (comp.), *A Guide to the Business Records in the . . . Virginia
State Library* (1983), 105–9.
[120] *HG*, 337–8, 340–1, 414; William St. C. Greever, *The Bonanza West* (1963), bibl.;
Ray A. Billington, *Western Expansion* (1982 edn.), bibl., esp. 810–23.
[121] Edwin G. Guddie, *California Gold Camps* (1975).
[122] See, e.g., Clarke C. Spence, *British Investments and the Mining Frontier, 1860–1901*
(1958), 272–3; William J. Trimble, *The Mining Advance into the Inland Empire*
(1914), 386–7; Marvin Lewis (ed.), *The Mining Frontier: Contemporary Accounts . . .*
(1967); Herbert Kraus and Gary D. Olson (eds.), *Prelude to Glory* (1974).

Bulletin is a most important source reflecting the significance of that city in the American mining industry and containing useful reports and editorials. The *Mining and Scientific Press* (San Francisco, from 1860; title varies) is also informative on Western mining. The *Mining Journal and Commercial Gazette: Forming a Complete Record of the Proceedings of all Public Companies* (London; from 1835 the *Mining Journal*; title varies) is also useful: indeed the large British investment in Western mining resulted in British newspapers and journals including data and news on British and other mining companies operating in the United States. Publications like the *Mining Journal* carried items on individual mines and companies as well as correspondence from British miners working in America. That journal, for instance, published intimate accounts of Lake Superior mines in 1859–61 written by Henry Buzzo, a Cornish mine manager in that area. English newspapers in areas from which immigrant miners came, like the *Cornish Telegraph*, the *Royal Cornwall Gazette*, and the *West Briton* also carry many informed reports and letters from the migrants.[123] Professional and technical journals, like the *American Journal of Science and Arts*[124] (from 1818; title varies; available in microform) and the *Transactions of the American Institute of Mining Engineers*,[125] and other specialist periodicals also contain localized data.[126]

County histories in mining areas and other contemporary histories, including those of individual mining communities,[127] are also useful, for often authors were writing of what was to them the recent past, when old-timers were still around. Contemporary accounts of particular rushes are also valuable,[128] and there are innumerable travel accounts relating

---

[123] John Rowe, *The Hard-Rock Men* (1974), 80–1, and *passim*; Arthur C. Todd, *The Cornish Miner in America* (1967), *passim*.

[124] E.g., A. S. Woolridge, "Geological and statistical notice of the coal mines in the vicinity of Richmond, Virginia," vol. 43 (1842).

[125] E.g., articles on the Midlothian Colliery, Chesterfield county, VA: vols. 1, 4, 5 (1871–3, 1875–6, 1876–7).

[126] E.g., "Notice of the Appomattox coal pits," *Farmers' Register*, 10 (1842).

[127] E.g., Lewis A. Kent, *Leadville* (1880).

[128] See, e.g., LeRoy R. Hafen (ed.), *Colorado Gold Rush* (1941).

to mining and mining districts.[129] Autobiographies, memoirs, reminiscences, letters, and diaries and journals,[130] published and unpublished, found in many libraries and record depositories, may provide additional insight and factual data.

Other types of contemporary published sources include general guides (like John S. Hittell, *Mining in the Pacific States of North America* (1861, repr. 1949)), and handbooks like Richard J. Hinton's *Hand-Book to Arizona: Its Resources, Towns, Mines . . .* (1878) and H. W. B. Kanter's *Hand Book on the Mines, Miners, and Minerals of Utah* (n.d.).[131] Containing more specific information about individual mines and companies are directories like Thomas B. Corbett's *The Colorado Directory of Mines . . .* (1879). And because of large-scale involvement of British companies and investment, British directories, like the annual *Mining Manual* (London, from 1887) and the British *Stock Exchange Year Book* (title varies),[132] may be useful.

The records of mining companies and ventures do not differ materially from general business records described above. Those of the Nevada Mining Company (1862–1901), for instance, include correspondence, receipts and disbursements, payrolls, bank books, time books, stockholders' statistics and accounts, reports on ore extracted, and assays.[133] For companies using slaves there may be records pertaining to them.[134] Reports to stockholders of large companies were often published. Collections of personal business papers relating to mining are to be found in the Library of Congress and in many depositories in areas where mining has been significant. Particularly important are collections at the Huntington Library, the Bancroft Library, University of California, Berkeley, and the University of Colorado libraries.[135] Some, like

[129] *HG*, 137–51; Rodman W. Paul, *Mining Frontiers of the Far West* (1963), 220; Billington, *Westward Expansion*, bibl.

[130] Walter Van T. Clark (ed.), *The Journal of Alfred Doten, 1848–1903* (1973).

[131] Cf. Calvin W. Gower, "Aids to prospective prospectors," *Kansas Hist. Q.*, 43 (1977).

[132] For details, see Stephens, *Sources for English Local History*, 131.

[133] *Guide to American Historical Manuscripts in the Huntington Library* (1979).

[134] Cf. Ronald L. Lewis, *Coal, Iron, and Slaves* (1979).

[135] See George Parkinson, *Guide to Coal Mining Collections in the United States* (1978); pp. 35–7.

the Bancroft Library, contain collections of photographs and pictures of mines and mining communities. Unpublished records relating to British companies operating in America are with the Registrar of Companies (London and Cardiff), the Companies Registration Office, Edinburgh (for Scottish companies), the Public Record Office, London (especially Classes BT 31, 34, 41) and in Guildhall Library, London.[136] The Bancroft Library has microfilms of some of these records.

Published prospectuses issued by mining companies were devised to attract investors, but are nevertheless valuable sources, sometimes including maps, mining byelaws, and so on. There were also many published reports, some of individual mines (like the *Report of Professor B. Silliman on the Emma Silver Mine* [Little Cottonwood Canyon, VT], 1872), others (like Richard E. Owen and E. T. Cox, *Report on the Mines of New Mexico*, 1865) of wider areas.

The volumes of the published federal censuses of manufactures, aside from those for 1810, 1820, and 1900, provide some statistics on mining and quarrying, though the strictures on the accuracy of industrial information in the censuses, noted in the previous section, should be kept in mind. The 1850 census gives data only at the state and territory level.[137] For 1840, however, there are quite detailed statistics at the level of counties, towns, and townships.[138] For 1860 gold mining, pig-iron output, and copper-smelting data are given for counties, and for some counties figures for iron-ore mining are distinguished from statistics of iron manufacture.[139] Descriptive accounts of coal and iron mining in the 1860 volume contain some local information.[140] The 1870 census published statistical data on mines and quarries by

136 For details see Stephens, *Sources for English Local History*, 133; Spence, *British Investments*, 269; W. Turrentine Jackson, *The Enterprising Scot* (1968), 370–1. Records once in London Stock Exchange are now at Guildhall, London. British consular reps. and correspondence may also be useful: see pp. 414–15.
137 Vol. II. Compendium vol. gives by counties and towns numbers employed in different kinds of mining.
138 Vol. II. For discrepancies with occupational statistics in the census, see SD 5 (28–2), ser. 449, 5–6.
139 Vol. III.   140 Ibid., clxiii–clxxvii.

counties – numbers of establishments, power, capital, and production – though not always accurately, and omitting smaller mines.[141]

The evidence provided in the 1880 census volumes is extensive, and though again defective, embraces much useful information.[142] Volume xv contains a very valuable directory of mines and metallurgical establishments east of the 100th meridian and of coal mines in the West. This names each establishment with its location and operator, and gives details of the product and statistics of output. For coal mines the markets and means of transportation are indicated and for iron-ore mines the uses of the product and where used may be given.[143] The volume also includes very detailed descriptions, with statistics, of mining areas, counties, and individual mines and smelting works, with many maps and plans. A very detailed index includes county entries. The mining of precious metals is dealt with separately in volume xiii which contains much information relating to individual counties and companies; a special appendix deals with the mines of Utah. Volume xiv is devoted to mining laws – federal, state, and territorial laws as well as local laws and regulations. The section on local laws contains very detailed information on counties and mining districts, including reports of miners' meetings. Volume x carries descriptive accounts of quarrying regions embracing local evidence. This volume also covers petroleum.

Volume vii of the 1890 census contains descriptive accounts of various mineral industries which embrace also statistical data with information, sometimes detailed, on individual counties, districts, and mines. Volume viii includes details of the mines of Alaska. A Census Bureau *Special Report, Mines and Quarries, 1902* (1905) contains much local information and some photographs in a series of sections on individual states and on particular minerals. Coal production is given by counties.

---

[141] Vol. iii, 770–90; Bureau of the Census, *Special Rep., Mines and Quarries, 1902* (1905), 5–6.
[142] *Special Rep . . . 1902*, 7.   [143] Pp. 857–988.

The original unpublished federal census schedules for industry cover metal and coal mining. Schedules for 1880 for quarries and small coal mines give the date of opening, area excavated or mined, location of chief market, methods of transportation, and data on accidents and on employees.[144] The original special schedules for mines have not survived.

The published federal population censuses will indicate where there were concentrations of miners in an area. Combination of occupational and personal data in the unpublished schedules with evidence from directories, newspapers, governmental records, and contemporary accounts can provide the basis for detailed analysis of the structure of mining communities.[145] Some state censuses – like that from Wisconsin in 1885 and 1895, and the Michigan census of 1894 – may also contain information on mining.[146]

Since the federal government played a significant part in the identification and surveying of mineral lands and in the supervision of mining developments, its archives, aside from the census, provide a considerable body of evidence. Mining lands in the public domain were the subject of complex federal legislation, of which a background knowledge is desirable before embarking on local studies. Such lands were variously, and at different periods, leased by the federal government, kept in its hands with permits granted for mining, and disposed of in the same way as land for agricultural settlement. In California and the Rockies, a blind eye was turned on those working the gold mines without formal rights, before extending the pre-emption system to allow them to purchase the land.[147] The records of the disposal of public-domain land and its later transference from individual to individual form an important body of evidence for mining history, as they do for agriculture and settlement. They are described in detail in

[144] RIP 67, 15–18.   [145] Cf. Ralph Mann, *After the Gold Rush* (1982).
[146] Dubester (1948).
[147] See J. W. Thompson (comp.), *United States Mining Statutes Annotated* (1915); Vernon Carstensen (ed.), *The Public Lands* (1963), various articles; Paul W. Gates, *History of Public Land Law Development* (1968), esp. therein Robert W. Swenson, "Legal aspects of mineral resources exploitation."

chapter 4, to which reference should be made – especially to what is said of the *Territorial Papers of the United States*, the *American State Papers: Public Lands*, Congressional "hearings," and petitions and memorials to Congress. Records of Congressional debates and legislation may contain local information. Memorials of territorial legislatures and others in the National Archives (RG 233) mention mining conditions in particular counties.[148]

The records of the General Land Office (RG 49) at the National Archives, Washington, DC, and its regional branches as well as in local land offices and other depositories, are a significant source. The nature of these records is explained in chapter 4.[149] A good proportion of the general correspondence concerned mining claims. From 1844 there is the out-correspondence of the Mineral Contest Division.[150] Very large numbers of plats showing mines and mining claims in many states and territories, particularly in the West, exist, some of them supplying patent and survey document numbers. In addition there are case files for some 47,500 mineral entries deriving from the Act of 1866 which opened mineral lands of the public domain to all citizens. These files contain applications for patents, field notes, records of litigation, and registers of mining claims, as well as copies of local rules and customs pertaining in self-governing communities before the Act. In addition there is a large collection of mineral contest dockets.[151] There are also the records of Army officers charged with leasing lead and copper lands in Illinois, Wisconsin, and Michigan, c.1824–47, and a record of

---

[148] Jane F. Smith, "The use of federal records in writing local history," *Prologue*, 1 (1969), 41–2.

[149] See also Harry P. Yopshe and Philip P. Brower (comps.), *Preliminary Inventory of the Land Entry Papers of the General Land Office* (PI 22, 1949), 4, 11–13 for coal, cash, and mineral entries.

[150] *GNA*, 372, 374.

[151] Ibid., 376; Jane F. Smith, "Settlement on the public domain as reflected in federal records," in Ralph E. Ehrenberg (ed.), *Patterns and Process in Historical Geography* (1975), 301–2; Richard S. Maxwell, *Public Land Records of the Federal Government 1800–1950* (RIP 57, 1973), 5. For self-governing mining communities, see Charles H. Shinn, *Land Laws of Mining Districts* (1884); Thomas M. Marshall, "The miners' laws of Colorado," *AHR*, 25 (1920); Harwood Hinton, "Frontier speculation," *Pacific Hist. Rev.*, 29 (1960).

land sales containing data on coal cash entries, following an Act of 1873.[152] The published annual reports of the GLO, described in chapter 4, contain much information on mineral lands and surveys and on mining activities.

Published reports of geographical and geological surveys, including those undertaken by the Interior Department, the War Department, and the Geological Survey,[153] provide evidence of mineral resources and mining and quarrying activity, sometimes with very specific local data:[154] as in a report of 1844 of a survey of Iowa, Wisconsin, and Illinois, a report of 1886 on Leadville, CO, and one of 1894–5 on mining at Cripple Creek, CO.[155] Among the unpublished records of the Geological Survey (NA, RG 57) are those of the Hayden, Powell, Wheeler, and King surveys, maps of mineral deposits, and field notebooks, some of which record the examination of individual mines.[156]

The records of the Secretary's Office of the Interior Department in the National Archives (RG 48) include territorial mine inspectors' reports on conditions, productivity, labor relations, and the like for New Mexico Territory (1892–1907), Utah Territory (1885–96), and Indian Territory (1893–1907),[157] and maps relating to coal and mineral lands and

152 *GNA*, 375; PI 187, 6; Smith, "Settlement," 295; RIP 57, 7; Jane Smith, "Comment," in Meyer H. Fishbein (ed.), *The National Archives and Statistical Research* (1973), 173.
153 *Checklist*, 467–9, 471, 1,267–70. Cf. James D. Hague, *Mining Industry* (vol. 3 of Charles King, *United States Geological Survey of the Fortieth Parallel*, 7 vols. and atlas, 1870–80, q.v.); John M. Nickles, *Geological Literature of North America* (Geological Survey Bulls. 746, 747 (1922, 1924)). And see pp. 47–9.
154 Cf. Smith, "Use of federal records," 32; Herman R. Friis, "The David Dale map of southwestern Wisconsin," *Prologue*, 1 (1969).
155 SD 407 (28–1), ser. 437; Samuel E. Emmons, *Geology and Mining Industry of Leadville, Colorado* (Geological Survey Monograph 12, 1886); *16th AR Geological Survey, 1894–5* (1895).
156 Robert Claus and Lester W. Smith (comps.), *Geologists' Field Notebooks, 1867–1939* (NA, Preliminary Checklist 46–9, 1945); Ralph E. Ehrenberg (comp.), *Geographical Exploration and Mapping in the 19th Century* (RIP 66, 1973), 13; *GNA*, 389, 391, 393. Records of the Mineral Resources Div., Geological Survey are in RG 70: ibid., 390, 408.
157 *Records of the Office of the Secretary of the Interior, 1833–1964* (NA, NNF-48, 1984), pt. 1, 98, 101 (T/S). Cf. *Interior Dept. Territorial Papers: New Mexico, 1851–1914* (PAM 364, 1962).

claims.[158] The published versions of these reports are in the Secretary's annual reports,[159] and sometimes contain much detail on individual mines. Thus we can learn of the Cannavan and Bailey Mine, one mile north-west of Gallup, Bernalillo county, NM, in 1895, the names of the owners, the kind of coal mined, the output and capacity, and the number of employees, together with various technical details, and that the Atlantic and Pacific Railroad hauled the output from Gallup station, and we are provided with a record of inspections.[160]

Other evidence in the National Archives on mining can be found in some State Department territorial papers (RG 59),[161] and in the correspondence of the Secretary of War (RG 107).[162] The records of the Chief of Ordnance (RG 156) include correspondence, leases, and other papers relating to mineral lands, among them a map of 1845 of such lands by Lake Superior.[163] There may be information in the published annual reports of the Secretary of War, but to search these large reports, with their inadequate or absent indexes, would be very time consuming. Authorized and unauthorized mining in Indian lands is recorded in the archives of the Bureau of Indian Affairs (RG 75) and in the Bureau's published annual reports.[164] Army records also provide some information on mining permits and mining activity in Indian lands.[165]

The Treasury Department published annual statistics of mineral production west of the Rockies for the years 1866–75.[166] These volumes have information on individual

---

[158] GNA, 370; Laura E. Kelsay (comp.), *Preliminary Inventory of the Cartographic Records of the Office of the Secretary of the Interior* (PI 81, 1955), 4; NNF–48, 160.

[159] *Checklist*, 439, 441. Also issued separately.

[160] HD 5 (54–1), ser. 3383, p. 675.

[161] GNA, 134. Cf. *State Departmental Territorial Papers: Arizona, 1864–72* (PAM 342, 1961).

[162] Smith, "Use of federal records," 38.

[163] GNA, 243, 245. Cf. Smith, "Use of federal records," 33–6.

[164] See pp. 234–7.

[165] In RGs 94, 108, 393: see Edward E. Hill (comp.), *Guide to the Records in the National Archives Relating to American Indians* (1981), 226–7, 229, 243, 310–11, 346.

[166] *Checklist*, 1,144–5. Cf. Paul, *Mining Frontiers*, 215–16, 218. See also *Mineral Resources of the United States East of the Rocky Mountains, 1867–8*, HED 273 (40–2), ser. 1343.

counties and mines, sometimes including yields and profits. From 1882 to 1931 annual reports on mineral production covering the whole Union were produced by the Geological Survey. These are very fruitful of statistical and descriptive detail on individual places and companies. Changes, as in the output of individual coal mines, can be followed from year to year. Another annual Treasury series, published from 1880 into the twentieth century, provides information by counties on the mining of precious metals, often with considerable details on individual mines and enterprises and indexes of localities.[167]

Aside from these there are among federal documents many reports on mining in different parts of the country. For instance, a report on local government for Utah Territory (1892) contains information by counties of coal, lead, silver, and gold mining; there is a report of 1842 of fraudulent sales of mineral lands in Wisconsin and Iowa; and a War Office document of 1838 contains correspondence about the sale of mineral land in Gallena, IL.[168] A very detailed account of the Alaskan gold fields (with maps) was published by the Bureau of Labor in 1898.[169] The *Report of the Industrial Commission* (1900–2) includes (especially in the testimony) much local and regional evidence on labor relations, working conditions, and capital in the mining industry. There is a list of witnesses and the index is worth searching under names of states, counties, and individual mines.[170]

Sometimes information is to be found in unlikely documents. A report of the Navy Department for 1844, for example, is concerned with American coals and provides details of different mines and companies.[171] Some early twentieth-century documents may contain retrospective information. Thus a report of 1907 on Goldfield, Bullfrog, and other mining districts in southern Nevada has information on

[167] For details of these series, see *Checklist*, 1,144–5.
[168] HD 943 (52–1), ser. 3044; HR 484 (27–2), ser. 408; HD 307 (25–2), ser. 329.
[169] *Bull. Bureau of Labor*, No. 16.
[170] Vol. xii: HD 181 (57–2), ser. 4342.
[171] SR 386 (28–1), ser. 436.

particular mines.[172] Mining activities are recorded in the series on the condition of banks throughout the United States (see last section), and the *Report of the Immigration Commission* (1910–11) contains evidence of immigrants working in coal, iron-ore, and copper mines.[173] The index to the US Serial Set should, therefore, be searched under, for instance, "mining," "mineral resources" and the names of particular products.

Litigation entered a great deal into mining history so that records of court testimony and reports of judicial decisions in both federal and state courts may be worth searching.[174]

State and territorial archives, published and unpublished, are likely to contain evidence on mining history, and catalogs of state records should be searched. Particularly relevant are state and territorial laws and statutes, legislative journals and reports of debates, and official reports of state mineralogists, geologists, mines inspectors, boards of agriculture, immigration commissioners, and bureaus of labor statistics. Thus, for instance, local mineral resources in California with descriptions of individual mines in 1887 are found in the annual report of the state mineralogist, while the state of Washington's mining districts are described in the report of the state geologist in 1891. Such reports are likely to be useful sources for individual mines, and often contain detailed plans and maps. A New York state document for 1899 includes a map of the location of iron-ore mines, statistics of iron-ore production in several districts, and descriptive notes on individual mines.[175]

Especially fruitful of data are likely to be the reports of state bureaus of labor statistics which may be the vehicle for mine inspectors' reports and much more. The Illinois Bureau of Labor Statistics biennial reports, for instance, carry statistics of mineral and quarry products with data on the employees and capital of mining enterprises. The 1886 report of the

---

[172] HD 56 (59–2), ser. 5160.
[173] SD 633 (61–2), ser. 5667–8 (pt. 1, 2 vols.), 17, 18, 19.
[174] Susan Chambers, "Western natural resources," *Prologue*, 21 (1989).
[175] *New York State, Museum Bull.*, 7 (1899).

Kansas Bureau of Labor and Industrial Statistics has a 110-page report on mines which includes totals of coal production by counties in 1885, returns from forty-nine mining establishments (indicating their locations, capital invested, numbers of employees, numbers of days operated, wages, and hours of labor), and selling prices of coal at Osage City, KS, annually from 1871 to 1886. It also prints returns from lead and zinc smelting works with data on capital, production, and wages.

For state lands the same sort of records as for public-domain land may exist. For Minnesota, for example, there are records of mineral-lease prospecting permits and a list of lands for which state mineral leases were issued.[176] The South Carolina state archives contain a record of licenses for phosphate mining, 1885–90, and other papers of the state board of phosphate commissioners, 1878–1900.[177] Among state records there may also be the licenses and records of incorporation of mining companies.

Records of the governments of counties, towns, and cities embracing mining communities may include general ordinances and byelaws, records of registers of deeds, and court records. The archives of Fremont county, CO, for instance, include indexes to mining claims, locators and lodes, location-certificate records, mining-deed records and affidavits of labor, providing much data on local mines and mining lands.[178]

176 Wirth, *Minnesota Iron Lands*, 224.
177 Marion C. Chandler and Earl W. Wade, *The Southern Carolina Archives* (1976 edn.), 39.
178 WPA, HRS, *Inventory of the County Archives of Colorado, No. 22, Fremont County (Canon City)* (1938), 49–50, 57.

CHAPTER 9

Maritime activity, communications, and the fur trade

This chapter is divided into two main sections. Source material for the study of rail, road, and internal waterway communications is treated in the second section, which also covers postal services. The initial section – on maritime activities – is chiefly devoted to sources of information on the coastal and foreign trade of the seaboard and Great Lakes ports, their shipping (including shipbuilding), and their fishing industries. These are activities which often had significance for the history both of the ports concerned and of the cities and regions served by them. There is necessarily some overlap between the two sections, especially regarding the underlying topic of trade. A brief note on the fur trade is appended.

TRADE, SHIPPING, AND FISHERIES

An enormous amount of secondary literature exists for the study of the maritime activities of port towns and their hinterlands.[1] For original evidence, federal records, published and unpublished, are a prime source. The records of debates in Congress contain data on trade, and in particular the federal censuses contain much evidence on local shipping and shipbuilding, and some on commerce. The published census of manufactures of 1810 includes by counties the tonnage of shipping constructed and its value.[2] The volumes of the 1860 and 1870 censuses provide more detailed county data on

---

[1] HG, 402–3, 405–6; Suzanne R. Ontiveros and Susan K. Kinnell (eds.), *American Maritime History: A Bibliography* (1986); Carman and Thompson (1962), 180–92; Robert G. Albion, *Naval and Military History: An Annotated Bibliography* (1972 edn.), esp. sections on shipping and commerce, U.S.; and see pp. 16–19.
[2] For this and other publ. censuses of manufactures, see pp. 354–61. For original schedules to these censuses which incl. shipbuilding, see pp. 354–7, 359–60.

numbers of shipbuilding establishments, and statistics of employees in that trade and their wages as well as details on raw materials and value of the ships produced.[3] The 1860 census volume on agriculture contains a great deal of statistical material on the shipping of agricultural produce from individual ports.[4]

The 1880 census prints a detailed report on shipbuilding containing descriptions of the construction of various types of vessel, embedded in which is much local information, including some of a statistical nature. For instance, there are annual totals of vessels (by type) built in the Portsmouth district of New Hampshire, 1800–78. There are also statistics by counties of the numbers, tonnage, and value of vessels built during the census year.[5] This census, in its volumes on "Social Statistics of Cities," contains, in addition, data for port towns on harbors, and sometimes, as for Buffalo, statistics of imports and exports and of vessels cleared and entered, built, and registered, enrolled, and licensed.[6]

The 1890 published census also contains local statistics for shipbuilding. It provides, too, very detailed statistics of coastwise, inland water, and Great Lakes commerce.[7] These are particularly valuable since the only annually published data on coastwise and inland trade are the tonnage statistics in the reports of the Commissioner of Navigation (see below), carriers by water not being required to report their business annually.[8] The 1900 census publishes data on shipbuilding in forty-two cities.[9] A Census Bureau Special Report on *Transportation by Water* (1906) includes data on trade and shipping for some individual ports.

As for fisheries, the 1840 census publishes by counties the numbers of men employed in them, and the 1860 census prints a descriptive essay, which includes statistical data for certain

[3] 1860, vol. III, table 1; 1870, vol. III, table XI.
[4] Vol. II: see introd. and index.
[5] Vol. VIII, 106–7, 254–8. See also vol. II, table V; vol. XXII, 7–17.
[6] Vols. XVIII, XIX: see index under "commerce and navigation."
[7] Vol. XIV (pt. 2), Transportation by water: see contents p.
[8] Cf. *The Federal Census. Critical Essays* (American Economic Assoc., Public. No. 2, 1899), 246–7.
[9] Vol. VIII, 1,085.

ports.[10] The 1870 and 1890[11] published censuses provide information only at state level, but in the 1880 census there is a
report on the oyster industry which includes the names of
vessels in the oyster fleet, their tonnage, size of crews, and
details of wages paid.[12] The original schedules of the manufacturing census of 1880 (see ch. 8) embrace fisheries.

A host of other federal documents contain information on
waterborne trade, shipping, shipbuilding, and fishing,[13] and
some of the more important may be noted. From 1867 a series
of annual lists of the *Merchant Vessels of the United States* (title
varies)[14] provides data on (in alphabetical order) sailing vessels, steam vessels, iron and steel vessels, and unrigged vessels
– giving for each the official number of the vessel, its rig (if
rigged), its name, tonnage (gross and net), its register dimensions, the year and place of its construction, and its home port.
The number and tonnage of ships built in each customs district, 1855–79, is given in an Agriculture Department *Report on
Forestry* (1880).[15]

A series of annual reports on trade and shipping runs from
1789. This begins with two volumes in the *American State
Papers* presenting annual statistics of exports and imports by
states (1789–1823), though with occasional information on
individual ports.[16] The reports do not usually provide data on
specific types of imported commodities, and while they give
valuations for goods subject to *ad valorem* duties they do not
give the quantities, and though they indicate quantities for
goods paying specific duties they omit their value. Most of the
reports on exports before 1817 do not give quantities.[17]

[10] 1840, vol. II, District tables (also in Compendium); 1860, vol. IV, 525–51.
[11] 1890, vol. VIII, 217–28, Alaska local details.
[12] Unnumbered vol. (see Dubester (1950), no. 156): also publ. as rep. of Fisheries Commission.
[13] See *CIS US Serial Set Index* (see p. 22). For some documents relating to canal and river trade, see next section.
[14] *Checklist*, 1,149, 1,185.
[15] HED 37 (46–2), ser. 1922, pp. 382–95.
[16] *American State Papers: Commerce and Navigation.*
[17] For shortcomings and for differences between valuations in this series and in the manifests (see below), see Jerome Finster, *Major Sources in Customs Bureau Records for Statistical Data on Exports and Imports of the United States to 1900* (RIP 49, 1973), 4–5.

Sources for U.S. History

This series does, however, provide, by ports, details of registered, enrolled and licensed shipping, and of vessels built, with an indication of how much was engaged in the coastal trade and fishing. These data are continued, into the twentieth century, in the annual *Reports on Foreign Commerce and Navigation*.[18] In this series imports and exports are analyzed by ports or customs districts only from 1856 onwards. The 1857 report, for instance, includes (by customs collection districts) the quantities of U.S. and foreign goods exported, as well as quantities of foreign imports. In addition, for the same districts, it provides much information on shipping: the numbers of U.S. and foreign vessels cleared and entering (with their tonnage and numbers of men and boys in the crew); the destinations of ships (foreign and U.S.) leaving and the numbers of such ships entering and from where; the tonnages of ships registered and enrolled[19] and of those under 20 tons' burden licensed, distinguishing coasting and cod-fishing vessels; divers details of steamships and ships engaged in coasting and in cod and mackerel fishing and whaling; and the numbers, class, and tonnage of vessels built. Later reports contain much the same sort of information, but with increasingly detailed information on exports and imports.[20]

Derived from the *Reports on Foreign Commerce and Navigation*, the annual *Statistical Abstract of the United States* (from 1878),[21] provides (retrospectively from 1856) valuations of imports and exports of merchandise and of gold and silver, and the tonnage of vessels entered and cleared[22] at the main ports, distinguishing U.S. and foreign ships.[23] From the 1894 report onwards the import and export data are provided for all

[18] See *Checklist*, 1,166–9.
[19] For distinction, see n. 49, below.
[20] For use of these reps., see Peter G. Albion, *The Rose of New York Port, 1815–1860* (1939) (drawn on in following pp.).
[21] *Checklist*, 1,184–5.
[22] Tonnages cleared annually appear from the 1882 rep., but they are given retrospectively, 1853–81.
[23] For tonnages entered and cleared from chief ports annually, 1867–1909, see National Monetary Commission, *Statistics of the United States, 1867–1909* (1910).

customs districts, with annual figures retrospectively back to 1879.[24]

Other noteworthy documents include a report on the wool trade and industry in 1887 giving statistics of wool imports, 1856–87, for various customs districts, and a similar report, for the years 1856–93, published in 1894.[25] The *Report of the Industrial Commission* (1900–2) has statistics of cotton exports from individual customs districts for 1898 and 1899,[26] much evidence on shipping registered and built at various ports, and a great deal of interesting testimony relating to canal, lake, and coastal trade.[27]

A Treasury document of 1870, dealing with the depressed state of American shipping, includes, by ports, information on steamer lines making regular trips between the U.S. and foreign ports, giving names of steamers (including whether British, German, or U.S. owned) and termini of routes. It also includes, for each year from 1850 to 1869, tables and graphs of tonnages of vessels coming from foreign countries into Boston, New York, Philadelphia, Baltimore, New Orleans, and San Francisco, distinguishing foreign and home-owned ships.[28] A report of 1874 on transportation routes to the seaboard includes statistics of exports from various ports.[29]

Other documents dealing with specific ports and districts include a Treasury document of 1838 which tabulates the value of trade between British North America and the districts of Passamaquoddy, Portland, Boston, and New York in 1828 and 1837. It details the value of imports and exports (distinguishing goods carried in U.S. and foreign ships and foreign and domestic produce) and the tonnage entered and cleared (distinguishing U.S. and British).[30] Another Treasury

---

[24] See also Bureau of Statistics quarterly reps., imports and exports, 1876–93: *Checklist*, 1,177–8.

[25] HED 550 (50–1), ser. 2570, table 2; HMD 94 (52–2), ser. 3110.

[26] Vol. VI: HD 494 (56–2), ser. 4168, p. 174.

[27] Vol. IV: HD 476, pt. 4 (56–1), ser. 3992.

[28] HED 111 (41–2), ser. 1417. See also HR 28 (41–2), ser. 1436, for similar inf. for various years between 1856 and 1869.

[29] SR 307 (43–1), ser. 1588–9, 2 vols.: see p. 424.

[30] HD 300 (25–2), ser. 329.

document, a report of 1852, is a mine of information and includes quantitative data on the trade of the Great Lakes ports, statistics of canal and railroad trade by states (1820–51), information on shipping moved at the chief Eastern seaports (1820–51), a review of the state of the deep-sea fisheries of New England with statistics for individual ports, details of exports and imports at various ports (mainly in the 1840s and 1850s), and data on river traffic.[31] A document of 1864 provides statistics of trade with Canada, and of internal overland, canal, Great Lakes, and Pacific coast trade for various years from the 1830s.[32]

Three documents of 1886–8, relating to disputes between British and American fishermen, contain much information on the fishing vessels of various U.S. ports and their activities.[33] The annual reports of the Fish Commission (1871–1903) provide, especially in "Accompanying Papers," much detailed evidence on fishing practices and individual U.S. fisheries, including some information on individual vessels.[34] And the first report of the Bureau of Animal Industry (1884) contains reports, with detailed statistics, on the livestock and meat trade of Chicago.[35]

In the National Archives, petitions to Congress and the papers of committees (including published and unpublished hearings) include information on commerce.[36] Many other federal records at the Washington headquarters and at the regional branches of the National Archives, as well as in other repositories, relate to imports and exports and to shipping, fishing, and water-borne traffic generally.

The records of the Solicitor of the Treasury (RG 206)

---

[31] HED 136 (32–2), ser. 651 (with vol. of maps).

[32] SED 55 (38–1), ser. 1176.

[33] HED 19 (49–2), ser. 2477 (1886); SR 1683 (2 pts.) (49–2), ser. 2456 (1887); SED 113 (50–1), ser. 2512 (1888). For fishery statistics for various areas, see statistical bulls. Fish Commission: *Checklist*, 408.

[34] *Checklist*, 406. *Statistical Bull.* 1 (1897), 2 (1897), deal with Florida and Lake Superior fisheries.

[35] HMD 25 (48–2), ser. 2311, pp. 245–61.

[36] For an example, see Charles E. South and James C. Brown (comps.), *Hearings in the Records of the U.S. Senate and Joint Committees of Congress* (SL 32, 1972), 10.

include letters relating to customs house bonds, to suits for the forfeiture of vessels engaged in the slave trade, and to ships and goods seized for various reasons, including as prizes during the Civil War. There are also case files, suit papers, and reports relating to customs matters, some of which include details of vessels and merchandise involved and so throw light on the nature and organization of trade.[37] The records of the Customs Division of the Treasury (RG 56) contain, for various dates, letters (including correspondence with customs collectors), memoranda, and abstracts of decisions relating to court cases on customs matters.[38] In RG 366 are the records of the special agencies of the Treasury, among them some concerning trade in occupied areas of the Confederacy during the Civil War.[39]

Among the records of U.S. district courts (RG 21), in regional branches of the National Archives,[40] are Admiralty case files. Most of those concern actions for damages relating to collision on the high seas and, especially after 1851, on the navigable waterways of the U.S.; breach of contract for services or goods; pilotage, towage, and wharfage fees; bottomry; and marine insurance. But some relate to prizes, salvage rights, smuggling, and illegal transportation of slaves. Arranged by date and names, they can provide much intimate detail about sea-going and other trade.[41] Common law cases in RG 21 include those concerned with the evasion of customs duties.

---

[37] George S. Ulibarri (comp.), *Preliminary Inventory of the Records of the Solicitor of the Treasury* (PI 171, 1968), 4–5, 9, 17, 23.

[38] For details, see Carmelita S. Ryan and Hope K. Holdcamper (comps.), *Preliminary Inventory of the General Records of the Department of the Treasury* (PI 187, 1977), 73–5, and see ibid., 19. Cf. Victor and Dorothy Gondos, "Material in the National Archives relating to Alexandria," *Virginia Mag. Hist. and Biography*, 57 (1949), 429–31. For microfilms of correspondence between Treasury and customs' collectors: *GNA*, 156; *MRR*.

[39] For details, see Munden and Beers, 233–41.

[40] *GNA*, 74–90; David R. Kepley, "An untapped treasure," *Pennsylvania Mag. Hist. and Biography*, 105 (1981), 313.

[41] See, e.g., *Admiralty Case Files of the U.S. District Court for the Eastern District of Virginia, 1801–1861* (PDM 1300, 1985); Robert J. Plowman, "An untapped source; Civil War prize case files, 1861–65," *Prologue*, 21 (1989).

Federal tax records may contain a little useful information. The records of the Pennsylvania direct tax of 1798 (in RG 58) give evidence on the location and dimensions of wharves.[42] Internal Revenue assessment lists for 1862–73 record duties on yachts.[43]

The records of consular posts in seaport towns overseas (RG 84) include documentation of arrivals and departures of U.S. vessels and their cargoes.[44] U.S. consuls abroad also sent despatches to Washington on commercial activity, including trade with America.[45] These (in RG 59) are basically descriptive but many contain references to the trade of specific ports and may provide the researcher with background information on trading conditions in foreign ports with known connections with the U.S. port being studied. From the early 1830s the consuls submitted semi-annual reports on the movement of all U.S. vessels in their ports. These indicate the name of the master of each ship, its tonnage, whence it came and whither it was bound, and sometimes data on the content and value of cargo. Extracts of the despatches were published as annual federal documents: *Commercial Relations of the United States with Foreign Countries* (1855–1902) and *Consular Reports* (1880–1903).[46] Though these mainly stress economic conditions in the foreign country concerned, some local information is to be found in them.

For the last decade or so of the nineteenth century the case files of the Interstate Commerce Commission (RG 134; from

---

[42] Hope K. Holdcamper, *Statistical Data on the National Wealth and Money Supply to be Derived from Internal Revenue Records* (RIP 55, 1973), 1; PAM 372, 2.

[43] For details, see pp. 101–2.

[44] *GNA*, 141–2; *Materials in the National Archives Relating to Transportation* (RIC 36, 1948), 16–17; R. L. Heiss, "Major quantitative sources among the foreign service post records of the Department of State, 1789–1935" (NA draft, 1968, unpubl.); Mark G. Eckhoff et al. (comps.), *List of Foreign Service Post Records in the National Archives* (SL 9, 1967). See also Alexander P. Mavro (comp.), *Preliminary Inventory of the Records of Selected Foreign Service Posts* (PI 60, 1953) (Amsterdam, Hong Kong, Winnipeg); R. H. Werking, "United States consular reports," *Business Hist.*, 23 (1981).

[45] Daniel T. Goggin and H. Stephen Helton (comps.), *Preliminary Inventory of the General Records of the Department of State* (PI 157, 1963), 21, 26.

[46] *Checklist*, 921–2, and see 907–8; Milton O. Gustafson, *Commerce Data Among State Department Records* (RIP 53, 1973), 1–3; *GNA*, 132.

1887) may be of use.[47] These (in WNRC) relate to disagreements between common carriers and their customers on such matters as rates of carriage, other complaints, and petitions. Such files provide the details of the complaint or dispute and petitions of carriers for relief. They include exhibits, testimony, reports, correspondence, and other legal papers. Among the general files of the Operating Division (in NA) are annual reports of carriers (1888–1914) (arranged alphabetically and then chronologically). They include data on their finances, business activities, and corporate organizations, and are available in microfilm.[48]

All merchant ships of 5 tons and over came under federal jurisdiction from the late eighteenth century, and this involved certification of vessels. The records of the Bureau of Marine Inspection and Navigation (RG 41) include surrendered copies of certificates of enrollment, license, and registry of American merchant vessels from 1815 to 1911.[49] These records provide information about a ship's owner or owners (place of residence, shares owned), master, date and place and material of construction, dimensions, rig and tonnage, home port, and date and place of (and reason for) issue and surrender of the certificate. They are arranged by port and then chronologically. Unfortunately many were damaged by fire in 1921. There are also master abstracts of enrollments and registry, arranged chronologically and by port of issue. These include the date of issue, name of ship, name of the person securing the certificate, name of the master, a reference to any preceding certificate, the vessel's tonnage, and place and date of surrender with reasons. In addition, for the period 1789–1811 there are abstracts of certificates of registry issued at Boston, New York, Philadelphia, and Baltimore. And also in RG 41 is a

---

[47] *GNA*, 553; Forrest R. Holdcamper *et al.* (comps.), *Preliminary Inventory of the Records of the Interstate Commerce Commission* (NC–64, 1964), 3. See also Leonard Rapport, "Interstate Commerce Commission case files," in Timothy Walch (comp.), *Our Family, Our Town* (1987), q.v. also for the Commission's publ. reps.

[48] T913.

[49] Vessels in foreign trade were registered, those in coastal trade and fishing enrolled or licensed according to tonnage (5–20 tons licensed).

collection of bills of sales and mortgages, dating mainly from 1850.[50]

A modern compilation drawn from records in RGs 36 and 41 lists over 26,000 vessels enrolled at New York, 1789–1867, with their tonnage, rig, year and place of construction, and date of first New York documentation.[51] Because of New York's commercial significance, many ships normally documented at other U.S. ports acquired new certificates on berthing there – resultant on change of ownership or transfer from coastal to foreign trading and vice versa. They appear in this list and, since the New York issuances indicate the date and port of issue of the preceding certificate, their entries may be used to provide data on the shipping of other ports. From 1867 there is the official annual *List of Merchant Vessels of the United States* (see above).

The records of the Bureau of Customs (RG 36), in the National Archives, Washington, DC, and its regional branches, provide the richest single source on shipping, shipbuilding, and imports and exports, and include data for coastal, Great Lakes, and river ports as well as those of the seaboard.[52] The records are arranged by customs collection districts. Each of these had a headquarters' port with customhouse, and there were also other ports of entry and delivery in the district. Boundaries of districts changed periodically, and although the main types of record for each district – the customs collectors' records – were similar, they were not identical. Records for Southern ports, for instance, include

---

[50] GNA, 483–4; Forrest R. Holdcamper (comp.), *Customhouse Marine Documentation: A List . . . Showing Ports for which Documents are Available* (NC–18, 1962); Forrest R. Holdcamper (comp.), "Preliminary inventory of the records of the Bureau of Marine Inspection and Navigation" (NA, unpubl., n.d.; not in Chadwyck-Healey, *National Inventory*); Forrest R. Holdcamper, "Registers, enrollments and licenses in the National Archives," *Am. Neptune*, 1 (1941), 275–80, and, for table by ports, 281–94. Many certificates of registry for 1791–1801 are in RG 36: see below.

[51] Forrest R. Holdcamper, *List of American-Flag Merchant Vessels that Received Certificates of Enrollment or Registry at the Port of New York, 1789–1867* (SL 22, 2 vols., 1968), q.v. for details and use of these records. Cf. WPA, HRS, *Louisiana, Ships' Registers and Enrollments of New Orleans* (several vols., 1941–2).

[52] Samuel E. Morison, "The custom-house records in Massachusetts as a source of history," *Procs. Massachusetts Hist. Soc.*, 54 (1920–1), 324–31.

slave manifests,[53] and other records relating to the enforcement of laws against the slave trade, while for districts along
the Canadian border there are records which relate to warehouses and transportation. Again, not all of these records have
survived and those for some ports are much more complete
than for others.[54] The most useful are noted here.

Outward foreign manifests consist of lists of vessels
engaged in foreign trade giving the name and rig of the ship,
its tonnage, the master's name, the port of embarkation, a
description, quantification, and valuation of the merchandise
exported, the names of the consignee and consignor, and the
date of clearance. Shippers' declarations are often attached
giving the same sort of information on shipments as do the
manifests. Inward foreign manifests provide details of the
vessel and the shipment as with outward manifests, the date of
departure, and the port of destination. There are usually shippers' declarations, invoices of goods, consular certificates of
goods taken on at foreign ports, with clearances, permits to
land, and reports of inspectors. Coastwise manifests contain
similar information to the foreign manifests. All are arranged
chronologically.[55]

Entry papers, filed with the customs officials by importers,
repeat the information in the inward manifests and may also
contain details of the costs and values of goods subject to
duties. Impost books (based on manifests) record, for each
shipment of dutiable goods, the name of the vessel, date of
entry, name of consignee, number of packages and their content, cost and value of goods, and the amounts of duty.[56]
Tonnage books record data on tonnages of vessels cleared.

There may also be quarterly returns or abstracts of vessel

[53] Cf. Paul Lewinson, *A Guide to Documents in the National Archives for Negro Studies*
(1947), 3.
[54] *Records of the Customs Service, 1881–1938* [with some earlier records] (NA, NNF–36,
1984); Forrest R. Holdcamper (comp.), *Preliminary Inventory of the Records of the
Bureau of the Customs* (NC–154, 1968) (not in Chadwyck-Healey, *National Inventory*), 9–10: these list collection district bounds and names of ports of delivery
and entry. See *GNA*, 169–72, for districts, records, and their location.
[55] NC–154, 11ff.; RIP 49, 1–3, q.v. for coverage of foreign manifests and entry papers
in 34 ports (apps. A, B): records for other ports do, however, exist.
[56] Ibid., 3–4, and app. C (for ports with large collections).

documentation records for goods carried in U.S. and foreign vessels (giving amounts and values of goods), abstracts of imports (giving totals for each type of merchandise), records of exports (giving dates, names of vessels, and types of goods), warehouse ledgers, records of tonnage duties paid by foreign vessels importing goods (with indication of goods and names of masters), coastwise slave manifests, records of fishing vessels entitled to bounty (paid to 1867, with names of ships and masters and type of fish), and fishing agreements (with dates, details of ships and crews, and quantities of fish caught).[57] Detailed perusal of the National Archives inventory for the port in which the researcher is interested may well reveal other useful records. For the port of Baltimore, for instance, there are eleven volumes recording duties on wine and liquor for various dates, giving dates of import, names of importers and quantity of wine, and the amounts of duty paid.

Other records in RG 36 consist of registers of the daily arrival and clearance of shipping.[58] These give some indication of how busy a port was but not the actual quantity or value of goods involved. Crew lists for outbound vessels are arranged by port of destination, and, for arriving ships, alphabetically by vessel name. They provide the sailors' names, ages, personal descriptions, and addresses.[59] This record group also contains records relating to the measurement and inspection of vessels, ships' logs,[60] and shipping certificate documents concerning ships seized or destroyed by French vessels in the war of 1789–1801. And among headquarters' records are case files, correspondence, and reports relating to collection of duties, smuggling, investigations, and so on, which may contain evidence on local trade.[61]

---

[57] NC–154, 11ff.

[58] Cf. *Registers of Vessels Arriving at the Port of New York from Foreign Ports, 1789–1919*, M1066; Federal Records Center, San Francisco, *Special List of Research Records* (1967), 5.

[59] There are usually quarterly abstracts of passenger lists.

[60] See, e.g., Elmer W. Lindgard (comp.), *Preliminary Inventory of the Records of the Collector of Customs, Puget Sound . . .* (PI 122, 1960), 9–18.

[61] *GNA*, 168.

Records of the collectors of customs of the Confederacy are found mainly in RG 365. These include ships' manifests, abstracts of duties collected, warehouse records, and correspondence. This record group also contains the archives of the Cotton Bureau of the Texas Customs Office which provide details of trade in cotton.[62] The War Department collection of Confederate records (RG 109) also embraces some customs and shipping materials for Southern ports.[63]

The archives of the Treasury Bureau of Accounts (RG 39), too, contain customs materials, including registers of customs collected, 1867–1911, together with ledgers of steamboat fees collected, 1871–96. Customs journals, arranged chronologically by names of collectors, are in that record group and in RG 217 (General Accounting Office).[64] The records of the Bureau of Fisheries (RG 22) contain data on fishing, sealing, and salmon packing, especially in Alaska.[65]

Aside from records on customs and shipping in the National Archives and its regional branches, similar records and much ancillary material are likely to be found locally. New York Custom House, for example, has records of collectors and other related material for the ports of Alexandria, Baltimore, Boston, New York, and Philadelphia.[66] For Baltimore there are among that city's records bonds for yachts and for ships involved in coastal and foreign trade, licenses, records of clearances and arrivals, and ships' manifests.[67] For Mobile, AL, there are ships' manifests, slave manifests, crew lists,

---

[62] Carmelita S. Ryan (comp.), *Preliminary Inventory of the Treasury Department Collection of Confederate Records* (PI 169, 1967), 11, 37–8, and see index under Henry P. Beers, *The Confederacy: Guide to the Archives of the Government of the Confederate States of America* (1968), 292–3 and see index under "customs"

[63] Elizabeth Bethel (comp.), *Preliminary Inventory of the War Department Collection of Confederate Records* (PI 101, 1957), 235–6; Beers, *Confederacy*, 126, 128, 133.

[64] Donald L. King and William F. Sherman (comps.), *Preliminary Inventory of the Records of the Bureau of Accounts (Treasury)* (NC–23, rev. 1963), 5. RG 217 also includes records of claims for steamboats and cargoes lost in Civil War: Munden and Beers, 195–6.

[65] *GNA*, 394–5: *Materials in the National Archives Relating to Labor and Labor Problems* (RIC 10, 1942), 6.

[66] Carman and Thompson (1960), 166–8.

[67] Richard J. Cox and Patricia Vanorney, "The records of a city," *Maryland Hist. Mag.*, 70 (1975), 304.

records of arrivals and clearances, records of tonnage cleared, monthly statements of quantities, values and sources of imported goods, and details of licensed vessels, as well as correspondence, bonds, warehouse records, bills of lading, invoices, and reports on coastal trade and fishing.[68]

Use of customs records is by no means straightforward. Not only is their survival patchy, but those that have survived may, as noted, be dispersed. Moreover, the records that are available must be used with circumspection and the system under which they were compiled studied. Statistics provided in them or compiled from them do not, of course, allow for smuggling or other illicit practices. But aside from that, by no means all vessels in the coastal trade were required to enter or clear at the customhouse and those exempted do not appear in arrival and clearance records (unofficial publications, however, record ships' movements). Again, some goods paid no customs duties and so either no record was kept of them or crude estimates were entered. And some goods paid duties at fixed rates which did not vary with actual value, while others paid *ad valorem* rates. Thus, as already remarked, for some commodities we have recorded quantities but no values and for others the reverse. There are also problems associated with the basis of valuation.

Especially in the earlier part of the nineteenth century, export manifest data were often based on careless statements by ships' masters, and collectors sometimes altered totals, resulting in differences in statistics totaled from the manifests and those forwarded by the collectors to the Treasury. Customs figures were generally more accurate after 1821, and after 1866 much more reliable.

It should be noted, too, that the foreign countries shown in import manifests and entries were the countries of invoice and not necessarily those of the goods' origin, while the ports where the entries were filed were not always those where the merchandise was landed. Similarly, destinations in export

68 WPA, Survey of Federal Archives, *Inventory of Federal Archives in the States, Series III: 2 Alabama* (1940).

manifests may be vague, unstated, or show only where the goods were to be landed – not their final destination.[69]

The assessment of the extent of a port's trade by the numbers of vessels involved is a very crude, though, as suggested above, perhaps not useless, measure. Tonnage data give a better picture, though it must be remembered that not all vessels were loaded to capacity, while the value of cargoes of the same volume varied enormously. Nor do all the records indicate exact tonnage, but provide instead only the type of vessel – which must be used as a basis for estimating tonnage. Data on commodities provide a more useful yardstick, especially for coastal trade, than tonnage statistics, for they include information on the value and type of goods involved.[70]

The archives of state and local government are also likely to provide much information on trade and shipping. It is not possible to be very specific here, but a few examples may be cited. For California, for instance, the annual messages of the governor, the transactions of the state agricultural society, harbor commissioners' reports, and reports of the board of horticulture, of the bureau of labor statistics, and of the state mineralogist, are all sources of information on the exports and imports of Californian ports, and some of the state censuses include data on trade and fishing. The state tax-valuation manuscripts for Massachusetts give "tons of vessels" in each town.[71] The Pennsylvania state archives contain many records of the wardens of the port of Philadelphia, among them reports and minutes, registers of vessel arrivals and clearances, monthly and annual tonnage reports, and wharf licenses.[72] For some states the annual reports of state boards of agriculture may contain information on trade – especially internal trade: records relating to the interest of states in canals are noted in the next section.

---

[69] Cf. Brock, 52–5; Meyer H. Fishbein, *Early Business Statistical Operations of the Federal Government* (RIP 54, 1973), 11–12; RIP 49, 6–7.

[70] Cf. Diane Lindstrom, *Economic Development in the Philadelphia Region, 1810–1850* (1978), 187–201.

[71] Ronald P. Formisano, *The Transformation of Political Culture* (1983), 355.

[72] Frank M. Suran (ed.), *Guide to the Record Groups in the Pennsylvania State Archives* (1980), 71–2.

Valuable evidence may also be found among local government records, especially in port towns, where city governments often owned piers, wharves, and docks and were responsible for maintaining navigation in harbors and rivers. Annual reports, sometimes published, and other records of harbor boards, harbor masters, port wardens, and the like, will be useful for the investigation of the organization of a port and the changing state of its economy. Records of dues collected for wharfage and other facilities may produce evidence on shipping and trade. The Philadelphia city archives contain records on shipping movements and a volume summarizing Philadelphia manufactures exported in 1882.[73] Again, ships, like land, were passed by deeds, and local government records of these transactions may give interesting details. Thus a vessel deeded at Williamsburg, VA, in 1872, was said to be engaged in the carrying trade between that town and Norfolk.[74]

To fill out the information on the commercial activity of an area or a particular port found in official records, and to provide the intimate detail needed to illuminate more fully the organization of local trade, the papers of individual merchants and firms, if they exist, should be examined. These will not differ greatly from those described in chapter 8 for business firms generally. They may, however, also include archives specific to shipborne trade, such as accounts of exported and imported goods, and records of bills of lading, which listed the contents of a shipment, the name of the consignee, and the names of the vessel and its master. Ships' manifests, found in customs records, may also be among private papers. The account book of a Baltimore merchant for 1818–21, for example, includes details of sales of cargoes, imports and exports, vessels, masters, and destinations of ships.[75]

Business correspondence may include letters between merchants and their agents, partners, factors, or correspondents in

[73] John Daly, *Descriptive Inventory of the Archives of the City and County of Philadelphia* (1980), 101, 138, 191.
[74] Colonial Williamsburg Foundation, Williamsburg city records, deed bk. 1 (1865–83), 286.
[75] Richard J. Cox and Larry E. Sullivan (eds.), *Guide to the Research Collections of the Maryland Hist. Soc.* (1981), 164.

other ports at home and abroad, and instructions to ships' masters as to what to buy and sell – revealing the intimate details of the nature and organization of commerce.[76] Some trade with America was carried out by foreign companies or partnerships of American and foreign traders, and the business papers of such companies and merchants, as well as those of shipping companies, may exist overseas.[77]

Where they exist, the records of marine and general insurance companies, including policies, inspectors' reports on vessels, reports on claims, and so forth, can also shed light on commercial activity. Ships' log books record details of voyages, and the reports of canal and railroad companies (see next section) may provide details of freight passing between different places.

Travelers' accounts, published narratives of sea-going voyages,[78] diaries and memoirs of merchants, and the like, may exist to fill out the picture. Important, too, are the files of local newspapers in port towns – particularly papers specializing in commercial affairs and marine intelligence. These will contain a great deal relating to the trade conducted in the port, including general marine news and reports on the state of trade, correspondence, news of accidents and ship sales, and notices of the arrival and departure of vessels, often with additional remarks. Many advertisements were in effect announcements of the arrival of ships with particular goods for sale. The semi-weekly *Shipping and Commercial List and New York Price Current* (title varies; 1815–1926) listed arrivals and departures at all the main U.S. seaports with analyses of cargoes arriving at New York. It carried, too, statistics of exports of the chief commodities, and frequent statements on freight rates, insurance, pilotage, and like matters. The various commercial and industrial directories[79] and handbooks,

---

[76] Cf. Henrietta M. Larson, *Guide to Business History* (1948), 22–3.

[77] See, e.g., B. R. Crick and Miriam Alman (eds.), *A Guide to Manuscripts Relating to America in Great Britain and Ireland* (1961), 87, 91–4, and index under "Business records," "Trade," port names; S. Marriner, *Rathbones of Liverpool* (1961); P. Mathias and A. W. H. Pearsall (eds.), *Shipping: A Survey of Historical Records* (1971), 114, 131, 139, 141.

[78] E.g., George Coggeshall, *Thirty-six Voyages ... 1799 [to] ... 1841* (3rd edn., 1858).

[79] See pp. 98, 381.

like *Hazard's United States Commercial and Statistical Register* (1839–42) and *Hunt's Merchants' Magazine and Commercial Review* (1839–70, title varies; available in microfilm), carry data on trade. The *New York Herald*, a general newspaper, includes special articles on maritime matters and annual summaries of commerce, shipbuilding, and so on, as well as intelligence from other ports.

In the port towns the annual reports of boards of trade, chambers of commerce, and like bodies also contain much statistical data on local trade and shipping – as, for instance, the *Annual Statement of the Trade and Commerce of St. Louis*, published by the St. Louis Merchants' Exchange. The annual reports of the New York Chamber of Commerce (from 1858–9) contain detailed figures of trade in various commodities, together with other statistics and accounts of the state of the market for the year.[80] The unpublished records of such organizations can also be fruitful of evidence. Those of the Chicago Board of Trade include figures of imports, exports, and storage of grain from 1859 onwards. The Baltimore Chamber of Commerce kept a record of ship arrivals and departures (available from 1886).[81]

Some useful records may exist overseas. Thus the minutes of the American Chamber of Commerce for the Port of Liverpool are full of information on commercial relations between that British port and New York.[82] The reports of foreign consuls in U.S. ports to their home governments may also contain interesting evidence on industrial and commercial conditions in their American stations.[83] In London, for instance, there are registers of shipping in New York covering the years 1858–1907, as well as other relevant papers, among them consular reports and correspondence from various places in the United States.[84] British consular reports in

---

[80] Albion, *Rise of New York Port*, 434.
[81] Owen Gregory, "The Chicago Board of Trade's archives," *AH*, 56 (1982); Cox and Vanorney, "The records of a city," 291.
[82] Albion, *Rise of New York Port*, 426. They are in Liverpool Public Library: Crick and Alman, *Manuscripts Relating to America*, 90–1.
[83] See articles in *Business Hist.*, 23 (1981).
[84] *Guide to the Public Record Office* (1963), vol. 2, 123–4, 130–1.

print,[85] and other published British Parliamentary Papers, are worth searching for the testimony of merchants and others with U.S. trade interests.[86]

COMMUNICATIONS

The history of railroad, canal, and river-navigation companies, their business activities and organization, and the history of road communications belong more to regional and national than to local history. It is often necessary, however, for the community historian to have a knowledge of regional communications. The impact of railroads and canals on the economy of local communities and districts was often considerable, and insofar as they were the carriers for local trade any investigation of the local economy will need to consider them. More particularly, the interest of some communities in the promotion of road, canal, and railroad developments was significant and very much part of their history – often with political as well as economic implications. The involvement of railroads in land settlement was important, too, and has already been noted (ch. 5). The sources for it will not be reconsidered here. Other local topics for consideration include the relationships between local farmers and transportation companies and the politics of regulation, the effects of rivalry between river, canal, and railroad companies, contests between local communities in an area over transportation projects, the significance of urban street railways,[87] and the nature and growth of postal services. Secondary works on the history of communications, including studies of individual railroad and canal companies, are legion.[88] County histories

---

[85] *Guide to the Accounts and Papers ... House of Commons, 1801–1852,* 199; ibid., *1852–1899,* 1,375–86.

[86] See, e.g., Norman S. Buck, *The Development of the Organisation of Anglo-American Trade, 1800–1850* (1969), 175, 181–3.

[87] For research topics in urban transportation, see Glen E. Holt, "Urban mass transit history," in Jerome Finster (ed.), *The National Archives in Urban Research* (1974).

[88] *HG*, 417–23; Prucha, 26 [C49]; Marion Codz, "Bibliography of railroads in the Pacific northwest," *Washington Hist. Q.*, 11 (1921); Library of Congress, *Railroads in the United States: A Bibliographical List* (1933); Charles W. Cheape, *Moving the Masses* (1980), guides cited 264–5; and see refs. pp. 16–18.

often provide local details, not otherwise available, of communications, especially roads.[89]

The importance of contemporary maps and plans, both published and unpublished, as sources for communications history cannot be overstressed. Many have been dealt with elsewhere in this volume,[90] and some will be mentioned below. Reports of law cases and court decisions and the records of legal cases in the various federal and state courts are also prime sources for transportation history, many containing information relating to local communities.[91] Thus, for example, the inhabitants of Mason county, KY, sought in the courts in 1851–2 to prevent county government investment in a local railroad.[92]

There is also a huge literature of contemporary publications providing both factual information and evidence of views and attitudes. This includes the writings of travelers and missionaries,[93] as well as other more specific publications, monographs, and journals.[94] Thus we have, for example, works like Christopher Colles, *A Survey of the Roads of the United States of America, 1789* (1789, repr. 1961), George Armroyd, *A Connected View of the Whole Inland Navigation of the United States* (1826, and later edns.), Henry S. Tanner, *Description of the Canals and Rail Roads of the United States . . .* (1840, repr. 1970), which deals with each canal and railroad, state by state, and Henry V. Poor, *History of the Railroads and Canals of the United States* (1860), also a state-by-state account, but confined to the Northern states. Morrison's 1903 history of steam

89 See use of them in Frederic J. Wood, *The Turnpikes of New England . . . [and] Virginia, and Maryland* (1919).
90 See pp. 45–60, 227–8; and also Andrew M. Modelski (comp.), *Railroad Maps of the United States: Bibliography of Original 19th-Century Maps in . . . Library of Congress* (1975); Andrew M. Modelski, *Railroad Maps of North America* (1984).
91 See pp. 25–6, 42–3.
92 Robert M. Ireland, *Little Kingdoms* (1971), 102. Cf. George H. Miller, *Railroads and the Granger Laws* (1965), table of cases, 260–2.
93 See pp. 34, 282.
94 See, e.g., Thomas R. Thompson, *Check List of Publications on American Railroads before 1841* (1842); Carman and Thompson (1962), 192–208; Library of Congress, *A List of Books . . . Relating to Railroads . . .* (1904); Library of Congress, *List of Works on Railroads in Their Relations to the Government and the Public* (1907); Library of Congress, *List of References on Transportation and Communication in the United States since 1860* (1924).

navigation cites and quotes many original documents, time schedules, newspaper notices, advertisements, and so on.[95] There are some useful foreign compilations, too, like the work of Guillaume-Tell Poussin,[96] Michel Chevalier,[97] and F. A. von Gernster,[98] and other more specifically regional publications such as Loammi Baldwin, *Report on Brunswick Canal and Railroad* (1836). More general works may also include data on transportation. Timothy Pitkin, *Statistical View of Commerce in the United States of America* (1835), for instance, gives stage-coach schedules.

Among useful periodicals are the *American Railroad Journal* (1831–74), the *American Railway Times* (1849–72, available in microfilm), the *Railroad Gazette* (1871–92), *De Bow's Review* (from 1846, available in microfilm) and *Niles' Weekly* (later *National*) *Register* (1811–49). The *American Railroad Journal*, in particular, published much detailed information of a local nature on all aspects of railroad development, some of it reproduced from local newspapers.[99] Journals primarily concerned with agriculture (see ch. 5) also contain information on communications.

Railroad manuals, like Henry V. Poor's *Manual of the Railroads of the United States* ... (from 1868) and Edward Vernon's *American Railroad Manual* ... (title varies; from 1873) are mines of statistical and descriptive detail on individual railroads.[100] *Cram's Standard American Railway System Atlas of the World* (various edns., 1890s), is also useful, as, too, are guides for customers like *A.B.C. Pathfinder Railway Guide* (Boston, 1872–1901) and the *American Railway Guide and Pocket Companion* (New York, 1850s), as well as local trade directories.

[95] John H. Morrison, *History of American Steam Navigation* (1903, repr. 1958).
[96] *Travaux d'Ameliorations Interieures, Projétés ou Executés par le Gouvernement des Etats Unis ... 1824 à 1831* (Paris, 1834), with atlas.
[97] *Histoire et Description des Voies de Communication aux Etats Unis* ... (2 vols. and atlas, Paris, 1840–1).
[98] *Die Innern Communicationen von Nordamerica* (2 vols., Vienna, 1842–3).
[99] Milton S. Heath, *Constructive Liberalism* (1954), 257, 432–3.
[100] First edn., 1860 titled *History of the Railroads and Canals of the United States* ... Inf. in National Monetary Commission, *Statistics of the United States, 1867 to 1909* (1910) is taken from Poor.

Local newspapers,[101] pamphlets, and other such contemporary partisan literature are extremely useful sources for the local history of communications, since road construction, canal building, river improvement, and, especially, the provision of railroads aroused great interest and controversy. This was particularly so over the involvement of state, municipal, and county governments in the promotion, financing, and regulating of these enterprises. All such matters were reported in the press and often generated other literature. Newspapers included reports on state and regional conventions held to discuss proposals for state support of internal improvements and these reveal the views expressed by local delegates and results of votes. Local meetings were similarly reported. The Boston *Daily Advertiser*, for instance, in January 1827 published a report of a citizens' committee on the need for a rail link between the city and the Hudson River,[102] and much other contemporary literature on the subject has survived.

Newspapers also often published much more detail on transportation debates, bills, amendments, and committee reports in the state legislatures, than are available in the official records, and, moreover, provide evidence of political implications. The results of local polls on such matters were always reported.[103] The press also carried letters from interested parties and pressure groups and editorial comment, as well as factual information on many aspects of transportation matters. They reported, too, on trade carried by road, rail, and water. Advertisements by carriers and others may be specially informative.

Important sources, too, are the publications of pressure groups and other interested parties (among them boards of trade, farmers' organizations, and political groups), as well as the promotional pamphlets of railroad and canal companies

101 For value of newspapers, see, e.g., Heath, *Constructive Liberalism*, chs. 10, 11.
102 Cited by Julius Rubin, *Canal or Railroad?* (Trans. American Phil. Soc., NS 51, pt. 7, 1961), 98.
103 Ireland, *Little Kingdoms*, 105–6; Harry N. Scheiber, "Urban rivalry in internal improvements in the old North West, 1820–1860," *Ohio Hist.*, 71 (1962), 238.

and the advertising literature of their land departments.[104]
There may also be autobiographies, memoirs, and collections
of private papers of those engaged in transportation developments.[105] The Brayman manuscripts at the Chicago Historical
Society, for instance, are an extremely valuable source for the
early history of the Illinois Central Railroad, gathered by the
company's solicitor.[106] Photographs relating to transportation
may be found in many collections.

The archives of turnpike, railroad, canal and river navigation companies, and records concerning them, may be very
extensive.[107] Some (a number of which are microfilmed)[108] are
in libraries and other depositories,[109] while others, particularly
those for railroads, remain in the hands of the companies
themselves or their successors.[110] Such archives may include
charters, minutes of directors' and stockholders' meetings,
annual reports to stockholders, correspondence, financial accounts, engineers' and surveyors' reports, contracts, leases
and other legal records, land department records (see ch. 5),
and perhaps newspaper clippings, photographs, brochures,
publications for passengers, circulars, and other occasional
publications.[111] Railroad company publications may well be
very numerous.[112] The annual reports of transportation

[104] Large collections of railroad pamphlets incl. those of John Crerar Library, 35 West 33rd St., Chicago, IL 60616; Hayes Memorial Library, 1377 Hayes Ave., Fremont, OH 43420.
[105] See, e.g., Keith L. Bryant, Jr., *History of the Atchison, Topeka and Santa Fe Railway* (1974), bibl.
[106] Paul W. Gates, *The Illinois Central Railroad and its Colonization Work* (1934), 334.
[107] Herbert O. Brayer. "I've been working on the railroad," *AA*, 7 (1974); Donald W. Meinig, "Railroad archives and the historical geographer," *Professional Geographer*, 7 (1955), 7.
[108] E.g., W. Thomas White, *Great Northern Railway Company Papers, 1862–1920; Northern Pacific Railway Company Papers*: microfilm (n.d.), University Publics. of America, 690 Cedar St., St. Paul, MN 55101.
[109] See pp. 35–6. Robert C. Post, "Manuscript sources for railroad history," *Railroad Hist.*, 137 (1977), draws mainly on *NUCMC* for details of 500 collections, provid- ing key for items on specific railroads.
[110] Bryant, *Atchison . . . Railway*, bibl.
[111] The Assoc. of American Railroads, 50 F St. NW, Washington, DC 20001 has large collections of stockholder reps. and railroad periodicals.
[112] See, e.g., Thelma M. Kistler, *The Rise of Railroads in the Connecticut River Valley* (1937–8), 272–6.

companies to their stockholders are obvious sources for the volume and nature of the freight they carried regionally and locally, as well as for evidence of relationships with state, county, and urban governments and the local mercantile community.

Copies in company archives of the valuation reports submitted by railroads to the Interstate Commerce Commission (see below) provide a very useful source for dates of construction and the beginnings of services of the parent company's lines and those of subsidiaries. They give precise dates, too, of amalgamations, reorganizations, and changes of name. The correspondence of general managers is likely to provide the best source for evidence on the economic reasons for the construction or otherwise of lines and their perceived commercial potential. Employees' timetables show the frequency and routes of scheduled (though not unscheduled, seasonal) freight and passenger services. Statistics of freight tonnages carried on individual lines are less readily available, but assiduous search in company records may reveal some.[113]

The 1850 published federal census contains general information on individual railroads and on telegraphs.[114] Brief data on railroads (including street railways) and canals and river improvements are published in the 1860 census.[115] The 1880 census, in its volumes on the social statistics of cities,[116] provides data of varying detail on street railways and communications generally for certain cities. More important, it devotes another whole volume (vol. IV) to communications. The wealth of statistical evidence provided in this last volume cannot be adequately summarized here, but sections deal with railroads, steam navigation, canals, and telegraphs and telephones – much of it concerned with individual areas and companies. Railroad statistics are fullest and cover construction, mileages, costs, revenue, tonnage, rates, employees, and physical characteristics. Both working and abandoned canals

---

[113] Meinig, "Railroad archives," 8.
[114] Abstract, 98–103, 106–13.
[115] Vol. IV, 323–6. See also Preliminary Rep. (Dubester (1950), no. 41), table 38.
[116] Vols. XVIII, XIX.

are dealt with individually. For 1890, too, are published similarly extensive statistical data on railroads and street railways,[117] and on transportation by water[118] – again too extensive to list fully here. Much information on particular railroad companies is provided, together with statistics for the street railways of certain named cities. Water-transportation information covers rivers, lakes, and canals, and also seaboard shipping. Both the 1880 and 1890 census volumes merit careful study. And the Bureau of the Census produced two special reports, covering, with much local detail, street and electric railways,[119] and another, *Transportation by Water* (1906), which includes some retrospective data.

Some of the federal documents noted in the previous section and in chapter 8 include information on canals, river navigation, and railroads. So many other federal documents are concerned with transportation that the index to the US Serial Set should be carefully consulted – under "bridges," "rivers," "roads," "canals," "railroads," etc., and under the names of specific companies or routes. There are, for instance, a few reports on roads and canals in Iowa Territory, 1839–40, on roads in Oregon, 1849–50, on a wagon road from Niobrara to Virginia City in 1865–6, on the Central Pacific Railroad in 1869, and on land-grant railroads in Nebraska in 1880.[120]

Records of Congressional debates may contain references to these matters, and records of legislation,[121] and of judicial cases in federal and state courts,[122] may also be worth consulting. There is, for instance, a report before a Maine court in 1891 which gives details of the passenger service provided by the steamer *Caroline Miller* between Bangor and New York.[123]

---

[117] Vol. XIV, pt. 1; Abstract (2nd edn.), tables 13, 14.

[118] Vol. XIV, pt. 2; Abstract (2nd edn.), tables 7, 8.

[119] *Street and Electric Railways, 1902* (1905); *1907* (1910).

[120] SED 598 (26–1), ser. 361; HR 348 (31–1), ser. 584; HED 58 (39–1), ser. 1256; SED 54 (40–3), ser. 1360; SED 135 (49–1), ser. 2340.

[121] See Schmeckebier and Eastin, 242–3 for refs. to laws on navigable waters, bridges, and railroads incl. those pertaining to specific localities. And see *Laws of the United States relating to the Improvement of Rivers and Harbors from 1790 to 1887*: SMD 91 (42–2), ser. 2451 (indexed).

[122] See pp. 25–6, 42–3; and Gaiselle Kerner (comp.), *Preliminary Inventory of the Records of the U.S. Court of Claims, 1783–1947* (PI 58, 1953), 92.

[123] *Atlantic Reporter*, vol. 22, 379.

Petitions, too, are sometimes relevant: one from a Samuel
Dickens and others in 1831-2 relates to a road from Memphis
to Little Rock.[124]

The *American State Papers: Miscellaneous* may be worth
searching. They contain, for example, a Treasury report
on public roads and canals which gives brief details of
individual turnpikes, canals, and other waterways, with some
maps.[125]

The annual reports of the Interstate Commerce Commission contain annual statistics of railroads from 1888: details
of companies, mileages, capital, income, costs, and so on.
Embedded in the reports and their appendixes is much about
individual routes and companies, and material for an understanding of transportation conditions.[126] Care is needed,
however, in using the statistics provided, which with some
exceptions cover steam railroads only, and which are arranged
by operating corporations regardless of the ownership or lease
by another railroad.[127] Data for steamer lines operating as part
of the railroad system are distinguished.

Annual *Reports on the Internal Commerce of the United States*
(1876-91)[128] do not provide consistently similar data from year
to year, but do present much quantitative and qualitative
evidence on traffic passing through certain places and on the
organization of such trade (embracing railroad, canal, and
river commerce). The reports for 1886 through 1891 give
special attention to particular localities.[129] The earlier reports
contain statistics on the communications of certain cities and
regions. The 1881 report, for instance, presents data on the
communications of Cincinnati, Chicago, and St. Louis. The
series is certainly worth combing. From 1892 to 1899 no

[124] HED 151 (22-1), ser. 151.
[125] Vol. 1, 724-921.
[126] *Checklist*, 558. N.B. esp. *16th AR* (3 vols., 1903): HD 253, pts. 3, 5, 6 (58-2), ser. 4699 (retrospective data on operations, tariffs, legislation, regulation).
[127] See Laurence F. Schmeckebier, *The Statistical Work of the National Government* (1925), 378-9.
[128] *Checklist*, 1, 167-8.
[129] 1886: Southern states; 1887: trade of the Mississippi, Ohio, and other rivers; 1889: AR, CO, Dakota, Indian Territory, KS, MO, MT, NB, NM, TX, WY; 1890: AL, AZ, CA, ID, NV, UT, WA; 1891: Great Lakes, Mississippi, and tributaries.

statistics on internal commerce were compiled except for a report of 1898 on lake commerce.[130]

Volume VI of the *Report of the Industrial Commission* (1900–2)[131] is devoted to the organization of the distribution of farm products, with much statistical and descriptive evidence, some of which has been noted in chapter 4. Included is much that is of value to community historians, although only a few examples can be given here.[132] For instance, there are statistics of the flour and grain trade from Chicago in 1891 by named railroads and by lake, details of the distribution of agricultural products in a number of important market centers, statistical data on the main stockyard cities, and a great deal on the costs and characteristics of transportation. Volume V, on transportation, includes a digest of evidence and testimony embracing information on individual places, railroads, canals, street railways, Great Lakes transportation, and the trade of various places (including Philadelphia). The index includes place-names. Volume XVII is concerned with railroad labor.[133] Volume VII includes information on street railways, and volume IX is mainly about railroad legislation and taxation.[134]

Other relevant federal documents include the annual reports of the Department of Agriculture and other documents noted in chapter 4. Indeed, any document dealing with the transportation and sale of farm produce may be of interest: as, for instance, the *Report of the Select Committee on the Transportation and Sale of Meat Products* (1889–90).[135] And a report of 1893 on wholesale prices, wages, and transportation has much on freight rates on particular rail routes.[136] The Cullom report of 1886 summarizes the railroad legislation of the various states and the work of state commissioners and in the testimony

---

[130] HD 277 (55–2), ser. 3679.
[131] HD 494 (56–2), ser. 4168.
[132] See also Schmeckebier, *Statistical Work*, 422–3.
[133] For railroads and trusts and combinations, see testimony in vols. I, XIII; and for railroad labor *5th AR Commissioner of Labor, 1889* (1890).
[134] For taxation of transportation cos., see also vol. XI (rep. on taxation of corporations).
[135] SR 829 (51–1), ser. 2705.
[136] SR 1394 (52–2), pt. 1, ser. 3074.

there is much local information and data on individual rail-roads and their traffic and freight rates.[137]

For inter-regional trade and communications various other documents may also be useful.[138] One, for example, records the tonnage of vessels in the coastal and Great Lakes trade from the 1830s.[139] The *Report of the Select Committee on Southern Railroads* (1867) deals primarily with the military use of Southern railroads during the Civil War and includes testimony and annual reports from the main companies.[140] The Pacific Railway Commission's report of 1887 provides in the report itself and in the testimony a great deal of information on railroads in that region.[141]

The Windom Committee's report of 1874 on transportation routes to the seaboard[142] contains detailed reports on the trade of certain routes with statistics of freight carried on a number of canals and railroads. Much local information is embedded in the report, its appendixes, and the testimony. For example, there are annual statistics of shipments of various cereals from Milwaukee by rail and lake, 1858–72. The Mississippi River Commission's report of 1883 has much detailed information and includes elaborate plans, and the report of the Deep Waterways Commission of 1897 provides a lot of evidence on trade communications in the Great Lakes and associated rivers and canals, with many maps.[143]

The preliminary report of the Inland Water Commission (1908)[144] contains retrospective information – for instance, it gives the annual tonnages of goods passing on the Erie Canal from the Western states and New York to Tidewater, from 1836.[145] Another early twentieth-century report on

---

[137] *Rep. Senate Select Committee on Interstate Commerce*: SR 46 (49–1), 2 pts., ser. 2356–7.
[138] See also documents cited in last section.
[139] SED 55 (38–1), ser. 1176.
[140] HR 34 (39–2), ser. 1306; HRs 3, 15 (40–2), ser. 1357. Cf. Munden and Beers, 72–3.
[141] SED 51 (50–1), ser. 2505–9.
[142] SR 307 (43–1), 2 pts., ser. 1588–9: detailed indexes.
[143] SED 32 (47–2), ser. 2075; HD 192 (54–2), ser. 3257.
[144] SD 325 (60–1), ser. 5250.
[145] P. 226. Cf. Douglas C. North, *The Economic Growth of the United States, 1790–1860* (1961), 251.

transportation by water is a most important source which it is difficult to do justice to here in the space available.[146] It is packed with statistical data and though a great deal of the information in it concerns the period about 1906, there is also much which relates to earlier years. Part I deals with general conditions and has an index of navigation companies and of navigable rivers and canals; part II presents much detail on the trade of individual river ports and on coastal and foreign trade: part III covers water terminals; and part IV deals with the control of water carriers by railroad and shipping consolidations, and has a detailed index. The final report of the Public Land Commission, *The Public Domain, Its History, with Statistics* (various edns. from 1880), gives brief details of land grants to individual railroad, wagon-way, and canal companies.[147] The annual reports of the Auditor of Railroad Accounts (from 1879) and of the Commissioner of Railroads (from 1881) include reports and accounts of some railroads in which the federal government had an interest.[148] The annual reports of the Supervising Inspector-General of Steamboats (from 1853) contain a little information on individual vessels.[149]

The Secretary of War's annual report for 1883[150] contains a report on transcontinental railways which includes maps and detailed descriptions on explorations and surveys, and an appendix gives factual details of Pacific railroads. Other War Department documents are also valuable. The annual reports of the Chief of Engineers[151] contain data on repairs and improvements to rivers and harbors and work on wagon roads. They embrace subordinate reports – as, for instance, on harbors on Lake Erie, on the Cumberland River, and, in the

[146] Bureau of Corporations, *Rep. Commissioner of Corporations on Transportation by Water* (4 vols., 1909–13): not in US Serial Set. See *NUC*, vol. 611, 137. Monographs publ. (1909–11) by National Waterways Commission contain retrospective data: see Schmeckebier, *Statistical Work*, 424–6.

[147] See *Checklist*, 1,523.

[148] In ARs Secretary of Interior: *Checklist*, 427–31, 549.

[149] *Checklist*, 1,185–6.

[150] HED 1, pt.2 (48–1), ser. 2182.

[151] N.B., *Index to Reps. Chief of Engineers . . . 1866–1912* (2 vols., 1915): HD 740 (63–2), ser. 6617.

1838 report, on funds needed to complete a road from Laplaisance Bay, MI, to intersect the Detroit–Chicago road.[152] From the 1870s they include statistics of trade on waterways improved by the Army, and, despite their fragmentary nature, are valuable because of the paucity of such evidence elsewhere.[153] The Chief of Engineers also made special reports, like the detailed survey of the Yadkin River, NC, in 1879 for navigation purposes, and a report on the Mississippi River and northern lakes which gives details of shipping and cargoes at ports on the Ohio River and the Great Lakes for 1841–2.[154]

The annual reports of the Corps of Topographical Engineers (in the reports of the Secretary of War) note surveys and constructions of roads and harbors and river improvements. The report for 1843 has figures on total traffic at lake ports for the years 1835–41 and on the quantities and value of goods moved at each port for 1841.[155] The annual reports of the Quartermaster General (also in the reports of the Secretary of War, but separately issued, too) include remarks about the state of the roads, means of travel in Western parts, and military transportation arrangements generally.

Records in the National Archives relating to transportation are extensive.[156] Those of the Senate (RG 46) include official communications, petitions, and memoirs on such transportation matters as railroad construction and operation, national roads, harbors, and canals. They contain many maps of military roads and of rights-of-way maps in the Midwest, Western, and Southern states, as well as "internal improvement" maps.[157] The records of the Department of the Interior (RG 48) include materials on railroad land grants (from 1849; among them indexed correspondence), surveys and maps of Western

---

[152] SD 1 (25–3), ser. 338.
[153] Schmeckebier, *Statistical Work*, 419–20.
[154] SED 35 (46–1), ser. 1869; HD 170 (27–3), ser. 422.
[155] Schmeckebier, *Statistical Work*, 420.
[156] The following draws without further citation on RIC 36, q.v. for further details and other sources.
[157] Patrick D. McLaughlin (comp.), *Transportation in Nineteenth-Century America: A Survey of the Cartographic Records in the National Archives* ... (RIP 65, 1973), 4, 6, and 11–13 for list of internal improvement maps in this RG; and see pp. 51n, 171.

wagon roads (1856–87),[158] and a large collection of annual reports (from 1878), correspondence, and maps relating to Pacific railroad surveys.[159] The archives of U.S. district courts (RG 21) contain records of court cases, including bankruptcy cases, involving railroads, shipbuilding companies, and so on.[160] Case files from 1855 among the U.S. Court of Claims records (RG 123), and, from 1868, among the records of the Department of Justice (RG 205) include those pertaining to railroads and other common carriers.[161]

The unpublished records of the Office of the Chief of Engineers (embracing those of the former Corps of Topographical Engineers; RG 77)[162] and its subordinate offices and boards (among them especially the Topographical Bureau, the Board on River and Harbor Improvements, the Office of Explorations and Surveys, and the Board on Internal Improvements) are mines of information. They include correspondence, surveys, reports, maps, and so on, relating to the construction and surveying of bridges, harbors, roads, railroads, and canals, and to river improvements.[163]

The special files of the Quartermaster General's Office (RG 92) include water transportation records (from 1834, but mainly from the Civil War period), and correspondence of the river, lake, and rail transportation division, 1863–70, and of

---

[158] *GNA*, 366, 370; "Records of the Office of the Secretary of the Interior, 1833–1964" (NA, NNF–48, T/S, 1984), pt. 1. 145–74; Laura E. Kelsay (comp.), *Cartographic Records of the Office of the Secretary of the Interior* (PI 81, 1955), 8–11; Munden and Beers, 512–14; Leslie E. Decker, *Railroads and Politics* (1964), 401; W. Turrentine Jackson, *Wagon Roads West* (1952), 379. N.B. M95, M620.

[159] RIP 65, 7; W. Turrentine Jackson, "Materials for Western history in the Department of the Interior archives," *MVHR*, 35 (1948), 68: many of these were used in publ. reps., themselves useful for travel conditions and topography. For details, see p. 52.

[160] *GNA*, 72–90; and see pp. 42–3.

[161] PI 58, 7–8, 18; Gaiselle Kerner and Ira N. Kellogg, Jr. (comps.), *Preliminary Inventory of the Records of the Court of Claims Section of the Department of Justice* (PI 47, 1952), 8–11.

[162] *GNA*, 236–41; Munden and Beers, 273–4; RIP 65, 4–5; Ralph E. Ehrenberg, *Geographical Exploration and Mapping in the 19th Century: A Survey of the Records in the National Archives* (RIP 66, 1973), 6–7. Engineer district records are in NA regional branches.

[163] See pp. 50–1. Some Pacific railroad surveys in the Topographical Bureau are in RG 94 (Adjutant General), and the records of the Coast and Geodetic Survey, 1806–1957 (RG 23), contain data on ship canals, harbors, bays, and anchorages: *GNA*, 233, 470–1.

the transportation branch, 1861–90. They also contain many records of the Office of the U.S. Military Railroads, 1861–5, which cover railroads operated as military lines during the Civil War. There is, too, material concerning indebted Southern railroads, 1865–8.[164]

Maps among the records of the Geological Survey (RG 57; from 1879) provide detailed information on the topography of roads, rivers, railroads, bridges, and so on.[165] Another collection of maps, plats, and diagrams (from 1830), in the records of the Bureau of Indian Affairs (RG 75), shows rights of way of railroads, canals, and roads across Indian reservations.[166] Records of the General Land Office (RG 49) include items (correspondence, ledgers, reports, pamphlets, legal briefs) on canal and railroad rights of way, subsidies of public lands to aid construction of canals, wagon roads, and railroads, and (from 1850) a collection of maps, plats, and diagrams. Early transit routes can be reconstructed from the township plats which are in this Record Group.[167]

The records of the Interstate Commerce Commission (RG 134) contain (from 1887) annual reports of railroads, correspondence, valuations, and case files relating to rates and discrimination, which include testimony, exhibits, and so on – all of which provide much detail on the companies' clients, trade, organization, finances, and property.[168]

In the records of the Commissioner of Railroads (1862–1904; RG 193) are reports of forty federal and state-aided railroads, reports of the government auditor of such railroads,

---

[164] Munden and Beers, 318–19; GNA, 247–8.

[165] GNA, 393–4; Edward E. Hill (comp.), Preliminary Inventory of the Records of the Bureau of Indian Affairs (PI 163, 1965), vol. 1, 59; and pp. 51–2. For publ. topographical Geological Survey maps, see pp. 47–8.

[166] Laura E. Kelsay (comp.), Cartographic Records of the Bureau of Indian Affairs (SL 13, 1977).

[167] RIP 65, 7–8; GNA, 374–6; Laura E. Kelsay (comp.), List of Cartographic Records of the General Land Office (SL 19, 1964); Decker, Railroads and Politics, 401; Jane F. Smith, "Settlement of the Public Domain as reflected in federal records," in Ralph E. Ehrenberg (ed.), Pattern and Process (1975), 301. And see pp. 52–3.

[168] GNA, 553: Rapport, cited n. 47 above, q.v.; Joseph B. Howerton (comp.), The Valuation Records of the Interstate Commerce Commission as a Source of Statistical Data Relating to American Railroads During the 19th Century (RIP 56, 1973). Cf. Kistler, Rise of Railroads, 270.

correspondence, and statistical statements.[169] Details of the costs of building national roads, including the Cumberland Road, and the financing of railroads can be found in the records of the Bureau of Accounts (Treasury) (RG 39; from 1897).[170] Records (1830–67) relating to the construction of the Alexandria, Chesapeake and Ohio, Dismal Swamp, Louisville–Portland, and Norfolk canals, among them the annual reports of these canal companies, are in the general records of the Treasury (RG 56). There, too, are letters, reports, and petitions about public roads and canals, and information on subsidies to certain railroads.[171]

Records of the Potomac Company and of the Chesapeake and Ohio Canal Company (from 1785) are among the records of the National Park Service (RG 79). They include correspondence, reports, ledgers, maps, minutes, materials on construction and maintenance, and records relating to traffic. These last include records of vessel registration, tolls, registers of passage of vessels, manifests, and statements of commodities transported.[172] Accounting records of loans to various Pacific railroads (from 1862) are among the records of the Bureau of Public Debt (RG 53).[173]

A few more sources in the National Archives may be mentioned. The records of the National Mediation Board (RG 13) now include material on the U.S. (Pullman) Strike Commission, 1894–6, and on labor disputes and agreements, and wage rates in various railroads, from 1898.[174] Statistical data on steamboat and barge traffic for Cleveland, OH, and on the Ohio and Mississippi rivers, 1835–6, are in the records of the Public Health Service (RG 90). Among the records of the

---

[169] Marion M. Johnson (comp.), *Preliminary Inventory of the Commissioner of Railroads* (PI 158, 1964), esp. 10–15; *GNA*, 411; Meyer H. Fishbein, "Business history research in the National Archives," *Business Hist. Rev.*, 38 (1964), 251–2.

[170] *GNA*, 166.

[171] PI 187, 6, 10, 86, 96; *GNA*, 154.

[172] Fishbein, "Business history research," 251; *GNA*, 401–2; Edward E. Hill (comp.), *Preliminary Inventory of the Records of the National Park Service* (PI 166, 1966), 29–44.

[173] Philip D. Lagerquise *et al.* (comps.), *Preliminary Inventory of the "Old Loans" Records of the Bureau of the Public Debt* (PI 52, 1953), 83–5; Munden and Beers, 188–9; *GNA*, 163.

[174] See p. 343.

Bureau of Ships (RG 19) are photographs and pictures of harbor facilities in coastal ports and inland waterways, and in those of the Bureau of Agricultural Economics (RG 83) are photographs of horse-drawn transport, railroads, and river vessels from 1897. There are photographs of Civil War railroads in the records of the National Archives and Records Service (RG 64); and those of the Bureau of Public Roads (RG 30) include some photographs on road transport from 1896, arranged by states, as well as correspondence from 1890 with state highway officials.[175]

Since state, municipal, and county governments were active in promoting, financing, and supervising internal improvements, their published and unpublished records are important. Much of their activity in this respect was also reported in the press, but for a detailed study governmental records are essential. Bibliographies of published and unpublished state records indicate that there is a vast amount of information in state documents and archives – a body of resources far too diverse to analyze here. State legislatures received petitions, debated and legislated on communications, and incorporated and regulated transportation companies, so that governors' messages, the journals of state legislatures, and published Acts and Statutes are full of relevant material. Especially interesting for the community historian are the reports in state legislative journals of votes in the legislatures on particular projects, on state policy, and on permissions granted to local governments to invest in transportation enterprises.[176]

State committees and commissions on specific communications matters were not infrequently appointed, and their reports may contain local as well as regional information. Thus we have, for instance, the report of a special committee on the railroads of New York state in 1879–80 (8 vols., 1879–80). Again, New Hampshire state documents include a number of reports on specific roads, canals, and turnpike

175 RIC 36, 5, 16, 17; *GNA*, 308; J. Eric Maddox (comp.), *Preliminary Inventory of Audio-Visual Records made by the National Archives . . .* (NC-121, 1965), 3–4; Truman R. Strobridge (comp.), *Preliminary Inventory of the Records of the Bureau of Public Roads* (PI 134, 1962), 9, 19.
176 See, e.g., Heath, *Constructive Liberalism*, 241–2, 250, 269, 280, 284.

companies. In the postbellum South the states gave direct aid to reconstruct railroads, so that state documents like auditors' and treasurers' reports may be useful – but the sources most likely to give useful information on these matters are the railroads' own annual reports, *Poor's Manual* and like works (noted above), and the commercial and general press.[177]

In addition, for most states, standing commissions, boards, and bureaus relating to transportation, and more general boards of public works, produced much published matter, including statistical, cartographic, and descriptive material. In particular, many states created canal commissions and railroad commissions (with varying titles) to develop, build, and supervise canals, and to oversee railroad standards of construction, freight rates, and so forth. In Pennsylvania both the journals and the annual reports of the canal commissioners were published. State railroad commissions often published reports submitted to them by railroad companies.[178] Such reports may well include detailed evidence on commodities despatched from various rail depots.[179]

Reports of transportation companies will also be found in other state documents. Thus, for New York state there are reports of plank-road companies submitted to the Secretary of State. For Virginia, annual reports of railroads were published by the Board of Public Works long before there was a railroad commission, and there are also data in the Board's reports on turnpike roads. In states generally, reports of state directors of canal and railroad companies were published as state documents. In some states documents were produced by boards or committees especially created to promote internal communications – like the Massachusetts Board of Directors of Internal Improvements. The Pennsylvania *Senate Journal* (1821–2), for example, contains the report of such a committee which

---

[177] Cf. Carter Goodrich, "Public aid to railroads in the Reconstruction South," *Political Science Q.*, 71 (1956); J. F. Stover, *The Railroads of the South, 1865–1900* (1953).

[178] William R. Brock, *Investigation and Responsibility: Public Responsibility in the United States, 1865–1900* (1984), ch. 7, app. 1, and (for checklist of reps.), app. 2.

[179] Cf. Michael P. Conzen, *Frontier Farming in an Urban Shadow* (1971), app. v.

Sources for U.S. History

includes a list of turnpike companies and bridges in the state, with accompanying factual data.

Annual reports of bureaus of labor and industrial statistics,[180] and of state boards of agriculture (especially in public-domain states), include both statistical and descriptive information on transportation matters. The report of the North Carolina Bureau of Labor Statistics for 1889 has a 77-page report by road supervisors giving the replies of J.P.s (the legal road supervisors in townships) to a questionnaire on the condition of public roads and the methods of working them, views of the J.P.s and of local people on these methods, and suggestions for improvement; as well as a 22-page report on roads by physicians in different parts of the state. Reports of state auditors may give useful evidence on the financing of transportation projects by state and local governments and other possible useful sources are the annual reports of state engineers. There are many state and municipal documents relating to street railways.[181] Of particular interest is a Massachusetts report of 1898 which provides data on such railways in fourteen cities.[182]

In addition to published documents, the unpublished records of state railroad and canal commissioners may exist, as they certainly do for New York and Pennsylvania,[183] as well as other unpublished materials relating to transportation. Illinois, for example, has voluminous records relating to the incorporation, financing, construction, maintenance, inspection, and supervision of the Illinois and Michigan Canal, as well as toll records, records of goods carried and of carriers and their vessels, surveys, plats, and engineers' papers. It has, too, the charters of incorporation of packet-boat companies, and the so-called "railroad record" – documents filed by railroad corporations which include byelaws, deeds, mortgages,

---

[180] See pp. 368–9; and e.g., Commissioner of Labor, *Index to all Reps. Issued by Bureaus of Labor Statistics . . . [before] 1902* (1902, repr. 1970).
[181] See [Boston Elevated Railway Library], *Reference List of Literature on Urban Electric Railways* (1927; suppl. 1930); Cheape, *Moving the Masses*, bibl.
[182] *Rep. . . . on Relations between Cities and Towns and Street Railway Companies* (1898).
[183] NY State Education Dept., *Guide to the Records in the New York State Archives* (1981), 63–6; Suran, *Guide to . . . Pennsylvania State Archives* (1980), 26–30.

leases, contracts, resolutions of shareholders, and articles of incorporation (which provide *inter alia* names of directors and details of stocks and shares).[184]

Not all railroad, canal, and turnpike company reports submitted to state governments were produced in full in state documents. Some survive unpublished among state archives, together with other related material. The Pennsylvania archives, for instance, include the annual reports of canal, navigation, and railroad companies, accounts of collectors along the state canal system, and accounts, contracts, and petitions relating to roads, while the letter books of the secretary of the commonwealth record much correspondence on internal communications matters.[185]

The records of urban and county governments also contain information on communications. They include those relating to turnpikes, other roads, bridges, railroads, and so on. Among them are records of committees with special responsibility for such matters, of turnpike directors, and of county and city engineers (including surveys, inspectors' reports, plats, etc.). For roads maintained by local government, county, and sometimes township, records may include complaints about road conditions, petitions for new roads, reports of viewers, plats, surveys, and decisions of county courts, boards of supervisors, or commissioners. For established roads there may be the reports and financial records and papers of road supervisors, viewers, or highway commissioners, and records of road labor services and taxes. The road survey record for McDonough county, IL, for example, contains plats, descriptions of roads, names of officers, the dates of surveys, and sometimes details of expenses.[186] Local records may also include records of the licensing of ferry operators and owners of toll roads and bridges, and contracts, litigation

---

[184] Victoria Irons and Patricia C. Brennan, *Descriptive Inventory of the Archives of the State of Illinois* (1978), 66–7, 395–426, 432–5.

[185] Suran, *Guide*, 59; Catherine E. Reiser, *Pittsburgh's Commercial Development, 1800–1850* (1951), 227; James W. Livingood, *The Philadelphia–Baltimore Trade Rivalry* (1947), 165.

[186] Roy C. Turnbaugh, Jr., *A Guide to County Records in the Illinois Regional Archives* (1984), 301.

papers relating to roads and transportation, and details of routes and schedules.[187] Records of local taxes on railroad companies provide details of the companies, including miles of track and data on property, rolling stock, and capital.[188] There may also be road-tax records.

When there was municipal or county investment in canals or railroads or when local governments themselves built and maintained harbors, bridges, and so on, treasurers' and auditors' reports and records, and the minutes of city councils, county commissioners, and their subcommittees, may be valuable.[189] There are also likely to be newspaper reports of related meetings. Opposition to such investment resulting in litigation will be detailed in court records and perhaps law reports.[190] There are often, too, county or city reports on communications in their localities (such as provided in a Baltimore city document of 1825), as well as records of committees concerned with particular developments – like the Philadelphia city committee on the Schuylkill canal.[191]

Since the mail was a federal responsibility, federal records provide the main source of information on postal services, though local evidence may also be available in newspapers, guides, directories, and so on.

The Post Office Department records in the National Archives (RG 28) contain postal route maps from 1839,[192] which not only indicate delivery routes, frequency of delivery, and the location of post offices, but, since they show roads and railroads, provide information on local communications generally. Records of the appointment of postmasters (from 1789) give dates of appointments and of the establishment and

---

[187] Cf. John H. Moore, "Local and state governments of antebellum Mississippi," *JMH*, 44 (1982), 111; Jones, 163.

[188] E.g., Turnbaugh, *Guide to County Records*, 23–5.

[189] See, e.g., Douglas E. Booth, "Transportation, city building, and financial crisis, Milwaukee, 1852–1868," *JUH*, 9 (1983); Heath, *Constructive Liberalism*, 275, 433.

[190] See, e.g., Ireland, *Little Kingdoms*, 102–3, 105–6, 165. State legislatures gave specific permission for such investment.

[191] Daly, *Descriptive Inventory of Archives of Philadelphia* (1970), 282.

[192] *GNA*, 358–63; Charlotte M. Ashby *et al.* (comps.), *Guide to Cartographic Records in the National Archives* (1971), 131; Ralph E. Ehrenberg, "Taking the measure of the land," *Prologue*, 9 (1977), 148–9.

closure of particular post offices. They are available in micro-form.[193] Geographical site-location reports (from 1837) (available in microform) give the whereabouts of each office and the exact location of the communities it served, including data on the physical features of the area, like rivers, creeks, railroads, and landmarks. From the 1870s they also show the number of persons served by each office.[194] Mail route (1814–80) and railroad route (1872–1928) registers have information on contracts with post riders, stage-coach companies, and railroads.[195] The mail route registers may illustrate develop-ment of postal services in individual townships and therefore of settlement, too.[196] Cases relating to post-office matters may be found in the records of the U.S. Court of Claims (RG 123).[197]

As for published material, the *Postal Guide* (various dates and titles from 1800)[198] lists all post offices. A great deal on local post offices, postal routes, and their traffic is found in the *American State Papers: Post Office Department, 1790–1833* (1834). The annual reports of the Postmaster General (from 1823)[199] often contain little local information. They may, however, be worth searching. The report for 1890–1 provides an alphabetical list of post offices indicating the numbers of

[193] Arthur Hecht and William J. Heynen (comps.), *Records and Policies of the Post Office Department Relating to Place-Names* (RIP 72, 1975), 13–16, q.v. for lists, tables, guides, and directories of post offices; RIP 65, 13–15; Forrest R. Holdcamper (comp.), *Preliminary Inventory of the Records of the Post Office Department* (PI 168, 1967), apps. 4, 5. See also Arthur Hecht et al. (comps.), *Preliminary Inventory of the Records of the ... Third and Fourth Assistant Postmasters General, the Bureau of Accounts, and the ... Chief Inspector of the Post Office Department* (PI 114, 1959), esp. apps. II, III, IV; and see p. 51. There is a catalog of rural delivery maps at NA: *Genealogical Research*, 261. Records Geological Survey (RG 57) incl. other postal route maps.
[194] Jane F. Smith, "Commentary," in Meyer H. Fishbein (ed.), *The National Archives and Statistical Research* (1973), 174–5; Richard W. Helbock, "Postal records as an aid to urbanization studies," *HMN*, 3 (1970); William E. Lind, "A general view of urban research possibilities in the National Archives," in Jerome Finster (ed.), *The National Archives and Urban Research* (1974), 32–3.
[195] Wesley E. Rich, *The History of the United States Post Office to the Year 1829* (1924), 176; RIC 36, 7.
[196] See, e.g., Smith, "Settlement on the public domain," 299.
[197] PI 58, 18.
[198] Before 1874 some were government publics., others not. For *Official Postal Guide*, from 1874, see *Checklist*, 848–51.
[199] *Checklist*, 839–40.

letters, postcards, and newspapers delivered and collected and numbers of carriers, together with much data on railroad post offices. There are other federal documents on postal matters, too, and the index to the US Serial Set may be worth searching.[200] A document of 1841, for instance, provides the revenue of each post office in 1840–1.[201] A *History of the Railway Mail Service* (1885) contains details of mailing practices for certain parts of the country, and provides dates of when services began.[202]

The biennial *Register of Officers and Agents, Civil, Military, and Naval, In the Service of the United States* (from 1816) lists each post office, its county, the name of the postmaster, and his compensation (salary). Since compensation was related to the amount of business, this evidence may be used to suggest the relative importance of the areas served and as an indication of changes in population and commercial activity – though with some caution, since the series contains errors.[203] The records of individual post offices may exist in other collections.[204] The Library of Congress has manuscript "Annals of the Post Office Department" dated about 1837,[205] and the National Museum of American History, Washington, DC, has records of the U.S. postal service and its predecessors.

A NOTE ON THE FUR TRADE

The fur trade is a specialized topic, the records for which cannot be treated in detail here.[206] Some local historians may, however, wish to investigate it and a few remarks may be

[200] See p. 22. For documents on telegraph and telephone services, see Schmeckebier, *Statistical Work*, 403–6.
[201] HD 65 (27–2), ser. 402.
[202] SED 40 (48–2), ser. 2261, app. A. For documents on the railway mail service, see *Checklist*, 863–70.
[203] Helbock, "Postal records," 11.
[204] E.g., Avril J. M. Pedley (comp.), *The Manuscript Records of the Maryland Hist. Soc.* (1968), 223.
[205] Rich, *History . . . Post Office*, 176.
[206] See *HG*, 335–7: Stuart Cuthbertson and John C. Ewers, *A Preliminary Bibliography of the American Fur Trade* (1939); David C. Wishart, *The Fur Trade of the American West, 1807–1840* (1979).

made. The larger trading companies were not local, but controlled the activities of agents, traders, and posts over large areas. Their unpublished records are widely dispersed.[207] Those of the American Fur Company, which dominated the trade in the first part of the nineteenth century, are in the Public Archives of Canada, Detroit public library, the libraries of the Missouri and New York historical societies, and in some other state and local depositories. The correspondence and records of receipts of furs and of their packing, as well as account books of various kinds, shed light on the trade over a wide area.[208] For smaller companies information is available mainly in the records of larger companies or in the private papers of those who did business with them.[209] Contemporary accounts and journal narratives may also be informative.[210] Details of the Alaskan fur trade are provided in the published federal census of 1890.[211]

The records of the Bureau of Indian Affairs in the National Archives (RG 75) contain a great deal on individual traders and companies. They include the records of the Office of Indian Trade (1806–24) – mainly correspondence and the financial accounts of the trading houses established to supply Indians with manufactured goods in exchange for furs and skins. These records provide evidence on such trade and on competition from private traders as well as on conditions among local Indians.[212]

The general correspondence of the Bureau includes a series of special files (1807–1904), which contain claims by traders

---

[207] Bruce M. White (comp.), *The Fur Trade of Minnesota: An Introductory Guide to the Manuscript Sources* (1977), drawn on in the following paragraphs; LeRoy R. Hafen (ed.), *The Mountain Men and the Fur Trade of the Far West* (1972), vol. 10.

[208] N.B. Grace L. Nute, *Calendar of the American Fur Company's Papers* (2 vols., *ARs* Am. Hist. Assoc., vols. II, III, 1944 (1945); covers 1831–49); Grace L. Nute, "The papers of the American Fur Company," *AHR*, 32 (1926–7).

[209] For a trader's own records, see Bert Anson, "Lathrop M. Taylor, the fur trader," *Indiana Mag. Hist.*, 45 (1949).

[210] See, e.g., Hiram M. Chittenden, *The American Fur Trade of the Far West* (2 vols., 1935, repr. 1986).

[211] Vol. VIII, 201–16.

[212] PI 163, vol. I, 23–30; Edward E. Hill (comp.), *Guide to Records in the National Archives . . . Relating to American Indians* (1981), 17–23; *GNA*, 377–8. Some are in microfilm: *MRR*.

over fur deals,[213] and letters sent to superintendents and agents and received from them. Among these letters are quarterly or annual lists of fur trade licenses, naming the traders and giving other information.[214] Field office records for particular superintendencies and agencies,[215] some of which are in regional branches of the National Archives, include correspondence which often relates to the fur trade. Army records include evidence on illegal trading and on the control of trading with the Indians.[216]

Other relevant collections are those of the Hudson Bay Company,[217] of McGill University, of the Bancroft Library, and of the Missouri and Minnesota historical societies.[218] The *American State Papers: Indian Affairs* has information on individual trading houses and factories.[219] The *American State Papers: Commerce and Navigation* includes a statement of furs and pelts received in 1804 and 1805 from certain Indian factories.[220]

[213] PI 163, vol. 1, 44. For the claim system, see James L. Clayton, "The impact of traders' claims on the American fur trade," in David M. Ellis, *The Frontier in American Development* (1969). NA, RG 217 (General Accounting Office) records payment to traders over claims against Indian tribes. N.B. Daniel T. Goggin (comp.), *Preliminary Inventory of the Records of Former Russian Agencies: Records of the Russian–American Company* (NC–40, 1963; and PDM 11, 1971).

[214] Publ. 1823–35 in ARs Secretary of War. See also Hill, *Guide to Records . . . American Indians*, 121.

[215] GNA, 386–7; Hill, *Guide to Records . . . American Indians*, 129–94; PI 163, vol. 2, 295–373.

[216] Adjutant General (RG 94); Continental Commands (RG 393): see Hill, *Guide to Records . . . American Indians*, index under "trade," "traders."

[217] In Provincial Archives of Manitoba, Winnipeg, Manitoba, R3C 1T5.

[218] McGill Univ., Montreal, Quebec, H3A 2T5; Bancroft Library, Univ. of California, Berkeley, CA 94720: State Hist. Soc. Missouri, Hitt and Lowry Sts., Columbia, MO 65201; Minnesota Hist. Soc., 690 Cedar St., St. Paul, MN 55101. See also Public Archives of Canada, *Union List of Manuscripts in Canadian Repositories* (2 vols., 1975). N.B. Museum Assoc. of American Frontier and Fur Trade, HC–74, Box 18, Chadron, NB 69337.

[219] Vol. 1, 768–73. For fur trade with Indians generally, see index under "trade."

[220] Vol. 1, 596.

CHAPTER 10

Education

Schooling was a matter of general concern in U.S. communities throughout the nineteenth century. The scope for local investigation is, therefore, considerable and the potential source material very extensive. Possible topics vary from the largely factual to the interpretation of the ideological basis of local educational changes and controversies. A solid investigation of education in a particular area or community should certainly include some statistical assessment of changes over time in the numbers of schools, academies, and colleges (and their division into private – including religious – and public) and of the numbers of students attending them. Other basic information to be sought includes, for the students, age and sex distribution, proportions they form of total age groups in the community, length of schooling experienced, and their social, religious, and ethnic mix.

To these may be added the nature of the curriculum and of classroom management and discipline, the kind of teachers (qualifications, ages, sex, ethnicity, length of service, salaries, and so on), and the organization, founding, and administration of public schooling in the district. The analysis of changing attitudes to schools on the part of parents, voters, employers, politicians, religious leaders, and others should lead to consideration of controversies over educational matters. These may include school funding, compulsory education, the place of the state and the churches in education, community control, child labor, and the rights of states and parents. The assessment of the extent and motivation of religious and political involvement in schooling (as social control, socialization, egalitarianism, and the fostering of national

439

unity), is another large topic for investigation. Other topics may include the significance of Sunday and evening schools, the treatment of girls as opposed to boys, and the experience of minorities – particularly immigrants, blacks, and Indians. Here may be embraced the impact of immigration on existing schools and the effects in the South of emancipation. The general level of literacy in a local community, and its relationship to other social phenomena, is also a worthwhile area of study.

The researcher into the history of education in a community will need to be aware of the general economic, religious, and political characteristics of the place, and may therefore need to use some of the sources described elsewhere in this volume in addition to those outlined in this chapter. He will also need to have a sound grounding in the subject generally and to be aware of recent views, controversies, and theories current among historians in this field. There are a number of bibliographies to assist here, some relating to particular states.[1] Many theses and dissertations also exist,[2] while

---

[1] *HG*, 501-2; Prucha, 195-7; Henry P. Beers, *Bibliographies in American History, 1942-1978* (1982), ch. v; William W. Brickman, *Research in Educational History* (1973); William W. Brickman, *Bibliographical Essays in Educational Reference Works* (1975); Jurgen Herbst (comp.), *The History of American Education* (1973), q.v. 1-2, for bibls., 22-4, for state histories of education; Francesco Cordasco and William W. Brickman, *A Bibliography of American Educational History* (1975), q.v. 3-12, for bibls., 86-96, for state histories; Michael W. Sedlak and Timothy Walch (eds.), *American Educational History* (1981); *Bibliographic Guide to Education* (G. K. Hall, 1978); *Education Index* (H. W. Wilson Co., 1929–); Ronald D. Cohen, "American public schooling," *Trends in Hist.*, 3 (1982); Lloyd P. Jorgenson, "Materials on the history of education in state journals," *HEQ*, 7 (1967), 8 (1968); ABC-Clio, *Social Reform and Reaction in America: An Annotated Bibliography* (1984); bibl. articles in *HEQ*. For higher education: Prucha, 196 [BB7, 8, 13]; William W. Brickman, "A bibliographical introduction to the history of U.S. higher education," in William W. Brickman and Stanley Lehrer (eds.), *A Century of Higher Education* (1962) (includes histories of individual institutions). For medical education: Francesco Cordasco and David N. Alloway, *Medical Education in the United States: A Guide to Information Sources* (1980). For agricultural education: articles by A. C. True in *Agricultural Yearbook* (1887, 1898, 1899), and see n.66 below; Fred Bateman, "Research developments in American agricultural history since 1860," *AgHR*, 31 (1983), 144-5; Paul W. Gates, *The Farmer's Age, 1815-1860* (1962), 439.

[2] See Prucha, 63-6; Phi Delta Kappa, *Research Studies in Education: A Subject and Author Index of Doctoral Dissertations* . . . (various vols., since 1953; prior to that see *Phi Delta Kappan*); Edward R. Beauchamp, *Dissertations in the History of Education*,

various compilations illustrative of educational records are available, too.[3] The indexes to the *Territorial Papers* are also worth searching, under "schools."

RELIGIOUS AND VOLUNTARY SOCIETY SOURCES

Especially in the larger cities, voluntary societies, like the New York Free School Society (later Public School Society), provided elementary schools for the poor and left published annual reports and other records. Some of these societies received money from local governments, so that evidence on them may be found in local government records. But throughout the century churches and religiously and charitably inspired organizations were most significant in establishing, supporting, and conducting schools. Aside from secular private schools, denominational schools were the main providers of elementary education before the public-school movement. The very extensive records of the various denominations, missionary societies, religious orders, and individual churches and congregations are, therefore, important sources for community educational history. They are described in detail in chapter 6,[4] and include, in particular, church and parish histories, denominational directories and almanacs, the records of conferences, conventions, synods, assemblies, local associations, and the like, those of church societies and committees, and diocesan reports and similar documents. Such records may provide factual data on schooling

---

1970–1980 (1985); Mary L. Lydon and Stanley B. Brown, *Research Studies in Education: A Subject Index of Doctoral Dissertations* (1953–); *Masters' Theses in Education* (1951/2– , Research Publics., Cedar Falls, IA); A. William Hogland, *Immigrants and their Children in the United States: A Bibliography of Doctoral Dissertations, 1885–1982* (1984); Arthur P. Young (comp.), *Higher Education in American Life, 1636–1986: A Bibliography of Dissertations and Theses* (1988).

[3] See citations *HG*, 503 (Knight), 508 (Hofstadter and Smith); Sol Cohen (ed.), *Education in the United States* (5 vols., 1974). See also Robert H. Bremner *et al.* (eds.), *Children and Youth in America* (2 vols. in 3, 1970–1); Herbst, *History of American Education*, 5–6

[4] See also pp. 471, 489–90, 507–9, 531.

and – for example, in correspondence and debates – evidence on attitudes towards education.[5]

Records of individual congregations often embrace those of day and Sunday schools connected with them or contain references to such schools. Parish and church histories, magazines, centenary publications and souvenirs, parish pamphlets, catalogs, and the like, can all provide useful evidence. Individual churches sometimes had their sessions incorporated as school trustees, and such incorporations are recorded in the Acts of state legislatures. Such records as published diocesan journals, too, contain much information on local parochial schools.

Academies and colleges maintained by various denominations, of which there were many, may not only have left their own published and unpublished archives, but be documented in the records of relevant church committees and other bodies and feature in annual reports of one kind or another. Church annual handbooks often contain factual data on academies, seminaries, and colleges connected with the particular denomination. The *United States Baptist Annual Register and Almanac* for 1833, for instance, provides details of the Virginia Baptist Seminary. The *Catholic Almanac* or *Catholic Directory* (later *Laity's Directory*)[6] contains a great deal of factual information, including pupil enrollment, on Catholic education throughout the country.

Some of the larger churches had their own associations and boards of education whose records are often useful. The annual report of the board of education of the Presbyterian Church, U.S.A. (Old School), for example, included in 1848–53 and 1866–8 lists of all known Presbyterian schools, and the reports sometimes contain other information on such schools, including some on individual establishments. Further details on particular schools are preserved in the executive and other manuscript records of the board.[7]

---

[5] See, e.g., Margaret B. DesChamps, "Presbyterians and Southern education," *JPH*, 31 (1953); Walter H. Beck, *Lutheran Elementary Schools in the United States* (1939; 2nd edn. 1965), pp. VII–VIII, 417–21.

[6] From 1817, title varies; annual from 1833.

[7] L. J. Sherrill, *Presbyterian Parochial Schools, 1846–70* (1932, repr. 1969), 49. Table IV, pp. 73–82, lists all "Old School" schools existing 1846–70.

Religious periodicals are another potential source. The monthly *Spirit of Missions* (from 1836; available in microfilm) printed reports of missions to the Board of Missions of the Protestant Episcopal Church, which include evidence on individual schools, including Sunday schools.[8] In 1848, for example, it reported two flourishing schools in the community of Black Hawk, Carroll county, MS, and moves to establish an academy. The *Religious Cabinet* (1842, and from 1843–9 called the *United States Catholic Magazine*; available in microfilm) contains a great deal on the history of Catholic schools. The *Biblical Recorder* (from 1834; available in microfilm) carried reports of associations and conventions, news notes, and advertisements of schools. The *Presbyterian Treasury* (1848–9, from 1850 called the *Home and Foreign Record*) included synopses of the annual reports of the board of education of the Presbyterian Church, U.S.A. (Old School). The *Southern Christian Advocate* in 1840 contained a report on the Georgia Conference Manual Labor School.[9] Religious and ethnic newspapers likewise carried information on the establishment and activities of church-controlled schools, as well as relevant advertisements, editorials, and letters.

Missionary work was often concerned with education as well as purely religious matters. The records of missionary societies, of individual missionaries and connected records have been described in chapter 6, and their work in the education of Indians and black Americans is noted below. Missionary societies were also active in the poorer areas of large cities and with whites on the frontier,[10] and their records contain much on Sunday and day schools, colleges, and seminaries in such communities. Similar work was undertaken by related bodies such as the Society for the Promotion of Collegiate and Theological Education in the West, the Ladies Society for the Promotion of Education in the West, and the

---

[8] See p. 283n.

[9] Edgar W. Knight, *A Documentary History of Education in the South before 1860* (5 vols., 1949–53), vol. 4, 138–9.

[10] See Polly W. Kaufman, *Women Teachers on the Frontier* (1984); Colin B. Goody-koontz, *Home Missions on the American Frontier . . .* (1939).

Board of National Popular Education, all of which from the 1840s published annual reports. The records of the American Education Society and a number of other mainly Congregationalist societies which supported colleges and individual students contain much relevant information on particular educational institutions.[11]

Quakers, Lutherans, and, particularly, Catholics were especially active in promoting schooling. Their records may, therefore, be given some attention here. Aside from the archives of trustees and committees and financial accounts of schools, Quaker records may include surveys of educational facilities in particular localities. Periodically, for instance, the Philadelphia Yearly Meeting collected returns from quarterly meetings of the numbers of Quaker boys and girls aged 5–16 at school, with details of schools run by Friends' meetings, of family schools, and of Quaker children at public schools, with details of those schools. The Educational Association of Friends in America produced a variety of publications including proceedings of various conferences and of their "Central" and "Eastern" departments.[12]

Catholic records are especially useful for education in the larger cities where there were concentrations of immigrants from Catholic countries in Europe.[13] Aside from directories, newspapers, pamphlet literature, parish histories, and publications of ethnic groups – all important sources for urban Catholic schools – official metropolitan, diocesan, and parish records, and records of Catholic societies and religious orders (see ch. 6) will also contain much data. The archives of individual parishes in the archdiocese of Boston, for instance, contain the records of many parish schools, academies, orphanages, and industrial schools. The papers of priests also, on occasion, contain information on the state of Catholic

[11] For details, see James Findlay, "The Congregationalists and American education," *HEQ*, 17 (1977).
[12] See, e.g., Thomas Woody, *Quaker Education in the Colony and State of New Jersey* (1923), 292–3; *NUC*.
[13] See John T. Ellis and Robert Trisco, *A Guide to American Catholic History* (1982 edn.).

education in various places.[14] There may also be annual reports of church superintendents of parish schools – as in the archdiocese of Philadelphia. Chancery records contain deeds relating to schools. Again, the original records of the teaching communities and orders, wherever preserved, may be useful.[15] Those of the Sisters of Notre Dame de Namur, who organized and staffed many Boston parochial schools, include school histories, attendance records, annals, memoirs, and examples of students' work.

Official Catholic correspondence with Europe may also provide information. Numerous letters from American priests, religious orders, and bishops in the Congregation de Propaganda Fide Archives and in the *Annales de la Propagation de la Foi*[16] are important for the study of Catholic education. Thus in 1859 a priest sought and received permission to establish a school at Opelousas, LA, and in 1879 the Archbishop of Boston made a special report to the Office of Propaganda explaining why he had not promoted parochial schools.[17]

CENSUS EVIDENCE

All the published federal censuses from 1790 (see ch. 2) have data on the age structure of local communities in varying degrees of exactness, distinguishing males and females. It is thus possible to hazard some idea of the school-age population. From 1880 the census provides details of child workers.[18] The 1840 census is the first to contain specifically educational information.[19] It publishes for counties, principal towns, wards, townships, etc., the numbers of universities and colleges, of academic and grammar schools, and of primary and common schools, with numbers of students in each

---

[14] James O'Toole (ed.), *Guide to the Archives of the Archdiocese of Boston* (1982), 52–60, 75, 79–85; James O'Toole, "Catholic church records," *New England Hist. and Genealogical Register*, 132 (1978), 256.

[15] Evangeline Thomas (ed.), *Women Religious History Sources* (1983); Mary J. Oates, "Organized voluntarism," *American Q.*, 30 (1978).

[16] See pp. 261, 286.

[17] Finbar Kenneally (ed.), *United States Documents in the Propaganda Fide Archives. A Calendar*, vol. 2 (1968), 243; vol. 5, 29; Oates, "Organized voluntarism," 657.

[18] See also *Census Bull.*, 68, 69 for the 1900 census.

[19] Vol. 1, District and District Recapitulation tables.

category, as well as the numbers of whites of twenty and over unable to read and write. The numbers of pupils at public charge in primary and common schools are also given. All these data, particularly the figures of students supported at public charge, may well contain inaccuracies and must be used cautiously.[20]

The 1850 census provides by counties the numbers of colleges, public schools, and of academies and other schools, with numbers of teachers and pupils in each category (such details having been returned by the schools).[21] Also given are the numbers of whites and free blacks attending school during the year, distinguishing the sexes, the numbers of native and foreign born attending school during the year (returned by families),[22] and the numbers of white adults who could not read and write, similarly distinguished.[23] Numbers of non-private libraries and of volumes in them are noted and broken down into public, school, college, and church libraries.[24] The 1860 census publishes educational data only at the state level. The 1870 census provides for counties and fifty principal cities (by wards) totals of children attending school, distinguishing native and foreign born, male and female, and white and black. It also gives similarly categorized statistics of those unable to write (in age groups) and totals of those of ten and over unable to read.[25] Other schooling statistics are provided only at state level. There is a map of illiteracy.[26]

The report on the "Social Statistics of Cities" in the 1880 census (vols. XVIII, XIX) provides information of a descriptive kind for some 200 cities. Data are sometimes, but by no means always, given on colleges of various kinds and on public schools, including numbers of schools, students and teachers,

---

[20] *Memorial . . . American Statistical Assoc. Praying . . . Correction of Errors in . . . Sixth Census*: SD 5 (28–2), ser. 449.

[21] Vol. I, table VII; Compendium, under states.

[22] Vol. I, table VIII. Numbers of pupils returned by schools do not always coincide exactly with those returned by families.

[23] Vol. I, table X; Compendium, under states.

[24] Vol. I, table XIII; Compendium, table CLXVI (twelve largest cities) for data on publics.

[25] Vol. I, tables X, XI; Compendium, table XXVII.

[26] Vol. I, 393.

and financial aspects of provision. Within sections on buildings there may be details on literary, scientific, and educational societies, orphanages, schools of various kinds, and libraries. Elsewhere in the 1880 census, statistical data on public schooling are provided only at state level, but very detailed information on the newspaper press in various counties and cities at different times is given.[27] An appendix presents by counties and larger cities a catalog of periodicals, 1879–80, with details, and a chronological history of the newspaper press arranged by states.[28] There is a useful index.

The 1890 census publishes, for cities of 25,000 population and above, numbers attending school during the year. These are broken down by sex and age groups, and for whites by nativity and parental nativity. For the same cities, data on the illiteracy of those of ten years and over are provided, distinguishing degrees of illiteracy, sex (for whites), and nativity, by age groups, and for those of ten and above numbers unable to speak English.[29] A special report on education, bound in the same volume, but separately paginated,[30] includes statistics by counties of the numbers of white and black pupils and teachers, by sex, in public schools in 1890 and the same information for cities of 10,000 population and over.[31] The volume of the 1890 census concerned with valuation and taxation contains details, for counties and municipalities, of taxation levied for public education. For each state there is an explanatory preamble outlining the nature of such taxation and its purposes. There are also statistics of revenue received by counties for school purposes from the state and from county funds or property and receipts for such funds by cities of 50,000 and upwards, together with details of expenditure on schools and libraries. Also included, by counties, are detailed accounts of public common-school finances, including breakdowns of

[27] Vol. VIII, 38–47, 61–4, 66–72, 98–9.
[28] Ibid., app. B, 199–355; app. C, 359–426.
[29] Vol. I (pt. 2), tables 25–30, 49–58, 68–70. See also Compendium (pt. 3), tables 42–6, 61–2, 70–2.
[30] Also publ. separately as *Report on Education in the United States* (Special Census Public., 1893). See also *Census Bulls.*, 11th Census, nos. 17, 36, 53, 84.
[31] Tables 8, 22. For cities of 25,000+, see Compendium (pt. 3), table 41.

revenue and expenditure, and a valuation of buildings and other property.[32] Preambles for each county add some refinement to the statistics, indicating, for instance, the nature of the tax sources (as state appropriation, poll tax, property tax), funds, and rents (which include rents from Section 16 lands).

The 1900 census publishes statistics of literacy and illiteracy for males of twenty-one upwards for counties and for cities of 25,000 or more inhabitants, distinguishing colored, negro, and native white.[33] A similarly categorized analysis for the same cities for those of age ten upwards distinguishes those who could read but not write and those who could do neither,[34] also classifying illiterates in the same categories, by age groups.[35] Somewhat less detailed data on illiterates of ten and over by counties are provided.[36] For cities of 100,000 upwards illiterate males of twenty-one and over are categorized by general nativity and citizenship.[37] For cities of 25,000 and over there are also statistics of those unable to speak English – for foreign-born males of twenty-one upwards (by citizenship).[38] For the same cities numbers attending school by sex and in age groups are given, classified by native whites (of native and foreign parentage), foreign whites, coloreds, and negroes. In addition there is an analysis of school attendance (by sex and in age groups) according to how many months in the year school was attended.[39] Numbers of teachers in proportion to the numbers in the population aged 5–24 are also given.[40]

Use of the original census returns, as opposed to the published volumes,[41] enables the researcher to get below the

[32] Vol. xv (pt. 2), 103–373, 478–557, 601–52.
[33] Vol. i, tables 81–2, 92.
[34] Vol. ii, tables 74–8; Abstract (1902), table 85.
[35] Vol. ii, tables 79–83. See also 12th Census, Special Rep., *Supplementary Analysis and Descriptive Tables* (1906), table xlviii (for age group 10–14).
[36] Vol. ii, table 84.
[37] Vol. i, tables xcvii, ciii.
[38] Vol. i, table 91.
[39] Vol. ii, tables 49–55. For comparison of school-age children and school attendance figures, see Abstract (1902), table 84.
[40] Special Rep. (1906) (as n.35 above), table xxix.
[41] For location and availability of microforms, see p. 80. The ICPSR data set (see p. 64) contains educational statistics for 1850, 1870, 1900.

county and city level to individuals, families, and institutions. It is necessary to distinguish the information found in the population schedules and that in the social statistics schedules. In the former (arranged by state or territory, and then by county and often minor subdivisions, as city, ward, township, parish, hundred, district), educational data first appear in 1840 when the householder was asked to indicate the number in the household attending universities or colleges and primary and common schools, the number educated "at common charge," and the number of white adults who could not read and write. Only the head of the household is actually named. No later census asked for this information in such detail.

The population schedules for 1850 through 1880 give names of household members but limit the data to whether they had attended day school in the year. For 1850 and 1860, whether each free adult could read and write is given, and from 1870, for all persons of ten and over, it is noted whether they could read and separately whether they could write. (No such data are given for slaves.) In 1870, too, for the first time all children had to be returned as either "at home," "attending school," or employed in a particular occupation. The 1890 returns are largely missing. Those for 1900 (available only in microfilm) give similar information on school attendance and literacy as in 1870 and 1880, and, for the first time, whether English could be spoken.

The social statistics schedules for the 1850 through 1870 censuses were based on official records, printed reports, and archives of educational institutions. In 1880 they were collected by experts and special agents. In them educational institutions are identified by type only (colleges, academies, common schools, etc.) with numbers of teachers and average numbers of students. Financial data include the revenue for each institution from endowments, taxation, other public funds, tuition, and other sources. Names of newspapers and periodicals and their circulation in each district (perhaps an indication of general levels of literacy) are listed and briefly described as scientific, literary, medical, religious, or agricultural.[42]

Published state censuses known to provide educational information (though not always below state level) include District of Columbia censuses of 1867 and 1878 (school attendance and literacy), and for Florida, 1855 (children 5–18 and numbers at school), Iowa, various 1859–69 (colleges, universities, students), 1875, 1885, 1895 (illiteracy), Massachusetts, 1865 (literacy), 1875, 1885, 1895 (school attendance, literacy), Michigan, 1884 (school attendance, literacy), Mississippi, 1840 (colleges, schools, literacy), Missouri, 1868 (persons "taught to read and write"), New York, 1845 (school attendance), 1855, 1865, 1875 (schools), North Dakota, 1885 (school attendance), and Rhode Island, 1865, 1875 (school attendance), 1885, 1895 (school attendance, literacy).[43] Even where school attendance figures are not given, many state censuses do provide numbers of children by age groups, so that where other evidence on schooling exists it may be related to the overall age-cohort figures. Some give statistics of child workers.

Information on schooling, literacy, and child labor in published censuses, and more particularly in the manuscript schedules (which provide data on named individuals), may be combined with other census evidence (and evidence in such sources as directories, school records, and local government and state records on education) to give greater insight into the place of schooling in the social life of local communities. Thus school attendance, ability to read and write, proficiency in English, full-time child labor, and so on, may be correlated with such variables as the age, sex, ethnicity, race, citizenship, long- and short-term residence, and occupation of parents and children, and the rurality or urbanity of the community. Further variables, like religion, may be derived from other

---

42 Carmen R. Delle Donne, *Federal Census Schedules, 1850–80* (RIP 67, 1973), 19. For location of originals and microfilms, see refs. pp. 81–2.
43 Dubester (1948), q.v. 67–73 for unpubl. returns.

sources.[44] The techniques involved in such correlation approaches are discussed in chapter 2. They offer considerable scope to the community historian interested in placing local educational history in its full socio-economic setting.

Census data, however, need to be used with care. Aside from the usual errors resulting from omission or incorrect transcription, the truthfulness of parental declarations of child school attendance may sometimes be doubted, especially where there was compulsory schooling. Comparison with evidence in state and local administrative and school records[45] may give a clue as to whether census figures are suspicious. Some check against child-labor statistics in the published censuses may also be useful. Evidence on literacy in the censuses also needs careful consideration.[46] Some persons no doubt claimed skills they did not possess (no test was involved); on the other hand, modesty may have resulted in some inaccurately declaring themselves illiterate; and some able to read in a language other than English may have been returned as illiterate. Moreover, it is unlikely that there was a clear-cut distinction between the illiterate and the literate.

Again, claims to basic literacy give no idea of comparative levels of literacy above the mere ability to read and write a little, and the same percentage of "literates" is consistent with quite different cultural levels in different communities. Certainly it is known that illiteracy figures in the 1840 and 1850 censuses were often underestimates and apparently improved

[44] For examples of such exercises, see Merle Curti *et al.*, *The Making of an American Community* (1959), 390–404; Carl F. Kaestle and Maris A. Vinovskis, "From fireside to factory," in Tamara K. Hareven (ed.), *Transitions* (1978), esp. app. on multiple classification analysis; Tamara K. Hareven, "Quantification, urbanization and the history of education," *HMN*, 8 (1974); Michael B. Katz, "Who went to school?" *HEQ*, 12 (1972); Selwyn K. Troen, "Popular education in nineteenth-century St. Louis," *HEQ*, 13 (1973); Joel Perlmann, "Who stayed in school?" *JAH*, 72 (1985). See also Maris A. Vinovskis, "Quantification and the analysis of American antebellum education," *JIH*, 13 (1983); Harvey J. Graff, "Notes on methods of studying literacy from the manuscript census," *HMN*, 5 (1971).
[45] Albert Fishlow, "The American common school movement," in Henry Rosovsky (ed.), *Industrialization in Two Systems* (1966), 66–7.
[46] See, e.g., Special Rep. (1906) (as n.35 above), 328–75. And see Harvey J. Graff, *The Literacy Myth* (1979), 329–33.

figures in later censuses were partly the result of more efficient data collection. From 1870 onwards greater reliance may be placed on the figures, which also distinguish between non-readers and non-writers.[47] Correlation of school attendance figures with illiteracy levels in a community is nevertheless fraught with difficulty. Before compulsory education was enforced, attendance figures embraced children of varying age ranges attending for varying periods within the year, and at schools of very different quality. The census merely indicated whether a person had attended school during the year – not at which school nor for how long.[48] Some idea of the average time spent at class, length of school terms, and extent of absenteeism may, however, be available in other sources, like state superintendents' reports.[49]

The researcher should be aware, too, of census weaknesses in other respects (see ch. 2) and should avoid uncritical application of statistical methods to bodies of evidence derived solely from this single source. The practice of linkage with other sources should be followed wherever possible. For instance, signatures (or marks) on marriage licenses and other records may give an indication of the extent of adult literacy in an area, to set beside the census evidence.

SOME FEDERAL SOURCES

Aside from the censuses, certain federal government sources may be useful. The annual reports of the U.S. Commissioner of Education (from 1867),[50] though described as "whole thick volumes of dullness,"[51] are mines of information on education in local communities, much of it statistical. They provide reports on educational conditions in various parts of the

[47] 1870 Census, vol. I, p. xxx; Special Rep. (1906), 332–3.
[48] A. Joel Perlmann, "The use of student records for the study of American educational history," HM, 12 (1979), 68.
[49] See below. Cf. Lee Soltow and Edward Stevens, "Economic aspects of school participation in mid-nineteenth-century United States," JIH, 8 (1977), 224, 228–30.
[50] N.B. Index to the Reports of the Commissioner of Education, 1867–1907 (Bureau of Education, Bull. 7, 1909, repr. 1970).
[51] World's Work (Dec. 1903), 4,174.

country, digests of state laws on education, summaries of state and city public-school systems, reports of committees and of professional meetings, and abstracts of state superintendents' reports. The volume for 1873,[52] for instance, provides a report on the condition of education in each state, covering instruction at all levels, with some statistics and mention of a number of individual places and institutions. Statistical tables give details for cities, towns, and villages of 2,500 population upwards, indicating population, legal school-attendance ages, numbers of children of school age, numbers over sixteen and under six, numbers enrolled at school, length of school year, and, for primary schools, numbers of male and female teachers and of pupils, and average attendance. Some detail for intermediate schools, grammar schools, high schools, and evening schools is also given, as well as similar information on private schools. Financial data on income and expenditure and salaries of teachers are supplied, too. Nor is that all – information on normal schools and on commercial and business schools is presented and there is statistical information on individual secondary institutions (location, date of charter and of organization, principal's name, religious denomination, numbers of male and female teachers and students, numbers preparing for college, and details of the curriculum, library, property, and finances). Similar statistical data are provided for preparatory schools, women's higher-education institutions, universities and colleges, and schools of science, theology, law, medicine, pharmacy, and dentistry. There is statistical information, too, on libraries, museums, reform schools, institutions for the physically handicapped, orphanages, and private kindergartens.

The 1888 report, as well as presenting similar information (for places of 7,500 inhabitants and over), carries abstracts of the reports of school officers of states, territories, and cities. The report for 1895 contains a lengthy study of parochial schools, and that for 1870 a survey of Jewish education in some

---

[52] HED 1 (43–1), ser. 1602.

large cities.[53] The Commissioner's reports are not, however, without fault and the statistical data in them, often questioned by contemporaries, should be used cautiously. Before 1889–90 the numbers given of public high schools are unreliable, and before 1900 statistics for higher education are flawed.[54]

The Bureau of Education produced some other relevant publications.[55] Its Bulletin 43 (1914), for instance, contains a survey of education in three Alabama counties, and there is a special report on technical education in 1869–70.[56] Bulletin 11 (1915) is a quantitative study of public schools in the southern Appalachians. The Bureau's Circulars of Information, published from 1870, include histories of education, stressing secondary and higher education, for thirty-five states.[57] Some Circulars include information on individual institutions. One for 1892 presents considerable detail on Southern colleges for women and institutions for blacks in the South.[58] In addition there is a collection of reports on colleges in various states in 1873 (1873[3]), and one on industrial education in the South in 1888 (1888[5]).

Some of the annual reports of the Commissioner of Labor contain data on the educational background of female workers and on child labor. For example, the 4th report, for 1888 (1889), deals with working women in twenty-one large cities, providing statistics of their prior attendance at public and other schools, together with workers' ages, nativity, and ages at which they began to work. The 8th report (1893) is devoted to industrial education and provides information on technical education and manual training in individual institutions

---

53 HED 1 (49–1), ser. 2381; HD 5 (54–1), ser. 3389, pp. 1617–76; HED 1 (41–3), ser. 1450.
54 Edward A. Krug, *The Shaping of the American High School, 1880–1920*, vol. 1 (1969), 451.
55 See *Bibliography of the Publications of the United States Office of Education, 1867–1959* (1971).
56 For details, see *Checklist*, 464.
57 See Herbst, *History of American Education*, 22–4; G. Stuart Noble, "State histories of education," *Rev. Educational Research*, 6 (1936), 374–5 (and 429–31 for similar works).
58 A. D. Mayo, *Southern Women in the Recent Educational Movement in the South*, 1892 (1).

arranged by states – some in great detail. Evidence is also included of particular universities, agricultural colleges, trade schools, and institutes of technology. The 11th report, *Work and Wages of Men, Women, and Children, 1895–6* (1897) gives details by industries and states of reasons for the employment of women and girls (as "more industrious and less liable to strike") but no specifically local information. The 17th report (1902) is concerned with industrial education and presents much detail and background history on trade and technical schools, including those for blacks in the South.[59]

Certain volumes of the *Report of the Industrial Commission* (1900–2) contain information on child labor.[60] Volumes x and xv include data on agricultural schools and volume xv on technical and industrial education and on black education in the South.[61] These volumes present extensive testimony which contains local information on individual institutions.

The *Report of the Immigration Commission* of 1910–11 includes five volumes (vols. 29–33) on the schooling of children of immigrants.[62] Volumes 30–3 provide tabular data on a number of individual cities. There are general investigations showing the situation of the public schools and their teachers (for forty-two cities), general investigations of parochial schools (for twenty-four cities) and intensive investigations of public schools (for twelve cities). The general investigations of public and parochial schools provide statistics of students in each grade by age and sex and by the general nativity and race of the father, analyzed in various ways. The intensive investigations include statistics of birthplaces, ages at arrival, school attendance abroad, rates of progress, father's citizenship, and father's ability to speak English. For the public schools the general investigations also provide statistics of teachers by sex and nativity and information on the numbers teaching each

[59] HR 388 (52–3), ser. 3269; SED 65 (52–2), ser. 3060; HD 341 (54–2), ser. 3545; HD 18 (57–2), ser. 4484.

[60] See, e.g. vols. VII, VIII, XII, cited p. 339. For rep. 1910–13 on women and child workers, see pp. 365–6.

[61] Vols. x (HD 179 (57–1), ser. 4340); xv (HD 184 (57–1), ser. 4345).

[62] SD 749 (61–3), ser. 5871–5; repr. 1970 by Scarecrow Press as *The Children of Immigrants in Schools*.

grade and teaching specified numbers of students. Volume 33 also includes data on immigrants in higher education.

The reports to Congress of territorial governors may also contain educational information. In the 1890s, for example, the reports of the Governor of Arizona Territory embrace reports of territorial immigration commissions which give numbers of schools, teachers, and pupils in each county.[63]

A search of the US Serial Set index may reveal other useful documents. For instance, there is a report of 1882 on industrial and agricultural education which provides very detailed evidence by states on individual land-grant colleges, other institutions, and schools (including Indian industrial schools).[64] Even more informative is a Senate report on instruction in "drawing as applied to industrial and fine arts," of 1879–80 (published 1885, 1891, 1897, 1898).[65] This contains (part 1), as well as general information, statistical data on industrial art instruction in named institutions all over the country. It also has (parts 1 and 2) details of experiments in industrial and manual training in public schools in Boston, New Bedford, Philadelphia, and a number of states over the country, with extracts of reports on industrial education in several cities. There are also descriptions of institutions in various cities (part 3) including art schools, technical institutes, drawing schools, teachers' colleges, museums and industrial schools, mechanics' institutes, schools of design, schools of art and industry, institutes of arts and sciences, mechanical drawing schools, and so on, many of which were concerned with the education of adolescents and adults. Part 4 contains reports on certain manual training schools, schools connected with technical industrial establishments, schools of science and engineering, and the land-grant colleges of agriculture and mechanic arts (including departments of universities).

The annual reports of the Commissioner of Agriculture carry reports on individual agricultural colleges, as do other

---

[63] AR Secretary of Interior, vol. 3: HD 5 (54–1), ser. 3383 (1895).
[64] Rep. relating to Industrial Education: SED 25 (47–2), ser. 2075.
[65] SED 209 (1) (46–2), ser. 1888, 1889 (1, 2, 3).

publications of the Department of Agriculture.[66] Some petitions to Congress from particular universities asking for land exist.[67]

Information in the National Archives on education at the local level, aside from the censuses, is not extensive. The records of the Office of Education (later Bureau) (RG 12) include among the letters sent by the Commissioner, "O" series, 1870–1908, correspondence concerning the allocation of federal funds to land-grant colleges under legislation of 1862 and 1890.[68] Details of land granted to states and territories for the benefit of schools and agricultural and mechanical colleges are found in agriculture scrip files, 1863–1908, in the General Land Office records (RG 49), and also in state land-office records.[69] Records concerning agricultural colleges (including those for black students) in the period 1890–1907 are in RG 48 (Department of the Interior).[70] Other records in the National Archives relating to labor and labor problems (described in chapter 7) sometimes contain information on education in particular places.[71] Records of hearings relating to committees on education and labor (1885–7), for instance, provide evidence on a school established by the Industrial Home Association of Utah.[72]

STATE AND LOCAL GOVERNMENT RECORDS

Education was primarily the concern of individual states, so that a vast array of state and local government records cover

[66] E.g., Alfred C. True, *A History of Agriculture in the United States, 1785–1925* (Dept. of Agric., Misc. Publ. 31, 1929); Alfred C. True, *A History of Agricultural Experimentation in the United States, 1607–1925* (Dept. of Agric., 1929).

[67] E.g., Transylvania Univ., KY: HD 103 (25–2), ser. 325.

[68] Carmen Delle Donne, *Preliminary Inventory of the Records of the Office of Education* (PI 178, 1974), 10. App. I provides a key. Most are in M635.

[69] Richard S. Maxwell, *Public Land Records of the Federal Government, 1800–1950* (RIP 57, 1973), 5, 18; *GNA*, 374. See, e.g., Nita K. Pyburn, *Documentary History of Education in Florida, 1822–1860* (n.d., pr. 1951), 10–11.

[70] Debra L. Newman, *Black History: A Guide to Civilian Records in the National Archives* (1984), 78–9; *Records of the Office of the Secretary of the Interior, 1833–1964* (NA, NNF–48, 1984), pt. I, T/S, 45, 56.

[71] See, e.g., *Materials in the National Archives Relating to Labor and Labor Problems* (RIC 10, 1942), 4.

[72] Charles E. South and James C. Brown (comps.), *Hearings in the Records of the U.S. Senate and Joint Committees of Congress* (SL 32, 1972), 9.

every aspect of the topic. Details of the framework within which local school organization was set by the state are to be found in the records of state constitutional conventions, state constitutions and amendments to them, and in state laws.[73] Related records include resolutions, petitions, debates, and litigation. Many of these sources will also contain information on individual educational institutions, particularly those above the elementary level. Acts of incorporation provided charters for academies and colleges, sometimes for other institutions like grammar schools,[74] manual labor schools, and mechanics' institutes, and for boards of town-school trustees and voluntary school societies. Petitions to legislatures and records of debates in the chambers may relate to particular educational institutions as well as to controversial matters on schooling policy – like compulsory education and the financing of schools. Thus the debate on the Bill to abolish the Massachusetts board of education in 1840, the course of the Bill and the record of roll-call votes can be followed in the journal of the Massachusetts House of Representatives.[75]

Litigation both in federal and state courts has been very influential in American educational history.[76] Aside from the significance of the legal decisions, the records of law cases can provide much incidental evidence on the organization of local school systems, on individual schools, and on the reasons for disputes between teachers, pupils, school boards, state officials, and so forth.[77]

Very significant for the community historian are the reports of state departments and officials. Of these the annual or

---

[73] See pp. 27, 300. ARs US Commissioner of Education contain digests of state education laws: e.g., *AR 1885–6* (1887), 47–214. See also reps. state superintendents of instruction (see below). For state child-labor laws, see refs. p. 340n.

[74] See, e.g., Edward D. Andrews, "The county grammar schools and academies of Vermont," *Procs. Vermont Hist. Soc.*, NS 4 (1936), app. H.

[75] Carl F. Kaestle and Maris A. Vinovskis, *Education and Social Change in Nineteenth-Century Massachusetts* (1980), 333.

[76] Useful are: John S. Brubacher, *The Law and Higher Education: A Case Book* (2 vols., 1971); J. Morgan Kousser, *Dead End: The Development of Nineteenth-Century Litigation on Racial Discrimination in Schools* (1986) (list of cases, 1834–1903). And see pp. 25–6, 42–3.

[77] See, e.g., Charles L. Coon, "School support and our North Carolina courts, 1826–1926," *North Carolina Hist. Rev.*, 3 (1926).

semi-annual reports of state superintendents of public instruction (or, variously, boards, committees, commissions of education, etc.) are usually mines of information on many aspects
of local schooling. It was not uncommon for these to contain
excerpts from reports of town, city, and county superintendents.

The report of the Virginia Superintendent of Public Instruction for 1889–90 may be taken as an example of the great
value of these records.[78] It provides an enormous amount of
statistical data. Various tables show by county and city details
of students (numbers enrolled, average monthly enrollment
and daily attendance, percentage of school-aged population
enrolled and in average attendance, numbers in higher
branches of schooling, and numbers issued with textbooks –
all distinguishing white and black, as well as teacher–pupil
ratios and average ages); numbers of schools (white and black)
with average periods of instruction and numbers of teachers
(white, black, gender) and their salaries; information on
graded schools (names of principals and local post offices;
white or black; attendance records; tuition costs); revenue
available (distinguishing state, county, district, and other
sources); expenditure and balances with details of how spent;
costs (distinguishing such items as teachers' and other salaries,
rent, fuel, insurance, textbooks for poor students); expected
yield of local funds (distinguishing district, county, and municipal levies); details of schoolhouses; statistics of the activities and salaries of local superintendents; and school
populations broken down into districts (with numbers of
schools, lengths of sessions, numbers of teachers and their
salaries, costs per pupil, numbers of indigent children supplied
with books – all distinguishing white and black, and, for
teachers, gender). This report also has tables of school populations (aged 5–21) by districts and cities broken down according to ability to read and write and according to attendance at
public or private schools, as well as numbers of non-attenders
– all distinguished by race. These figures were based on the

[78] *Virginia School Rep. 1890* (1891).

1890 census and were not an annual feature. These statistical data were followed by digests of the reports of county and city superintendents, reports on institutes (conferences) and on textbooks, and the general report of the state superintendent commenting on both the matters presented statistically and others. Finally there are individual annual reports on the University of Virginia, the College of William and Mary, the Hampton Institute, and on a military institute, an agricultural college, a female normal school, a medical college, an institution for the deaf, dumb, and blind, and a normal and collegiate institute.

As they became more influential, state education departments produced many other publications. For instance, the Massachusetts Board of Commissioners of Common Schools issued a publication on child labor: *Education and Labor, 1842* (1842), and another Massachusetts document, on *Factory Children*,[79] was also concerned with the schooling of child workers.

The reports of state bureaus of labor are likely to contain information on manual training, institutional schools, child labor, half-time and evening schooling, apprenticeship, and sometimes on education generally. The second report of the Massachusetts Bureau of the Statistics of Labor (1871) includes a 110-page report on the work and life of factory operatives, based on oral testimony, which gives special attention to child factory workers and half-time schools. The fifth report of the same bureau (1874) has a twenty-page report on education and child employment, including statistics provided by school committees of school-age workers and details of evening schools in thirty-seven towns and cities. The thirteenth report of the Massachusetts bureau (1882) includes information on child labor and on the illiteracy of mill operatives in Fall River. Again, the second report of the Rhode Island Bureau of Industrial Statistics (1888) includes details provided by employers on wages of child workers in twelve industries and a report on the effect of child labor on school attendance and truancy. The

[79] Massachusetts SD 50 (1875).

fourth report of the Virginia Bureau of Labor and Industrial Statistics (1901) provides figures for individual counties and cities in various years between 1889 and 1899 of the numbers of free schools (white and black) and employed teachers (by race and sex). The first report of the same bureau (for 1898 and 1899) includes a synopsis on schooling in each of the state's principal cities. Other publications of state labor bureaus, especially factory inspectors' reports, and related unpublished material in state archives, are likely sources for child labor.

Many other series of state documents may also contain material on local education. Revenue and taxation documents and the annual reports of state auditors are likely to provide information if the state was in any way responsible for funding schools. The reports of the state auditor of Delaware, 1833–90, for example, contain tabular statements of numbers of schools in certain counties, with numbers of students and of weeks operating, together with financial data on each school. State boards of health reports may include evidence on the hygienic condition of schools. The Tennessee board's reports include from the 1880s statements on school health conditions, with descriptions of individual schools.

Educational information is commonly found from time to time in other state documents. The Kentucky Senate journal of 1822 published a solicited account of education in South Carolina in that year.[80] A Maine document of 1829 consists of returns of trustees of incorporated literary institutes relating to their establishments, and another of 1850 lists incorporated colleges and academies, with the funds received from Maine (and from Massachusetts prior to separation).[81] A South Carolina legislature committee report of 1852 surveys all public education by districts and parishes, providing numbers of schools, teachers, and pupils as well as financial data.[82] Again, a Massachusetts report of 1845 on labor laws has details of child labor in Lowell taken from workers' testimony.[83] The

---

[80] Lowell Harrison, "South Carolina's educational system in 1822," *South Carolina Hist. and Genealogical Mag.*, 51 (1950).

[81] Hasse, Maine, 34, 37.

[82] *Reps. and Resolutions of the . . . Senate of South Carolina* (1852), 229–30.

[83] Massachusetts HD 50 (1845): *Documents, 1845* (1845), 10.

annual messages of the Governor of Maine in 1881–2 and 1883–4 gave the number of towns having no school districts, the number of school districts in the state, and the number of towns having free high schools. Various of his other reports contain historical sketches of the state schools and systems. Quite often, too, entire state documents were devoted to particular places: there are, for instance, many reports on common schools in New Castle county, DE.[84] Sometimes, too, reports of special committees and commissions on educational matters were documented – like the Massachusetts' *Report of the Commission on Industrial and Technical Education* (1906).

In addition, states produced many publications relating to state educational institutions. For Missouri, for example, they include publications relating to establishments for the handicapped, the state normal school, the Lincoln Institute, the military school, the school of mines, a girls' industrial school, a boys' reform school, the Missouri Teachers' Association, and the University of Michigan.

State archive collections are likely to contain extensive unpublished material on education, and catalogs and guides to such collections should be searched. Where extant the archives of state departments of education and superintendents of public instruction may well be more informative than their published reports.[85] For Illinois, for instance, the records of the Superintendent of Public Instruction are voluminous, including reports from county superintendents and much correspondence. The latter covers a multitude of matters, especially buildings, textbooks, the interpretation of school laws, curricular matters, discipline, school inspections, child labor, teachers' certification and employment, parental inquiries, school-board elections, statistical data on schools, and so on. There are also the minutes of the Illinois State Board of Education from its inception in 1857, and an enormous quantity of

---

[84] Hasse, Delaware, 52–3.
[85] Not all ARs were publ. (e.g. some for MA were not).

material on Illinois State Normal University.[86] Where records
are aptly filed or indexed the task is easier. The correspondence of the Louisiana Department of Education (at Louisiana
State University), for example, is arranged by parishes.

Search of state archives should not, however, be confined to
those of education departments. Much may be found in other
state records. The Massachusetts senate files for 1825, for
example, contain the reports of a committee on the education
of industrial child workers with returns of information from
individual communities. These record, for instance, that at
Brinfield five boys and ten girls worked twelve hours a day,
but noted that there was a good school which they attended
"as their parents judge proper."[87]

Since the administrative structure of public schooling varied
from state to state, within states over time and sometimes
from area to area, local records relating to public education
vary greatly. They include those generated by county, city,
district, and individual school authorities, but it is difficult to
generalize about their whereabouts. They may be found in
state archives, with county or city records, in the hands of
successor school districts, in existing schools, or in state historical societies' and other libraries, as well as in private
hands.[88] They may even be held by local colleges or universities. The College of Education of Ohio State University,
Columbus, for instance, has hundreds of report cards from
schools, 1851–1940.[89] Where state funds for local schools
exceeded money raised from local taxes, there is a tendency for
the more important records relating to public-school administration to be filed with state archives.[90] Often, however, states
devolved responsibility for administering the system to
county authorities.

Certainly local records relating to educational matters in

---

[86] Victoria Irons and Patricia C. Brennan (eds.), *Descriptive Inventory of the Archives of the State of Illinois* (1978), 135–7, 389.

[87] MA Senate files, 1825, 8074. Abstracts publ. in John R. Commons *et al.* (eds.), *Documentary History of American Industrial Society* (1910–11), vol. 5, 60.

[88] See WPA, HRS vols. For many school, college, county, and private records (in many states), see Carman and Thompson (1960), 182–94.

[89] Krug, *Shaping of the American High School*, vol. 2 (1972), 354.

[90] Donald D. Parker, *Local History* (rev. E. Josephson, 1944, repr. 1979), 54.

particular communities are very diverse and where they have survived can shed much light on the way the public-school system worked, and on the relationships between counties and states over such matters. Moreover, where records provide the names of those involved in the local administration of public schooling, as many records described below do, they may be linked with census, directory, and other evidence to provide some analysis of the social, religious, economic, and political characteristics of such persons.

Sometimes county boards administered the schools directly. More often responsibility was devolved to township trustees and beneath them to directors of school district boards. At all events the minutes, reports, and other records of such authorities (some of which may be published) are important sources. So, too, are those of the county superintendents of public instruction, who usually existed however devolved the system, and of other county officers.

Board minutes can be prolific of evidence on administrative and financial matters. Those of the trustees of an Indiana township, for instance, include items on school buildings, teachers' contracts, election returns, censuses of school-age children, taxes, and the distribution of funds to districts.[91] Minutes of a Michigan school board give details of textbooks used for various subjects.[92] Other matters often covered include evidence on the length of school terms and teachers' appointments and salaries. There may also be minutes of annual meetings of school district voters.

Annual reports of county boards and county superintendents were often published,[93] and these provide data for the public schools of each district – such as numbers of pupils by age and sex, attendance figures, numbers of male and female

[91] George Billman and Donald F. Carmony, "Public schools in Congressional township 13, Range 7 East, Shelby county, Indiana, 1829–52," *Indiana Mag. Hist.*, 58 (1962). Others were less full: Arthur R. Hogue (ed.), "The records of an Indiana school district," *Indiana Mag. Hist.*, 48 (1952).

[92] Dominic P. Paris, "The Newburg school, 1831–1918," *Michigan Hist.*, 39 (1955).

[93] James G. Hodgson, *The Official Publications of American Counties, A Union List* (1937).

teachers (perhaps with their qualifications and salaries), valuations of school properties, and details of school libraries. Sometimes information on the literacy of children of school age and reasons for illiteracy are given, and occasionally statistical data on pupils at parochial and other private schools are included. Where the board's financial accounts survive they include records of expenditure and sources of income. Annual reports of township trustees and school district boards giving the same sort of information may also exist. There may be, too, official diaries of the superintendents' activities and correspondence with school boards, officers, principals, teachers, and others.

In states which received federal land grants for educational purposes, there should be records relating to the lease or sale of the sections. There may be petitions from potential purchasers or lessees, and county deed registers will document the conveyancing of the land. The policy pursued with regard to such land and the subsequent level of funds available may be significant for the history of local education.

Information on the financing of public education at the local level is to be found in the records of county and township treasurers, town budget accounts, tax records, and the like. County treasurers' records, for example, should show the distribution of school taxes and state education funds to school boards. Tax lists will show not only totals received but the basis of the tax and whether or not it was related to the extent parents made use of the schools. Some thus include the names of inhabitants with children at school and the names and ages of the children.[94]

Various depositories may yield records relating to teachers and other personnel, containing data on their terms of employment and salaries and on certification. Teachers' contracts indicate salaries and conditions and incidentally may give an insight into how a school was run – as, for example, the length of the session, teaching hours, and the

---

[94] E.g., "Records of Pennsylvania school children, 1802–1809," *National Genealogical Soc. Q.*, 50 (1962); Cohen, *Education in the United States*, vol. 2, 1,030.

curriculum.[95] School vouchers, representing certified accounts for teaching school, and in Florida sworn in county probate courts, include lists of students and their attendance records.[96] Other registers of school attendance and of school officers may also exist. School censuses, lists of children of school age, are frequently found, though they may not always be as accurate as federal and state census evidence where that is available.[97]

Records deriving from the inspection or visitation of schools sometimes exist and, especially where the same school is recorded over a number of years, can be very useful. In Illinois, superintendents' visitation records provide evidence on the numbers of students present and enrolled, personal details of teachers, and remarks on the performance and skills of teachers and pupils, as well as details of textbooks and equipment.[98]

In Michigan, many inspectors' reports are extant from 1858 well into the twentieth century. They may be used as an example of the content of such records.[99] They include the name and post office of the director of the school district, the number of school-age children in the district, and the number attending school in the year and the average attendance of such scholars; the number of months taught by a qualified teacher; the number of books added to the library in the year and the number in the district library; and detailed information on the construction of school buildings. In addition the inspector noted whether each school was a graded school, the number of visits made by county superintendents and directors, the number of qualified teachers and the aggregate number of months taught by all such teachers. Male and female teachers are distinguished and their salaries given. For each school district there is a detailed analysis of income and expenditure,

[95] See, e.g., Frederick Eby, *Education in Texas* (1918), 94; Cohen, *Education in the United States*, vol. 3, 1,139.
[96] See, e.g., Pyburn, *Documentary History*, 158–9.
[97] Kaestle and Vinovskis, *Education and Social Change*, 306.
[98] Roy C. Turnbaugh, Jr., *A Guide to County Records in the Illinois Regional Archives* (1984), 257.
[99] Philip P. Mason, "Manuscript sources of Michigan educational history," *Michigan Hist.*, 39 (1955), 334–6.

showing the kind of taxes supplying funds, the amount raised from tuition, and other sources of income, as well as lists of textbooks used, and remarks on the condition of township libraries. Some of the earlier reports also comment on the general condition and progress of the schools as far as discipline, morals, behavior, scholarship, and attendance were concerned.

Populous cities, frequently the focus of strong political and ethno-religious controversies over education and possessing concentrations of schools, often developed their own school administrations with records similar to those of counties and districts, but in many cases more extensive and professionally compiled. The annual reports of their school committees, boards, and superintendents may have been published as city documents and are commonly very comprehensive. The annual reports of the Board of Public Schools of St. Louis, MO, for instance, provide evidence on attitudes and policy, school curricula, school buildings, and duties of directors and teachers, and a wealth of detail on students, parents, the impact of legislation, and the general development of the city's school system.[100] Sometimes even the reports of sub-committees were published – indeed they may be most important. Such a document for Boston in 1828, for instance, initiated discussion on various improvements in the system of instruction in the city.[101] Petitions from religious and other groups and other submissions to city authorities and their education boards abound in the larger cities, where there were often controversial school issues.[102] City ordinances outline the school systems and their development, and municipal handbooks provide basic data on schools and administrators. Sometimes special reports were made, like the one in Chicago in 1838 on common schooling. Auditors' and finance committee reports give an indication of how money was raised for education and spent.

---

[100] Selwyn K. Troen, *The Public and the Schools* (1975), 238–9.
[101] Repr. Cohen, *Education in the United States*, vol. 2, 989.
[102] E.g., NY City, Public Docs., vol. VII, no. 19: *Petition . . . Catholics of . . . New York Relative to the Distribution of the School Fund* (1840).

Many of the records described in the paragraphs above abound in figures, and it should be stressed that, as with the censuses, statistical data on school enrollment found in state and local records need to be used with caution. Some returns were not very carefully compiled, while comparison over time or between places may be made difficult by changes in the basis of figures or in the efficiency of compilation. Thus, for example, unless average attendance rates and some idea of the length of the school session and the ages of pupils are available, comparison of raw enrollment figures may be misleading.[103]

OTHER RECORDS

The records of individual schools, however, may provide some insight into the nature of the statistics in government records as well as much more evidence for the community historian. Some school administrations preserved students' records long after they left school. At Providence, RI, for instance, the public-high-school pupil records are complete from 1857. Teachers' daily records or registers and school register books and the like may provide for each student the name, sex, age, previous school, dates of entry and leaving, parents' places of birth and occupations, general comments, record of achievement, behavior, and attendance, and details of courses followed.[104] Linked with census materials, directories, and tax and vital records, published lists of graduates, newspapers, and so on, school records can give an indication of the characteristics of those attending school and of those who did not. They may also shed light on any differences in the kind of students attending different types of school. It may be possible, too, to link schooling data with later biographical material to indicate relationships between education and

[103] Maris A. Vinovskis, "Trends in Massachusetts education, 1826–1860," *HEQ*, 12 (1972).

[104] Perlmann, "Use of student records"; Kaestle and Vinovskis, *Education and Social Change*, 55; Dean May and Maris A. Vinovskis, "A ray of millenial light," in Tamara K. Hareven (ed.), *Family and Kin in American Urban Communities, 1800–1840* (1976); Carl F. Kaestle and Maris A. Vinovskis, "From apron strings to ABC", *Am. Jnl. Sociology*, 84, Supplement (1978), pp. S 54–5.

economic and social mobility in a community.[105] There may also be school correspondence, records of subscriptions to school funds, examination results, and tuition accounts.

School textbooks used in a particular school may survive, though rarely. If, however, the titles of texts used are revealed in any of the sources noted here, then copies of the books may be tracked down in libraries,[106] so providing possible evidence of what went on in the classroom. Some books, like the McGuffey readers, were very commonly used.[107] Surviving pupils' exercise, note, and copy books can also be illuminating, though extant items may not always be representative of general standards: there is a greater tendency to preserve the best than the less good.[108]

Photographs of school students and their teachers and of exteriors and interiors of schoolhouses can be subtly informative, even when formally arranged.[109] They may give not only an indication of numbers, ages, and sexes of pupils and teachers and the physical characteristics of school buildings, but also provide evidence on such matters as racial composition and perhaps, by implication from the arrangement of the personnel, of teacher–pupil relationships. The examination of extant school, college, and university buildings, or pictures of them, can, too, to the practiced eye, provide suggestive evidence of organization, teaching methods, and, particularly, the image the institution wished to portray – though conclusions based solely on such evidence should be tentative.[110]

School souvenir publications and centennial and other school histories, though often hagiographical, may contain

[105] Perlmann, "Use of student records"; Katz, "Who went to school?," 436; Selman Berrol, "Who went to school in mid-nineteenth century New York?," in Irwin Yellowitz (ed.), *Essays in the History of New York City* (1978).
[106] See Charles Carpenter, *History of American Schoolbooks* (1963); Charles F. Heartman, *American Primers, Indian Primers, Royal Primers* (1935); *AR U.S. Commissioner of Education, 1897–8* (1899), 799–868; Ruth M. Elson, *Guardians of Tuition* (1964), bibl. and list of schoolbooks. See also Herbst, *History of American Education*, 6–7.
[107] The Library of Congress has a collection of McGuffey readers.
[108] Carman and Thompson (1960), 183–94: refs. to such records in a number of states.
[109] See, e.g., Wayne E. Fuller, *The Old Country School* (1982); Andrew Gulliford, *America's Country Schools* (1984).
[110] Ronald E. Butchart, *Local Schools: Exploring their History* (1986), 85–8.

details of teachers and students and other factual information not available elsewhere. Academies, grammar schools, high schools, colleges, normal schools, universities, and other institutions of higher and adult education, are more likely than elementary schools to have produced their own publications. There may have survived yearbooks, faculty and student handbooks, catalogs or prospectuses, giving details of incorporation, make-up of the governing body, situation and buildings, organization, rules and discipline, tuition charges, curricula, names of principals and teachers, details of textbooks and equipment, and numbers and names and perhaps biographical details of students.[111] Such publications, of course, present the characteristics of the institution as it wished them to be seen. There may also be news sheets, journals, or school magazines, which if extant for a run of years can be most useful sources of information. Separately printed rules for teachers, parents, and students may survive. Such institutions are also likely to have kept detailed manuscript records. Minutes and reports of committees and governing bodies may exist, as well as annual reports of various kinds and detailed student records. These last may embrace records concerning tuition and enrollment books – giving information on parents and on graduation, and perhaps indicating whether a student went on to college or university. If school correspondence has survived, it can be very useful. A large collection of parents' letters to the principal of a North Carolina boarding school, for example, gives great insight into the school's curriculum and organization.[112] Alumni records, too, should not be overlooked. Linkage of such student data with biographical information on parents may help to illuminate the social-class structure of secondary and higher education in a community and give some clue as to the role of such education in social mobility.[113]

[111] See, e.g., Theodore Sizer, *The Age of the Academies* (1964), 175–80.
[112] Marion H. Blair, "Contemporary evidence – Salem Boarding School, 1834–1844," *North Carolina Hist. Rev.*, 27 (1950).
[113] See, e.g., Reed Ueda, "The high school and social mobility in a streetcar suburb," *JIH*, 14 (1984).

As noted above, information on particular universities and other institutions of higher education may appear in state documents and other governmental records. For the domestic archives of such establishments there may be catalogs or details of them may appear in other catalogs of records.[114] Such material may not only form the basis of house histories and give intimate details of student life,[115] but may also contain information on relationships with local secondary schools. After 1870 the practice of university accrediting of high schools produced reports of visits to high schools by faculty, and much correspondence. Such records, for instance, survive at the universities of Michigan and Wisconsin.[116] Again, the archives of the Hampton Institute (now University), Virginia, include correspondence from schools connected with it, and biographical details of alumni, many of whom became school-teachers. Records of college and university alumni, like the records of the alumni of secondary schools, can provide evidence of social and occupational mobility.[117]

In some large cities, prior to the establishment of school boards, what were virtually public-school systems were set up by voluntary societies (sometimes receiving a degree of public funding), like the New York Public School Society.[118] Records of such societies are, therefore, a prime source for elementary education in such places.

Information on the activities of various pressure groups and societies to promote education are to be found in their records, where they have survived,[119] and these are likely to contain general evidence on local developments and contemporary attitudes. Many educational societies were state institutions. Some, like the Educational Association of the State of Florida,

[114] N.B., *Directory of College and University Archives in the United States and Canada* (Soc. Am. Archivists, 1980); *AA*, 13 (1950), 343–50; *University Archives in ARL Libraries* (Assoc. Research Libraries, 1984); *NUCMC*.
[115] See, e.g., Sarah Gordon, "Smith College students," *HEQ*, 15 (1979).
[116] Krug, *Shaping of the American High School*, vol. 1, 449.
[117] Hanley P. Holden, "Student records," *AA*, 30 (1976); Cynthia H. Requardt, "Alternative professions for Goucher College graduates, 1892–1910," *Maryland Hist. Mag.*, 74 (1979).
[118] Records in New York Hist. Soc. See also p. 441 above.
[119] The *NUC* is useful for tracing their publics. For religious socs., see above.

the Educational Society of Connecticut, and the Alabama Educational Association (which had local and county branches),[120] published annual reports or proceedings of their meetings. Some, like the Educational Association of Virginia, also produced other publications, such as circulars to teachers and reports and minutes of conventions. The reports of some of these societies were printed in the annual reports of state superintendents of education. This, for instance, was the case with the Delaware State Teachers' Association for the Education of Colored People.

Less well-known organizations than state-wide and city-orientated societies also existed and may have been locally significant. Search may reveal published and unpublished records. The proceedings of the semi-annual meetings of the Education Society of Lewis county, NY, for example, were published, while the activities of the Providence Association of Mechanics and Manufacturers, an artisan society pressing for free schools in its city, are documented in its unpublished records.[121] Some Sunday-school organizations have also left records.[122] In larger towns light may be thrown on middle-class self-education by the records of cultural associations – philosophical, scientific, literary and musical societies, subscription libraries, and the like.[123]

It is worth searching, too, for the publications of state teachers' associations. The Alabama State Teachers' Association (for black teachers), like others, published its own proceedings. Others had them published in their own or other state educational journals. Some, like those of the Mississippi Teachers' Association, may exist in an unpublished state.[124] Associations of this kind also existed below the state level and may have left useful material. In 1833, for instance, the Essex

---

[120] Stephen B. Weeks, *History of Public School Education in Alabama* (1915), 76, 121.

[121] With Rhode Island Hist. Soc., Providence: William G. Shade, "The 'working-class' and educational reform in early America," *Historian*, 39 (1976–7).

[122] Anne M. Boylan, *Sunday School: The Formation of an American Institution, 1790–1880* (1988), 213.

[123] See, e.g., John T. Guertler (ed.), *The Records of Baltimore's Private Organizations* (1981).

[124] G. Stuart Noble, *Forty Years of the Public Schools in Mississippi* (1918).

County Teachers' Association, Massachusetts, published a report on local schoolhouses.[125]

At the national level, the National Education Association of the United States' *Journal of Addresses and Proceedings* (1858– , title varies)[126] records events and discussions at its annual conventions, and the Association has left many other publications.[127] Its records have been said to provide the best source for the history of education through the eyes of teachers and their representatives.[128] Some published proceedings of the Education Association of the Confederate States of America also exist. The extensive papers of the American Sunday School Union are at the Presbyterian Historical Society in Philadelphia and are also available in microfilm.[129]

Also possibly worth consulting are the published transactions of regional associations of colleges and secondary schools. Such organizations existed for New England, the Middle states with Maryland, the North Central states, and the Southern states. Some of these transactions were also reported in educational journals.[130] Again, the activities of all sorts of other educational societies and local pressure groups and benevolent societies with educational interests are likely to be recorded in local newspapers. The *Raleigh Register* (NC) in 1822, for example, provided information on the Raleigh Female Benevolent Society which set out to instruct poor girls in spinning and weaving.[131]

Indeed, newspapers are a most important source for local educational history, particularly where other evidence is sparse.[132] They not only published factual information on the

125 Kaestle and Vinovskis, *Education and Social Change*, 337.
126 Includes, 1866–70, Procs. American Normal School Assoc.
127 See also Martha F. Nelson (comp.), *Index ... to the Publications of the National Educational Association ... 1857 to 1906* (1907); Krug, *Shaping of the American High School*, vol. 1, 453–4, 456.
128 Brock, 299. See also Edgar B. Wesley, *NEA: The First Hundred Years* (1957).
129 Boylan, *Sunday School*, 213.
130 For details, see Krug, *Shaping of the American High School*, vol. 1, 454.
131 Charles L. Coon, *The Beginnings of Public Education in North Carolina* (1908), vol. 1, 208–9.
132 See, e.g., Vera M. Butler, *Education as Revealed by New England Newspapers Prior to 1850* (1935, repr. 1969); Walter Moffatt, "Arkansas schools, 1819–1840," *Arkansas Hist. Q.*, 12 (1953).

establishment, extension, and closure of individual institutions, on their activities and achievements, on examination results and on faculty, but also acted as a forum for news reports, features, editorials, letters, and obituaries, shedding light on individuals, opinions, matters of controversy,[133] school taxes, and the role of education in local politics.[134] Advertisements in the press for teachers and for students can provide information on tuition, curriculum, size of schools, expected qualifications of teachers, and so on. Those seeking to recruit child workers provide evidence on another side of child life, often an alternative to education. The use of lotteries for school funding may be recorded in advertisements, and the annual reports of schools run by philanthropic societies may also appear in newspapers.

Sometimes letters to the local press were used by education officials and boards as the easiest way to explain to the public such matters as school organization, school taxes, and the implications of state laws and recent litigation for the local community.[135] As well as the results of elections to school boards and like, the record of votes on proposed school laws and reports of debates on such matters are also likely to be found in local newspapers. Radical newspapers sometimes carried descriptions of child labor. The *Mechanics' Free Press*, for instance, in 1830 published comments on the educational condition of Philadelphia child factory workers.[136] Indeed much evidence on child labor in particular places is to be found in local and other newspapers.[137] The religious press (see ch. 6) is important for periods of controversy over parochial schools and the like.

Local directories often give information on the existence of public and private schools and school teachers, and may

133 See, e.g., James C. Carper, "A common faith for the common school?," *Mid-America*, 6 (1978).
134 See, e.g., Elinor M. Gersman, "Progressive reform of the St. Louis school board, 1897," *HEQ*, 10 (1970); and ch. 7 for other sources.
135 See, e.g., Pyburn, *Documentary History*, 148–50.
136 See Commons, *Documentary History*, vol. 5, 61–3.
137 See, e.g., Elizabeth H. Davidson, *Child Labor Legislation in the Southern Textile States* (1930), bibl.

well provide more detail on high schools, grammar schools, academies, seminaries, colleges, and universities. They may present information on the residence and occupation of members of school boards, school trustees, and so on, and, like the manuscript census schedules, help in the identification of the parents of students.[138] Some early-twentieth-century directories of private schools provide retrospective information. General periodicals, like the *Atlantic Monthly* (from 1857, available in microform), carried advertisements for private schools.

Educational journals, some connected with societies mentioned above, are also a fund of information.[139] The *Educational Journal of Virginia*, for instance, included in its pages educational reports on cities and counties in the state. Indeed, many educational journals were state based, like the *Pennsylvania School Journal*, the *Alabama Teachers' Journal*, and the *Ohio Educational Monthly*. Some were connected with particular cities, like the St. Louis *Journal of Education*, useful for the history of the public-school movement in Missouri. There were also numerous national educational journals, some of which contain local information. The *Journal of American Education* (1826–30), which became the *American Annals of Education* (1830–9) (title then varies; available in microfilm),[140] for example, carries in its 1828 volume items on New York high schools, infant schools in Philadelphia, the Boston primary-school system, female high schools in New York, schools in Springfield, MA, and the primary schools of Maryland. In addition a feature, "Intelligence," carried news of individual schools, academies, colleges, and universities. In the 1833 volume there is a very detailed description of school discipline at Mount Vernon School, by the principal, and a report on manual labor schools in Georgia. In the 1830s this journal

[138] Burchart, *Local Schools*, 72–3.
[139] See Sheldon E. Davies, *Educational Periodicals During the Nineteenth Century* (Bureau of Education Bull. 28, 1919; repr. 1970); Frank L. Mott, *A History of American Magazines, 1885–1905* (1957), 267–73; H. F. West, "Common School Advocate – the earliest Indiana school journal," *Indiana Mag. Hist.*, 6 (1910). For educational jnls. in microform, see Hoornstra.
[140] There are annual indexes.

published the statistics of school attendance in Massachusetts' mill towns from the returns of the Massachusetts legislature. The *Common School Journal* (1838–52, title varies; available in microfilm)[141] and the *American School Board Journal* (from 1891) are among other useful journals containing letters and articles about individual schools, normal schools, and education generally in various communities, as well as reporting teachers' institutes and conventions. *Education* (from 1891)[142] and the *Educational Review* (1891–1915) contain occasional college advertisements and references to individual institutions, but on the whole are less worth searching.

For secondary schooling, the *School Review* (from 1893), formerly the *Academy* (1886–91) and *School and College* (1892), has little on individual schools but the discussions reported illustrate the views of identifiable principals and professors on many aspects of education. Very useful is Barnard's *American Journal of Education* (1855/6–1882).[143] Volume 3, for instance, contains articles on a preparatory school in New Jersey and an academy in Pennsylvania. Local journals of a non-educational kind may also sometimes contain information on educational matters. The *Evangelical and Literary Magazine* (1818–28), for instance, served as a forum for discussion on public schooling in Virginia in the 1820s.[144]

In addition, some other contemporary publications may be regarded as primary sources. Visitors' writings may include information on schooling, particularly on academies and colleges. Natchez Academy, MS, is, for example, described by a traveler in 1835.[145] County and other local histories usually have information on schools, especially in their early days, some of which may not now be available elsewhere; and similarly with early histories of school societies and school

---

[141] Mostly concerned with MA. Vols. indexed.
[142] Available in microfilm. Index vols. 1–65 (1946).
[143] Available in microfilm. Classified index in vols. 17, 26. See also *Analytical Index to Barnard's American Journal of Education* (1892).
[144] J. L. B. Buck, *The Development of Public Schools in Virginia* (1952), 33–4. Available in microfilm.
[145] Joseph H. Ingraham, *The South West by a Yankee* (1835), vol. 2, 38–40. And see p. 34.

systems.[146] Works on the condition of slum children in the larger cities, like Jacob A. Riis's *The Children of the Poor* (New York, 1893), may also be useful.[147]

Occasionally childhood reminiscences, published and unpublished, may exist to give an extra dimension.[148] General autobiographies, too, may have interesting material, especially where the subject was active in the educational affairs of the community. Oral and written testimony collected earlier in the twentieth century may be preserved to shed light on nineteenth-century conditions.[149] The personal papers of educationists, clergymen, local politicians, benefactors, teachers, and others may also be useful.[150] And the James B. Angell papers at the Michigan Historical Collection, University of Michigan, contain not only letters concerning the N.E.A. Committee of Ten, but correspondence from high school principals in Michigan and other Midwest states detailing the curricula and organization of their schools.[151] Again, Trinity College, Hartford, has the papers of Henry Barnard, which include reports from school districts and school visitors, letters, and other material from different states.[152] Sometimes teachers' diaries and letters written by students, especially by those at boarding schools to their parents, may survive, and can give considerable insight into the daily life of

---

[146] E.g., Joseph M. Wightman, *Annals of the Boston Primary School Committee . . . 1818 to . . . 1855* (1860).

[147] Cf. Francis H. Nichols, "Children of the coal shadow," *McClure's Mag.*, 20 (1903) (re PA coal counties); Charles Brace, *The Dangerous Classes of New York and Twenty Years' Work among Them* (1872).

[148] Geraldine J. Clifford, "Home and school in 19th century America," *HEQ*, 18 (1978); Geraldine J. Clifford, "The use of personal-history documents in the history of education," *Hist. Education*, 7 (1978). N.B., Barbara J. Finkelstein, "Schooling and schoolteachers: selected bibliography of autobiographies in the nineteenth century," *HEQ*, 14 (1974).

[149] See, e.g., Florence E. Paton, "History of schools of Portage township in the copper country," *Michigan Hist.*, 2 (1918); Colleen M. Elliott and Louise A. Moxley (eds.), *The Tennessee Civil War Veterans Questionnaire* (5 vols., 1985).

[150] See, e.g., Coon, *Education in North Carolina*, vol. 1, 94–7; Kaufman, *Women Teachers on the Frontier*.

[151] Krug, *Shaping the American High School*, vol. 1, 449. For syllabuses of forty named high schools from this source, see ibid., 47–51.

[152] Information from Margaret F. Sax, Watkinson Library, Trinity College, Hartford, CT 06106, who is (1990) compiling a catalog.

a school, covering such topics as the curriculum, textbooks used, teaching methods, food, general activities, and so forth.[153]

Local controversies over educational matters, for instance taxation, common-school systems, the place of religiously affiliated schools, and the use of English as the medium of instruction, are likely, especially in the larger towns, to have generated pamphlet material.[154] Some pamphlets, like those published by the Anti-Bennett Law State Committee in Wisconsin in the 1850s,[155] contain very detailed factual information. Child labor, embracing the education of child workers, is another topic which generated much polemical material. Early twentieth-century publications on this topic often contain retrospective data.[156]

Many other types of records are potential sources for local educational history, though not all can be treated here. We may note, however, that fire-insurance records can provide details of school buildings,[157] some business archives related to schools (including Sunday schools) for child workers,[158] wills and estate inventories can provide evidence of the possession of books, and may include bequests to schools. Evidence of signature literacy is found in wills, deeds, marriage records, petitions, and business papers. Registers of convicts may include data on ability to read or write. Local plans and maps may show the existence and location of educational establishments. Voting returns may be studied with a view to identifying those who voted for and against local educational proposals.[159]

---

[153] See, e.g., Geraldine J. Clifford, "Saints, sinners and people," *HEQ*, 15 (1975), 269; Stanton C. Crawford and John A. Nietz, "Student life in schools in the Ohio Valley ninety years ago," *Western Pennsylvania Hist. Mag.*, 23 (1940).

[154] E.g., William H. Ruffner, *Circulars, Public Education Documents, Pamphlets, and Miscellaneous Material on Public Education in Virginia* (1870–82).

[155] Roger E. Wyman, "Wisconsin ethnic groups and the election of 1890," in Robert P. Swierenga (ed.), *Quantification in American History* (1970), 245.

[156] See Davidson, *Child Labor*, bibl.

[157] E.g., Colonial Williamsburg Archives, Williamsburg, VA, Mutual Assurance Soc., 21, 322, 1860.

[158] E.g., Bremner, *Children and Youth*, vol. 1, 178.

[159] E.g., Michael B. Katz, *The Irony of Early School Reform* (1968).

BLACK EDUCATION

Much has been written about black education[160] and some of it is very controversial.[161] Many of the specific sources and types of sources already cited in this chapter contain information relating to the education of black Americans – especially the federal censuses, the reports of the U.S. Commissioner of Agriculture and other federal records noted above. The reports of state superintendents of education, other state, city, county, township, and school district records and other archives relating generally to education are likely to contain information on facilities for blacks. Since schooling was usually segregated, there may be distinct parallel records for black and white schools: for Washington and Georgetown, DC, for instance, there are reports of a Superintendent of Colored Schools. Records of individual schools and colleges will, of course, be similar to those described above. Useful, too, for black education will be some of the sources described in chapter 3.[162] Nevertheless, because of the peculiar history of black education in America, especially in the South and where there were concentrations of blacks in the North, certain sources of information need special attention here.

The background for the legal situation of blacks with regard to schooling is to be found in state constitutions and state legislation. The laws of individual Southern states before the Civil War, for instance, introduced bans on the instruction of slaves and free blacks. Postbellum constitutions need to be studied for the situation then, especially with regard to segregation.[163] The journals, debates, and proceedings of state

---

[160] See Leo McGee and Harvey G. Neufeldt (comps.), *Education of the Black Adult in the United States: An Annotated Bibliography* (1985); Frederick Chambers, *Black Higher Education in the United States: A Selected Bibliography...* (1978); Cohen, "American public schooling," 9–11; and see general bibls., pp. 135, 440.

[161] Vincent P. Franklin, "Historical revisionism and black education," *School Rev.*, 8 (1973); Vincent P. Franklin and James D. Anderson (eds.), *New Perspectives on Black Educational History* (1978).

[162] See also Walter L. Fleming, *A Documentary History of Reconstruction...* (2 vols., 1906–7).

[163] Useful are Perley Poore, *The Federal and State Constitutions, Colonial Charters and Other Organic Laws of the United States* (2 vols., 1878); inf. on state laws on black education in ARs U.S. Commissioner of Education for 1871, 1901; *American Jnl. Education*, 19 (1870), 301–402.

legislatures, and of state constitutional conventions after the Civil War, will provide evidence of attitudes towards black schooling, segregation, and so forth. City ordinances, too, may record the regulation of and the attitudes to black schooling. In addition, conditions of blacks in large cities were sometimes the subject of surveys. There was one for Cincinnati in 1835 and several Philadelphia censuses of blacks.[164]

The reports of the U.S. Commissioner of Education, described above, are full of data on black schooling in various places. The report for 1902, moreover, contains a retrospective report on the work of Northern churches in promoting the education of freedmen from 1861. A special report of the Bureau of Education, on colored education in the District of Columbia (1871, repr. 1969), contains also a factual summary of the legal status of black schools in each of the thirty-five states around 1870, with information on some individual schools. The Bureau's state histories of education (see above) contain for the Southern states much on the education of freedmen. Indeed federal documents relating to black schooling, other than those already noted with reference to schooling generally, relate mainly to the Southern and border states in the Civil War and Reconstruction periods. Thus the reports of the Joint Committee on Reconstruction and of the Select Committee on the Condition of Affairs in the Late Insurrectionary States, as well as the reports of the commanders of the five military districts, 1867–70 (in the annual reports of the War Department) are full of information on white Southern attitudes to black schooling and evidence of violence towards black and Yankee teachers and black schools.[165] There is also a report of the Board of Education for Freedmen, Department of the Gulf, for 1864 (1865),[166] which contains reports on individual schools. The volumes of the *War of the Rebellion: A Compilation of the Official Records of the Union and Confederate Armies* (1880–1910) contain evidence on schooling for white and black children during the war.

[164] See pp. 85–6. [165] See pp. 136–7.
[166] For copies, see *NUC*, under "U.S. Army, Dept. of the Gulf." Not in US Serial Set.

Education

The published and unpublished records of the Bureau of
Refugees, Freedmen, and Abandoned Lands are an enormous
storehouse of evidence on the education of freedmen in the
Southern and border states during the war and its aftermath,
sometimes also providing restrospective antebellum material.[167] The published annual reports of the Commissioner
(which include the reports and memoranda of assistant commissioners and inspectors) and such reports of assistant commissioners as were separately published, all described in
chapter 3, contain much local evidence on black schooling. A
report of the Assistant Commissioner for Alabama, for instance, provides a table of locations of freedmen's schools,
1865–6, with numbers of pupils and teachers. Additional are
the published six-monthly reports of the Revd. John W. Alvord, the Bureau's General Superintendent of Education.[168]
These are useful for Bureau-assisted schools and their teachers, but should be used with caution since they were edited to
portray Bureau activities in a good light. The original unpublished reports, on which they were based, described below,
should be preferred.[169]

The unpublished records of the Bureau in the National
Archives (RG 105) are an essential source for any detailed local
study of black schooling in the South during the War and
Reconstruction periods.[170] A good number are available in
microfilm.[171] They may be divided into Washington headquarters' records and those of field offices. Of the headquarters' records those of the Education Division of the Bureau
consist largely of correspondence and school reports covering

---

[167] Barry A. Crouch, "Freedmen's Bureau reports," in Robert L. Clarke (ed.),
   Afro-American History (1981), 89–90.
[168] John W. Alvord, *Semi-Annual Reports on Schools and Finances for Freedmen, 1866–
   1870.* Not in US Serial Set.
[169] Henry L. Swint, *The Northern Teacher in the South* (1967), 9–10.
[170] See, e.g., William T. Alderson, "The Freedmen's Bureau and negro education in
   Virginia," *North Carolina Hist. Rev.*, 29 (1952); Martin Abbott, "The Freedmen's
   Bureau and negro schooling in South Carolina," *South Carolina Hist. Mag.*, 57
   (1956); William P. Vaughan, *Schools for All* (1974).
[171] NA, *Black Studies: A Select Catalog of National Archives Microfilm Publications*
   (1984).

the years 1865–71. [172] The correspondence includes both letters received and copies of letters sent and is mainly with the officers of the benevolent societies cooperating in the establishment and maintenance of schools for freedmen, with private individuals, and with the Bureau's superintendents of education in the various states. Occasionally there are letters on educational matters from assistant commissioners. The correspondence is arranged mainly chronologically and there are various registers and indexes. Also included is a report to Commissioner Howard on freedmen's schools in late 1865.

With the correspondence are reports of school inspections, lists of teachers sponsored by societies, contracts and specifications for schoolhouses, price lists of books, and working papers relating to expenditure. Some letters from state superintendents include reports on schools not found in the main collection of school reports described next.

The collection of school reports from state superintendents in the headquarters' records consists (for 1865–70) of monthly, consolidated quarterly, semi-annual, or annual narrative and statistical reports. [173] The statistical monthly reports provide the names and locations of schools, names of their supporting societies, whether day or night, and whether the buildings were owned by freedmen or others. For students, numbers are given, broken down by sex, race, age, degree of literacy, and whether ex-slave or not. Numbers learning different subjects, like writing, arithmetic, geography, needlework, and "higher branches" are indicated, as well as details of the level of tuition paid by the freedmen and the financial expenses of the schools. The narrative monthly reports include comment on local attitudes towards freedmen's education, particular problems, suggestions for improvement, and so on. The periodic consolidated reports are also statistical or narrative, conflating the monthly reports, and, in the case of narrative reports,

[172] For details, see Elaine Everly (comp.), *Preliminary Inventory of the Records of the Bureau of Refugees, Freedmen, and Abandoned Lands: Washington Headquarters* (PI 174, 1973, repr. 1981), 27–30; Elaine Everly, *Statistical Records of the Bureau of Refugees, Freedmen, and Abandoned Lands* (RIP 48, 1973); NA, *Black Studies*, 23–9.
[173] For a key, see NA, *Black Studies*, 28–9.

including more detailed recommendations. There is also an indexed collection of synopses of school reports and a register of school reports giving dates and types of reports by states.

Also among the headquarters' records is a register of rents paid by benevolent societies (arranged by societies) indicating the contribution of the Bureau, and including lists of teachers (by states) with names of schools and their location. Other lists of teachers, arranged by teachers' names, show their employing society and the state in which they were employed. Some give the city where the teacher's school was located. In addition there are, mostly for 1869–70, quarterly, semi-annual, and annual accounts with societies relating to the rents of school buildings. Claims by societies for support indicate the location of schools, teachers' names, number of months each teacher was employed, average student attendances, and monthly rents.

Some information on schooling can be found in other headquarters' records of the Bureau. The correspondence of the Commissioner contains letters on the establishment of schools and authorizations of payment for school buildings, as well as reports of school inspections. The correspondence of the Chief Quartermaster includes letters relating to the acquisition and repair of schoolhouses and the transportation of teachers, as well as registers of moneys spent on rent, repairs, and construction.[174]

Of the records of the Bureau's field offices, which are arranged by states,[175] those of its state superintendents of education are the most important for local history. They include correspondence on many aspects of education and drafts and copies of the reports on schools sent forward to the Commissioner (described above). The latter form the basis of educational data in the annual reports of assistant commissioners. There may, too, be special reports (as, for instance, on tours of inspection in Alabama in 1866 and 1867). There are also the

---

[174] For details, see PI 174, 5–6, 9, 30–2.

[175] For details, see Elaine Everly and Willna Pacheli (comps.), *Preliminary Inventory of the Records of the Field Offices of the Bureau of Refugees, Freedmen, and Abandoned Lands* (NM–95, 1973–4, T/S, 3 vols., available NA, Washington, DC); NA, *Black Studies*, 32–62, q.v. for those available in microfilm.

monthly school reports submitted by the officers of subdistricts. These include both statistical information on schools in their areas and general comment on local attitudes towards the education of freedmen and indigent whites, any need for additional schools and teachers, and the efforts and ability of societies and the freedmen themselves to meet such a need. In addition, there are monthly or weekly reports by individual teachers indicating subjects taught in day, night, and Sunday schools, and giving details of numbers of pupils, their attendance, tuition charged, and comments. Some seem to relate to schools not supported by the Bureau. There may be, too, detailed financial records for individual local schools (arranged by towns and cities), as for Georgia, 1869–70, and Alabama, 1867–8, and covering school buildings, equipment, and salaries.

Other items among the records of the Bureau's state superintendents of education may include teachers' records (letters of appointment, receipts for salaries, transportation certificates), lists of missionaries and society agents, and deeds and copy deeds relating to school sites (as for Maryland, Delaware, and West Virginia, 1866–70). Some items are unusual. For Tennessee there are monthly reports submitted by Fisk University, the Colored Baptist Institute, Nashville, and other institutions. For Texas there is a list of 1869 of freedmen's schools closed through lack of funds. The records for Louisiana embrace some very detailed archives of the antebellum state Board of Education, 1864–5.[176]

Educational evidence is sometimes to be found in Bureau field office records other than those of superintendents of education – especially among the correspondence of the assistant commissioners and in reports of subassistant commissioners. For Louisiana there is also, in the Assistant Inspector General's reports, 1866–8, record of numbers of schools and pupils arranged by plantations. And generally the records of subordinate field offices, where extant, contain local evidence. For Demopolis, AL, for instance, there is a list of contri-

---

[176] For details, see NA, *Black Studies*, 51–2.

butions to a black school and also an individual teacher's records which include a pupil roll giving names, ages, fees paid, and days attended. For Lincolnton, NC, there are reports on local schools.[177] The signature books of the local branches of the Freedmen's Savings and Trust Co., which provide data on the ability of blacks to sign their names, are among the records of the Comptroller of the Currency (RG 101).[178]

Other Record Groups in the National Archives may occasionally provide local information on education. Thus evidence on agricultural colleges for black students is found among the records of the Office of Experiment Stations (RG 164), 1888–1937, and in the records of the Department of the Interior (RG 48) (including for 1890–1907 correspondence, college catalogs, and news clippings). Some correspondence in the Department of Justice records (RG 60) provides information on education, including data on Howard University, while evidence on the schooling of black youths in the District of Columbia is in the records of the House Select Committee on Reconstruction (RG 233).[179]

Information in state archives on black schooling is to be found mainly in the reports and records of state superintendents and boards of education, but also in reports and papers of state auditors, governors' messages, petitions, special committee reports, and so on.

Other important sources of information on local black education include newspapers and pamphlet literature. Locally published pamphlets and broadsides concerning controversies and law cases relating to black schooling are abundant, particularly in the larger cities, and provide much evidence on the course of such controversies, local attitudes, and so forth. Such material is preserved mainly in local libraries, historical societies, and universities.[180] Less polemical and more fruitful of information, though nevertheless frequently partisan, are reports, letters, and editorials in local newspapers. These also

---

[177] NM–95, 19.

[178] See, e.g., Carl R. Osthaus, *Freedmen, Philanthropy, and Fraud* (1976), 86–7.

[179] Debra Newman (comp.), *Black History: A Guide to Civilian Records in the National Archives* (1984), 78–9, 121, 216, 300.

[180] Some have been reproduced: e.g., by Garland Publishing.

contain evidence of the existence of black schools and colleges and details of their organization and activities. Though given little space here, newspapers must be regarded as a very significant source for this topic. Similarly educational journals, like those noted in the last section, often include information on the schooling of blacks, particularly after the Civil War.

Other contemporary published material includes local and regional periodicals. *De Bow's Review*, for instance, provides examples of Southern postbellum attitudes to black education and to Yankee teachers. Descriptions of Southern life published by travelers and other observers, mainly from the North and abroad, can also be of interest. Whitelaw Reid's work, for example, contains descriptions of black schools immediately following the end of the Civil War.[181]

Diaries, autobiographies, memoirs, letters, and other papers of those who had a special interest in black education – politicians, missionaries, teachers, ex-slaves, and the like – are to be found in collections of private papers and if they exist can be very useful for the community historian.[182] Some may have been published. The *Narrative of the Life of Frederick Douglas as an American Slave Written by Himself* (1845) cites several cases of secret black schools.[183] Ex-slave narratives, detailed elsewhere, may contain information on the education of slaves.[184]

In particular the experiences of Yankee teachers working in the South during the War and Reconstruction, recorded in letters, diaries, and reminiscences, can be very valuable sources.[185] Since schooling, particularly in the South, was for long a concern of religious bodies, and since missionary societies and religiously inspired abolitionist and freedmen's aid societies were so concerned with the education of black

[181] Whitelaw Reid, *After the War* (1866), 246–58.
[182] Cf. Vaughan, *Schools for All*, 162; Larry W. Pearce, "Enoch K. Miller and the freedmen's schools," *Arkansas Hist. Q.*, 31 (1972); Richard L. Morton (ed.), "A 'Yankee' teacher in North Carolina," *North Carolina Hist. Rev.*, 30 (1953).
[183] Bremner, *Children and Youth*, vol. 1, 517–20.
[184] See pp. 157–9; Thomas L. Webber, *Deep Like Rivers* (1978).
[185] E.g., Mary Ames, *From a New England Woman's Diary in Dixie in 1865* (1906); Rupert S. Holland (ed.), *Letters and Diary of Laura M. Towne* (1912); "Journal of Miss Susan Walker," *Publics. Hist. and Phil. Soc. Ohio*, 7 (1912).

children, the multitudinous records of such churches and societies are likely to be very fruitful sources for the local history of black education. The records of specific churches and denominations and of individual congregations have been described in chapter 6, and this should be consulted for details.

The Quakers were very active in education and welfare and their records are especially worth searching: for instance, the Friends' Association of Philadelphia published annual reports, censuses, and other papers relating to blacks in that area;[186] Friends' records in Indiana document the despatch of missionaries to found an orphanage at Helena, AR; a Friends' committee in Virginia made a report in 1862 on the condition of black refugees in different parts of the state; and the reports of the Baltimore Association of Friends to Advise and Assist Friends of the Southern States (1866) provide information on Sunday schools for blacks.[187]

The extensive published and unpublished records of freedmen's aid and emancipation societies are also likely sources. The Rutherford B. Hayes Library, Fremont, OH, has correspondence relating to the Slater Fund for Negro Education, which contains references to many communities, schools, and colleges, 1881–7.[188] The records of the Peabody Fund give much local information on public education in the South.[189] The American Freedmen's Union Commission, a society supporting teachers for ex-slaves, has left minutes, financial accounts, letters, and teachers' testimonials.[190] The archives of

[186] Theodore Hershberg, "Free blacks in antebellum Philadelphia," in Hershberg, *Philadelphia*; Swint, *Northern Teacher in the South*, 202.
[187] Thomas C. Kennedy, "Southland College," *Arkansas Hist. Q.*, 42 (1983); Alrutheus A. Taylor, "The negro in the reconstruction of Virginia," *JNH*, 11 (1916); Emma King, "Some aspects of the work of the Society of Friends for negro education in North Carolina," *North Carolina Hist. Rev.*, 1 (1924).
[188] See Louis D. Rubin, *Teach the Freeman: The Correspondence of Rutherford B. Hayes and the Slater Fund for Negro Education, 1881–1887* (2 vols., 1959) for selection (index inadequate).
[189] See *Procs. Trustees of the Peabody Education Fund* (6 vols., 1875–1916). And see J. L. M. Curry, *A Brief Sketch of George Peabody and a History of the Peabody Education Fund...* (1898, repr. 1969).
[190] In Olin Library, Cornell Univ., Ithaca, NY 14853–5301.

the American Missionary Association,[191] perhaps the most active of Northern societies sending teachers to the South during the Civil War and after (providing in collaboration with the Freedmen's Bureau education for blacks in some thousand schools and eight institutes of higher education), contain much data on individual communities, schools, and other educational institutions.[192] Very interesting are their teachers' monthly school reports, returned on printed forms.[193] There are also published annual reports.

Another important society, the American Home Missionary Society, has left a substantial archive of unpublished papers,[194] and published reports. Other significant missionary and aid societies which published annual reports (giving details of schools and communities) include the American Baptist Free Mission Society, the American Baptist Home Mission Society, the Freewill Baptist Home Mission Society, the Methodist Episcopal Freedmen's Aid Society, the Massachusetts Society for the Religious Instruction of Freedmen, the Presbyterian Committee on Missions for Freedmen, and the Protestant Episcopal Commission of Home Missions to Colored People.

Some of these societies were particularly active in education. The Methodist Episcopal Freedmen's Aid Society, for instance, was engaged in schooling in Tennessee, Georgia, Alabama, Mississippi, Louisiana, Kentucky, West Virginia, Virginia, and Florida, and also supported fourteen institutions for the higher education of blacks. It published the *Christian Educator* (1889–1931) which contains information on both

[191] See pp. 285–6. Formerly at Fisk and Dillard univs., now at Tulane Univ., New Orleans: see Amistad Research Center, *Author and Added Entry Catalog of the American Missionary Association Archives. With Reference to Schools and Mission Stations* (3 vols., n.d.). Some available in microform.
[192] Larry W. Pearce, "The American Missionary Association and the freedmen in Arkansas, 1863–1878," *Arkansas Hist. Q.*, 30 (1971); Larry W. Pearce, "The American Missionary Association and the Freedmen's Bureau in Arkansas," *Arkansas Hist. Q.* 30 (1971), 31 (1972); Clifton H. Johnson, "Some archival sources on negro history in Tennessee," *Tennessee Hist. Q.*, 28 (1969), 11–12; and see *American Missionary* cited below.
[193] See, e.g., Joe M. Richardson, "The American Missionary Association and black education in Civil War Missouri," *Missouri Hist. Rev.*, 69 (1975), 447.
[194] See p. 284.

schools and colleges. Other societies had similar journals which carried news of educational establishments of all sorts with which they were associated. The *Baptist Home Missionary Monthly* is an example.[195] Indeed, journals sponsored by missionary societies and abolitionist and aid societies are very useful for local information.[196] The *American Missionary* (1846–1934), the *Freedmen's Journal* (1865–6), and the *National Freedman* (1865–6) (all available in microform), and the *Freedmen's Record*, for instance, published data on black schools and letters and reports from individual teachers and agents on local educational activities. The *American Freedman* (May, 1868) describes the first black school in Richmond, VA, after the city's surrender. Other religious journals, including those associated with particular denominations, should also be consulted.

INDIAN SCHOOLING

Some native American children in the nineteenth century attended regular schools, but many received education in special establishments connected with churches and missions or provided by the federal government. The history of these schools is not often treated by local historians, but some brief guidance may be given for those who wish to do so.[197]

Travelers' accounts,[198] newspapers, reminiscences, and the like, sometimes mention Indian schools, but the chief sources of information about them are missionary records and those of the federal government. Catholic and Protestant organizations in the nineteenth century established missions and schools practically everywhere where Indians were located.

---

[195] Johnson, "Some archival sources," q.v. for other educational activity by missionary socs.

[196] See pp. 153–4, 283, for details.

[197] For secondary works, see esp. Evelyn C. Adams, *American Indian Education* (1946), 108–14; Brewton Berry, *The Education of American Indians – A Survey of the Literature* (1969); Francis P. Prucha, *A Bibliographical Guide to the History of Indian-White Relations in the United States* (1977), ch. 13, and *Supplement* (1982), ch. 11.

[198] E.g., Charles F. Meserve, *A Tour of Observations among Indians and Indian Schools in Arizona, New Mexico, Oklahoma, and Kansas* (1894).

For missionary sources chapter 6 should be consulted,[199] but it may be mentioned here that the Board of Foreign Missions of the Presbyterian Church in the United States, for instance, ran many schools for Indians, and at the library of the Presbyterian Historical Society in Philadelphia there is a collection of "American Indian Correspondence." Correspondence is also extracted in the Board's annual reports (1838–93).[200] Missionary periodicals, too, are important for information on individual schools.

Federal documents containing data on the education of Indians[201] include the *American State Papers: Indian Affairs* (1834), which provides a list of schools in 1833 with locations, dates of establishment, numbers of pupils, and amount of federal grant. Also worth searching are the indexes to the *Territorial Papers of the United States* under "schools" and "Indians." The main published federal sources, however, are the annual reports of the War Department before 1824 and from then the annual reports of the Commissioner of Indian Affairs (embracing reports of the Superintendent of Indian Schools) – successively published in the reports of the War Department to 1849 and then in those of the Interior Department. A publication of the Bureau of Indian Affairs in 1903 gives much information on specific schools of various kinds.[202]

In the National Archives the records of the Bureau of Indian Affairs (RG 75) are a prime source. They embrace records inherited from the Office of the Secretary of War for the period before the Bureau existed. Among these are letters about mission schools and the use of the Civilization Fund,

---

[199] See also Robert F. Berkhofer, Jr., *Salvation and the Savage* (1965), esp. bibl.; Francis P. Prucha, *The Churches and the Indian Schools, 1888–1912* (1979), bibl.; Philip C. Bantin and Mark G. Thiel, *Guide to Catholic Indian Missions in Mid-West Repositories* (1984). See also the Propaganda Fide records (pp. 261, 445).

[200] See Michael C. Coleman, "The responses of American Indian children to Presbyterian schools in the nineteenth century; an analysis through missionary sources," *HEQ*, 27 (1987).

[201] See Steven L. Johnson, *Guide to American Indian Documents in the Congressional Serial Set. 1817–1899* (1977), under "education," "schools."

[202] *Statistics of Indian Tribes, Agencies and Schools* (1903, repr. 1976).

established in 1819 to support such schools,[203] and correspondence of the Superintendent of Indian Trade, which contains information on Indian education.[204] The "General Records" of the Bureau contain correspondence from the 1820s and other material which provide for individual schools details on location, establishment dates, numbers of students and teachers, and much other information. The records of the Bureau's Finance Division contain evidence from the 1830s on support of schools and school buildings. The Land Division's records include from the 1850s schedules of land allotted for schools. The Bureau's cartographic collection has some maps showing schools, and the Employees section records contain from 1848 registers of teachers and others in school service, as well as inspectors' reports on them.[205]

The records of the Bureau's Education Division[206] and its predecessors include much useful correspondence, compilations of "statistics," and reports from agents and school superintendents, mainly from the late 1870s. These last contain a great deal of information on individual schools: numbers of students and teachers, religious denominational support, financial data, attendance and achievement details, salaries, and details of buildings. For 1887–1911 there are records of contracts with public-school systems and missionary societies relating to individual schools. Sometimes accompanying testimony provides retrospective information. The so-called field office records of the Bureau consist of records created by certain superintendencies, agencies, area offices, and non-reservation schools. They are now held in regional branches of the National Archives and include correspondence and reports

[203] Edward E. Hill (comp.), *Guide to the Records in the National Archives Relating to American Indians* (1981), 16–17. N.B. Cynthia G. Fox (comp.), *American Indians: A Select Catalog of National Archives Microfilm Publications* (1984).

[204] Hill, *Guide*, 21.

[205] For details see Edward E. Hill (comp.), *Preliminary Inventory of the Records of the Bureau of Indian Affairs* (PI 163, 2 vols., 1965). And see Gaston Litton, "The resources at the National Archives for the study of the American Indian," *Ethnohistory*, 2 (1955), 196. For refs. in the Chickasaw Removal Records, see Hill, *Guide*, 71.

[206] PI 163, 205–16; Hill, *Guide*, 30, 41, 101, 104–8.

on schools and sometimes on particular children.[207] The detailed records of a few individual schools are filed separately.[208]

Some unpublished military records also include evidence on Indian schools. The Quartermaster General's records (RG 92), for instance, give some details of a proposed school for interpreters at Fort Snelling, Wisconsin Territory.[209] Some information may be found, too, in correspondence in the records of the Indian Division of the Department of the Interior (RG 48).[210] The records of the House of Representatives (RG 233) have correspondence on the Cherokee educational fund.[211]

Some published annual reports of the U.S. Commissioner of Education also contain information on Indian schools. The report for 1870 (1875), for example, includes a survey of the general condition of Indian education with some mention of particular schools and the attitudes of various tribes towards schooling. The Bureau of Education also issued a special report on Indian education in 1888 and a survey of schooling in three Alabama counties in 1914.[212] Evidence of provisions for Indian education is to be found, too, in various treaties with the Indians,[213] and a report of 1882 gives the annual amount spent on Indian education in particular schools and areas in the years 1877–81.[214]

The unpublished federal census schedules for the 1880 census include information on the education of Indians living near military reservations.[215] The published 1890 census includes

[207] See *GNA*, 386–7.
[208] See refs. in PI 163 and Hill, *Guide*; Robert Svenningsen (comp.), *Preliminary Inventory of the Pueblo Records Created by Field Offices of the Bureau of Indian Affairs* (PI 192, 1980).
[209] See *Territorial Papers of the United States*, xxvii, 1,062.
[210] Hill, *Guide*, 197–8.
[211] Ibid., 363; Rowland Buford *et al.* (comps.), *Preliminary Inventory of the Records of the House of Representatives* (PI 113, 1959), 211.
[212] Office of Education, *Indian Education and Civilization* (1888); *Bull.*, 43 (1914); and see *Circular*, 4 (1884); Hill, *Guide*, 388.
[213] See p. 234; Washburn, *The American Indian* (cited p. 235n), index, 3,055–6.
[214] SED 113 (47–1), ser. 1330.
[215] In RG 29 in 4 vols.: Katherine Davidson and Charlotte M. Ashby (comps.), *Preliminary Inventory of the Records of the Bureau of the Census* (PI 161, 1964), 101.

details of financial aid to individual listed Indian schools, 1888–90, taken from the reports of the Commissioner of Indian Affairs, while quite detailed information on individual schools is contained in the descriptive reports on Indians in various parts of the country – including, for example, types of buildings, teachers' salaries and other expenses, and accommodation and attendance figures, together with ages and sex of pupils.[216] Four Extra Census Bulletins for the 1890 census also provide details of education in various tribes.[217] Local data on Indian education and literacy in the volumes of the 1900 census are limited. Numbers of literate and illiterate Chinese, Japanese, and Indian (not distinguished) males over twenty-one are given by counties.[218] And, for the same racial groupings, numbers aged ten and upwards (by sex) unable to speak English are given for cities of 25,000 population upwards.[219]

[216] Vol. x: see index.
[217] Listed Schulze (1983), 267–8, 400–10; Dubester (1950), 240.
[218] Vol. i, table 92.
[219] Vol. ii, table 90. A number of tables give educational inf. for "colored" people, which included Indians.

CHAPTER 11

Poverty, health, and crime

The existence in Michigan of a Board of State Commissioners for the General Supervision of Charitable, Penal, Pauper, and Reformatory Institutions, and in Massachusetts of a board that covered public health, lunacy, and poor relief, was not unique. It testifies to the fact that the treatment of the poor, and treatment of the physically and mentally handicapped, the sick, and the delinquent, were frequently linked in nineteenth-century thought and practice. And since poverty did, indeed, often result from ill health or disability or was itself a cause of such conditions, and was in its turn not infrequently a spur to crime, this is not surprising. Again matters of public health – sanitation, water supply, medical practices – were to some extent connected with the problems of the poor. It is, therefore, convenient to treat these related topics in a single chapter, the more so since some of the records for their study are common ones.

It must be said, however, that often, except in the cases of public health and the relief of poverty, the scope for a purely local treatment will for some places be limited. Many of the institutions of welfare and correction were state establishments concentrated in state capitals, while much organized charity was exclusive to the larger cities where social problems were more threatening than in less populated places. Nevertheless the topics covered in this chapter embrace a wide spectrum of life and for many places there are likely to be some interesting matters for community historians to investigate. Moreover, since they cannot be dealt with in a vacuum but need to be related to the demographic, social, economic, and political structures of local communities, and to local religious and maybe educational activity, among other things, the researcher will often need to combine the sources discussed here with those outlined in other chapters.

With all such topics the likelihood of change over time and the reasons for it merit consideration, as does the extent to which the local picture fits with the regional or national one. Much has been written on the topics discussed here, but it has often been at the national or state level and necessarily generalized, based on the writings of reformers, legislation, and official reports, without much investigation (except in the great cities) of what actually happened in particular communities and institutions. Thus it has been noted that the history of poorhouses has been neglected[1] and that we know less of their reality than of ideas about them.[2] And poor-relief organization, facilities for the care of the sick, and public health arrangements could vary from one county to another in the same state.

THE POOR, THE SICK, AND THE HANDICAPPED

The field of inquiry for the treatment of the poor, the sick, and the physically and mentally handicapped is certainly wide.[3] It comprehends the local organization of relief of paupers (including the nature and extent of outdoor and indoor relief, the auctioning of paupers, the role of institutions, and private as well as public involvement), its financial basis, the detailed history of individual institutions (almshouses, workhouses, hospitals, and so on) and of charities and their administrative organization, and local attitudes towards the unfortunate (embracing religious, humanitarian, political, and economic outlooks).[4] It could involve the identification and socio-political

---

[1] Michael B. Katz, *Poverty and Policy in American History* (1983), 57, 90.

[2] Glenn C. Altschuler and Jan B. Salzgaber, "Clearinghouse for paupers," *JSH*, 17 (1983–4), 573.

[3] Cf. Merle Curti, "The history of American philanthropy as a field of research," *AHR*, 62 (1957).

[4] See, e.g., Priscilla F. Clement, *Welfare and the Poor in the Nineteenth-Century City: Philadelphia, 1800–1854* (1985). For philanthropy as "social control," see also works cited in Glenn C. Altschuler and Jan M. Salzgaber, "The limits of responsibility," *JSH*, 22 (1988), 532–3; Marvin E. Gettelman, "Philanthropy as social control in late nineteenth-century America," *Societas*, 5 (1975); Walter S. Trattner (ed.), *Social Welfare or Social Control?* (1983); Clarke A. Chambers, "Towards a redefinition of welfare history," *JAH*, 73 (1980), 419n.

analysis of those groups interested in promoting, supporting, and carrying out welfare activities, and their relation to local social and political elites.[5] The role of women and those of particular religious groups may be included here. Similar analysis can be applied to the social, economic, and demographic characteristics of paupers. Other topics include the relationship of poverty, physical and mental handicap, and ill-health to urbanization, industrialization, seasonal work, child and female labor, changes in the role of the family, economic (including agricultural) depression, production for the market and the spread of wage labor, immigration, and the Civil War and emancipation. The particular treatment of pauper children, the widowed, the aged, the able-bodied, the lunatic, the feeble-minded, the blind, the deaf, the dumb, the vagrant, the members of racial and ethnic minorities,[6] the immigrant, the debtor, and so on are worthwhile subjects for research. Also pertinent are variations between local urban and rural communities and different parts of large cities. Again, the typicality or otherwise of periodic dependency in working-class life and the characteristics of the recipients of long- as opposed to short-term relief can be looked into.[7] The study of the nature of institutions for the poor, the ill, and the handicapped can embrace daily routines, admission policies, the employment of inmates, profit making, discipline, finance, efficiency, and the like – for apparently similar institutions varied greatly.[8] For hospitals and institutions for the handicapped, the nature and effectiveness of medical treatment is another subject for inquiry. More complex questions involve the extent to which poverty was alleviated, and medical

---

[5] See sources and methods discussed ch. 2; and also, e.g., Kenneth L. Kusner, "The function of organized charity in the Progressive Era," *JAH*, 60 (1973); Dorothy G. Becker, "The visitor to the New York poor, 1843–1920," *Social Service Rev.*, 35 (1961).

[6] See, e.g., Howard N. Rabinowitz, "From exclusion to segregation," *Social Service Rev.*, 48 (1974).

[7] Cf. Joan U. Hannon, "Poverty in the antebellum Northeast: the view from the New York state's poor relief rolls," *JEH*, 44 (1984).

[8] Cf. Susan Tiffin, *In Whose Best Interest?* (1982), 66–7.

aspects of welfare. Difficulty arises, for instance, in dealing with contemporary categorization of idiocy, feeble-mindedness, insanity, and lunacy, and in the identification of particular diseases and causes of death.

The assessment of the living standards of those at the lowest economic levels of local societies can be undertaken using the sources described elsewhere,[9] together with those relating to housing conditions dealt with in the next section. Assessing the extent to which "poverty" existed or was alleviated is more difficult, since it involves a definition of what poverty was at a particular time, and the determination of a "poverty line." Methods used by historians in such tasks have often involved the use of known nineteenth-century working-class budgets,[10] the construction of model family budgets based on evidence of actual expenditure, or the assessment of income needed for goods and services, and the comparison with wages. These methods are fraught with difficulties and the problem may well be insoluble. Certainly the complications of family incomes as opposed to merely fathers' earnings need to be considered, as well as the likelihood of cyclical or seasonal unemployment, and poverty related to the family life-cycle. The subject is too complicated for further discussion here, but those contemplating investigations of this sort should familiarize themselves with the literature,[11] and also consider the more easily undertaken, and perhaps more plausible, assessment of "relative" levels of working-class living conditions at various times. The secondary literature on the treatment of the poor and handicapped is very

---

[9] Pp. 337–51, 355–79, 395–6.

[10] For refs. to budget samples in reps. U.S. and state bureaus of labor, etc., see Jeffrey G. Williamson, "Consumer behavior in the nineteenth century," *Explorations in Economic Hist.*, 2nd ser., 4 (1967), app. A, 125–30. Carroll D. Wright's studies incl. those in ARs Massachusetts Bureau of Statistics (6th, 1875); U.S. Commissioner of Labor (6th, 7th, 1890, 1891).

[11] E.g., John F. McClymer, "The historian and the poverty line," *HM*, 18 (1985); Michael B. Haines, "Poverty, economic stress and the family in a late nineteenth-century American city," in Hershberg, *Philadelphia* (and see ibid., 233–5); Joan U. Hannon, "The generosity of antebellum poor relief," *JEH*, 44 (1984).

extensive.[12] Federal and state censuses may seem an obvious source of information on the poor and handicapped, and they certainly provide many statistics. The published volumes for the federal censuses of 1830 and 1840 present statistics of deaf and dumb (in age groups) and blind, all by race, for counties, towns, townships, and other minor divisions. In 1840 numbers of "insane and idiotic," by race, and whether maintained at public or private charge, are also given.[13] The 1850 census provides such details at national and state levels only, but does give for thirty-four towns the numbers of paupers supported during the year and the cost of their upkeep.[14] For 1860 the only local details are for hospitals and other institutions for the blind, deaf and dumb, and insane.[15] The 1870 volumes contain nothing below the state level, but a whole volume for the 1880 census is devoted to "the defective, dependent and delinquent classes." Local data include statistics by counties of the mentally handicapped, the blind, and for cities of 50,000 or more, of the insane, blind, deaf and dumb – all by race, sex, and nativity.[16] There is similar and additional information for specific institutions for the blind, deaf and dumb,[17] and the mentally handi-

---

[12] *HG*, 481–8; Gerald N. Grob, *American Social History before 1860* (1970); Robert H. Bremner, *American Social History Since 1860* (1971); Benjamin J. Klebaner, *Public Poor Relief in America, 1790–1860*, pt. III (1976) (lists works on relief in particular states); ABC-Clio, *Social Reform and Reaction in America: An Annotated Bibliography* (1984). See also Russell Sage Foundation, *Rep. Princeton Conference on the History of Philanthropy* (1956), bibl.; Roy Lubove, *The Professional Altruist* (1965), bibl.; Robert H. Bremner, *From the Depths* (1950), bibl. and notes; James Leiby, *A History of Social Welfare and Social Work in the United States* (1978), refs. and guide to the literature (366–7, for works on particular states); Michael B. Katz, *In the Shadow of the Poorhouse* (1986), 293–4; Sophonisba P. Breckinridge, *Public Welfare Administration in the United States* (1938 edn.); Robert H. Bremner *et al.* (eds.), *Children and Youth in America*, vols. 1, 2 (1970–4). Henry M. Hurd (ed.), *The Institutional Care of the Insane in the United States and Canada* (4 vols., 1916–17) is useful on individual states and institutions. For hospitals, see citations in next section; Leonard K. Heaton, *New England Hospitals, 1790–1833* (1957), 243–4: histories of individual hospitals.

[13] 1830, vol. I, "Aggregate Amount" tables; 1840, vol. I.

[14] Compendium, *Statistical View* . . . (Dubester (1950), no. 33), table CLXXII.

[15] Vol. I, pp. liv–cvii. See also 1860, Preliminary Rep. (Dubester (1950), no. 41), 33, 41–5, 49.

[16] Vol. XXI, tables III, IV, XXXV, XXXVI, LXVI, LXVII, LXXXV.

[17] Ibid., tables LXIX, LXXXI, LXXXVII, CI, CII. See also Compendium, tables CL, CLI.

capped.[18] The report on "Social Statistics of Cities" in the 1880 census includes information on charitable and healing institutions.[19] The 1890 census has a volume devoted to "crime, pauperism, and benevolence," carrying data at county level on institutionalized paupers (and on counties and towns without almshouses),[20] as well as on inmates of benevolent institutions (by race, sex, nativity, and parental nativity).[21] It also has a volume on "the insane, feeble-minded, deaf and dumb, and blind" giving numbers in those categories by counties,[22] and (with more detailed information) by cities of 50,000 and over, and for individual institutions.[23]

More detailed information is available in the unpublished census schedules. In the population schedules for 1830 and 1840 numbers of handicapped persons were collected from families and from 1850 they were named. In 1850 and 1860 data on individual paupers in families were also collected, as well as on paupers and handicapped in institutions. Questions on poverty were dropped from the 1870 population census. Social statistics schedules for 1850 through 1870 provide, for counties and subdivisions, details of poor-relief taxes, numbers (but not names) of foreign and native paupers supported, and the cost, derived from official records and the records of institutions.[24]

For 1880 supplemental schedules "for the defective, dependent, and delinquent classes" provide names of "idiots," "deaf-mutes," and "blind," and details of their afflictions, as well as data on "homeless children" in institutions and on "paupers and indigent inhabitants in institutions ... or boarded at public expence in private houses," with an indication of the cause of their misfortune. Statistical data on institutions are also given. Persons named in these schedules

[18] Vol. XXI, tables VI, XXV–XXX, XXXVIII, XXXIX, LIV. See also Compendium, tables CXLVI–CXLVIII.
[19] Vols. XVIII, XIX.
[20] Vol. III, pt. 2, tables 202–4, and pp. 697–9.
[21] Ibid., table 282.
[22] Vol. II, tables 152, 154, 173, 190, 224.
[23] Ibid., tables 153, 174–6, 191–2, 200, 225, 246.
[24] See Carmen R. Delle Donne, *Federal Census Schedules, 1850–80* (RIP 67, 1973), 19–20. The 1870 population schedules did not include pauper data.

are cross-referenced to their entry in the population schedules, permitting identification with particular families.[25] The Census Office administrative records (RG 29) include for 1890–1 lists of institutions for the poor, handicapped, and sick.[26]

Some state census records,[27] like those for 1865, 1885, and 1895 for Minnesota, and those for New York for 1825, 1835, 1845, 1865, and 1875, also contain data on handicapped persons.[28]

Despite the availability of all this published and unpublished census material, it must be admitted that many of the figures, particularly before 1880, are of very dubious validity.[29] Aside from the fact that "glaring and remarkable errors"[30] could result in the published volumes from inefficient compilation of statistics from the manuscript returns and from printing errors, incorrect information was often collected in the first place, especially from family heads. The American Economic Association in 1899 cast considerable doubt on the accuracy of the figures for outdoor paupers in the 1880 federal census and, indeed, on census statistics of poverty and disablement generally throughout the nineteenth century.[31] Following the 1890 census it was admitted that "it was impossible to obtain the statistics of [outdoor] pauperism."[32] This is why, in the 1900 census, coverage was restricted to the institutionalized poor. Again comparability between one census and another is difficult because of the changing definitions used for various categories.[33] Thus, while the historian must consider census

[25] RIP 67, 20–1. For location of social statistics schedules, 1850–70 and of supplemental schedules, 1880, see ibid., app.; Source, 108–9. For an example, see Katz, Poverty and Policy, 146–7.
[26] GNA, 466.
[27] See Dubester (1948), for details.
[28] Information from Dallas R. Lindgren, Minnesota Hist. Soc.; Marilyn Douglas and Melinda Yates, New York State Census Records, 1790–1925 (1981), 48–9.
[29] Katz, Poverty and Policy, 134–42; Albert Deutsh, "The first U.S. census of the insane and its use as pro-slavery propaganda," BHM, 15 (1944); Margo J. Anderson, The American Census: A Social History (1988), 28–9.
[30] Memorial Am. Statistical Assoc., 1844: SD 5 (28–2), ser. 449, pp. 9–17.
[31] The Federal Census: Critical Essays, Am. Economic Assoc. Publics., NS 2 (1899), 184–203. Cf. Amos G. Warner, American Charities (1894), 162.
[32] Charles R. Henderson, "Outdoor relief," Procs. National Conference of Charities and Corrections (1894), 110.
[33] See, e.g., Harry Best, Blindness and the Blind in the United States (1934), 125–6.

evidence, it should be used with considerable caution. The safest evidence is that for institutions.

Aside from the censuses, federal records relating to welfare matters are sparse. Most important, for the South, are the records of the Freedmen's Bureau described in detail in chapters 3 and 10. Later in the century an interest in the housing conditions of large cities, particularly immigrant centers, resulted in federal publications noted later in this chapter. Some of these contain information on aspects of poverty other than housing conditions. The *Report of the Immigration Commission* (1910–11) includes information on immigrants as charity seekers in 1908–9 in forty-three cities.[34] Records of debates in the two Houses may contain data relating to federal aid for asylums for the handicapped.[35] Records relating to federal institutions for the handicapped are in the Department of the Interior records (RG 48).[36]

Since the poor and handicapped were generally a state responsibility, state records are a more fruitful source. The following discussion stresses published documents, but the possible existence of related unpublished archives should be checked from catalogs of state records. State constitutions and laws provide the framework for public action at both state and local levels including the public regulation and support of private charity.[37] The Acts and Statutes of state legislatures and the records of debates and decisions in their journals or minutes are, therefore, prime sources. The existence of state legislation covering public welfare is unlikely, however, to result in community historians merely reproducing the same tale for place after place. The law often allowed scope for local variations, while local administrations sometimes did not conform with the law either in letter or spirit. Moreover, laws specific to certain counties, townships, and municipalities

[34] Vols. 34, 35: SD 665 (61–3), ser. 5868.
[35] For examples, see Breckinridge, *Public Welfare Administration*, 172–84.
[36] *Records of the Office of the Secretary of the Interior, 1833–1964* (NA, NNF–48, T/S, 1984), pt. I, 85–106; *GNA*, 365; William R. Crawford, "Sociological research in the National Archives," *Am. Sociological Rev.*, 6 (1941), 212.
[37] See, e.g., James Leiby, "State welfare administration in California, 1879–1929," *Pacific Hist. Rev.*, 41 (1972), 169–70.

were often passed.[38] Again laws and statutes may contain much detail on the treatment of individual paupers in particular counties.[39] State legislation also established state institutions for the poor and handicapped, and sometimes granted charters for private charitable societies and institutions. During the Civil War special legislation for aiding veterans and their families was sometimes passed.[40]

The published law reports of the various states are also valuable,[41] not only for the interpretation of the law, but, since they provide details of individual cases in particular localities, they also illustrate the treatment of individuals and the working of the poor law. Much litigation records differences between townships or counties over settlement and relief of the transient poor.[42] Recent compilations of the law may refer to important cases.[43]

Many state documents relate to the topics discussed in this section. States not infrequently commissioned special reports on aspects of welfare which often contain local material. For example, New York state published special reports on public poor relief in 1824, 1857, and 1874–5.[44] In Massachusetts the Quincy report on poor law matters (1821) provides much detail on conditions in particular places.[45] Thomas R. Hazard's report on relief of the insane and poor in individual towns in Rhode Island in 1850 (1851) is extremely detailed,[46] while a

---

[38] E.g., Benjamin J. Klebaner, "Employment of paupers in Philadelphia's almshouse before 1861," *Pennsylvania Hist.*, 24 (1957), 143; Benjamin J. Klebaner, "Some aspects of North Carolina public poor relief, 1760–1860," *North Carolina Hist. Rev.*, 31 (1954), 479–80, 486.

[39] E.g., Emil McK. Sunley, *The Kentucky Poor Law, 1792–1936* (1942), 8.

[40] William F. Zornow, "State aid for indigent soldiers and their families in Florida, 1861–1865," *Florida Hist. Q.*, 34 (1956).

[41] See p. 26.

[42] Cf. Martha Branscombe, *The Courts and the Poor Laws in New York State, 1784–1943* (1943).

[43] See, e.g., Grace A. Browning, *The Development of Poor Law Legislation in Kansas* (1935), app. II.

[44] *New York Senate Jnl.*, 1824 (repr. in *The Almshouse Experience: Collected Reports* (Arno Press, 1971)). Cf. Hannon, "The generosity of antebellum poor relief," 811–16; Katz, *Poverty and Policy*, ch. 2, pt. II.

[45] *Rep. Massachusetts General Court Committee on Pauper Laws* (1821).

[46] See Margaret Creech, *Three Centuries of Poor Relief Legislation* (1936), 196–204.

Louisiana report of 1857 on charitable institutions provides information on a score of homes for children.[47]

Dorothea L. Dix was the author of a number of detailed submissions, published as memorials to various state legislatures as official state documents.[48] These represent very detailed and illuminating reports on individual jails and poorhouses in various counties and cities. They have particular relevance for the relief and treatment of the insane poor, but are also mines of information on the poor generally. As well as these, many other reports by private institutions concerned with the poor and handicapped were published as state documents.

More generally important are regular periodic returns of local government officers to state legislatures. In many states the annual reports of state establishments (hospitals, almshouses, blind institutions, and so on), which are discussed below, were published as state documents. Where, as in New York state, there were emigration commissioners, their annual reports provide information on poor immigrants, including children. Especially important are the periodic reports of county or town overseers of the poor, which are dealt with below. Often such reports are unpublished and to be found in state as well as local archives. Frequently, abstracts of them are published in annual state documents of one kind or another.[49] Not all state legislatures, however, always required such reports to be returned, nor when requested did all counties submit returns.

By the later nineteenth century many states had set up state boards of charities and correction (the nomenclature varied) whose main function was to advise on public charities and inspect public institutions. Some had wider powers (like responsibility for the enforcement of legislation and for managing certain institutions) and some were closely associated with

[47] Repr. Bremner, *Children and Youth*, vol. 1, 604–6.
[48] For a list, see Helen E. Marshall, *Dorothea Dix* (1937), 272–3.
[49] E.g., Massachusetts, Secretary of the Commonwealth, *Abstract of the Returns of the Overseers of the Poor*.

private charities.[50] Their interests embraced poor-houses, general poor relief, hospitals for the insane, and, since they were also concerned with "correction," reformatories and prisons. Their reports, annual or biennial, are mines of information on local matters and include reports on the extent and nature of local poverty, on county institutions and charities, local systems of indoor and outdoor relief, policy changes, and funding – often with statistical data, and other local material. Details were not, however, always accurate.[51]

Where they exist the unpublished archives of the state boards may provide intimate detail on individual paupers. In New York, for instance, local almshouses sent annual schedules of examinations of paupers to the state board.[52] The records, particularly the annual reports, of other state boards and officials may also contain information on welfare locally. The annual messages of state governors, for instance, may give details of the work of state institutions in the context of general political circumstances. The reports of state bureaus of labor and statistics[53] may also embrace reports and data on individual institutions and provide information on private associations and charities: the report of the California Bureau of Labor Statistics for 1891–2, for example, gives a detailed account of women's organizations of this kind in the state. Useful, too, may be the reports of state boards of health, dealt with fully in the next section. A report of the Maryland Board of Health for 1876–7 carries extremely detailed reports on each county almshouse as well as on county jails, state hospitals, institutions for the handicapped, reformatories, and prisons. In California, in the absence of a board of charities, the state board of health and other state agencies collectively covered welfare matters in their reports.[54] Grants and subsidies to

---

[50] See William R. Brock, *Investigation and Responsibility* (1984), ch. 4, for the variety of powers and interests of various boards.

[51] Warner, *American Charities*, 164.

[52] Katz, *Poverty and Policy*, 95–7.

[53] See pp. 341, 345, 368; and *3rd Special Rep. U.S. Commissioner of Labor*, cited fully, p. 341n; U.S. Dept. of Labor, *Index of All Reps . . . by Bureaus of Labor Statistics . . . to 1902* (1902) (not in US Serial Set).

[54] Frances T. Cahn and Barry Valeska, *Welfare Activities of Federal, State, and Local Government in California, 1850–1934* (1936).

charities and other institutions, and funds spent on state institutions, may be traceable in the financial records of states. Petitions to state legislatures, for the extension of outdoor relief, the establishment of asylums, and so on, may also exist.

At the local level the records of the ruling bodies of counties, New England towns, municipalities, and sometimes townships, and those of officials and bodies entrusted with the responsibility for the poor and the handicapped, are often rich sources for all aspects of local welfare. Thus the minutes, proceedings, or journals of the meetings of county supervisors or commissioners, county courts, selectmen, city councils, boards of aldermen, county police boards – or whatever was the ruling body – may contain much information, sometimes on individual cases, as may the minutes of town meetings. Such records can shed light on attitudes to poverty and its extent and nature, methods of relief, individual institutions, and on relations with private charities and religious institutions. There may be local financial accounts specific to expenditure on poor relief, hospitals, and asylums, and records of poor taxes. Annual reports and addresses of mayors, published in the larger cities, often contain references to poor relief and various welfare institutions.

Crucial for community study are the periodic reports (often called returns or accounts), usually unpublished,[55] made to local or state governments by appointed or elected bodies or officials directly responsible for the relief of the poor (called variously guardians, overseers, commissioners, wardens, trustees, directors, superintendents, departments of poor relief, or poor committees – but for convenience here referred to as overseers of the poor). These provide much intimate detail of local organization, treatment, practices, and attitudes, with statistics of numbers relieved in various ways and accounts of money expended. Those for Monroe county, WV, for instance, show the expenditure on indigents, giving names of individuals, date of expenditure, and comments on

[55] But see above for abstracts publ. in state docs.

each case.[56] Similar reports were submitted by superintendents of local public almshouses, county homes, poorfarms, hospitals, and institutions of various kinds.

Other records of the overseers include their minutes, which illuminate the day-to-day working of the system and its costs, the treatment of individual paupers, placement of pauper children, and so on;[57] registers or rolls of relief recipients, or "pauper lists," which again give details of support given to individuals;[58] correspondence; petitions about policy or particular cases; and indentures of the apprenticeship of pauper children.[59] There may also be the financial accounts of the overseers, which provide evidence on all sorts of matters, including the working of poorfarms, the food and supplies purchased for almshouses, and so on.[60] Vendue contracts for those who bid to support individual paupers and handicapped persons, and bonds of former slave owners, guaranteeing assistance for their emancipated slaves, may also exist.[61]

For larger cities, where there were numerous poor and handicapped, more extensive, often published, records will exist. There may be special reports, like that of the Philadelphia poor guardians in 1827 on conditions in some other large cities,[62] and a Boston report on the city's institutions in 1892.[63] Departments of public charities and correction, as in New York City, or of poor relief, as in Atlanta, GA and Richmond, VA, are likely to have left much more extensive records than county poor overseers: annual reports of both these bodies were published in city documents.[64] In such cities, too, public

---

[56] WPA, HRS, *Inventory of the County Archives of West Virginia, No. 31, Monroe County (Union)* (1938), 38.

[57] See, e.g., Susan Grigg, *The Dependent Poor of Newburyport* (1984), 54–8.

[58] These may form the basis of reps. to local and state governments.

[59] Lawrence W. Towner, "The indentures of Boston's poor apprentices, 1737–1805," Colonial Soc. Massachusetts, *Publics.*, 93, Trans. 1956–63, 435–68.

[60] Altschuler and Salzgaber, "Clearing house for paupers," 579, 597n; Grigg, *Dependent Poor*, 116–17n.

[61] Benjamin J. Klebaner, "Pauper auctions," *Essex Institute Hist. Colls.*, 91 (1955), 200; Merle Curti *et al.*, *Making of an American Community* (1959), 285; Klebaner, "Some aspects of North Carolina public poor relief," 490–1.

[62] Repr. in *The Almshouse Experience*.

[63] *Rep. Special Committee . . . to Inspect the Public Institutions* (1892).

[64] David M. Schneider, *History of Public Welfare in New York State* (1938), 380n; Rabinowitz, "From exclusion to segregation," 350n, 353n.

works schemes employing the poor may be documented in the records of the city departments responsible.[65] Unpublished correspondence and other records of city clerks' departments and those of committees may also reveal actions and attitudes on welfare matters.

Other local government records include details of removal cases which are found in petitions to sheriffs, in constables' records, and in the records of county courts, where removal orders were issued. Probate court records can be searched for charitable bequests in wills,[66] and for the treatment of orphans, lunatics, and others whose care came under the court's jurisdiction. Bonds, reports, and accounts provide details of periods of guardianship.[67]

Much philanthropic work was carried out by societies and organizations that were private, though some of these acquired quasi-public status through the receipt of aid from state governments. The records of such organizations (associations for preventing poverty, improving the condition of the poor, relieving widows, pregnant women and children, hospital societies, ethnic organizations, emigrants' aid societies, citizens' associations, temperance societies,[68] provident associations, children's aid societies, and religious societies of many kinds – see ch. 6)[69] are, therefore, likely to provide evidence for the study of welfare and attitudes to the poor and the handicapped, especially in the larger towns where such organizations were active. Most were city- or state-wide and of varying degrees of permanence. In times of crisis, short-term emergency societies were often created and record of their activities may exist.[70]

Many of the long-standing societies published annual

[65] Benjamin J. Klebaner, "Poor relief and public works during the depression of 1857," *Historian*, 22 (1960), 273–4.
[66] Merle Curti, "Tradition and innovation in American philanthropy," *Procs. Am. Phil. Soc.*, 105 (1961), 147–8. Significant bequests may be noted in older local histories, directories, etc.
[67] Jones, 145–6.
[68] E.g., Earl Taylor and Roberta Songhi, *Massachusetts Temperance Societies' Publications* (1984).
[69] Cf. John T. Guertler (ed.), *The Records of Baltimore's Private Organizations* (1981).
[70] Katz, *Shadow of the Poorhouse*, 59.

reports, sometimes as pamphlets, and these may have been reproduced or summarized in local newspapers. The reports vary in content, some being perfunctory and limited to financial data and unusual events. Others were very full, providing evidence on goals and methods and local views,[71] as well as accounts of activities and personnel. Some even give detailed accounts of actual welfare cases. The minutes of managing, subsidiary, and special committees provide much the same sort of evidence, but often more fully, and shed light on day-to-day activities, salaries and duties of officials, and so forth. Society charters, articles of association, constitutions, and rules provide some indication of aims and attitudes, and qualifications for membership.[72] Lists of officers, directors, or members, if extant, are important for determining the types of persons involved in philanthropic activity.[73] Financial records can give evidence on the scale of activity and its nature, while correspondence may yield useful detail. The correspondence of the New York Association for Improving the Condition of the Poor contains reports on individual cases from its visitors.[74] Case records generally represent rich evidence of the day-to-day work of the societies, and the attitudes of their workers and clients.[75] Societies also published many pamphlets: some of these contain accounts of societies' origins. Many illustrate attitudes and activities and name the voluntary personnel involved. Some represent substantial investigations of local conditions: the New York State Temperance Society, for instance, published in 1834 a report on county poorhouses and jails in the state and in some counties in other states.[76]

To the records of societies specializing in particular aspects of welfare may be added those of "Charity Organization Societies" (such as the New York Charity Organization Society, the San Francisco Associated Charities, and the

---

[71] Tiffin, *In Whose Best Interest?*, 297; Roy Lubove, "The New York Association for Improving the Condition of the Poor," *New York Hist. Q.*, 43 (1959).

[72] Becker, "The visitor to the New York City poor," 382–4, 386–8.

[73] Cf. Blanche D. Coll, "The Baltimore Society for the Prevention of Pauperism, 1820–1822," *AHR*, 61 (1955–6).

[74] Becker, "The visitor to the New York City poor," 391–2.

[75] Katz, *Shadow of the Poorhouse*, 299n, 304n.

[76] Ibid., 296n.

Associated Charities of Cincinnatti) which emerged in the later nineteenth century to provide an integrated approach to local welfare needs by encouraging the cooperation of "issue-specific" charities. Where they exist, their reports and publications are valuable sources.[77]

Other sources are the published proceedings of state conferences of charities and correction and those (and other publications) of the Conference of Boards of Public Charities (later called the National Conference of Charities and Correction). The annual proceedings of the National Conference of Charities and Correction (1874–1917)[78] are mines of information on local matters, including evidence on individual institutions, systems of outdoor relief, charitable work, treatment of the mentally handicapped, juvenile delinquency, and so on. They carry a useful section on "Reports from States" and a list of state institutions.

The charitable activities of churches and religious organizations can be investigated though the sources noted in chapter 6,[79] particularly denominational archives, journals, reports of religious societies and religiously run institutions, biographies, church handbooks, religious and ethnic newspapers, and the records of city missions and missionary societies. The American Home Missionary Society, for instance, did much work among urban immigrants, especially after 1883,[80] and many city missions were run by churches.[81] Charity sermons, published as pamphlets and reported in newspapers and periodicals, provide clues as to local attitudes towards poverty.

---

[77] See, e.g., Alvin B. Kogut, "The negro and the charity organization in the Progressive Era," *Social Service Rev.*, 44 (1970).

[78] Titled: *Conference of Charities* (1874–9), *Conference of Charities and Correction* (1880–3), *National Conference of Charities and Correction* (1884–1917). An index was publ. 1906.

[79] And see John O'Grady, *Catholic Charities in the United States* (1930, repr. 1971), bibl.; Timothy L. Smith, *Revivalism and Social Reform in Mid-Nineteenth Century America* (1957), ch. XI; Evangeline Thomas (ed.), *Women Religious History Sources* (1983); Stella O'Connor, "The Charity Hospital at New Orleans," *Louisiana Hist. Q.*, 21 (1948), 100.

[80] See pp. 284, 488.

[81] Paul Boyer, *Urban Masses and Moral Order in America, 1820–1920* (1978), 134. Cf. Nathan I. Higgins, *Protestants against Poverty* (1971).

Another significant body of sources exists in the records of private and public institutions: almshouses, workhouses, asylums, foundlings' homes, houses of refuge, orphanages, reform schools, hospitals, and so on. Their annual reports may survive as original records locally or in state archives, reported or abstracted in state documents,[82] or embedded in the annual reports of the local government agencies or of the private or religious societies or denominations responsible for them. For instance, Episcopal Church hospital reports were printed annually in the Convocation journal of the Missouri District of Oklahoma and Indian Territory (1895–1908). Such reports chart the affairs of the institution in varying degrees of detail, providing information at least on all important events and developments, and usually giving numbers of inmates and staff details. Annual reports of institutions for the poor and handicapped describe daily routines, provide descriptions of inmates and note their treatment. Reports of child-care institutions indicate current attitudes and perceived causes of poverty and delinquency.[83]

Fuller details of administration and its problems may be revealed in the minutes of the meetings of committees of managers, supervisors, directors, commissioners, and the like, responsible for the running of institutions. In large establishments minutes of sub-committees may exist: at Philadelphia Almshouse these included a board of physicians, a hospital committee, and a committee on manufacturing. Auditors' accounts, published or unpublished, are another informative source.[84]

More intimate data will be manifested in the working records of institutions. These include the correspondence of officers, daily statistical and categorical lists of inmates, schedules of regulations, punishment records, and registers of admission and discharge (giving such data for inmates as sex, age, birthplace, residence, ethnicity, education, literacy,

---

[82] See *NUCMC*; *Source*, 321–4.
[83] David J. Rothman, *The Discovery of the Asylum* (1971), 305, 307, 309; Bremner, *Children and Youth*, vol. 1, 747–50 for an example.
[84] Clement, *Welfare and the Poor*, 186n, 213.

marital status, occupation, state of health, nature of handicap, cause of poverty or handicap, personal habits, names of children or parents).[85] Orphanages may have matrons' and masters' reports and files on inmates containing details of residential and parental background and perhaps of eventual discharge or apprenticeship. Hospital registers, admission ledgers, case record books, and clinical records provide not only information on individual inmates and their treatment but on the characteristics and incidence of particular maladies.[86] Discharge and death records (giving cause) were also kept by some hospitals. Financial accounts (day books, ledgers, payrolls, etc.) show details of income and expenditure on food, clothing, furniture, buildings, medical care, salaries, and so on. When manufacturing was carried on by inmates there may be separate financial accounts for that activity as well as related material. Almshouse registers and other records may provide details of indenturing and placement of pauper children. Records of the examination of paupers, to establish whether they were legal residents, give interesting biographical information on the poor. Some institutions kept "books of daily occurrences."[87]

Newspapers and the periodical press form another important source. In the editorials, news columns, and correspondence of newspapers is evidence on attitudes towards relief, provision for the handicapped and sick, views on methods, advice to the unemployed, data on disputes and developments, and factual information on institutions and societies, and on public relief. Sometimes meetings of boards of supervisors were reported, and the annual reports of poor law officers, private charities, hospitals, and institutions of various kinds were published. Some papers periodically reported almshouse admission or residential figures and numbers on

---

[85] Roy C. Turnbaugh, Jr., *A Guide to the County Records in the Illinois Regional Archives* (1983), 311, 313, 316; Katz, *Poverty and Policy*, ch. 2, pt. 1, and for examples, 70–1, 74–5, 118.

[86] John H. Warner, "Power, conflict, and identity in mid-nineteenth-century American medicine," *JAH*, 73 (1987).

[87] See, e.g., Creech, *Three Centuries of Poor Relief*, 18; Clement, *Welfare and the Poor*, 212–14; Grigg, *Dependent Poor*, 59–66; Klebaner, "Employment of paupers," 146.

outdoor relief. In most Western states the reports and accounts of county poor officials are found only in the newspapers.[88]

Reports on individual institutions may sometimes be found in national publications. *Niles' Weekly Register*, for instance, in 1827 published a report on the poorhouses of Baltimore, Boston, New York, and Providence.[89] *Harper's Magazine* (vol. 64, 1882) carried an article on the Wilson Industrial School and Mission in New York City. The activities of various religious and ethnic philanthropic societies may well be documented in newspapers and periodicals associated with such groups. Missionary magazines and denominational newspapers in particular carry accounts of humanitarian projects.[90]

The files of specialist journals are also worth exploring. Philanthropic journals dating from the last part of the century are useful for welfare, child labor, crime and its treatment, and social agencies. They include *Lend-A-Hand* (1886–97), associated with the Boston area, the *Kingdom* (1896–1906; Western coastal states), and the *Commons* (1896–1905; Chicago). The Charity Organization Society of New York published the *Charities Review* (1891–1901: merged in 1901 with *Charities*, 1897–1905, another useful journal).[91] Another such journal was the *Monthly Register of the Philanthropic Society for Organizing Charitable Relief and Repressing Mendicants* (1897–1900). Medical journals, too, may be useful (see next section). The *American Journal of Insanity* (from 1894), for instance, periodically published abstracts of reports from individual asylums,[92] and its volumes are full of information on particular institutions as well as on conventions. Local medical periodicals should also be searched. The *Buffalo Medical Journal*, for instance, has detailed reports on the Erie County Poorhouse in

---

[88] Warner, *American Charities*, 164.
[89] Repr. Bremner, *Children and Youth*, vol. 1, 639–42.
[90] Smith, *Revivalism and Social Reform*, 242–3; and see pp. 282–3.
[91] *Charities* was later the *Survey*. See also Leiby, *History of Social Welfare*, 120; Leiby, "State welfare administration," 174n.
[92] Vols. 18–22 (1862–6).

1856 and 1875,[93] and the *New England Journal of Medicine and Surgery* frequently reported on individual hospitals.

In addition to the sources already discussed there are many other published sources of information. Local directories and guide books may contain factual information on charities and institutions, and especially in the large cities there may be special directories of charities. There is, too, much contemporary literature in the form of books and pamphlets, detailed guidance to which cannot be supplied here:[94] local libraries should be searched. Pamphlet literature varies from controversial and polemical tracts to factual accounts of the origin, organization, and purpose of local charities, societies, and institutions, with information on their sponsors, officers, members, and activities.[95] Among collections of such pamphlets may be found annual reports and accounts of less-well-known and ephemeral societies.

Old county and city histories frequently provide factual information on welfare matters, and these and older institutional histories may contain data no longer available elsewhere, and sometimes give insight into particular outlooks on social problems. Thus Charles Lawrence's *History of the Philadelphia Almshouses and Hospitals* ... (1905) and Thomas G. Norton's *History of the Pennsylvania Hospital, 1751–1895* (1895) include extracts from many original documents, correspondence, and statistics. Centenary celebrations often gave rise to such publications. Histories of missions, religious orders, and churches, and biographies of religious leaders may contain evidence on hospitals, asylums, and other institutions with which they were associated. Other contemporary literature of possible use includes the writings of travelers. E. S. Abdy, for instance, in his *Journal of a Residence and Tour in the United States of North America* (3 vols., 1835, repr. 1969), mentions the treatment of the poor, houses of refuge, asylums for the handicapped, prisons, and so forth.

[93] Katz, *Poverty and Policy*, 61–8.
[94] For the former Russell Sage Library and other significant collections, see Clarke A. Chambers, "Archives of social welfare," *Encyclopedia of Social Work* (17th edn., 1977), 82–3.
[95] Cf. *The Jacksonians on the Poor: Collected Pamphlets* (Arno Press, 1971).

The private papers, including diaries, of those involved in social work, social reformers and local politicians, can be very useful sources and should be searched for.[96] The private papers and diaries of A. G. Byers, secretary of the Ohio Board of State Charities (1867–90), are, for instance, full of intimate information on individual institutions.[97] Autobiographies and memoirs of such people, published and unpublished, are also useful. Many settlement workers, for example, wrote memoirs,[98] while reminiscences of others may also exist.[99] The medical notebooks, journals, and case books of hospital physicians, perhaps to be found in personal collections or hospital records, can shed much light on types of malady and medical practice.[100]

The medical and health care of slaves can be studied from plantation and family records (see chs. 3, 5). Doctors' itemized bills, accounts, and ledgers, plantation diaries, ledgers, day books, accounts, correspondence, and prescription books, record the existence of illness among slaves, their medical treatment, and causes of death. Contents of medical chests may also have been listed. Sometimes there are inventories and other records of slave hospitals.[101] Other relevant sources include newspaper advertisements relating to runaways with deformities. Succession (i.e. appraisal) records, filed in county courts, list the physical and mental impairments (as blind, dumb, insane, etc.) as well as the illnesses of slaves (as heart disease, rheumatism).[102]

PUBLIC HEALTH

Until the second half of the century matters of public health – water supply, sanitation, nuisances, epidemics – were

[96] Chambers, "Archives of social welfare," 80–2.
[97] Brock, *Investigation and Responsibility*, 96–7.
[98] See Allen F. Davis, *Spearheads for Reform* (1967), 253.
[99] See, e.g., Bremner, *Childhood and Youth*, vol. 1, 277–8.
[100] See, e.g., Earl D. Bond, *Dr. Kirkbride and His Mental Hospital* (1947); Eaton, *New England Hospitals*, 240.
[101] Todd L. Savitt, *Medicine and Slavery* (1978), 316–21; John Duffy, "Medical practice in the antebellum South," *JSoH*, 25 (1959); Richard H. Shryock, "Medical practice in the old South," *South Atlantic Q.*, 29 (1930), 173–4.
[102] William D. Postell, *The Health of Slaves on Southern Plantations* (1970), 158–63.

primarily the concern of local authorities. Some towns, cities, and counties had boards or commissioners of health from before 1800, though these virtually confined their activities to combating epidemics and dealing with unusually bad nuisances. Many communities, however, had no health boards until as late as 1875. By that date ten states had established state boards of health and by 1900 forty states had. These central boards promoted the development of active local boards of health, though even when these were required by state laws they were not always to be found.[103]

Since public health was so much a local matter and since conditions and public action varied so greatly, there is much scope for community historians to investigate this and the allied topic of slum housing, particularly for the larger cities where the problems were most concentrated. The nature and incidence of local disease patterns, the charting of the course and effect of epidemics, and their relation to mortality statistics,[104] form basic subjects for research. So, too, does the tracing of the development of public health facilities and their effectiveness and the relationship between state and local health authorities.

Particularly interesting for study is the relationship between the social demography of city districts (embracing ethnic, racial, wealth, and occupational classifications) and the incidence of disease and the availability of good water supplies and sanitary and transport facilities. The relationship of these factors to population density is a connected topic.[105] Such investigations will involve linkage of the records and methods outlined in chapters 2 (demography), 7 (local government –

---

[103] For the history of state boards of health, see Brock, *Investigation and Responsibility*, ch. 5.

[104] See pp. 72–4, 82, 94–6. Though notoriously inaccurate and often incomplete, they did improve over time and can be of use for local health matters: see, e.g., Rose A. Cheney, "Seasonal aspects of infant and childhood mortality," *JIH*, 14 (1984); Joseph A. Waring, *A History of Medicine in South Carolina. 1825–1900* (1967), 62–5; Barbara G. Rosenkrantz, *Public Health and the State* (1972), 227–8; Richard A. Meckel, "Immigration, mortality and population growth in Boston, 1840–1880," *JIH*, 15 (1985).

[105] See Clayton R. Koppes and William P. Norris, "Ethnicity, class, and mortality in the industrial city," *JUH*, 11 (1985).

utilities), and 9 (communications) with those on public health and working-class housing conditions considered below.

Since public health was also often a political issue,[106] the use of the types of sources outlined in chapter 7 (politics section) in conjunction with the sources described in this chapter may also be necessary. Another topic of interest may be changing local attitudes to public health action, including the part played by reformist groups and professional associations. Investigation of this may involve looking into the characteristics of both supporters and opposers of reform. Other worthwhile topics, especially for the larger cities, are the characteristics of working-class housing, especially slum and ghetto conditions, and the attempts of government, private enterprise, and philanthropic and cooperative housing associations to provide better shelter.[107] Connected with this is the part played by lodging houses, the significance of housing in the life-cycle, and the impact of immigration from abroad and from elsewhere.[108]

There is a great deal of secondary literature on public health, housing, disease, and allied topics.[109] For medical matters, including epidemics, the National Library of Medicine (formerly the Library of the Surgeon General's Office, the Army Medical Library, and the Armed Forces Medical

[106] Jane M. Russell, "Politics, municipal services and the working class in Atlanta, 1865 to 1890," *Georgia Hist. Q.*, 66 (1982); George Rosen, "Politics and public health in New York City (1838–1842)," *BHM*, 24 (1950).

[107] See works cited John F. Bauman, "Housing the urban poor," *JUH*, 6 (1980); Eugene L. Birch and Deborah S. Gardner, "The seven-percent solution," *JUH*, 7 (1981).

[108] These topics are too broad for detailed treatment here. In addition to sources cited below, building permits, builders' records, building trade publics., tax records, family papers, physical and photographic evidence, and the use of family reconstitution techniques (see pp. 96–7) may be useful. See also Jules Tygiel, "Housing in late nineteenth-century American cities: suggestions for research," *HM*, 12 (1979).

[109] See refs. above, p. 498n; *HG*, 440–2; Prucha, 212 [EE15]; Grob, *American Social History*, esp. 88–95; Bremner, *American Social History*, esp. 74, 98–101; Rosenkrantz, *Public Health*, note on sources; James Ford *et al.*, *Slums and Housing*, vol. 2 (1936, repr. 1971), bibl.; Richard O. Davies, "One-third of a nation," in Jerome Finster (ed.), *The National Archives and Urban Research* (1974), works cited; Charles E. Rosenberg, *The Cholera Years* (1962), bibl.; Suellen M. Hoy and Michael C. Robinson, *Public Works History in the United States: A Guide to the Literature* (1982), for sewers, water supply, parks.

Library) has an enormous collection. Its multi-volume catalogs provide a guide both to recent and contemporary
materials.[110] The *Bulletin of the History of Medicine* and the
Journal of the History of Medicine and Allied Sciences, as well as
the usual journals on social history, carry articles on the history of American medicine.

Turning to primary sources, state archives are very important. The records of state boards of health and of those local
boards, bureaus, commissions, or departments which have
survived (mainly those in larger cities) provide the basic data
on the growth of health services and on the incidence of disease
and state of sanitation. Particularly important for such information are the annual reports of state and municipal boards,
usually published, which also include reports on individual
hospitals and asylums and, in the case of state boards, reports
from local boards and from their own districts. Some were
vehicles for the publication of vital statistics (see ch. 2).

The annual reports of the Massachusetts state board included investigations of such matters as housing, alcoholism,
water supplies, slaughter houses, disease, and density of population, and embraced much statistical data. They shed much
light, too, on local attitudes and political outlooks. Such
records carried reports from local boards of health and detailed
accounts of proposals for legislation, outbreaks of disease, and
so on.[111] The 1879 report of the Illinois board contained a
register of physicians, and that for Wisconsin in 1891 a compendium of state health laws.[112]

The unpublished archives of boards of health, where they
have survived, will provide more detail.[113] Particularly important here are board minutes, correspondence, and other

[110] U.S. Army, *Index Catalogue of the Library of the Surgeon General's Office* (1880–
1961); *Armed Forces Medical Library Catalogue* (1950–4); *National Library of Medicine
Catalogue* (1955–65); *National Library of Medicine Current Catalogue* (1966–). See
also annual bibls. in *BHM*, 1940 through 1966 (vols. 8–40); the *Bibliography of the
History of Medicine* (National Library of Medicine, annually from 1965); periodic
bibls. in *Isis*; *Current List of Medical Literature* (from 1941); Wellcome Historical
Medical Library, London, *Current Work in the History of Medicine* (from 1954);
Quarterly Cumulative Index Medicus (from 1927); and see citations, Prucha, 212–16.
[111] Rosenkrantz, *Public Health*, 225–6.
[112] Brock, *Investigation and Responsibility*, 132, 134.
[113] Ibid., ch. 5, notes the location of some.

working papers (as reports, resolutions, petitions, minutes of committees). The state boards and those of the larger cities published many broadsheets, reports, statistical pamphlets, and miscellaneous papers. The Massachusetts state board, for instance, produced a *Weekly Bulletin* (1883–1903) listing outbreaks of disease. It should be noted that sometimes state boards of health, like that of Massachusetts in 1879, were merged with boards of charity, details of which are given in the previous section. Even before such mergers the records of the boards of charity may be worth searching for public health and housing matters.

The records of state legislatures and the proceedings of city councils include petitions, memorials, proposals, debates, and resolutions on matters of public health. The framework within which boards of health performed and regulations on health matters are found in state laws and city ordinances and byelaws – though it must not be assumed that legislation was always enforced or adhered to.

In times of epidemics, or when pressure groups or others forced attention on sanitary matters, special legislation or regulations might result and sanitary surveys be commissioned by local or state governments or private agencies. The resultant reports often illuminate not only the particular matter at hand, but also the general health and living conditions of communities.[114] Thus in 1849 Boston, New York, and Philadelphia issued special reports on the increase of cholera, and in 1854 New Orleans one on yellow fever. New York state legislature in 1857 published a report on tenement houses in New York and Brooklyn. Most famous are the reports by Griscom in New York City, and Shattuck in Massachusetts.[115]

Additional information on sanitary and domestic conditions in the slum districts of certain cities may be found in city and state reports on immigration, sewerage, and housing, and in the annual reports of city baths' departments and the

---

[114] For publics. of some states, see Hasse, under "public health."
[115] John H. Griscom, *The Sanitary Condition of the Laboring Population of New York . . .* (1845); Lemuel Shattuck, *Report of a General Plan for the Promotion of Public and Personal Health . . .* (1850).

like, and occasionally in those of state bureaus of labor statistics.[116] The New Jersey bureau of labor statistics, for example, examined, in 1888–91, the effects on employees' health of work in pottery, hat-making, and glass blowing.[117]

County records of the certification of medical personnel may suggest the availability of medical services at various times.[118] For Montgomery county, IL, for instance, there are such records for physicians, midwives, accoucheurs, and dentists, from the 1870s.[119] Probate inventories which list items like washstands may possibly be used to indicate the spread of hygienic practices.[120]

Federal records relating to public health are few and not often useful for the community historian. The reports of the Commissioner of Indian Affairs and the records of the Bureau of Indian Affairs contain data on health conditions in Indian Territory.[121] The reports of the Surgeon General of the Army provide estimates of mortality caused by malaria and information on the ravages of other diseases. And a report of 1856 gives details of the physical characteristics of localities where forts were situated relevant to the prevalence of certain diseases, with statistics (mainly for the period 1839–54).[122]

Towards the end of the century several reports of the Commissioner of Labor are relevant. His 7th Special Report, *The Slums of Baltimore, Chicago, New York, and Philadelphia* (1894, repr. 1970), contains data on the physically defective and on the sanitary condition (including sleeping accommodation) of tenement dwellers in those cities.[123] His 8th Special Report,

[116] See p. 368, n. 69 above.
[117] Cited Bremner, *From the Depths*, 283.
[118] For the regulation of medical practice, see Brock, *Investigation and Responsibility*, ch. 5.
[119] Turnbaugh, *Guide to County Records in the Illinois Regional Archives*, 67–8, 71.
[120] Richard L. and Claudia L. Bushman, "The early history of cleanliness in America," *JAH*, 74 (1988), 1,227.
[121] See pp. 234–7; and, e.g., Bernice N. Crockett, "Health conditions in Indian Territory, 1830 to the Civil War," *Chronicles of Oklahoma*, 35 (1957). N.B. Mark V. Barows et al., *Health and Disease of American Indians North of Mexico: A Bibliography, 1800–1969* (1972).
[122] SED 96 (34–1), ser. 827 (see pp. 498–508 for the location of the forts).
[123] HED 257 (53–2), ser. 3228. For conditions in some cities, see rep. on sweated trades (1892), cited p. 364.

The Housing of the Working People (1895),[124] provides much detail on model housing for a number of cities. The 9th annual report of the Commissioner of Labor (1894) presents data by state, county, and city on named building and loan associations and on state legislation on these organizations.[125] The 14th annual report (1899) has evidence on water, gas, and electric light plants under private and municipal ownership.[126] Epidemics were the subject of some federal reports: one of 1875 on the cholera outbreak of 1875 and another of 1878 on the yellow fever epidemic of that year contain much local data.[127]

In the National Archives, RG 90[128] includes the records of the National Board of Health (effective 1879–83), which contain a report on the yellow fever epidemic of 1878 and correspondence with state, county, and municipal boards of health.[129] It also contains the records of the Marine Hospital Service (founded 1798) which became the Public Health Service in the twentieth century. The Marine Hospital Service was concerned mainly with its own hospitals and matters of quarantine relating to shipping. Its records embrace statistics of patients in eleven hospitals and correspondence which may contain local information.[130] Publications of the Public Health and Marine Hospital Service include a series of weekly mortality reports and information on quarantine and the relief of sick sailors. In 1901, for instance, there is a report on plague in San Francisco.[131]

In RG 105 in the National Archives, for the years 1865–8, there are monthly reports of sick and wounded refugees and freedmen from the Freedmen's Bureau Hospital in Atlanta,

124 HED 354 (53–3), ser. 3325.
125 HED 209 (53–2), ser. 3227.
126 HD 713 (56–1), ser. 4004.
127 HED 95 (43–2), ser. 1646; U.S. Board of Experts, *Procs. Board of Experts . . . to Investigate the Yellow Fever Epidemic of 1878 . . .* (New Orleans, 1878): not in US Serial Set.
128 *GNA*, 502–3.
129 Charles Zaid (comp.), *Preliminary Inventory of the Records of the National Board of Health* (PI 141, 1962), 7–8, 11–12.
130 Forrest R. Holdcamper (comp.), *Preliminary Inventory of the Records of the Public Health Service* (NC–34, revised 1966).
131 For details, see *Checklist*, 1,127–40, 1,147–8; PI 141, 3–4, 10.

GA. Also in the National Archives, the records of the Public Housing Administration (RG 196), from 1895 to the early twentieth century, contain some photographs of slum housing in various cities, and the economic data files of the Department of Housing and Urban Development (RG 207) include some evidence from the 1850s onwards.[132]

The published federal census for 1850 provides numbers of dwellings and families in each county for whites and free blacks.[133] That for 1860 gives only the number of dwellings in each ward of New York City and Philadelphia.[134] The 1870 census provides the number of dwellings and families with the number of persons per dwelling for fifty cities,[135] and that for 1880 has similar information for 100 large cities.[136] The 1890 census gives statistics, for counties and places of 2,500 inhabitants upwards, of numbers of dwellings and families, and persons to a dwelling and to a family, and a more detailed analysis for cities of 100,000 and over.[137] In a volume devoted to farms and homes, the 1890 census also provides much on home proprietorship in cities and farms of various sizes and in some counties.[138] The 1900 census gives for cities of 25,000 and more the numbers of families and dwellings and the number of persons per dwelling and family. For cities of 50,000 and over an analysis by wards is presented of the number of dwellings with given numbers of families living in them. Totals of families and dwellings by counties and places of 2,500 and more are also given.[139] Statistics of the proprietorship of homes are given by counties, places of 8,000 upwards, and

[132] *GNA*, 521; Jerome Finster, "Some aspects of urban housing records in the National Archives," in Jerome Finster (ed.), *The National Archives and Urban Research* (1974), 73, 77.
[133] Vol. I, State Tables, IV, and see pp. xcv–cii. See also *Statistical View* (Dubester (1950), no. 33), table XCIX.
[134] Vol. IV, p. 339.
[135] Vol. I, table XXI. See also Compendium, table XLVII.
[136] Vol. I, table XXV. See also Compendium, table CIX.
[137] Vol. I (pt. 1), tables 88–9, 91, 93–5. See also Abstract (1896 edn.), Farms and Homes, table 5; Compendium, pt. 1, Dwellings and Families, tables 3, 4, 6, 8–10.
[138] Vol. XIII. See contents pages, and esp. tables 12–13, 94, 98–100, 103–5, 122, 130, 140, 148, 151, 154, 160–1, 164. See also Abstract (1896 edn.), Farms and Homes, tables 4–5.
[139] Vol. II, tables LXXIX, XC, 96, 98, 100, 101 (and see 102), 103–4; and Abstract, table 89. For cities of 100,000+, see vol. II, tables XCI, XCII, XCIV–XCVIII.

certain cities. For cities of 100,000 and more statistics analyzing proprietorship by sex, race, and age are provided.[140]

The 1880 census volumes on "Social Statistics of Cities" provide, for some of the cities covered, information on cemeteries, waterworks, drainage, garbage disposal, infectious diseases, municipal cleansing, pollution, sanitary authorities, and hospitals.[141] The 1890 census gives statistics of death rates, population density, families and dwellings, water supply, sewers, parks, and cemeteries – by wards in twenty-two cities of 100,000 or more inhabitants.[142]

A great deal of privately published nineteenth-century material on public health and housing also exists. Newspapers are a particularly fruitful source for local health affairs. They reported outbreaks of disease, news of water and sewerage undertakings, the establishment of boards of health, hospital foundations and extensions, and other public-health matters. They often published articles on health, notices of local officials, official health reports and, during epidemics, daily health bills.[143] Their columns carried editorial comment, letters, news reports, and articles on and perhaps by public health reformers and their adversaries. Since sanitary reform cost money and was a political matter, and health offices could be political appointments, bias needs to be suspected.[144] The editor of the *Columbian Centinel*, for instance, was an active politician and President of the Boston board of health.[145] As well as the local press, periodicals like *De Bow's Review* (1846–80, available in microfilm), *Niles' Weekly* (later *National*) *Register* (1811–49, available in microfilm), carried news of health matters in various places, especially relating to mortality statistics and epidemics. For the larger cities, local directories and manuals may contain factual information on boards of health and their personnel.

---

[140] Vol. II, tables 106–7, 111–13, 115. See also Abstract (1902 edn.), tables 89–90.
[141] Vols. XVIII, XIX.
[142] Vol. IV (pt. 2). There are useful maps.
[143] Webster Merritt, *A Century of Medicine in Jacksonville and Duval County* (1949), 192–4.
[144] Judith W. Leavitt, *The Healthiest City* (1982), 276–7.
[145] John B. Blake, *Public Health in the Town of Boston, 1630–1822* (1959), 261.

Particularly in heavily populated localities, large numbers of contemporary pamphlets and monographs on sanitation and medical matters generally were published. Some were polemical, reflecting the views of protagonists over reform.[146] Some were issued by societies, local government health agencies, and well-informed medical men, engineers, and the like. Many accounts of epidemics were published,[147] and some unpublished ones survive in depositories.[148] Older general histories of health matters may also exist – like *Medical Annals of Baltimore, 1608–1880* (1884) by John R. Quinian, M.D.

Housing conditions in the slums and ghettoes of the large cities were the subject of much contemporary literature, a great deal of it by reformers. The works of Jacob A. Riis are well known,[149] but there were many others,[150] some particularly informative. The *Annals of the American Academy of Political and Social Sciences*, volume 20 (1902), for example, carries a number of articles on housing problems in various places. Travelers' writings sometimes touched on sanitary conditions, especially in the great cities,[151] and those of missionaries at times attest to health conditions on the frontier.[152]

Medical journals, some published by state and local medical societies,[153] are an important source for informed local opinion and of factual data on local health matters. Thus the *Southern*

---

[146] Cf. John B. Blake, "Lemuel Shattuck and the Boston water supply," *BHM*, 29 (1955), 554–62.

[147] E.g., G. D. Armstrong, *The Summer of Pestilence: A History of the Ravages of Yellow Fever in Norfolk* (Philadelphia, 1856).

[148] E.g., Joseph Y. Porter, "Report of yellow fever in Key West ... 1875 ... 1878," Florida State Board of Health Library, Jacksonville.

[149] *How the Other Half Lives* (1890); *Children of the Poor* (1892); *Out of Mulberry Bend* (1898); *A Ten Years' War* (1900); *The Battle with the Slum* (1902); *Children of the Tenements* (1903).

[150] Ford, *Slums and Housing*, vol. 2, bibl.

[151] E.g., Basil Hall, *Travels in North America in the Years 1827 and 1828* (3 vols., Edinburgh, 1829).

[152] Peter T. Harstad, "Disease and sickness on the Wisconsin frontier," *Wisconsin Mag. Hist.*, 43 (1960), 259; Crockett, "Health conditions in Indian Territory."

[153] Collections of nineteenth-century medical series are in the National Library of Medicine, New York Academy of Medicine, Boston Medical Library, Library of the College of Physicians of Philadelphia. For lists of such jnls., see John Duffy, *A History of Public Health in New York City, 1825–1866* (1968), 597–8; Madge E. Pickard and R. Carlyle Biley, *The Midwest Pioneer* (1945), 311–13; Rosenkrantz, *Public Health*, 229–30. For series in microform, see Hoornstra, 246–7.

Medical Reporter, 2 (1851) has an article on sanitary conditions in New Orleans, the *Buffalo Medical Journal*, 13 (1857–8) a commentary on a report on that city's health, and the *Charles Medical Journal* in the 1850s data on health conditions in various localities. National journals, too, sometimes published material of local interest: the *American Journal of the Medical Sciences*, 10 (1845) prints an article on diseases in Godsden county, FL. Many of these journals carried reports on current epidemics.

Aside from journals, local medical societies also at times produced other publications. The Medical Society of the District of Columbia in 1860, for instance, published a report on the sanitary condition of Washington and Georgetown. Other societies, too, professional and reformist, produced much material. The New York Association for Improving the Condition of the Poor published its first report on sanitary conditions of the local working class in 1853, and similar reports were published by the Sanitary Association of the City of New York in 1859, 1860 and later, and the Citizens' Association of the city in 1865. The City Homes Association of Chicago published a report by Robert Hunter on Tenement Conditions in Chicago in 1901. And the *Proceedings of the Engineers' Society of Western Pennsylvania* (April 9, 1893) published an analysis of the water supply of two cities.

Finally, private papers of ordinary people as well as of medical men,[154] public health officials, reformers, and politicians – correspondence, diaries, reminiscences, financial accounts – can add an extra dimension. Diaries and letters may be particularly useful for periods of epidemics.[155]

CRIME AND ITS TREATMENT

Topics relating to adult crime, juvenile delinquency, policing, and imprisonment that lend themselves to local inquiry are numerous. They include the types of crimes prevalent at

[154] For doctors' letters, see William Barlow and David O. Powell (eds.), "Frontier medicine and life," *Western Pennsylvania Hist. Mag.*, NS 61 (1978).
[155] See, e.g., G. Canby Robinson, "Malaria in Virginia in the early nineteenth century," *BHM*, 32 (1958); Harstad, "Sickness and disease," 90.

various times in a community, the relationship of crime to local economic and social conditions (demographic structure, urbanization, industrialization, frontier conditions, poverty, and so on), and the geography of crime within city neighborhoods and rural areas. Analysis of the characteristics of local criminals and juvenile delinquents (race, ethnicity, sex, age, occupation, etc.), the identity of reformers, and of those who made up juries and vigilante groups, and the characteristics of police officers – all these can be fruitfully examined by linking the types of sources discussed in this section with those outlined in chapter 2. The sex, age, occupational, and racial and ethnic composition of convict communities, and the family background of juvenile delinquents,[156] can be similarly researched. Other interesting lines of inquiry include attitudes of local elites and others towards the problems of crime, vagrancy, and delinquency, the organization of police forces and sheriffs' offices and their relationship with local politics,[157] the reasons for the development of police forces (such as disorder, crime, growth of bureaucracy), and police attitudes towards racial and ethnic groups. Additional topics include conviction rates, types of punishments for different crimes, the relationship of local criminal justice with political ideology in the area, the treatment under the law of different ethnic, racial and class groups, the size and organization of prisons, reform schools and the like, and the treatment of convicts and institutionalized children.

Not all these topics are possible for every locality – many areas, for instance, had no police force for much of the period, while the relevant records have too often been inadequately cared for. Again some topics are very complex. Determination of changing patterns in crime rates and types of crime is fraught with difficulty. Nineteenth-century statistics of crimes committed, arrests, and convictions are very defective.[158] Moreover, rises in numbers of arrests, indictments,

---

[156] Cf. Robert S. Pickett, *House of Refuge* (1969), 189–90: Barbara M. Brenzel, "Domestication or reform?," *Harvard Educational Rev.*, 50 (1980).

[157] Cf. Eugene J. Watts, "The police in Atlanta, 1890–1905," *JSoH*, 39 (1973), 175–6.

[158] Philip D. Jordan, *Frontier Law and Order* (1970), 112.

and convictions may result from increased police efficiency, changes in police policy, alterations in the law, and so forth, rather than from an increase in real crime rates.[159] Again, in treating the subject of compulsorily confined children, it should be noted that some children were placed in work-houses, houses of refuge, reformatories, and even jails, be-cause they were perceived as potential rather than actual criminals, and included the neglected, abandoned, and vagrant.

The sources for the study of crime and punishment overlap with those for the poor and handicapped and the first section of this chapter should also be consulted. Some bibliographical aids to the subjects of this section are cited below.[160]

Federal records contain little for the history of crime and punishment at the community level.[161] There is a report on convict labor in the annual report of the U.S. Commissioner of Labor for 1886[162] and the Industrial Commission made a similar report in 1900.[163] The Bureau of Education issued a circular in 1875 containing descriptions of some reformatory schools and the like.[164] A volume devoted to immigration and crime forms part of the *Report of the Immigration Commission* of

---

[159] For this and possible methodological approaches, see Peter C. Hoffer, "Counting crime in premodern England and America," *HM*, 14 (1981); Maris A. Vinovskis, "Cops and corpses," *HM*, 16 (1983); Roger Lane, "Crime and criminal statistics in nineteenth-century Massachusetts," *JSH*, 2 (1968); Michael Hindus, *Prison and Plantation* (1980); Eric H. Monkkonen, *Police in Urban America, 1860–1920* (1981).

[160] Grob, *American Social History*, section xv; Bremner, *American Social History*, section E; *HG*, 492–6; Francesco Cordasco and David N. Alloway, *Crime in America: Historical Patterns and Contemporary Realities: An Annotated Bibliography* (1985); ABC-Clio, *Crime and Punishment in America: A Historical Bibliography* (1984); Blake McKelvey, *American Prisons* (1936), 32–3, 62–3, 114–15, 148–9, 196, 216, 233; Jack K. Williams, *Vogues in Villainy* (1959), 150–2; and bibl. inf. in: Rothman, *Discovery of the Asylum*; Tiffin, *In Whose Best Interest?*; Joseph A. Hawes, "Society versus its Children" (Univ. of Texas diss., 1969, available Univ. Micro-films); Robert M. Mennell, *Thorns and Thistles: Juvenile Delinquency . . . 1825–1940* (1973).

[161] Federal institutions are not dealt with here.

[162] HED 1 (pt. 5) (49–2), ser. 2497. See also Commissioner of Labor, *Convict Labor* (Bull. 5, 1896).

[163] *Rep. Prison Labor*: HD 476 (pt. 3) (56–1), ser. 3991. See also *Procs. National Convention of the National Anti-Convict Contract Assoc.* (1886).

[164] *Circular of Information, No. 6*: see Bremner, *Children and Youth*, vol. 2, 269–71, for an extract.

1910–11,[165] while a report of 1910–13 on women and child workers devotes a volume to juvenile delinquency in certain large cities.[166] Federal records relating to law and order in the South during the aftermath of the Civil War are dealt with in chapter 3, and among the unpublished records of the Department of Justice (NA, RG 60) are letters to the Attorney General from unruly Western areas which shed light on conditions there.[167]

No statistics of crime or convicts appear in the published federal census volumes before 1850 and from then through 1870 the data are only by geographical divisions. The 1880 census gives statistics of prisoners (by race, sex, nativity) in counties that contained 50,000 or more people.[168] The volumes on the "Social Statistics of Cities" for that census include for some places data on police forces and on penal and reformatory institutions.[169] The 1890 census provides statistics of prisoners in each state prison, county jail, city prison, workhouse, or house of correction – by race, and nativity,[170] and details of expenditure on police in cities of 50,000 and over.[171]

The manuscript population schedules from 1850 provide for counties and subdivisions the names of prisoners in penal and reformatory institutions, and for 1850 and 1860 of those convicted of crimes and residing with their families. The social statistics schedules for 1850–70 include numbers of prisoners (native, foreign) in institutions. The 1880 supplementary schedules for the defective, dependent, and delinquent classes provide by county and subdivision names of prisoners with reasons for their detention, details of crimes and sentences,

[165] Vol. 36: SD 750 (61–3), ser. 5876.
[166] Vol. 8: SD 45 (61–2), ser. 5692.
[167] Stuart M. Traub, "Rewards, bounty hunting and criminal justice in the West: 1865–1900," *Western Hist. Q.*, 19 (1988). For records relating to use of the Army to pursue outlaws and quell civil disorder, see Elaine C. Everly, "State and local history sources in the Military Archives Division," in Timothy Walch (comp.), *Our Family, Our Town* (1987), 31.
[168] Vol. XXI, table CXVI. For data on named institutions, see tables CXVIII, CXIX. See also Compendium, tables CLIII–CLVI.
[169] Vols. XVIII, XIX.
[170] Vol. III, tables 9–11, 15–17, 21–3, 27–9.
[171] Vol. XV, table 12.

work undertaken in jail, names of institutions, and prisoners' home addresses with cross-references to the population schedules.[172]

Newspapers are a most important source for contemporary attitudes, the organization of policing, individual crimes, statistics of crimes and arrests, the activities of various institutions and societies, trials, court and jail commitments, and news of criminal gangs. Editorials and correspondence comment on the state of law and order, police activities, expertise and attitudes,[173] and the nature of punishment. Newspapers often campaigned for changes – for new jails or houses of correction, for expansion of police forces, and so on. As always, newspapers do have drawbacks: they often reflected certain political attitudes, and stories about crimes, criminals, and jails were not always accurate. Nor is the extent or character of lawlessness reflected exactly in the press: some newspapers had a greater interest in such topics than others.[174]

There is a great deal of other relevant contemporary published material. Older county and city histories may include information on crime, prisons, and law and order, which may be used judiciously. Travelers' writings may also touch on such topics, though some were prone to exaggeration and repetition of hearsay, and they need to be used with considerable caution.[175] Charles Dickens (in *American Notes*) and other foreign visitors reported on institutions for juvenile delinquents,[176] and many foreigners made reports on American penal establishments. Among the most useful for information on many individual institutions are William Crawford's report of 1834 to the British government,[177] Gustave de Beaumont and Alexis de Tocqueville, *On the Penitentiary System in the United States and Its Application to France* (trans. Francis

---

[172] RIP 67, 5, 10–11, 19–21. For location of the non-population schedules, see ibid., app.; *Source*, 108.

[173] See, e.g., Howard N. Rabinowitz, "The conflict between blacks and the police in the urban South," *Historian*, 39 (1976–7).

[174] Williams, *Vogues in Villainy*, 144.

[175] Ibid., 141–4.

[176] See, e.g., Bremner, *Children and Youth*, vol. 1, 683–5.

[177] *Rep. . . . on the Penitentiaries of the United States . . .* (1834, repr. 1969).

Lieber, 1833, repr. 1964, 1976), which covers penitentiaries
and establishments for juvenile delinquents, but not rural jails,
and E. S. Abdy's *Journal* (cited in the first section of this
chapter), which has unique information on a few institutions.
There are home-produced reports, too. Details on individual
prisons may be found, for example, in Samuel J. Barrows,
Prison Systems of the United States (1900) and in the various
volumes by Hubert H. Bancroft on a number of Western
states. Official reports are treated below.

Contemporary accounts and histories of penal institutions
and police forces exist and may well contain data now no
longer available elsewhere. Examples include Gershom
Powers's *A Brief Account of the Construction, Management &
Discipline . . . of the New-York State Prison at Auburn* (1826) and
William E. S. Fales's *Brooklyn's Guardians* (1887).

Crime, its prevention and its punishment, were the subjects
of a plethora of pamphlets and other contemporary literature,
some of it containing valuable factual data but generally most
useful for illustrating attitudes. Many of these publications
were of a general nature, but many, too, were locally orientated, particularly towards populous areas. Some were
specific to particular institutions: like *Notes on Inmates in the
Female Department of the House of Reformation of South Boston*
(1834).[178] A large number were published by local societies,
like the Philadelphia-based Pennsylvania Prison Society.[179]
There were, too, many popular and detailed accounts of
crimes, trials, and executions. Speeches and writings of politicians, judges, preachers, and reformers – very often partisan
– also appeared in pamphlet form. The correspondence, autobiographies, diaries, and reminiscences of those interested in
prison reform,[180] of lawyers,[181] and of workers in the police or

[178] Repr. in David J. and Sheila M. Rothman (eds.), *Women in Prison, 1834–1928* (1985).
[179] See Negley K. Teeters, *They Were in Prison* (1937), 515–20.
[180] See, e.g., Bremner, *Children and Youth*, vol. 2, 444. For the papers of William Roscoe of Liverpool, England on American prisons, see B. R. Crick and Miriam Alman (eds.), *A Guide to Manuscripts Relating to America in Great Britain and Ireland* (1961), 89.
[181] Williams, *Vogues in Villainy*, 138–9.

prison service, may exist.[182] Recollections and private papers of former inmates of penal institutions are rarer.[183]

Many societies existed to prevent crime, help children at risk, reform juvenile delinquents and convicts, support prison reform, and to run institutions of various kinds.[184] Their published and unpublished records, especially the minutes of their general and committee meetings, are an important source. More likely to be available, and also valuable, are their published annual reports: those of the New England Society for the Suppression of Vice, for instance, exist from 1880. Such reports and the occasional publications of societies like these may sometimes include official data no longer extant elsewhere. Thus the Massachusetts Temperance Society published a report in 1834 containing otherwise unavailable statistics from police court and reformatory records.[185]

Particularly important are the records, published and unpublished, of various prison societies (as the New York Prison Society, and the Philadelphia Society for Alleviating the Miseries of Public Prisons). Their annual reports (often published) are important for contemporary attitudes as well as providing very detailed information on individual prisons and their inmates. A report of the Boston Prison Discipline Society in 1834[186] contains evidence of this kind and information on conditions in many Massachusetts county jails and houses of correction.[187] The unpublished papers of the prison societies, including, especially, correspondence, also contain evidence on individual jails.[188] And, as well as many pamphlets, some societies published their own journals: the [Pennsylvania] Journal of Prison Discipline and Philanthropy

---

[182] E.g., Zebulon R. Brockway, *Fifty Years of Prison Service* (1912, repr. 1969); B. K. Peirce, *A Half Century with Juvenile Delinquents* (1869); Gideon Haynes, *Pictures from Prison Life* (1869).

[183] E.g., J. C. Powell, *The American Siberia* (1891, repr. 1970); Eddie Guerin, *I Was a Bandit* (1929); Bremner, *Children and Youth*, vol. 2, 516–18.

[184] See also socs. discussed in first section of this chapter.

[185] Roger Lane, *Policing the City* (1967), 227.

[186] The reps. of this soc., 1826–54 were publ. 1855 (repr. 1972).

[187] See J. M. Moynahan and Earle K. Stewart, *The American Jail* (1980), 46–9, for extracts.

[188] See examples in ibid., 52–7.

(Philadelphia, 1845– ; available in microform), for instance, was published by the Pennsylvania Prison Society, and the Boston society published the *Prisoners' Friend* (1851–).

The *Proceedings* of the Annual Congress of the National Prison Association (title varies; from 1872) includes papers which incidentally contain information on different institutions and evidence of the declared views of those connected with them. For instance, the 1873 volume carries a detailed description of the Detroit House of Shelter, and the 1890 volume has information on the condition of prisoners working in mines belonging to the Tennessee Coal, Iron and Railroad Company.

The reports and other records of the children's aid societies, found in the larger cities, shed much light on juvenile delinquency and living conditions of poor children. The "placing-out" policy of such societies often brought them into conflict with the Catholic Church,[189] so that Catholic records (ch. 6) may provide ancillary evidence. Some of these societies produced journals, like the *Child and State*, a valuable source on philanthropic activity, published by the Boys' and Girls' Aid Society of San Francisco.[190]

Officially recognized as well as illegal vigilante or vigilance committees existed throughout the nineteenth century aimed variously at combating crime (on the frontier and in the city) and unfair practices (as in mining districts), preventing slave risings in the South, and in the North fighting slavery and assisting slaves.[191] They also existed, as in 1812, at times of perceived danger from outside.[192] They sometimes held trials and meted out punishment. Their existence, membership, and activities are recorded in newspapers, older histories, biographies, reminiscences, pamphlets, papers of territorial governors, records of court cases, state legislation, and so on, as well

[189] Tiffin, *In Whose Best Interest?*, 90–1.
[190] Leiby, "State welfare administration in California," 172.
[191] See citations, *Source*, 207, 211; Anthony S. Nicolosi, "The rise and fall of the New Jersey vigilant societies," *New Jersey Hist.*, 86 (1968); John H. Moore, "Local and state government of antebellum Mississippi," *JMH*, 44 (1982), 119–22; Patrick B. Nolan, *Vigilantes on the Middle Border* (1987).
[192] See, e.g., "The vigilance committee: Richmond during the War of 1812," *Virginia Mag. Hist. and Biography*, 7 (1900).

as in their own records – membership lists, journals, and the like. Many small groups, however, have left no records.[193]

Basic to the study of penal institutions are the minutes of the meetings of supervising committees, commissions, boards of visitors, and the like, and their annual reports, or the annual reports of governors, superintendents, wardens, jailers, and so on.[194] Some of these remain unpublished, like those of the Virginia State Penitentiary, but many for state and municipal institutions are likely to have been published as official documents. They may be printed in full or abstract form in various municipal documents, or in state legislative journals, in the reports of state boards of charities and correction, state boards of prison commissioners, or state inspectors of prisons, or in messages of territorial governors. A good run of such minutes or reports can provide the basis for the study of an institution, providing evidence of every aspect of the history of the establishment, the impact of changing attitudes and policies, treatment of inmates, details of contract work and attached labor camps,[195] and even biographical data on individual convicts.[196]

Internal records of prisons and reformatories include journals, admission (or commitment) and discharge books, and registers, rolls, or lists of prisoners, "sentence books," and convict record books.[197] All these contain details of individual inmates, such as age, sex, race, nativity, residence, sentence, sentencing and admission dates, crimes committed, reasons for discharge, and maybe physical description, data on education, occupation, religion, habits (temperate or intemperate), marital state, family connections, and so on. Separate files for different categories of prisoner may have been kept: on runaway slaves and indentured servants, prisoners convicted in federal courts, prisoners of war, military and ship

[193] Richard M. Brown, *Strain of Violence, Historical Studies of American Violence and Vigilantism* (1975), app. 3, lists all known vigilance committees (excl. Northern anti-slavery groups) by county and place with dates, membership numbers, etc. For the Ku Klux Klan, see pp. 136–7, 146.
[194] Cf. Edward L. Ayers, *Vengeance and Justice* (1982), 277–8.
[195] Paul W. Keve, *The History of Corrections in Virginia* (1986), 74–82.
[196] Rothman, *Discovery of the Asylum*, 303.
[197] For details, see *Source*, 301–9.

deserters, escaped prisoners, debtors, those convicted of particular offences or in particular courts, and so forth.[198]

There may also be reports of jail physicians and chaplains (of which some were published as state documents), records of medical treatment, of daily routine, and of discipline, files of death warrants, petitions for clemency, pardon records, rules and regulations, financial accounts, and warden's correspondence. Where convicts were contracted out for work there may be details of contracts with railroad companies, mines, state bureaus, and so on, and reports and other material on labor camps. Much interesting work on the nature of local crime and criminals and on their treatment can be based on such material.[199]

The archives of institutions catering for juvenile delinquents and the like may include, as well as annual reports, minutes of directors or controlling committees, and of committees of visitors, treasurers' records, and superintendents' journals, and records of indenturing children. From these an overall picture and details of day-to-day administration may be culled.[200] Extremely valuable, if extant, are detailed records, often called case books, "histories of subjects," and record books, of individual children and their treatment.[201]

Large numbers of state documents relate to county jails, prisons, crime, and allied topics, and catalogs should be carefully searched. The reports of private institutions, like the New York Society for the Reformation of Juvenile Delinquents, were often published as state documents. The published laws, statutes, and penal codes of the several states, and city codes and ordinances, provide the framework for a study of crime and punishment. Acts of incorporation of societies concerned with crime and criminals, and of particular

---

[198] See, e.g., Richard J. Cox and Patricia Vanorney, "The records of a city," *Maryland Hist. Mag.*, 70 (1975), 301–2.
[199] See, e.g., Nicole H. Rafter, *Partial Justice* (1985), pt. II.
[200] See, e.g., Pickett, *House of Refuge*, 209.
[201] See, e.g., Barbara M. Brenzel, "Lancaster Industrial School for Girls," *Feminist Studies*, 3 (1975); Barbara M. Brenzel, *Daughters of the State* (1983), 1–3, 197; Barbara M. Brenzel, "Domestication or reform?"; Stanley K. Schultz, *The Culture Factory* (1973), 244–7.

institutions may outline their structure. Law Reports, described in chapter 1, provide sworn testimony and other details of particular cases. State legislative journals may record petitions about jails, convictions, pardons, and so on. Pardons for young convicts in Georgia in 1895 give details of the offender, and where convicted.[202]

Special reports on particular penal institutions or on aspects of correctional policy were commonly published as state documents.[203] The results of many investigations of New York state prison, for example, were so published.[204] Of wider significance is the report to the New York legislature on prisons generally in the United States.[205] This contains very detailed descriptions of the organization and condition of individual workhouses and jails and includes information on juvenile reform schools. The State of Connecticut, *Contract Convict Labor Commission* (1880) reports not only on convict labor in Connecticut but includes a summary of the reports of similar investigations in other states.

Aside from the reports on individual institutions in the reports of bodies like boards of charities and correction (see above), other regular state and municipal documents may contain relevant information. In particular, reports of bureaus of labor and statistics may embrace reports and data on individual institutions as well as on private associations.[206]

Criminal statistics and other information on crime are to be found in various kinds of state reports.[207] We may take Massachusetts as an example. The report of the Massachusetts Bureau of Statistics of Labor for 1882, for instance, gives details of numbers of arrests in various towns for each of eight years, analyzed by the nativity of the father of the arrested.[208] From 1830 reports of the Inspector of the state prisons include the number, county of residence, offenses, and sentences of

[202] Bremner, *Children and Youth*, vol. 2, 444.
[203] For Dorothea L. Dix's reps., see p. 503.
[204] A rep. of 1883 was repr. 1974.
[205] Enoch C. Wines and Theodore Dwight, *Rep. on Prisons and Reformatories of the United States and Canada* . . . (1867, repr. 1976).
[206] See p. 368, n. 69 above.
[207] See Lane, "Crime and criminal statistics."
[208] Donald B. Cole, *Immigrant City* (1963), 213.

convicts. The annual reports of the constables of the commonwealth provide county arrest statistics and figures for stolen
property. From 1841 the abstracts of the annual returns of
county jail keepers and overseers of houses of correction (see
above) give the numbers of offenses and the sex of those
committed to penal establishments. Numbers of homicides
were reported in annual registers of deaths – but these are of
doubtful validity. From 1833 reports of the Attorney General
include summaries of high-court cases in which he was involved, including all capital cases, abstracts of cases handled
by district attorneys, and abstracts of criminal cases (by counties) heard in the lower courts. The reports of city as well as
state police forces provide more information. Those of Boston
summarize causes of arrest and details of those arrested (sex,
resident or not, citizen or foreign), amounts of money stolen,
and numbers of illegal liquor shops, gambling dens, and
brothels. They provide maps of the boundaries of police
districts.[209]

Searches in other official documents may also be worth
while. For Pennsylvania, for instance, the reports of the Superintendent of Schools include data on the literacy of inmates
in county jails and poorhouses.[210] State and local government
financial accounts may provide such evidence as the costs of
policing and of maintaining individual institutions. The
reports of the Louisiana State Auditor give information on the
leasing of convicts.[211] Again, reports and other records of state
administrative agencies, like civil and engineering bureaus,
commissioners for public buildings, and boards of public
works, may provide information on the costs of building and
maintenance of penal establishments.[212] On the frontier, the
records of territorial governors and legislatures, including
petitions and correspondence, contain evidence on problems

---

[209] Lane, *Policing the City*, 225–6, 228, 230–6. Cf. Roger Lane, *Violent Death in the City*
(1979), 125–6.

[210] Lee Soltow and Edward Stevens, *The Rise of Literacy and the Common School in the
United States* (1981), 154.

[211] Mark T. Carleton, "The politics of the convict lease system in Louisiana, 1868–
1901," *Louisiana Hist.*, 8 (1967).

[212] See, e.g., David Kohn and Bess Glen (eds.), *Internal Improvements in South Carolina, 1817–1828* (1938).

of law and order,[213] and details of individual cases are sometimes reported in *Territorial Papers*.[214]

Details of the organization, personnel, and methods of police forces can be obtained not only from the reports noted above, but also from other police records. The minutes of boards of police commissioners provide information on routine operations and administration, and sometimes details of arrests, charges, testimony, and verdicts on police disciplinary charges. The working records of police departments can yield intimate detail on arrests, those arrested, offenses, and sometimes outlines of court cases. Orders record all the administrative regulations and commands under which the department worked, while roster and record books give details of police officers. Reports of officers on patrols may sometimes be available. Police reports in antebellum New Orleans provide details of those held in jail, employed in chain-gangs, and so on.[215] Not all police department records, however, have survived: those for New York City, for instance, were mostly sold for waste about 1914.[216]

Other relevant material may well exist in the unpublished archives of cities and states. In particular the files of state governors, attorney generals, and other state officials, of their correspondence with mayors, sheriffs, magistrates, jailers, constables, and private individuals, may provide a wealth of detail. They may include letters on such matters as pardons, convict labor, particular institutions, the administration of justice, and so forth. The South Carolina "State Penal Papers," covering 1800 to 1859, may be taken as an example of a collection of unpublished official records.[217] They consist of letters between governors and law officers, reports and accounts of jailers, constables, coroners, prison physicians, court solicitors, and court witnesses. They include the

[213] Robert V. Haynes, "Law enforcement in frontier Mississippi," *JMH*, 22 (1960); Traub, "Rewards, bounty hunting."
[214] Carter, *Territorial Papers* (see p. 19), e.g., vol. 4, 368; vol. 8, 196; vol. 21, 1,059.
[215] Heartman Collection of Manuscripts relating to the Negro and Slavery, Xavier Univ., available in microfilm.
[216] James F. Richardson, *The New York Police* (1970), 291.
[217] Williams, *Vogues in Villainy*, 137.

petitions and miscellaneous accounts of citizens, such as jurors and posse members. Also in the South Carolina archives are pardon papers and militia and posse papers, as well as letters and papers relating to the execution of the law, including the full presentments and indictments of grand juries.

The records of sheriffs, as county peace officers and servants of the courts, are also important. County jails and their records came under the sheriff's department. As an officer of the county courts of record he kept process and execution documents which provide details of court cases and judgments.[218] Such records, especially jail registers, provide much evidence on criminals and their offenses, offering possibilities of correlation with data from censuses, directories, newspapers, and judicial records, for investigation of the relationship to crime of social and economic factors.[219]

As well as the reports of law cases noted above, court records are one of the basic sources for the study of crime and punishment. To make the best use of them, familiarity with legal terminology and the organization and procedures of the courts is desirable.[220] The main types of court records are case files, court journals, minutes, orders, judgments, witness lists, indexes and dockets, and grand-jury records.[221] Perhaps the most significant of these are case files, which include the original transcripts of summonses, writs, affidavits of witnesses, bonds, depositions, exhibits, declarations, jury lists, witness lists, indictments, warrants, verdicts, dismissals, and details of coroners' inquests. Often the detail in the files is not available in other court records.

Court minute books (act books, court records, journals, or proceedings) record in summary the cases and all the actions taken by the court, with brief details of cases, lists of juries,

---

[218] See, WPA, HRS, *Inventory of the County Archives of Kansas: No. 35, Gray County (Cimarron)* (1939), 158–9.

[219] Harvey J. Graff, "Crime and punishment in the nineteenth century," *JIH*, 7 (1977), 478–9, 481, 484–5.

[220] See Seymour V. Connor, "Legal materials as sources of history," *AA*, 23 (1960); *Source*, ch. 6, both drawn on in the following account.

[221] Nomenclature varies from state to state. The WPA, HRS vols. devoted to local government records are a good starting point for research.

and listings of grand-jury indictments (see below). Court orders to sheriffs, marshals, constables, and so on, include short descriptions of cases and indicate judgments or sentences to be carried out. There may be official indexes to court case records (usually filed by names of litigants). Dockets of various kinds, often the best-preserved criminal court records, detail pending cases, their progress, and judgments, and may also be used as indexes to court minutes and orders. Witness lists, which record names and sometimes addresses, may be useful when dealing with testimony.[222] The minutes of preliminary grand-jury (or indictment-jury) investigations prior to indictment in trial courts provide descriptions of cases, with records of testimony, reports, and the jury's findings.

The records of the court of the coroner, whose duties were to investigate all violent and mysterious deaths, provide not only data on the types and causes of such deaths, but considerable insight into the state of law and order, the attitudes of the local community (as, for instance, over lynching) and the general flavor of local life. Coroners' records may include dockets (detailing inquests, listing victims, jurors, and witnesses, and recording verdicts), inquisitions determining the facts of the case, depositions of witnesses including medical evidence, death certificates providing personal details of the deceased, and maybe annual reports. These last list the numbers of deaths (by cause, sex, race) and in some cases (as in Philadelphia) may have been published as official documents or printed in the newspapers.[223]

---

[222] David J. Bodenhamer, "The efficiency of criminal justice in the antebellum South," *Criminal Justice Hist.*, 3 (1982), 83; Eric Monkkonen, "Systematic criminal justice history," *JIH*, 9 (1979), 451.
[223] Lane, *Violent Death*, 149–51; *Source*, 171–3; Jones, 164–5.

Index

The names of individuals, states, places, institutions, publications, etc., introduced simply as or in examples, have been indexed only selectively (with an emphasis on states and large cities). The same applies to citations in the text of authors, depositories, books, journals, etc. which do not differ in nature from those cited in the footnotes.

Index

Index

541

Index

censuses (*cont.*):
use of, 86–92, 111, 113–14, 291–2,
450–2, 500–1
chambers of commerce, 131, 221,
376–7, 414
Champonier, P. A., 230–1
charities, 132, 312, 313, 321, **494–514**
passim, **529–33** *passim; see also*
societies, charitable and philanthropic
Charleston, SC, 81n, 364
*Checklist of United States Public
Documents, 1789–1909*, 20, 21, 22
Chesapeake and Ohio Canal Company,
343, 429
Chevalier, Michel, 417
Chicago, IL: Board of Trade, 376–7,
414; buildings, 15; City Homes
Association of, 524;
communications, 58, 422;
Congregational Association, 267;
education, 306–7, 467; elections, 331;
Italians in, 122, 127, 130, 132; labor
troubles, 339, *and see* U.S. (Pullman)
Strike Commission; meat industry,
402; slums, 519; sweated trades, 364
child labor, 65–72 *passim*, 79, 129, 139,
242, 339, 358–68 *passim*, 372, 378,
445, 450–62 *passim*, 474, 478, 512,
527
children, 13, 65–86 *passim*, 89–90, 92,
200, 503; *see also* child labor;
education; orphanages; reformatories
Chinese, in U.S., 71, 149n, 493
Christian Church, *see* Disciples of
Christ
Church of Jesus Christ of Latter-day
Saints, 241, 257, 258, 266–7
churches and church records, 156–7,
239–94; blacks and, *see* blacks,
religion and; charitable work, 132,
509; Civil War, effects on, 242, 247,
253, 292; and education, 132–3,
261–2, 278, 441–5; and immigrants,
132; and organized labor, 242;
Southern, *see* Southern states,
churches; types of records, 253–63;
vital statistics, 96, 257–8; *see also*
buildings, church; denominations;
histories, church and parish;
missionary work; religion
Cincinnati, OH, 364, 422, 480, 509
CIS US Serial Set Index, 20, 22; *see also*
US Serial Set
cities:
finances, *see* local government,
finances
governmental organization, 299,
300–1, 307, 312
records, 11 (state of), 27, 45, 302–3,
305–10, 369; auditors', 434, 467;

baths' depts., 518; on blacks,
151–2, 480; charters, 300–1, 305,
369; clerks' depts., 507; on
communications, 433–4; council,
151, 369, 434 (debates, minutes,
resolutions), 308–9, 323, 467, 518
(petitions, memorials); engineers',
433; health boards, 515, 517–18,
520; on housing, 518; on
immigration, 518; laws,
ordinances, 305–6, 369, 467, 480,
518, 533; on poor, handicapped,
criminal, 506–7, 532; port, 412;
school boards and officers, 459,
460, 467; tax, *see* taxes, city and
county; treasurers', 434; voting,
319; *see also* censuses, city; local
government; manuals, official
Civil War, 12, 134–9 *passim*, 145, 146,
189, 310–11; and agriculture, 164,
189; battlefields, 50; and blacks, 154,
286, 480–8; and churches, 242, 247,
253, 292; maps, 50–1, 54;
photographs and prints, 34; prizes,
403; veterans, 502
claim clubs, 222–3
Claims, Commissioners of, *see*
Southern Claims Commission
Cleveland, OH, 128, 429
climate, 32, 173–4, 184, 201, 229
Coast and Geodic Survey, 427n
Colorado: censuses, 79, 82, 84, 207,
359; forestry, 191; labor troubles,
341; land claims, 167; mining, 387,
392, 396; Populism in, 226
Colored Farmers' National Alliance,
226
Columbus, OH, 122, 131, 367
*Commercial Relations of the United States
with Foreign Countries*, 404
Commons, John R., collection of,
348–9
Commissioner of Corporations on
Transport by Water, 424–5
communications, 31, 69, **415–36**;
census evidence on, 420–1; federal
records on, 169, 339, 363, 420–30,
434–6; local government records on,
306, 433–4; newspapers and
periodicals and, 417–18; research
topics, 415; state records on, 430–3;
see also canals; internal
improvements; maps and plans,
communications; postal services;
railroads; railways, street; river
navigation; roads; telegraphs and
telephones
Comptroller of the Currency, Bureau
of, 147–8, 382, 383, 485

Index

Index

communications, 46, 50–3 *passim*, 57–8, 171, 416, 422, 424–8 *passim*; county, 56, 58, 59, 227–8; cyclists', 60; exploration, 46–7, 50, 52; fire-insurance, 59–60, 104, 383; forest, 190–1; geological, 48–9, 58; illiteracy, 446; industrial, 376; internal improvement, 46, 50, 51, 57–8, 171, 426, *and see this entry*, communications; immigrants, 58; Indians and Indian lands, 51, 52, 54, 191, 236; land (and landownership), 52–4, 55, 56, 59, 171, 174, 227–8; military departments, 50; mines and mineral lands, 52, 391–3, 395; plantations, 228; postal, 51, 91, 434; public domain, 52–4, 174–6, 178; real estate, 104; religion, 245, 247, 253n, 290; rights of way, 426, 428; Sanborn, 59; school lands and districts, 55, 491; Southern states, 49–56 *passim*, 201, 228; street, 31, 99; topographical, 47–8, 50, 51; town and city, 31, 49, 55, 56, 58, 308; township, 52, 53, 54, 304, 428; townsite, 52, 55, 178; tax assessment, 59; war, 49, 50–1, 54; ward, 57, 104, 332; West, 47, 50, 228, *and see this entry*, public domain; *see also* atlases, *and under state names*

Marine Hospital Service, 520

Marine Inspection and Navigation, Bureau of, 405–6

maritime activity, 397–415

market gardening, *see* horticulture

marriage records, *see* vital statistics, marriages

Maryland: blacks, 484, education, 473, 475, 484; elections, 331; health, board of, 504; land offices, 208; land system, *see* states, original thirteen, land system; maps, 50; taxes, 100–1; *see also* Baltimore, MD

Massachusetts: banks, 382; censuses, 361; child labor, 460–3; communications, 432; crime and prisons, 534–5; education, 450, 456, 458, 460, 462, 463, 472–3, 476; elections, 331; health and housing, 517, 518; immigration, 123; industry, 368, 461; labor laws, 461; land offices, 208; land system, *see* states, original thirteen, land system; literacy, 450; maps, 58; political parties, 348; poor, handicapped, and delinquent, 494, 502; taxes, 100–1; Society for the Religious Instruction of Freedmen, 488; Temperance Society, 530; vital statistics, 93, 95;

see also Boston, MA; Newburyport, MA

McCormick collection, 221

McLane, Louis, 362–3

mechanics' institutes, 456, 458

medical records, 514; *see also* hospitals

memoirs, *see* autobiographies and memoirs

Memphis, TN, 136, 306, 364, 422

Mennonites, 272

Merchant Vessels of the United States, 399

Methodist Episcopal Freedmen's Aid Society, 488

Methodists, 253, 257, **272–3**; missionary work, 285–6, 288, 488–9

Mexico, 181; records in, 28n, 261; war with, 50

Michigan: blacks, 150; censuses, 361–2, 390; county government, 296; education, 450, 464, 466–7, 477; elections, 331; immigration, 127; industry, 361–2; land claims, 167; literacy, 450; mining, 361–2, 390, 391; *see also* Detroit, MI

microforms, 19; *and cited in footnotes, passim*

migration, *see* geographic mobility; immigrants and immigration

military posts, 237

Military Railroads, Office of U.S., 428

military reservations, 173, 179, 182

militia, 85

Milwaukee, WI, 128

mining, 173, 179, 236, 375, **385–96**; and banks, 382–3; censuses and, 355–6, 357–8, 361–2, 388–90; convict labor in, 531, 533; in Indian lands, 393; inspection of, 343, 344, 392; labor relations in, 339–40, 343, 392, 394; local government records and, 396; maps, 46, 48, 52, 58, 392; and newspapers and periodicals, 385–6; slave labor in, 155, 387; state records and, 395–6

Minnesota: censuses, 500; land records, 176; Lutherans, 270; mining in, 396; Populism in, 226

missionary work, 154, 156–7, 254, 260, 267, 274–5, 277, 278, **281–9**, 292, 443–5, 513, 523; city, 131, 242, 286–7, 509; Indian education, 489–90; *see also under names of missionary societies*

Mississippi: education, 450, 488; elections, 325; land claims, 167; maps, 51; Reconstruction, 137

Mississippi River, 429

Mississippi River Commission, 51, 424

Mississippi Valley, Superintendency of Freedmen in the, 145

Index

Missouri: education, 462; labor troubles, 338; land claims and records, 167, 176, 211; literacy, 450; maps, 51 197; slaves, 197; *see also* St, Louis, MO
Missouri River Commission, 51
Mobile, AL, 81n
mobility, *see* geographic mobility; social mobility
Montana, 191
Moravians, 253, 273–4
Morgan, Thomas J., 349
Mormons, *see* Church of Jesus Christ of Latter-day Saints; Reorganized Church of Jesus Christ of Latter-day Saints
Morrison, John H., 416–17
mortality records, *see* vital statistics, deaths
mortgages, 104, 151, 196, 208, 212, 213, 220, 304, 308; *see also* liens
mulattoes, 149n
municipalities, *see* cities
Museum Association of American Frontier and Fur Trade, 438n
museums, 14, 149n, 220, 436, 438n, 453, 456
music, 13
muster rolls, 307

National Archives, 37–42, *and passim for records therein*
National Archives and Records Administration, *see* National Archives
National Association of Cotton Manufacturers, 376
National Board of Health, 148
National Cartographic Information Center, 47n
National Conference of Charities and Correction, 509
National Education Association of the United States (NEA), 473, 477
National Farmers' Alliance and Industrial Union, 225–6
National Historical Publications (and Records) Commission, 19
National Inventory of Documentary Sources, 36n
National Library of Medicine, 516
National Mediation Board, 343, 429
National Museum of American History, 149n, 436
National Park Service, 343, 429
National Prison Association, 531
National Register of Historic Places, 15, 247
National Reporter System, 26

National State Papers: Texts and Documents, 22
National Union Catalog, 17
National Union Catalog of Manuscript Collections, 35
National Waterways Commission, 425n
naturalization records, 124, 126, 304
Naval Records, Office of, (RG 45), 139n, 191
Navigation, Commissioner of, 398
Navy, Dept. of the, 394; *see also* Engineering (Navy Dept.), Bureau of; Yards and Docks Dept. (Navy Dept.); Naval Records, Office of
Nebraska: agriculture and lands, 209; censuses, 82, 84, 207, 359; Populism in, 226
Nevada: labor records, 349; mining, 387, 394–5
New Bedford, MA, 456
New England: Congregationalists, 267; counties, 296; educational associations, 473; fisheries, 402; Freedmen's Aid Society, 283; Lutherans, 270; maps, 227, 228; Society for the Suppression of Vice, 530; towns, 90, 296, 297–8, 302–5, 505; *see also under names of states, places*
New Hampshire: communications, 430–1; industry, 362–3, 398; land records, 170; land system, *see* states, original thirteen, land system
New Jersey: censuses, 75, 362; county government, 296; health, 519; immigration, 189; industry, 362; land system, *see* states, original thirteen, land system; Lutherans, 270; political parties, 348
New Mexico: censuses, 82, 84, 207, 359; forestry, 191; labor troubles, 343; land claims, 167; maps, 50; mines, 343, 388, 392, 393
New Orleans, LA, 307; banks, 381; blacks, 88, 138, 151; censuses, 81n, 88; city government, 312; convicts, 536; health, 518; trade and shipping, 180, 364, 401; Reconstruction, 311
New York, NY, Association for Improving the Condition of the Poor, 131, 524; blacks, 88; censuses, 85, 88; Chamber of Commerce, 414; charities, 157, 506, 508; Charity Organization Society, 508; Citizens' Association, 524; cotton exchange, 364; Custom House, 409; education, 471, 475, 477, 512; Federation of Churches . . . 157; German Society,

Index

Index

(historical); housing, 516; immigrant aid, 57, 131, 507–8; Jewish, 268, 269; medical, 524; missionary, 240, 242, 259, 281–9, 441–5, 486–9, 509, *and see* missionary work, *and under names of missionary societies*; musical, 472; political, 131; prison, 529, 530–1; professional, 131, 321; provident, 157, 507–8; religious, 131, 157, 225, 254, 258, 276, 288–9, 441–4, 507–8, 512 (*and see this entry*, Bible and tract; denominational (historical); Jewish; missionary); scientific, 447, 472; temperance, 287, 507–8, 530; *see also under names of associations, societies, etc.*

Society of Friends, *see* Friends, Society of

Society for the Promotion of Collegiate and Theological Education in the West, 443–4

Society for Propagating the Gospel among the Indians and Others in North America, 285

Society for the Propagation of the Faith, 262

sociology, 5, 11

Soil Conservation Service, 191, 238

Soundex, 80–1

South Carolina: civil parishes, 296; education, 461; elections, 325; Land Commission, 150; land system, *see* states, original thirteen, land system; penal papers, 536–7; peonage in, 344; Reconstruction, 137; *see also* Charleston, SC

South Dakota: county government, 296; maps, 228; *see also* Dakota territory

Southern Baptist Convention, Home Mission Board, 285

Southern Claims Commission, 41, 54, 138, 147, 187–8, 325

Southern states: churches, 156, 240–56 *passim*, 265–6, 270, 272, 273, 275, 283, 292, (*and see* blacks, missions to; blacks, and religion); county government, 296–7; education, 454 (*and see* blacks, education; blacks, laws on); maps, 49–56 *passim*, 201, 228; peonage in, 344; railroads, 424, 428, 430; Unionists of, 188; *and passim. See also* Civil War; Southern Claims Commission; Reconstruction; slaves and slavery

Spain, 261; land grants, 168

State, Dept. of (RG 59), 41n, 125, 127n, 129, 393

state governments, records, 26–7, **44–5** administrative records:

manuals, 299–30, 331, 332

permanent boards, bureaus, departments, officers, etc.:
adjutants general, 345; agriculture, 190, 209, 210–11, 367–8, 395, 411, 432; arbitration, 344; attorneys general, 535, 536; auditors, 209, 382, 344, 431, 432, 461, 485, 535; banking, 382; charities and correction, 503–4, 518, 532, 534; civil and engineering, 210, 432, 535; comptrollers general, 209; entomologists, 211; factory inspectors, 367, 461; geologists, 395; governors, 150, 211, 326, 345, 461–2, 504, 536; health, 106, 461, 504, 515, 517–18, 520; immigration, 32, 123–4, 125, 132, 211, 225, 289, 395; institutions, 460, 461 (educational), 503, 504, 533–4 (penal and welfare); internal improvements, communications, 155, 423, 430–3, *and see this entry*, public works; labor bureaus, etc., *see* labor, state bureaus of; land offices, 208–9, 223; lumber inspectors, 367; mine inspectors, 395; mineralogists, 395; police, 302, 535; prisons, 532, 534–5, 536, *and see this entry*, charities and correction; public instruction, 209, 453, 458–60, 462–3, 466–7 (school inspectors), 472, 485, 535; public works, 209, 431, 535; surveyors, 209; treasurers, 382, 431

special reports: banking, 381–2; censuses, *see* censuses, state; education, 460; housing and public health, 127, 518; immigrants, 126; poor and handicapped, 502–3

constitutional records: constitutional conventions, 27, 150, 300, 319, 458, 479–80; constitutions, 149, 300, 479, 501; local government organization, 296–302

courts, *see* courts, state; law reports law records, 27, 149, 209, 300–2, 381, 430, 501–2; agricultural matters, 190, 209; blacks, 149, 479; communications, 423, 430; education, 453, 458, 479; health, 518; incorporations, 293, 300, 369, 396, 430, 442, 458; labor, 339, 340, 343, 344, 351, 365–6, 461; land,

Index